Measurement
and
Evaluation
in
the
Schools

Louis J. Karmel

Marylin O. Karmel

MEASUREMENT AND EVALUATION IN THE SCHOOLS

Second Edition

MACMILLAN PUBLISHING CO., INC.
New York
COLLIER MACMILLAN PUBLISHERS
London

41125

Macmillan Publishing Co., Inc.
866 Third Avenue, New York, New York 10022

Collier Macmillan Canada, Ltd.

Library of Congress Cataloging in Publication Data

Karmel, Louis J
  Measurement and evaluation in the schools.

  Bibliography: p.
  Includes index.
  1. Educational tests and measurements.
I. Karmel, Marylin O., joint author. II. Title.
LB3051.K16   1978   371.2'6   76-52429
ISBN 0-02-362000-5

Printing: 1 2 3 4 5 6 7 8   Year: 8 9 0 1 2 3 4

Preface

This *second edition* of Measurement and Evaluation in the Schools *retains the prime objective of presenting measurement and evaluation concepts in simple and direct language. Like the first edition, it is directed to students of guidance, counseling, and psychology as well as to the classroom teacher. It is not, however, a book for the advanced or theoretically oriented student of measurement. The emphasis is on essential concepts needed in actual testing situations. Thus, it is best used with beginning and practically oriented students of educational and psychological testing. This practical orientation is expressed through clear everyday language and real-life cases that translate measurement theories and concepts into the reality of the world. Accuracy and scholarship have not been neglected in attempting to simplify and make measurement usable.*

The present edition is significantly enhanced by the addition of Dr. Marylin O. Karmel as co-author. She brings to the text a point of view developed from experience as a public school teacher and a college professor. She also brings theoretical knowledge of developmental psychology.

The authors have revised each chapter in an attempt to incorporate suggestions of students and colleagues. This has resulted in changing the order of some chapters, adding new chapters, and expanding others. The reorganization resulted in placing statistics before validity and reliability so that statistical concepts could be applied. Ethics, standards, and procedures follow. The chapter on sources of text information has been placed at the end of the book, which lends to its being used as a reference. The organizational plan is intended to increase, not to discourage, student interest. Historical and scientific information is integrated throughout the text in relevant sections.

Two new chapters have been added, "Informal Techniques" and "Criterion-Referenced Testing." The chapter on informal techniques is devoted to informal procedures of observation, self-report, and peer report as sources of information about an individual. These include anecdotal records, rating scales, checklists, behavior modification, and unobtrusive measures. The chapter on criterion-

referenced testing attempts to place in sharp focus the differences among norm- and criterion-referenced tests and concepts such as criterion, mastery testing, individualized instruction, and published criterion-referenced tests. In addition, the chapter on achievement tests has a section on criterion-referenced grading.

The remaining chapters have been updated, and new material has been added when needed. The chapter on contemporary issues and problems, which has been so well received by critics, students, and colleagues, has been infused with the latest research findings on topics such as race and IQ and the influence of genetics on intelligence. As in the first edition, an attempt has been made to present scientifically all aspects of issues.

New material on developmental and preschool tests has been added to Chapters 6 and 8. This reflects a trend in society for younger children to be placed in organized group situations. In the area of intelligence testing, new material on a Piagetian framework for such testing has been added. The chapter on college entrance examinations has been extensively updated, including a discussion of falling College Board scores. In all chapters citing tests, the lastest editions and illustrations are used.

The appendix of representative tests (C) has been greatly expanded, and the most recent editions and reviews in the Mental Measurements Yearbook are cited. The other appendixes have also been updated, and a new appendix has been included on the significance of correlation coefficients. We are grateful to the Literary Executor of the late Sir Ronald A. Fisher, F.R.S., to Dr. Frank Yates, F.R.S. and to Longman Group Ltd., London, for permission to reprint Table VII from their book Statistical Tables for Biological, Agricultural and Medical Research (6th edition, 1974).

The authors would like to thank their students as well as colleagues who have been so generous with their comments and suggestions. These have been extremely helpful and have been incorporated into this new edition.

L. J. K.

M. O. K.

Contents

Tables

Figures

ONE

Reasons for Testing and Contemporary Issues

The Reasons We Give Tests

chapter 1

The last rain drops of the thunderstorm fell slowly on the cement walkway. The people in the building hardly noticed, for they were engrossed in an informal dissection of a human being—a fifth grade student.

Ms. Love, a fourth-grade teacher, spoke in a rapid and determined cadence. "John is always counting on his fingers. I tried last year to stop him but he insists on doing it his way. He won't listen to anyone. Heaven knows I tried."

"He won't listen to anyone. I tried to tune in to him, but I couldn't," says Ms. Hip the student teacher.

"You know, ladies, I think the boy has exhibited maladaptive behaviors in all areas and needs some modification," states Mr. B. Mod the school counselor.

"Do you think he may be retarded or just a slow learner?" At this question, by the fifth-grade teacher, there was shocked silence. Mr. B. Mod was the first to speak, after observing his colleagues with a cold gaze.

"You obviously have not been observing and recording your observations in a scientific manner. Otherwise you would know, as I do, that our student is not retarded or a slow learner, but has been programmed to respond to your expectations, which are zero, and is then reinforced by your 'I knew it' attitude."

Did you notice, Mr. or Ms. Reader, that everything that was said in the preceding discussion had to do with subjective judgment? Should our evaluations be only subjective or can we help people by being objective as well in our analysis of weaknesses and strengths of people? Tests were created to help make teacher judgment objective —that is, to supplement, not to replace, teacher opinion. Tests are an independent method of assessing student behavior.

Parents, too, are concerned about their children's assessment. They want to know about tests and why the school uses them. "I am beginning to think our children are tested to death," states an irate parent. Another parent asks why the school gives tests when, "We all know they aren't very good." The critics of testing add to the concern by such statements as, "Tests are culturally biased," "Tests penalize the creative child," or, "Tests invade the privacy of the individual." Other thoughtful voices raise the issue of teacher-made tests and their relevancy for measuring student learning.

These questions are of legitimate concern and need to be answered in an objective and meaningful manner. This chapter will attempt to provide a general basis for the answers to these and other questions; Chapter 2 will deal with specific issues and problems.

It is very difficult to generalize about testing in the school situation without taking into consideration certain variables such as the philosophy and objectives of a particular school, its resources, and its geographic location. A school should administer many different types of tests because no one test can measure all the varied facets of a child's ability, interests, and personality. In the process of educational and personal development, changes occur which must be considered in any meaningful picture of a human being. Even in one single area, such as intelligence, more than one test is needed over a period of years to obtain a reliable estimate of ability.

Basically, schools use tests as educational tools to promote individualized instruction. Individualized instruction is the major reason for testing. It implies that the school's basic duty to the child is to know him or her as an individual. Inherent in this is a recognition of the dignity and worth of the individual and his unique qualities. The basic premise for giving tests is the assumption that individuals differ and that education must be geared to these differences so that each person may develop his or her own unique potential.

If we accept this assumption of individual differences, then we must also make certain other assumptions. We must realize, for example, that some children are ready to read at four, whereas others are not ready until they are six or eight. Some children find school a "snap," and others find it a "drag." Certain children find mathematics easy, and others are lost. The child who finds math difficult may excel in English, whereas his mathematically superior peer may find English his most difficult subject. Some children may be academically superior in all subjects; others may be slow to learn in all areas. Some children may reveal a great deal of promise but obtain poor grades in school. Other children may have personal problems that interfere with academic success.

We will now turn our attention to the nature of tests, how they help in identifying some of the children previously mentioned, and how they can be used to individualize instruction. Before we begin our discussion of the reasons for testing, we must first know the meaning of the term *test*.

Webster's *New Collegiate Dictionary* defines the word *test* as "any critical examination or trial . . . means of trial . . . subjection to conditions that show the real character of a person or thing in a certain particular," and "that with which anything is compared for proof of genuineness." According to Webster, the use of *test* in education means, "Any series of questions or exercises or other means of measuring the skill, knowledge, intelligence, capacities or aptitudes of an individual or group."

Generally, when we use the word *test*, we mean to appraise something or someone. That is, to test is to evaluate or measure something or someone against given criteria in order to obtain data that reveal relationships between our subject and our frame of reference. For example, in our space program, the vehicles and men are subjected to simulated conditions of space before the actual launching. They are being *tested* to ascertain their future performance in outer space. In a school setting, the child is *tested* in order to discover the degree of learning that has taken or may take place. Mary failed her spelling test. Johnny got 100 on his history test. Billy's test scores reveal a high potential for school success. Ruth's test scores show average potential for success in secretarial tasks. Mary and Johnny's past learnings are being measured; Billy and Ruth's future chances of success are being evaluated, that is, tested.

Teacher-Made Tests

In the classroom the teacher may approach testing in many different ways. He or she may, for example, ask the students to write "in your own words the meaning of the Fifth Amendment of the United States Constitution." Or the teacher may say, "Discuss the implications of the Magna Carta on the United States political system." Such questions are generally referred to as essay tests.

In addition to or instead of the essay examination, the classroom teacher may use the objective test. The word *objective* encompasses many different types of tests. *Objective*, as used in testing, means that the scoring is not influenced by the opinion, knowledge, or skill of the person scoring the test, or whether or not the person taking the test and the person scoring the test "communicate." Thus any test that has predetermined correct answers may be called objective. For example, in the two previously mentioned essay questions, the correct answer is subject to interpretation by the teacher. The scoring is, therefore, subjective. On the other hand, the objective test leaves little, if any, latitude for interpretation of answers because there is only one correct answer.

The true-false question and the completion and multiple-choice item are examples of the objective test. The following are items illustrative of these tests.

True-False: The scoring of an essay test is subjective. T_____ F_____

Multiple Choice: In *objective testing,* the term *objective* refers to the method of

1. Identifying learning outcomes.
2. Selecting test content.
3. Presenting the problem.
4. Scoring the answers.

Completion: According to the author of your text, schools use tests as educational tools to promote _____ _____.

Why Do Teachers Use Tests?

The teacher's primary role in the classroom is to teach; whether he or she succeeds may be ascertained by the intellectual growth and development of the pupils. In order to gauge this progress, the teacher must institute evaluative techniques. These techniques include essay and objective tests and informal procedures such as day-to-day classroom observations and teacher judgment based on professional experience and intuition. All of these procedures aid the teacher in evaluating pupil progress. Our attention, however, will be focused on the reasons for using formal evaluative instruments called tests.

Certification of Pupil Achievement

Many educators are dissatisfied with our present system of grading. It is true that poorly constructed tests may make our present system even worse. It is also true, however, that students must be evaluated in some manner, whether it be by marks, letters of recommendation, or comments on academic levels of proficiency. The test, if properly conceived and executed, can be of assistance in the verification of pupil progress. The teacher, for example, needs to know if pupils have learned enough in first grade to warrant promotion to second grade. The teacher needs to know about pupil achievements in order to certify these accomplishments to other educational institutions, to the world of work, and to parents.

The consistent use of classroom tests provides the teacher with an objective appraisal of each student's learning progress that can then be transmitted to parents and others. Tests provide the teacher with a student's actual school achievement instead of an intuitive generalization based on observation. Diagnostic evaluation of a student's actual knowledge, skills, and achievement in one specific area can be ascertained by the use of criterion-referenced tests. Specific behaviors of the student can be measured and reported to the parents and child. These objective data about students combined with appropriate professional judgment can lay the foundation for educational decisions by parents and teachers.

Measuring Outcomes of Instruction

Tests aid in determining the learning outcomes of classroom instruction. The teacher-made test is a reflection of what the individual teacher considers important. If a teacher-made test stresses concepts or understanding over factual recall, this is indicative of the teacher's basic educational objectives. The teacher can then evaluate the success or failure of classroom learning in relation to the test results. An analysis of student responses to the test can be helpful to the teacher in adjusting the level and direction of classroom instruction.

In preparing for an instructional unit, the teacher asks questions such as, "What kinds of learning behaviors do I want to encourage?" "What cognitive processes should be stimulated?" That is, what information and understandings should the student possess? What changes in the affective and cognitive domains should have taken place? In essence, we are asking what kind of learning outcomes are desired. In answering our questions, we will identify instructional objectives. These objectives are the basis for evaluation of learning outcomes, and without them proper evaluation is impossible. Evaluation is therefore an integral part of instruction.

The measurement of instructional objectives not only is necessary from a theoretically "good" point of view but also is becoming a legal necessity as more and more states pass laws requiring teachers and other educational persons to answer for what takes place in the classroom. Educational accountability laws usually require evaluation of learning outcomes, although they differ from state to state.

Incentive

Well-constructed tests that reflect classroom instruction can increase student learning by helping to develop study habits and to direct intellectual energy toward the desired educational objectives. Test results can reveal areas of strength and weakness of individual students and act as motivating devices for future study. Of course, poorly constructed tests that are used as disciplinary instruments may have the opposite effect and discourage student incentive.

Teacher-made tests are an important aspect of classroom instruction and can increase or decrease academic progress, depending on their quality and relevance. A detailed discussion of various types of teacher-made tests and specific suggestions concerning their construction will be found in later chapters.

Programmed Instruction

Programmed instruction and testing are wedded to each other. Testing is central to programmed instruction. The *linear* programs help the learner to progress at small intervals. In these small steps, the questions are usually answered correctly, thereby reinforcing the learner to want to continue. On the other hand, the *branching* program is constructed to allow the student to follow the path that is best for him. After each segment, questions are asked that determine if the pupil should proceed further. In this area, testing is used basically as an analytic device to ascertain progress. It enables the bright student to go through the program with the least number of intervals while the slow student can repeat and go back as much as needed. Whether programmed instruction is in the form of teaching machines, workbooks, textbooks, or computer-assisted instruction, there is a direct and obvious need for evaluation.

Standardized Tests

Most people have had some experience with a standardized test in school, in the armed services, or in the process of applying for employment. In educational and psychological measurement, *standardization* means a fixed or uniform procedure in the administration and scoring of tests. A standardized test may be administered to a group or to an individual, but always under the same conditions. The allotted time is always the same and the answers to the questions are always scored in the same manner.

Standardized tests are the direct result of the early efforts of persons concerned with testing who sought a uniform method of measuring children's abilities and educational progress. The evaluation of academic achievement in the United States before 1860 was mainly by oral examination. Teachers or visiting examiners would present oral questions to the student. There was no method of objective evaluation of the replies nor did each student of the same grade receive the same questions. Only one student at a time was tested. The oral examination was time-consuming and revealed little indication of differences among students in areas of specific achievement, because each student was presented with a different task. There was no uniformity in questions or in the evaluation of responses.

The oral examination was gradually replaced in the last half of the nineteenth century by the written examination. Colleges began using the written test as a basis for admission. These tests were similar to our present essay test. All students were presented with the same questions and asked to respond in written discourse. This procedure had the advantage of uniformity of tasks and completion time as compared to the oral method. However, the scoring or grading of the student's responses was still highly subjective. The scorer's standards, bias, mood, and other factors, such as neatness and clarity of handwriting, could play a part in the final evaluation.

Although these early essay tests were not standardized, they were the first attempts at standard procedures in educational testing. At the same time that educators were working on uniform school examinations, modern experimental psychology was developing. Wilhelm Wundt in 1879 established the first [1] formal psychology laboratory in Leipzig, Germany. Most of his work was devoted to the senses, especially vision. The quantitative relationship between a stimulus and the ensuing experience was of particular concern to the early experimental psychologist and remains today of great importance to educational and psychological measurement. The actual studies dealing with such sensory processes as the relationship between light or sound waves and the experienced intensity of the sensation are not of particular interest to educational and psychological measurement. However, the experimental procedures that the early psychologists developed—and indeed, the discovery, that there was a difference in the perception of identical phenomena by different people—are important. Their experimental methods provided a legacy of careful attention to experimental methods, statistical techniques, and precision in the standardization of testing instruments.

The authors and publishers of standardized tests attempt to evaluate their instruments by many of the same rigorous scientific techniques that were developed in experimental psychology.

Another way of thinking about a standardized test is to equate it with a recipe in cooking. If you are planning to make a crepe suzette or a chocolate cake, you will need instructions that have proved successful. If you follow these instructions *exactly*, your efforts should be rewarding. You should be able to reproduce the flavor and texture of the original recipe. The elaborate kitchens of many of the leading flour companies have a laboratory atmosphere. The exact ingredients, procedures for mixing, and conditions of baking are repeated over and over again to assure you, the consumer, of an accurate recipe. In the same way, a standardized test is subjected to rigorous experimentation on different groups of people. The conditions of testing, the reading of directions, and the scoring are always the same. The person who is being tested with the X Test of Mental Abilities in Greensboro, North Carolina, will receive exactly the same directions, questions, and time to complete the examination as the person who is being tested with the same standardized test in New York City or London, England. Scoring of the test will be the same no matter where the test is administered. The correct answers are fixed, and no deviation from this format because of geography, culture, or subjective opinions of the test administrator is permitted.

If there are changes in the standardized directions, then the test ceases to be standardized and its value is severely impaired or completely obviated.

---

[1] It should be noted that experimental psychology did not begin with Wundt at Leipzig. He established the *first modern formal* psychology laboratory, but many of his areas of study had been pioneered by others. Plato, Aristotle, St. Augustine, and others left their mark on the history of psychology. It was Descartes who in the seventeenth century introduced the concept of reflex action. E. H. Weber's experiments in physiology in the middle of the nineteenth century under experimental controls and quantification of these data constituted the beginnings of laboratory psychology. Also in the mid-nineteenth century G. T. Fechner amplified Weber's findings in a book on psychophysics (1860). Psychophysical methods invented by Fechner laid the groundwork for psychology's first laboratory procedures.

This is similar to the changing of a recipe. If you put in three cups of sugar rather than one, the chocolate cake may be more to your liking than the original recipe, but it is no longer the same cake. This is true also of the standardized test. You may change the directions, time, or scoring and thereby make the test more appropriate for your group of students. What you will have then is a classroom test, maybe an excellent one, but not a standardized test that will allow you to compare your students with other children of similar age or grade throughout the country.

The chief value of the standardized test is to provide teachers and students with an objective educational yardstick that can measure abilities or achievements free of subjective error. Let us look at some common evaluation problems found in the classroom.

Mary is a ten-year-old in the fifth grade at Jones Elementary School. She is very neat in her appearance and work. Her teachers have always found her to be a "doll" and more than willing to help with projects in the classroom. Mary's grades have always been excellent. Last fall Mary and her classmates were given a battery of standardized tests. Mary's teacher was surprised to find that Mary was only of average ability and achievement according to the test results.

Peter, who is also ten years old and in the same class as Mary, is quite a different person. Peter has done poorly in school, barely passing each year. His appearance and written work are very sloppy. When his teacher asks him to help with projects he is quite reluctant and sullen in responding. Peter's teacher was also surprised at Peter's test scores. The standardized tests revealed that Peter was of superior ability and above average in achievement.

Mary and Peter present us with the classical cases of possible teacher bias. Mary is a "model" child and the teacher likes her. Peter is sullen and difficult to teach; furthermore, he is untidy in appearance and work. Is it possible that the teacher's personal feelings have entered into the evaluation of their classroom work?

Mary and Peter's teacher, being human, cannot help being subjective in the grading of her students. The standardized test assists her by presenting data free of subjectivity. Mary and Peter may now be viewed from another frame of reference. The teacher can weigh her subjective feelings with the objective evidence and make appropriate teaching decisions.

It should be noted in our example that no definitive suggestions were made as to the new course of action open to Mary and Peter's teacher. It is still up to her to make the final educational decisions. No claim is made or intended for the infallibility of the standardized test over teacher evaluation. The standardized test is only an educational tool to be used along with other educational techniques. It provides another aid in helping the teacher and student make sound educational decisions.

Let us return for a moment to our example of cooking. In our discussion of recipes and their scientific standardization, we must not lose sight of two factors. One is that the application of experimental procedures is as new in cooking as it is in educational and psychological measurement. Old recipes that our grandmothers used were as subjective as oral examinations in school. For example, if you read old cookbooks you might find this direction in a recipe: "Add enough flour to make a stiff dough." How much skill in cooking did our grandmothers need to interpret "enough" and "stiff dough"? This is not to state that our grandmothers could not bake or that their results were not as good as or better than those of our present cooks. The basic point is that grandmother had to interpret recipes intuitively or subjectively, whereas present-day cooks may follow exact directions of procedure and measurement of ingredients.

Many of grandmother's teachers were able to match the quality and reliability of many of our present standardized tests. But, as in cooking, one doubts that they were able to produce their results consistently without subjective error.

The second factor to be noted is that, of course, a standardized test is not as reliable as a recipe produced in one of our modern experimental kitchens. The human variables involved make this impossible. However, standardized tests generally appraise human behavior and capacity in a more accurate manner than subjective devices, such as a teacher's evaluation.

In essence, then, the standardized test is a scientific instrument that has been exposed to rigorous experimental controls. Its main features are uniformity of administration and scoring. It consists of questions that are factual in the sense that there is an agreed upon correct answer. Each test is subjected to careful investigation by a preliminary administration, and questions that have been found to be poor are eliminated. The actual construction and criteria that must be met in producing a standardized test will be discussed in ensuing chapters.

The reader should remember that standardized tests *are not free of error*. They are not substitutes for teacher evaluation. The teacher's own tests, as well as ratings on class projects and daily classroom performances, are as important as they ever were. Nevertheless, they add to the educational arsenal of teaching devices and enhance teacher effectiveness.

Why Do Schools Use Standardized Tests?

The reader has now been exposed to the differences between teacher-made and standardized tests. A general overview of the reasons for testing has been presented. Let us now explore some of the specific reasons for using standardized tests in the school.

Grouping

The school may use the information provided by standardized tests to group pupils within a particular classroom or to form classroom groups. Thus tests can help the teacher handle individual differences in students by indicating which children have the same or similar level of skill in a particular subject. Students in education and psychology are constantly exposed to the concept of individual differences. The arrangement of students within the classroom or the assignment of students to certain classroom groups according to ability and skill is in line with our awareness of individual differences.

In the classroom the teacher observes and experiences individual differences among her students. Teachers are often frustrated by their inability to give proper instruction to the bright child and the slow student at the same time. If the teacher is able to use an objective instrument, such as an intelligence test, along with subjective criteria, he or she can group children within a class according to their individual ability and teach accordingly.

If a school's philosophy is in agreement with homogeneous grouping of classes, then standardized tests can help in arranging classroom groups. For example, the knowledge gained from a mathematics aptitude test may assist the junior or senior high school staff in placing some students in algebra and others in general mathematics.

Let us, for illustrative purposes, look at two students, Robert and Mike, who are to begin ninth grade next fall. Robert and Mike have taken a battery of standardized tests that will be used along with other data in their classroom assignment at Glen High School. Glen High School groups its pupils into three categories—slow, average, and advanced—for instruction in English, foreign languages, mathematics, and science. Robert's tests revealed high general ability, high achievement in English, high aptitude for foreign languages, but only average achievement and ability in science and mathematics. Mike's scores showed average general ability, poor English achievement with little chance of success in foreign languages, and poor skills and ability in mathematics and science.

Robert is advised to enroll in the "advanced" foreign language class (choice of specific language is his own decision), the "advanced" English class, the "average" algebra class, and the "average" science class.

Mike is advised to wait until the tenth grade before beginning his language studies. The school also advises the "slow" English class along with general mathematics and the "slow" science course.

The school's recommendations for classroom placement are based on a variety of factors; these include school record, teacher recommendations, and results of standardized testing. Tests add the objective dimension to the important decision of where to place pupils.

The reader should note two important facts. (1) Children should *never* be assigned to classroom groups or within a class solely on the basis of tests. The test adds an objective dimension to intelligent planning. It should *not* be used in lieu of teacher opinion, but only as another measure. The combination of teacher opinion and standardized test results gives us the best basis for intelligent decisions. Either one used alone decreases the probability of sound educational planning. (2) It should also be stated that, even if the class has been grouped according to ability, there will still be a wide range of talent within the class. For example, students placed in the "average" algebra class will probably present abilities and achievements ranging from barely average to very high average. The barely average pupil will probably have difficulty in mastering the material, whereas the very high average student may find some of it very boring. Yet both are in the average group. To think that with grouping we have completely eliminated the problem of varying abilities is to misunderstand the process. Grouping does cut down the spread of talent; it does not, however, eliminate it.

Special Study and Remedial Instruction

It is, many times, very difficult for a teacher to distinguish between general low intellectual ability and a specialized problem in a particular skill such as reading. If a teacher finds that a student is doing poorly in mathematics, he or she may think the student is not capable of the work. If, however, there is objective evidence that the child is capable, then the teacher may concentrate on the subject matter and the specific difficulty within it. If, on the other hand, evidence reveals limited ability, instruction may proceed according to the child's ability and the teacher may not expect as much as from a more gifted youngster. If the teacher suspects a reading deficiency, a reading test may be utilized to ascertain the degree of deficiency. Materials and instruction may then be provided at the child's reading level. The utilization of tests that measure both achievement and ability assists in selecting from within the classroom those students who have a remediable deficit.

Evaluating Capability and Accomplishment

Some students who seem to lack intellectual ability as indicated by their poor grades may actually be of superior intelligence but, because of certain family problems and/or emotional conflicts, may not be achieving up to their capacities. Tests can assist in providing an objective measure of capability without being indebted to classroom achievement or subjective appraisal.

Some examples of the use of tests in evaluating discrepancies between potential and achievement are found in every school system. As a school psychologist in the public schools, one of the authors had occasion many times to work with pupils who had been "discovered" through the use of standardized tests. Donald S. was one such youngster. Donald S. was a fifteen-year-old ninth-grade boy who was failing English and algebra and barely passing in his other subjects. The teachers and guidance counselor suggested placing Donald in the slow-learner's English class and substituting general mathematics for algebra.

Upon reviewing Donald's test record it was found that Donald was in the top 1 per cent of his age group in intelligence. That is, Donald's intelligence test scores revealed he had more ability than 99 per cent of children his age as measured by the test.

Tests, in this case, provided another measure of Donald's ability. Armed with the objective evaluations of Donald, the school staff was able to institute appropriate measures. This author worked with Donald and his teachers for over a year. In the counseling sessions, certain family problems were revealed and seemed to be the cause of Donald's underachievement. Progress with Donald was slow, but by his senior year he was in advanced classes. The last the author heard from Donald he was a sophomore in college and doing well. If standardized tests had not been used at Donald's school, it is doubtful that Donald's problems would have been uncovered. He would have been placed in a slow-learner's group, with the probability of college quite remote. More importantly, Donald may have never realized his own potential.

Academic Reality

Tests can assist the counselor or teacher in helping to present to the student a realistic picture of his strengths and weaknesses. Mary wants to be a physician. Mary's grades are average. Her test scores indicate weakness in science and mathematics. Her general school ability, as measured by standardized tests, is slightly below average. Is it realistic for Mary to pursue a career in medicine? Clerical speed and accuracy tests show that Mary is talented in office skills. Should Mary pursue a career in office work? Charles is an eighth-grade boy who is deciding which courses to take in ninth grade. He wants to take algebra, German, and biology. His guidance counselor notes that his general school ability as measured by standardized tests is in the superior range. Algebra and language aptitude and science achievement tests reveal excellent potential. Charles' school grades, however, are only average. The counselor may feel that Charles has the ability but has not yet mastered study habits; therefore, he may advise waiting until the tenth grade to take biology. In any case, standardized tests have helped provide information with which sound and realistic decisions may be made.

Educational and Vocational Goals

"Shall I go to college?" "Should I be a secretary?" "Should I go into a printing trade or auto mechanics?" These are only a few of the questions asked by youngsters. Standardized aptitude and interest tests provide meaningful information to help answer these questions.

The boy or girl who is not sure whether to go to college can be greatly assisted by a scholastic aptitude test.[2] The College Board Examination (SAT) is an example of a scholastic aptitude test. This test, as well as the American College Testing Program (ACT), assists students in deciding whether to go to college and in the choice of the college most appropriate to their abilities

[2] A test designed to measure a person's potential ability to succeed in school.

and needs. At the same time, the college may itself select students who will profit most from the kind of education it provides.

Even with the best methods and skills in classroom evaluation, a limited and often distorted view of a student's ability and achievement results when the class standing and comparison are restricted to one school. Schools vary throughout the United States in their standards and range of student abilities. It is difficult to determine how a student stands in any subject or ability unless one knows the group to which he is being compared.

It is important to remember that Joan may be at the top of her class at Park High School, but if she were to attend Horace High School she might be only an average student. A standardized scholastic aptitude test enables the student and college to view academic ability nationally rather than at the local level only.

In the area of work, standardized aptitude and interest tests help students select vocations that are in line with their abilities and interests. James has decided not to go to college. He feels his abilities and interests lie in a mechanical occupation. His aptitude tests show good eye-hand coordination and finger dexterity. His scholastic aptitude test scores are about average. The interest inventory reveals interest in mechanics and science. His interests and plans correspond to the objective test data. James is, therefore, probably pursuing appropriate goals.

Transfer Students

Many schools, of course, may assign transfer students on the basis of previous school achievement, grade, and age. This is, however, a difficult procedure in some instances. Schools differ, as has been previously mentioned, and a child of ten in fifth grade at X school should not necessarily be placed in fifth grade at Y school. Standardized tests may aid the school in placing the new student in the grade and group appropriate to his or her needs and level of achievement. It also should be stated that some schools are remiss in keeping sound records and/or forwarding them in time for placement. Thus a school may find it necessary to make an evaluation of a new student for placement with little or no record of his or her former achievement.

Discovering Educationally and
Socially Maladjusted Children

In every school there are some students who present severe problems of educational or social adjustment. These include the withdrawn, the unhappy, the mentally retarded, and others who are not adjusting to the pattern of the school. The standardized test renders assistance to teachers and counselors in their attempts to understand and help these children. The following case is only one among many different possible uses of tests in this area.

Albert is a seven-year-old boy in the second grade. His teachers report that he is an isolate without any school friends. During recess he is usually found sitting alone on a swing or on the school steps. His academic progress is poor. Albert never creates any classroom problems. He usually sits in the back of the room with a stoical expression on his face. No matter what the teacher does, Albert reveals little emotion. Albert's teacher is not sure she will be able to promote him to third grade. Is Albert mentally ill? Is he "just passing through a stage"? Is he mentally retarded? Or is he an eccentric individualist?

The school psychologist is asked to evaluate Albert and make appropriate recommendations. A good portion of the school psychologist's evaluation will rest on the basis of special personality and intelligence testing. The test results will produce answers to the school's questions about Albert. The school may then institute appropriate actions which will help Albert realize his maximum potential for academic and personal actualization.

Research Uses

"The individual child is our primary concern." This statement has been voiced by almost all American educators no matter what their particular philosophical orientation. This concern is reflected in measurement devices and goals. Our discussion thus far has been directed to this objective, that is, the direct measurement of factors that will help the school individualize instruction and provide educational guidance for each individual pupil.

The use of measurement instruments to assess the educational environment for future curricular changes does not immediately affect individual students. Research into all areas of the curriculum is designed to understand and develop new approaches to serve each individual student in a more effective manner. Often these investigations have little immediate significance but can serve as a piece or pieces of the educational puzzle that need to be fitted together in order to serve our students better. Let us briefly review some examples of educational research that utilize standardized testing.

McKee and Brzeinski (1966) undertook a six-year longitudinal study in which they found that with a well-designed program children could learn to read at the age of five in kindergarten. They also discovered that by the time they were in the fifth grade the children who were exposed to the same program in reading in the first grade surpassed those who were given an early exposure in kindergarten but placed in regular classes in first grade. The children who began reading in kindergarten and continued in this type of program until fifth grade revealed the greatest achievement in reading, vocabulary, language, and social studies. Trends in higher achievement in arithmetic and science were also noted, although the consistency was not as great. No significant effects on spelling were evident.

The implications from this study for educational development and change are self-evident. Standardized testing was of paramount importance in that it produced objective criteria with which to ascertain achievement differences in groups. Instruments such as reading readiness tests, scholastic aptitude tests, and special achievement tests in reading, vocabulary, social studies, and other areas of instruction provided an objective appraisal of student ability and progress.

Vincent, Bright, Dickason, and Bussey (1976) used the Metropolitan Reading Test and the California Achievement Test to investigate the influence of a reading readiness program for preschoolers on their later academic achievement. The program was designed at the Western Institute for Science and Technology. The subjects were disadvantaged children, and the study extended over a three-year period. The hypothesis was that children participating in the preschool readiness groups would show greater reading readiness in the first grade than would those not participating. Results supported this hypothesis. Two out of three of the experimental groups did significantly better in first-grade reading than did the subjects not participating in the readiness experiences. Success generalized to other subject areas in many cases.

Smith and Hansen (1976) used the reading subtest of the Sequential Tests of Educational Progress (Series II, Form 4A) to study the effects of student-selected and teacher-selected writing assignments that dealt with a short story as the reading selection. Subjects consisted of 464 fourth graders. Results showed that good readers, as measured by the reading test, enjoyed the task more than poor readers. The good readers also preferred reading the story to writing about it (whether self- or teacher assigned). Girls preferred to have the task assigned by the teacher, whereas boys preferred choosing their own, indicating that girls may be less self-reliant and more dependent than boys.

Another research area of indirect immediacy for contemporary pupils but of direct importance for future students is the investigation of testing in professional education. Many of the graduate students of today will be the teachers and professors of tomorrow. Obviously, selection is important if we are to present future generations with the best possible educational instruction. McGuire (1968) reviewed the literature in this area covering aptitude, achievement, attitude, interest, and personality tests, as well as research into new types of tests and follow-up studies. His conclusion is a challenge to future investigators: "As of this date it appears that at the level of professional education much effort has gone into the development and fragmented study of predictors of success without comparable attention either to the construction and validation of reliable criterion measures or to the investigation of environmental influences on success. The challenge is clear!" (p. 58).

The utilization of standardized tests in the area of school curricula should proceed with the utmost caution. In evaluating curriculum and/or curricular experiments, the school should keep in mind the objectives of the school and that of the tests. For example, if a program in modern mathematics is instituted, a test of modern mathematics should be used to evaluate progress —not a test used to measure competence in traditional mathematics.

If tests are used with intelligent application to educational objectives, they can serve as valuable guide posts in measuring educational outcomes. It should also be noted that in any curriculum, modern or traditional, there are common basic skills that are necessary.

Some other areas of research that utilize standardized testing are evaluation of school children in terms of psychological and educational development and growth; the psychological growth and educational development of retarded and gifted youngsters; and, of course, continual evaluation and testing of the instruments used to assess the skills, abilities, and other topics presented in this chapter.

In essence, then, standardized testing is a valuable tool in research endeavors that attempt to provide answers to educational questions. Testing, by its very nature, is wedded to research and an ongoing appraisal of what is and what may be.

Areas Where Standardized Tests Should Not Be Used

The reader should be aware that the "red light" areas of testing that will be discussed are not agreed upon by all authorities. It is safe to state, however, that most would at least consider them "yellow light" spheres which are to be cautiously considered.

Assigning Grades

Teachers should never use standardized test results as evaluative consideration in assigning grades. Standardized test content is general and not specifically related to the local school curriculum.

Evaluating the School

It is true that standardized tests may help in assessing schools and classes in terms of aptitude and background characteristics, for they may function as a beacon to focus on strengths and weaknesses of specific schools and classes. This is a dangerous procedure, however, for there is a strong tendency of central administrations to use the results in a judgmental or punitive manner. This may promote the "teaching for tests" syndrome, which is undesirable. It is undesirable because the local school system loses its autonomy in developing its own educational objectives. The development of curricula is then turned over to testing people. Teaching for tests also tends to be superficial, emphasizing "correct answers" rather than understandings.

As previously stated, schools in particular geographic areas with particular students have particular needs and need to develop their own particular curricula. National standards cannot and should not be educational yardsticks for all school systems. This is not to say that there are not underlying common denominators in the basic skills, or that national standards are meaningless. They do provide us with a common frame of reference that is necessary in guiding individual students in educational and vocational goals, particularly when they will be competing with students from a broad geographical area. They do, however, lose much of their significance when we use them to judge the local school rather than to aid in individual guidance.

To illustrate, let us look at two very different schools. School A is situated in an urban setting with the majority of students from a disadvantaged background. The educational objectives of this school are to enrich the impoverished lives of its students and to teach basic methods of living in a twentieth-century urban complex. In addition, this school teaches the classical academic subjects and skills. To assess its educational worth by the use of a nationally standardized achievement test is to measure only one aspect of its total program. Certainly the standardized test is applicable as individual guidance for the students of School A. For example, those students who desire to go on to college must know their chances of success based on national standards rather than on the local norms, where competition may not be as difficult.

Let us now turn our attention to School B, which is the exact opposite of School A. It is situated in an upper-middle-class suburban community. The majority of the students are above average in intelligence and achievement. To judge the worth of the whole school on the basis of nationally standardized tests would be to inflate unrealistically the school's accomplishments. One would expect School B to be above the national standards, given its setting and student body. This school must develop its own internal methods of judging its particular curriculum. Of course, it must be stated that for individual guidance the national test helps the individual student gain a realistic picture of how he compares to other students throughout the country. He may be only average at School B, but above average on a national scale. This would have special meaning in planning educational and vocational objectives. It would not, however, give the central administration meaningful data to assess its whole school system or curriculum.

Teacher Evaluation

School administrators should never use the results of standardized tests to evaluate the competence of individual teachers. This procedure is wrong on several counts. First, it does not take into account the fact that class achievement is, in part, the result of previous educational history. It is not educationally valid or fair to judge a teacher who has taught a class for a semester or a year as solely responsible for the students' academic performance. Second, innate intelligence and family cultural experiences contribute greatly to educational achievement. Third, as has been mentioned previously, an achievement test measures only a small portion of the objectives of most schools. Fourth, it is likely to cause teachers to teach for tests rather than pursue the local educational and curriculum goals. Teachers, being human, will tend to neglect areas of the curriculum that are not conducive to measurement—such areas as citizenship, discussion, and speaking ability. Skills and learning that are easily testable and found in many standardized achievement tests often become the focal point of teaching.

Evaluating teachers on the basis of test results not only blunts the horizons of teaching effectiveness but also demoralizes teachers. Teachers react to evaluative pressure in many ways. Some teach for the tests by securing old tests and concentrating on areas that are covered. Others "prepare" their students by drilling them on exact questions or similar questions that are to be presented. Still others are so pressured that they give the exact questions and answers that are to be asked and require students to memorize them. Though these procedures cannot be condoned, they are certainly understandable when the administration places the burden of teacher evaluation on class test scores.

Finally, it should be mentioned that not only is this kind of evaluation wrong for teachers and their students, but it also leads to poor testing practice. The value of the test is lessened, if not destroyed, by excessive evaluative emphasis. The basic purpose of testing is to render educational assistance to the student, the teacher, and the school.

In summary, it can be stated that tests are useful educational instruments in helping children develop and realize their own individual potential. Standardized tests should be used as objective evidence to supplement the teacher's subjective judgments. They are only one of many educational tools in helping children. They are not substitutes for teacher evaluation. The teacher's own tests, ratings on class projects, and a child's daily classroom performance are as important as they ever were. Standardized tests, used properly, can be of immense assistance to the teacher and to his pupils.

Contemporary Issues and Problems

chapter 2

Major Criticisms

The critics of testing have voiced their positions loud and long. Psychologists, educators, sociologists, and scholars from other disciplines, as well as lay people, have been critical of testing. Many of the criticisms have been characterized by half-truths, personal bias, and misunderstanding of testing principles and objectives. The criticisms fall roughly into three categories—those that deal with the effect of testing on the individual, the effect of testing on institutions, and the effect of testing on society in general. Let us look at some of these criticisms and see what the charges are.

Testing and the Individual

There are several charges against testing that deal with the effect of testing on the individual. The first of these charges that we shall consider is that tests damage an individual's self-esteem.

DAMAGED SELF-ESTEEM

The critics of testing feel that testing may predetermine an individual's social status and harm that person's self-image. They state that testing places people in intellectual slots. In addition, they think it may injure educational motivation. The child, for example, may feel, "I am not very smart. Why should I try harder? What's the use?"

The critics who are concerned with damage to a person's self-esteem through testing usually are referring to intelligence tests. These instruments are popularly called IQ tests.

The student of testing should be aware of the fact that there *is no device or measurement instrument, at this time, that can measure with absolute certainty permanent general ability to learn.* Today's intelligence tests measure many aspects of human behavior, including the influence of an individual's cultural background, school achievement, and motivation to learn and do one's best while taking a test. To state that the results of an intelligence test are a measure of innate intelligence is to do a disservice to the individual and to measurement in general. Later in this chapter a full discussion of what IQ is and what it is not will be presented. The important point to remember, for now, is that *psychologists do not know whether intelligence tests do, or do not, measure innate intelligence or capacity to learn, but they do know that an individual's past experiences are reflected in test scores.*

If the results of intelligence tests are not thought of as permanent or immutable, then the criticism that they assign individuals to fixed intellectual or social slots is not appropriate. What is relevant is the use and interpretation of the results. If intelligence tests are used to stamp children into intellectual and social molds, then it is not the fault of the test but of the user. Psychologists, educators, and test publishers continually alert and warn test users against the erroneous assumption of test infallibility. On the other hand, it is true that some people use tests as if they were divinely inspired and free from human error. The critic, bearing this in mind, may concede the point that competent psychologists or counselors may effectively use tests; however, he will then state that most test users are not psychologists, counselors, or individuals trained to understand the limitations of tests. Therefore, such a critic will state, because most people do not know how to interpret tests properly, no one, or at the very most only psychologists, should use them. This critic's position, simply stated, is that the improper use of tests does more harm than good and therefore all intelligence tests should be abandoned.

The answer to this last criticism is obvious and can be answered by quoting an old folk saying, "Don't throw out the baby with the bath water." In essence, the criticism of damage to self-esteem and social cataloguing is not a basic criticism of the test per se but of the utilization and interpretation of tests. What is needed, therefore, is more education in the proper methods of test administration and interpretation. The improper interpretation of test results may harm an individual's self-esteem. It is also true that most things improperly used may be harmful to an individual. For example, milk is an excellent food and recommended as an essential part of children's diets. Yet we know that some children and adults may have severe gastrointestinal problems as a result of drinking it. No one seriously proposes banning milk because some people cannot digest it.

The student of measurement should understand the possibility of harm to a child because of testing and should be aware that testing is only one phase of the educational process and that if it is used properly it may be of great value to most children.

LIMITED EVALUATION

The criticism of limited evaluation of tests recognizes that a human being is a complex organism consisting of many different aspects including talent, personality, and motivation. The charge is that the use of one type of test, usually the kind dealing with verbal and quantitative skills, taps only a small portion of the abilities of most individuals. The implication is that this is the only measure used by schools and colleges in sorting students and therefore much talent is lost to the society.

Modern educators are quite aware of the fact that many students have talents that are neither verbal nor quantitative, and contemporary education thus envisions more than "reading and 'rithmetic."

The answer to this test criticism again lies in the intelligent utilization of tests. A good evaluative program uses many measures in the evaluation of an individual. In the area of college admissions, for example, the college that has an admission or scholarship award policy based only on verbal and quantitative test scores is using testing improperly. The publishers of these tests have stated repeatedly that scores on these tests should not represent the sole consideration for admission or scholarship awards.

The proper procedure is the utilization of many different kinds of measures. In a complete evaluation of an applicant, college admission officers would want to know a candidate's past test scores in educational areas other than the linguistic and mathematical. They would want to know about the candidate's school record in terms of grades, courses, extracurricular activities, and teacher ratings before making their final decision. In this way the verbal-quantitative test is only one measure among many criteria in the selection process. This principle applies, of course, at all levels of educational evaluation.

ABRIDGMENT OF HUMAN CHOICE

The third criticism of tests dealing with the effect on the individual is of a philosophical nature, and reflects our general fear that machines may rule man. *Tests reduce people to numbers*, state the critics of testing. They go on to warn that the use of tests may reduce human choice and action. This is a serious charge. Human freedom of choice is essential to our form of government and underlies most, if not all, of our educational philosphies. Any procedure or instrument that would take away this precious right is a danger to our society. Do tests constitute such a danger? Are they in fact a menace to human freedom of choice?

Let us look at the situation as objectively as possible. If we do this we must admit that tests could pose such a menace if used improperly. Of course, most things, if used improperly, could endanger freedom. The United States government, for example, has data on each of us that could be used by the wrong people in a punitive and dictatorial manner. Yet these data are necessary to run the government and provide services to the whole society. There is no doubt that these data could provide the means to abridge freedom, as could some offices of government. Tests are no different. Used improperly, without proper respect for the individual and knowledge of the inherent limitations of tests, grievous wrongs, such as the limitation of freedom of choice, could occur.

To some, the use of mental tests implies that human behavior is as measurable as the dimensions of a table top. Given this frame of reference, the task of the test author would be relatively simple. Tests could be developed around finite goals, and the factors that contribute to these objectives could be isolated and then measured. When factor X was mixed with factor Y, the outcome would always be XY. Human behavior could be predicted, measured, and controlled with the same certainty and facility that one finds inherent in chemical solutions and reactions.

If the preceding were true, that is, if human behavior were as measurable as a table top, then the danger of eliminating human choice would be great indeed. These things are, of course, not true. Our testing instruments are far from perfect. Psychologists cannot isolate all the variables that contribute and give direction to human actions.

Under these circumstances the problem of testers playing God or of impersonal evaluation becomes quite remote. Of course, it must be recognized that the improper education of test users could contribute to the improper use of measurement instruments. If the tester does not know the limitations of his instrument and is afflicted with megalomania, he may indeed act out the role of a deity and assign youngsters to given educational slots on the basis of test results. Again, the answer to this criticism is the proper education of the test user and consumer.

Psychologists and educators are painfully aware of the limitations of tests. They know and appreciate the fact that a great proportion of decision making must be made in the maze of uncertainties, desired outcomes, and methods of achieving these outcomes. They also know that mistakes will be made.

Testing and Institutions

"The professional testers are controlling educational curricula and the destinies of our children," state the critics. This criticism of testing has created an almost paranoid quality and anxiety to the critical vendettas aimed at testing. Is there any reality to the charge? The answer is not easy. The writers have observed a subtle form of undue test influence in duties as a counselor and psychologist in the public schools. Teachers have been seen teaching for tests and principals bragging about their school's test record, in a state where the Department of Education requires certain prescribed tests from kindergarten to twelfth grade. Is it true, therefore, that testing people control educational goals and the destinies of individuals?

Today, the answer is no, but if proper measures, such as the education of those who use these instruments, are not instituted, the answer in the future may be yes. American education at the present time is too decentralized and loosely organized to control the lives of its students. In some European countries, of course, this is not true, and testing (usually of the subjective essay type) is of paramount importance in the lives and destinies of students.

In the United States, tests usually follow rather than lead in curricular change. Though tests may affect a phase of a student's educational experience, it can be stated with some certainty that they do not determine his destiny.

Let us explore the basic problem of control and what it means in measurement terms. The teacher and/or principal who provides an atmosphere or situation of competitiveness on tests is laying the groundwork for future control. For example, Mr. Jones, principal of Northern High School, gives his teachers a testing pep talk:

Mr. Jones: Ladies and gentlemen, last year Northern's test scores in mathematics and social studies were, on the average, the lowest in the county. We must be doing something wrong in these fields. Our kids are as smart as those in the other schools and I know our faculty takes a back seat to none.

Well, I think I've got the answer to help our kids make a better showing. I've asked our director of guidance to secure some old mathematics and social studies tests which are similar to the ones we give our kids in the spring. I want you to study them and gear your teaching accordingly. I know the other schools must be doing the same thing and I feel sure if we do we may even beat them. OK, let's give it our best and show the other schools what kind of teachers and students Northern has.

The preceding illustration is a realistic possibility, although most principals would probably be more subtle in their exhortations. The teachers of Northern are now caught up in the teaching-for-the-test syndrome. If they do not gear their teaching for the prescribed tests and their students do poorly, they open themselves to the possible loss of their position; at the very minimum, they may incur the wrath of the administration.

This kind of situation does a major disservice to measurement, education, and local control over curriculum. An accurate picture of individual and group performance is compromised by concentrating on the format and content of these tests. A true picture of the educational level of the students is at best tentative. Educational goals and objectives are reduced to recognition, memorization, and ability to respond to a test rather than true learning, which incorporates not only memorization of data but also integration of these data into the student's thinking and behavior.

Of even more serious concern is the relinquishing of local and regional curriculum control. The task of devising the curriculum is handed over to a national testing center. This center, no matter how sincere and dedicated, is in no position to formulate educational objectives for all schools throughout the United States. Not only do individuals differ, but so do regions and schools. The curriculum at an upper-middle-class suburban school may not be appropriate for an urban school in a disadvantaged area.

In addition to individual differences our educational system has traditionally been based on local control by the citizens of the school district. Schools in a democracy are intended to reflect the needs and desires of the community. If the school bases its standards on the content of national tests, this tradition is seriously compromised.

Educators and psychologists are very much aware of the fallacy of using tests to measure the worth of a school. They know that conditions and objectives differ from school to school. They are also painfully aware of the limitations and fallibility of standardized tests. No responsible educator or psychologist advocates the use of tests alone to judge teachers or schools. The problem again lies not with testing, but with the improper use of tests.

In essence, then, educational personnel using tests must be aware of the limitations of measurement and proceed with the utmost caution in deriving inferences from test scores. This does not mean, of course, that national tests are of no value. Certainly, there are basic skills and data that students at given grade levels should know no matter where they reside. If test scores are evaluated within the educational objectives of the school and are interpreted in the light of the local school setting, they will add to the total evaluation. *The important point to remember is that tests are only one method of evaluation and must be considered in the light of the student population and the school curriculum.*

Thus we may state that the criticism of test control of education and people is generally not true today. In some isolated cases, however, it is true that uninformed teachers and principals allow tests to exert an undue influence within their schools. The solution to this situation, as in others, is more measurement education for test consumers. At the same time, all of us—psychologists, teachers, principals, and test publishers—must maintain a constant vigil against the encroachment of tests dictating educational policy.

Testing and Society

Another area of criticism attacks the entire testing movement and often has as its goal the abandonment of *all* testing. Let us examine these general charges in detail.

TESTING AND MINORITIES

The critics state that testing is geared to middle-class values and is, therefore, unfair to children of less fortunate environments. They cite the lack of enriching developmental experiences of disadvantaged children compared with their more fortunate middle- and upper-class peers. To these critics, our present tests are culturally biased. The tests, according to them, not only reflect middle-class concepts but also use middle-class language and assume all students have been exposed to middle-class experiences.

The heat engendered in this critical area was increased by the civil rights movement. The 1960s and 1970s saw a proliferation of psychological studies dealing with the issue of *cultural bias* and fairness to minorities. In recent years such professional organizations as the American Psychological Association (Cleary, Humphreys, Kendrick & Wesman, 1975) have appointed groups to investigate and clarify the fairness and unfairness of educational tests with disadvantaged students. Let us hear from some of the experts and professional associations as to their findings and recommendations. Loretan (1966), former Deputy Superintendent of Schools for New York City, was instrumental in eliminating the use of IQ tests in the New York City schools. His basic reason for dropping IQ tests was the problem of cultural bias. He states, "the vocabulary and concepts in most of the group IQ tests are foreign to many children in our large and varied country (and certainly to many children in New York City). We have not been able to extract cultural biases from our tests, and yet we use these tests with children who are culturally different" (p. 6).

Rosenberg (1966), in an address at the 1966 District of Columbia Psychological Association meetings, applauded the New York City school system's decision to eliminate intelligence testing. He stated,

> I feel that there has been some recent heartening news from such areas as New York City, where, as you all know, intelligence testing was essentially thrown out of the school system. This may sound like an extreme measure, but if the abuses in the New York School System were anywhere as bad as the abuses that occur in the Baltimore City School System, then I say, "Better throw out the baby with the bath" and start again, if there is the slightest chance we may produce something better. To continue to damage children by inaccurate decisions based on our inadequate procedures is to contribute to what might well be called the scientific racism of the 1960's.

Rosenberg goes on to state that Drs. Wechsler and Anastasi (both well-known and highly respected psychologists) are correct in their assessment that "intelligence tests are correct, what is wrong is in society." However, he feels that they do not go far enough. He feels that the labeling of "deprived-area children with low IQ's condemns them to a status where they will be offered much less in our school systems." Rosenberg states further, "it seems to me that our assumption must be that in the poverty area the intelligence of children is actually distributed normally as it is at higher socioeconomic levels."

Anastasi (1966b) questions the logic of eliminating items that differentiate groups of people. She asks,

> where shall we stop? We could with equal justification proceed to rule out items showing socioeconomic differences, sex differences, differences among ethnic minority groups and educational differences. Any items in which college graduates excel elementary school graduates could, for example, be discarded on this basis. Nor should we retain items that differentiate among broader groups, such as national cultures, or between preliterate and more advanced cultures. If we do all this, I should like to ask only two questions, in conclusion.

First, what will be left? Second, in terms of any criterion we may wish to predict, what will be the validity of this minute residue? (pp. 456–57)

Anastasi (1976) warns that, "If we rule out all cultural differentials from a test, we may thereby lower its validity as a measure of the behavior domain it was designed to assess. In that case the test would fail to provide the kind of information needed to correct the very conditions that impaired performance" (p. 58).

Fitzgibbon (1972) states that "one could say that we have not been so much culture biased as we have been 'culture blind'" (p. 3). By this he means that white, middle-class test authors violated the "feelings of the test-taker without even knowing it" (p. 2).

Cleary et al. (1975), in their report on educational tests and disadvantaged students for the APA, conclude,

> *Although an intelligence test is a behavioral measure of current intellectual status, it is unjustified to conclude that the score reflects merely middle-class learning experiences. The correlation of .50 between parent and child IQs is too low to support this restrictive view. It is difficult to explain on the basis of privilege how the children of fathers whose IQs are 140, plus or minus one or two points, will have an average IQ of 120 and show a standard deviation around this mean almost as large as the IQs of children in general (87% as large). Tests are indeed culturally bound, but the bind is not as tight as critics imply. (p. 23)*

Rosenberg and others who have voiced their criticism of the cultural bias of tests are correct in one sense. That is that *all* of our present tests *are culturally biased*. If they were not they would have little value in our school system.

The problem that besets this area of debate is twofold: (1) the absence of a common frame of reference in definitions of terms and (2) the inability of the critics to face reality. Rather than do this they cloud the issue with the illusion of how one would like things to be.

Let us look at the first problem, definition of terms. The labeling of group tests of school ability as intelligence tests is a grave error. This gives the impression to many people that what is being measured is innate intelligence, when in fact what is measured is *chance of success in school*. Psychologists have recognized for some time that the term *intelligence test* may be a misnomer. Today we say that intelligence tests are tests of scholastic aptitude. Nothing concerning innate intelligence is stated or implied in this label.

The second major problem is unwillingness of the critic to face reality. Statements such as Rosenberg's that we should assume that the children in poverty areas have the same distribution of intelligence as those in higher socioeconomic levels seems to be an unscientific supposition. These data we have already gathered scientifically. We do not need an assumption based on wishful thinking. The data indicate that the two populations have different distributions of intelligence. The interpretation of these data, however, leaves room for varying opinions.

It could be stated that a disadvantaged environment tends to inhibit the growth of intellectual functioning and this blockage begins from the time of birth. The constitutional theorist may, on the other hand, state with equal fervor that there is a tendency in nature to "breed true to type." That is, people who for one reason or another are unsuccessful tend to choose mates of similar backgrounds, thus perpetuating their own type, whereas those who rise above the poverty syndrome marry people with similar strivings or those that are already in a more privileged environment. Later in this chapter we will deal in detail with the question of the relationship between intelligence and such variables as genetics, environment, and ethnic background.

The writers would not make a definitive statement concerning the distribution of intelligence in a disadvantaged area because of the many factors that impinge on this type of evaluation. It is easy, however, to state quite definitively that there are no data to support Rosenberg's claim of a normal distribution of intelligence; on the contrary, the clinical evidence and "intuition" of many authorities would lead one to the opposite position.

The important point to remember is that it is easy for our subjective predilections to interfere with our objectivity. In the long run, this interference can hurt the very cause and people we want to help.

What is cultural bias in tests? First, the language used is reflective of the culture. Second, the required test tasks are reflective of the skills and objectives of our schools, which in turn *should* be reflective of the skills and objectives of our general society. If they were not they would give few useful data to the school. The school needs to know the chances of a student's success in a school system that is, in fact, oriented to middle-class values. If the schools were oriented to another system, then our tests might not be culturally biased, but they would be inappropriate.

The basic purpose of scholastic aptitude tests is not to obtain a measure of innate intelligence, but to measure a student's potential for academic achievement in our school system. Thus the answer to the charge of cultural bias is, "Yes, tests are culturally biased, but how valuable would they be if they were not?"

Wesman (1972) presents the case quite well when he states,

> You don't cure malnutrition by throwing out the scale that identifies babies who are underweight. You don't win a war killing the messenger who brings news of defeat in a skirmish. If tests reveal that the disadvantaged have been deprived of opportunities to learn fundamental concepts, the remedy is to provide those opportunities—not do away with the source of information.
>
> To make tests the scapegoat for the ills of the disadvantaged is not only unfair to test publishers and authors, it is unfair to a society that needs to know and to grow. (p. 401)

The reader should not infer from the preceding that our present tests cannot be improved, nor should he infer that the writers are unaware of, or unsympathetic to, the problems of disadvantaged children. Our present tests need a great deal of improvement, but this improvement lies in better test construction and use rather than in test elimination. Cultural handicaps will not be removed by changing our tests; only changing the conditions within our society that promote these deprivations will do that.

TOO MUCH TESTING

Some critics complain that children are being "tested to death." In answering this charge, it is very difficult to define how much is too much; it should be remembered that tests are not always correct in their assessment of ability. The more information we have on a student, the better we are able to assist him and the less is the chance of error. The important question is what information is needed to help children develop themselves to their fullest potential.

Let us look at two four-year high schools in two different settings and review their standardized testing programs. The outline on p. 32 presents these schools and their testing programs. Hess is a suburban high school located in an upper-middle-class area, whereas Washington is a city high school situated in an underprivileged setting.

(Before reading further, read and review the two testing programs cited with the following questions in mind:

1. Is there too much testing at Hess, at Washington, or at both?
2. If there is too much testing, what tests would you eliminate and why?

If you feel that your knowledge is insufficient to enable you to judge, remember that most critics of testing are no more prepared than you, and a great many do not have as good a background as yours. Discuss your feelings and thoughts with your classmates and see what they have to say. After you have done this the following discussion of the issues and problems of "testing too much" should be more meaningful.)

Let us start our discussion and analysis of Hess and Washington schools with one of the basic premises of measurement: What information is needed? Hess administers seventeen tests and test batteries over a period of four years, whereas Washington administers twenty tests and test batteries over the same period. Is either of them, or are both, testing too much? It is obviously impossible to add the number of tests and declare the school with the most the winner of the "too many tests" trophy. The appropriate and most valid method of appraising a school's testing program is to start with the school and its educational goals and objectives. Note that the present analysis will deal only with the question of the quantity and necessity of tests, not with the "ideal" program. For a more complete and detailed discussion of testing programs, see Chapter 18. The answer to our question is that Hess High School is testing too much. There is no need to give a school ability test every year. This is especially true in an advantaged area. A school ability test given in ninth and eleventh grades would be more than enough. The majority of children at Hess will be going to college and will take one of the national college aptitude tests, another form of a school ability test in the eleventh and twelfth grades. Clearly, Hess is in error in administering so many school ability tests.

There is also no need to administer achievement tests every year, especially in the Hess environment. The teachers and administration may want some general assessment of how their students compare nationally. This is valid and could be accomplished by testing twice, either in the ninth and eleventh grades or in the tenth and twelfth grades. Local tests constructed by the faculty would more adequately reflect the progress of the Hess students.

The inclusion of art and music aptitude tests in the general testing program is generally not warranted in any school's standardized testing program. Again, this is especially true at Hess. High school students from middle-class homes usually do not need these tests. They generally know their artistic interests and propensities by the time they are in the tenth grade. If a student needs or wants objective verification, then these tests may be administered individually.

The use of personality tests in a general testing program is open to serious question. They can have an important function but should be used only when individual cases indicate they are needed. The exception, of course, is for research purposes.

A general review of the Hess testing program reveals that there is too much duplication and that some of the tests that are being given throughout the school could be given on an individual basis.

Now let us look at Washington. Although one might challenge the value of one or two of the tests in Washington's program, on the whole it would be valid to state that the tests administered are necessary and meaningful. Therefore, Washington does not give too many tests.

In the ninth grade a general estimate of scholastic aptitude is gained by the administration of different types of ability tests. Note that three of the six tests are school-ability-related instruments. The administration of these instruments is especially important in an underprivileged setting. In a different area, three school ability tests in the same year would be too many. At Washington this is not the case. The school ability test helps gauge these students in comparison to other ninth graders throughout the United States. Although most research evidence does not indicate that the culture-fair test is generally a better indicator of ability to learn for disadvantaged groups than the regular school ability test, it may be of help for certain children. Even if it helps only a few children the expenditure of time and money will have been a small price to pay. The general school and vocational aptitude tests are a measure of ability in various vocational tasks, such as clerical skill and mechanical comprehension; in addition, they constitute another, less culturally oriented, measure of school ability.

One might question the administration of reading tests in the ninth, tenth, and eleventh grades; however, in an underprivileged setting, reading skills are seriously impaired and the school must endeavor to bring them up to

Hess High School	Washington High School
Ninth grade: 1. School ability test 2. Interest test 3. General school and vocational aptitude test battery 4. Achievement tests in mathematics, social studies, and English	Ninth grade: 1. School ability test 2. Culture-fair test * 3. Interest test 4. General school and vocational aptitude test battery 5. Achievement tests in mathematics, social studies, and English 6. Reading test
Tenth grade: 1. School ability test English 2. General personality test 3. Achievement tests in mathematics, social studies, and English 4. Music and art aptitude tests	Tenth grade: 1. Vocational aptitude tests in specialized areas such as mechanical aptitude, manual dexterity, and stenographic aptitude 2. Reading test 3. Attitude questionnaire
Eleventh grade: 1. School ability test 2. Achievement tests in mathematics, social studies, and English 3. National college aptitude test 4. General school and vocational aptitude test battery	Eleventh grade: 1. School ability test 2. Culture-fair test 3. General school and vocational aptitude test battery 4. Reading test 5. National college aptitude test 6. Achievement tests in mathematics, social studies, and English
Twelfth grade: 1. School ability test 2. Achievement tests in mathematics, social studies, and English 3. National college aptitude test 4. National scholarship test 5. Advanced interest test	Twelfth grade: 1. General Aptitude Test Battery (produced by Bureau of Employment Security, U.S. Department of Labor) 2. National college aptitude test 3. National scholarship test 4. Attitude questionnaire 5. Advanced interest test

* Culture-fair test is an instrument that attempts to measure experiences that are equally familiar or unfamiliar to *all* groups of people.

at least an average level. The ninth-grade student who cannot read above the fifth-grade level may expect serious trouble. The administration of reading tests each year would be a reflection of the added emphasis Washington gives to reading.

In summary, it can be stated that our most important concern in judging whether a school tests too much is not quantity, but the appropriateness of the tests for a particular school in a particular geographical area with a particular student body and their own particular educational goals and objectives. In the preceding example, we saw that the school that gave the most tests was not testing too much, whereas the school that gave less tests was indeed subjecting its student body to more tests than necessary.

Problem Areas

In addition to the major criticisms previously discussed, there are several issues relating to testing that present problems to many people. Often these problems are compounded by a lack of communication and a misunderstanding of the factors involved.

Intelligence and Intelligence Tests

A major problem area in testing and one that antagonizes certain groups is concerned with intelligence, intelligence testing, and IQ. Many of the problems are created by a lack of understanding of what these terms mean and what they do not mean. Let us examine these concepts and terms more closely.

INTELLIGENCE

It is very difficult to define the word *intelligence*. Many psychologists and educators have defined intelligence as a concept that is synonymous with learning ability. Others have narrowed their definition to a self-evident fact, namely, intelligence is what intelligence tests measure.

The student of measurement should keep in mind that the term *intelligence,* as used in psychology, *has no absolute meaning.* It is frequently defined to meet the needs and orientation of the person defining it. Binet, the pioneer of intelligence tests, described intelligence as a unitary characteristic, that is, the human organism's ability to adapt and critically perceive his environment. Terman (1916), who pioneered Binet's test in the United States, defined intelligence as "an individual's ability to carry on abstract thinking" (p. 42). Wechsler (1960) stated that "intelligence is the aggregate or global capacity of the individual to act purposefully, to think rationally, and to deal effectively with his environment" (p. 7). Cleary et al. (1975), in an APA report on testing, define intelligence as "the entire repertoire of acquired skills, knowledge, learning sets, and generalization tendencies considered intellectual in nature that are available at any one period in time" (p. 19).

It is evident from these different concepts of intelligence that there is no general agreement among theorists concerning the essence of intelligence, and the preceding concepts by no means exhaust the thinking on the subject. The interested reader can find further discussion of intelligence by referring to the works of Spearman (1927), Thorndike (1927), Thurstone and Thurstone (1941), Matarazzo (1972), and Cronbach (1975).

IQ: What It Means and What It Does Not Mean

There is a difference between intelligence as conceptualized by the theorists and the measurement of intelligence. It is evident that the measurement of intelligence is related to the ability of a person to perform or function in a given test setting. Thus, within this frame of reference, the only intelligence we know about is the specific performance of an individual on a specific test. Intelligence as an inherited quality is an abstraction when related to a specific measurement instrument. It can only be surmised from behavioral responses to a test based on what someone considers "intelligence."

The student of measurement, if he understands the tentative basis of the term *intelligence*, will be in a better position to evaluate meaningfully the literature concerning the relationship between intelligence and such variables as heredity, environment, race, and culture.

The most simple definition of IQ is, of course, intelligence quotient. The *Dictionary of Psychology* (Warren, 1934) states that IQ is "the ratio of an individual's intelligence, as determined by some mental measure, to normal or average intelligence for his age" (p. 141).

For some people, IQ has been a magic term that is all-encompassing and definitively accurate. Since the inception of the first IQ test, many teachers and parents have unreservedly labeled children as bright or dull on the basis of their IQ. The danger of this assumption is enormous. Good (1966) states, "The term IQ has been so grossly abused and it is so inappropriate to the shifting values yielded by various tests that we probably should abandon it altogether" (p. 179). As our definition stated, IQ is the ratio of the individual's intelligence as determined by a test. That is, intelligence is defined as that "something" which is measured by a mental test. This definition does not allow for differing types of intelligence, nor are psychologists certain of what they mean by this kind of intelligence. Hebb (1958), a noted psychologist, states that Binet "learned how to measure something without any very clear idea as to what it was he was measuring." Today, more than sixty years later, we measure it a bit more satisfactorily, and now it can be measured with a great variety of techniques, but we are still somewhat uncertain about what "it" is.

In addition to our uncertainty of what intelligence is, there are many variables inherent in the construction and administration of tests that limit further our equating IQ with innate intelligence, that is, errors in test construction, sampling of population, scoring, and physical and psychological conditions of the test setting. Factors such as previous schooling and cultural environment also play their part in the IQ test score.

The IQ (based on the 1973 Stanford-Binet) fixes the mean (average) at 100 with a distribution of sixteen points on either side; that is, the range of average or normal intelligence is roughly defined as falling between 84 and 116. Because this distribution is considered within the normal range, the IQ can be interpreted to indicate a child's relative position in a group. Children, for example, with scores on an IQ test above 116 would be considered above average, whereas children with scores below 84 would be considered below average, with specific numerical classifications defining more precisely their degree of deviation from the average. The IQ, then, is a method of reporting a test score related to other test scores in a given group in the same way, though more precisely, that one grade in a classroom is related to other grades.

The accuracy of the reported IQ is directly related to the worth of the test per se and its purposes and format, as well as to environmental and cultural factors. The group intelligence test that reports a test score in the form of IQ is evaluating, to some degree, different aspects of "intelligence" than an individual intelligence test. The boy, for example, who reads poorly will have this deficit in achievement reflected in his group IQ score. On the other hand, the same child taking an individual intelligence test will not be penalized because little, if any, reading is required. The two IQs may then mean two different things, although they are both expressed in the same symbolic structure.

Neither the individual nor the group intelligence test is completely accurate. The IQ symbol representing the results of these instruments should be viewed in the same light. That is, a reported IQ is only a relative indication of how an individual compares to others taking the same test. IQ must be considered along with other evaluative criteria such as other types of tests, classroom performance, and the observations of the teacher. A more definitive examination of test score interpretations will be presented in subsequent chapters. The important thing to remember at this point is that *intelligence tests are only one measure of ability, and IQ is only a symbol of this ability.*

Heredity Versus Environment

The relative influence of heredity and environment on an individual's behavior has been a constant source of controversy for many years. Views have ranged from those of the constitutionalists, who feel that all a person is and does is determined genetically, to those of the environmentalists, who feel that development is determined solely by a person's experiences. Some people have, of course, taken the middle ground, that an individual is the result of a combination of hereditary and environmental influences. The development of the intelligence test intensified the debate. In the years since the development of individual and group tests of intelligence, enormous amounts of data have been compiled that have made possible comparisons among, for example, different racial, socioeconomic, and cultural groups. Basic to all of these comparisons is the search for clues that would provide the reason for differences among these groups. Are group differences the result of heredity, environment, or a combination of these factors?

In spite of the countless studies over the last forty years, the answer to this question is as difficult and as elusive as it has always been. The debate and investigations continue today, though to some they may seem useless and rather academic. It must be stated, however, that the relative influences of heredity and environment are of fundamental importance to psychologists and educators. It is obvious that if a person's potential for achievement were determined solely by inherited abilities, our educational system would have a different philosophy than it would in an environmentally oriented structure.

HEREDITY

Let us look at the evidence for the genetic position. Psychologists have been interested in the question of the influence of heredity on intelligence since the nineteenth century. Sir Francis Galton published a study of "hereditary genius" in 1869. In this study Galton introduced the concept that intelligence is distributed in a population in the same way as are physical characteristics such as height. We now call this a normal distribution. Galton, through studying families, concluded that the basis for this distribution was genetic.

With the advent of IQ tests in the twentieth century studies have been conducted on the relationship of measured IQ to genetic kinship. These studies have dealt with IQ as measured by our current tests and not necessarily innate intelligence. There is currently no scientific way to measure directly the effect of genes on behavior. Thus the data are primarily correlational [1] and do not permit a direct statement of cause. A large number of studies have been conducted with different tests and different populations. Some investigators of genetic factors in human differences have studied unrelated children from similar socioeconomic backgrounds. Identical twins have been excellent sources for study because of their identical genetic characteristics. Critics have pointed out, however, that twins are exposed to the same environment and, therefore, that environmental factors may be the dominant variable. Consequently, comparisons have been made between identical twins who lived together and those raised separately, as well as between siblings raised together and those reared apart.

Although studies may differ in particulars, the usual method is to obtain IQ measures on persons of varying degrees of familial relationship and to compute the correlation. The range of situations representing a control of

---

[1] Correlation in measurement means the degree of relationship of two variables. A correlation coefficient (r) has as its possible limits $+1.00$ and -1.00; for example, a coefficient of $+0.90$ is very high, whereas a $+0.20$ coefficient is very low. For a more detailed explanation and discussion of correlation see Chapter 3.

hereditary and environmental factors are the following: identical twins reared together, identical twins reared apart, fraternal twins reared together, fraternal twins reared apart, siblings reared together, siblings reared apart, adopted children reared together, and unrelated children reared apart. Correlations have also been obtained on natural parents and their children and foster parents and their children.

If unrelated persons are randomly chosen the correlation of their measured IQ is 0.00, that is, there is no correlation. This is to be expected. The data have consistently shown that the highest correlation between measured IQ and kinship is for identical twins and that as genetic relationship decreases so does the correlation with IQ. Erlenmeyer-Kimling and Jarvik (1963) reviewed data from fifty-two studies of consanguinity and measured IQ. These data are consistent in the direction of the correlation: the greater the degree of genetic relationship, the higher the correlation. Following is a compilation of these studies showing the median correlation for relationship and IQ.

identical twins reared together	0.87
identical twins reared apart	0.75
fraternal twins (both sexes)	0.53
siblings reared together	0.49
unrelated children reared together	0.23
unrelated children reared apart	0.01
parent-child	0.50
foster parent-child	0.20

The data consistently show that unrelated persons with the same environment obtain correlations in the .20s and those persons with identical heredity obtain correlations in the .70s. For many people these data show the stronger influence of heredity. The environmentalists, however, use the same data to show the influence of the environment in modifying basic genetic endowment. Certainly, a correlation of .20 to .30 is not insignificant in terms of performance and measured IQ.

Factors such as socioeconomic level have been studied and a positive correlation has been found between social class and IQ. Cleary et al. (1975) note, however, that correlations between the social class of parents and the IQs of their offspring are lower than the correlations of parent and child IQ. They state, "there may be an intellectual advantage that accrues to privilege per se, but it is far from certain that even the moderate correlations between parents and children are entirely the result of privilege" (p. 23).

Attempts have been made to remove children from "poor" environments to "good" environments and then to measure the change, if any. Much of this research has been characterized by inadequate scientific control and poor statistical procedures and results have lacked any clear trend.

ENVIRONMENT

Let us now look at environment, which for the purposes of this discussion will be divided into two categories, physical and psychological.

Physical. In the physical area some of the factors that relate to the future development of the individual are (1) prenatal environment and conditions of birth, (2) dietary conditions of pregnant women, (3) disease during pregnancy, and (4) nutritional climate and physical health of the child.

In the prenatal period of development several environmental agents influencing later intellectual growth are known. Among these, the most notable is German measles, which if contracted by the mother during the early stage of pregnancy will often attack the fetus and cause mental retardation.

Certain factors operating at the time of birth have been shown to have a relationship to mental impairment. Some of these factors are anoxia (oxygen deficiency), mechanical injuries, anesthesia, prematurity, and abrupt births.

Mental development may be impaired in early childhood by physical trauma to the brain, poisons, and certain viruses and bacteria. Gross protein starvation has also been noted in some cases of mental retardation. The future may reveal relationships between chemical additives in our food and mental functioning.

Psychological. A number of studies have shown that chronic psychosocial factors, such as mother-child separation, maternal neglect, and personality problems of the mother, influence the mental development of the child. Another factor that has been widely studied is the effect of a restricted environment upon mental development.

A study that compared children living in an isolated mountain environment with children living in a valley community was conducted over forty-five years ago by Sherman and Key (1932). The mountain children lived in an isolated valley in the Blue Ridge mountains; the village children lived at the foot of the mountains in a less isolated environment. Both groups were from disadvantaged settings, but the schools for the mountain children were less adequate. Both groups scored, on the average, lower than the national average on a group test of intelligence, and the scores of the mountain children were lower than those of the valley children. Decreases in scores were apparent in the older children of both groups; however, the decreases were much less for the valley children than for the mountain group.

Newman's (1940) intensive studies of identical twins who were reared in different environments reveal that when one of the twins has been exposed to a more favorable cultural and educational climate, there is a strong tendency for intelligence test scores of the twin with the advantaged environment to be significantly higher.

Newman does not claim, however, on the basis of his findings that environment is more important than heredity. He holds only that when educational and cultural opportunities are unusually good or poor for either of the twins, there will be definite effects on intelligence test scores (p. 189).

CONCLUSION

Our discussion thus far has revealed the difficulties involved in formulating a definitive stand at either extreme of the heredity and environmental continuum. Let us review some of the inferences, implications, and opinions of a few investigators.

Lewontin (*Greensboro Daily News*, 1976), a Harvard biologist, explained to the press at a meeting of the American Association for the Advancement of Science that it is incorrect to talk of groups having lower or higher genetic potential. He stated, "What I don't know and don't understand is when we're going to stop trying to find an intellectual difference based on genetics" (p. A6). Dr. Lewontin went on to say that the National Institutes of Health published an advisory to scientists that "studies of the hereditability of IQ are not worth doing" (p. A6). On the other hand, Dr. Bernard Davis of Harvard Medical School said he was uncomfortable with the notion of ending research on the subject (p. A6).

Erlenmeyer-Kimling and Jarvik (1963),[2] in a review of all the twin data of the last fifty years, demonstrate the remarkable consistency in the genetic influences on intelligence as measured by an IQ test. The data also indicate that environment plays an important role in mental development.

Jensen (1968) states,

> *That individual differences in mental abilities are largely hereditary in origin is well established. We still do not know all the causal links in the chain from genes to mental test scores, but this is another matter and not a necessary condition for establishing the heritability of a trait.*
>
> *The polemics of the heredity-environment question have largely revolved around certain unfortunate misconceptions. One misconception is the idea that heredity-environment is a dichotomy—that a given trait is the result of either heredity or environment. Actually, the concept of heritability refers to the genetically determined proportion of variance in individual differences in a trait. Heritability is a continuous variable, taking values between 0 and 1. (p. 5)*

Jensen goes on to state that in order to improve education we should be aware of the child as both a biological and a social being. It is his feeling that if we do not recognize the biological basis of educability we will "restrict our eventual understanding and possible control of the major sources of diversity in human capacities and potentialities" (p. 39).

Nichols and Broman (1974) are dubious about the twin studies that point to heritability because of the inclusion of severely retarded children, which may significantly increase the correlation in IQ scores of twins.

---

[2] The reader who is interested in exploring the area of twin studies further is also referred to the extensive work of Vandenberg (1966).

Stone and Church (1973), after presenting a highly critical view of IQ tests and a very strong environmentalist position in the nature versus nurture controversy, admit that research evidence points to an hereditarian view of intellectual differences (p. 338). For example, they state, "The critic has no ready answer to the finding that foster children often (although by no means invariably) are more like their real parents than their adoptive parents in measured intelligence except to say that nobody has yet sufficiently studied the psychology of adoption and the possible problems of identification involved" (p. 339).

Many contemporary psychologists feel that differences between people have a strong genetic basis. Caspari (1968), a biologist concerned with the issue of heredity and environment, feels that there is strong evidence for a genetic influence on intelligence. He feels evidence for this view is provided, in part, by genetic conditions which can lower intelligence (for example, phenylketonuria and galactosemia). He states, "There seems to exist a large number of genes influencing this character [intelligence], since almost all chromosomal aberrations found in man are accompanied by mental deficiency" (p. 51).

He goes on to discuss the ratio between heredity and environment and concludes that one cannot state which is most important unless we study a specific cultural environment. The more important question to Caspari is the interaction of heredity and environment in the production of intelligence. He concludes by stating,

The challenge to education appears to me to reside in the problem of how to create educational methods and environments which will be optimally adjusted to the needs of unique individuals. The main contribution which a geneticist can make to educational research is to stress the fundamental biological fact that every human being is a unique individual and that his genetic individuality will be expressed in the way in which he reacts to environmental and educational experiences. (p.54)

One approach to investigating the effects of heredity versus environment has consisted of the studies of brilliant and retarded persons. These investigations have revealed that such traits occur more often in certain families, which seems to indict heredity as a predisposing factor.

A contemporary aspect of the age-old nature-nurture controversy is the application of heritability estimates to IQ scores. Basically, a heritability index reveals the ratio of genetic factors to the total variance of a given trait in a specific group under prevailing circumstances. Thus, for example, the heritability of a given IQ score among urban American high school students may be 70. This would mean that 70 per cent of the variability found in these scores is related to hereditary factors and 30 per cent is attributed to environmental factors (Anastasi, 1976).

The limitations of heritability indexes were clearly understood by Jensen (1969), although he used them as a basis for his tilting to a genetic position. Anastasi (1976) lists three limitations of the indexes:

1. "the concept of heritability is applicable to populations, not individuals" (p. 351).
2. "heritability indexes refer to the population on which they were found at the time. Any change in either hereditary or environmental conditions would alter the heritability index" (pp. 351–52).
3. "heritability does not indicate the degree of modifiability of a trait. Even if the heritability index of a trait in a given population is 100 per cent, it does not follow that the contribution of environment to that trait is unimportant" (p. 352).

Herrnstein (1971, 1973) concludes that 80 to 85 per cent of the variability in IQ is due to genetic factors. Eysenck (1971), an English psychologist, agrees with Herrnstein's position.

Biehler (1974) recommends that "instead of attempting to arrive at a definite decision regarding the nature and extent of differences in IQ, it would seem more constructive to use intelligence test scores to individualize instruction by taking into account types of intellectual operations and cognitive styles" (pp. 614–15).

It was noted in the first edition of this text that a stirring among psychologists to investigate heredity and environment would once again take place. Since that time (1970) controversy has in fact marked this area as one that is still far from resolved. More will be said on this topic in the next section. Let us conclude by stating that it is generally believed today that heredity provides the structure within which mental growth takes place. The environment, on the other hand, is influential in determining the form and growth of certain abilities that might be developed. For example, Mozart and Einstein probably would have been outstanding in a primitive culture, but they would not have been outstanding in music and mathematics if these disciplines did not exist. On the other hand, it is very difficult to conceive of an environment that could create an Einstein or a Mozart without the genetically determined raw material that these men possessed.

Test Score Differences Between Races and Social Classes

The question of differences in test scores for different racial and socio-economic groups is, of course, closely related to our previous discussion of heredity and environment. If heredity determines intelligence or is at least a predisposing agent, are there significant differences between races and socioeconomic groups? If environment is the key to intellectual ability, then cultural and educational opportunity should be the determining agent in test scores. Let us look at the past fifty years of research to see if any conclusions can be drawn.

Modern-day discussions of IQ scores and race inevitably must include the name of Dr. Arthur R. Jensen, professor of educational psychology at the

University of California at Berkeley. Jensen's now famous 1969 paper (123 pages) in the *Harvard Educational Review* set the stage for the public and professional rebirth of controversy on IQ scores, race, and social classes.

The twenty years before Jensen's paper had seen little research on racial differences in ability, although some psychologists' studies had shown that blacks scored lower on tests than whites. These psychologists interpreted their findings as revealing a biological basis, but their work was not taken seriously. During the 1960s, traditional social mores were challenged, and the society tilted to a strong environmental bias.

In an attempt to eradicate the differences in intellectual performance presumed to emanate from differing environments, the Head Start program for disadvantaged children was begun. This program has generally failed to live up to its promise of compensation in the area of intellectual stimulation. Likewise, other hasty large-scale programs failed to live up to advanced billing. Thus a questioning of the strict environmentalists' position began among psychologists, educators, biologists, and other scientists. Jensen's 1969 article was the catalyst that gave the established stage and actors their cue to begin their lines. This scholarly work cited a great many studies and presented Jensen's conclusions that the whole subject of racial differences had been taboo. "[The] importance of genetic factors in racial behavioral differences has been greatly ignored, almost to the point of being a tabooed subject, just as were the topics of venereal disease and birth control a generation or so ago" (p. 80).

Even before 1969, Jensen was questioning research on racial differences. Jensen (1968) asked if an "official decision" had been made to create an impression that the issue of social variations has been scientifically tested with conclusive results. A publication of the U.S. Office of Education (1966) stated, "It is a demonstrable fact that the talent pool in any one ethnic group is substantially the same as that in any other ethnic group." The Department of Labor (1965) report on the Negro [3] family concluded that, "Intelligence potential is distributed among Negro infants in the same proportion and pattern as among Icelanders or Chinese, or any other."

These writers have never seen anything in the literature that supports, with scientific certitude, the statements of the U.S. Office of Education and the Department of Labor. Jensen (1968), in reviewing these statements, states, "Such statements entirely lack a factual basis and uncritical acceptance of them may unwittingly harm many Negro children born and unborn" (p. 23). The discussion that follows will be an attempt to look at some of the data— not to "make" a case for one side or the other.

---

[3] The reader will note the word *Negro,* rather than *black,* was generally used to designate persons of African descent before 1970. In order to be historically and scientifically accurate, the authors have used the terminology of the study cited. The term *black* to designate persons of African descent has been used when the authors are themselves referring to this group or when a study used this designation.

RESEARCH FINDINGS

After the first intelligence tests were developed, studies were made comparing children and adults of different groups. The basic concern was to find differences, if any, in various groups of individuals. Comparisons were made between different age groups; racial, social, and national groups; urban and rural groups; and income levels. The findings indicated appreciable group differences. Children living in rural areas and in the Southern or southwestern United States, as well as Indian and black children, exhibited generally lower scores than children living in Northern urban areas.

In the area of social and economic levels many studies reveal, on the average, that children belonging to upper socioeconomic levels do better in intelligence tests than children from the lower strata (Tyler, 1956; Fifer, 1966; Davis, 1951). This seems to be true in England and Russia as well as in the United States (Johnson, 1948). These studies, however, do not clarify the reasons for differences. Some studies inject the additional variable of motivational differences. These investigations point to the possibility that middle-class children try harder on tests than their lower-class peers (Eells et al., 1951). The interpretation of these investigations has generated conflict and confusion among scientists and lay people alike.

The first large-scale studies of group differences were the result of massive testing in World War I. The Army, at the beginning of the war, asked the American Psychological Association to help construct a method for classifying soldiers according to their mental ability. Robert Yerkes headed a committee which developed a group test of intelligence called the Army Alpha Test. The development of this test drew heavily upon the work of Arthur Otis. (Otis, a former student of Terman's, had been experimenting with a group test of mental ability.) In addition, the committee devised a test for illiterates called the Army Beta Test. Almost 2 million soldiers were examined using these instruments (Chauncey and Dobbin, 1966).

The Army Alpha was a test of ability that examined the person's knowledge, simple reasoning, arithmetic, and ability to follow directions. The Army Beta was a nonverbal test. Directions were in pantomime and removed the effect of differences in language ability from the score. The Beta was administered to all men who fell below a given score on the Alpha. This group was composed of men who were handicapped by a foreign-language background or illiteracy, as well as those who performed poorly on the Alpha for any other reason.

The Alpha and the Beta have gone through many revisions since World War I and are still in use today. Since their development they have served as models for most group intelligence tests.

The results from testing nearly 2 million men using both the Alpha and Beta revealed racial and regional differences. Native-born whites achieved significantly higher average scores than Negroes. Northern Negroes achieved significantly higher average scores than Southern Negroes (Yerkes, 1921).

Myrdal (1944) noted that Negroes (on the Army Alpha test) from Pennsylvania, New York, Illinois, and Ohio averaged higher scores than whites from Mississippi, Arkansas, Kentucky, and Georgia.

Klineberg (1935, 1944) and Montagu (1945), in their analysis of Yerkes' data, focus their attention on the superiority of Northern Negroes over white groups from certain Southern states.

Garrett (1945) has stated that these comparisons have been made to demonstrate that education and economic opportunity are of more importance than race. He further states that all psychologists would agree that these data clearly indicate the importance of education; however, he feels it is doubtful that any definitive conclusion concerning race differences can be made on the basis of these results alone.

Garrett (1945) reported that Negroes from Ohio, Pennsylvania, Illinois, and New York scored below white soldiers of these states in the same proportion as they scored below the whites in the whole country. Garrett concludes from this that given a better education, the Negro does improve his score but not his position relative to the white. He notes that white Southerners, even though they had educational deficits, did approximately as well as Northern Negroes. Thus he infers that if Southern whites had the same advantages as Northern Negroes, they would do better on the test.

Studies since World War I have shown some indications that improvement in educational opportunities can result in an increase in IQ scores. Lee (1951) found that Southern-born Negro children who moved to a Northern city and entered school as first graders improved their average IQ scores from 86.5 to 93.3 by the end of the sixth grade.

Klineberg's (1935) investigation of Negro children in New York City revealed that Negro children who spent a longer time in New York City tended to have higher IQ scores than Negro children of more recent residence.

Kardiner and Ovesey (1951) attempt to explain lower Negro intellectual performance on the basis of psychiatric findings. They see a loss of efficiency in Negro intellectual functioning because of a focusing of attention on factors unrelated to performance. That is, there is a great temptation to adjust to symbols rather than strive for the real objective. This approach may lessen frustration, according to the authors, but it also may convey the impression of less intellectual ability.

Fifer (1966) and his associates attempted to devise tests that would be "as free as possible" of cultural bias and to present these tests in a testing situation under optional conditions. Four ethnic groups were studied—Chinese, Jews, Negroes, and Puerto Ricans. Each group was divided into middle- and lower-class designations. Examiners for each group were of the same ethnic group as the one being tested. The children were tested in four areas—verbal ability, reasoning, numerical ability, and ability to deal with spatial concepts. The data showed test performance differences between middle-class and lower-class groups regardless of ethnic origin. These differences varied from group to group. Of the middle-class groups, the Jewish middle class had the highest average scores, whereas the Puerto Rican middle class had the lowest average scores. The investigators felt their study revealed "strong evidence of differential patterns of mental abilities among four . . . ethnic groups" (p. 489).

A special note on a very important study on the *Equality of Educational Opportunity* (United States Department of Health, Education, and Welfare, 1966) merits attention in our discussion of race and test score differences. This study was undertaken in accordance with Section 402 of the Civil Rights Act of 1964, which directed the United States Commissioner of Education to "conduct a survey and make a report to the President and the Congress, within two years of the enactment of this title, concerning the lack of availability of equal educational opportunities for individuals by reason of race, color, religion, or national origin in public educational institutions at all levels in the United States, its territories and possessions, and the District of Columbia" (p. iii).

The survey focused on six racial and ethnic groups—Negroes, whites, American Indians, Oriental Americans, Puerto Ricans (living in the continental United States), and Mexican Americans. The study was conducted in the fall of 1965 and involved 4,000 public schools and 645,000 pupils.

The test results revealed that, with the notable exception of Oriental Americans, the average minority student scored much lower on the battery of standardized achievement tests in every area than the average white pupil. In addition, it was found that this lower achievement for minority groups is progressively greater as the educational level increases.

In the first grade the Negro group's median (average) score in the "nonverbal" test was lower than that of any other group, whereas the Oriental Americans' score was the highest of any of the six groups. In the "verbal" area the Puerto Rican group was lowest, followed closely by the Negro group; the white pupils obtained the highest scores.

In the twelfth grade the Negro group obtained lower scores than any other of the six groups in the following tests:

1. Nonverbal.
2. Verbal.
3. Reading.
4. Mathematics.
5. General information.
6. Average of the five tests.

Although the white group obtained the highest average scores, followed closely by Oriental Americans (United States Department of Health, Education and Welfare, 1966, p. 20), it was also found that students in the South, both white and Negro, had lower test scores than their counterparts in the North. [The interested reader, in addition to referring to the preceding source, may also want to read an excellent review of the survey by Borgatta and Bohrnstedt (1968).]

Martin Jenkins, an early Negro investigator of racial differences, studied gifted children of both races in the 1930s. He found that a considerable number of Negro children were within the range of the highest 1 per cent of white children, that is, an IQ of 130 or above. He further reported that sixteen published investigations presented data showing Negro children with IQs above 130, and twelve of these were above 140.

Jenkins (1964), in discussing gifted Negroes, states,

> *I am not attempting here to show that approximately as many Negro children as white are to be found at the highest levels of psychometric intelligence. There appears little doubt that the number of very bright Negro children is relatively smaller than the number of bright white children in the total American population. Nevertheless, it is apparent that children of very superior psychometric intelligence may be found in many Negro populations, and that the upper limit of the range attained by the extreme deviates is higher than is generally believed. (p. 88)*

Spuhler and Lindzey (1967) conclude that both sides of the controversy agree in one important area, that the existing research suggests the average IQ score of the American Negro is 85 or 86 whereas that of the typical American white is 100. This is a fact of testing life. The question, of course, is why. For example, Brown (1976), in his text on measurement, states matter-of-factly, "blacks score about one standard deviation below the mean of whites on intelligence tests" (p. 345). This means that whites score fifteen to sixteen points, on the average, higher than blacks.

Some researchers have questioned the basic assumptions of intelligence testing. Schwartz and Elonen (1975) conducted a sixteen-year longitudinal study of intelligence. They concluded that the concept of intelligence accepted by the public and professionals alike was mistaken. The authors claimed that their data refuted the underlying premises of Jensen; that is, that IQs are entities in and of themselves and have real and complete meaning rather than being a partial picture of intelligence. "Application of the clinical process to test construction should be a starting point to direct us away from a mechanistic view of intelligence . . . and quotients as well as the belief that everything need be measured or, in fact, can be measured" (Schwartz and Elonen, 1975, p. 694).

Cleary et al. (1975), commenting on the results of racial differences on tests throughout the years, state,

> *The intellectual deficit among Negroes as measured by present instruments is not restricted to verbal tests. Nonverbal tests of intelligence show an equally large deficit. Furthermore, if general intelligence is broken down into the various component abilities, there are minor differences among them in the size of the racial difference, but the nearly uniform size of the differences is more striking than the differences in size. The mean intellectual deficit is quite general and not narrowly restricted to specific skills involving standard English.*
>
> *With regard to academic achievement, the mean for Negroes is also about one standard deviation below the Caucasian mean, and the discrepancy is not appreciably greater at the end of the twelfth grade than it is at the beginning of the first grade. The deficit, in other words, is of long standing in ontogenetic development. (p. 16)*

The studies that have been cited are only a very small sampling of the hundreds of investigations that have been concerned with racial and socio-economic differences. The interested student who desires to explore this subject further will find an excellent resource in Shuey's (1966) exhaustive treatment of the multitude of studies on Negro and white test differences since World War I. Although Shuey has a "point of view" it does not distract from her excellent scholarship and ability to present both sides of the controversy.

In the next two sections of this chapter an attempt will be made to integrate all the previously mentioned data with the educational objective of assisting all children within our school system. Let us conclude this section with some general statements by knowledgeable authorities and organizations. Shuey (1966) states,

The remarkable consistency in test results, whether they pertain to school or preschool children, to children between ages 6 to 9 or 10 to 12, to children in Grades 1 to 3 or 4 to 7, to high school or college students, to enlisted men or officers in training in the Armed Forces—in World War I, World War II, or the Post Korean period—to veterans of the Armed Forces, to homeless men or transients, to gifted or mentally deficient, to delinquent or criminal; the fact that differences between colored and white are present not only in the rural and urban south, but in the Border and Northern states; the fact that the colored preschool, school, and high school pupils living in Northern cities tested as far below the Southern urban white children as they did below the whites in the Northern cities; the fact that relatively small average differences were found between the IQ's of Northern-born and Southern-born Negro children in Northern cities; the fact that Negro school children and high school pupils have achieved average IQ's slightly lower in the past twenty years than between 1921 and 1944; the tendency toward greater variability among whites; the tendency for racial hybrids to score higher than those groups described as, or inferred to be, unmixed Negro; the evidence that the mean overlap is between 7 and 13 percent; the evidence that the tested differences appear to be greater for logical analysis, abstract reasoning, and perceptual-motor tasks than for practical and concrete problems; the evidence that the tested differences may be a little less on verbal than on nonverbal tasks; the indication that the colored elementary or high school pupil has not been adversely affected in his tested performance by the presence of a white examiner; an indication that Negroes may have a greater sense of personal worth than whites, at least at the elementary, high school, and college levels; the unproved and probably erroneous assumption that Negroes have been less well motivated on tests than whites; the fact that differences were reported in practically all of the studies in which the cultural environment of the whites appeared to be similar in richness and complexity to that of the Negroes; the fact that in many comparisons including those in which the colored have appeared to best advantage, Negro subjects have been either more representative of their racial group or more highly selected than the comparable whites; all taken together, inevitably point to the presence of native differences between Negroes and whites as determined by intelligence tests. (pp. 520–21)

Jensen (1969) concluded that the average performance of the disadvantaged as compared to the norm is not a direct result of discrimination or inequalities in education. The evidence to him tilts in the direction of a genetic explanation, although he does not exclude the influence of the environment. In a later publication Jensen (1972) addresses himself to the problem of scientific censorship closing the door on investigation of racial differences without scientific data. "Speakers and writers on intelligence, mental retardation, cultural disadvantage, and the like . . . state, often with an evident sense of virtue and relief, that modern psychology has overthrown the belief in fixed intelligence" (p. 11).

On the other side of the argument, it is of interest to note that in September 1961, at the American Psychological Association's convention, the Society for the Psychological Study of Social Issues stated the following:

> *The evidence of a quarter of a century of research on this problem can readily be summarized. There are differences in intelligence when one compares a random sample of whites and Negroes. What is equally clear is that no evidence exists that leads to the conclusion that such differences are innate. Quite to the contrary, the evidence points overwhelmingly to the fact that when one compares Negroes and whites of comparable cultural and educational background, differences in intelligence diminish markedly. The more comparable the background of white and Negro groups, the less the difference in intelligence. There is no direct evidence that supports the view that there is an innate difference between members of different racial groups.*

Garrett (1962), in reviewing the preceding, declares that Negro-white differences in mental tests are so regular that he feels they suggest a genetic basis.

Cronbach (1975), in an excellent historical review of the testing movement, presents the relationship of the popular currents of the day and the acceptance of scientific data. The difficulty that the genetic advocate has today was also experienced by those who were attempting to provide an environmental explanation of racial and social-class differences in the post-World War II era. For example, during that time, Davis, a sociologist, contended that tests underestimate working-class children. Commenting on Davis' inability to get his point across, Cronbach (1975) states, "The Davis campaign failed for several reasons. He challenged the testers when they were in public favor. He concerned himself with persons of low status, and there were no militant voices to take up that cause. And if it were true that his new tests identified potentially able children for whom someone ought to invent better schooling, that advice was too abstract for public debate or action" (p. 8).

Cronbach (1970) defends tests but uses them as his basis for inferring that slum children are culturally handicapped rather than being born inferior. He states, "To interpret IQ's as inherited and fixed is unfair" (p. 303).

Jensen (1968, 1969, 1970, 1972, 1974a,b), Herrnstein (1971, 1973), and Shockley (1971) have been subjected to a great deal of intellectual and emotional abuse for their genetically oriented views on racial differences. Some critics have called for the censorship of their views and demanded that their work not be discussed. This attitude has alarmed many scientists and led a group of fifty eminent scientists to sign a document that was published in the *American Psychologist* (1972). This document begins with a very brief history of civilization and the periods of censorship of scientific research and teaching. Examples such as Galileo's suffering in orthodox Italy and scientists being punished in Hitler's Germany were presented. These scientists contend that today "censure, punishment and defamation are being applied against scientists who emphasize the role of heredity in human behavior. . . . A large number of attacks come from nonscientists, [and] academics committed to environmentalism in their explanation of almost all human differences . . . it is virtually heresy to express an hereditarian view. . . . A kind of orthodox environmentalism dominates the liberal academy and strongly inhibits teachers, researchers, and scholars from turning to biological explanations or efforts" (p. 660).

The resolution of these scientists calling for openness should be strongly considered by every student and scientist in all fields of scientific inquiry. The resolution is reproduced below for your review.

> *Resolution: Now, therefore, we the undersigned scientists from a variety of fields, declare the following beliefs and principles:*
> 1. *We have investigated much evidence concerning the possible role of inheritance in human abilities and behaviors, and **we believe such hereditary influences are very strong.***
> 2. *We wish strongly to encourage research into the biological hereditary bases of behavior, as a major complement to the environmental efforts at explanation.*
> 3. *We strongly defend the right, and emphasize the scholarly duty, of the teacher to discuss hereditary influences on behavior, in appropriate settings and with responsible scholarship.*
> 4. *We deplore the evasion of hereditary reasoning in current textbooks, and the failure to give responsible weight to heredity in disciplines such as sociology, social psychology, social anthropology, educational psychology, psychological measurement, and many others.*
> 5. *We call upon liberal academics—upon faculty senates, upon professional and learned societies, upon the American Association of University Professors, upon the American Civil Liberties Union, upon the University Centers for Rational Alternatives, upon presidents and boards of trustees, upon departments of science, and upon the editors of scholarly journals—to insist upon the openness of social science to the well-grounded claims of biobehavioral reasoning, and to protect vigilantly any qualified faculty members who responsibly, teach, research, or publish concerning such reasoning.*
> *We so urge because as scientists we believe that human problems may best be remedied by increased human knowledge, and that such increases in knowledge lead much more probably to the enhancement of human happiness than to the opposite.* (American Psychologist, 1972, p. 660)

In reviewing all the literature, one thing is quite clear: the vast majority of studies reveal very significant differences between test scores of different racial, ethnic, and socioeconomic groups. These writers' own position on the conflictual studies and interpretations is in agreement with Spuhler and Lindzey (1967), "What we can say with confidence is that racial groups differ in intelligence as measured by existing instruments. The extent to which these differences are to be attributed to biological factors (race) rather than to experiential (particularly cultural) factors remains largely unknown" (pp. 391–92).

Educational Reality and the Disadvantaged

In order to assist an individual in his choice of and preparation for education and meaningful work, we must know his past achievements, present capabilities, and future potential. One method of evaluating these is by testing. Are these tests useful in guiding the disadvantaged? First, let us focus our attention on the achievement test, the area of testing that is the least controversial when dealing with the disadvantaged. Lennon (1964) states,

> It is axiomatic that the school and the teacher must know the present status of each child, and the progress he is making, with respect to certain concrete goals of instruction. . . . Whatever advantages or limitations a child brings to his school learning tasks, the school and the teacher still must be concerned with how successfully he is attaining the goals of instruction; and this is one of the contributions that the standardized achievement test makes, whether in the case of the culturally disadvantaged or the more fortunate pupil.

The school needs to know the present status and progress of both its advantaged and disadvantaged children.[4] Thus we may answer part of our question: *yes*, achievement tests are useful in guiding disadvantaged children. The teacher, of course, is in an excellent position to know whether the achievement test is appropriate for his or her particular students and should share this information with the school administration.

Proper test administration is very important, especially with disadvantaged children. Many articles and books have been written about the alienation of culturally disadvantaged youngsters. The test situation, unless properly handled, could reinforce this alienation. Test administrators must be especially careful to convey to children their concern and interest. Explanations concerning the purposes of testing should always be made clear before the examination begins. Disadvantaged children need to know that testing is not another obstacle or method of "getting them."

In testing these children the gravest question is, "Are IQ tests fair for the disadvantaged?" In order to address ourselves to the question of fairness or unfairness of IQ tests for the disadvantaged, we must first briefly review why IQ tests are given. In general terms, IQ tests are given in order to determine

[4] The following discussion of reality and the disadvantaged is based in part upon a previous publication of one of the authors. See Karmel (1967).

what an individual is capable of doing. What are Bill's chances for success in school? Will he need special attention? If so, what kind of instruction? Is he mentally retarded or gifted? If an IQ test can help to show that Bill needs special attention and that attention is then given, Bill has obviously received immense help.

Present performance may be gauged by school grades, teacher opinion, and standardized achievement tests. Future potential cannot be ascertained in the same way, because the teacher's judgment is already reflected in grade evaluation and opinion. Another evaluative technique must be used to make sure that Bill is not being judged by factors that may be unrelated to his academic potential, such as teacher bias or poor academic background.

Thus, in using a test of future potential, along with the teacher's opinion and data from objective achievement tests, we have a situation similar to the checks and balances in our government. The teacher's opinion and evaluation are checked and weighed against what a child may accomplish on standardized achievement tests, in which his performance is compared to that of children all over the country, not just those in his classroom.

If IQ tests and other data help the school to understand each individual (as an overwhelming number of studies show), then certain inferences must be made. These inferences are drawn from an interpretation of the test results. *If the test data do not discriminate between individuals, teachers or guidance counselors cannot make inferences, nor can they help the individual student.*

In attempting to facilitate learning, the school is concerned with what a pupil can and will do. A pupil's race or socioeconomic status is not important in educational planning. What is important is the individual's present status and future potential, that is, what he or she has attained and what he or she may become.

We are living in a middle-class-oriented society, and the school is a reflection of this society. In judging a student, the school is not evaluating him or her in terms of ability to "get along"; it is appraising his or her ability to function and grow in an educational setting.

In discussing this problem in a previous publication (Karmel 1967), one of the authors has stated the following:

> *If IQ tests are uniformly unfair to Negroes and other groups, then so are our schools and perhaps more importantly our educational aspirations for our children are in need of radical replacement. We seem to be in a quandary concerning the basic rule of education. On the one hand we demand higher and higher standards of excellence from our students and on the other hand there are those who say that we are unfair to have standards, and it is of as much value for a child to know the codes of the city street. Does recognition of a child's cultural deprivation and different mores mean one should accept, condone, and perpetuate them?*
>
> *The value we place on educational achievement may be contested by some, but most educators and lay people, both Negro and white, would agree on the efficacy of educational advancement as a key to the enrichment of the individual*

and his society. The methods in achieving this goal may differ, but in learning one must have the "stuff" to learn with no matter what the learning technique. Thus, the question of the fairness of the IQ test is directly related to the educational mores of our society for in the last analysis the IQ test is measuring the potential of Johnny to succeed in a school system oriented to society. If it was not aimed in this direction it would have little value. (pp. 11–12)

In essence, then, the variables of genetics, environment, race, socioeconomic status, and cultural bias are academic questions when we are considering the practical educational reality of how well a pupil will do and how the school can best serve the individual student with his own unique potential to learn. The student of measurement should not infer from this that these variables are unimportant. On the contrary, they are extremely important when considered in their proper context. If our goal is to predict the chances for an individual pupil to succeed in our present school system, then we must have tests that reflect this system. The reasons that an individual may or may not be able to learn constitute an issue beyond that of testing. Testing is not geared, nor should it be, to treatment. It may be used to facilitate treatment by providing data that the school may use to render individual educational planning and guidance. To illustrate this point, let us look at Smith Junior High School.

Smith Junior High School is located in a predominantly disadvantaged neighborhood. Mr. Lowell, the principal, is concerned about the appropriateness of group IQ tests for his students. This concern is shared by many of his teachers. Many feel that IQ tests are unfair because of their cultural bias. These concerns prompt Mr. Lowell to call in Mr. Fields, a testing consultant, to help guide the school in its educational planning. The faculty meeting is open for discussion and the science teacher poses the first question:

Science Teacher: Is it fair to say that one of our students is dumb because he gets a low IQ or test score? I feel it isn't, because the tests are made up for middle-class kids and our kids don't have the same exposures.

Mr. Fields: I agree it is not fair to say your kids are dumb. It is fair to say, however, that the chances of success in school are not too good for your kids who obtain low scores on IQ tests.

Science Teacher: What do you mean by not too good?

Mr. Fields: Studies have shown that there is a high relationship between IQ scores and school success. That is, children who score at the average level or above have a better chance of staying in school and graduating and they are able to do the work required.

Social Studies Teacher: I agree with the studies but it still doesn't seem fair to label these youngsters.

Mr. Fields: I agree, these youngsters should *not* be labeled. The purpose of testing is to aid not hinder educational growth.

Mr. Lowell: Are you saying that IQ tests are not indicative of innate intelligence?

Mr. Fields: No, I am not saying that they are not indicative of innate intelligence, nor am I saying that they are able to identify innate intelligence. We truthfully do not know. What we do know is that they are very helpful in predicting school success. This is why we prefer to call them scholastic aptitude tests rather than intelligence tests.

Math Teacher: Well, that may all be true but I know they are used to label and since they are not perfect or near perfect how can you defend them?

Mr. Fields: I cannot defend their exclusive use but in conjunction with teacher evaluations they enhance educational prediction.

Mr. Lowell: What about using a culture-free test?

Mr. Fields: There are no such tests. Yes, some tests are labeled culture-free or culture-fair, but research does not bear out the promise of their titles. They too, in some measure, reflect the culture.

Librarian: If we could have a test that was free of cultural bias would you recommend its use?

Mr. Fields: It would depend on several factors. First, what is its predictive utility? Second, how would you use it? That is, if it predicted school success as well as or better than our present instruments without penalizing youngsters because of cultural background, then of course I would use it. If it didn't predict school success but could be used as an aid in detecting youngsters with ability who could be educationally salvaged by intensive teaching, then I would still use it.

Even though your children come from disadvantaged homes you will still find some who do well on tests and you can advise these children accordingly. On the other hand, without these tests a child in your school may think he is doing quite well and not know of his standing with youngsters from different areas of the country.

Let us leave Smith Junior High School and direct our attention to individual cases. John, a six-year-old black child, is evaluated by an IQ test. The test reveals that he is on the borderline between dull normal and mentally retarded. This is a situation where the knowledge of cultural bias would be important. There is no doubt that John's test results should be received with more skepticism and caution than if he were white. The school should weigh other factors and not rely solely on this score. If, however, John were twelve years old and tested at the same level, the results in terms of educability and reality would be less suspect. This is not to say that there might not still be error, but the chance of making up for the cultural deprivation would be less.

The student of measurement should remember that the interpretation of IQ scores, as is true of the scores of other tests, must be made on the basis of many factors, including culture, but in the final analysis the scores should be interpreted in accordance with the objectives of testing. Whether the child is advantaged or disadvantaged, he or she competes and lives in a society geared to middle-class objectives and values.

American education must face the problem of how best to educate the disadvantaged. Alleviation of this problem, however, will not be found in eradication of the instrument that gauges its existence. The IQ test is only an instrument to gauge what is, not what should be. Thus the answer to cultural and socioeconomic deprivation lies in rectifying and treating the etiological agents that create the disadvantaged community, not in doing away with an instrument that helps us know of its presence. To do away with IQ tests because they measure social problems is as logical as throwing out medical procedures that indicate cancer because a treatment today is not available.

A Practical Approach to the Use of Standardized Tests

The reader has now been exposed to what an IQ is and what it is not; what "intelligence" is and what intelligence tests are; discussion of the part heredity and environment may play in human behavior; test score differences in black and white children and adults; and interpretations of test scores for the disadvantaged. The question before us is how to translate these facts, findings, interpretations, and points of view into sound educational policy.

Sound educational decisions emanate from sound educational policy. Educational policy must be based on the best available information gleaned from experimental investigations and empirical observations. Although the issues, conflicting data, and different interpretations seem confusing, there are areas of agreement that can be used as a basis for sound educational policy. They are the following:

1. Tests are not infallible, but, used along with other methods of evaluation, such as teacher judgments, they are very useful in helping individuals to realize their own unique potential.
2. Educators must understand the limitations as well as the advantages of tests.
3. Tests should never be used as an excuse to avoid human judgment or contact.
4. The number of tests used is determined by the amount of information needed.
5. The existence of hereditary differences does not alter the fact that most investigators recognize the importance of environment in shaping the child's intellectual ability.
6. Tests should always be used in conjunction with educational objectives. Interpretation of test scores is meaningful only when applied to educational and individual goals.

TWO | **Testing the Test**

Statistics, Norms, and Standard Scores

chapter 3

In previous chapters, we have discussed why we give tests and some of the issues involved. In this chapter the ways in which test results are communicated will be discussed. The information here is not intended for statisticians or for mathematically oriented teachers (although they may read it too). It is intended to convey in simple terminology basic statistical insights and techniques in order to better understand testing.

If the reader has been exposed to basic statistics either in course work or in other readings, he could skip statistics and go on to norms and standard scores.

As educators and psychologists, there are three different kinds of information that you may need to know. First, you may want information concerning the performance of an entire group. Second, you may want information concerning a particular individual. Third, you may want to compare groups or individuals on two or more measures. Numbers are simply the shortest, easiest, and least confusing way to convey such information, provided that those giving the information and those receiving the information speak the same language.

Rationale for Statistics

At this point let us pause and examine feelings that many of you may have toward statistics. Some of you may be saying, "What good are they? I won't be using them anyway." If you have encountered difficulty with mathematics, you are apt to be anxious. On the other hand, those of you who have experienced little difficulty or have found mathematics fun and exciting may be eager to begin. It is necessary, however, that all of you, no matter what your mathematical ability, learn simple shorthand techniques in elementary statistics. These are the tools of the trade. You will need to know simple statistical procedures in order to give meaning to your standardized testing programs; in order properly to evaluate standardized tests of scholastic aptitude, achievement, and so on; and in order to read professional books and journals intelligently.

If you are one of those who finds numbers confusing, you may take comfort from the following:

1. It is said that Charles Darwin frankly admitted trouble with statistics.
2. Sir Francis Galton, who was instrumental in introducing statistics into psychology, at times had to ask others to help or to do some of his mathematical problems.
3. The advanced statistics that require mathematical insight and skill need not concern the teacher and school counselor.
4. Elementary statistics requires no more than an average seventh-grade understanding of arithmetic.
5. The advent of the computer enables the student to concentrate on the use rather than on the *mechanics* of statistics. Thus those of you who are mathematically unsophisticated need not be greatly concerned. The important thing today is understanding when to use a certain technique or method.

Language

A number of symbols and shorthand devices have been developed in order to enable us to describe the characteristics of groups and individuals in comparison with other groups. These symbols are similar to the symbols you are now putting together in order to read this page. That is, we translate our neurological impulses into *learned word symbols* which we call thoughts. These thoughts are further translated into learned letter symbols which are put together to form *learned word* or *thought symbols*. These symbols you recognize as words on paper, but more importantly they communicate ideas or "thoughts" to you.

In communicating the information necessary to understand tests and test results, we use a different language, the language of statistics. Thus with a single number, letter, or symbol an idea may be conveyed that would require a paragraph, or even a page, of verbal discourse.

The objective of statistics in testing is to *describe* a score, a set of scores, and the various relationships between them. A score on any measure or test has little or no meaning in and of itself. Meaning is given to a score by its relationship to other scores in a given measure. Let us consider for a moment what information you need on a score or set of scores:

1. The highest and lowest score (range).
2. How often a particular score was obtained (frequency).
3. The pattern of scores between high and low (distribution).
4. The average score (mean).

Why do we need this information? Obviously, if you give a test of 100 items to your students and no one gets more than ten correct, this is not a good test for your class. A test, classroom or standardized, *must* distinguish between those students who have mastered the subject or possess a given characteristic and those who have not mastered the material or do not possess the characteristic. Carried further, the test should tell us the relative degree to which the student has these skills or abilities.

Even if we have a wide range of scores on our 100-item test, but most of the students receive the same score, this test is not distinguishing among students.

All this information can be conveyed quickly and simultaneously by using numbers arranged in certain ways.

Distribution

In measuring any aspect of any group of individuals, you will obtain a variety of individual scores; that is, you will have a distribution of scores. One function of statistics is to describe this distribution. We may describe this distribution in a variety of ways. Some of these ways are ranking, frequency distribution, class interval, or graphic representation. Let us look at these methods.

Ranking Scores

One way to see quickly the range of scores is to arrange them in order from highest to lowest. Let us assume for a moment that we are all teachers of English. One of us has recently administered a vocabulary test to ten ninth-grade students. At this time we are primarily interested in scores (not in total number of questions on the test). Table 1 presents the scores from highest to lowest. A simple inspection of the scores in Table 1 reveals that

Table 1. Scores on Vocabulary
Test for Ninth-Grade Students

85	65
70	50
70	50
65	40
65	30

they range from 30 to 85, whereas all other scores are between these extremes. These scores are *ranked,* or we may say that they are arranged in *rank order.*

Frequency Distribution

We can simplify our picture of these scores by putting all scores that are the same together. But to account for the number of students having the same score, we need a new column of figures that will tell us how many students received that score.

The column for scores we head X; the column that represents the number of people obtaining that score we head *f.* N is used to designate the number of subjects tested.

Using our small group for illustrative purposes, let us look at our vocabulary scores through shorthand. (Obviously, the small number cited does not require shorthand; however, when the numbers are increased a hundredfold or more, the need becomes more apparent.) Table 2 shows that three students scored 65, two students scored 50, two scored 70, and scores of 85, 40, and 30 were obtained by three different students.

The numbers and letters are arranged to form a *frequency distribution* of scores. *Frequency* means number of occurrences. *Distribution* means the way in which something occurs. When we put these two words together we have *frequency distribution.* Our frequency distribution shows the number of raw scores and the number of students obtaining a given score. Our shorthand system allows us to use X to represent *raw score.* Raw score means simply the number of items or questions right. The letter *f* represents the number or *frequency* of students obtaining a given score.

Class Interval

We can further simplify our presentation of a set of scores by grouping several together to form fewer groups. This is necessary when there is a

Table 2. *Frequency Distribution of Scores on a Vocabulary Test for Ninth Graders*

X	f	
85	1	
70	2	
65	3	X = score
50	2	f = frequency
40	1	N = number
30	1	
N =	10	

Table 3. *Scores on an IQ Test*

125	133	135	137	155	127	140	133
134	129	144	136	122	151	129	121
133	142	115	136	141	120	125	138
115	127	127	133	146	110	116	134
146	121	119	126	119	117	124	121
139	128	147	118	127	128	129	132
114	116						

large number of scores. For example, you have been given the set of IQ scores listed in Table 3. Scores presented in this manner do not convey much useful information because there are too many data to comprehend them in a meaningful way. To make these data useful, we need to know the average score in the group, how much the scores varied from this average, and how the scores were distributed. The first step in organizing these scores is to set up a frequency distribution.

Because we have many scores, we will bunch several adjacent scores together and call this a *class interval*. The *class interval* may be defined as an arbitrary tool for arranging data in groups. Each possible score must be accounted for within the range from highest to lowest, even if no one received that score.

The first thing to be decided in constructing the class intervals for these data is the size of the class interval or group. The size of the class interval is determined by the rule that there should be not less than ten nor more than twenty intervals. The usual grouping is fifteen. In dealing with small numbers of scores, fewer class intervals are favored because of convenience. In grouping data, certain minor errors are introduced into the calculations. The cruder the grouping—that is, the smaller the number of groups—the greater the chance for error. In determining the size of the class interval, we are guided by the need to reduce our data to the number of groups chosen.

Let us now look at our scores in Table 3; 155 is the highest and 110 is the lowest. Thus our range is from 110 to 155. Because we have a small number of scores, we will arrange them in ten groups. Now our question is how many scores will be in each group. In determining this we obtain the range of scores, add 1 to the highest score, and subtract the lowest score ($155 + 1 - 110 = 46$). We then divide 10 into 46, which is 4.6, round it off to the nearest whole number, and our class interval is 5. If we had chosen fifteen groups, our computation would have yielded 3.06 and our class interval would have been 3. You should remember that the basic purpose of grouping scores is to make a convenient representation.

With class intervals of 5, we find that the lowest interval extends from 110 to 114, the second from 115 to 119, and so on. In order to cover all possible scores, the first interval actually extends from 109.6 through 114.5, and the second interval from 114.6 through 119.5. This continues through the intervals, with the highest interval being 154.6 through 159.5. Class

Table 4. *Frequency Distribution of IQ Scores with Scores Grouped by Class Intervals*

Scores	Tally Marks	Frequencies (f)
155–159	I	1
150–154	I	1
145–149	III	3
140–144	IIII	4
135–139	THL I	6
130–134	THL II	7
125–129	THL THL II	12
120–124	THL I	6
115–119	THL III	8
110–114	II	2
		$\Sigma f = 50 = N$

intervals are usually stated in whole numbers, but it is understood that they extend from half a number above to half a number below.

In summary, the following steps were involved:

1. Add 1 to the highest score and subtract from this the lowest score ($155 + 1 - 110 = 46$).
2. Divide the range by number of groups desired ($46/10 = 4.6$).
3. Round off to nearest whole number ($4.6 = 5$).

Table 4 shows our data grouped in class intervals of 5. In order to obtain the frequencies, we have used a system of tallies. Each mark in the column marked "tally marks" represents one individual having a score in that five-point range. For example, in the range 140–144, we see that four scores fell in this range. We do not know the exact score for any of these individuals, that is, whether a score was 140, 141, 142, 143, or 144. We have to assume that they were evenly distributed.

After the tallies are made they can be counted and the number placed in the f (frequencies) column. A frequency distribution is an important first step in organizing any set of data. In itself it gives useful information and in addition is the basis for other statistical calculations such as standard deviations.

Graphic Representation

We may also show a set of scores by "drawing a picture" of them.

Histogram and Polygon

The first two pictorial representations of data that we will consider are the histogram and the frequency polygon. Let us again refer to the data in

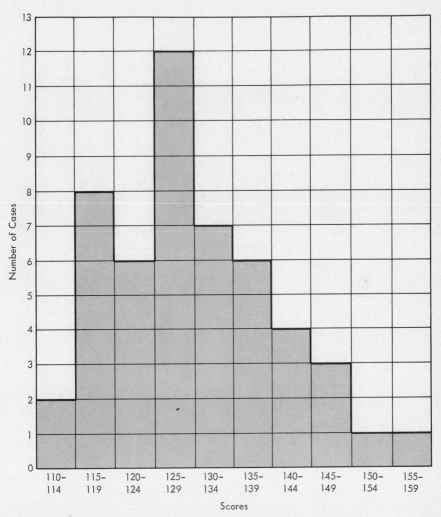

Figure 1. Histogram of fifty IQ scores.

Table 4. An inspection of the distribution shows us that the most frequent scores occur in the interval 125–129, and that the very low and very high scores are less numerous. The greatest cluster of scores is in the lower half of the range. Following are two different representations of the same data in pictorial form.

In Figures 1 and 2 the frequency of the IQ scores can be more readily viewed than in Table 4. The histogram (Figure 1) is sometimes referred to as "piling up the bodies," because each square represents an individual who obtained that score. When more than one score falls in a given class interval, it is represented by making that pile another square higher. The score intervals can be seen along the abscissa (horizontal baseline). The ordinate

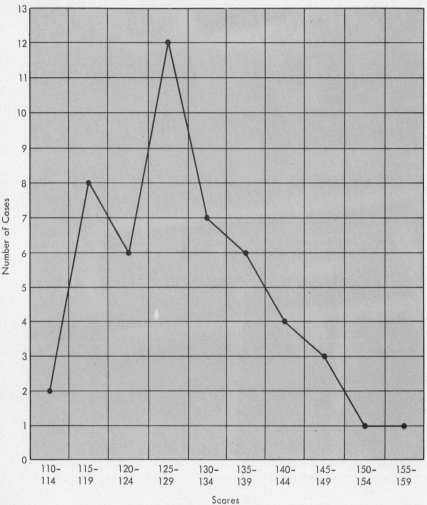

Figure 2. Frequency polygon of fifty IQ scores.

(vertical height) represents the frequencies. Thus we read from the histogram that seven individuals scored in the range 130–134 and so forth.

The same data are pictured in Figure 2 in the form of a frequency polygon. In this figure, the midpoint of each of the score intervals has been plotted. The height of the point equals the frequency in the interval. These points have been connected to show graphically the distribution of scores. The histogram and frequency polygon are generally similar devices to illustrate the same facts. There are, however, advantages and disadvantages to both. On the whole, the frequency polygon is generally preferred to the histogram because it gives a better showing of the shape of the distribution. The student who is interested in pursuing this area in more depth should consult one

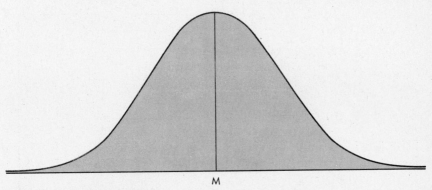

M

Figure 3. A normal curve.

of the many statistics texts which offer a more definitive treatment of the subject (see, for example, Chase, 1974; Popham and Sirotnik, 1973).

Normal Curve

A very important graphic representation of data is the theoretical normal curve. The normal curve is a mathematical construct, not necessarily a representation of actual data. In psychological testing, however, the assumption is often made that measured characteristics are distributed normally in a given population. That is, a graphic representation of the data would resemble a normal curve. Data on a group are often evaluated on how closely they approximate a normal curve.

Let us look at the characteristics of this type of distribution. A normal curve is symmetrical and bell shaped. Figure 3 represents a normal curve. You will note that the curve reaches its greatest height in the center, indicating that the greatest number of cases fall at the center. Each side is identical and slopes with the same degree and distance.

When a distribution differs significantly from the normal curve, it is said to be *skewed*. A curve may be skewed negatively (to the left) or positively (to the right). Figure 4 illustrates positively and negatively skewed curves as compared to a normal distribution.

The height of a normal curve is also exactly determined by theoretical considerations. Thus the same percentage of cases always falls at the center. In actual distributions, this height may sometimes be higher or lower. This characteristic of distributions is referred to as peakedness or *kurtosis*. A curve with a high peak and a narrow middle is called leptokurtic, while a curve with a low peak and a broad middle section is called platykurtic. A curve with a middle level of peakedness is called mesokurtic.

Figure 5 illustrates three levels of peakedness in three curves. Note that the curve with the highest peak has shorter tails, and the curve with the lowest peak has longer tails. This is because a curve always represents 100

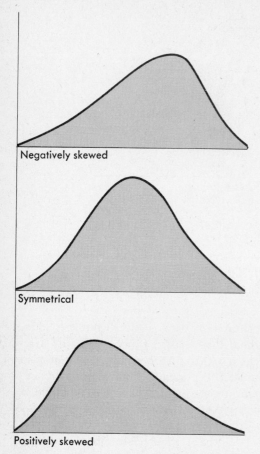

Negatively skewed

Symmetrical

Positively skewed

Figure 4. Skewed and symmetrical curves.

per cent of the cases involved in a distribution. Therefore, if there are more cases in the center, there are fewer at the tails, and the tails are shorter. In a similar manner, if there are fewer at the center, there are more represented in the tails, and the tails are longer.

In a normal curve there is an exact proportion of cases represented in each segment of the curve. We will discuss this concept in more depth in relation to standard deviation.

Measures of Central Tendency

A basic difference between psychological measurement (such as intelligence) and physical measurement (such as length) is that in physical measurement one begins with zero and measures up to find an absolute length, whereas in psychological measurement one can begin not with zero, but with the

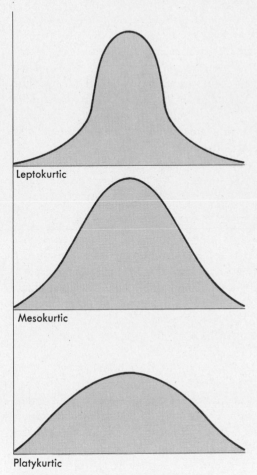

Leptokurtic

Mesokurtic

Platykurtic

Figure 5. Kurtosis of curves.

middle (the average), and measure to each end of the distribution. Thus, in communicating the results of psychological tests, one important kind of information is what happens at the center, which we refer to as measures of *central tendency*. Averages give us clues to the characteristics of the center of a group. They do not tell us about the exceptions on either side of the average. Averages represent a typical score for a group. With a typical score or average, one group can be quickly compared with another. Similarly, an individual's score can be compared with the typical score of the group.

These statistics are called measures of central tendency rather than averages because the word *average* is a general term. Since there are different types of statistical averages, it is a meaningless word without proper reference to the kind of average being described.

Many people think of an "average" as the sole product of an arithmetic process, but there are different types of averages that are useful in portraying the typical of a given group. Each of these is calculated by a different procedure. These averages are the *mode*, the *median*, and the *mean*. Thus these three measures that indicate a typical condition or the average performance of a given group are what we mean by *measures of central tendency*. For example, in describing a group's reading level at the national *median* for seventh-grade students, not only are you signifying that they are typical or average in performance, but also you are stating how this average was computed. You are stating your statistical frame of reference. Let us look at these three measures of central tendency in terms of what they mean and how they may be derived.

Mean $(\overline{X})$

The mean [1] is one of the most widely used measures of central tendency; it is the arithmetic average that you have been using for years in computing your grade averages in school. For example, let us suppose that you have been asked by the Dean of Pedagogy to submit your overall undergraduate grade average for evaluation. This is a rather simple procedure for you. You sit down and count the number of A's, B's, C's, D's, and F's and their hours of credit. Let us suppose that at your college an A is equal to 4 points, a B to 3 points, a C to 2 points, a D to 1 point, and an F to zero. Let us also suppose that all your 120 hours were made up of three-hour courses. Thus you would have taken forty three-hour courses ($120 \div 3 = 40$).

Now let us use the frequency distribution to help compute your grade average. Remember $X =$ raw score and $f =$ frequency of these scores. Upon inspection of your transcript, you find that you earned the following grades: (1) ten A's, (2) twenty B's, (3) five C's, (4) two D's, and (5) three F's.

Here we have introduced some new symbols. You remember that N equals

Grades and Their Values in Tabular Form

X	f	fX
4	10	40
3	20	60
2	5	10
1	2	2
0	3	0

$N = 40 \quad \Sigma fX = 112$

[1] It should be noted that two other types of measures of central tendency are also used. These are the *geometric mean* and the *harmonic mean*. These are rarely used by teachers, guidance counselors, or psychologists and need not concern the beginning student.

number; in this case N = number of courses. In other situations it may equal number of scores, number of persons, and so forth. Our new symbol is Σ, which is called the summation sign ("adding up" or "sum up"). In your situation, then, N equals the number of courses you have taken and Σ equals the total frequency of these grades multiplied by the weighted grade. Thus, *fX* is frequency times grade weight or scores. A is equal to four points. You received ten A's. Ten times the weighted grade of A equals 40. Let us continue to figure out your grade average. We know that you had forty courses (N = 40) and the sum of these times their frequency (Σ*fX*) after weighting equals 112. You know that in order to find the average you must now divide the total or sum of the weighted scores by the number of courses. Your arithmetical procedure is the following:

$$
\begin{array}{r}
2.80 \\
40\ \overline{)\ 112.00} \\
80 \\
\hline
320 \\
320 \\
\hline
00
\end{array}
$$

Thus your undergraduate grade average is 2.80, or a B—. Those D's and F's hurt your grade average and worked against the effect of ten A's and twenty B's. On the other hand, the A's and B's helped you in making up for the three failures and two near failures.

The following frequency distribution allows us to look at your grade average through the symbols of statistics:

Frequency Distribution of College Grades and Steps in Calculating Grade Point Average

X	f	fX
4	10	40
3	20	60
2	5	10
1	2	2
0	3	0

N = 40   Σ*fX* = 112

$$\overline{X} = \frac{\Sigma fX}{N} = \frac{112}{40}\text{, or } \overline{X} = 2.80.$$

You have just completed your grade average, or, in statistical jargon, the *mean* or *arithmetic average*. The mean grade from forty different grades is therefore 2.80.

The mean uses more of the available information in a distribution than the mode and median. Less information is used in computing the others in that the mean uses all the scores. In most cases the mean provides a more sensitive index of central tendency. There are situations, however, when the use of every score can be a disadvantage. For example, you are attempting to find out the average income in your school district. There are 10,000 wage earners, most of whom earn salaries in the $8,000 to $12,000 range. There are, however, ten people whose income is $100,000 or more, and one person is reputed to earn close to $1 million a year. The arithmetic average would not, of course, be the appropriate statistic to use. The few wage earners with much greater incomes would distort the final average and would make your school district's typical income much higher than it really is. In such cases, a median is a better representation of the average.

Median (Mdn.)

In our previous illustration the case of a few high incomes was shown to distort the usefulness of the mean. The median would not be so affected because when computing it we would give equal weight to all the scores. That is, an income of $1 million would have an equal place with an income of $8,000. This is because we count frequencies up or down in calculating the median. The median is the midpoint of a set of scores. We may also say it is the score below which 50 per cent of the cases fall and above which 50 per cent of the cases fall.

Let us simplify our income data for illustrative purposes. Table 5 shows

Table 5. *Average Incomes of Nine Wage Earners Using the Mean and Median*

Wage Earner	Annual Income	Median Procedure	Mean Procedure
Jones	$100,000	(1) Counting down five cases	18,000
Smith	9,000	(2)	9 ⌐162,000
Leslie	8,500	(3)	9
Stern	8,300	(4)	72
Foster	8,000	(5) Median	72
Stevens	7,500	(4)	0
Shoemaker	7,200	(3)	
Marty	7,000	(2)	Mean = $18,000
Nelson	6,500	(1) Counting up five cases	Median = 8,000
N = 9	$162,000		

nine wage earners, one earning $100,000 a year and the rest earning under $10,000. This table illustrates the use of the median as well as how the mean can give a distorted picture of a set of numbers or scores. In this case note how Jones' income changes the mean but has little influence on the median.

In computing the median, we count up or down to exactly half of the scores or in this case the wage earners. Thus, with nine salaries represented, the median would be the fifth, which is $8,000. The mean income for this group is $18,000. We see that the mean is $10,000 more than the median. Both the median and the mean are "averages," but for these data the median is a more accurate representation of the typical wage of the group.

Theoretically, in a normal distribution curve the mean, median, and mode will all fall on the same point. If you have a large discrepancy between any of these three measures of central tendency for a group of data, a visual inspection may help to determine what is distorting the figures.

Mode (Mo.)

The mode is a very crude statistic and generally not very useful. However, it is easy to find and gives a quick and rough measure of central tendency. For example, you have fifty English test scores and you want to know five minutes before a department meeting what the typical score was. You might look at the score that occurs most frequently and have a rough approximation; this most frequent score would be the mode. It is, of course, very possible that the mode may not indicate anything at all and be far removed from the average score. Therefore, it is recommended that you never use it except in the most pressing cases and use it then with the utmost reservations.

Measuring Variability

In describing a set of scores, it is desirable to have some data on *variability*, or on how scores vary from the measure of central tendency expressed as the mean. In terms of the previous discussion of graphic representation, variability is a description of the tails of our curve, that is, of the spread of scores. The most commonly used index of variability is called the *standard deviation*.

Standard Deviation

Generally, the term *standard deviation* is used to describe how scores vary from the mean. Popham (1973) describes it quite well when he says, "Actually the standard deviation is somewhat analogous to the mean. While the mean is an average of the scores in a set, the standard deviation is a sort of average of how distant the individual scores in a distribution are removed from the mean itself" (p. 15). Put another way, it is a statistic that expresses the average distance from the mean a set segment of scores

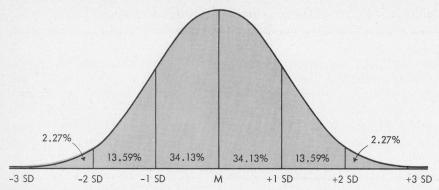

Figure 6. A normal curve showing standard deviations and percentages of cases in each.

fall. A large standard deviation indicates a wide spread of scores, whereas a small standard deviation reveals less score spread. If we turn our attention to a distribution, we may perceive standard deviation more clearly.

In a normal curve the area on both sides of the mean in which approximately 68 per cent of the scores fall is designated as plus and minus one standard deviation from the mean.

Figure 6 reveals the normal curve with the standard deviations and the percentages of cases in each deviation. The whole area of the curve represents the total universe or total number of scores in the distribution. Vertical lines have been drawn to the base line at the mean and at intervals designated as +1 to +4 on the right and −1 to −4 on the left. The areas between these lines contain the percentages of cases or people to be found under that section of the curve. In the theoretical normal curve there is an exact relationship (mathematical) between the standard deviation and the ratio or proportion of cases. This relationship always remains constant.

In an IQ test with a normal distribution that has a mean of 100 and a standard deviation of 15, 34.13 per cent of the scores would fall somewhere between the mean and +1 standard deviation, or between 100 and 115 IQ points. In the same way, 34.13 per cent of the scores would fall somewhere between the mean and −1 standard deviation, or between 85 and 100 IQ points.

It can thus be seen that 68.26 per cent of cases shown on a "normal curve" occur somewhere between +1 and −1 standard deviations from the mean. This means that approximately two-thirds of all scores in a normal distribution lie between ±1 standard deviation from the mean. Similarly, a little over 95 per cent (95.44) of scores will fall between +2 and −2 standard deviations from the mean, and almost all the scores (99.9 per cent) will be somewhere between +3 and −3 standard deviations from the mean. The percentage of cases included in each standard deviation is illustrated in Table 6. This exactness of percentage of cases in each deviation is an

Table 6. Standard Deviations and Percentile Equivalents *

Standard Deviations				Percentile Equivalents
+3				99
+2				98
+1				84
0 (X̄)	68%	95%	99%	50
−1				16
−2				2
−3				0.1

* Note that percentiles are rounded.

important property of a normal curve and one that will be referred to in the section on standard scores. Standard deviation may be used as a way of reporting test scores. For example, you may state that John scored at the +2 standard deviation from the mean in the X test of intelligence. This communicates that he scored at the 98th percentile, or better than 98 per cent of the people taking the test.

The exactness of the number of cases that will always be found in a normal curve between ±3 standard deviations from the mean enables us to use it as a gauge to compare groups and individuals. All distributions, of course, are not "normal," and the exact relationships will not always hold. It is true, however, that many distributions are close enough to the normal curve that we may make use of this property of the normal curve.

Previously, we discussed peakedness and spread of curves. An understanding of standard deviation enables us to communicate quickly both the shape of the curve (group performance) and an individual's relative standing within the group. From the standard deviation we know whether our scores were bunched at the center or whether the spread was great.

If you have a student who is +1 standard deviation from the mean on a test (if, of course, the group at least approximates the "normal" distribution), you can state that he is at the 84th percentile compared to the group of people that the test producer used in determining the distribution. Put another way, you can say that he surpasses roughly 84 per cent of the group to whom he is being compared (50 per cent below the mean and 34 per cent between the mean and +1 standard deviation).

In terms of scores, the standard deviation becomes greater as the scores are more widely spread. That is, the larger the standard deviation, the wider the spread of scores. Thus we have some idea of the variability of a set of scores by the size of the standard deviation.

For example, a standard deviation of 3 would indicate a sharply peaked curve with a short tail, whereas a standard deviation of 32 would indicate a lower curve with longer tails. A standard deviation of 3 would indicate that 68 per cent of the cases were within six points of each other. In such a case, a twelve-point spread would cover 95 per cent of cases, and 99 per cent of cases are covered by eighteen points. This test would yield little discrimination among individuals, particularly in the range ±1 SD (plus and minus one standard deviation).

On the other hand, a standard deviation of 32 yields much more discrimination among individuals. With this standard deviation, we know that the middle 68 per cent of cases were spread over 64 points, whereas 95 per cent of cases were spread over a range of 128 points. To account for 99 per cent of cases, our range would be 192. Later in this chapter, we shall discuss standard scores in relation to the normal curve.

Correlation

Another statistic for which you will have a great deal of use is a correlation coefficient. A correlation coefficient is a mathematical measure of a relationship between two or more variables. In statistics, we attempt to replace a subjective judgment that may vary from person to person and day to day with a precise mathematical number that will not vary regardless of who calculates it.

You may suspect that students who do well in high school are most likely to succeed in college. Your suspicion, however, is not enough on which to base decisions. You need some method to evaluate the strength of the relationship. This will help you to decide how much confidence you can place in a stated relationship. One method of increasing confidence is to obtain a correlation coefficient.

We will address our attention to the Pearson product-moment coefficient (*r*). There are other kinds of correlations that you can review in any elementary statistics text (Popham and Sirotnik, 1973).

A correlation may be expressed on a continuum ranging from +1.00 to —1.00. A coefficient of +1.00 indicates a perfect positive relationship. This means that on two measures the highest individual on measure X was also highest on measure Y, and that this relative relationship continues throughout the entire population. A coefficient of —1.00 indicates a perfect negative relationship. In this situation the subject who scored highest on measure X scored lowest on measure Y and so forth throughout the distribution. A coefficient of zero means that there is no systematic relationship between the two sets of scores. Seldom, however, is a relationship either +1.00 or —1.00. In a more usual case it will be reported in terms of decimals.

Table 7 presents two sets of scores, one set on test X and one on test Y. These scores were made by the same students, each student having one score on both test X and test Y. If we inspect Table 7, we note that the student who made the highest score on test X made the highest score on test Y. The student who made the second highest score on test X made the

Table 7. Scores of Ten Students on Two Tests

Students	Test X	Test Y
James	12	14
Mary	13	15
David	16	18
Joe	17	19
Kim	18	20
Cathy	20	22
Lou	21	23
Lynn	24	26
Sue	26	28
Beth	27	29

second highest score on test Y, and the exact correlation continues throughout the scores. This illustrates a perfect $(+1)$ correlation.

Figure 7 reveals the scores of Table 7 in a *scatter diagram* format. Note the class intervals that we talked about before are now used in this diagram. The scores have been grouped in class intervals of two. Each column in the diagram intersects with every row. This creates a cell at each intersection. Every cell signifies a unique combination of one of the scores of test X with one of the scores of test Y. For example, Mary has a score of 13 on test X and a score of 15 on test Y. Look at Figure 7 and locate at the top the class interval containing Mary's X test score. This is in the second column from the left. Move down this column until you locate, on the left margin, the interval containing Mary's Y test score, which is in the third row from the bottom. Thus our tally is placed in that cell which has been made by the intersection of the row and column.

Note that all the tallies fall along a straight line. This form of relationship is an indication of a linear correlation. There is a direct and high relationship between the two sets of scores.

The teacher and counselor should remember that correlation is a measure of mutual relation. Our basic question is, "What is the relationship between two or more variables?" As you know, correlation coefficients have many uses. Of special importance to the student of measurement is its use with reliability, validity, and prediction. It is a basic tool in estimating these very important factors.

How do you interpret a correlation coefficient? Or, how high is high? This depends on the use that you will make of a coefficient. For one purpose, .50 might be fine, while for another a .90 would be more desirable. One measure of a correlation coefficient is to determine whether it is statistically significant. One can never be absolutely sure in judging data or results of experiments whether your data represent a real relationship or whether

Scores on Test X

Scores on Test Y	11–12	13–14	15–16	17–18	19–20	21–22	23–24	25–26	27–28
29–30									I
27–28								I	
25–26							I		
23–24						I			
21–22					I				
19–20				II					
17–18			I						
15–16		I							
13–14	I								
11–12									

Figure 7. Scatter diagram from Table 7.

they represent a chance occurrence that would rarely happen. Mathematicians have prepared tables that give the probability that your results were a chance occurrence. The convention that has been adopted is that data must be significant at least at the .05 level of confidence. This number indicates the risk you are willing to take that generalizations from your data are wrong. A .05 significance means that in 95 cases out of 100 there would exist a true relationship, whereas in 5 out of 100 the data could have occurred by chance and an actual relationship does not exist. A .01 significance means that you are taking a risk that one out of a hundred times you would erroneously report a significant relationship.

See Appendix D for a table that reports the correlation coefficient that must be found and the risk of reporting an erroneous relationship. In using this table, you need to know the number of pairs of subjects. Subject pairs are indicated in the column labeled *df* (degrees of freedom). Enter the table at the number of pairs minus two and read across to the desired level of confidence. There you will find the coefficient required at the risk you are willing to take. As you use more subjects, it takes a lower correlation to be significant.

One final word about correlation. Correlation does *not* tell us the cause of a relationship, only that two variables occur either together (positive correlation) or inversely (negative correlation). The cause of both variables may be something else. You will need to understand correlation in judging tests. Both validity and reliability are reported as correlations.

Norms

We have been discussing ways in which we can describe the performance of a group on tests. Another use for statistics in testing is to describe and communicate the performance of an individual in relation to the group.

Mrs. Stone was so proud of her son Robert because he had an IQ of 100. Mrs. Stone thought, of course, that 100 was a perfect score. She did not know that an IQ of 100 was average. As future teachers or counselors, you should remember that no score is meaningful unless you know on what basis it was derived. In one test, for example, a score of 200 would really mean that the student did not answer even one question correctly. Always ask, then, for the frame of reference of the child's test scores. A number is meaningless without it. Even a simple raw score which indicates the number of items answered correctly is not meaningful unless you know how many questions were asked and what the factors are that indicate a good showing.

In order to convey meaningful information about test performance and scores we translate the raw score into *norms*. These norms are reference points that compare raw scores with different factors. For example, a raw score of 10 on a given test may indicate a gifted child at the first-grade level, whereas the same score for an eighth-grade child may indicate retardation. Thus a raw score is given meaning only when we refer it to the appropriate norms.

There are two kinds of reference groups we can use to understand the performance of an individual. We may compare a child to all other children of the same age or in the same grade in school (developmental norms). We may feel, however, that simply living a certain number of years does not afford enough similarity for a valid comparison. Thus we may want to compare a person to a group with similar characteristics. For example, it is more useful to compare a high school senior who is going to college to other seniors who are going to college than to all other high school seniors. Therefore, we use group norms for more exact meaning and more clearly defined statistical application. Developmental norms include grade and age equivalents, mental age, and infant developmental quotients. Group norms use the statistical concepts of percentiles, standard scores, and deviation IQ. An important concept in using any of these methods of interpreting scores is equality of units.

Age Norms

Age norms compare a child to other children who are the same age. This type of norm is the major one used with infants and is sometimes referred to as the developmental norm. In evaluating the physical growth of an eight-month-old infant, length, weight, and motor development would be compared to norms developed from a representative sample of eight-month-old children. Age norms are most useful with very young children. As children live longer, their life situations and experiences become more responsible for differences among them. Therefore, with older children, variables such as socioeconomic group, education of parents, and career aspiration reflect life experiences, and are used as a basis for selection of reference groups. Except, perhaps, for height and weight, simply being a certain age becomes less important as a normative source. Rarely is age alone used with older children. Obviously, there is a relationship between age and grade in school because most children begin first grade at age six and throughout the years children in the same grade are generally about the same age.

Grade Norms

The grade norm (also called grade-placement norm) is obtained by finding the average scores for students at different grade levels. A test is administered to a representative sample (normative group) of youngsters from different schools, from different geographical locations, and of different ages. Average scores are obtained for each grade level. The raw score of a particular pupil can be compared to these norms and a grade equivalent score can be derived.

The chief advantage of grade norms is that comparisons are made among children who have had the same amount of educational exposure. The standard method of expressing grade norms is by assigning a number to each grade—for example, the number 6.0 would indicate average performance at the beginning of sixth grade; 6.5 would indicate average performance in the middle of the school year or grade. The tenths of grade placement for any testing date may be ascertained by an inspection of Table 8.

Table 9 presents a hypothetical distribution of raw scores and their grade equivalents, which would be similar to normative data presented in a test manual. Thus if Ray Gold, an eighth-grade student, had a raw score of 25, his grade equivalent or grade placement score would be 10.8.

Most measurement authorities today question the advisability of using grade norms, especially in reporting test results to parents. This is because they seem to be so simple that misunderstandings often result from their

Table 8. Grade Placement at Time of Testing *

Date of Testing	Sept. 1 Sept. 15	Sept. 16 Oct. 15	Oct. 16 Nov. 15	Nov. 16 Dec. 15	Dec. 16 Jan. 15	Jan. 16 Feb. 15	Feb. 16 Mar. 15	Mar. 16 Apr. 15	Apr. 16 May 15	May 16 June 15
Month of Grade Placement	0.0	0.1	0.2	0.3	0.4	0.5	0.6	0.7	0.8	0.9
Week of Instruction In Grade	1–2	3–6	7–10	11–14	15–18	19–22	23–26	27–30	31–34	35–38

* Reproduced from *Stanford Achievement Test*, Advanced, Directions for Administering. Copyright © 1972 by Harcourt Brace Jovanovich, Inc. Reproduced by special permission of the publisher.

Table 9. Raw Scores and Their Grade Equivalents for the X Test of Social Studies for Junior High Students

Raw Score	Grade Equivalent	Raw Score	Grade Equivalent
30	12.5	15	6.8
29	12.0	14	6.6
28	11.8	13	6.3
27	11.6	12	6.1
26	11.2	11	5.9
25	10.8	10	5.5
24	10.3	9	5.0
23	9.7	8	4.5
22	9.2	7	4.0
21	8.7	6	3.5
20	8.4	5	3.0
19	8.0	4	2.5
18	7.7	3	2.0
17	7.3	2	1.5
16	7.1	1	. . .

use. At first glance, one is apt to interpret our previous example as indicating that the student is advanced enough to work at a higher grade than he is actually able to do. This assumption could be entirely untrue. Thus Ray Gold's score indicates that he has obtained a score equal to the average score earned by children in the tenth grade. This may only mean that he has mastered most of the work at or below his grade level. The average eighth-grader, on the other hand, will of course miss more of the items.

Durost (1961b) illustrates quite well the basic point of our discussion when he states,

> *A fifth-grade child who has really learned to compute accurately may do ten straight computation examples without error, while the average child who has not mastered all his number combinations or is unsure in borrowing or carrying will miss several of these problems. The higher score earned by the first child will result in his receiving a grade equivalent substantially beyond his grade placement; yet he could not work at that level successfully because he has not been exposed to the new processes and learnings normally taught in the higher grade. (p. 1)*

Percentile Norms

Percentiles are as easily understood as grade norms and do not suffer from the same limitations. A percentile norm rank indicates the proportion of students who fall below a given score. *It does not mean the percentages of questions answered correctly.* It means the percentage of people whose performance a student has equaled or surpassed. Thus if 75 per cent of the students to whom Betty is being compared score lower than she, she is at the 75th percentile. That is, on a given test, Betty has done better than 75 per cent of the students taking the test, and 25 per cent have scored higher than she.

Tables 10 and 11 present percentile norms for the Differential Aptitude Tests. The norms in these tables are for tenth-grade students in their first semester (fall of the year). The test manual presents similar norm tables for boys and girls from grade eight through grade twelve. Note that Table 10 presents norms for girls and Table 11 gives norms for boys. The reference, or "norm," group is especially important for accurate and meaningful test interpretations. The teacher or counselor inspecting these tables is immediately given data to assist him in knowing to whom he is comparing his students.

An inspection of Tables 10 and 11 reveals raw scores under the various tests in the battery with percentile rankings for each score. Let us suppose we want to find the percentile rankings for two students on the verbal reasoning test. Both Susan and Wyatt have a raw score of 40. Looking at the numbers under Verbal Reasoning for boys, we find that a raw score of 40 is equivalent to the 90th percentile. Wyatt's percentile norm for Verbal Reasoning is therefore at the 90th percentile level. Susan has the same raw score as Wyatt. Do you think her percentile level will therefore be the same? If Susan were a boy, her percentile level would be the same. Susan is a girl, however, and on this test we must compare her to other tenth-grade females. Table 10 presents norms for girls similar to Susan. That is, they were tested in the tenth grade during the first semester in the fall of the year. Looking under Verbal Reasoning, we find Susan's raw score of 40 equivalent to the 85th percentile. Thus both Wyatt and Susan have the same raw scores, that is, number of correct answers, but Wyatt is at a higher percentile ranking because of normative sexual differences. When we say that Wyatt is at the 90th percentile, we are correct if we have explained the reference group beforehand, that is, if we have defined "those taking the test."

It should be noted that not every percentile is given in Tables 10 and 11. More detailed tables would reveal percentiles for each score; Tables 10 and 11, except for the extreme top and bottom, present percentiles in steps of five. Several raw scores are often equivalent to a single percentile. Though we could be more exact, this type of estimation is sufficient in most cases.

Percentiles are extensively used because they are easy to interpret and do not have the glaring shortcomings of age and grade norms. They have been and are being used today to report test scores on a wide variety of measurement instruments such as intelligence, aptitude, achievement, and interest tests. Percentiles can be used with almost any group. There are, however, certain limitations in their use.

First of all, the group that is being used as a reference point presents some problems. This has been seen already in our discussion of Wyatt and Susan's test scores. The discrepancy between the raw scores and percentile equivalents on the girls' and boys' norms was noted. It is obvious that we need different norm groups for such factors as sex, age, and grade. The group to which you compare a pupil *in every case must be* the group to which he or she belongs. It is, for example, of no value to compare a college applicant's academic aptitude scores to the scores of the general high school population. His scores must be compared to those of other college applicants in order to get a meaningful picture.

A good illustration of the test score differences reflected in various norm groups is seen in the United States Army classification tests. The norms for these tests are based on the general population of males, which ranges from those who have not completed elementary school to those who have obtained a college or advanced degree. No distinction, at least in the past, was made according to educational background. That is, Smith, who is a college graduate, and Jones, who did not complete high school, would be in the same normative group, with no distinctions made for different educational backgrounds. For the Army's general purposes, of course, there would be no need to divide the norms according to educational level. In fact, it could be harmful. Smith might not make the officer corps because he was being compared only to college graduates. On the other hand, Jones might qualify for the corps because he was the highest in his group. Thus *normative groups must be relevant for the decisions to be made.*

There must be many sets of norms for a given test. The test user may then choose those most pertinent to his situation and needs. There are practical limits, however, to the number of norm groups that can be supplied by a test publisher. Schools, therefore, need to provide their "local norms" to supplement the published percentile norms. The use of "local norms" helps the school to determine the relative standing of pupils in its own system. In some situations this comparison is often more significant than the use of national norms. Let us look, for example, at three different high schools.

Stuart High School is a secondary school located in a upper-middle- to

Table 10. *Percentile Norms for Girls for the Differential Aptitude Test, Forms S and T, Fall (first semester) Tenth Grade* *

Girls (N = 6,750+)

Per-centile	Verbal Reasoning	Numerical Ability	VR+NA	Abstract Reasoning	Clerical S and A	Mechanical Reasoning	Space Relations	Spelling	Language Usage	Per-centile
99	48–50	38–40	85–90	48–50	73–100	59–70	53–60	97–100	56–60	99
97	46–47	36–37	81–84	46–47	67–72	56–58	49–52	95–96	53–55	97
95	43–45	34–35	76–80	45	63–66	53–55	45–48	93–94	50–52	95
90	41–42	32–33	71–75	43–44	60–62	50–52	42–44	91–92	47–49	90
85	38–40	30–31	67–70	41–42	57–59	48–49	39–41	88–90	45–46	85
80	36–37	29	64–66	40	55–56	47	37–38	86–87	43–44	80
75	34–35	27–28	60–63	39	53–54	45–46	34–36	84–85	41–42	75
70	32–33	26	57–59	38	52	43–44	32–33	82–83	39–40	70
65	30–31	24–25	53–56	37	51	42	30–31	80–81	37–38	65
60	28–29	23	50–52	36	49–50	41	28–29	77–79	36	60
55	25–27	22	47–49	35	48	39–40	26–27	75–76	34–35	55
50	23–24	21	44–46	34	46–47	38	25	73–74	32–33	50
45	21–22	19–20	41–43	32–33	45	37	23–24	70–72	31	45
40	19–20	18	38–40	31	43–44	35–36	22	67–69	29–30	40
35	17–18	16–17	35–37	29–30	42	34	20–21	64–66	27–28	35
30	15–16	15	31–34	27–28	41	32–33	19	61–63	26	30
25	13–14	13–14	28–30	25–26	39–40	31	17–18	58–60	24–25	25
20	11–12	12	25–27	21–24	37–38	29–30	16	54–57	22–23	20
15	10	10–11	21–24	16–20	35–36	27–28	15	50–53	19–21	15
10	8–9	9	18–20	12–15	32–34	24–26	13–14	45–49	16–18	10
5	7	7–8	15–17	9–11	26–31	21–23	11–12	40–44	13–15	5
3	6	6	13–14	7–8	17–25	19–20	10	35–39	11–12	3
1	0–5	0–5	0–12	0–6	0–16	0–18	0–9	0–34	0–10	1
Mean	24.8	21.2	46.0	31.9	46.9	38.7	27.4	71.7	33.1	Mean
SD	12.2	8.7	19.6	10.9	11.9	9.9	11.1	16.7	11.3	SD

Raw Scores

* Reproduced by permission. Copyright © 1973, 1974 by The Psychological Corporation. New York, N.Y. All rights reserved.

Table 11. Percentile Norms for Boys for the Differential Aptitude Test, Forms S and T, Fall (first semester) Tenth Grade *

	Boys (N = 6,400 +)			Raw Scores							
Per-centile	Verbal Reasoning	Numerical Ability	VR+NA	Abstract Reasoning	Clerical S and A	Mechanical Reasoning	Space Relations	Spelling	Language Usage	Per-centile
99	48–50	38–40	85–90	48–50	68–100	66–70	57–60	97–100	53–60	99
97	46–47	37	81–84	47	62–67	63–65	53–56	94–96	50–52	97
95	43–45	35–36	77–80	45–46	57–61	61–62	50–52	90–93	46–49	95
90	40–42	33–34	72–76	44	54–56	59–60	46–49	86–89	43–45	90
85	38–39	31–32	68–71	42–43	52–53	57–58	43–45	82–85	40–42	85
80	36–37	29–30	64–67	41	50–51	56	40–42	79–81	38–39	80
75	33–35	28	60–63	40	49	55	38–39	76–78	36–37	75
70	31–32	26–27	57–59	39	48	54	36–37	73–75	34–35	70
65	29–30	25	54–56	38	46–47	52–53	33–35	70–72	32–33	65
60	27–28	23–24	50–53	37	45	51	31–32	68–69	31	60
55	25–26	22	47–49	35–36	44	50	29–30	65–67	29–30	55
50	23–24	20–21	44–46	34	43	48–49	27–28	62–64	27–28	50
45	21–22	18–19	41–43	33	41–42	47	25–26	59–61	26	45
40	20	17	38–40	31–32	40	45–46	23–24	57–58	24–25	40
35	18–19	15–16	34–37	30	38–39	43–44	22	54–56	23	35
30	15–17	14	31–33	28–29	37	41–42	20–21	52–53	21–22	30
25	13–14	12–13	28–30	25–27	35–36	39–40	19	49–51	19–20	25
20	12	11	25–27	21–24	33–34	36–38	17–18	46–48	17–18	20
15	10–11	9–10	22–24	17–20	30–32	33–35	16	43–45	15–16	15
10	9	8	19–21	13–16	27–29	29–32	14–15	39–42	13–14	10
5	7–8	7	16–18	10–12	21–26	25–28	12–13	34–38	11–12	5
3	6	5–6	14–15	7–9	10–20	22–24	11	29–33	9–10	3
1	0–5	0–4	0–13	0–6	0–9	0–21	0–10	0–28	0–8	1
Mean	25.0	21.2	46.2	32.4	42.4	47.4	29.6	63.6	28.6	Mean
SD	11.9	9.3	19.8	11.0	11.7	10.9	12.2	17.6	11.2	SD

lower-upper-class suburban community. The children who attend Stuart have been exposed to a great many cultural and educational advantages. On a standardized test of academic ability, the average pupil's score at Stuart is at the 75th percentile level (in the national population, the average child is, of course, at the 50th percentile level). It is obvious, therefore, that Stuart must develop its own norms in order to have more meaningful comparisons and to place children in appropriate classes.

On the other hand, Lincoln High School is a secondary school located in a large urban complex referred to as the "inner city." The average student at Lincoln on the same test of academic aptitude scores at the 35th percentile. Thus Lincoln needs to develop local percentile norms for the same reasons as Stuart.

Pearson High School is also located in a large metropolitan area. However, Pearson draws students from diverse socioeconomic backgrounds. The average student at Pearson scores at the 55th percentile level on the same academic aptitude test. For Pearson the national percentile norms supplied by the test publisher seem to be appropriate and a valid reference point.

Another caution in the use of percentiles involves the interpretation of differences in percentile rankings. A student, for example, who ranks at the 95th percentile may get five or six more items correct than his classmate who is ranked at the 90th percentile. The student, however, who is at the 55th percentile may get only one or two more items correct than his friend who is at the 50th percentile.

Percentile units are *unequal*. Remember, an equal percentile difference does not necessarily represent equal raw score differences. The inequality of percentiles may be seen in Figure 8. Note alongside the "percentile equivalents" the closeness of percentiles and the distance at both extremes. See, for example, how far apart the 95th and 99th percentiles are, or the 1st and 5th percentiles, as compared to percentiles in the 20th to 80th percentile range.

To summarize, we may state that percentile norms are reference points that provide us with a basis for interpreting a score of an individual in relation to his status in a given group. It is important that the group is relevant to the individual and to our purposes for comparison. It is also important to bear in mind that percentile units are unequal and that at the extremes of the normal curve five percentile units are not equivalent to five percentile units in the middle.

Standard Scores

In our previous discussion of raw scores the rationale for converting scores into agreed upon or standard units was presented. The use of standard scores

Figure 8. A normal curve showing percentiles and standard score scales. (From *Test Service Bulletin,* No. 48, Psychological Corporation, 1955.)

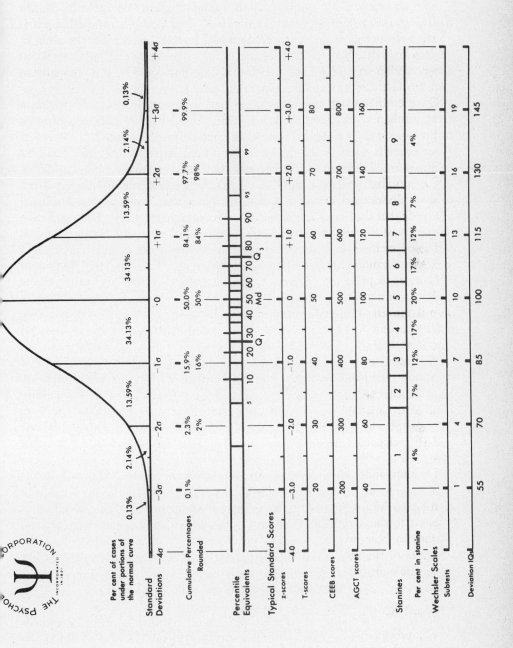

is another method to provide comparability to the meaning of a raw score. Thus the tester in Rich Square, North Carolina, and the tester in Tokyo, Japan, would both have a similar frame of reference. This standard frame of reference is the normal curve. A standard score is based upon the number of standard deviations a given score is from the mean. Typical standard scores can be seen in Figure 8. Before continuing, turn back to the section on standard deviation and review the concept. An understanding of the standard deviation is very helpful in attaining insight into the standard score mechanism because standard scores reflect an individual's performance as distance from the mean in terms of the standard deviation.

In Figure 8, the first standard scores are the z-scores, which are equivalent to the standard deviations. Inspecting our normal curve in Figure 8, we can see that a standard z-score of +1 has between it and the mean 34 per cent of the cases. A standard z-score of +1 is then equivalent to the 84th percentile and a standard z-score of −1 is equivalent to the 16th percentile. This relationship is always the same with standard scores for any normal distribution. If we look further we can see that −4 and +4 standard scores are equal distances below and above the mean. Thus the standard score does not suffer from the same defect of unequal units as do the percentile equivalents.

It should be noted that z-scores may be computed for any type of distribution by equating the mean to 0.00 and the standard deviation to 1.00. The z-score equivalents in Figure 8 are correct only for a normal distribution.

The use of z-scores presents some difficulties. First of all, a standard score of zero is incorrectly interpreted by some to mean a very poor performance rather than the mean or average performance. The z-score has two other disadvantages: Half are negative value, and many involve decimal fractions. To eliminate these awkward and time-consuming disadvantages, different standard score systems have been developed. An inspection of Typical Standard Scores in Figure 8 reveals three other types of standard scores that do not suffer from these disadvantages.

T-scores are expressed in whole numbers with a mean of 50 and a standard deviation of 10. A T-score of 75 would be equivalent to a z-score of +2.5. The T-score method usually eliminates negative numbers and decimal fractions.

The CEEB (College Entrance Examination Board) has a mean of 500 and a standard deviation of 100. This eliminates both decimals and negative numbers. A high school senior, for example, who obtains a score of 600 on one of the tests would be in the 84th percentile.

The AGCT (Army General Classification Tests) scores, as can be seen in Figure 8, have a mean of 100 and a standard deviation of twenty points. This scale was developed during World War II. The United States Navy, on the other hand, expresses its test results in T-scores.

Stanines are another type of standard score; they were developed by the United States Air Force in World War II. The word *stanine* was taken from

"STAndard NINE-point scale" (Durost, 1961a). Thus a stanine scale is a nine-point scale with a mean of 5 and a standard deviation of 2. The distribution of stanines, as can be seen in Figure 8, is based upon the normal curve. Note that just below the stanines are percentages which indicate the per cent of the total found in each stanine.

The stanine score is considered by many testing authorities as the preferred method of explaining test results to students and parents and is gaining wide acceptance in our schools today. This is because stanines are easily understood and are broader in scope than other devices, yet they are precise enough for the purpose of reporting test scores. It should also be noted that in the area of research, stanines are easy to use because they are one-digit numbers. When computers are used, they are economical as well because they require only one column to signify a score on a punch card. They immediately tell the test user the standing of the pupil. For example, a student with stanines of 7, 8, or 9 is far above average in whatever measure is being sought. On the other hand, stanines of 2 or 3 indicate he is well below average. Figure 9 presents a ladder of stanines with the percentage of children reaching each rung.

Though the stanine scale is an excellent method of reporting test results, it has technical limitations. Magnusson (1967) states,

> The T-scale allows finer differentiation among individuals than the stanine scale. So long as a sufficiently high reliability justifies a stricter differentiation, we will lose a certain amount of information about the individuals by giving their results as stanine scores. For a reliability of 0.91 the standard error will be 0.3s, and for a reliability of 0.96 the standard error will be 0.2s. For a T-scale where s = 10, these figures indicate standard error of 3 and 2 units respectively. The standard error is so small that the scale can be said to differentiate so accurately that one would lose valuable information if the results were to be given on a stanine scale instead of a T-scale. (p. 241)

The reader who is interested in pursuing the techniques of stanine interpretation to parents and other lay persons should see Durost (1961a), Engelhart (n.d.), and Karmel (1966).

The important thing to remember about standard scores is that they are based on a normal distribution and should not be used for other data. Standard scores are meaningful only in relationship to a particular group. The standard deviation of a particular reference group and an individual's score is represented as the number of standard deviation units from the mean of the group. The main difference of the standard score over percentile rankings is that they are presented in equal steps or units.

Intelligence Quotients

The abbreviation for intelligence quotients is IQ. There are two different kinds of IQ: a ratio IQ and a deviation IQ. These two types reflect the way in which the score is derived.

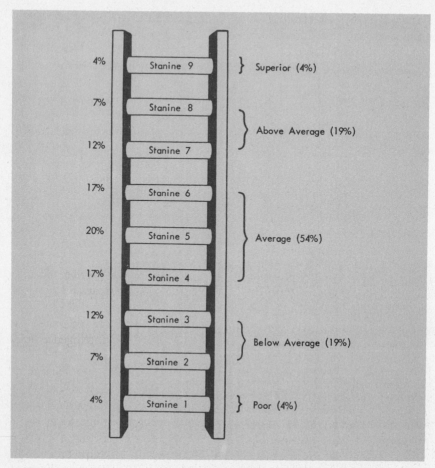

Figure 9. Stanine ladder. (Reproduced from L. J. Karmel, *Testing in Our Schools.* New York: The Macmillan Company, 1966. Copyright © 1966 by Louis J. Karmel.)

RATIO IQ

A great deal of confusion, misunderstanding, and emotionalism has clouded the concept of the intelligence quotient. Basically, the intelligence quotient is no more than a formula for obtaining a type of score that was found convenient for classification of individuals. The classical formula is

$$\text{Intelligence Quotient (IQ)} = \frac{\text{Mental Age (MA)}}{\text{Chronological Age (CA)}} \times 100.$$

Theoretically, the intelligence quotient will be 100 for the average person. That is, if a ten-year-old child does as well on an intelligence test as average ten-year-olds in the normative group, his mental age will be 10. Translated into the formula, we have the following:

$$100 \times \frac{10}{10} = 100$$

If, on the other hand, a ten-year-old does as well on an intelligence test as the average twelve-year-old, we have the following:

$$\frac{100 \times 12}{10} = 120$$

Let us look at one more example, that of a ten-year-old who has a lower mental age than his chronological years.

$$\frac{100 \times 8}{10} = 80$$

Thus our first ten-year-old is perfectly average (IQ = 100). Our second ten-year-old is above average (IQ = 120), whereas our third ten-year-old is below average (IQ = 80).

The intelligence quotient using a ratio IQ was developed originally by Wilhelm Stern for use with the Binet test of individual intelligence (see Chapter 6).

In working with the American version of the original Binet (Stanford-Binet) using ratio IQ, it has been found that the standard deviation is approximately 16 with a mean of 100. This deviation, however, is not consistent for different age levels. Thus an IQ of 110 at age 11 may be equal to an IQ of 120 at age 13. The convenience of reflecting a concept of IQ in a single number outweighs this ambiguity of interpretation.

Another problem with the ratio IQ is equating a measure of two different tests. The reader should bear in mind that an IQ on X test of intelligence is not necessarily equal to an obtained IQ on Y test of intelligence. It is possible, for example, that on X test the highest obtainable IQ would be 138, whereas on the Y test the highest obtainable IQ might be 164. Again, scores must be interpreted on the basis of relevant norms. The meaning of an IQ must be interpreted in the light of the test from which it was derived.

The reader should not conclude from this discussion that IQ scores derived from MA/CA are worthless. They are not, and they still may serve a valuable function. They give us some relative information if the user bears in mind the standard deviation and range differences, and they can be useful tools.

Another word of caution is indicated. Do not confuse the previous discussion of IQ with other methods of obtaining IQ scores. The Wechsler tests of intelligence report results in an IQ format. The method used to compute IQ in these tests, however, is very different from the classical formula previously presented. The shortcomings of the IQ based on mental age have been eliminated through the use of the deviation IQ.

DEVIATION IQ

The deviation IQ is actually a standard score, and, as such, the term *IQ* may be misleading. Nevertheless, because of many years of use, the term conveys a useful concept. Remember, mental testing is a young field and the search is still for equal units and uniform reporting. The deviation IQ is another step in this direction. Research on the Stanford-Binet demonstrated generally a standard deviation of 16. The Wechsler Intelligence Scales report IQ in terms of deviation. These are standard scores with a mean of 100 and a standard deviation of 15.

Let us look back at Figure 8. At the bottom, you will see the Wechsler Scales, and below them the deviation IQs. You can see that your knowledge of standard scores will be useful in understanding these scores. A person's raw score on each of the subtests is translated to a standard score using relevant norms. This standard score, as you can see, is based on a mean of 10 and a standard deviation of 3. The total standard scores (verbal scale, performance scale, and full scale—see Chapter 6) are then converted into IQs. An inspection of Figure 8 shows that these IQs are based on a mean of 100 and a standard deviation of fifteen points. Thus roughly 68 per cent of the IQs are between ±1 standard deviation. Among testing people, this type of estimation of IQ is known as the *deviation IQ*.

It should be noted that the deviation IQ does not differ from other standard score procedures. A given IQ in the distribution will always have the same relative position. A final note on this subject is of particular importance. The 1960 revision of the Stanford-Binet substituted the deviation IQ for the mental age concept. As you will recall, the formula of 100 × MA/CA was originally constructed for use with the Binet. The trend in testing today is to use the standard score whether we call it IQ or T-score. The *Standards for Educational and Psychological Tests* (American Psychological Association et al., 1974) states the following, "When standard scores are used, the system should be consistent with the purposes for which the test is intended and should be described in detail in the test manual. The reasons for choosing one scale in preference to another should also be made clear in the manual" (p. 23).

Practical Usage of Norms

There are two essential things to remember when trying to understand individuals by testing them. The first is the appropriateness of the test for the person, the second is to know how others have performed on the test. The "best" and most appropriate test that is valid and reliable will yield meaningless scores unless it is compared with other scores (Seashore and Ricks, 1950). Norms provide us with a frame of reference for comparison.

Norms are only meaningful if they are relevant. It does little good to compare the quality of apples with that of oranges. Similarly, when Mary is compared to a normative group, it should be composed of individuals of similar backgrounds. *Standards* (American Psychological Association et al., 1974), for example, cites as an essential requirement that, "Norms presented in the test manual should refer to defined and clearly described populations. These populations should be the groups to whom users of the test will ordinarily wish to compare the persons tested" (p. 20). In illustrating this essential requirement, *Standards* goes on to state,

> *It should be noted that "populations" are plural; in nearly all instances of tests developed for other than purely local use, the user needs to know the applicability of the test to different groups. For tests developed with a view to widespread use in schools or industry, information is needed about differences or similarities of normative data for appropriate subgroups such as sex, ethnic, grade, or age groups. Users need to be alert to situations when norms are less extensive for one group than another.*
>
> *For example, the manual for an occupational interest inventory, or for an aptitude test particularly useful in certain occupations, should point out that a person who has a high degree of interest or aptitude in a curriculum or occupation when compared to people in general will usually have a lower degree of interest or aptitude compared to persons actually engaged in that field. Thus, a high percentile score on a scale reflecting musical interest, in which the examinee is compared with people in general, may be equivalent to a low percentile where the examinee is compared with professional musicians. (p. 20)*

Teachers and counselors are often called upon to advise students about college and their chances for admission. Sound and meaningful advice is based on several factors, such as the student's high school grades, college admission test scores, and the academic caliber of students at the desired college. In a sense, most of these are norms, that is, comparison of relevant factors of the student with relevant factors of the college. Put these together and we have meaningful comparisons.

Look at Tables 12 and 13 and note the differences in median scores in each table.

Table 12 presents a general population of high school seniors. Table 13, on the other hand, is a selected group composed of high school seniors planning to go to college.

If a student had a standard score of 18 in English, 16 in mathematics, 17 in social studies, and 19 in natural science, he or she would be average or above (60th percentile, 57th percentile, 51st percentile, 64th percentile) compared to the "unselected" seniors found in Table 12. If, on the other hand, we look at Table 13, we find a dramatically different picture. Comparing this same student to "college-bound" seniors, we find he or she is a great deal below average (34th percentile, 28th percentile, 28th percentile, 39th percentile).

Thus, in guiding a youngster or adult we must have appropriate norms.

Table 12. Percentile Ranks of Unselected High School Seniors *

	Standard Score	Test 1 English	Test 2 Mathematics	Test 3 Social Studies	Test 4 Natural Sciences	Tests 1–4 Composite	Standard Score
	36						36
	35		99.9				35
	34		99.8				34
	33		99.6		99.9		33
	32		99.2	99.9	99.5	99.9	32
	31		98	99.3	98.8	99.7	31
	30	99.9	97	98	98	99.4	30
	29	99.6	96	96	96	99.1	29
	28	98.9	95	94	95	98	28
136 school	27	98	93	92	93	97	27
systems in	26	96	91	90	90	95	26
thirty-nine	25	93	89	86	87	92	25
states	24	91	87	83	83	89	24
9,370 students	23	87	84	79	79	86	23
	22	82	80	74	75	82	22
	21	77	76	70	71	78	21
	20	72	72	66	68	73	20
	19	66	68	61	64	68	19
	18	60	65	56	59	63	18
	17	54	61	51	55	58	17
	16	46	57	46	49	52	16
	15	38	52	42	44	46	15
	14	32	47	38	39	41	14
	13	26	41	33	35	35	13
	12	22	36	28	30	30	12
	11	17	30	23	26	24	11
	10	13	25	19	22	18	10
	9	10	20	14	17	13	9
	8	7	16	10	13	9	8
	7	5	12	7	10	6	7
	6	4	8	4	7	4	6
	5	3	6	3	5	2	5
	4	2	5	2	4	1	4
	3	1	4	2	2		3
	2		2	1	1		2
	1						1
Median score		16.5	14.5	16.8	16.1	15.6	

* From *Using ACT on the Campus,* © 1965 by American College Testing Program, Inc. Used by permission of the American College Testing Program, Inc.

Table 13. *Percentile Ranks of College-Bound High School Seniors* *

	Standard Score	Test 1 English	Test 2 Mathematics	Test 3 Social Studies	Test 4 Natural Sciences	Tests 1–4 Composite	Standard Score
	36		99.9				36
	35		99.8				35
	34		99.3	99.9	99.9		34
	33		98.5	99.8	99.6		33
	32		97	99.2	98.9	99.9	32
	31	99.9	95	98	98	99.6	31
	30	99.7	93	96	96	98.8	30
	29	99.1	91	93	93	97	27
	28	98	88	89	89	95	28
882,080 students	27	96	85	85	84	91	27
	26	92	81	80	79	87	26
	25	88	77	74	73	82	25
	24	81	72	69	67	75	24
	23	74	66	63	60	68	23
	22	67	61	57	55	61	22
	21	59	56	51	49	53	21
	20	51	51	45	44	46	20
	19	42	46	38	39	38	19
	18	34	40	33	33	31	18
	17	27	34	28	27	25	17
	16	21	28	22	22	19	16
	15	16	22	17	18	15	15
	14	13	18	13	15	11	14
	13	10	14	10	11	8	13
	12	7	10	8	9	5	12
	11	5	8	6	7	4	11
	10	4	6	4	5	2	10
	9	3	4	3	3	1	9
	8	2	3	2	2		8
	7	2	2	2	2		7
	6	1	2	1	1		6
	5		1				5
	4						4
	3						3
	2						2
	1						1
Median score		19.9	19.8	20.8	21.1	20.5	

Table 14. Percentile Ranks for College Freshmen Enrolled in Junior Colleges and Technical Schools *

	Standard Score	Test 1 English	Test 2 Mathematics	Test 3 Social Studies	Test 4 Natural Sciences	Tests 1–4 Composite	Standard Score
	36						36
	35						35
	34						34
	33						33
	32		99				32
	31		98	99	99		31
	30		97	98	98		30
	29		96	96	96	99	29
	28	99	94	94	93	98	28
	27	98	92	91	90	96	27
93 colleges	26	96	90	88	86	94	26
27,646 students	25	93	87	84	82	91	25
	24	89	83	80	77	86	24
	23	84	79	75	72	81	23
	22	78	75	70	66	75	22
	21	72	71	65	62	69	21
	20	64	65	59	56	62	20
	19	56	59	53	50	54	19
	18	48	53	47	44	46	18
	17	40	46	41	38	39	17
	16	33	39	34	32	31	16
	15	26	33	27	27	25	15
	14	21	27	22	22	19	14
	13	17	22	17	18	14	13
	12	13	18	13	14	10	12
	11	10	14	10	10	7	11
	10	8	10	8	8	5	10
	9	6	7	5	6	3	9
	8	5	6	4	4	2	8
	7	4	5	3	3	1	7
	6	3	3	2	2	1	6
	5	2	2	1	1		5
	4	1	1	1	1		4
	3	1	1				3
	2						2
	1						1
Median score		18.2	17.6	18.5	18.9	18.5	

Table 15. *Percentile Ranks for College Freshmen Enrolled in Doctoral-Granting Institutions* *

	Standard Score	Test 1 English	Test 2 Mathematics	Test 3 Social Studies	Test 4 Natural Sciences	Tests 1–4 Composite	Standard Score
	36						36
	35						35
	34		99				34
	33		98		99		33
	32		96	99	98		32
	31		94	97	97	99	31
	30		92	94	94	98	30
	29	99	88	91	90	96	29
	28	97	84	86	85	93	28
44 colleges	27	94	81	82	79	89	27
53,177 students	26	90	76	75	73	83	26
	25	84	70	68	65	76	25
	24	77	65	63	59	68	24
	23	68	59	56	52	60	23
	22	59	53	50	45	51	22
	21	51	48	44	40	43	21
	20	42	42	37	35	35	20
	19	33	36	31	29	28	19
	18	25	30	26	24	21	18
	17	19	25	20	19	16	17
	16	14	20	15	15	11	16
	15	10	16	11	11	8	15
	14	7	12	8	9	5	14
	13	5	9	5	6	3	13
	12	4	7	4	5	2	12
	11	3	5	3	3	1	11
	10	2	4	2	2	1	10
	9	1	3	1	2		9
	8	1	2	1	1		8
	7	1	2	1	1		7
	6		1				6
	5		1				5
	4						4
	3						3
	2						2
	1						1
Median score		20.9	21.3	22.0	22.8	21.8	

* From *Using ACT on the Campus,* © 1965 by American College Testing Program, Inc. Used by permission of the American College Testing Program, Inc.

Using "unselected high school seniors" as our frame of reference, we would probably advise college or at least junior college for our student. If we compare this student to the appropriate norms, "college-bound high school seniors," our suggestions would be quite different.

One more illustration of the importance of relevant norms can be seen in Tables 14 and 15. Table 14 presents norms for high school seniors who later attended junior colleges or technical schools. Table 15, on the other hand, is made up of high school seniors who enrolled at institutions that offer bachelor's, master's, and doctor's degrees; these institutions are primarily large public and private universities (The American College Testing Program, 1965).

An inspection of Tables 14 and 15 reveals differences in median scores. Again we see that the normative or reference group is extremely important.

Guidelines. Good norms are based upon representative and random samplings of the population for which the test has been constructed. The sheer quantity of the sample does not mean the norms are appropriate. A test, for example, based on 200,000 pupils in New York City would probably be good for New York, but would not necessarily be relevant for other geographical regions. Thus, in your review of a test manual, do not accept alleged national norms unless they are supported by a cogent and complete analysis of the sample of people they represent. Expect and look for specific relevant evidence to support the test author's claim for representative samplings.

School systems and other users of test data should develop their own local norms. These local norms should be revised periodically. This is especially relevant in the use of achievement tests. "Local norms are more important for many uses of tests than are published norms" (American Psychological Association et al., 1974, p. 33). Many test manuals describe the process of computing local norms. These local norms may be calculated by the same procedure used in determining national norms.

A list of some of the essential normative data that you should look for in a test manual follows [2]:

1. Scales used for reporting scores should be thoroughly documented and explained in the test manual in order to facilitate test interpretation.
2. Standard scores generally should be used for reporting raw scores.
3. Tables for converting grade norms to standard scores or percentile ranks should be provided.
4. Norms should in most cases be published in the test manual at the time of distribution.

[2] Based on *Standards for Educational and Psychological Tests* (American Psychological Association et al., 1974).

5. Standard scores or percentile ranks should reflect the distribution of scores in an appropriate reference group.
6. Normative groups should be clearly defined and described.
7. Method of sampling should be reported.
8. Achievement test norms should report number of schools as well as number of students tested.
9. Score variance because of such variables as age, sex, and education should be reported.

Validity and Reliability

From the foregoing chapters you are perhaps convinced that testing is a necessary and useful part of the educational enterprise, but still have questions such as, "How do I know if the test is any good?" This question is pertinent and extremely important. Let us turn our attention to this and other questions relevant to test selection.

How to Evaluate a Test

There are general considerations in test evaluation that are always important. The foremost of these is whether the test measures what it is supposed to measure. Next in importance is whether the test measures consistently and accurately. In addition to these factors, one is always concerned about the "practical" aspects of the test. Is it convenient to use? Is it economical and easy to administer and interpret? What about the time factor?

Three criteria for evaluating a test have already been mentioned. They are validity, reliability, and practicality. Let us now turn our attention to these specific test-selection factors.

Validity

The most important variable in judging the adequacy of a test is its validity. Here the question is, "What does the test measure?" Stated in other terms, a knowledge of the validity of a test can tell us what we can infer about a person from a score on a test. Thus validity data tell us how we can appropriately interpret test results.

The test author's basic purpose in constructing the test, for example, may have been to measure reading comprehension. The test buyer's concern is that the test does, in fact, measure reading comprehension. If it does, to what degree? If it does to a large extent, it is considered valid. To the degree that the test measures something else—for example, spelling—its validity as a measure of reading comprehension is impaired.

A test constructed with the aim of predicting success in high school algebra is valid to the degree that those who achieve the highest scores on it also achieve the highest grades in algebra. A test designed to measure artistic aptitude is valid to the extent that it can distinguish between those who will succeed and those who will fail in artistic endeavors.

You, as a user of tests, should judge the test in terms of your purposes. The *Standards for Educational and Psychological Tests* states, "It is the basic responsibility of the test user to read, understand, and evaluate the manual, the research, and the literature to show the appropriateness of the test for the intended use" (American Psychological Association et al., 1974).

It is important to know that validity is not measured directly, but is inferred from other data. Thus it is a judgment of the test user as to whether evidence of validity is adequate, marginal, or unsatisfactory. In a similar manner, it is the judgment of you, the test user whether the purposes of the test are appropriate to your needs for information on your local situation. Remember that validity is a matter of degree. A test is almost never completely valid, nor is it usually entirely invalid. The primary questions, then, in selecting a test are the following: How valid is it? Will it serve your needs? If it does, to what degree?

Tests are used for different evaluative needs, and for each need a different method of investigation is necessary to establish validity. Different kinds of tests are used for various measurement purposes. It should be noted, however, that the purposes of many tests overlap. For example, the major purpose of an intelligence test may be to measure mental ability, but it also may be used for determining personality aberrations and brain damage. Therefore, it is necessary to gather different validity data within one test as well as to secure validity information on different types of tests. In our example, three different uses of an intelligence test were cited. Thus validity data would be needed in each of the three because of their differing goals. It is important to remember that the *nature of the data to be secured is dependent on the objective or objectives of testing rather than on the kind of test* (American Psychological Association et al., 1974).

We will discuss four kinds of validities agreed upon by a joint committee of the American Psychological Association, American Educational Research Association, and National Council on Measurement in Education. These validities are (1) concurrent and (2) predictive criterion-related validities; (3) content validity; and (4) construct validity.

Criterion-Related Validity

Criterion-related validity is shown by comparing scores on a test with outside criteria, such as teachers' grades or job success. Evidence of criterion-related validity is necessary when you wish to infer performance on another variable from a test score. The other variable then becomes the criterion. There are two kinds of criterion-related validity: concurrent and predictive. Concurrent validity involves using a test to estimate an individual's present performance on a criterion. Predictive validity involves using a test to predict an individual's future performance on a criterion. Both concurrent and predictive validity are reported as correlations between the test score and the criterion measure. These measures of correlation are subject to the interpretation of correlation discussed in Chapter 3.

A major goal of psychology is to predict behavior, and a major tool for predicting behavior is a good test with a high predictive validity. There are problems, however, in applying results published by a test publisher to your own situation. Let us look briefly at how validation studies are conducted. After the test is constructed and written in its final form, an experimental study is designed in which the test is administered to a *representative* sample of subjects. To gather evidence of concurrent validity, a criterion is chosen reflecting the subjects' *present* status on some other measure, for example, current grades in high school subjects or job rating by a supervisor. The correlation of these two measures is the estimate of concurrent validity. Predictive validity, on the other hand, requires the passage of time. To gather evidence of predictive validity, a representative sample of subjects is given the test. If the criterion is grade-point average in college, the test constructor must then wait to see what grade-point average the subjects obtain. The correlation between the two measures is calculated, and generalizations of prediction can be made. Please note that you *cannot predict future performance from evidence of concurrent validity*. In judging criterion-related validity, obviously the criterion used is extremely important. As a test user, you need to judge that this criterion is actually what you want to predict and that it is appropriate to your group. Let us look more carefully at the criterion.

THE CRITERION

Thus far our attention has been directed to what criterion validity is and the various methods to establish it. It has been stated that in order to possess this form of validity, test scores must match with a criterion measure. Some may ask, "How do we know if the criterion measure is any good? What would we gain if we had a positive correlation between test scores and a poor criterion?" These are relevant questions. One of the most difficult problems that faces the educator and test maker is deciding on a satisfactory criterion. This is especially true in fields that have many variables that impinge on success or failure. How does one establish, for example, a suitable criterion basis for effective teaching? Does one use supervisory ratings? If so, what about their quality? The chance of variance from supervisor to supervisor is great. The atmosphere of the school and the level of ability and interest of the students might affect the teacher's attitude and instruction. In the area of vocational selection the same problems exist in defining successful performance. Conditions of work and managerial evaluations differ. It is obvious that ratings are not always consistent and that there are many factors that affect performance.

There are other criterion measures that may also be used. A college English proficiency examination given to entering freshmen may be validated in terms of its ability to predict future test scores on a comprehensive English examination given a year later. The criterion measure here is the comprehensive English examination. The most common criterion is a measure of success such as grades in training or educational programs. Selection tests for physicians, for example, may be validated against grades earned in medical school. This procedure is open to question because of several problems. First of all, grades tend to be unreliable; but even if they were not, their validity as a basis for the criterion variable would not be very high. Teachers more than anyone else know that grades have drawbacks even in terms of success in the actual training program.

We must face the fact that no criterion measure is ever perfect. The ultimate criterion is a constellation of many factors that may only be seen after a man has finished his productive work life. What is professional success and by whose measure do we gauge it? The reader can supply the other obvious philosophical questions and problems. The more important thing to remember is the imperfectness of criterion measures and their relative validity. Magnusson (1967) states, "The only way to make the criterion data more valid is to refine the analysis of the variable we wish to measure and as far as possible relate the criterion measurement to what we consider to be the genuine criterion" (p. 127).

The *Standards* give the following requirements for criterion (American Psychological Association et al., 1974).

1. All measures of criterion should be described completely and accurately in the manual.
2. The criterion measure itself should be studied for evidence of validity.

EXPECTANCY TABLE

Remember, as a test user, *you* must judge the test. Sometimes the best use may be made of tests by using your own local criteria. You can construct an expectancy table for your own population of students. This is especially important if your school is skewed with a high or low socioeconomic group, if it contains a high proportion of ethnic students, if you desire a comparison of male and female performance, or if for any other reason you think your student population may differ from the sample used in the standardization of the test.

The expectancy table is a simple device that can be used to communicate criterion-related validity to test users with little statistical knowledge. The expectancy table is a grid (see Figure 10) containing a number of cells with test scores along the side; at the top are final course grades, supervisor's rating, or any other criterion of success that is desired. For each person a tally is placed that shows, vertically, his test score and, horizontally, his rank on the criterion. After the completion of the tallying, the tallies in each cell are added and recorded in the cell. The figures in each row of cells are added and the sum is placed at the right of each row; then the numbers in each column are added and the sum is recorded at the bottom of each column.

Table 16 presents the data from Figure 10. The sum of each cell has been converted to a percentage basis by totaling the number of tallies in its row. Thus of the twenty-two cases with scores between 60 and 69 on the Sentences

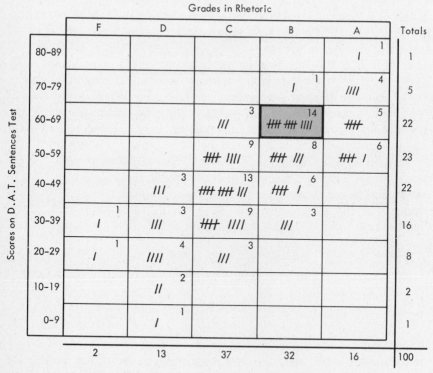

Figure 10. Expectancy grid showing how students' grades in rhetoric and previously earned scores on the DAT Sentences Test are tallied in appropriate cells. (From A. C. Wesman, Expectancy tables: A way of interpreting test validity. *Test Service Bulletin,* No. 38, New York: The Psychological Corporation, 1949.)

Table 16. Expectancy Table Prepared from the Grid in Figure 10 *

Total Number	Number Receiving Each Grade					Test Scores	Per Cent Receiving Each Grade					Total Per Cent
	F	D	C	B	A		F	D	C	B	A	
1					1	80–89					100	100
5				1	4	70–79				20	80	100
22			3	14	5	60–69			14	63	23	100
23			9	8	6	50–59			39	35	26	100
22		3	13	6		40–49		14	59	27		100
16	1	3	9	3		30–39	6	19	56	19		100
8	1	4	3			20–29	13	50	37			100
2		2				10–19		100				100
1		1				0– 9		100				100
100	2	13	37	32	16							

* The left-hand table summarizes the frequencies as they appear in the original grid. The right-hand table shows these frequencies converted into per cents. From A. G. Wesman, *Expectancy Tables—A Way of Interpreting Test Validity.* Test Service Bulletin, No. 38. New York: The Psychological Corporation, 1949.

Test, 23 per cent (five) earned a grade of A, 63 per cent (fourteen) earned a B, and 14 per cent (three) earned a C. Not one of the cases in this group received a grade lower than C. From these data, one might state that future students in rhetoric who attain scores of 60 to 69 on the DAT Sentences Test will probably be better-than-average students because only 14 per cent earned grades lower than A or B. Similar interpretations may be made for other scores and individuals (Wesman, 1949).

This example of an expectancy table reveals the predictive value of only one predictor at a time. A great many decisions in college admissions and guidance are made on the basis of more than one predictor. The double-entry expectancy table is useful when decisions are made on the basis of two predictors.

Table 17 shows the use of a double-entry expectancy table with 294 junior high school boys and girls. The Academic Promise Tests (APT) were administered at the beginning of a course in science. After the completion of the course, the grades received were: 31 A's, 65 B's, 123 C's, 40 D's, and 35 E's. Raw scores (number right) on the APT numerical section and APT langauge usage section were used in constructing the table. The numbers in the cells reveal how many pupils in each of the two-test category groups received each of the five grades. For example, the number 5 at the top of the upper right-hand cell signifies that five pupils whose APT numerical score was 40 or higher and whose APT language usage score was also 40 or more received A's in their science course (Wesman, 1966).

The advantages of the double-entry expectancy table are similar to those of

Table 17. Relationship Between APT-N and APT-LU Scores and Grades in Science of 294 Seventh-Grade Students *

Numerical Score	Language Usage Score				Row Total
	19 and Below	20–29	30–39	40 and Above	
40 and above	A B C D E	A B C 2 D E	A 6 B 6 C 1 D E	A 5 B 2 C 1 D E	A 11 B 8 C 4 D E
30–39	A 1 B C 2 D E 1	A 1 B 7 C 8 D E	A 4 B 12 C 12 D E	A 5 B 10 C 3 D E	A 11 B 29 C 25 D E 1
20–29	A 2 B 3 C 9 D 8 E 3	A 3 B 7 C 25 D 6 E 7	A B 6 C 17 D 1 E	A 1 B 8 C 2 D E	A 6 B 24 C 53 D 15 E 10
19 and below	A 1 B 2 C 22 D 19 E 19	A 1 B 2 C 18 D 6 E 4	A 1 B C 1 D E 1	A B C D E	A 3 B 4 C 41 D 25 E 24
Column total (by grade)	A 4 B 5 C 33 D 27 E 23	A 5 B 16 C 53 D 12 E 11	A 11 B 24 C 31 D 1 E 1	A 11 B 20 C 6 D E	Grand Total A 31 B 65 C 123 D 40 E 35

* From A. G. Wesman, *Double-Entry Expectancy Tables*. Test Service Bulletin, No. 56. New York: The Psychological Corporation, 1966.

the single-entry table. Double-entry tables are easy to prepare and understand and require little statistical knowledge. The basic advantage of the double-entry table is that it allows simultaneous display of relationships between two predictors and a criterion.

Other kinds of expectancy tables may also be constructed to answer such questions as, "How do we choose the best job applicants?" or, "What are the chances that an office worker will obtain an average rating or higher?" (For a more detailed analysis and application see Wesman, 1949, 1966; Anastasi, 1976, pp. 100–102.)

The expectancy table is especially useful in interpreting test predictions to teachers and school administrators. There are limitations, however. The primary drawback is the small number of cases used, which allows less confidence than do measures using large numbers of cases. It should be remembered that the average score of a class is a more reliable figure than any individual score.

VALIDITY COEFFICIENTS

The most common method of reporting test validity is by the use of a validity coefficient, which reveals the correlation between the test and criterion. This estimation of validity by a correlation coefficient is called the *coefficient of validity*. It demonstrates the relationship between test and criterion data. The *coefficient of validity* provides an overall index of the validity of the test. It is also more consistent and less prone to sampling error than the expectancy table percentages because it utilizes all the cases in the group.

There are no test manuals at the present time that report validity coefficients near or at +1.0. All fall short of perfect prediction. We would, of course, like to have higher coefficients; however, any positive correlation signifies that predictions from the test will be better than guesses.

The most important thing to remember when evaluating a validity coefficient is the extent to which it may allow for the improvement of prediction and judgment. If the validity coefficient is zero, knowledge of a test score does not allow us to predict a student's score on the criterion with any accuracy at all. As the correlation between test scores and the criterion measure increases, so does our ability to predict. Thus a person who scores in the top quarter on the test will probably be in the top quarter on the criterion measure. It should be noted, however, that some of our predictions will be in error because some of those obtaining test scores in the top quarter will be in the second quarter on the criterion measure, whereas a smaller number will be in the third quarter, and we may even find a few in the lowest quarter. The larger the validity coefficient, the less chance of predictive error.

Remember, the validity coefficient is a correlation coefficient and should be high enough to be statistically significant at the .05 or .01 level of confidence. (See Chapter 3.)

STANDARD ERROR OF ESTIMATE

The *standard error of estimate* [1] is a statistical technique used to account for the number of individuals for whom statistically calculated predictions are wrong, and the magnitude by which the estimates are in error. If, for example, validity is perfect, then the standard error of estimate is zero; if, on the other hand, validity is zero, the standard error of estimate is maximal. Thus the standard error of estimate decreases as validity increases. Statements con-

---

[1] The reader who is interested in pursuing this area in more depth can find detailed discussion in Anastasi (1976, pp. 165–66); Nunnally (1972, pp. 117–18); Magnusson (1967, pp. 138–41); Games and Klare (1967, pp. 403–405).

cerning "improvement over chance" refer to the extent to which the standard error of estimate is reduced.

The teacher or counselor who is deciding on the selection of a test should always note with caution statements by test authors or publishers that their test is valid. It is important always to ask yourself, "Valid for what?" The sheer magnitude of a validity coefficient does not assure validity for every situation or need. What you want to know is what the test measures and what you want measured.

What to Look for in the Test Manual

The following guidelines are presented for your assistance in reviewing a test manual. The fact that not all of them may be mentioned in a test manual should not surprise you. The better tests, however, will discuss the majority of the following either in the test manual or in a technical supplement.[2]

1. There should be an accurate description of all criteria measures. Attention should be drawn to the aspects of performance not reflected in the criterion.
2. Validity of the test for each criterion about which a prediction is to be made should be given.
3. Many test-criterion correlations should be reported.
4. Time periods in the test administration and collection of criterion data should be stated.
5. The criterion score should be determined independently of test scores.
6. Tests that report validity for grade predictions should clearly state the way performance is measured. (Is it in line with your procedures?)
7. There should be measures of central tendency and variability for the validation sample. (See Chapter 3 for a discussion of these concepts.)
8. The manual should describe variables such as sex, age, socioeconomic status, and level of education when these factors are related to what is being tested. For educational tests, reference should be made to the nature of the community and selection policy, if any, of the school.

Content Validity

Content validity is especially important to teachers. The teacher who gives an examination that covers the materials and objectives of instruction within her classroom has probably given a test that has content validity. How does the teacher know that a test has content validity? Before an answer can be forthcoming, certain questions must be asked. Consider for illustrative purposes a test in American history. What are the facts, skills, and concepts

---

[2] For a complete listing and discussion of the recommendations, see *Standards for Educational and Psychological Tests* (American Psychological Association et al., 1974, pp. 25–48).

that have been stressed in the classroom? What are the curricular objectives? How does the content of the test match these? Does the test require knowledge and insight beyond the scope of the course and the stated instructional objectives? To answer these questions, one must match test content against course content. If the instructional goals of the course are represented in the test, we may say the test has content validity. It sounds easy, but is it? The analysis of the test and the course is largely a "logical" and subjective judgment. In order to make our assessment as "rational" as possible, we must have an itemized list of course objectives to compare to an itemized list of test content.

Note that there are no numbers reported in terms of content validity. In criterion-related validity, we could say that the predictive validity of a test is .80 or .75. Content validity, however, is a judgment you make based on the information given in the manual regarding the universe of subject matter and the processes and objectives sampled. You then must judge if the test is a *representative* sample of all possible questions, processes, and behavior.

It is important to remember that *content validity* is especially vital for achievement measures as well as for tests of adjustment based on observations. A standardized achievement test is judged as having content validity when its content represents the curricular goals of those using the test. Whether the test is a national standardized instrument or a local classroom test, we can say it has content validity only after we have asked ourselves: Do the tasks of this test typify the educational objectives we feel are important in this area of learning? Are they the educational objectives that we have stressed in our classroom and school system? If the relationship is good, we may say the test is valid.

Test authors and publishers who produce tests for national use strive to determine the generally accepted educational aims of instruction in the area in which a test is to be constructed. They do this by surveying textbooks, class syllabi, and subject-matter specialists to determine the entire range of skills, knowledges, processes, and behaviors covered in successive grade levels in subject-matter areas. Thus constructing a nationally standardized achievement battery is a monumental task. If you do not want testmakers dictating curricula, then you should carefully check that specific tests sample the skills and objectives your school wishes to develop in students and to evaluate by test scores.

What to Look for in the Test Manual

The following guidelines should be of assistance in evaluating content validity. Not all test manuals will include all these guidelines, but the better tests and manuals will include a majority of them.

1. The subject matter covered and the extent of the sampling should be described. For example, a manual of a test of English usage might describe the types of items used and the range of subject matter as

well as illustrating to what degree responses to test items indicate accomplishments in such areas as spelling, grammar, and punctuation.

2. A short résumé should be presented of the credentials of specialists who have been consulted to evaluate the appropriateness of questions and scoring procedures, and a short description of how they arrived at their judgments.

3. If the test items have been selected by a group of experts, the manual should reveal the degree of agreement among them.

4. Statements in the manual that relate to sources of information should be dated. Courses of study and methods of instruction change, and what was a very good reflection of these yesterday may be a poor shadow today.

Construct Validity

Construct validity is ascertained by investigating what traits a test measures, that is, what the test score tells us about a person. Does it relate to some abstract construct that will give us insight into the person? Some examples of such constructs are neuroticism, anxiety, and intelligence. Construct validation requires a step-by-step accumulation of data from a great many different sources. It requires a combination of logical and empirical methods of examination. Basically, when studies of construct validity are made, they are instituted to check on the actual theory that is indigenous to the test. Thus the investigator asks, "From this theory, what hypotheses may be made concerning the behavior of individuals with high and low scores?" Data are then secured in order to test these hypotheses. Inferences based on the evidence are then made concerning the theory's adequacy to account for the collected data. If the investigator finds that the theory is inadequate to render an explanation for the data, he will (supposedly) change the test interpretation, restate or revise the theory, or completely refute the theory. New evidence, of course, would be needed to show construct validity for a revised interpretation (American Psychological Association et al., 1974).

Cronbach and Meehl (1966) discuss at great length the complexities of *construct validity* and recommend its investigation "whenever no criterion or universe of content is accepted as entirely adequate to define the quality to be measured" (p. 70). They go on to state that the determination of psychological constructs that account for test performance is a good practice for almost any test.

Construct validity because of its broad range of meanings and use can create some misunderstandings. Cronbach and Meehl (1966) in their discussion of construct validity state,

> *A construct is some postulated attribute of people, assumed to be reflected in test performance. In test validation the attribute about which we make statements in interpreting a test is a construct. We expect a person at any time to possess or not possess a qualitative attribute (amnesia) or structure, or to possess some degree of a quantitative attribute (cheerfulness). A construct has*

certain associated meanings carried in statements of this general character:
Persons who possess this attribute will, in situation X, act in manner Y (with
a stated probability). The logic of construct validation is invoked whether the
construct is highly systematized or loose, used in ramified theory or a few simple
propositions. . . . (p. 94)

The knowledge that the investigator has concerning *content* and *criterion-related* validity would be used in analyzing *construct* validity. For example, criterion-related validity in a college admissions test may be established by correlating test scores with college grades, but the selection of grades as the criterion may have come about through a consideration of what constructs are most likely to provide a base for devising a good selection test. Furthermore, a validity coefficient revealing a relationship between the test and grades (or any other criterion) gives us no meaningful information about the reason or reasons for the extent of the correlation. In order to be meaningful, it must be grounded in the context of some theoretical proposition. Thus *construct validity* is commonly investigated when we wish to increase our knowledge of the qualities that the test is measuring.

Construct validation is useful and important at times for every kind of psychological test. For example, the degree to which a certain intelligence test is free of cultural bias would be a task for construct validation. The following are some techniques and procedures used to determine *construct validity*. (For a more complete account see Cronbach and Meehl, 1966; Anastasi, 1976; American Psychological Association et al., 1974.)

1. *Correlations with other tests.* The newly constructed test is correlated with established tests that are already accepted measures of the quality or trait being examined. The Stanford-Binet, for example, has served as a criterion for validation of group intelligence tests for many years. (It is also used in *criterion-related validity*.) The construct to be measured is intelligence. The assumption is that the Stanford-Binet measures intelligence; therefore, a high correlation between the new test and the Binet means the new test also measures intelligence.

2. *Factor analysis.* This statistical procedure is of particular importance to construct validity. Basically, factor analysis is a technique used for analyzing the interrelationships of psychological data. Its major purpose is to simplify behavioral description by the reduction of the number of categories from a starting multiplicity of measurement (test) variables to a few traits. After these traits have been identified, they may be used to describe the factorial composition of a test. Thus a test may be identified in terms of the major factors determining its scores as well as the weight of each factor (Anastasi, 1976).

3. *Experimentally induced effects.* In order to discover how a test would respond to changes in external conditions, experimentally induced variables are presented. For example, a test of anxiety could be administered to an individual under conditions of stress. The anxiety test scores

could then be correlated with physiological and other gauges of anxiety during and after testing.

What to Look for in the Test Manual

The following guidelines, as in the cases of content and criterion-related validity, are based on the *Standards for Educational and Psychological Tests* (American Psychological Association et al., 1974).[3]

1. If the test is to measure a theoretical variable such as creativity or anxiety, the proposed interpretation should be stated clearly and completely; that is, a definition of the construct to be measured should be given. Thus one might say "creativity" is that ability or trait that leads to original contributions.
2. The manual should signify the degree to which the proposed interpretation has been proved.
3. Evidence concerning the effect of speed on test scores and on their relationship with other variables should be stated.

A Last Word on Validity

The reader should bear in mind that the three aspects of validity—*content, criterion-related,* and *construct* validity—are only conceptually independent. It is very rare that only one of them is important in a specific situation. In most cases, a comprehensive and thorough study of a test would involve data on all types of validity.

Remember that statements in the test manual concerning validity should be specific and focused on the types of validity for the kinds of interpretations to be made. *No test is valid for all purposes, situations, or individuals.* The intended use of the test is the determining factor in the kind of evidence that is needed. Let us briefly examine each, utilizing the basic kind of validity evidence needed, as well as its overlap with other types of validity.

1. *Criterion-related validity.* Criterion-related validity is of primary importance in intelligence or scholastic aptitude tests to reveal the ability to predict school or college success. The kind of aptitudes measured is evaluated many times by the *content* of the test items and correlations with other tests.
2. *Content validity.* Content validity is of primary importance in achievement tests. A test publisher consults with a group of subject-matter experts who help devise and arrange test items they feel cover the topics pertinent to the area represented by the test (content validity). Criterion-related validity is also necessary to check against a later criterion of performance. An achievement test may be used for a selection program.

[3] For a complete account and discussion see pp. 29–31 and 46–48 of the *Standards*.

A theoretical analysis of what is being measured by the achievement test requires a consideration of *construct* validity. For example, is a score on a mathematics test reflective of mathematical ability, understanding, or memorization of data?

3. *Construct validity.* Construct validity is of primary importance in personality tests, especially where projective techniques [4] are used. If a diagnosis is to be made, other criteria such as psychiatric opinion (*criterion-related* validity) are used at the time of testing or afterward.

It is obvious from our discussion that *validity* is a broad term encompassing many different factors. Our first question—"What does the test measure?"—is the one whose answer the classroom teacher, test author, and publisher needs to know. After this question has been answered, our next inquiry concerns the accuracy of the test. Let us, then, turn our attention to reliability.

Reliability and Measurement Error

The second most important variable in judging a test is reliability. The question here is not what the test measures, but how much of the score reflects a true measure of the individual and how much is due to error and extraneous factors. In reliability, we are concerned with consistency and the stability of a score. If we measure the same person again, how similar will the test scores be? Thus when Mrs. Gold's eighth graders take the "Jones Test of School Ability" on two different occasions, are their scores approximately the same or have they changed? If they are approximately the same, we may say the test is reliable. Henry received a score of 60 the first time he took the test and a score of 62 the second time. His scores are *consistent*. On the second administration of the same test his class, on the average, received approximately the same scores they did on the first administration. The test seems to be reliable in that there was consistency in the results obtained when testing was repeated on the same students. A lack of consistency would have been evident if the students in Mrs. Gold's class had not obtained similar scores or held the same relative test score positions. The determination of reliability on standardized tests, of course, involves many more classes and individuals, but the principle remains the same.

Reliability is a general term referring to many different types of evidence. Each kind of evidence suggests the consistency to be expected among similar observations. Specific types of errors or inconsistencies are explained by different kinds of evidence. There is no single measure of test reliability that is always preferable. The choice is dependent upon the intended utilization of the test scores. Although there are various methods of estimating

[4] See Chapter 7 for a discussion of projective techniques used in personality testing.

the reliability of psychological and educational tests, the most commonly used are based upon two measurements of the same subjects. The two measurements may be obtained by three different techniques:

1. *Retesting* subjects with the same test.
2. *Alternate form* of the original test, that is, correlation of original test scores with scores on another independent test (different form) having an item content similar to the original test.
3. *"Split-half,"* or *"odd-even,"* [5] correlation, which involves a division of the test into two parts, one part being the odd-numbered questions and the other being the even-numbered questions. The correlation between scores on the odd-numbered and the even-numbered items yields a reliability coefficient for the entire test.

It is apparent from our brief discussion so far that different methods of obtaining reliability take into consideration different sources of error. There are various factors that contribute to "unreliability" or inconsistency. They include (a) differences in the condition of the individual being tested—for example, mood, physical state, and so on; (b) differences in the test content or test situation; (c) variations in test administration, such as noise or differences in the administrative skill of the tester; (d) mistakes and differences in scoring and recording scores as well as variations in the process of observation (American Psychological Association et al., 1974).

Up to this point we have discussed what reliability is and some of the general considerations in estimating its presence. Let us now return to the three specific techniques mentioned earlier: (1) retesting, (2) alternate forms, and (3) "odd-even."

Retesting

Testing individuals with the same test they have taken earlier is known as retesting. If a physician, for example, wanted to check on the accuracy of a nurse's ability to measure patients' weight and height, the physician might ask the nurse to measure each patient twice, using the same procedures. An even better technique would be to have someone else do the second measuring, so that the nurse's recall of the first measurements would not influence the second ratings. The physician, of course, might also want to know the exact weight and height of a patient each day and how the measures vary. These two instances provide us with two separate but related investigations, measures of (1) individual variance and of (2) variation caused by the procedure of measurement.

[5] The American Psychological Association et al. statement of *Standards* (1974) refers to these types of reliability as *matched-half* and *random-half*. It also suggests estimate of reliability from a single administration if a test by analysis of variance.

The reliability of measurement in height and weight assessments is less complex than it is in standardized testing. However, the same principle is involved. Let us take as an example a test of English and the procedures for finding reliability under the retesting technique. The English test is administered to a class and is immediately readministered. Measurement here is contaminated because children are able to remember questions and do not spend as much time with the second test. The children who were not able to finish the first time will certainly be in a better position to complete the test the second time.

It is important not only to determine the degree of variation of individual response from one occasion to the next but also to know the extent of sampling variance involved in deciding on a given set of items. That is, there is no reason to think that one set of fifty English usage items is superior or inferior to another equivalent set of fifty. Suppose that one set of questions deals with a unit recently covered by some of the children being examined. These items would be especially easy for them. The test might then overestimate their level of English usage. It would do so consistently on both testings because the items would remain the same. A given set of test items is not equally valid or reliable. The point to remember, then, is that although the retesting method of determining reliability provides data regarding a particular set of items used, it is possible to obtain a very different reliability estimate if another set of items is used.

Retesting with an identical test may account for errors in answer differences to a test at a specific moment and variation in individuals from time to time. It cannot rule out, however, the variation arising out of the specific set of items chosen.[6]

The major drawback to retesting is overestimation of the reliability resulting from subjects' remembering their previous answers. *Standards* (American Psychological Association et al., 1974) is quite clear on this point:

> *Aside from practical limitations, theoretically, retesting is not ordinarily a desirable method of estimating reliability because the examinee may remember his or her responses to items from one testing to the next. Hence, memory becomes a systematic source of variance and the correlation of the two sets of scores may be higher than the correlation of two sets of scores based on two different but parallel sets of items drawn from the population of items in the same way. (p. 48)*

Alternate Forms

The alternate forms measurement of reliability attempts to establish reliability by correlating scores, obtained by the same individuals, on two different forms of the same test. These alternate or equivalent forms are con-

---

[6] Although the retest technique is not appropriate for most psychological tests, there are some motor and personality tests that are not greatly influenced by repetition and are amenable to the retest method (Lindeman, 1967).

structed with the same basic purposes in mind. They contain items of similar difficulty and cover the same areas of knowledge or skills even though they use different questions. Individuals may be tested with one form initially and then retested with the other form. The resulting correlation between the scores on the two forms is the reliability coefficient. This type of coefficient represents two aspects of test reliability—time stability and response consistency to different samples of items.

Thus alternate or equivalent test forms are variations on the same test theme. They are individually constructed tests created to meet the same specifications. Each form should contain the same number of items covering the same kind of content and arranged in the same format. All aspects of the test—including the degree of content difficulty, instructions, time limits, and so forth—must be comparable. Thus two equivalent intelligence tests should contain items and questions of the same difficulty and should cover the same kinds of areas, for example, numerical ability, abstract reasoning, and vocabulary.

Once we have established the equivalence of our alternate forms, we may administer them either "back-to-back" (that is, with the second form immediately following the completion of the first if we are not concerned with time stability) or separated by a time interval if time is a consideration.

Alternate form reliability, like any other technique, is not free of problems. There is the problem of practice effect, as in retest reliability. Although the use of equivalent forms will reduce the effect of practice, it will not eliminate it. Another limitation is the *real* difference between the forms; the concern here is with the degree of difference between test items.

The lapse of time between the first and second administrations of the test will introduce another possible source of variation in score, and thus another error in measurement.

Given the limitations of the alternate form technique, it is still the most appropriate method for most educational tests. Therefore, it is recommended that the teacher or counselor give it the greatest amount of weight in investigating the reliability of a test.

One final note of practicality is in order. The administration of a second form of a test is expensive and time-consuming; therefore, many test authors and publishers have resorted to other devices. Sometimes they are satisfactory, but more often they are poor compromises.

"Odd-Even" and "Split-Half" Reliability

If it is not practical to do testing on two different occasions or if it is desired only to sample the content consistency without taking into account individual response variation from one time to another, the "odd-even" or "split-half" technique may be used. A test of 100 items may be divided into two sets of fifty items each. One set contains all the even-numbered items, whereas the other set contains all the odd-numbered items. The relationship between scores on the even and odd sets is an "odd-even" or "split-half" correlation. The correlation coefficient for the whole test of 100 items may then be estimated by the Spearman-Brown formula. This formula thus makes it possible to obtain an estimate of reliability from one administration of one test.

The correlation obtained by comparing the odd-even test items is actually the correlation between two tests, each of which is one half the length of the original test. At this juncture, a correction is made by using the Spearman-Brown formula. On our 100-item test, a coefficient of 0.70 was obtained from the odd-even method. The formula is as follows:

$$\text{Reliability of entire test} = \frac{2 \, (\text{reliability of } \frac{1}{2} \text{ test})}{1 + (\text{reliability of } \frac{1}{2} \text{ test})}$$

The actual process using our obtained coefficient of 0.70 derived from our correlating the fifty odd items with the fifty even items is

$$\text{Reliability of entire test} = \frac{2 \, (0.70)}{1 + (0.70)} = \frac{1.40}{1.70} = 0.82.$$

The correlation coefficient of 0.82, then, presents us with an estimate of reliability of an entire test where the half tests provided us with a correlation of 0.70.

The ease and convenience of the "split-half" method have led some test authors and publishers to use it when more appropriate techniques, such as the alternate form method, are indicated. Some cautions in the use of the "split-half" technique are indicated. First, the variation of an individual from day to day is not recorded in this type of estimated reliability. Second, it should not be used with a speed test, which is an examination made up of relatively easy items that most individuals, if given enough time, will answer correctly. The objective in many speed tests is to see how many items can be responded to correctly in the indicated time. In computing "odd-even" scores on a speed test, the two scores tend to be similar and the reliability coefficient may be close to +1, or perfect. For illustrative purposes, let us say a 100-item test depends entirely on speed, so that individual differences in score rest completely upon number of items tried, rather than upon errors. If Robert has a score of 84, he will have forty-two correct odd items and forty-two correct even items; if Jim obtains a score of 64, he will have thirty-two odd and thirty-two even correct. Thus, with the exception of accidental errors on a few questions, the correlation would be perfect (+1.00).

Most of our tests are not speed tests—and though they may be timed, the results will generally not be as severely affected when the "split-half" technique is used with them.

The important thing to remember is that the "split-half" procedure is a measure of the consistency of content sampling. Stability of individual scores over time does *not* enter into this estimation because both halves of the test were taken at the same time (Anastasi, 1976).

Other methods of dividing a test into two halves may be used. These are matched-half and random-half. In a matched-half, each half of the test is matched in terms of content by expert judgment. According to *Standards* (American Psychological Association et al., 1974), in this method all questions that are experimentally dependent should be placed in the same half of the test. For example, in a reading test there may be several questions about the same paragraph. These questions are experimentally dependent on the same material and should be placed together. If the two halves of the test do not have exactly the same number of items, appropriate procedures can be used to equate them. In random-half, the two halves of the test are selected by an appropriate randomizing procedure.

Before leaving this area of reliability, one other method of estimating internal consistency should be noted. It is the formula developed by Kuder and Richardson (1937). It does not require the division of the test into halves and rescoring and calculating a correlation coefficient. This formula is based on the assumption that every item in a test measures the same general factors as do the others. This procedure leads to a reliability coefficient that may be interpreted in the same manner as the "odd-even" coefficient. This formula has drawbacks similar to those of the Spearman-Brown formula mentioned in our previous discussion, in that (1) it is not appropriate for speed tests and (2) it does not measure individual variance from one time to another.[7]

A final method of calculating reliability using one test administration is by analysis of variance using a computer. In this method the correlation between every possible combination of halves is calculated, and the reliability coefficient is the mean of all these coefficients.

Standard Error of Measurement

In our discussion of testing thus far, we have seen some of the factors that affect the accuracy of a test score. To state, then, that no test is perfectly accurate should not surprise the reader, nor should anyone at this point think that a person's test score is determined only by his ability or knowledge. It is true, of course, that usually a person is the primary determiner of his own score, but the score is also a reflection of the inaccuracy of the test itself.

In interpreting a test score, it is extremely important to take into account how much of the score is due to error and how much is due to qualities or skills the individual actually possesses. It is also useful to know the source

---

[7] The formula most commonly used is called the Kuder-Richardson "formula 20." It is stated as

$$r_{tt} = \frac{n}{n-1}\left[1 = \frac{\Sigma pq}{\sigma^2}\right]$$

For a more complete discussion and statistical treatment, see Cronbach (1970), Nunnally (1972), and Magnusson (1967). For those with a good mathematical background, Lord and Novick (1968) is an excellent advanced treatment of tests and statistical theories.

of these errors. A statistical technique which accounts for this test error and allows us to estimate the margin of error in the test score is the *standard error of measurement*. It is especially useful in the interpretation of individual scores when attempting to estimate the expected degree of variation in a student's test score. If Mary, for example, obtains an IQ of 116, how much confidence can we place in this score? Will she obtain an IQ of 128 next testing session or an IQ of 104?

It is true that the reliability coefficient gives an estimate of accuracy, but it does not assist specifically in interpreting individual scores. The numerical value of the coefficient is dependent to a great degree on the range of scores in the group being examined. That is, if a group has a small spread in the ability being measured, the coefficient will be low, whereas if the group has a large spread in a particular field, it will be higher. The standard error of measurement does not have these difficulties.

Let us look at an actual school situation where knowledge of the standard error of measurement would be used. An intelligence test has been administered to the ninth-grade classes at Stevens Junior High School. Mrs. Olson, a teacher, is asking the counselor about one of her students.

Mrs. Olson: How did Donald Smith do on the test?

Counselor: Let's see. His IQ is around 110.

Mrs. Olson: What do you mean, "around 110"? Is it 110 or is it not?

Counselor: The score he obtained was 110, but we can't be sure that 110 is his "true" score.

Mrs. Olson: I see, but what is a "true" score?

Counselor: The true score does not actually exist, but it is the theoretical actual measure of Donald's IQ. A test score, however, reflects his actual ability plus the inaccuracy of the test to measure that ability. This inaccuracy is called the standard error of measurement.

Mrs. Olson: Hold on, I'm getting a little confused. What is this "standard error"?

Counselor: We know that every test is inaccurate to some degree, but we have no way of measuring that inaccuracy directly. Thus we must estimate this error. Let us suppose that Donald took an IQ test like this one every day for a year. If we plotted these 365 scores, the data would resemble a normal curve. The average of all these tests would be Donald's true score. If we then computed a standard deviation on these scores, that number would be the standard error of measurement of the test. Obviously, there are not 365 forms of an IQ test, nor is it feasible to retest one person so many times, so an estimate of standard error is arrived at mathematically. That is why it is an estimate rather than an empirical fact. The standard error of this test is 6. That means that for 68 per cent of the people taking this test their true score will be within ± 6 points of the obtained score. For 95 per cent of the people taking the test, their true score will be within ± 12 points of the obtained score.

Mrs. Olson: That is very interesting, but you said that this was a very reliable test.

Counselor: Yes, it is. Our reliability coefficient is .90, which means that the correlation between two forms or two halves of the test was less than perfect, but good; 1.00 would indicate a perfect correlation. As you have probably already guessed, as the reliability coefficient goes up, the measurement error goes down; as the reliability coefficient goes down, the error goes up.

Mrs. Olson: Then why can't we just use the reliability coefficient?

Counselor: While they do generally have an inverse relationship, they measure somewhat different things. Reliability, remember, is a correlation coefficient, while an estimate of measurement error is mathematically derived and also takes into account the standard deviation. As a math teacher, you can see this from the formula.

$$SE^m = SD \sqrt{1 - r} \quad {}^8$$

Therefore, it is not always accurate that a test with a higher reliability will have a lower error of measurement.

Mrs. Olson: Good, but what about Donald? What does a score of 110 tell us.

Counselor: What we have said explains why we report test results as a range rather than a number. How wide a range we give depends how much risk that we are wrong we are willing to take. If we assume that Donald is in the 68 per cent whose true score is within six points of the obtained score, we will say Donald's IQ is between 104 and 116. If we assume that he is in the 95 per cent whose true score is within twelve points of the obtained score, we will say Donald's IQ is between 98 and 122.

Mrs. Olson: That is a wide range.

Counselor: Yes, it is. That is why it is better to tell you that Donald's IQ is solid average to high average. He should have no difficulty with the work in your algebra class. You will not be pushing him beyond his ability to see to it that he does his work.

Mrs. Olson: Thank you. That is what I really wanted to know.

Now that Mrs. Olson knows something about standard error of measurement, she would not be shocked to find that on another testing her student may obtain an IQ of as high as 122. The standard error should make us cautious in attaching meaning to minor elevations or depressions in test scores. Remember that in actual practice we do not know an individual's "true" IQ: we know only the IQ obtained on one test and the probabilities that another administration of the same test would yield a score that varied by so many points.

The standard error of measurement is one of the reasons that one test score should never be thought of as a fixed number but as a score *within the band* where the true score lies. A large standard error means the band is broad; consequently, we would have less confidence in our obtained score than if the standard error were smaller. For example, what if Mrs. Olson's

---

8 SE^m = Standard error of measurement.
  SD = Standard deviation of obtained scores.
  r = Correlation coefficient.

student obtained an IQ of 110 on a test with a standard error of ten points? The band where his "true" score might be (one standard error) would be between 100 and 120. How comfortable can the teacher or counselor feel with a band that reveals there is a good chance that the student's true IQ is average (100) or superior (120)? If we carry it out to two standard errors, the band where the true score might be found is increased from the lower limits of average (90) to the very superior range (130). If, on the other hand, the standard error is two points, the teacher can feel fairly comfortable (carried out to two standard errors) that her student's obtained IQ of 110 will fall on either side of his true IQ by four points, or from 106 to 114. This range would indicate solid average ability.

Table 18 presents the relationship between the reliability coefficient and the standard error of measurement. The standard errors of measurement for different reliability coefficients and standard deviations can also be seen in Table 18. Note that as the reliability coefficient increases, the standard error decreases. It is obvious, then, that the higher the reliability, the smaller the error in individual test scores.

Table 18. Standard Errors of Measurement for Given Values of Reliability Coefficient and Standard Deviation *

	Reliability Coefficient					
SD	.95	.90	.85	.80	.75	.70
30	6.7	9.5	11.6	13.4	15.0	16.4
28	6.3	8.9	10.8	12.5	14.0	15.3
26	5.8	8.2	10.1	11.6	13.0	14.2
24	5.4	7.6	9.3	10.7	12.0	13.1
22	4.9	7.0	8.5	9.8	11.0	12.0
20	4.5	6.3	7.7	8.9	10.0	11.0
18	4.0	5.7	7.0	8.0	9.0	9.9
16	3.6	5.1	6.2	7.2	8.0	8.8
14	3.1	4.4	5.4	6.3	7.0	7.7
12	2.7	3.8	4.6	5.4	6.0	6.6
10	2.2	3.2	3.9	4.5	5.0	5.5
8	1.8	2.5	3.1	3.6	4.0	4.4
6	1.3	1.9	2.3	2.7	3.0	3.3
4	.9	1.3	1.5	1.8	2.0	2.2
2	.4	.6	.8	.9	1.0	1.1

* From J. E. Doppelt, *How Accurate Is a Test Score?* Test Service Bulletin, No. 50. New York: The Psychological Corporation, 1956.

This table is based on the formula $SE_m = SD \sqrt{1 - r_{tt}}$. For most purposes, the result will be sufficiently accurate if the table is entered with the reliability and standard deviation values nearest those given in the test manual. Be sure the standard deviation and the reliability coefficient are for the same group of people.

A great many test manuals report both the reliability coefficient and standard error of measurement. If the standard error of measurement is not given, Table 18 would enable you to make an approximation.

To obtain the standard error for a test from Table 18, note the reported reliability coefficient and standard deviation as given in the test manual and match them with or near the coefficients and standard deviation (SD) in the table. Let us suppose, for example, that you find that the Brown Test of School Ability has a reliability coefficient of .87 and a SD of 12. The first thing you would do is find the appropriate coefficient, which is .85 (because it is nearest to .87), and then go down the row (.85) until you are next to the SD row of 12. The number 4.6 (under the .85 column and directly across from the number 12 under SD) is the approximate standard error of measurement. It should be restated that the standard error of measurement and the reliability coefficient are both methods of demonstrating test reliability. The standard error is not directly comparable from one test to another and is independent of the variance of the group on which it is computed.[9]

Remember, a reliability coefficient and the standard error of measurement have a reciprocal relationship. As one goes up, the other goes down. *Standards* (American Psychological Association, 1974) states,

> *Reliability coefficients have limited practical value for test users. The standard error of measurement ordinarily is more useful; it has great stability across populations since it is relatively independent of range of talent, and it may be used to identify limits that have a defined probability of including the true score. Test users may use reliability coefficients in comparing tests, but they use standard errors of measurement in interpreting test scores. Information in a test manual about a standard error of measurement may often be more important than information about a reliability coefficient. (p. 50)*

Factors Affecting Reliability

Let us turn our attention to four specific influences on test reliability.

LENGTH OF TEST

In our discussion of the Spearman-Brown formula it was seen that the length of a test may affect the reliability coefficient. The chance of measurement errors decreases proportionately with the length of the test. That is, the longer the test, the greater the chance that the score is a reflection of the person being tested and that it is a more accurate estimation of his ability, achievement, or any other characteristic being measured. This is logically true because we have increased the number of samplings of the characteristic

---

[9] The reader who is interested in a more thorough statistical treatment of the standard error of measurement should see McCollough and Van Atta (1965), Magnusson (1967), Games and Klare (1967), Nunnally (1972), and Popham (1975). For a little less statistical and more verbal discussion of this subject, see Doppelt (1956) and Cronbach (1970).

we wish to measure. If, for example, in an American history course you administer a test consisting of one essay question concerning the Civil War period, how reliable will your results be? The students who happened to know that particular area would get a perfect score, whereas those who were weak in that area would get zero. Let us suppose you increased the number of questions to five, could you then feel more comfortable in evaluating your students' knowledge of the Civil War? Undoubtedly you would say yes, but with the reservation that even more questions—say, ten or fifteen more, or 100 multiple-choice—would be an even better device. Thus by increasing the size of our sample and thereby lengthening the test, we increase the reliability of our instrument.

Of course there are practical limitations to increasing the length of a test. Factors such as time available for testing, number of good questions one is able to write, and student fatigue all limit the length of the test. If you must have short tests, then a more frequent testing schedule would provide a greater sampling of what you want to measure and would consequently be more reliable. In interpreting standardized test results, be wary of subtest scores based on relatively few items. If no reliability data are given for them, the best thing is to use only the total score or scores.

RANGE OF TALENT

The reliability coefficient, as we have stated before, varies with the extent of talent in a group, even though the stability of measurement is not affected. A wide range of talent yields high coefficients, whereas a small range produces low coefficients. Thus, to interpret a coefficient properly, a measure of the variability of the group is needed.

Table 19 illustrates this range effect or spread of scores on two forms of an arithmetic test administered to twenty students. Note that changes in rank from one form to the other are rather insignificant. These data would produce a fairly high coefficient. However, if we examine only the five highest students and their ranks, the importance of the changes becomes greater. Student C's change in rank from third to fifth in the larger group represents only a 10 per cent shift (two places out of twenty). The same shift in the smaller group is a 40 per cent change (two places out of five). If we use the twenty on which we calculate the reliability of the test, it is evident that going from third on form X to fifth on form Y still leaves the student in the top part of the distribution. On the other hand, if the estimation of reliability is only on the group of the top five students, this change from third to fifth means a drop from the middle to the bottom of the distribution. If we based our coefficient on these five cases, it would be very low. Again, it should be noted that it is not the smaller group which brings about a lower coefficient, but the narrow range of talent. If you take five other cases such as A, E, J, O, and T, who rank from first to twentieth, a coefficient as great as that based on all twenty students would be produced (Wesman, 1952).

Table 19. *Raw Scores and Ranks of Students on Two Forms of an Arithmetic Test* *

Student	Form X		Form Y	
	Score	Rank	Score	Rank
A	90	1	88	2
B	87	2	89	1
C	83	3	76	5
D	78	4	77	4
E	72	5	80	3
F	70	6	65	7
G	68	7	64	8
H	65	8	67	6
I	60	9	53	10
J	54	10	57	9
K	51	11	49	11
L	47	12	45	14
M	46	13	48	12
N	43	14	47	13
O	39	15	44	15
P	38	16	42	16
Q	32	17	39	17
R	30	18	34	20
S	29	19	37	18
T	25	20	36	19

* From A. G. Wesman, *Reliability and Confidence.* Test Service Bulletin, No. 44. New York: The Psychological Corporation, 1952.

This example illustrates why the reliability coefficient may vary although the test items and the students' performances are unchanged. Remember that *you need to have information on the range of ability in the tested group before you can correctly interpret the reliability coefficient of the test.*

ABILITY LEVEL OF THE GROUP

The ability level of the group is a factor similar to the one just discussed. When you interpret a student's test score, remember that the most meaningful reliability coefficient is one which rests on the reference group that is comparable to that of the student. Of course, it is impossible for a test manual to present reliability for all possible group memberships.

The appropriate comparison group is based on what we want to know. If we are testing ninth-grade boys for mechanical aptitude, we should have reliability coefficients based on the scores of ninth-grade boys. The coefficients are less meaningful when they are based on "all high school" boys taking the test. They become even less pertinent when the coefficient rests on all high school and college students taking the test. The coefficient of reliability becomes increasingly meaningful the closer we can come in comparing the group we want to know about with the original group on which the coefficient was based.

METHOD USED

It is very important to consider the procedures used in obtaining the reliability coefficient when comparing two different tests. The size of the reliability coefficient is related to the methods used. Different procedures treat various sources of variance differently.

It cannot be said that because procedure A obtains a higher coefficient that it is better than procedure B, which yields a lower reliability coefficient. For example, the "split-half" operation usually produces the highest reliability coefficient. We know that it is not the best technique and that speed may unduly influence the value of the coefficient it produces. (See the previous section on "odd-even" and "split-half" procedures.) On the other hand, the most demanding and generally most appropriate procedure—that is, the alternate or equivalent form method—when used with a time interval between test and retest, yields the lowest reliability coefficients. Do not be impressed by the sheer elevation of the coefficient. The value of the reliability coefficient should be considered, but remember that the methods used are reflected in the coefficient and warrant your attention.

All methods by their very nature introduce some error in measuring the "true" score. The sources of these errors are discussed in the *Standards for Educational and Psychological Tests* (American Psychological Association et al., 1974). When the retesting method is used, the subjects may remember the questions (and the answers they gave) from the previous administration. Thus memory is a source of error in this method. In using parallel forms of the same test, error arises from the fact that, although the items are similar, the subjects are not asked to perform exactly the same task. Another source of error in this method is that there must be a time lapse between the two administrations. Many things happen to change individuals during this time. Thus time lapse becomes a source of error. The third method of estimating reliability, the split-half method, represents the other side of the coin. Reliability is concerned with how a measure holds up over time; thus a source of error for split-half is that it does *not* sample individual variation over a period of time. In addition, while all items come from the same test, the two halves of the test do not require identical tasks. The principle is that there is error in all estimates of reliability. What you need to know to interpret tests is how much error and what kind.

Height of Reliability Coefficient

A reliability coefficient should be as high as possible. Unfortunately, perfection is not now possible, so we must settle for the best we can get.

The degree of reliability should be determined by the purposes and situations for which we intend to use the measurement instrument. The school psychologist who must decide on the possibility of placing a child in a mentally retarded class or state institution needs the most reliable instruments available. The counselor attempting to ascertain parental attitudes toward educational policy is of course not as concerned with reliability, because only the average figures need to be highly accurate, not the individual parental responses.

If an instrument with low reliability (and a high standard error of measurement) is the "best" or only device, and you need to use it, be careful in making evaluations. Obtain all types of data and use the test results with this information on a tentative basis. As we stated in our discussion of validity coefficients, even a poor but significant coefficient is better than nothing. The basic principle to keep in mind is that the importance of the decision is equal to the need for precision in measurement. The greater our need for confidence in the stability and consistency of the test, the more we need higher reliability.

Again, remember that a reliability coefficient is a correlation coefficient and should be significant at the .05 or .01 level of confidence. At the .05 level of confidence, you are willing to risk that five times out of 100 this reliability coefficient is in error.

What to Look for in the Test Manual

The following guidelines will in most cases be familiar to you from our recent discussion of reliability. They are intended only as a quick checklist to help you in evaluating a test's reliability. They represent some of the most important features and are based largely on the recommendations in *Standards for Educational and Psychological Tests* (American Psychological Association et al., 1974). The reader is referred to *Standards* for a complete and detailed description.

1. Reliability evidence should be reported to the extent that you may judge whether scores are dependable for the recommended purposes of the test. If any important data have not been obtained, this should be mentioned.
2. Every score, subscore, or combination of scores should be judged by the standards for reliability.
3. Reports on reliability or error of measurement should be given in enough detail to permit you to judge if the data are applicable to the types of persons you desire to examine. For example, in a mechanical comprehension test, is there evidence that indicates that reliability was obtained for girls as well as boys?
4. The reliability analysis for an intelligence or achievement test intended to be used to make differentiations within one school grade should be based on pupils only within the actual grade. It should *not* be based on many grades with a broader range of ability.

5. The test manual should state if there are significant changes in the error of measurement from score level to score level.
6. Test authors and publishers should report reliability investigations in standard statistical terms (for example, standard error of measurement and reliability coefficients). It is their job to communicate with you. Do not be awed by unconventional statistics. If the statistical usage is unusual the test author should present a complete explanation of why and what these statistics mean.
7. Reliability is very important but it is not a replacement for validity. Reliability does not demonstrate validity; it can only support it.
8. If two forms of a test are used, both of which are intended for the same subjects, averages and spread of scores as well as the coefficient of correlation between the tests should be given.
9. Sometimes measures of internal consistency are most appropriate; however, they should not be thought of as substitutes for other measures. If alternate forms are available, they should be used, and alternate form reliabilities should be reported as the preferred technique. This does not mean coefficients resting on internal analysis should be omitted. It only means that alternate forms have first preference.
10. In most cases estimates of internal consistency should be based on the "split-half" or Kuder-Richardson technique. Any deviation from this should be clearly explained in the test manual.
11. Careful attention to a review of reliability coefficients based on internal analysis, especially on time factors, is important. If speed is a factor the coefficients will be exceptionally high and tend to be insignificant.
12. The test manual should indicate to what degree test scores are likely to change after a given amount of time has elapsed. The mean and standard deviation of scores and correlation at each testing should also be reported.

Practical Concerns

Until now our attention has been focused on the technical and theoretical aspects of testing. These, of course, are of primary importance in selecting tests; however, practical considerations cannot be overlooked. Financial aspects of testing and test time are necessary concerns of the school administrator and his staff. In addition, ease of administration and scoring are important factors, because teachers generally have a minimum amount of experience and training in testing.

Economic Aspects

Money is a very important consideration when formulating educational policy. Testing must take its turn in the line of educational needs awaiting financing. Fortunately, testing is relatively inexpensive, especially when compared to other educational needs. In addition, federal and state allowances almost guarantee every school district in the United States enough funds to maintain an adequate standardized testing program.

Because funds are not unlimited, it is desirable to save money when possible. One of the first places where it is possible to save is in the reuse of test booklets that have separate answer sheets. Thus the only yearly expenses are answer sheets and occasional replacements of worn-out booklets. Test booklets with separate answer sheets, however, should not be used in the primary or lower elementary grades. The end of the fifth grade or beginning of the sixth is probably early enough to begin using separate answer sheets. However, there may be situations where the children's sociopsychological, intellectual, and motor skills are very well developed, in which case an earlier grade would be appropriate. On the other hand, in some settings junior high school would be early enough.

Administrative Aspects

Tests are generally administered by teachers or other educational personnel with limited measurement training. The ease of administering a test is facilitated by simple and clear directions. Giving a test with a great many subtests which require exact (stopwatch) timing and new directions for each section is an exacting job. This may produce a situation for possible errors in directions and timing which could affect the final results. Validity and reliability of the test scores would then be of questionable value.

Time Aspects

Saving time in test administration should be approached with extreme caution. In our discussion of reliability, it was stated that the reliability of a test is dependent on the length of the test. Thus shortening the test time is generally accomplished at the expense of test reliability. This is particularly true of some "quickie" tests on the market that claim to produce a reliable IQ score in fifteen or twenty minutes. Some tests are efficiently constructed, but in most cases reductions in testing time mean loss of reliability.

Scoring Aspects

There are many teachers who have viewed testing with horror because of tedious hours spent hand scoring. To make matters worse, many times the directions for scoring required a test specialist to interpret. Today, by the use of separate answer sheets and machine scoring, this problem has at least been reduced for those teachers who teach upper elementary grades and beyond. In addition, most contemporary test manuals go to great lengths to present scoring procedures in simple and easy-to-understand terms.

Tests for children in the primary grades (K–3) must of necessity involve more time in scoring because young children may find separate answer sheets confusing. By the middle elementary grades (about the middle or end of the fourth grade), there are techniques, such as answer spaces at the right side of the page which can be scored with an answer key, that lessen the scoring burden. (See Chapter 5, section on scoring, for more details.) There is every reason to choose a test that is easily scored over one that is difficult to score if this does not sacrifice validity or reliability.

Interpretive Aspects

There is no point in an elaborate testing program if the results are not meaningful in educational planning. Test results that are hard to understand or easy to misinterpret are not only a waste of time but in some cases are harmful to the children we are attempting to help.

The manual should present cogent and clear statements concerning the meanings of scores. Do not administer any test, even if it has all the positive features we have discussed, until you are sure you know what to do with the results. Tests are constructed to tell us something. If they do not do this, they are a meaningless exercise in the consumption of time.

Test Ethics, Standards, and Procedures

chapter 5

What are the basic ingredients of a psychological test? Maybe 2 pounds meaty veal knuckles, 3 quarts water, 1 large onion stuck with 2 cloves, 2 leeks, 1 carrot, and so on. No, you say? Those are some of the ingredients to make white veal stock. These ingredients define the "dish"; that is, the content vividly relates to the entree. This is not true with a psychological test.

The basic purpose underlying the construction and use of psychological tests is to sample some aspect of an individual's behavior. This is true whether the behavior is mental ability or personality characteristics, whether the objective is to evaluate reading progress or interest patterns, whether the purpose is to measure attitudes or possible brain damage, creativity or musical talent. The list of possible behavioral samples is lengthy. The point to remember is that a psychological test is not defined by content as much as it is by function.

The psychological test is an instrument that attempts to measure an aspect of behavior in an objective and standardized manner. (See section on standardization, Chapter 1.) The primary intent is to sample human behavior without introducing human subjectivity. This goal, of course, has never been fully reached on any psychological test, because perfect standardization and objectivity have not yet been attained. On the other hand, a reasonable amount of success in this area is evident with the majority of tests.

Teacher-made tests are not generally considered psychological tests because they usually do not fulfill the requirements of objectivity and standardization. Our discussion of ethics, standards, and procedures in this chapter will be focused on psychological tests.

The major criticisms and controversies of testing were discussed in Chapter 2. One of the most obvious conclusions from a review of test criticism is that many times the attack should not be directed at the test per se, but at the use of tests. In this chapter, an attempt will be made to give the student some guidelines for proper test usage.

Some History

The development of an official body of standards for testing is relatively new. It was not until 1954 that an official statement on test procedures was published.[1] This statement represented a consensus of data that was considered most beneficial to a test consumer. In the period before 1954, test standards and quality varied according to the ethics, standards, and knowledge of individual test authors and publishers. In order to understand more fully the importance of standards in testing, let us briefly review the major periods and issues.

The first use of the term *mental test* in the psychological literature was in an article by Cattell (1890). The article discussed the use of tests of muscular strength, speed of movement, reaction time, sensory discrimination, and other measures used to determine intellectual levels of college students. Other investigators, such as Ebbinghaus (1897), devised tests of arithmetic computation, memory span, and sentence completion to measure school children's intelligence. Many more investigations could be cited, but the important point is that these early efforts were to lead to the development of the Binet intelligence scales.

In 1905 Binet, along with Simon, developed the first intelligence test similar to our present tests. The 1905 scale was a tentative instrument without an objective method for deriving a total score. The second scale (1908) introduced the term *mental age*, which compared children to normal children of the same age. (For example, a mental age of five years means a child passed all the items normal five-year-olds would pass.) In Chapter 6 we will deal with Binet's first efforts in more detail.

The work of Binet was reviewed with earnest enthusiasm in the United States and his tests were translated from French into several English versions, the most noteworthy of which was the Stanford-Binet.

The Stanford-Binet Intelligence Test was developed at Stanford University by L. M. Terman (1916). It was in this test that the term *IQ* was first used.

The genesis of modern testing may be considered to be from 1900 to 1916. This is the period during which Binet and his co-workers were developing the first scales. It was during this time that Terman (1916) and others such as Kuhlmann (1912) were translating and revising the Binet Scale.

The next fourteen years, 1916–1930, may be viewed as the "fad" period

---

[1] The first official declaration on testing standards was called *Technical Recommendations for Psychological Tests and Diagnostic Techniques*, written and published by the American Psychological Association in 1954.

in test development. The Binet tests and revisions were individual tests in that they could be administered to only one person at a time. This next period saw the emergence of group testing.[2] The development of group testing, as you will recall from our discussion in Chapter 2, was brought about by the entry of the United States into World War I. The need for swift intellectual classification of over a million recruits led to the development of the Army Alpha and Beta tests. After the war, these tests were released for civilian use and served as the models for other group intelligence tests.

During this period, large-scale testing programs were instituted with optimistic naïveté. Standardized tests were developed for most of the content areas of the school curriculum. The examination of college applicants for admission became routine. Instruments for evaluating many different school skills were developed and used extensively. In short, the American public became test conscious. Not only was the public aware of testing, especially IQ tests, but it and many professional educators tended to deify tests. Tests were the instruments from the promised land. This attitude of blind acceptance of testing, of course, led to many serious abuses. The fact that measurement was in its infancy was often forgotten in the rush to "be with it."

Americans are noted for their tendency to jump on the bandwagon of something new, and testing was no exception. However, educators, psychologists, and others after a time became more critical of tests and of the uses made of them. Thus Anastasi (1976) states that, "When the tests failed to meet unwarranted expectations, skepticism and hostility toward all testing often resulted. Thus the testing boom of the twenties, based upon the indiscriminate use of tests, may have done as much to retard as to advance the progress of psychological testing" (p. 12).

This mounting criticism of testing had the beneficial effect of forcing the test producers and consumers to reconsider their methods. This period of reappraisal and broadened prospective extended from about 1930 to 1946. The exacting standards of test construction and usage which we know today owe much to this period of test development.

The successful use of tests and test batteries [3] during World War II gave rise to a measurement renaissance after the war ended. From about 1946 to 1961 may be considered the period in which testing experienced a rebirth— not so much in the construction of new tests, but in the widespread use of tests and test batteries. Large-scale testing programs in local school systems were launched and those administered by the College Entrance Examination Board were expanded. During this time a new college entrance examination, called the American College Testing Program, was founded.[4]

This renaissance of measurement also saw the birth of test standards. It

[2] A group test may be administered to one or more individuals at a time.

[3] A group of several tests that are comparable, the results of which are used individually, in various combinations, and/or totally.

[4] This is a federation of state programs founded in 1959. Objectives are similar to the College Board program. (See Chapter 11.)

was in this period that the American Psychological Association (1954) and the American Educational Research Association and the National Council on Measurements Used in Education, Committee on Test Standards (1955) first published recommendations for the construction and use of tests.

In the early 1960s, as in the 1930s, a negative reaction to testing became evident. This time, however, the bulk of test criticism was voiced by lay critics. Most of these critics had little knowledge of testing and did little research to back up their attacks (see Chapter 2).

The period from 1962 to the present may be characterized as the "illegitimate criticism" era of test history. This may be contrasted to the "legitimate criticism" period of the 1930s and early 1940s. Whereas the first period was initiated, directed, and pursued by professionals who were earnestly attempting to rectify past errors in order to produce better tests, the present critical period sees nonprofessionals attacking tests in a sensational and non-scholarly manner.[5] A destructive rather than a constructive approach is evident.

In the light of test history and the recent barrage of critical attacks on measurement, the importance of standards cannot be overemphasized. As a student of measurement, it is particularly important for you to be aware of the code of test ethics and standards we are about to discuss.

Ethics

The history of psychological measurement has witnessed rigorous adherence to the scientific method, personal dedication, and creativity. On the other hand, there has been needless duplication, intrusion of profit motivation, and improper scientific attitude and procedure. To combat the misuses of psychological tests, professional organizations concerned with measurement have developed ethics and standards. In 1963 the American Psychological Association published an article entitled "Ethical Standards of Psychologists."[6] Testing is a major area of concern in this document, which codifies the professional ethics of the association. The proper use of psychological tests is also featured in *Ethical Standards* (American Personnel and Guidance Association, 1974), which is the code of professional ethics of the American Personnel and Guidance Association. The American Psychological Association (1973), in order to produce even more clarity on ethics (especially conflicts of value, e.g., science's progress and individual protection), published *Ethical Principles in the Conduct of Research with Human Participants*, and in 1977b *Standards for Providers of Psychological Services.*

[5] A notable exception is *Testing, Testing, Testing* (American Association of School Administrators, Council of Chief State School Officers, and National Association of Secondary-School Principals, 1962), a brief booklet which attempts to take a critical look at testing in a coherent and productive manner.

[6] Amended by the American Psychological Association's Council of Representatives in September 1965 and December 1972.

Three professional organizations (American Psychological Association, American Educational Research Association, and National Council on Measurement in Education) concerned with measurement joined together in 1966 to produce a document on standards for tests. This "bible" for test standards was called *Standards for Educational and Psychological Tests and Manuals.* The problems and issues in testing such as admissions to institutions of higher learning and employment screening were soon outdated. The three professional organizations, therefore, revised the 1966 edition in 1974. Let us briefly review some of the main points pertaining to ethics and standards as formulated by these professional organizations.

Distribution and Sale

One of the most important points in the ethical use of psychological tests is that the sale and distribution be confined to qualified users. The qualifications of the purchaser should be commensurate with the type of test being sold. For example, the school counselor may be qualified to administer, score, and interpret tests of educational ability, achievement, and interest, but he may not have the training to administer an individual test of intelligence such as the Stanford-Binet or a personality device such as the Rorschach. The codes of ethics of both the psychological and guidance associations are quite clear on this point. The American Personnel and Guidance Association (1974) states, "Different tests demand different levels of competence for administration, scoring, and interpretation. It is therefore the responsibility of the member to recognize the limits of his competence and to perform only those functions which fall within his preparation and competence" (p. 208).

The American Psychological Association (1977a) states, "Psychologists associated with the development or promotion of psychological devices, books or other products (tests) offered for commercial sale make every effort to insure that announcements and advertisements are presented in a professional, scientifically acceptable, and factually informative manner" (p. 22).

Test Interpretation

One of the basic concerns of both professional workers using tests and the general public is test interpretation. Principle 8 of "Revised Ethical Standards of Psychologists" (American Psychological Association, 1977a) is explicit in placing the responsibility on the writer and publisher to state in the manual all material needed for interpretation, including, "the development of the test, the rationale, and the evidence of validity and reliability . . . applications for which the test is recommended and . . . special qualifications required to administer the test and to interpret it properly" (p. 23). Responsibility for interpretation rests on the psychologist. "In reporting test results, psychologists indicate any reservations regarding validity or reliability resulting from testing circumstances or inappropriateness of the test norms for the person tested.

Psychologists strive to insure that the test results and their interpretations are not misused by others" (p. 23).

Many of the abuses and misuses of tests have resulted from the use of tests by persons with little or no training. Test results should be released only to qualified personnel, and adequate facilities for further counseling should be available if the results are particularly disturbing to the individual. For example, John Smith, a senior at Exodus High School, is in the upper quarter of the class. His college entrance examination scores are very low and he is understandably very depressed and despondent over the results. At this point, further counseling is certainly indicated. The counselor or psychologist could probe for the possible personal reasons for the low scores and discuss possible measurement factors that could account for the discrepancy.

If John Smith does not receive appropriate counseling he may decide against going to college, and his self-concept could be appreciably lowered. In some cases, extreme disappointment could lead to attempts at suicide. Thus even the most seemingly innocuous test results must be handled by qualified personnel who are trained to counsel as well as interpret test results.

Test Security

Test security is another ethical concern of psychologists and educators. Control of the distribution and sales of tests is needed not only to prevent unqualified persons from using tests but also to prevent public familiarity with test items that could interfere with test validity.

It is apparent that if a high school senior obtained a copy of a college admissions examination or the answers to many of the questions, the test would no longer be a measure of college aptitude for him. One of the consequences of such a situation might be admission to a college where the candidate has little chance of success.

Many times tests are invalidated by persons acting in good faith. Almost every teacher and counselor has witnessed examples of this. For example, during a school district's eighth-grade testing, the author witnessed a counselor instructing children in algebra before administering an algebra aptitude test. "Boys and girls," he said, "last year the eighth-grade had a lot of trouble with this kind of problem and I think if you understand how to do it your scores will be higher." (Walking to the board the counselor wrote a simple equation.) "Now when $X = 3$ and $Y = 3 \ldots$." He proceeded to explain how that type of problem was worked.

The example problem the counselor used was not an exact duplicate of the test item, but the only difference was the numbers used. The counselor "meant well" and felt that he was "helping the kids." But was he? He was in fact hurting them. The purpose of the test was to select children for ninth-grade algebra and general math. Those students not ready for algebra who did well on the test would be in for some academic shocks. The validity of the test to predict behavior in ninth-grade algebra had been compromised, by how much it is impossible to tell.

Invasion of Privacy

Another important ethical problem to the testing profession as well as the lay public is "invasion of privacy." This problem is especially relevant to personality tests. Some individuals, without knowing they are doing so, may reveal personal characteristics. The psychologist who uses these tests has an important responsibility to the individual being tested. *No person should be tested under false pretenses.* It is very important that the examinee know how the test results will be used. The code of ethics is very clear on this issue. "The client has the right to have and the psychologist has the responsibility to provide explanations of the nature and the purposes of the test and the test results in language that the client can understand . . ." (p. 23).

In the area of confidentiality, the code is also quite explicit. "Information obtained in clinical or consulting relationships, or evaluative data concerning children, students, employees, and others are discussed only for professional purposes and only with persons clearly concerned with the case" (p. 22).

Standards

Earlier in this chapter it was stated that until 1954 there was no official guide representing a consensus concerning test standards. Although this is true, it should be noted there were informal test standards before that date. These standards could be found in textbooks and other publications. Test publishers and authors interested in quality have generally adhered to these. It is also true, however, that less dedicated or knowledgeable authors and publishers produced tests that fell short of these informal standards. In order to lessen the occurrence of inadequate tests, professional associations concerned with testing produced official statements of measurement standards. The discussion of testing standards that follows will be generally based on *Standards for Educational and Psychological Tests* (American Psychological Association et al., 1974).[7] Our attention will be particularly focused on areas of concern to the user of tests.

Advertising

Test publishers should present their tests in an accurate and complete manner. Beware of extravagant claims in promotional materials. For example,

---

[7] A copy of *Standards for Educational and Psychological Tests* may be obtained by sending $1.50 to the American Psychological Association, 1200 Seventeenth Street, N.W., Washington, D.C. 20036.

an advertising brochure for an achievement test may state that, "This instrument measures the modern day educational objectives of American history." This, of course, is very difficult, because curricular objectives differ from school to school and from teacher to teacher. The statement suggests that the test is suitable for all classes in American history. It may indeed be an excellent test, but the potential user cannot be sure, without detailed inspection, that the test is in line with the curricular objectives of his school.

Test Age

There is no specified period that a test and manual may be used without revision. It is recommended (American Psychological Association et al., 1974), however, that a publisher should withdraw a test from use if the manual is fifteen years old or more. Society and educational objectives change with time. For example, a test to predict algebra aptitude might be completely outdated by the "new math," or one to measure "new math" outdated by reversion to older methods.

The relevant questions concerning test age are: What is the relationship of the test to current educational practices and to the contemporary society? How recent is the date of publication and/or revision? Are there new data with the new revision? Are there dates given for the collection of the new data and new norms?

Test Manual

The test, the manual, and all other accompanying material should be geared to helping test users evaluate test results. It is very important that the users of test know what the results mean. One method of facilitating this is making sure that all material dealing with the interpretation of the test is clear and correct. This means that it should have meaning to a school teacher as well as to a measurement specialist. This is extremely important. If the user is not able to read the manual with understanding, he will not be able to interpret the test scores adequately.

The manual should stress the vulnerability of the test and discuss factors other than the test score that need to be considered in interpreting the results. The test manual should assist the test user by stating precisely the basic purposes and uses for which the test is intended.

It is very important that the test manual indicate to the prospective purchaser and test seller the qualifications required to administer and interpret it. If a test may be used for different purposes, the manual should state the amount of training needed for each use.

Be careful of statements in manuals that do not have a statistical basis. If, for example, you read that such and such a score indicates "psychotic tendencies," look for statements that tell you what proportion of people obtaining that score have later been identified as pyschotic.

It is essential that every test manual contain the *validity* of the test for each interpretation to be made. It is incorrect to say "validity of the test"; one can, however, speak of the validity of particular interpretations. For example, the manual for an English test of mechanics of expression may state that the test is appropriate for high school juniors and seniors planning to go on to college. However, is it able to discriminate among those students in honors classes who are planning to matriculate at highly selective colleges?

It is essential that every test manual contain the *reliability* of the test. The manual should report the evidence of reliability and the method used in obtaining it. The yardstick for reliability should apply to every score or combination of scores. For example, a test yields a verbal and nonverbal score; reliability for both scores should be reported.

Test manuals should contain directions for administration that you can understand and practice. Be sure that the directions are clear enough that your students will understand the tasks that are required. The scoring procedures should also be presented in detail and with clarity so as to eliminate scoring errors.

Norms should be presented in every test manual. They should refer to specific populations so that the children being tested may be compared to these reference groups.

Testing and Scoring Procedures

The most obvious and primary consideration when discussing testing procedures is the need for rigorous adherence to standardized testing conditions as outlined in the test manual. It is unfortunate but true that many teachers and sometimes even counselors violate this basic rule. Almost all test manuals are quite explicit about the need to read the directions verbatim and follow the time limits with precision.

It is impossible in a book such as this to outline all the various techniques in test administration and scoring of all psychological tests. For example, certain tests such as the Stanford-Binet and the Rorschach require specialized training, including special courses, texts, and intensive supervision. The primary purpose of the following discussion is to assist school teachers and counselors who will be called upon to administer and score group standardized tests.

Administering the Test

THE TEST ADMINISTRATOR

The administration of a group test is not a complicated procedure. Any teacher and most secretarial personnel can be trained to perform this function through an in-service program (see Karmel, 1965). The relative simplicity of administering group tests leads many teachers and school administrators to the erroneous conclusion that little advance preparation is necessary. This, of course, is not true. No matter who administers the tests and no matter how many years of testing experience they may have had, examiners need to know the peculiarities of the specific tests they are to administer. An in-service program attended by all faculty members during the first month of the school year should promote good test administration.

The first session should include a general orientation that encompasses the reasons that tests are given, what the tests mean, and the specific implications for pupil growth and educational development. The time period for this phase of the session should be no longer than forty minutes, with at least fifteen minutes devoted to questions and discussion. After approximately forty minutes, an informal coffee break to continue the discussion is a good idea.

A second session for faculty who are to administer and proctor [8] the tests should also be planned. This session should be scheduled within two to five days of the school testing dates. The main purpose of this session is to thoroughly familiarize the test administrators and proctors with the specific tests to be used. Stress should be placed on directions for the administration of the test, especially standardizing procedures. The importance of the following test procedures should be emphasized:

1. *Test directions should always be followed without any deviation.*

This means that the test administrator does not change the directions even slightly. If the directions are poor, this should be considered when choosing the test. Test administrators should understand the importance of reading directions *verbatim*. No matter how good your memory may be, never rely on it when administering a test.

2. *Student questions should be answered within the context of the test directions.*

This may mean repeating or paraphrasing test directions, or it may mean going over practice examples to clarify procedures. Students must understand the directions before testing begins. For example, look in on the administration of an arithmetic test. Miss Hart is reading the directions.

Miss Hart: In this part of the test you will have an opportunity to show your ability to work with numbers. Look at your test booklet and you will see three sample problems. Problem number one asks you to add 15, 17, and 10. Note that on the right-hand side of the problem there are four possible answers. Choose the one that you think is right. *(Pause.)* Circle the letter of the right answer. *(Pause.)*

---

[8] A proctor is an assistant to the test administrator who helps by passing out test materials, keeping order, and answering student questions.

Student: Can we circle the number?

Miss Hart: Choose the answer that you think is right and circle the letter (*with emphasis*) of the right answer.

Student: What if none of the answers are right?

Miss Hart: Look at sample problem two and you will see next to one of the letters the words *none of these*. Remember, you are to *circle* the letter next to the answer you think is right. Has everyone finished sample problem number one? (*She looks around to see if everyone has.*) Good, now go on to sample problems two and three.

Student: I don't understand problem number three.

Miss Hart: You don't understand problem three?

Student: Well, what I mean is, how could you get 25 when—OK, I see my mistake; never mind, I understand.

Miss Hart: Does everyone understand the sample problems? Are there any questions before we start? (*She looks around the room not only for raised hands but also for possible problems by the expressions of the students. Seeing that there are no questions, Miss Hart continues her reading of the directions.*) Remember to choose the answer you think is right and circle the letter next to it. Do not spend too much time on any one problem. Any questions? (*Miss Hart looks around once again.*) All right, begin.

During the testing session Miss Hart and her proctors maintain a constant vigil, always available to help any student with a problem. Miss Hart knows that once a test begins, questions are not to be encouraged. She knows, of course, that neither she nor her proctors may assist a student on specific items or provide clues as to the correctness of a pupil's response.

Let us return to Miss Hart and the test setting. A student has just raised his hand and Miss Hart has silently gestured for him to come to her desk.

Student: I don't understand the meaning of this question.

Miss Hart: You don't understand the meaning of the question?

Student: No, I don't.

Miss Hart: You don't?

Student: Well, what I mean is I don't remember how to do this part of it. Can you just tell me what (*student points to a section of a test problem*) I should do here?

The reader should note that up to this point Miss Hart has been non-directive; that is, she has reflected the student's questions. To do more would obviously have entailed answering the test question or giving important cues, which would have the same result. Now, however, Miss Hart must be directive and make it quite clear to the student that he will have to work out his own problems:

Miss Hart: Jim, I am very sorry. (*Miss Hart smiles warmly.*) I can't answer your question. If you are stuck on that question, go on to the next item. Just do the best you can.

3. *Time limits must be strictly observed.*

"Don't ever trust one clock," said an experienced teacher-tester. They seldom teach that in graduate school, or in measurement texts, but let us pass on this advice. It really does make sense. Your watch may stop running, but more likely you may be holding it and inadvertently change the time (that has happened). Or if you rely on the school clock, the electricity could be temporarily shut off and there you are in the middle of an examination not knowing "the time of day." The following are two basic rules that should be of help: (a) if a test has sections with short time limits, five minutes or less, each examiner should have a stop watch to ensure accurate timing; (b) most tests will require only an ordinary watch with a second hand. When using a watch, write down the time you begin and the time testing is to stop. (Remember to use a second time piece such as the school clock to insure reliability.)

4. *The examiner and his assistants should check, infrequently, on the progress of the examinees.*

The word *infrequent* is used because there is often too much circulating around the room by proctors. In a great many cases, this does not serve the interest of the students and tends to make them more anxious. On the other hand, some "circulating" is necessary. The best procedure, of course, to assure student compliance with the test format is to be sure all students understand what is expected of them and how they are to respond to the test items before testing begins.

A few minutes after testing has begun, the examiner and proctors should silently move around the room to check that students are working on the correct pages and that they are marking their responses in the appropriate place. After the proctors have completed their "rounds," they should return to strategically located posts where they may be available to help individual students. They should not circulate again until a new test or subtest is begun.

A final note of caution is in order. Remember, it is not the duty of the examiner, nor is it necessarily beneficial to the examinee, to encourage or prompt students during the test. An exception to this rule is in the examination of young children, where it may be necessary to encourage children in the first six grades to keep working or to check their work after they have finished.

The in-service training program should be a yearly occurrence. In most schools, major testing occurs in the fall. If tests are also given in the spring, it is not necessary to repeat both sessions. However, a refresher review is desirable, followed by concentration on the tests to be given in the spring. Only those faculty members who will be administering the tests need be involved. The spring session should be no longer than one class period, or approximately forty-five minutes.

PHYSICAL SETTING

Thorndike and Hagen (1969) list four desirable conditions for testing. They state that the subjects should be "(1) physically comfortable and emotionally relaxed, (2) free from interruptions and distractions, (3) conveniently able to manipulate their test materials, and (4) sufficiently separated to minimize tendencies to copy from one another" (p. 542).

Anastasi (1976) suggests a room free from distraction, with adequate lighting and ventilation. Although all these recommendations seem appropriate, they really do not seem to affect test scores. For example, one of the authors worked one summer in a test center at a major university where construction was going on and the temperature was over 95 degrees. After completing the test (a graduate admissions examination), a designated committee of these students approached the test director to complain about the hideous conditions of testing. Their complaint was so obviously justified that the director agreed to allow them to take the same examination in another setting on the following day. The new setting was in an air-conditioned building free of noise or other distractions. A comparison of test scores indicated few significant changes. In fact, two students scored several points lower on the second administration.

Super, Braasch, and Shay (1947) presented a number of distractions to graduate-student groups during the administration of a vocational and scholastic aptitude test. The experimental group was subjected to trumpets blaring in the next room, sudden opening of the door by "irate" students who would then argue noisily outside the door, and a timer that went off five minutes early. The experimenter then told the annoyed students to go on for five minutes more. Guess what happened? There were no significant differences in test scores between the experimental group with all of the distractions and the control groups that completed the tests under "ideal" conditions.

It is the feeling of this writer that psychological conditions are more important than the physical setting. Nevertheless, *one should strive for optimal testing conditions.* The following are nine conditions that, although not always possible to achieve, are desirable.

1. Maintain adequate lighting and ventilation (as good as those in the classroom setting).
2. Try to use the classroom for testing, especially with young children.
3. Post signs on the doors indicating that testing is in progress.
4. Make arrangements with the administration to suspend the class bells, fire drills, or public announcements.
5. See to it that everyone has had a chance to use the bathroom. (This is especially important with young children.)
6. See that each examinee has two usable pencils, and that there are extras for those who will need more.
7. Have desks or tables that facilitate the manipulation of test materials.

8. Try to separate the children so that they are not tempted to look at a neighbor's paper.
9. Have at least one proctor for every twenty-five students.

PSYCHOLOGICAL SETTING

The psychological climate is of primary importance; much of it is dependent on the physical conditions and the test administrator's ability to establish rapport. The psychological setting varies with the attitude of the examiner. For example, is the examiner a threatening or supporting figure? Is he the kind of person students rebel against or want to please, or are they indifferent to him?

The various methods for achieving rapport will differ somewhat according to the type of test and the ages and grades of the students. Preschool and primary school children (nursery through third grade) especially need to be treated in a warm and friendly manner. The examiner should be relaxed and "cheerful" so that the children are not threatened by the test. Children at this level should enter testing with feelings similar to those they feel when a new game is initiated. On the other hand, the older school child should be treated more realistically. That is, he should be told once again (a pretest orientation has already exposed him to the reasons for testing) to do his best and that the examination is to help him. It is always helpful to state that "hardly anyone ever finishes or is able to answer all the questions correctly."

The importance of the psychological setting has been demonstrated in numerous research studies (see Sarason, 1950; Sacks, 1952; Wickes, 1956; Sarason et al., 1960). These studies have revealed that testing must be interpreted in the light of the test situation and that good relations with the examiner produce better test results. For example, Wickes (1956) found that the examiner's behavior had a significant effect upon test scores. It has also been shown that it is beneficial to know the children before testing them. Sarason and his associates (1960) theorize that some children perceive the "objective" examiner as a rejecting figure because of their own dependency needs.

The preceding factors make it very difficult to suggest concrete guidelines for producing the right psychological test atmosphere for all children and for all test situations. There are some general rules, however, that would be appropriate for most testing situations and most students.

1. A pretest orientation for the students should be scheduled. This meeting should include the purposes and reasons for testing. All students who will be tested should attend.
2. The test administrator should maintain a relaxed and empathetic manner throughout testing. Directions should be read in a warm (not sugary) and clear voice.
3. The examiner should convey his objectivity to the examinees without coldness or aloofness.

4. The test administrator and his proctors should refrain from any autocratic or authoritarian manner. At the same time, the students must understand that testing personnel are in charge and certain procedures must be carried out in order to safeguard test validity.
5. Every effort should be made to provide the best physical conditions for testing.

Scoring Procedures

The primary consideration of teachers and counselors in test scoring is economy of time. Few things make school personnel more hostile to testing than the laborious hand scoring of tests. Teachers and counselors should not have to be concerned with this clerical task.[9] Their time can be spent more profitably in other educational endeavors; moreover, there are more accurate and reliable methods of scoring. Almost every section of the country has access to commercial test-scoring services located at university test centers or private agencies. If the school cannot afford such services there are many other methods available. Let us briefly review some of these.

Scoring Stencil

The scoring stencil is a cardboard answer sheet with the correct answers punched out. It is applicable to tests with a multiple-choice or true-false item format. The stencil is placed over the answer sheet and the number of black pencil marks that are visible is equal to the number of correct answers obtained. That is, the placement of the stencil over the student's answer sheet immediately reveals the number of right answers. Some sample items from a test that uses a scoring stencil [10] may be seen in Figure 11. This test is concerned with "word meaning"; students are requested to read the beginning part of each sentence and decide which word is best. They are then instructed to fill in the circle which has the same number as the one they have chosen.

The Self-scoring Answer Sheet

The self-scoring answer sheet is another method of scoring found in some tests. An example of this type may be seen in Figure 12. In this example from the Kuder Preference Record, a pin-punch answer pad is used. The student is given a metal pin that he uses to punch holes in circles on the answer sheet. The inside of the answer booklet contains printed sets of circles. The student's score is computed by tallying the number of holes punched in the circles.

A variation of the same principle is found in the self-scoring carbon pad. This form requests the student to mark his responses on the outside of an answer booklet with a pencil. The booklet is self-contained and cannot be

---

[9] This is not always true, of course, when primary teachers might want to check for difficulties in certain tasks and gear their future teaching accordingly.

[10] Items may also be answered on a separate answer sheet for machine scoring.

14 **The traditional ways a society does things are often called its —**
   5 species   7 language
   6 technology   8 culture   14 ⑤⑥⑦⑧

15 **Which one of these would *least* likely be found in the ruins of an ancient Mayan city?**
   1 jade objects
   2 wagons
   3 wooden carvings
   4 stone tablets   15 ①②③④

16 **Man's learned, socially influenced behavior is called his —**
   5 religion   7 culture
   6 technology   8 species   16 ⑤⑥⑦⑧

17 **The slogan "Remember Pearl Harbor" was popular during —**
   1 World War II
   2 World War I
   3 the Korean War
   4 the Vietnam War   17 ①②③④

Figure 11. Sample questions from Test 9, Social Science, of the Stanford Achievement Test, Intermediate Level II, Form A. (Reproduced from the *Stanford Achievement Test, Intermediate Level II, Form A,* copyright © 1973 by Harcourt Brace Jovanovich, Inc. Reproduced by special permission of the publisher.)

opened without tearing. Squares or circles underneath the correct answers record the responses through the carbon backing onto the answer sheet. Scoring is accomplished by counting the number of marks in the squares or circles.

MACHINE SCORING

The scoring of a large number of answer sheets by machine is faster and requires less manpower than scoring by hand. There are many machine-scoring plans from which to choose. Figure 13 illustrates an IBM-type answer sheet that has been used widely in the last twenty years. The IBM answer sheet may be scored by hand or by the 805 International Test Scoring Machine. Special electrographic pencils are needed for this answer sheet. Figure 14 reveals the newer MRC answer sheet, also used in machine scoring. The MRC answer sheet is scored on electronic test equipment at Measurement Research Center, Iowa City, Iowa. Ordinary soft-lead pencils are used with this answer sheet.

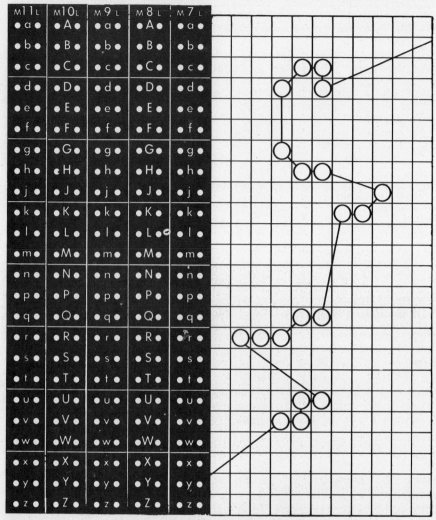

Figure 12. Front and inside views of a portion of the Pin-Punch Answer Pad of the Kuder Preference Record—Vocational Form CP. (From *Kuder Preference Record Vocational, Form* CP by G. Frederic Kuder. Copyright ©1948, G. Frederic Kuder. Reprinted by permission of the publisher, Science Research Associates, Inc.)

The school district should make its choice of scoring method on the basis of individual needs and financial capacity. The following are some of the major plans.

Package Plan. A school district contracts with a test publisher for tests, answer sheets, scoring, and statistical analysis of scores. This plan, though

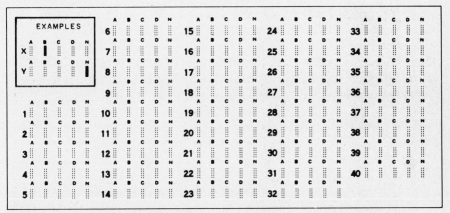

Figure 13. A section of an IBM 805 answer sheet used with the Differential Aptitude Tests. (Reproduced by permission. Copyright © 1972, 1973 by the Psychological Corporation, New York, N.Y. All rights reserved.)

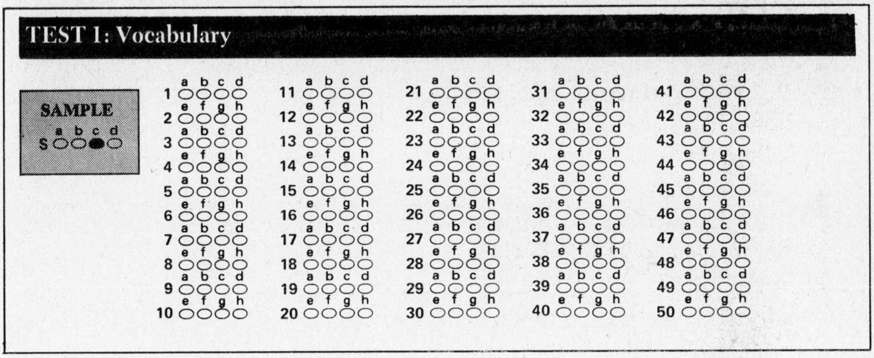

Figure 14. A section of a MRC answer sheet used with the Iowa Silent Reading Tests. (Reproduced from *Iowa Silent Reading Tests,* Copyright © 1973 by Harcourt Brace Jovanovich, Inc. Reproduced by special permission of the publisher.)

very convenient, sometimes leads schools to purchase tests they normally would not use. Important test factors, such as the suitability of the test for the local system, are often overlooked because of the administrative ease of the plan.

Test-Scoring Plan. The test-scoring plan leaves the school district a great deal more freedom to choose tests. A school makes arrangements for test scoring with a test publisher, university testing bureau, or a company such as Testscor whose primary business is scoring tests. It is also possible to make arrangements with most of these companies to obtain a statistical analysis of the school's results.

Test-Scoring Equipment. Obtaining test-scoring equipment involves renting or purchasing machines to score tests at the local school district. Smaller school districts often join together to share the cost and use of the machines. This plan is the most inexpensive if the machines are kept busy. There are several problems, however, with this plan. First, one must train personnel in the use of the machine. Second, the problem of machine breakdown can cause delays and expense. In addition, one must add to the cost of the machine itself the expense of special help in the form of machine operators and clerical assistants.

SCORING ERRORS

No matter what type of scoring method is utilized, one must constantly be alert to the possibility of error. This means that the original machine scoring should always be rechecked by randomly selecting and rescoring by hand approximately every twenty-fifth paper. The reader should note that "every twenty-fifth paper" is an arbitrary choice; every tenth or thirty-fifth paper will also do. Each hand-scoring operation should always be independently checked. This means every hand-scored answer sheet must be scored at two different times to assure accuracy. Ideally, this involves two different scorers; however, this is sometimes very difficult to manage. If two different scorers cannot be arranged, then the next best thing is to rescore the papers on a different day. Rescoring does not mean a simple checking of counting and addition. It means carrying out all scoring operations from placing the key over the student's responses to deriving his score.

Personnel assigned to scoring tests should be well trained for the specific operations needed in the tests to be used. They should be cautioned to be especially careful in adding part scores (that is, adding different subsections) to make a total score, and in going from raw [11] to converted [12] scores. Remember the old saying that "a chain is only as strong as its weakest link"; this is also true in testing. The most sophisticated research, test design, and other important test construction factors are rendered meaningless if the scorer makes a simple mistake in addition.

Factors Affecting Test Performance

Motivation

In testing ability the a priori assumption is always made that the person being examined is "doing his best." If the conditions of uniformity of testing are to be maintained, every person should be motivated and expected to "do his best." The importance of motivation to the examinee's test behavior

---

[11] Raw score is the number of correct answers.
[12] Converted score is the symbolic representation of the raw score translated into percentiles, stanines, or grade equivalents.

has been demonstrated in a number of studies. Incentive studies offering rewards for submission to authority figures have failed to produce significant score increases on ability tests compared to scores earned in a regular test setting (for example, see Benton, 1936). On the other hand, when the student is concerned over his test score, increases of scores may be seen. (See Hurlock, 1925; Gustad, 1951; Eells, 1951; and Flanagan, 1955 for interesting investigations and discussions of this problem.)

The emotional climate of the test setting and personality problems of students being examined may influence the motivation of some students. Gordon and Durea (1948) administered the Stanford-Binet to eighth-grade students and retested these same children two weeks later in an atmosphere designed to lower self-esteem and produce discouragement. The second tests revealed significantly lower scores than those of another group of eighth-grade children who were retested under normal conditions. Goldman (1971) states that,

> *clients who see the forthcoming test as potentially useful to them but not threatening are likely to exert optimal amounts of effort.* Lack of effort *may come from various sources: In some cases it may represent lack of interest in the test and lack of any expectation that it has something of value to offer. In other cases, lack of effort may represent just the opposite perception, that the tests are terribly important and even threatening. In such a case lack of effort may play a defensive role, permitting the individual to say afterward, "I didn't really try, because I wasn't interested in the results of this test, and they won't affect my plans in any way. (p. 117)*

McClelland (1966), after experimentally investigating the role of motivation in achievement and test scores, reports that, regardless of innate ability, a person who has little or no motivation to learn is not going to obtain a high intelligence test score. Regarding intelligence test scores, he states,

> *There are two places where motivation enters into an intelligence test score: one in the accumulation of knowledge that the subject shows on the intelligence test or achievement test, and the other in the attention he gives at the time he takes the test. We know that people who have high achievement motivation will actually do better in the testing situation. So there is an intertwining here of achievement motivation and the intelligence measure. (p. 537)*

Many studies have revealed that achievement motivation is related to social values and child training. These in turn relate to ethnic group, religion, social class, and other factors (see McClelland, Atkinson, Clark, and Lowell, 1953; McClelland, 1955; Rosen, 1956; Winterbottom, 1958). These studies focus on the importance of a child's background in determining the proportion of abilities he will use in a test situation.

An analysis of many of the investigations indicates that a family environment that stresses early responsibility and independence of children as well as the social values of competition and hard work leads to achievement orientation and motivation.

Atkinson (1957), in his investigation of "risk-taking behavior," found that an individual who feels there is little chance for advancement may reveal correspondingly low levels of motivation. The implications from these findings, if valid, are especially relevant in testing the culturally disadvantaged. That is, there is a strong possibility that disadvantaged groups may do poorly on tests in part because they lack the incentive to capitalize on those talents that they do have.

The student of measurement should pay close attention to the role of motivation in testing. Special caution is especially indicated in interpreting the test scores of emotionally and culturally disadvantaged youngsters.[13] On the other hand, it is also obvious that most American school children are not disadvantaged and are generally sophisticated about tests and motivated to do well in academic and test situations. These children are easily motivated and their cooperation in testing situations is not difficult to obtain. Therefore, if the classroom teacher follows the instructions of the test manual and is psychologically supportive of her pupils, it is fairly safe for her to assume that most of her students will be doing their best. The teacher who is in a disadvantaged setting will, of course, want to stress the positive importance of testing and to provide optimal motivational conditions. She will also want to consider motivational factors in her analysis of the test results.

Anxiety

Test anxiety and free-floating anxiety[14] are closely related to test-taking motivation. The highly motivated student, for example, may be so anxious to do well that his very desire may interfere with a good score. The person who is tense makes errors he would not normally commit. The student of measurement knows from his own personal experiences and observations that there is a great deal of anxiety and tension during testing.

Gaudy and Spielberger (1974) reviewed the literature as well as their own studies in an attempt to relate anxiety and educational achievement. Spielberger (1972) edited a book of readings on contemporary theories and research attempting to present all facets of this highly complex and interesting subject.

DeLong (1955) studied the behavioral reactions of elementary students in a normal classroom setting and during the administration of tests. He reported that during testing the children reacted in an anxious and disturbed fashion.

The relationship of anxiety to test performance is not all one-sided. There

---

[13] In addition to emotional and cultural factors that may interfere with optimal test performance in a school setting, special motivational problems are encountered in testing prisoners or juvenile delinquents and mentally ill patients in institutional settings (see Sears, 1943; Rosenzweig, 1949; Sarason, 1954).

[14] Free-floating anxiety is a state of general uneasiness or dread for which there is no objective reason.

are some studies that reveal that a degree of anxiety or tension enhances test performance. Review the following research and compare it with your own thinking on this subject.

A great many investigations into the problem of anxiety and test performance have been made by S. B. Sarason and his colleagues (Mandler and Sarason, 1952; Sarason and Mandler, 1952; Sarason, Mandler, and Craighill, 1952; Sarason and Gordon, 1953; Sarason, Davidson, Lighthall, and Waite, 1958; Waite, Sarason, Lighthall, and Davidson, 1958; Sarason, Davidson, Lighthall, Waite, and Ruebush, 1960). They developed a questionnaire to ascertain test anxiety. This instrument [15] contained such questions as: While taking a group intelligence test, to what extent do you perspire? Do you worry a lot before taking a test? If you know that you are going to take a group intelligence test, how do you feel *beforehand*? While you are taking a test, do you usually think you are not doing well?

Sarason et al. (1958), in a study of 600 children in second to fifth grade, found that test anxiety increased with grade advancement. They also found that children with the greatest anxiety tended to perform at a lower level. In an earlier study (Mandler and Sarason, 1952), similar findings were reported; however, it was noted that the lessened performance caused by high anxiety tended to be overcome with time. This study and a later investigation (Waite et al., 1958) led Sarason and his associates to conclude that test anxiety tended to impair test performance. They also found that social class was a factor in test anxiety. Upper- and middle-class subjects had less test anxiety than those of lower class. They interpreted this to mean that at higher social levels there is less family pressure on intellectual achievement. Sarason et al. (1960) found that with elementary school children anxiety was more pronounced in verbal than in nonverbal tests and was greater on new and different types of tests.

Sinick (1956) concluded that "a high level of anxiety, whether existent or induced in Ss, generally brings about impaired performance, but occasionally causes improvement" (p. 317). Grooms and Endler (1960) concur that for some individuals anxiety is an inhibitory factor that lowers performance.

After years of studying the problem of test anxiety, Sarason and his associates (1960) state, "The most consistent finding in our studies is the negative correlation between anxiety and intelligence test scores: the higher the test score on anxiety, the lower the IQ" (p. 270). They further state that the source of the anxiety is only partly lower ability. The vast majority of subjects who made up the negative correlation were within the average range of intelligence (90–110) and should not have had academic problems. They feel that "in the case of the intellectually average but anxious child, the estimate of potential based on conventional tests may contain more error than in the case of most other intellectually average children" (p. 270).

Goslin (1963) makes a very practical point when he says that the place of

---

[15] It should be noted that there was more than one form of the basic questionnaire; for example, there was one form for children and one form for older students.

anxiety on test performance is difficult to ascertain because often the child whose level of test anxiety is high is difficult to identify. Those who have taught will readily see the truth of this statement. It is also interesting to note that Sarason's data seem to reinforce Goslin's statement. The problem is further complicated because people react differently to anxiety. There are certain highly anxious persons who demonstrate an exceptional mental alertness whereas others become intellectually frozen.

What does all this mean to you, the potential test user? It means that caution must be used. It is impossible to know each individual being tested and to know whether a little tension would be appropriate. The following "do's" and "don'ts" are practically oriented to school, teacher, and child and are based on research findings and personal experiences.

DO'S

1. Do read the test manual's directions verbatim.
2. Do prepare students for testing either individually or in groups. This orientation should include the purposes of testing and the uses that will be made of the results.
3. Do be alert to the influence of anxiety on test scores in individual interpretations.

DON'TS

1. Don't offer incentives of any kind.
2. Don't orient students about testing on the day you plan to administer the tests.
3. Don't generalize and use anxiety as the only reason for low test scores.

A final word of caution has to do with your attitude while administering the test. Assume a matter-of-fact attitude.

Practice and Coaching

It has been known for many years (see, for example, Casey, Davidson, and Harter, 1928) that IQ scores can be significantly increased if children are coached on specific items they have missed and then given the same examination again. Contemporary research (Dyer, 1953; Dempster, 1954; Longstaff, 1954; Vernon, 1954; Wiseman, 1954; French, 1955; Lipton, 1956; French and Dear, 1959) reveals that coaching and practice may be of value to persons who have not had experience with a certain type of test or who have not had recent exposure to certain subject matter of a particular examination. The effects of coaching and practice must be broken down into various situations in order to have practical import for the test user. The following are questions and answers based on the extensive research findings of over forty years.

1. Are coaching and practice helpful in raising a person's test score?
   Answer: Yes, with certain qualifications.

2. What qualifications?

   Answer: Qualifications dependent on specific individuals and specific tests.

3. What about tests used to assign students to certain schools and grades?

   Answer: British psychologists have conducted many studies in this area because of their concern over assignment of children to different types of secondary schools. They found that improvement of scores is dependent upon ability, the kind of tests, and the type and amount of coaching given.

   The investigations revealed that subjects with poor educational backgrounds are more apt to benefit from intensive coaching than those who have had excellent educational preparation (see Wiseman and Wrigley, 1953).

4. That's interesting, but I am especially interested in college entrance tests. Can you study for them?

   Answer: The College Entrance Examination Board, noting the concern of parents in the United States over their children's test performance, has over the years conducted a series of studies to determine the effects of coaching on its Scholastic Aptitude Test (Dyer, 1953; French, 1955; French and Dear, 1959; College Entrance Examination Board, Trustees, 1959; College Entrance Examination Board, 1968; Angoff, 1971; Pike and Evans, 1972). These studies reveal slight increases in scores but none that are significant.

5. What do I advise my students?

   Answer: Advise students individually. If a student has not had mathematics recently or has not been exposed to testing, a review of the former and some practice tests may be of help. For most students, however, the following statement by the College Entrance Examination Board is appropriate [16]:

The trustees of the College Entrance Examination Board have noted with concern the increasing tendency of secondary school students to seek the assistance of special tutors or of special drill at school in the hope of improving thereby scores earned on College Board examinations. The Board has now completed four studies designed to evaluate the effect of special tutoring or "coaching" upon the Scholastic Aptitude Test, the basic test offered. Three other studies have been conducted independently by public high schools. These studies being completed, we now feel able to make the following statement:

The evidence collected leads us to conclude that intensive drill for the SAT, either on its verbal or its mathematical part, is at best likely to yield insignificant increases in scores. The magnitudes of the increases which have been found vary slightly from study to study, but they are always small and appear to be independent of the particular method of coaching used and of the level of ability of the students being coached. The results of the coaching studies which have

[16] *College Board Score Reports: A Guide for Counselors and Admissions Officers.* Copyright, 1966, by the College Entrance Examination Board. Used by permission of the College Entrance Examination Board.

thus far been completed indicate that average increases of less than 10 points on a 600 point scale can be expected. It is not reasonable to believe that admissions decisions can be affected by such small changes in scores. This is especially true since the tests are merely supplementary to the school record and other evidence taken into account by admissions officers.

The conclusion stated here has been reached slowly and with care, although the atmosphere in which the problem has been studied has not been entirely calm. In recent years newspapers and even radio advertisements advancing the claims of the drillmasters have increased in number and boldness. Parents, already disturbed by exaggerated notions of the difficulties of students in gaining admission to college, have demanded that the schools divert teaching energy and time to a kind of drill that is obnoxious to educators of every philosophy.

With parental concern so great, each completed study yielding negative findings with regard to the usefulness of coaching has led only to speculation that under some other set of circumstances some other set of students might make important score increases as a result of coaching for the test. The time has come to say that we do not believe it.

Tutors often show apparent good results mainly because students and scores do change with the passage of time. Our studies have simply shown that the scores of students who are left alone change in the same directions and to nearly the same degree as do scores of students who are tutored. The public, though, is disconcerted to see any change in a measure of "aptitude" which is regarded as unchangeable. As the College Board uses the term, aptitude is not something fixed and impervious to influence by the way the child lives and is taught. Rather, this particular Scholastic Aptitude Test is a measure of abilities that seem to grow slowly and stubbornly, profoundly influenced by conditions at home and at school over the years, but not responding to hasty attempts to relive a young lifetime.

In addition to changes due to growth, other changes occur because the test, while dependable, shares a characteristic common to all tests in that it cannot be made to give exactly the same score for each student each time the test is taken. Changes due to this lack of complete dependability are uncontrollable. Thus, with scores being affected by both the imperfect nature of the testing process and the student's growth, about one student in four will find that his scores actually decrease from one year to the next, while most other students will have small to moderate increases. About one student in fifteen [17] *will find that his scores increase by 100 points or more between junior and senior years in high school, and this is true whether he is coached or not. It is not surprising then that tutors are often able to point to particular students who have made large increases in their scores.*

It is possible to predict the size and number of fluctuations in scores that will occur within large groups, but fluctuations of individual scores cannot be predicted. Yet it is upon individuals that interest properly focuses, so that unexpected changes are easily, though erroneously, attributed to coaching, to the school, or to some other visible agency.

We have said nothing about the tests of achievement in specific school subjects. These have not been studied in the same way as has the aptitude test. We do know that these tests do a modest but useful job of measuring learning of the material tested. We suspect that the question of coaching for these tests is a matter of choosing a method of teaching the subject. We cannot

---

[17] College Entrance Examination Board in a personal communication to the author states that fifteen has been extended up to twenty. That is, "About one student in *twenty* will find that his scores . . . ."

believe that drill on sample test questions is the most productive method available.

Finally, we worry very little when parents of comfortable means decide that at worst tutoring can do no harm and therefore use their money for coaching toward College Board examinations. We are very concerned when parents purchase coaching they cannot afford or, failing to do so, feel that an unfair advantage has gone to those who have had a few weeks or months of tutoring. But we are concerned most, and have been moved to make this statement, because we see the educational process unwillingly corrupted in some schools to gain ends which we believe to be not only unworthy but, ironically, unattainable.

6. Can you practice for intelligence tests?

    Answer: A great many investigations reveal that, on the average, scores will increase upon retesting if the same examination is used (see Crane and Heim, 1950; Heim and Wallace, 1950). If *parallel forms* [18] are used, elevations in test scores are less pronounced. The author's experience suggests that, on the whole, most children and adults tend to obtain the same general scores no matter how much testing or practice they have had.

Other Factors

Brief statements on the following variables will be made not because they are unimportant but because they are mentioned in different sections of the text and need not be elaborated upon at this time.

RESPONSE SETS

Response sets are a tendency to choose a certain direction in responding to test items. For example, some people tend to answer no to all personal problems. Another type of response set is found in individuals who tend to guess freely, or who are afraid to guess (Goldman, 1971).

Teachers, counselors, and psychologists should not be particularly concerned with this factor, because it is the primary responsibility of the test constructor. The test user should note, however, the tendency of some tests to produce response sets and weigh this factor before purchasing a given test. (For detailed discussion of this factor, see Cronbach, 1950, 1970; Goldman, 1971.)

CHEATING

The problem of cheating is as old as mankind. It is obvious that if a person knows the answers in advance, looks at another person's paper, starts before the signal to begin, or finishes after time is called, his score will not be a reflection of his own ability and therefore will be an invalid evaluation.

---

[18] Parallel forms are tests measuring the same subject matter at the same level of difficulty, using different questions.

One form of cheating is making oneself look "good" on interest and personality inventories. It has been found that most of these tests lend themselves to making false responses (Cross, 1950; Garry, 1953; Gehman, 1957; Noll, 1951).

The best way to avoid cheating is to be sure that you have a good test orientation. This will help convince students that an honest score is in their own interest. Another method of avoiding cheating is to be sure that the examiner has enough assistance to observe the students being tested.

THREE

Individual Tests of Intelligence and Personality

Individual Tests
of Intelligence

chapter 6

"The Greeks had a word for it, but the Romans had a word with better survival properties. Regardless of the word, what is now called intelligence has been talked about for at least 2,000 years. And as long as 2,000 years before the advent of attempts to measure intelligence, there seems to have been recognition of the fact that individuals differ in intellectual ability" (McNemar, 1966, p. 180).

The teacher and counselor will rarely administer and interpret individual tests of intelligence such as the Stanford-Binet. They may, however, use these test results in many ways to facilitate learning in the classroom. In addition, group tests of intelligence (more appropriately termed *scholastic aptitude tests*) that the teacher or counselor will administer, and in some cases score, are based in large measure on the validity of the individual test of intelligence.

In this chapter we will discuss in detail two of the most widely used individual tests of intelligence, the Stanford-Binet and the Wechsler series (WPPSI, WISC-R, WAIS), as well as nonlanguage, culture-fair, and infant tests. In Chapter 2, we discussed the problem of defining intelligence. You will remember that intelligence is defined differently by various psychologists and that the term *intelligence* has no absolute meaning. The meaning of IQ was also discussed in general terms and later in Chapter 3 the mathematical derivation was presented. Before reading further, it may be beneficial for you to review relevant sections of Chapters 2 and 3.

Stanford-Binet Intelligence Scale

History

In about 1890 the French psychologist Alfred Binet became interested in investigating reasoning and judgment. He wanted to know the ways in which "smart" and "dull" children differed. In his attempts to study these differences, he used many types of measures, including size of cranium, tactile discrimination, and digit recall. These measures produced little relationship to general mental functioning.

In 1904, Dr. Binet was appointed to a commission that was to study and recommend to the educational leaders of Paris a procedure for ascertaining which children were unable to profit from a regular school setting. This commission was interested in picking out pupils who were in the mentally retarded range and placing them in a school which would provide instruction at their level of ability.

Binet was asked to produce a method to distinguish these retarded children from "normal" pupils. His first scale, published in 1905 in collaboration with Simon, drew on the knowledge gained in his earlier studies. This scale, called the 1905 scale, was designed to cover various functions which Binet considered components of intelligence. These included comprehension, reasoning, and judgment. Children between three and six years of age were called upon to give their names, copy figures, point to their right and left ear, and obey simple commands. Some of the tasks older children were asked to do were to name the months of the year, make up sentences, define abstract words, and name various coins.

In 1908 and 1911, revisions of the 1905 scale were published. Chauncey and Dobbin (1966), in discussing Binet's work, made an important observation not only on Binet's procedures but on intelligence tests in general. They state,

> No test or technique measures mental ability directly. What Binet did, and what all other "intelligence test" builders after him have done, was to set up some tasks for the young intellect to attack and then to observe what happened when the intellect was put to work on them. His method was truly scientific and remarkably like the method used by physicists forty years later to detect and measure the forces released by the atom. The cloud chamber does not permit the physicist to see the atom or its electrically charged components, but it does reveal the tracks of ionizing particles and thus permits the scientist to deduce the nature of the atom from which the particles emanate. (p. 5)

Lewis M. Terman, an American psychologist, began to experiment with the Binet tests in 1910. In 1916 he produced the Stanford Revision of the Binet Scale (Terman, 1916). This revision attempted to provide standards of intellectual performance for "average" American-born children from ages three to sixteen. Intelligence ratings were arrived at by mental age scores. Terman increased the number of tasks from Binet's original 54 to 90. The 1916 scale, for the first time, included detailed instructions for administering and scoring each subtest.

The 1916 scale was used for clinical diagnosis and research purposes during the 1920s and early 1930s. It was found that certain tests had low validity and that below the mental age of four and at the young adult levels the sampling had been inadequate. In addition, instructions and scoring lacked the precision needed for objective appraisal. In order to eliminate these faults, a second revision of the Stanford scale was produced.

The second revision, published in 1937, utilized the results of past studies, personal experiences, and a ten-year research and standardization project. Dr. Maud A. Merrill coauthored the 1937 revision with Terman (Terman and Merrill, 1937). This revision retained many of the characteristics of the earlier tests, such as age standards. It provided a broader sampling but remained a test of "general intelligence" rather than a test of specific kinds of abilities. Two Forms—Form L and Form M—were used. In terms of sampling and statistical techniques, the 1937 scale was much more sophisticated.

The third revision, Form L-M, was published in 1960. This revision combined the best features and subtests of the 1937 scale into a single form. The most radical change in the 1960 scale was in the IQ tables, which give deviation, or standard score, IQs. This was a departure from the previous method of MA/CA $\times$ 100 (see Chapter 3). The revised IQ is a standard score with a mean of 100 and a standard deviation of 16 (Terman and Merrill, 1960).

Rather than another revision, a restandardization of Form L-M was accomplished in 1972 (Terman and Merrill, 1973). The test items are basically the same,[1] but the norms were obtained from 2,100 new subjects examined during the 1971–1972 school year. The test publishers were able to utilize the large-scale norming of the Iowa Tests of Basic Skills, the Cognitive Abilities Test, and the Tests of Academic Progress that was done in 1970.

Samples of about 20,000 individuals in each age group were tested. These were taken from a great number of communities that were selected in terms of population, geographical region, and economic status. The entire sample of 200,000 pupils in grades 3–12 was taken from representative communities selected by stratified sampling techniques including not only geographical regions, economic status, and size but also racial (black) and ethnic (Mexican-American and Puerto Rican) cases.

The students to be examined with the Stanford-Binet were chosen by their scores on the verbal battery of the Cognitive Abilities Test. This was done so that the distribution of scores in the subsample corresponded to the national distribution of the whole sample. Only children who came from

[1] Two small exceptions: age II "doll card" was updated; and age VII has the word *charcoal* instead of *coal* in the Similarities Test.

families in which English was the basic spoken language were included. Ages two to eight were obtained by matching siblings of the group-tested children. In this age group, subjects were selected by the score of the older brother or sister on the Cognitive Abilities Test.

These 1972 norms are obviously based on the most representative sample to date. In addition, they are reflective of possible effects of contemporary cultural changes on test behavior. It should be noted that these norms indicate some increase in test scores at all ages. The increase ranges from substantial at the preschool ages to a small but significant increase at ages fifteen and over.

Characteristics

The Stanford-Binet Intelligence Scale begins with tests for the average two-year-old and progresses to levels that differentiate between average and superior adults. In order to illustrate the actual content of the test, excerpts from four different age levels are presented with brief explanations.[2]

Year Two

1. Three-Hole Form Board [3]
   (Material: Form board 5 in. × 8 in. with three insets for circle, square, and triangle.)
   Procedure: The board is presented with the blocks in place. The Examiner [4] tells the child to watch him and he proceeds to remove the blocks placing each on the table before its appropriate recess on the side toward the child. E then says, "Now put them back into their holes."
   Score: To receive credit, child must place all three blocks correctly in one of two trials.
2. Delayed Response
   (Material: Three small pasteboard boxes and a small toy cat.)
   Procedure: E: "Look, I am going to hide the kitty and then see if you can find it again."
   Score: The child watches the E place the kitty under each box and is asked to find the kitty. If on any of the three trials the child turns over more than one box that trial is scored as a minus.
3. Identifying Parts of the Body*
   Procedure: E: "Show me the dolly's hair." ("mouth," etc.—large paper doll.)
   Score: The child must identify the parts on the paper doll.
4. Block Building: Tower
   Procedure: Twelve 1-inch cubes are placed in erratic order before the child. The E proceeds to build a four block tower saying, "See what I'm making!" He then pushes the rest of the blocks toward the child, saying, "You make one like this."

---

[2] Lewis M. Terman and Maud A. Merrill. *Stanford-Binet Intelligence Scale: Manual for the Third Revision, Form L-M 1972 Norms Edition.* Copyright, © 1973, by Houghton Mifflin Company. Excerpts are reprinted with the permission of Houghton Mifflin Company.

[3] From this point on, an asterisk (*) will denote that the task is used at two or more age levels.

[4] From this point on, *Examiner* will be designated by the letter E.

Score: Child must build a four or more block tower in response to E's request.

5. Picture Vocabulary*

   Procedure: "What's this? What do you call it?" (Eighteen 2 in. × 4 in. cards with pictures of common objects.)

   Score: Recognition, e.g., plane, telephone.

6. Word Combinations*

   Procedure: Notation of child's spontaneous word combinations during interview.

   Score: Combinations of at least two words. For example, "Mama bye bye" and "all gone" are scored plus while one-word combinations such as "bye bye" or "night-night" are scored minus.

Year Six

1. Vocabulary

   Procedure: "When I say a word, you tell me what it means. What is an orange?" (Words like "tap" and "gun" are given to the child. Forty-four words are given. E stops after six consecutive words have been failed.)

   Score: Six words must be correctly identified at this level.

2. Differences*

   Procedure: This area requires the child to differentiate between objects. This, for example, may be seen in the question: "What is the difference between a bird and a dog?"

   Score: Two out of three must be answered correctly for credit.

3. Mutilated Pictures

   Procedure: Five pictures with a part missing are given. The child is asked, "What is gone in this picture?" or, "What part is gone?"

   Score: Missing part must be named or described verbally. Credit is not given for pointing. Four out of five must be correct for credit.

4. Number Concepts*

   Procedure: (Twelve 1-in. cubes) "Give me three blocks. Put them here."

   Score: Five different number combinations of blocks are requested.

5. Opposite Analogies*

   Procedure: Statements such as, "A table is made of wood; a window of ——?"

   Score: Four analogies are given. Three out of the four must be answered correctly for credit.

6. Maze Tracing

   Procedure: Mazes are used that have start and finish points marked. E says, "This little boy lives here, and here is the schoolhouse. The little boy wants to go to school the shortest way without getting off the sidewalk. Here is the sidewalk. Show me the shortest way."

   Score: Credit is given if the right path is chosen and if marking is more inside than outside the boundaries of the path. The Maze Tracing score is obtained when the child is able to correctly trace two out of three of the mazes.

Year Eleven

1. Memory for Designs*

   Procedure: "This card has two drawings on it. I am going to show them to you for ten seconds, then I will take the card away and let you draw from memory what you have seen. Be sure to look at both drawings carefully." (Card is shown for ten seconds.)

   Score: Degrees of accuracy represented in full and half credits.

2. Verbal Absurdities*
   Procedure: Statements are read and after each the question, "What is foolish about that?"
   Score: Three "foolish" statements are read and quality of insight into the absurdities is recorded and evaluated. For example, "The judge said to the prisoner, 'You are to be hanged, and I hope it will be a warning to you.' "
3. Abstract Words*
   Procedure: This area is concerned with the child's ability to handle abstract or hypothetical constructs, for example, a question such as "What is connection?" may be asked.
   Score: Five words are given and response is evaluated on meaning.
4. Memory for Sentences
   Procedure: "Now listen, and be sure to say exactly what I say."
   Score: E reads aloud two statements (separately) and child is to give back statement verbatim. In order to receive credit, statements must be exactly correct with no omissions or additions or change in order of words.
5. Problem Situation
   Procedure: "Listen, and see if you can understand what I read."
   Score: Statement is read and child is asked question about it.
6. Similarities*
   Procedure: "In what way are ——, ——, and —— alike?"
   Score: Three things are presented and a response that reveals understanding whether basic or superficial is scored correct.

Superior Adult Level Three

1. Vocabulary*
   Procedure: "I want to find out how many words you know. Listen, and when I say a word, you tell me what it means. What is an orange?" (begins at six-year level).
2. Proverbs
   Procedure: "Here is a proverb, and you are supposed to tell what it means. For example, this proverb, 'Large oaks from little acorns grow,' means that great things may have small beginnings. What does this one mean?" (Three proverbs are then given.)
   Score: List of possible interpretations that are correct and incorrect.
3. Opposite Analogies*
   Procedure: "A rabbit is timid; a lion is ——."
   Score: List of correct and incorrect responses. Three analogies are given.
4. Orientation
   Procedure: The person is given a card on which two problems concerning directions are given. He is not allowed to use pencil and paper.
   Score: Correct responses.
5. Reasoning*
   Procedure: Person is presented with card and reads problem while E reads it aloud. Pencil and paper are not allowed.
   Score: Time limit and possible correct answers through different mathematical methods (2) are given.
6. Repeating Thought of Passage*
   Procedure: "I am going to read a short paragraph. When I am through you are to repeat as much of it as you can. You don't need to remember the exact words, but listen carefully so that you can tell me everything it says."
   Score: Accurate reproduction of component ideas.

The preceding illustrations are representative of some of the tasks in the Stanford-Binet. You can see that sometimes the tasks at different age levels are completely different, whereas in other cases they are the same. (The asterisk denotes usage at more than one level.) Many of the tests at the lower age levels deal with objects and pictures, whereas at the upper levels the tests are more abstract and verbal. Such abilities as judgment, interpretation, memory, past achievement, and abstract reasoning are evaluated.

The examiner, in administering the test, begins at a level where the child is likely to succeed with some effort. Remember that the tasks at a given age level reflect the average child's ability at that age. If the child is unable to pass the tasks at the level first tried, the examiner will go back to an easier level. If the child is successful at the initial level, the examiner will continue, level by level, until the child fails all tests at a specific level. Once this level has been established, the examiner credits the child with the basal age, which is the highest age level at which all of the tests are passed. For example, if all tests up to and including the fifth year are passed, and one test for the sixth year is not passed, the basal age is five years. The examiner also credits the child with tasks passed at more advanced levels. Thus, if there are six tests at each year-age level, a child passing a single test obtains credit for two months of mental age. For example, Ted S. passed all tasks at the five-year level, three of six tasks at the six-year level, one of six tasks at the seven-year level, and failed all tasks at the eight-year level. Thus, the following computation to derive his mental age would be made:

1. Passed all tasks at five-year level = five years basal age.
2. Passed three of six tasks at six-year-level = six months credit.
3. Passed one of six tasks at seven-year level = two months credit.
4. Failed all tasks at eight-year level = o.
Mental age = five years, eight months.

Ted's mental age describes the level at which he is performing. This, of course, does not take into account his life age. Ted's performance in relation to children of his own age is then expressed as an IQ. An IQ has the same meaning at one age as at any other. In order to find Ted's IQ, the examiner would consult a table to convert the mental age to IQ.

Classifying Binet IQs

The distribution of the 1937 standardization sample, as illustrated in Table 20, is still used as a frame of reference in the 1973 revision. It presents a basis for statistical classification of IQs. As Terman and Merrill (1973) state,

The classificatory terms used carry no implications of diagnostic significance for IQ categories. "Average or normal" has statistical meaning as designating

Table 20. *Distribution of the 1937 Standardization Group* *

IQ	Per Cent	Classification
160–169	0.03 ⎤	
150–159	0.2 ⎬	Very superior
140–149	1.1 ⎦	
130–139	3.1 ⎫	
120–129	8.2 ⎭	Superior
110–119	18.1	High average
100–109	23.5 ⎫	
90–99	23.0 ⎭	Normal or average
80–89	14.5	Low average
70–79	5.6	Borderline defective
60–69	2.0 ⎤	
50–59	0.4 ⎬	
40–49	0.2 ⎬	Mentally defective
30–39	0.03 ⎦	

* From Lewis M. Terman and Maud A. Merrill. *Stanford-Binet Intelligence Scale: Manual for the Third Revision Form L-M,* 1972 norms ed. Copyright © 1973, by Houghton Mifflin Company. Reproduced with the permission of Houghton Mifflin Company.

the middle range of IQ's. So, too, IQ's 60 and below indicate "mental deficiency" with respect to average mentality on the scale and carry no necessary diagnostic implications such as are usually attached to the term "feeblemindedness." "Very superior" is applied to subjects whose IQ's fall well within the top 1.5 per cent of the group. . . . The table serves as a "frame of reference" to indicate how high or low any specific score is in relation to the general population. (pp. 17 and 19)

Wechsler Scales

History

Wechsler's first test of intelligence, the Wechsler-Bellevue Scale, was developed primarily for adults. In constructing the first scale, Wechsler analyzed various standardized tests of intelligence that were already being used. He evaluated each test's claim to validity on the basis of correlations with published tests and empirical ratings of intelligence. The ratings included teacher's estimates and ratings by army officers and business executives. In addition, Wechsler attempted to rate the tests on the basis of his own and other psychologists' clinical experience. Two years were devoted to experimental work in trying out various tests on different groups with varying intellectual abilities (Wechsler, 1958).

In revising the first scale, Wechsler also changed the name to the Wechsler Adult Intelligence Scale (WAIS). The WAIS is a revision and complete standardization of Form I of the Wechsler-Bellevue Intelligence Scale (W-B) and provides more efficient measurement of the intelligence of adolescents and adults between the ages of sixteen and seventy-five. Wechsler (1955) states, "The extension of the *Wechsler-Bellevue Scales* and the standardization of the modified instrument are represented by the new *Wechsler Adult Intelligence Scale*" (p. 2).

The WAIS, like its predecessor, the W-B, consists of eleven tests. The Verbal Scale contains six tests; the Performance Scale has five tests. All the tests in both the Verbal and Performance Scales are combined to make the Full Scale. Following are the tests in each scale,

VERBAL TESTS	PERFORMANCE TESTS
1. Information	7. Digit Symbol
2. Comprehension	8. Picture Completion
3. Arithmetic	9. Block Design
4. Similarities	10. Picture Arrangement
5. Digit Span	11. Object Assembly
6. Vocabulary	

The Wechsler Intelligence Scale for Children (WISC) was developed by Wechsler in 1949 before the WAIS. It was an outgrowth of the W-B Scale, and in some aspects the two are identical. The main differences were the additions of easier items and independent standardization of the WISC. A revised edition, WISC-R, was published in 1974. The WISC-R has the same Verbal, Performance, and Full Scale format. There are ten basic and two alternative tests:

VERBAL TESTS	PERFORMANCE TESTS
1. General Information	7. Picture Completion
2. General Comprehension	8. Picture Arrangement
3. Arithmetic	9. Block Design
4. Similarities	10. Object Assembly
5. Vocabulary	11. Coding or Mazes (alternate)
6. Digit Span (alternate)	

Digit Span and Mazes (or Coding) are considered supplementary tests to be added if time permits or if one of the tests has been invalidated.

It should be noted that in the WISC-R, a special effort was made to make the content more oriented to children. For example, in one subtest *cigars* was changed to *candy bars*. In addition, the revised edition has more female and black subjects in the pictorial subtests.

The standardization group for the WISC-R included a sample of 100 boys and 100 girls at each year from six and one-half through sixteen and one-half totaling 2,200 children. The sample was based on the 1970 U.S. census in terms of geographical area, domicile (urban-rural), occupation (of head of the house), and race. Examinations were given in thirty-one states, including Hawaii, and Washington, D.C. The mean IQ obtained in this standardization of the WISC-R is similar to the mean obtained for the 1972 Binet.

The Wechsler Preschool and Primary Scale of Intelligence (WPPSI) published in 1967 is for children between four and six and one-half years of age. The WPPSI, like the WISC-R, consists of a series of ability tests that attempt to obtain evidence of various dimensions of the young child's intellectual competence. The WPPSI contains six verbal tests (one an alternate) and five performance tests.

Verbal Tests	Performance Tests
1. Information	7. Animal House
2. Vocabulary	8. Picture Completion
3. Similarities	9. Mazes
4. Comprehension	10. Geometric Design
5. Arithmetic	11. Block Design
6. Sentences (alternate)	

Eight of the eleven tests are similar to the WISC-R and provide the same measures as the WISC-R. Sentences, Animal House, and Geometric Design are new subtests in the Wechsler series.

The standardization of the WPPSI utilized a national sample of 1,200 children—100 boys and 100 girls at half-year age intervals from four and one-half to six and one-half. The 1960 census was used to select representative subjects in reference to geographical area, domicile (urban-rural), race and occupation of father.

Characteristics

The Wechsler approach of grouping certain items in subtests under two basic scales (Verbal and Performance) is a radical departure from the Stanford-Binet plan of grouping items according to difficulty. Binet and Terman organized their material in successive age levels whereas Wechsler organized types of tasks in the various subtests. Let us now turn our attention to the various subtests and their content. The following items are similar to those found in the WISC-R and WAIS. The subject is expected to give a generalized and direct answer.

INFORMATION

How many toes do you have? (WISC-R)
How many days in a month? (WISC-R)
Where does syrup come from? (WAIS)
Who wrote *Crime and Punishment*? (WAIS)

COMPREHENSION

What should you do when your nose bleeds? (WISC-R)
Why should people be honest? (WISC-R)
Why does an airplane have a motor? (WAIS)
What does this statement mean? "A watched pot never boils." (WAIS)

ARITHMETIC

Seven blocks are presented in a row before the child and he is asked to count them with his finger. (timed—WISC-R)
At 5¢ each, what will four apples cost? (timed—WISC-R)
A woman with $20 spends $8.50. How much does she have left? (timed—WAIS)
The price of frozen green beans is three packages for 45¢. What is the price for nine packages? (timed—WAIS)

SIMILARITIES

For subjects under eight years of age and suspected mental defectives, four "analogies" such as "Water is blue but grass is _____" are given. If two of the four items are passed the examiner continues on to the more difficult items. (WISC-R) For example, "In what way are a pear and apple alike?"
WAIS items are similar but more difficult.

DIGIT SPAN (WAIS)

"I am going to say some numbers. Listen carefully, and when I am through, say them right after me." The examiner starts with three digits and continues until nine digits or until subject misses two trials on a series. For example, 58264 was missed, another five digits are given and if subject misses again test is stopped. If correct response is given test continues.
After completing this first series of digits subject is asked to repeat numbers backwards. For example, the examiner says "683" the subject should answer "386." Test is discontinued in same manner as previous series. WISC-R uses this same format for alternate test.

VOCABULARY

Words such as *wagon* and *ruby* are presented to the subject on the WISC-R while words such as *spring* and *digress* are included in the vocabulary section of the WAIS. There are forty words on both the WISC-R and WAIS. After the subject has had five consecutive failures (no credit) this test is discontinued.

Picture Completion

"I am going to show you some pictures in which there is a part missing. Look at each picture and tell me what part is missing." Subject may verbalize part that is missing or point to it.

Block Design

"You see these blocks have different colors on their different sides. I am going to put them together to make something with them. Watch me." Four blocks are arranged according to a design on the examiner's card. Subject is required to make the same design using the blocks as the model. If he is successful he is shown card number 2, which has a design that he is to copy by arranging the blocks in the same manner. Starting with designs that require four blocks and continuing (if subject does not have three consecutive failures) up to nine blocks the subject is required to accurately reproduce the model designs on the cards presented to him. Bonus credits are awarded for speed in completing tasks on more difficult designs.

Picture Arrangement

A series of comic-like pictures are presented to the subject and he is asked to put them in the correct order so they will tell a story. Bonus credits are given for speed on completing tasks.

Object Assembly

"These pieces, if put together correctly, will make a girl. Go ahead and put them together." The examiner presents subject with cut up (puzzle-like pieces) parts and asks subject to put them together. Time bonuses for speed are given.

Digit Symbol (WAIS)

"Look at these boxes. Notice that each has a number in the upper part and a mark in the lower part. Every number has a different mark. Now look here where the upper boxes have numbers but the squares beneath have no marks. You are to put in each of these squares the mark that should go there. . . ." Each square that is correctly completed is counted as one point while reversed symbols are given half credit. See Figure 15 for items similar to WAIS Digit Symbol Test.

Coding (WISC-R)

Similar to digit symbol of the WAIS. Two sections, one for young children

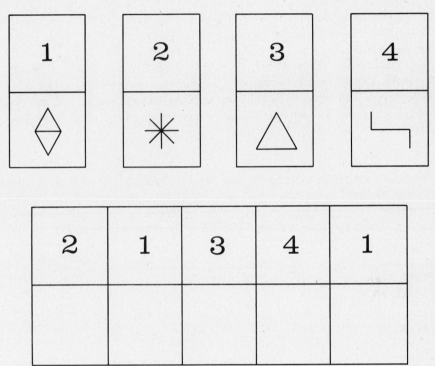

Figure 15. Example of items similar to tasks on Digit Symbol Test of the Wechsler Adult Intelligence Scale.

with symbols such as a ball and triangle, are used, while the same format as the WAIS is used for older children.

MAZES (WISC-R)
Child is requested to keep pencil on paper and plot way out of maze. "This is a maze. You are to start here and find your way out here without going up any blind alley or crossing any lines."

What Wechsler Scores Mean

Raw scores on each subtest are converted into "scaled scores." These "scaled scores" or standard scores have a mean of 10 and a standard deviation of 3. They are added together to produce three IQs—Verbal, Performance, and Full Scale. The Verbal and Performance IQs are added together to produce the Full Scale IQ. Wechsler was the first to introduce standard-score IQs. He chose to place the mean at 100 and the standard deviation at 15. (The Stanford-Binet, you will recall, has a standard deviation of 16.)

The IQs for verbal and performance tests reveal different abilities. The performance tests taken as separate units are not reliable; however, when combined in the Performance Scale, there is a very high reliability.

The reliability for the Full Scale IQ of the WAIS is .97; for Verbal IQ .96; Performance IQ .93 (Wechsler, 1958). The reliability of the WISC-R Full Scale, Verbal, and Performance IQs ranges from .90 to .96. The reliability for the Full Scale WPPSI IQ is between .92 and .94; for Verbal IQ it ranges between .87 and .90; and for Performance IQ it is between .84 and .91.

Table 21. *Intelligence Classifications for the Wechsler Scales, Theoretical and Actual* *

Statistical Basis of Intelligence Classification (Theoretical)		
Classification	Limits in Terms of P.E.	Percentage Included
Retarded	—3 P.E. and below	2.15
Borderline	—2 to —3 P.E.	6.72
Dull-normal	—1 to —2 P.E.	16.13
Average	—1 to +1 P.E.	50.00
Bright-normal	+1 to +2 P.E.	16.13
Superior	+2 to +3 P.E.	6.72
Very superior	+3 P.E. and over	2.15

Intelligence Classification of W–B I IQ's—Ages 10 to 60 (Actual)		
Classification	IQ Limits	Percentage Included
Retarded	65 and below	2.2
Borderline	66–79	6.7
Dull-normal	80–90	16.1
Average	91–110	50.0
Bright-normal	111–119	16.1
Superior	120–127	6.7
Very superior	128 and over	2.2

Intelligence Classification of WAIS IQ's—Ages 16 to 75 (Actual)		
Classification	IQ	Percentage Included
Retarded	69 and below	2.2
Borderline	70–79	6.7
Dull-normal	80–89	16.1
Average	90–109	50.0
Bright-normal	110–119	16.1
Superior	120–129	6.7
Very superior	130 and above	2.2

* From Joseph D. Matarazzo, *Wechsler's Measurement and Appraisal of Adult Intelligence,* 5th ed. Copyright © 1972, The Williams and Wilkins Co. Reproduced by permission.

The concurrent validity of all three Wechsler tests is excellent, when the Stanford-Binet is used as the criterion. The Wechsler Scales and the Stanford-Binet seem to measure the same ability. The reported correlations are in the .80's. The Verbal Scale of the Wechsler seems to be most closely related to the Binet test.

Construct validity, however, seems to present a weaker picture. According to Anastasi (1976), the problem is a lack of empirical data on this type of validity. She states, "The factor-analytic studies contribute to a classification of the constructs in terms of which performance on the Wechsler scales may be described but even these studies would have been more informative if they had included more indices of behavior external to the scales themselves" (p. 264).

In general terms, various scores on a Wechsler scale indicate a certain degree of intellectual functioning. Table 21 presents classification of intelligence on both a theoretical and an actual basis. Note that the actual measured intellectual distribution closely approximates the theoretical. Matarazzo (1972) states,

> Such a classification is symmetrical, comprising as many classes above the mean as there are below it. In the case of categories described by IQ's below the mean, it has been fairly easy to take over the terms now in general use. In the case of categories above the mean there were and are some for which no ready terms are available, in particular the one to describe the group falling in the interval +1 P.E. to +2 P.E. above the mean. Since the individuals composing this category form a group of subjects who are as much above average as the dull-normal are below the average, a logical term that suggested itself was that of bright-normal. The term is rather clumsy but better than most that come to mind. As a second choice there is the somewhat long but descriptive term high-average to superior. It should be noted that this phase does not have the same denotation it has in the Terman classification. (pp. 125–126)

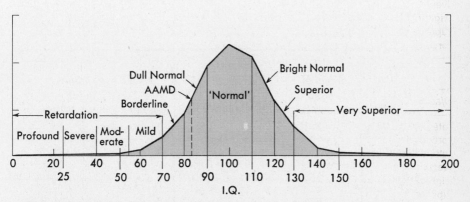

Figure 16. Graphic representation of intelligence classifications. (From Joseph D. Matarazzo, *Wechsler's Measurement and Appraisal of Adult Intelligence,* 5th ed. Copyright © 1972, The Williams and Wilkins Co. Reproduced by permission.)

Figure 16 graphically illustrates these intelligence classifications for the Wechsler Scale. This representation approximates the normal curve, with normal in the center, defective on the left, and superior on the right.

MENTAL RETARDATION

According to the classifications in Table 21, the lowest 2.2 per cent of the population is classified as mentally retarded. The American Association on Mental Retardation (AAMR) has subdivided this 2.2 per cent into four classifications: mild, moderate, severe, and profound. Table 22 presents these classifications plus a borderline category. Note that this table indicates the standard deviation as well as both Stanford-Binet and Wechsler scores. Bear in mind that while Stanford-Binet and Wechsler scores are roughly equivalent *they are not identical.* In general, you may consider that a score at or below —2 standard deviations on either test indicates retardation. In a similar manner, this includes roughly 2 per cent of the population.

The WISC-R for children over eight years of age or the WAIS for adolescents and adults (sixteen to seventy-five years of age) is an excellent instrument for ascertaining mental retardation. It should be noted, however, that accepted practice is not to rely on one test in deciding if a person is retarded; a series of tests are given—including intelligence, achievement, and personality—and are considered along with past grades and opinions of school teachers.

It should be noted that sometimes a child will have emotional problems so severe that they interfere with his intellectual functioning and cause him to score in the range of mental retardation when in fact he may possess an average or even superior intelligence. Teacher observations can also be valuable in finding these children. A sensitive teacher may notice that a child

Table 22. Classification of Mental Retardates by Word Description, Deviation, and IQ Range *

Word Description of Retardation in Measured Intelligence	Level of Deviation in Measured Intelligence	Range in Standard Deviation Units	Corresponding IQ Range for	
			Stanford-Binet SD 16	Wechsler SD 15
Borderline	—1	—1.01 to —2.00	68–83	70–84
Mild	—2	—2.01 to —3.00	52–67	55–69
Moderate	—3	—3.01 to —4.00	36–51	40–54
Severe	—4	—4.01 to —5.00	20–35	25–39
Profound	—5	below —5.00	below 20	below 25

* From Joseph D. Matarazzo, *Wechsler's Measurement and Appraisal of Adult Intelligence,* 5th ed. Copyright © 1972, The Williams and Wilkins Co. Reproduced by permission.

occasionally performs well, thus denoting ability, even though his usual performance is far below average.

Other Diagnostic and Clinical Features

The Wechsler Scales are more than tests that produce a psychometric IQ, important as that may be; they also assist in evaluating personality character-istics and organic brain disease. It has been found, for example, that in the majority of mental disorders impairment of functioning is greater in the performance section than in the verbal area. A fifteen-point difference or more between Performance and Verbal IQs is considered significant (Mata-razzo, 1972).

ORGANIC BRAIN DAMAGE

Those who are brain-damaged consistently do better on verbal than on performance tests. They do very poorly on the Digit Symbol and Block Design tests. Memory impairment is reflected in a poor memory span (Digit Span).

SCHIZOPHRENIA [5]

The schizophrenic usually does relatively well on Information and Vocabu-lary and does poorly on either Similarities, Picture Completion, or both. Some schizophrenic patients do well on one or several of the tests that are failed by the typical schizophrenic.

ANXIETY TYPES

The tests most sensitive to those suffering from anxiety, whether it be pathological or of less severity, are Arithmetic, Digit Span, and Digit Sym-bol. It has also been noted that these people tend to have lower Performance Scores than Verbal Scores.

OBSESSIVE-COMPULSIVE NEUROSIS

Those suffering from obsessive-compulsive neurosis are characterized by perfectionism, rumination, and rigidity. For example, they never outgrew "touching all the lines on the sidewalk." The quality of verbalizations is generally the most reliable sign of obsessive-compulsive trends on the Wech-sler Scales. Schafer (1948) cites several examples of their verbalizations: "There is a good deal of dispute as to who invented the airplane but the Wright Brothers get credit for it." "If I were lost in the forest in the day-time I might follow the sun . . . or go by the moss on the north side of the trees . . . or maybe follow a stream. Do I have a compass? If I had one I'd . . . "(p. 25).

---

[5] *Schizophrenia* is a general term that refers to a related group of mental disturbances, all characterized by a loss of touch with reality. The classical divisions are (1) catatonic, (2) hebephrenic, (3) simple, and (4) paranoid.

HYSTERIA

Hysteria is generally characterized by impulsiveness, egocentricity, tendency towards histrionics, and in severe cases conversion hysteria such as paralysis of a limb with no apparent physical cause. Those with hysteria generally obtain performance scores that equal or exceed the verbal level. On the verbal section, one finds relatively good scores in Comprehension and a poor showing in Information. Among the performance tests, Digit Symbol is usually well performed.

GENERAL NEUROSIS

In the area of general neurosis one may see children or adults with obsessive-compulsive, hysteric, and phobic reactions. These people usually reveal themselves by doing poorly on relatively easy items in Information, Vocabulary, Digit Span, Arithmetic, Picture Completion, and Block Design, while passing the more difficult items in these tests. These individuals have much higher verbal than performance scores (Schafer, 1948).

It should be remembered that none of these diagnostic signs is true in all situations. They are only rough generalizations that reveal to the skilled clinical or school psychologist some clues to the overall characteristics of the person being examined. They are, of course, used along with other tests and forms of evaluation such as interviews and day-to-day behavioral records. The various syndromes mentioned do not represent all the possible diagnostic categories, nor are they complete in any sense. They are intended as illustrations of the broad range and use of the Wechsler Scales that go beyond the psychometric IQ usage.

Two illustrative cases dealing with brain damage and anxiety follow to show how the Wechsler is used in actual clinical practice (Wechsler, 1958).[6]

W-BI

Vocabulary	7
Information	8
Comprehension	9
Arithmetic	7
Digits	6
Similarities	9
Verbal	39
Picture Arrangement	6
Picture Completion	1
Block Design	1
Object Assembly	2
Digit Symbol	5
Performance	15

Case o-2. White, male, adolescent, age 14. Brought to hospital because of marked change in personality. Had been normal boy until 6 months prior to admission. Illness first manifested by failure at school and increased irritability. Physical and neurological examination on admission essentially negative. Case presented to illustrate value of Scale in detecting possible organic brain conditions prior to manifestation of neurological symptoms. Psychometric organic signs are: Verbal much higher than Performance; very low scores on *both* Object Assembly and Block Design; large discrepancy between Digits forward and Digits backward. On the qualitative side, subject

[6] The following two cases are taken from David Wechsler, *The Measurement and Appraisal of Adult Intelligence.* (4th ed.) Baltimore: The Williams and Wilkins Company. ©, 1958, David Wechsler. Used by permission of David Wechsler.

Verbal IQ	91
Performance IQ	50
Digits forward	6
Digits backward	3

WAIS

Information	12
Comprehension	11
Arithmetic	10
Similarities	15
Digit Span	10
Vocabulary	14
Digit Symbol	11
Picture Completion	15
Block Design	11
Picture Arrangement ...	14
Object Assembly	11
Verbal IQ	118
Performance IQ	116
Full IQ	121

showed common organic manifestation of being able to reproduce designs if presented with a model of assembled blocks (200), after failing completely with the usual form of presentation.

Case An. 4. 16-year-old white male student who was admitted to a psychiatric out-patient clinic; revealed the typical adolescent problems: tension with his family, particularly in his relationships with his mother and sibling, difficulty in school, and struggling to find a value system, perhaps a sense of identity. His difficulties in school forced him to leave school shortly before his admission to the out-patient clinic.

On admission patient gave a two year history of epigastric pain with an ulcer demonstrated radiologically at different stages of healing or activity. The present episode began three weeks prior to admission when an active ulcer was demonstrated by x-ray and was treated medically. He was referred to a psychoanalyst who saw him 3 times prior to admission. He was admitted in a state of acute anxiety. Diagnosis: anxiety state.

Psychometrically, this patient did not show too large inter-test variability but it is significant that the lowered scores on the Verbal part of the examination were on Arithmetic and Digit Span. The Digit Symbol was not so much out of line on the Performance part of the examination but was still one of the lower scores. In this case we seem to be dealing with an individual with chronic anxiety and a great deal of aggression directed inward. This would be better indicated by his projective technique tests. The high scores on the Similarities in contrast with the low score on Comprehension also suggests a possible schizoid trend. This case suggests a much more complicated diagnosis than the one assigned it clinically; it has been added to illustrate the presence of anxiety (along with other symptoms) revealed by the psychometric pattern.

Diagnostic Cautions

The student of measurement must be very judicious in accepting the preceding data as definitive. They are far from that, and, as we have stated, diagnosis must be made in conjunction with other sources of information. Many psychologists do not feel the Wechsler scales are very authoritative in clinical assessment. They would use it only as a "rough gauge" of behavioral dysfunction.

Matarazzo (1972), the heir-apparent to Wechsler, after reviewing count-less studies and revising Wechsler's definitive book on intelligence as well as the Wechsler tests, states, "despite the many empirical findings reviewed throughout this book, psychological assessment is still primarily an art" (pp. 506–507).

Evaluation of the Binet and Wechsler

The Stanford-Binet and the Wechsler Scales have few, if any, test peers. They are both standard equipment in the psychologist's battery of tests. Though he may augment them with other devices, he puts his greatest faith and reliance on them.

The Stanford-Binet test is essentially a standardized method of observing behavior and provides a single psychometric score that describes present level of general intellectual ability. Its psychometric vintage, mellowed by years of numerous investigations, provides data to which the examiner can turn for interpretive assistance. It excels especially at the lower age levels, and until the recent advent of the Wechsler Preschool and Primary Scale of Intelligence had no competitive peers.

The Binet deliberately concentrates on verbal and educational abilities. This is, of course, an advantage for predicting school success and a deficit (for certain kinds of predictions) for use with disadvantaged groups. The Binet does not measure all facets of "intelligence," nor does it necessarily measure inborn capacity. (This means only that we are not certain of all the ramifications of what it measures.) It is an important and excellent tool and if used properly may help in the educative process.

The Wechsler Scales seem to be, generally, as valid for prediction as the Stanford-Binet. The Wechsler covers a broader range of various abilities than the Binet. It is also more useful in clinical evaluation, especially in the diagnosis of brain and neurological disorders. The examiner need not be as highly trained in test administration, and the time to administer the tests is generally shorter. Most psychologists prefer to administer the WISC after the age of eight or nine and the WAIS to adults over sixteen years old because they feel they are more useful clinically than the Binet. On the other hand, most would not trust the WISC-R below eight years of age.

Thorndike and Hagen (1969), in reviewing the merits of the Wechsler and Binet, state,

Most psychometricians would probably agree now in preferring the WAIS as a measure for adolescents and adults, though its relation to academic success is perhaps not as clearly established as is the Binet's . . . for children from 7 to 15, a decision between the two tests is not an easy one. The Binet is reported to be somewhat more difficult and time-consuming to give. The usual Binet procedure of carrying the examinee through to the point where he encounters a long series of failures is judged to be a seriously upsetting matter for some emotionally tense children. . . . The ultimate basis for choice will be the validity of the inferences that can be made from each in the situations in which they are actually used. Prediction of academic success can apparently be made about equally well from either test. It seems likely that the two tests are about equally useful for children with mental ages of 7 or above. (p. 305)

It is obvious from our discussion that the Stanford-Binet and the Wechsler Scales are the best individual measures of intelligence presently available. They are time-consuming and expensive, however, in that only one person at a time may be examined and only highly trained individuals such as clinical or school psychologists may properly administer them. (See Merrill's "Training Students to Administer the Stanford-Binet Intelligence Scale.")

In our schools today both the Wechsler and Binet are given only when other tests and information seem unreliable or in special cases that require intensive and thorough information, as for placement of a child in a special class for retarded, emotionally disturbed, or perceptually handicapped youngsters. When used for these special purposes and administered and interpreted by a trained psychologist, they are extremely useful tools in helping to provide individualized instruction. Teachers and school administrators should be certain, however, that the Binet or Wechsler results that they consider are based on the report of a trained clinical or school psychologist. (This means more than a course or two in individual testing.) This is important not only because of the highly complex nature of the tests, but also because of the clinical skills in observation needed to evaluate the psychometric scores.

Nonlanguage Tests [7]

Most intelligence tests contain, to some degree, tasks that are verbally oriented. This is not surprising because the vast majority of learning and conceptualization takes place in a language context. Use of language in testing is not only natural but desirable, because academic progress is developed through language, and tests having this orientation are thus in the best position to predict scholastic potential. Nonlanguage tests have been developed primarily to evaluate those individuals who, because of certain handicaps, cannot be properly measured with instruments containing linguistic tasks. Nonlanguage tests are especially useful with individuals who speak a foreign language or who come from a culturally different environment, as well as with those who have physical deficiencies in hearing and speech.

A good example of an individual nonlanguage test is Form I of the Arthur Performance Scale (Arthur, 1933, 1943). There are nine tests in the Arthur Scale.

---

[7] There will be no specific distinction made between "nonlanguage" and "performance" tests in this section. Nonlanguage will suffice for both.

1. *Knox Cube* is a test of immediate recall. The examiner taps four cubes in a specified series and instructs the subject to do the same. The procedure is repeated each time with the series of taps becoming greater in complexity and length.
2. *Seguin Form Board* (originally devised for use with mental defectives) consists of ten geometric figures that are to be placed in their appropriate holes in the board. The subject is told to place them in the holes as fast as he can.
3. *Two-Figure Form Board* is a more difficult form board than the Seguin. Cut-up pieces are to be placed into a square and cross.
4. *Casuist Form Board* is similar to the Two-Figure Form Board but more difficult because of the closer similarity of the pieces.
5. *Manikin* is a wooden figure of a man that is cut up into arms, legs, trunk, and head and is to be assembled by the subject.
Feature Profile consists of cut-up wooden pieces to be assembled to form a face.
6. *Mare and Foal* is a picture-completion-type test which has cut-outs that are to be assembled or fitted into place.
7. *Healy Picture Completion I* is a rural scene from which ten small squares have been removed. The subject is to select the correct square from a number of pieces before him to complete each part of the picture.
8. *Porteus Mazes* is basically a simple pencil maze requiring the subject to trace with a pencil the shortest path from the entrance to the exit without lifting the pencil from the paper.
9. *Kohs Block Design* consists of designs to be reproduced using colored cubical blocks similar to children's blocks.

The Revised Form II of the Arthur Performance Scale (Arthur, 1947) is an alternate to Form I with added features such as special instructions for deaf children, revisions of the Knox Cube, Seguin Form Board, Porteus Mazes, and Healy Picture Completion. A new test called the Arthur Stencil Design Test I was also added. This test calls for the subject to reproduce designs that are presented on cards by superimposing cut-out stencils upon a solid card.

The subject is given points for his performance on each subtest of the Arthur Scale. These points are summed, and the total score is converted to a mental age equivalent. An IQ may be obtained by the classical formula of MA/CA.

Another nonlanguage test of special importance to teachers and counselors is the Goodenough Draw-A-Man Test in which the child is asked to "make a picture of a man; make the very best picture that you can." Teachers have used this test in primary grades for many years as an estimation of intelligence and readiness for reading. This test was first standardized in 1926 and was not revised until 1963. It is now called Goodenough-Harris Drawing Test (Harris, 1963). The revision follows the original in putting emphasis on the child's observational acuity and on the growth of conceptual thinking rather than on artistic ability. The production of specific anatomical features, dress, perspective, and other features is scored.

The revised scale also requires children to draw a picture of themselves and a woman. The Self scale is more accurately a projective device (see Chapter 7 dealing with projective techniques), whereas the Woman scale is scored similarly to the Man scale. Norms on both Man and Woman scales were established on 300 children at each year of age from five to fifteen. These subjects were chosen according to father's occupation and geographical area.

Figure 17 shows drawings made by kindergarten children taken from Goodenough's (1926) chapter on scoring samples. Though there is an elaborate scoring system, the experienced scorer can grade "forty to fifty papers an hour, although in the beginning he may not have been able to score more than five or ten an hour" (p. 87).

These writers have chosen the early scoring samples as illustrations in Figure 17 because (1) they are mentioned as basic criteria by Harris (1963), and (2) they present a balanced view of different IQ levels.

The important thing to remember is that the Draw-A-Man Test is not scored on esthetic or technical qualities but on the completeness and developmental maturity of the drawing. For example, a clear indication of the neck as separate from the head and body is scored a plus, not a "mere juxtaposition."

There are more nonlanguage tests available for school use. A good many of these may be given in groups as well as individually. Among some of the more noteworthy are the Pintner Non-language Test, in which all instructions may be given by pantomime, and the Nebraska Test of Learning Aptitude, which was standardized on deaf and near-deaf children (individual test).

Culture-Fair Tests

In Chapter 2 we discussed the issues surrounding the problem of cultural bias in tests. This section will not deal with the controversial aspects of cultural test bias but only with a discussion of the efforts to develop culturally fair instruments. Not too many years ago the term used was *culture-free*; however, this designation was soon dropped when measurement people, after reviewing years of experimentation and clinical data, realized that no test is "culture-free." The aim today is not to produce an instrument free of culture but an instrument relatively fair to different cultures. For example, the American test that assumes a basic American background in football and baseball and uses items that reflect this exposure would not necessarily be fair for an English or German student and certainly would not be appropriate for an African village boy or girl.

Culture-fair tests are similar to nonlanguage tests in that they are almost

Boy, American, age 4-7, kindergarten.
Total score 10. M.A. 5-6. IQ 120.

Boy, American, age 5-10. kindergarten.
Total score 15. M.A. 6-9. IQ 116.

Girl, American, age 5-6, kindergarten.
Total score 8. M.A. 5-0. IQ 91.

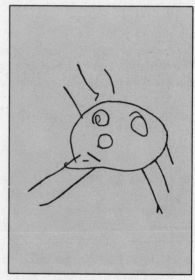

Girl, Italian, age 6-0, pre-school.
Total score 6. M.A. 4-6. IQ 75.

Figure 17. Four drawings by children showing age, score, MA and IQ. (From *Measurement of Intelligence by Drawings* by Florence L. Goodenough, copyright, 1926 by Harcourt Brace Jovanovich, Inc., renewed 1954 by Florence L. Goodenough. Reproduced by permission of the publishers.)

always nonverbal. They must, of course, be more than nonverbal; they must also be free of cultural bias. The Army Beta (see Chapter 2) is a nonlanguage examination; however, the Picture-Completion Test in it has items such as a violin, a gun, and a pocketknife, which are cultural products.

One of the first attempts to develop a culture-fair test was the Cattell Culture Free Intelligence Test. This test is based on the underlying assumption that general intelligence is a behavioral act of seeing relationships in the things with which we have to deal and that this aptitude to view relationships may be tested with simple diagrammatic or pictorial material. In addition, if the test is to be used in different cultures, the pictures or forms of objects should be universal and not confined to any cultural group. There is no evidence that, in fact, the test is useful for different cultures (Thorndike and Hagen, 1969).

Another "culture-free" test, developed in Great Britain by Raven (1938, 1947, 1962), is the Progressive Matrices. It is a nonverbal test series requiring the subject to solve problems presented in abstract figures and designs. The 1938 form consists of sixty matrices (designs) from each of which a part has been removed. The subject is required to choose the missing insert from six to eight alternatives. The 1947 form contains the two most elementary sets from the 1938 edition plus additional items. The 1962 form is a thirty-six-problem series designed for people with above-average intelligence. All forms have norms obtained from an English population. The Progressive Matrices, though useful in a clinical setting, is not supported by any substantial research data in terms of validity or reliability.

A great deal of research has taken place since Cattell first introduced the Culture Free Test. Since then numerous tests purporting to be culturally free or culturally fair have been constructed and tested with little positive results (see, for example, Fowler, 1955; Coleman and Ward, 1955). Their predictive validity has not been as good as that of other "culturally biased" instruments, yet they do not eliminate this "bias." The research continues to demonstrate that lower-class children perform generally as poorly on "culture-free" instruments as on other less culturally controlled devices.

Wesman (1968) feels that the search for the culture-free or culture-fair instrument is "sheer nonsense." He states,

> The implicit intent in the attempt to create culture-free or culture-fair tests is somehow to measure intelligence without permitting the effects of differential exposure to learning to influence scores. This contains the tacit assumption that "native intelligence" lies buried in pure form deep in the individual, and needs only to be uncovered by ingenious mining methods. If we recognize that intelligence comprises learning experiences, it becomes clear that our attempts are not ingenious, but ingenuous. (p. 269)

The reader must remember that tests are reflections of culture and therefore culture *should* be reflected in test scores (see Chapter 2). There is no single test that *can be* or *should be* "fair" to all cultures. Anastasi (1976) puts the matter in perspective when she states, "Cultural differences become cultural handicaps when the individual moves out of the culture or sub-culture in which he was reared and endeavors to function, compete, or succeed within another culture" (p. 346). Thus a culturally disadvantaged person is one who attempts to compete in a different or alien culture, using that culture's game rules.

Infant and Preschool Tests

In spite of all our democratic conceptions, and misconceptions, about every-body being equal, there is scarcely a home in which parents and grandparents do not take a natural interest in the "smartness" of their particular baby or preschooler (Ilg and Ames, 1955, p. 189).

Infant Tests

Gesell (1940) was one of the first to design tests based on observation of the child's perceptual, postural, and manipulative responses. His first tests were a rattle, a ring on a string, a cup and spoon, a 1-inch cube, a small sugar pellet, and a pencil and paper. The child's first reaction to the pellet occurs at about four months of age, when he sees it on a table top or other piece of furniture propped before him. This initial reaction is visual only. Three months later, at seven months, he will take it awkwardly with his hands; by one year he will handle it with precision (Ilg and Ames, 1965).

Some of the questions asked by Gesell (and by psychologists today) about a child are the following: Does he sit up, stand up? If so, at what age? Does he walk and if so at what age? Does the child turn to look at a light? Does he notice a face? Can he use his hands to pick up a block, spoon, or tiny pellet? What kind of grasping motion does he use?

In 1927 Gesell began his famous longitudinal study of the normal develop-mental stages of the human infant. Repeated observations of 107 infants constituting a generally "normal" sample were made. The children were judged healthy with no known problems. They came from American-born parents of Northern European extraction and were considered of middle-class status in terms of socioeconomic and educational level. The infants were examined at the ages of four, six, and eight weeks and at four-week intervals until fifty-six weeks of age. Follow-ups were made later at eighteen months, at two, three, four, five, and six years. Over a ten-year period, re-examinations were made when possible. The Gesell Developmental Schedules were constructed from the data obtained (Gesell and Amatruda, 1938; Gesell et al., 1949). (See Figure 18, which presents the materials used in testing.)

Gesell and Amatruda (1947, pp. 5–6) outlined four major areas for deter-mining the child's level of behavioral development. They are, in brief summary,

Figure 18. Gesell Developmental Schedules materials. (Reproduced by permission of Nigel Cox.)

1. *Motor behavior:* Postural reactions, head balance, sitting, standing, creeping, walking, manipulation of objects, and so forth.
2. *Adaptive behavior:* Eye-hand coordination in grasping, reading, and manipulation of objects.
3. *Language behavior:* Facial expression, gestures, postural movements, and speech. Also, comprehension of other people's speech is noted.
4. *Personal-social behavior:* Feeding, toilet training, play, smiling, and so forth.

The Gesell Developmental Schedules are for the most part observational "tests." Approximate developmental levels in terms of months in each of the four areas are scored.

Another widely used infant scale is the Bayley Scales of Infant Development. This instrument is designed to assess the early mental and psychomotor development of infants from two months of age to the young child of two and one-half years. The instrument yields a Mental Development Index and a Psychomotor Development Index. In addition, there is a composite rating called Infant Behavior Record that gives an overall evaluation as well as qualitative ratings of infant behavior.

The Bayley Scales were standardized on 1,200 children. The sample was chosen on the basis of age, sex, race, residence (urban-rural), and education of head of household. The scores are reported as standard scores for fourteen groups from two months to thirty months.

This scale is in the tradition of developmental schedules begun by Gesell. It uses some items from the Gesell schedules but is based largely upon the monumental studies of the Berkeley Growth Study directed by Bayley and her co-workers.

In recent years, infant tests have changed focus from primarily intellectual to assessing development in a more global sense. The Denver Developmental Screening Test (DDST) was designed to assess delayed development. It can be used for children six weeks to two years and covers four areas: gross motor, fine motor-adaptive, language, and personal-social. It was developed by selecting items from twelve existing infant and preschool tests and eliminating items ambiguous or lacking discrimination. The instrument is inexpensive and can be administered by personnel with little training.[8] In scoring this test, development is rated as adequate, inadequate, or questionable. It does *not* yield an intelligence score, nor is information given of its prediction of later intellectual performance. It was developed in a medical setting and is useful for screening abnormal development. It does not, however, appear to be as sensitive to slow development as the Bayley Scales or the Cattell Infant Scale (Frankenburg, Camp, and Van Natta, 1971). A weakness of the DDST is in the standardization. Developed in Denver, it used only children living in Denver in the proportions represented in the 1960 census.

The DDST is widely used by Head Start and other preschool evaluation programs and is a valuable addition as an instrument to identify those children who need special help at a time that the developmental sequence is amenable to intervention.

The Learning Accomplishment Profile (LAP) (Griffin, Sanford, and Wilson, 1975) is another instrument designed to pinpoint developmental delay in children from one to six years. This instrument was developed through research at the University of North Carolina at Chapel Hill and will be available for general use in the near future. It is a synthesis of several approaches of the past and can be used with either handicapped or normal youngsters. The objective of the authors was to develop an instrument to diagnose developmental problems without stigmatizing the child. The instrument covers five areas: gross motor, fine motor, self-help, cognitive, and language/cognitive. According to the authors, it can be used for both diagnostic and prescriptive purposes.

These developmental screening tests will yield more research in the future, as more data are gathered on children. This is specially true and important in the area of predictive validity.

---

[8] This may not be true, however. A study by Furuno and Connor (1970) reported a correlation of only .30 between DDST scores administered by aides with less than high school training and Stanford-Binet scores administered by psychologists or a pediatrician's clinical evaluation.

Other infants tests such as the Cattell Infant Intelligence Scale, California First-Year Mental Scale, and the Kuhlmann-Binet are more in the classic tradition of individual intelligence tests, although they all have items in common with the Gesell as well as the Binet scales.

Validity and reliability data on infant tests are generally quite low (Bayley, 1949, 1970; McCall, Hogarty, and Hurlburt, 1972). Bayley (1949) studied the relationship of test results in the first year of life with later scores, using the California First-Year Mental Scale, the California Pre-School Scale, and the Stanford-Binet. The results were very disconcerting. For example, scores obtained by infants tested at ten, eleven, and twelve months correlated at .20 with scores obtained at five, six, and seven years of age.

McCall et al. (1972) reviewed many studies of infant and childhood intelligence. Correlations were computed for infant tests administered from one to thirty months with retests administered in childhood from three to eighteen years. The results indicated that tests administered in the first years of life have little or no predictive value for intelligence in later childhood. These correlations range from .01 to .33. The correlation increases somewhat when the infant is between nineteen and thirty months, indicating that intelligence, as measured by our tests, obtains some degree of stability around two years of age. These correlations, however, range only from .41 to .54, not outstandingly high coefficients.

Infant tests do have a use as a rough gauge, especially when used with other data such as parental report and observations. The infant tests seem to be more reliable in predicting performance when there is retardation and/or neurological impairment (Werner, Honzik, and Smith, 1968; Ireton, Thwing, and Gravem, 1970). They are most useful, however, in assessing current neurological or sensory defects, and environmental deficits.

The final word is not in on infant intelligence. The low correlations with later functioning indicate that we have yet a lot to learn about infant intelligence. Our present tests need to be used with caution. Many investigators are attempting to identify, define, and measure infant intelligence using other approaches. The most promising at this point is those studies using the theoretical framework of Piaget. We will discuss these later in the chapter.

Preschool Tests

The decade of the 1960s saw a fervent attempt to design and implement educational programs for preschool children. In large measures these were designed for the children of low socioeconomic families and were an attempt to compensate for real or imagined deficits in the intellectual environments these families provided for their children. Because these programs were primarily designed to stimulate intellectual growth, they needed instruments to measure the growth, or lack of it, which had taken place. The preschooler is generally considered the child between the ages of two and six years. In this section we will consider tests of intelligence for children of this age.

The most venerable instrument for the measurement of intelligence in the preschool child is the Stanford-Binet. This test was discussed earlier in the chapter. Closely behind the Stanford-Binet is the Wechsler Preschool and Primary Scale of Intelligence. This test has also been reviewed previously.

The Merrill-Palmer Scale (Stutsman, 1931) is one of the best-known tests designed for preschool children. The age range is from two to four. There are thirty-eight tests, which yield a total of ninety-three scorable test areas. Only four call for verbal responses. Some of the tasks are "standing on one foot," "building a block tower," and "cutting with scissors."

The Minnesota Preschool Scale (Goodenough and Maurer, 1942) is another widely known preschool test. There are two forms, each containing twenty-six tests, with a format very similar to the Binet. Some of the tests are the following:

Test 5: Imitative Drawing. The examiner draws a vertical stroke and then a cross. The child is to imitate each.
Test 8: Imitation. A set of four cubes, on which examiner taps in a certain manner and child is requested to imitate the sequence of taps.
Test 14: Colors. Child is asked to name the color of cards that are red, blue, pink, white, and brown.
Test 20: Paper Folding. Examiner takes paper and folds it in three consecutive folds and then asks child to copy his actions.

The most outstanding features of the Minnesota Preschool Scale are the careful procedures that were followed in the standardization. It has been found to be especially relevant for children between the ages of three and five years.

A more recently developed instrument is the McCarthy Scales of Children's Abilities published in 1972. This test is for children between two and one-half and eight and one-half years of age. It has eighteen tests grouped into six overlapping scales: Verbal, Perceptual Performance, Quantitative, General Cognitive, Memory, and Motor. The General Cognitive score comes closest to the usual general measure of intellectual development. It is based on fifteen of the eighteen tests (three motor tests are excluded). The scores are expressed as a General Cognitive Index (GCI), which is a standard score with a mean of 100 and a SD of 16. The term IQ was not used, although GCI and IQ are in the same traditional units because, according to the manual, IQ has had a misleading history.

Kaufman and Hollenbeck (1973) discuss the extensive standardization procedures of this test. The initial selection was based on studies in developmental psychology, clinical experience, and factor-analytic research. It should be noted that the first factor analyses were substantiated during the final version of the battery (Kaufman, 1975). It is also interesting to note that no significant sex differences have been found (Kaufman and Kaufman,

1973b), and ethnic comparisons (Kaufman and Kaufman, 1973a) showed no significant differences.

Piagetian Scales

There are as yet very few measurement instruments designed to measure the intelligence of the young child from the framework of Piagetian theory. There is, however, much research currently being conducted, and several scales are being prepared. These will no doubt be available in the near future; at present, they are available only for research purposes. The Piagetian approach to intellectual development is that the infant or child passes certain points of development that mark a qualitative difference in intelligence. All children pass through these stages, but perhaps at different times. In addition, children's thinking about space, causality, time, and the physical world differs from adult thinking. Piagetian scales are designed to measure the attainment of various qualities of thinking, for example, object permanence in the sensorimotor stage and conservation in the concrete operational stage. These scales generally assume an orderly sequence of development and may be considered criterion-referenced rather than norm-referenced. However, norms for difference groups will probably be published with the scales.

One published test based on a Piagetian approach is the Concept Assessment Kit—Conservation. It is for children four to seven years old and measures the qualitative change in thinking about physical objects that a child attains in moving from the preoperational stage to the stage of concrete operations. The child is shown two physical objects, such as two glasses of water. One object is then changed in appearance (as one glass of water is poured into a different-shaped glass). The child has attained conservation when he knows the quantity remains the same, even though it looks different. The younger child attends to perceptions, while the older child can override perceptions to make a logical conclusion with concrete objects. This test has three forms: Form A, Form B, and Form C. Forms A and B both have six subtests: Two-Dimensional Space, Number, Substance, Continuous Quantity, Weight, and Discontinuous Quantity. Form C has the six subtests mentioned in addition to Area and Length.

The standardization sample was relatively small (560 children) and was restricted to one area of the country. A wider sample would give the test more generalizability. The studies and statistical data are generally acceptable and indicate a promising instrument.

Several large-scale studies are under way to develop scales. Laurendeau and Pinard (1962, 1970) are working to this end in Montreal, Canada, and Uzgris and Hunt (1975) are working at the University of Illinois. In addition, work is being done at Piaget's Institute in Switzerland to develop standard scales for general use. This approach shows great promise in the assessment of the intellectual area of young children.

Projective Techniques

"It's a Martian creature who has been injected with super powers that cannot be destroyed. I see black wings and a nose like—what's his name? You know, the old guy with a funny nose. Damn, I can't think of it. Anyway, this bat—no, I mean Martian animal—is going to eat us all up. I know he'll devour you and me. Can't someone stop him? Look at those big teeth! Wow!! That's all."

The preceding quotation could be a verbalized response to a projective device.

Projective techniques are not tests in the true sense, because there are no right or wrong answers. One cannot obtain a perfect score or fail. Certainly there are "right" answers in the sense that a group of certain kinds of responses reveals to the trained examiner personality traits that may be pathological. There are, however, no definitive raw scores that point to mental illness or the absence of disturbance.

Projective techniques are used in personality testing in order to explore the individual's world of make-believe. To accomplish this, material that is indefinite and vague is presented to the person who then is to respond in his own unique manner.

Frank (1939) introduced the term *projective techniques* long after the actual instruments had been in use. He thought of them as similar to the X-ray methods of medicine. Frank and others have distinguished the projective technique from other personality instruments by focusing on the ambiguity or unstructuredness of the stimulus material, thereby allowing the subject almost complete freedom of response. With an objective personality test (see Chapter 10), on the other hand, the subject responds to a limited number of predetermined responses.

Another distinctive characteristic of projective techniques is their *indirectness*; that is, the subject being examined is not completely aware of how his responses are going to be evaluated and is therefore less inclined to fake or resist answering. For example, if someone asked you, "Do you love your mother?" how would you answer? Obviously, social and personal (at the conscious level) forces would exert a strong influence. If, on the other hand, the name *mother* was stated as one word in a group of words that you were to respond to ("first thing that comes to your mind"), you would not have time to be as defensive or control your response.

Levy (1963) does not agree completely with the distinctions between projective techniques and objective personality testing. He states,

> we are forced to conclude that the identity of projective techniques as a unique class of techniques is on very shaky grounds if these are either the amount of freedom of response offered the examinee or the ambiguity of the stimulus presented to him. At best, tests might be ordered along such continua. But that such an ordering would result in a bimodal distribution, with conventionally designated projective tests making up one hump and non-projective tests the other, seems quite unlikely. (p. 201)

The reader of this book need not concern himself at this point with the nuances of psychological pedantry.[1] The teacher and counselor need to know that a projective technique or device attempts to elicit free and unguided responses through unstructured material. It is true that in a sense anything can be called a projective technique. That is, predictions may be made from a sample of behavior. The psychologist who reports his findings from intelligence testing has more to say than what the subject's IQ is. He observes the quality of performance and behavior of the person during the test and generalizes from these impressions in the same or similar manner that one does in interpreting responses on projective devices.

Projective techniques have their rationale in everyday observations. For example, did you ever notice how one person will view an accident, play, or painting in a manner unique to himself? The manner in which a person perceives things depends upon his background, and this, of course, varies with each individual. The more vague the material presented to a person, the more opportunity he has to project himself into it. Projective tests take advantage of this situation. An ink blot, a picture, or a word may suffice as a means of finding out about the person's feelings and thoughts.

The projective device originated within a clinical setting and is the favorite personality test of the clinician and to a somewhat lesser degree the school psychologist. Most projective devices have as their theoretical base the psychoanalytic system of human behavior. Psychologists, of course, with other orientations also utilize projective techniques. Projective techniques

---

[1] Ainsworth (1951), Murstein (1961), and Cronbach (1970) discuss in great detail the assumptions and problems in projective techniques. The teacher who is interested in pursuing this subject further is referred to their discussions.

are not only used in ascertaining personality characteristics, but also in un-covering intelligence, creativity, attitudes, and social traits.

In our schools, projective devices are administered only after other informa-tional sources such as classroom behavior, teacher opinion, objective tests, and interviews have failed to provide enough information. The school psychologist is usually the only school person trained to use the projective technique, and he uses it with only a small number of students who present serious emotional and/or intellectual problems. *Projective tests are never given to all students.* In addition, when the school psychologist does ad-minister a projective device, in almost all cases, he obtains parental consent.

The number and various types of projective techniques are quite large. An in-depth review of them is beyond the scope of this book. We will, therefore, focus our attention on a few that you as a teacher or counselor may encounter in the schools. (For a thorough and extensive survey and evaluation of projective techniques, see *The Mental Measurements Year-books.* These volumes have a separate section devoted to projective tech-niques.)

In the remainder of this chapter, we will focus our primary attention on the Rorschach, Holtzman Inkblot Technique, Thematic Apperception Test, and Draw-A-Person.

Rorschach

Overview

The *Rorschach* is one of the basic diagnostic tools of most psychologists. This test is sometimes referred to as the inkblot test. It consists of ten cards, each having a different inkblot; five are printed in black and white and five in color. Figure 19 illustrates an inkblot similar to a Rorschach blot.

The psychologist shows one card at a time to a child (or adult), asking him to tell what the inkblot makes him think of and what it may mean to him. After the initial instructions, the psychologist does not directly help or instruct the subject except to show him the cards. After the ten cards have been given, they are presented a second time. In this phase the psychologist attempts to find out what in the inkblot made the person answer as he did. For example, the psychologist may state, "What in card one made you think of a bat?" In this manner the psychologist gains insight as to where in the inkblot the person saw the "bat," as well as what in the person's background made him think of a bat.

Throughout the Rorschach examination, the psychologist records in detail the person's responses. After the test is completed, an analysis of the record is made. The scoring and interpretation of the Rorschach record are a long and complicated task, and the psychologist needs a great deal of training and experience to do it competently. Thus the administration and scoring

Figure 19. An inkblot similar to a Rorschach card.

of a Rorschach should not be undertaken by a teacher, counselor, or even some psychologists who have not undergone special training. The Rorschach should be administered only by trained clinical or school psychologists and only to students who are in need of it.

History

The earliest use of inkblots that we know of was recorded in a book entitled *Kleksographien,* published in Germany in 1857. The author, Justinus Kerner, recounts that he accidentally found out about the inherent possibilities in inkblots by noting the bizarre configurations they seemed to take on as he observed them. Kerner's most interesting finding was that it seemed almost impossible to reproduce inkblots according to a preconceived plan. He had experienced the interplay between the objective aspects of the inkblots per se and the individual perception of the observer. Kerner did not realize the significance of his observations as a method of personality diagnosis (Klopfer and Kelley, 1946).

Alfred Binet was one of the first to recognize the possible applications of the inkblots to personality diagnosis. A series of investigations made by Binet and other psychologists followed, with the focus of their attention on the content of the subject's responses to the inkblots. The inkblots were used as stimulus material for free associations (Klopfer and Kelley, 1946). It remained in this domain until Herman Rorschach, a Swiss psychiatrist, published the results of ten years of inkblot experimentation in various psychiatric hospitals in Switzerland. These findings were published in 1921 in a monograph entitled *Psychodiagnostik* (Rorschach, 1942). The chief characteristic of Rorschach's findings over those of previous investigators was the focus of attention on the manner of handling the stimulus material rather than just what was seen.

Unfortunately, Dr. Rorschach died a few months after the publication of his findings. Oberholzer, Rorschach's colleague, took over and became a leader of the Rorschach technique. Oberholzer was responsible for the first publications of the technique in the United States and also trained Americans, such as David Levy, in its use. Under Levy, Samuel Beck wrote the first doctoral dissertation, in 1930, on the Rorschach technique in the United States.

Since Beck's dissertation, the Rorschach has grown in influence and acceptance among American psychologists. It is now a basic tool in the evaluation of personality characteristics.

Test Administration

The relationship between the examiner and subject is extremely important. Usually other tests are given first and rapport is established before the Rorschach is administered. The behavior of the subject during the administration is noted and is used in completing the diagnosis. On the other hand, Klopfer et al. (1954) state, "Although it is desirable to have 'good' rapport, it is unnecessary to assume that this is essential in order for the test report to be valid. It seems more important that the relationship, whatever it is, should be clearly perceived and understood by the examiner" (pp. 3–4).

The actual examination consists of three basic phases. Let us briefly review these in the context of an actual examination, using only one of the ten cards as an example. The reader should note that, in the examination, each phase is continued until the completion of the ten cards and then the next phase is initiated.

Performance Phase—Card I

Examiner: I have some inkblots to show you and I want you to tell me what they make you think of, what you see, and what it might mean for you. Remember, this is not a test in the usual sense of failing or passing. You can't get a "hundred" or a "zero" as you can on a test in the classroom. People see all kinds of things in these inkblots. Now tell me what you see and what they make you think of.[2]

---

[2] It should be noted that the language is, of course, varied according to the subject and situation, although the basic instructions remain the same.

Subject: It looks like a bat with large wings. It's . . . ah . . . it's flying.
Examiner: Anything else; remember, tell me what you see and what it makes you think of.[3]
Subject: Just a bat flying—nothing else. (*Subject is given the next card and responds; this procedure is followed until ten cards have been administered.*)

Inquiry Phase—Card I

Examiner: You did very well. Now we are going to go back and look at the cards again and I want you to tell me *what in the cards* made you think of what you said. In card 1 you saw a bat flying; now tell me what in the card made you think of a bat.
Subject: It just looks like a bat.
Examiner: It just looks like a bat?
Subject: Yes, it looks like a bat; it has wings, a body, and face and its shape, just looks like a bat to me. (*Procedure is followed until ten cards are completed.*)

Testing of the Limits—Card I

Examiner: You said you saw a bat in card 1?
Subject: Yes, because of its shape.
Examiner: Any other reason?
Subject: No, just its shape.
Examiner: What about the color black?
Subject: Yes, that's right, I think black and death and bats all are the same. Like vampires—black is the color—but also the shape was important. (*This phase only used on cards in which the examiner needs more information.*)

Summarizing, then, the three basic phases and their modes of operation are

Performance. Nondirective and free association period where subject gives the first thoughts that come into his mind.
Inquiry. Some nondirective prodding to find out what made the subject respond as he did. This phase makes scoring possible and gives the subject a chance to supplement and complete his original responses.
Testing the limits. Degrees of pressure exerted to find out what in the card made the subject respond as he did. Used when two other phases have not produced rationale for responses. This phase *is not scored*, but used as clinical evidence.

---

[3] After this prompting the examiner will not say anything else throughout this phase of the examination.

Scoring

There are two widely used and different procedures for scoring the Rorschach (Beck, 1961; Klopfer and Kelley, 1946; Klopfer et al., 1954). The scoring procedure we will discuss is based on the Klopfer technique. The examiner, in scoring the Rorschach, has the option of using the quantitative method and/or content analysis. Let us look at the quantitative procedure first.

First, the examiner looks for the location of the response. Where in the blot did the subject see, for example, the bat. If he used the whole blot, the response is scored W. If he used a large part of the blot, it is scored D. If he only used a small unusual part of the blot, it is scored Dd. Use of the white space rather than the black ink blot is scored S.

The next concern of the scorer is the determinant for the subject's response—the characteristic of the blot that prompted the response. The primary determinants are figures in human-like action (M), animals in animal-like action (FM), abstract movement (m), shading (k), and color (c). In addition, each response is evaluated on its relevancy to the blot.

The third category is content. This area is focused on what actually is seen in the blot. Among some of the frequent content responses are human figures (H), human details (Hd), animals (A), objects from animal parts, like fur (A obj.), man-made objects (obj.), and so forth.

Each response is also analyzed to determine if it is original or popular. The definitions of original and popular response depend on the classification system used. In general terms, however, a popular response is one given by a majority of subjects, whereas an original response is one that is rarely if ever seen.

Interpretation

The interpretation of a Rorschach record is a difficult and laborious process requiring rigorous training and clinical experience. A detailed analysis here would be at best an incomplete statement. Several textbooks dealing only with the Rorschach are usual for the serious study of the technique. Therefore, the reader should note that what follows is a simple and extremely brief summary of some of the key features of interpretation.

QUANTITATIVE ANALYSIS

In quantitative analysis, the interrelationships between various scoring classifications previously mentioned (e.g., W, FM, A, P) are noted and studied. Some of the possible interpretations, for example, are

1. A great many human responses (M) that are appropriate for the given inkblot and are sufficiently explained is a sign of high intellectual endowment.

2. When M's appear in optimal relationship with animal responses (FM), this is a sign of self-acceptance.
3. Color responses, shading, and texture give evidence of the subject's emotional life.
4. The location areas that the subject chooses may suggest his typical approach to problems and situations with which he deals in everyday life.

CONTENT ANALYSIS

Certain responses may be interpreted symbolically; for example, snakes and totem poles may indicate sexual feelings. The absence of human figures may indicate the subject has little empathy for people. Animal responses in young children are quite normal; however, an adult who gives a great many may be infantile. In addition, certain cards usually evoke certain responses; the absence or avoidance of these may reveal characteristics of the subject.

SYNTHESIS

The proper interpretation of the Rorschach requires the examiner to bring to bear all the features mentioned in an analysis of the quantitative and content relationships and their frequency; of the consistency of the various hypotheses that are derived and of how well they go together with the behavioral notations and the subject's case history. This process requires not only training and skill but also an intuitive approach called clinical judgment. This dependence on clinical feeling is one of the major hurdles to be overcome in the statistical validation of the Rorschach.

Dependence on clinical skill has not prevented years of statistical research. These research findings have in many instances been negative or at best inconclusive. Some positive results, of course, have also been noted. For example, Goldfried, Stricker, and Weiner (1971) found that when the Rorschach is used as a measure of thinking processes and perceptual organization, it has a great deal of promise.

The Rorschach has been investigated not only with adults but also with children. Levitt and Truumaa (1972) review data from fifteen studies and quantitative Rorschach indexes for intelligence by age up to sixteen years.

It should also be noted that the computer has been utilized in Rorschach interpretation. Piotrowski's Automated Rorschach (PAR) was made operationally available in 1974. The reports are organized differently according to the special needs of clinics, penal institutions, and industry.

Evaluation

The Rorschach is a very difficult instrument on which to establish statistical validity because of its inherent reliance on the clinical experience of the person scoring and interpreting the record. The various studies and investigations do not reveal empirical validation for the scoring system of the Rorschach. The Rorschach has been found to have little predictive validity when compared to psychiatric diagnosis and other criteria. The studies that do reveal validity have been criticized on methodological grounds. Thus it must be stated that from a statistical and experimental viewpoint the Rorschach is no better than an interview device. On the other hand, it must also be stated that a great many clinical and school psychologists view the Rorschach as a valid and reliable instrument based on their professional experiences. In addition, psychiatrists rely heavily upon the psychologists' findings, which are based largely though not completely on the Rorschach.

In the experience of one of the authors as a clinical and school psychologist, the Rorschach has been found to be invaluable. Although recognizing its limitations, the author feels it is valid if administered and interpreted by a trained and experienced person. Its chief limitation to the clinical user is that it is time-consuming. The average administration, scoring, interpretation, and write-up of the Rorschach take between six and eight hours.

The Rorschach is used by the school psychologist only when other devices are inadequate and when parental permission is obtained. In these circumstances it can be of invaluable assistance.

Holtzman Inkblot Technique

The Holtzman Inkblot Technique (HIT) is an attempt to present a projective technique that meets the technical standards of testing while incorporating the advantages of projective devices. It, of course, utilized the Rorschach as its model (Holtzman, 1968, 1975a).

The HIT presents two parallel forms of forty-five cards (blots) each. These ninety blots include some that are asymmetric, some in one color other than black, and some with visual textures. Only one response to each blot is elicited. The experienced psychologist may select a smaller number of blots from either or both forms in order to obtain multiple responses and investigate more thoroughly special areas of concern in a specific situation.

The computer has been utilized in the analysis of hundreds of protocols. This has led to the "Scoring Guide," which enables results to be reproducible from one scorer to another. Scores are obtained for twenty-two response variables based on eight groups, normal and pathological. These include normal subjects ranging from five-year-olds to adults, and clinical groups such as alcoholics, mental defectives, and schizophrenics (Hill, 1972).

Evaluation

The reliability of the HIT is excellent, especially for a projective device. Split-half and alternate-form reliabilities have yielded very satisfactory results. There is also a group form of HIT that uses slides.

Validity data on this device have been considerable (Gamble, 1972;

Holtzman, 1968, 1975a). At this point the findings look good, but more data are necessary to prove the diagnostic significance of the scores and the construct validity of the behavioral variables evaluated by this device (Anastasi, 1976).

Thematic Apperception Test

Another projective technique in wide use is the Thematic Apperception Test (TAT). It was developed in 1935 by two psychologists, H. A. Murray and C. D. Morgan, of the Harvard Psychological Clinic (Murray, 1938, 1943). The TAT is almost as widely used as the Rorschach. Clinical and school psychologists use it as one of the basic instruments in their psychological test battery. In addition to its years of service in the diagnostic test battery, it has also served as a model for later instruments that have the same story-type format (see, for example, Varble, 1971).

Test Administration

The TAT consists of a set of pictures showing human figures in different poses and actions. Some of the pictures are only for boys, others for girls, some for adults (over fourteen years of age), and others for all individuals. There are nineteen pictures for a particular age and sex, and one blank card. The psychologist, in most cases, does not administer all twenty cards but selects only those he considers particularly appropriate for a given person.

The psychologist instructs the subject to tell him a story based on the picture presented. He requests a past, present, and future for each of the stories. The exact instructions sometimes vary, but they always include the request for a past, present, and future in the subject's story. Generally, the instructions are the following,

> *I am going to show you some pictures. I'd like you to tell me a story about what is going on in each picture, what has led up to it, what is happening now, and what may happen in the future. Remember that there are no right or wrong stories, only what you see. Here's the first picture—now tell me a story about what has happened and what is happening and what you think will happen.*

The TAT stories are either taped or taken down verbatim by the psychologist. No time limits are given and the subject may tell a short or long story, depending on how he feels.

Scoring

The scoring of the TAT is not quite as time-consuming as that of the Rorschach. Many different scoring techniques have been advocated for the TAT. Shneidman (1951, 1965) presents many of the methods commonly used by recognized experts. These range from an emphasis on the content of the stories (interpersonal relations, parent-child, etc.) to a statistical-normative approach. Whatever method is used in interpretation, the examiner attempts to obtain a whole picture by analyzing all the cards administered rather than by drawing conclusions from only one card.

Let us examine one commonly used method, a content analysis of the stories. This is a clinical method whereby the examiner attempts to discover the psychodynamic causes of disturbed behavior or of the level of adjustment. The first step is to read the record for a general impression. Second, the examiner summarizes each story and obtains its salient features. Third, each story is analyzed for possible conflict, mother-child relationships, sexual identity, hostility, aggression, defenses (for example, rationalization and projection), and so forth. After these analyses have been made, they are put together to form a general picture. Themes such as anxiety, sibling conflicts, and other disturbing features that recur on more than one card are looked for. As Lasaga (1951) states,

> If a person has extremely intense worries or conflicts, these worries or conflicts will show up again and again in a large number of the stories of the test, possibly in most of them. This means that every TAT certainly reflects several aspects of the whole personality of the subject being tested, but, when one or more intense conflicts exist in the subject's life at the moment the test is made, what will appear first of all in the TAT will be these conflicts. (p. 145)

Let us look at the story of an eleven-year-old boy in the fifth grade. The story is in response to a TAT card that presents a boy of about the same age sitting down and looking at a violin and bow with his hands supporting his face.

> Well, this is the past. He was going with his mother to buy a violin and dropped it and tripped over it and fell flat on his face and blood came gushing out. After he had gone to the doctor, he came home and was crying because the violin was broken. Probably some day, he'll fall again, and he'll get his violin fixed. I didn't mean to say he'll fall again.

The boy who gave the preceding response was referred to this writer because of academic and social difficulties. He would not play with other children and felt inadequate with them. "I am not as good as other kids." When asked about school he stated, "I am so far behind. I am dumb."

What do you think about this boy? Read his story again. The other TAT stories as well as his Rorschach responses and other tests revealed a child who lacked social alertness and was unable to deal with social situations. More importantly, strong trends indicating possible criminal behavior as he grew older were noted. Psychotherapy was recommended.

Lasaga (1951) states that conflicts may appear at the conscious, partially conscious, or unconscious level while the subject is taking the test. Thus Lasaga (1951) concludes that, "When a test presents stories other than those totally objective or completely trivial, which cannot be explained literally by conflicts or facts of the patient's life; then it is to be supposed that such stories express in a symbolic or metaphoric form worries and happenings in his real life" (p. 145).

Evaluation

The TAT has been used in many research investigations. Little and Shneidman (1955), in an attempt to study the clinical validity of the TAT, found that even among expert interpreters a great range of validity coefficients are obtained.

There are a great many scientific data which reveal that physical and social conditions such as sleep deprivation, hunger, social frustration, and test failure may significantly alter TAT responses (Atkinson, 1958). The many different techniques of interpretation of the TAT may limit its reliability. This, plus the differences in length of stories, makes generalization of scores difficult (Entwisle, 1972; Veroff, Atkinson, Feld, and Gurin, 1974).

It must be admitted, as with the Rorschach, that the TAT is not an objective test and that its validity and reliability in statistical terms do not warrant its use. Although statistical techniques have not supported the claims of TAT advocates, clinical day-to-day experience has shown its wide and beneficial use in clinics, hospitals, and schools, as well as in industrial appraisal for executive employment.

Other Projective Story Techniques

Make a Picture Story (MAPS)

The MAPS test was developed by Shneidman in 1947 and has been referred to as a "younger brother" of the TAT. It is different from the TAT in that it varies the material by separating the figures and backgrounds and allows the subject to select and place his choice of figures on a blank background before he relates a story.

The materials for the MAPS consist of twenty-two background pictures (8½ by 11 inches) printed achromatically on cardboard. With two exceptions, there are no figures in any of the pictures. Some of the unstructured backgrounds are a stage and a blank card; others are semistructured, such as a forest and desertlike landscape; and others are structured, such as a medical scene and bathroom.

There are sixty-seven figures with various facial expressions and various types of dress. Among these are males and females, children, blacks, Orientals, Mexicans, and animal figures. See Figure 20, which presents the figures used.

Figure 20. Make a Picture Story materials. (From E. S. Shneidman. Reproduced by permission of The Psychological Corporation.)

Shneidman (1951) illustrates a typical administration of the MAPS:

What I am going to do is show you pictures like this, one at a time. [Living-room background picture was placed directly in front of the subject.] *You will have figures like this* [at this point all the figures were poured out of their envelope onto the table top] *and your task is simply to take one or more of any of these figures and put them on the background picture as they might be in real life. We might start by sorting the figures so that you can see each one. Spread them out on the table.*

[After all of figures had been placed on the table by the subject, the examiner states,]

I would like to go over the instructions . . . all you are to do is take one or more of any of these figures, put them on the background as they might be in real life, and tell a story of the situation which you have created. In telling your story, tell, if you can, who the characters are, what they are doing and thinking and feeling, and how the whole thing turns out. Go ahead. (p.19)

The MAPS is essentially an unstandardized test investigating psychosocial areas of fantasy. A formal scoring system has been developed, but there are no statistical data that support its validity or reliability. As with the Rorschach and TAT, its primary role is in clinical, rather than objective, evaluation.

The Blacky Pictures

The Blacky Pictures (Blum, 1950) were originally constructed to test certain psychoanalytic concepts. They consist of ten cards that display cartoonlike drawings. These cartoon drawings center around the "adventures" of a dog called Blacky.

Blacky can be of either sex, depending on the projection and identification of the subject. The test may be used with children but was originally designed for adults. The main theme of the cartoons centers on psychosexual development. The method of administration is like that of the TAT except that the subject is asked, in addition to telling a story, to answer a set of standardized questions. School psychologists must be especially careful in administering this test because of the overt sexual connotations. As in all personality assessment, parental permission must be granted before the test is given.

The Blacky Pictures can be a useful tool with many research advantages. It is not, however, an objective or standardized instrument. Used by competent clinicians, it can be of diagnostic assistance.

Symonds Picture-Story Test

The Symonds Picture-Story is basically a projective technique designed to study the personality characteristics of adolescent boys and girls. It has the same test format as the TAT, but it uses a set of pictures constructed to study adolescent fantasy. The administration and scoring are similar to those for the TAT procedures. There are twenty pictures that may be given to boys or girls.

Symonds (1948) suggests that the examiner's main task in the content analysis is to record the principal psychological forces in the stories. He lists fourteen forces which should be noted in the content analysis:

> (1) *Hostility and aggression, (2) love and erotism, (3) ambivalence, (4) punishment, (5) anxiety, (6) defenses against anxiety, (7) moral standards and conflicts, (8) ambition, striving toward success, (9) conflicts, (10) guilt, (11) guilt reduction, (12) depression, discouragement, despair, (13) happiness and (14) sublimation. (pp. 10–12)*

The Symonds test, like other clinical instruments, has little statistical validity but may be useful to the skilled examiner. A full explanation and detailed aspects of the test can be found in Symonds' *Adolescent Fantasy* (1949).

Children's Apperception Test

The Children's Apperception Test (CAT) is very similar to the TAT, but animals rather than people are employed. This substitution is based on the assumption that children can more readily identify with animals than with people (Bellak, 1975). The animals are pictured in typical activities of humans in the same manner as in books for children. The CAT is designed to stimulate fantasies centering around possible areas of conflict, such as eating, sibling rivalry, aggression, toilet-training, and other developmental experiences of childhood.

The administration and scoring of the CAT, as well as its validity and reliability, are similar to those of the previously mentioned picture story techniques. However, several studies have shown no significant differences between the story responses of children exposed to human and animal figures (see Armstrong, 1954; Furuya, 1957). Most psychologists use the TAT for both children and adults, and only occasionally use the CAT as a replacement for the TAT.

Other thematic apperception tests have been published. They include the CAT-H (human modification of the CAT) for children with a mental age of 10 or more (Bellak and Hurvich, 1966); the Senior Apperception Technique (Bellak, 1975; Bellak and Bellak, 1973); and the Gerontological Apperception Test (Wolk and Wolk, 1971). The aged devices feature one or more older people and illustrate problems of the aged.

Other Types of Projective Techniques

Word Association Test

Word association tests attempt to reveal associative connections between certain prescribed words and the free verbal responses of the subject. This technique has a long history dating back to Galton and Wundt and carried forward by the well-known psychoanalyst Dr. Carl Jung (1910). Jung used words that were common to emotional fixations. He would state a word and then record the subject's verbal reaction word and the time taken to respond. The words, reaction time, and behavioral mannerisms while responding were recorded and an analysis was then made.

Kent and Rosanoff (1910) designed a free-association test as a psychiatric screening instrument using common, "normal" words. These words tended to stimulate common associations rather than atypical responses. Frequency tables were developed that contained the number of times a response to a given word was found in 1,000 adults. If a subject replied with a different response, that is, if it was not found in the table, his response was labeled *idiosyncratic.* This test's validity was obviated somewhat when other variables in addition to mental illness, such as age, sex, culture, and education, were found to influence responses. On the other hand, the test is still widely used in research on verbal and personality behaviors throughout the world (Postman and Keppel, 1970).

Sentence Completion Tests

The Rotter Incomplete Sentences Blank is a good illustration of a sentence completion test. The Rotter comes in three forms—High School, College, and Adult. All three forms have forty stems such as "The happiest day" and "I love." The High School and Adult forms differ slightly in the wording of a few items. The College form was used in the initial standardization. The subject is asked to express his true feelings in completing each stem.

Clinical interpretations of the content of the sentences are made. In addition, numerical scores can be obtained. The scoring method is predicated on three categories: conflict or unhealthy responses, neutral responses, and positive or healthy responses. There is no time limit.

Draw-A-Person Test

Karen Machover is responsible for the well-known Draw-A-Person projective device. It is her feeling, as well as that of many others, that a drawing of the human figure is tied up with the personality of the individual doing the drawing. Machover (1949) states,

> When an individual attempts to solve the problem of the directive to "draw a person," he is compelled to draw from some sources. External figures are too varied in their body attributes to lend themselves to a spontaneous, objective representation of a person. Some process of selection involving identification through projection and introjection enters at some point. The individual must draw consciously, and no doubt unconsciously, upon his whole system of psychic values. The body, or the self, is the most intimate point of reference in any activity. We have, in the course of growth, come to associate various sensations, perceptions, and emotions with certain body organs. This investment in body image as it has developed out of personal experience, must somehow guide the individual who is drawing in the specific structure and content which constitutes his offering of a "person."
>
> Consequently, the drawing of a person, in involving a projection of the body image, provides a natural vehicle for the expression of one's body needs and conflicts. Successful drawing interpretation has proceeded on the hypothesis that the figure drawn is related to the individual who is drawing with the same intimacy characterizing that individual's gait, his handwriting, or any other of his expressive movements. (p. 5)

Administration of the Draw-A-Person Test (DAP) is relatively simple. The subject is given a sheet of paper (8½ by 11 inches) and a medium-soft pencil with eraser and told to "draw a person." If the subject is anxious about his drawing skill, the examiner reassures him that "this is not a test of artistic skill." After completing the first drawing, the subject is given another sheet of paper and told to draw a person of the sex opposite to the figure in his first drawing. If the first drawing was of a man, he is told "now go ahead and draw a woman." The examiner may sometimes question the subject after the completion of the drawings for "associations," asking what the person is doing or what his age is.

Interpretation of the DAP is based mainly on psychoanalytic theory (Machover, 1949). The drawing analyst looks for many things, including the size of the figure and where it is placed on the sheet. Shading, erasures, and background also lend themselves to analysis. For example, Machover states that "if the fist is clenched he may literally be expressing his belligerence" (p. 35). The types of clothing, nose (large or small), feet, neck, head, lips, and so forth, are also considered.

Research studies that have attempted to validate the DAP have yielded conflicting data. The DAP, as in the case of its projective brothers, is not easily quantified. It must almost be taken on faith. It is the type of instrument in which after years of usage one may have great confidence but little scientific evidence with which to prove some of its claims. It has been the senior author's experience that it is a very valuable diagnostic tool when used by the skilled diagnostician as one of many measurement tools.

House-Tree-Person Test

The House-Tree-Person Test (HTP) was devised by J. N. Buck with certain preconceived ideas of what a house, tree, and person should mean to an individual. It is assumed by Buck that a house should evoke feelings concerning the subject's home, that a tree is symbolic of life and of an individual's capacity to enjoy his environment, that a person is seen as activating feelings about and needs in interpersonal relations (Buck, 1964).

Administration of the test is similar to that of the DAP. The subject is asked to draw a picture of a house and then the same instructions are repeated for the tree and person. After the drawings have been completed, certain questions, some of which are standardized, are asked. The scoring is both clinical and statistical and highly time-consuming. Validation studies do not substantiate Buck's basic rationale (see Fisher and Fisher, 1950).

The Bender-Gestalt Test

The Bender-Gestalt Test is not considered a projective technique in the same sense as is the TAT, although similar elements are present. Cronbach (1960) sees the Bender-Gestalt as a "stylistic" test, that is, a technique which focuses on the subject's style of handling a problem, as contrasted to the TAT, which examines the "whole person"—his emotions, attitudes, thinking, and so forth.

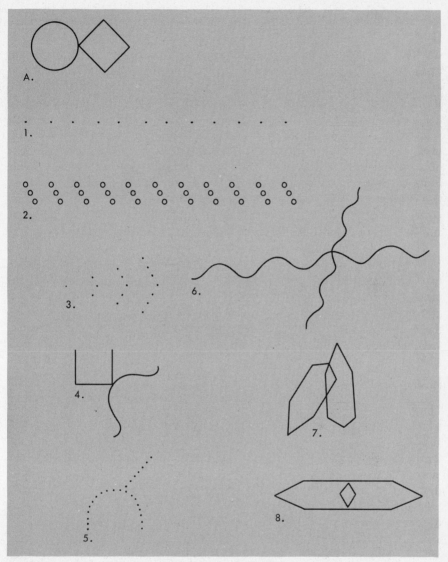

Figure 21. Designs of the Bender-Gestalt Test. (From Lauretta Bender,
A Visual Motor Gestalt Test and Its Clinical Use: Research Monographs,
No. 3. Copyright © 1938 by the American Orthopsychiatric Association, Inc.
Reproduced by permission of the publisher.)

The Bender-Gestalt is based on the classical teachings of the Gestalt school
of psychology. Bender (1938) chose nine of the original Wertheimer (one of
the founders of the Gestalt school of psychology) patterns for her test. Figure
21 presents these nine patterns.

The Bender-Gestalt is used as a clinical instrument to evaluate intelligence, maturation, psychological disturbances, and brain damage. It is easily administered. The instructions generally are the following: "I have here nine simple designs (or figures) which you are to copy, free hand, without sketching—on this paper. Each design is on one of these cards which I will show you one at a time. There is no time limit to this test" (Pascal and Suttell, 1951, p. 11).

The rotation of the paper and reproduction of the figures are noted by the examiner. There are quantitative methods of scoring; however, most psychologists today use the qualitative or clinical integration of all the responses in evaluating the subject's reproductions.

This will probably change as more standardization and reliable objective data of the test become available. For example, Koppitz (1975) attempted to standardize the Bender-Gestalt Test with children. This adaptation (Bender-Gestalt Test for Young Children) was constructed as a nonverbal developmental scale for children from five to ten years old. Norms on 1,104 kindergarten to fourth-grade children in eastern and midwestern schools were obtained.

Koppitz (1975) presents high validities in evaluating school readiness and success in the first grade. Data also indicate that the Bender-Gestalt developmental score has good validity with mentally retarded children and their subsequent school achievement. The user of the Bender-Gestalt Test must remember that the test is a rough gauge of possible organic brain damage and an indicator of behavioral dysfunctions when used with other diagnostic instruments. Cronbach (1970), commenting on this, states, "As to brain damage the overlap of brain-damaged and normal groups is considerable; poor Bender performance, especially when a child appears normal or superior on conventional ability tests, does signal the need to check on possible brain damage" (p. 633).

Evaluation of Projective Techniques

Our review of projective techniques has shown the wide variety of methods used to obtain a sample of conscious and unconscious behavioral characteristics. We have seen that most projective techniques have little, if any, statistical verification. It is obvious that evaluation of many, if not all, of the projective devices falls short. However, some studies do appear to present validity data, and the supporters of projective techniques feel that someday their views will be statistically established.

The authors believe that projective devices do not lend themselves to quantification any more than the clinical judgment of the psychiatrist or family physician can be experimentally justified. This does not prevent us from seeking help from these professionals. The positive experiences of clinical and school psychologists and their professional co-workers such as psychiatrists and social workers are testimony to the effectiveness of the projective method. Psychiatrists, by and large, do not make final disposition of a case, whether it be legal or medical, until they have seen the report of the psychologist, whose analysis and diagnosis of personality characteristics are based on projective techniques. Psychiatrists respect the analysis because they have found a high correlation between the projective findings and their own evaluations and, more importantly, between patient recovery and future behavior. Remember, the psychologist uses a battery of tests, and his opinions are based on the total picture presented by all test data, the person's history, and personal interviews.

Thus we can state that although the projective techniques generally do not meet the requirements for scientific test evaluation, from a clinician's or pragmatist's viewpoint they work. Until we have better instruments or research validation, we shall have to continue to use these devices for personality assessment.

Many schools that lack the services of a qualified full-time psychologist may have to refer a student to an outside agency. It is important to be sure of the qualifications of the person doing the testing. Certification by the state and reference statements from professional sources should be checked. School authorities should also guard against the administration of these tests without both parents' consent. In summary, projective techniques used discriminately by qualified people can be of assistance in ascertaining behavioral problems.

FOUR | Group Standardized Testing

Scholastic and Special Aptitude Tests

chapter 8

Individual tests of intelligence and personality, important as they are, represent only a small fraction of the tests being used today. Most of the testing in our schools as well as in other settings is on a group basis. These group instruments are similar to objective school examinations and differ from individual tests primarily in that they may be administered to more than one individual at a time. Later in this chapter we shall discuss the advantages and disadvantages of group tests as compared with individual tests. Let us now turn our attention to the scholastic aptitude test commonly referred to in past years as the group intelligence test. For illustration only certain tests will be named and examined; this should not be construed as an endorsement, nor should the omission of a test be interpreted as a negative evaluation. The *Mental Measurements Yearbooks* (see Chapter 19) present critical test evaluations.

Scholastic Aptitude Tests

The reason that we now use the term *scholastic aptitude test* rather than *IQ* or *general intelligence* or *group intelligence* test can be found in what these tests actually measure. Authorities differ in their interpretations of the results of these tests. Some feel that they are measures of innate intelligence, whereas others feel that they fall short of this because of their reliance on factors such as culture, educational exposure, and achievement. Most authorities, however, would agree that they measure with some accuracy, though not perfectly, an individual's chance of success in school, because they measure the skills required for educational progress. One of their main reasons for being is to help the school understand and plan appropriate instruction for individual students.

The issue of whether they in fact measure innate ability or intelligence is primarily of theoretical interest. The educator is concerned with educating students and meeting their needs. If the tests predict chances of success or failure in the school setting, they are useful. (See Chapter 2 for a more complete discussion of this issue.) The educator can then make alterations or additions in the curriculum and tailor individual programs of study for children with special educational needs.

Investigations over a period of more than forty years have shown a positive correlation between scores on group intelligence tests and academic success. Although these studies have not shown a perfect or near perfect correlation, there is enough evidence to demonstrate their usefulness in educational planning.

Measurement experts, realizing that the group intelligence test is not necessarily a measure of innate intelligence but is a good indicator of school success, have changed the title to convey more accurately what it really measures, that is, a person's scholastic aptitude. Today most test publishers and consumers agree with this reasoning; however, because terms are not easily changed, the terms *IQ* or *general intelligence tests* can still be found.

The administration of group tests to children should not begin before the age of five or six (kindergarten or first grade). Below the age of five, individual tests should be used because of the importance of assessing test behavior and the need for controlling the child's attention and motivation (see Chapter 6). Even with five- and six-year-old children careful attention to their test behavior and understanding of directions such as how to turn pages correctly is extremely important if valid results are to be obtained. For example, in the *Handbook* for the Cooperative Primary Tests (Educational Testing Service, 1967), a pilot test is given youngsters before the scorable tests are administered, so that the children will know how to respond. Even with the pilot test, however, some children are still not sure of what they are to do.

>   While experience with the Pilot Test in pretesting and norming situations has indicated that almost all children can answer almost all items on the practice test, or at least understand what they are supposed to do, the teacher may occasionally find a child who does not seem to be able to handle the tasks it presents. If, after a second trial with the Pilot Test at a later time, this still seems to be the case, the teacher is probably well advised not to go ahead to administer other tests in the series to this child. Interpretations from the other tests might be more misleading than helpful. (p. 7)

Figure 22. Sample items and directions for administering the Verbal Meaning Test. (From *PMA Primary Mental Abilities, Examiner's Manual,* for Grades 2–4. © 1963, Thelma Gwinn Thurstone. Reprinted by permission of the publisher, Science Research Associates, Inc.)

Directions for Administering the Verbal Meaning Test

The examiner must have a copy of the test booklet opened to the appropriate page to use for demonstration purposes.

Since the children already have their individual PMA 2–4 test booklets, say:

> Open your test booklet to the first page of pictures and fold it back like this. *(Demonstrate.)* In the first row there are pictures of a flower, a toy windmill, a leaf, and a Christmas tree. Put an X on the leaf like this.

Demonstrate on the blackboard by making an X like this
X to indicate the answer chosen.

> Each time you mark a picture, your mark should look like this.

Inspect each child's booklet. If a child's mark is incorrect or too light, mark the booklet for him. Then say:

> Are there any questions? *(Pause to answer questions.)*

When all questions have been answered, say:

> Now look at the second row of pictures. In this row there are pictures of some bread, fruit, a plant, and a pea pod. Put an X on the picture of the fruit. *(Pause.)*
> In the third row find the picture that finishes this story: Tommy doesn't like vegetables. He ate all of his lunch except the _____. Mark it with an X. Which picture did you mark? That's right—the carrot.
> Move down to the next row of pictures. Mark the picture that finishes this story: Anne was going to her music lesson. Her mother told her not to forget to take her _____. Mark it. That's right—the violin.

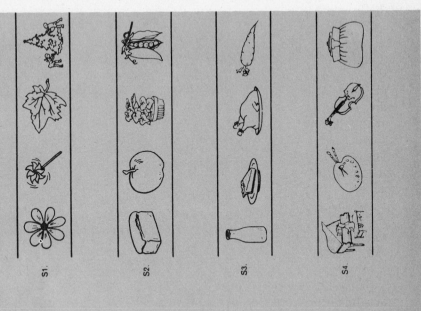

S1.

S2.

S3.

S4.

Group tests for the first two or three grades require no reading. The instructions are given orally, and usually one or two examples are presented before the testing starts. The child marks his answer in the booklet with a soft pencil or crayon.

A good example of the scholastic aptitude test in the lower grades is the Science Research Associates, Primary Mental Abilities Test for grades 2–4 (Thurstone, 1963). This test attempts to measure four "mental abilities." These are defined in the *Examiner's Manual* (Thurstone, 1963) as follows:

V—*Verbal Meaning: The ability to understand ideas expressed in words. In the later school years this is the most important single index of a child's potential for handling academic tasks. At the lower levels it is tested by a vocabulary test in picture form; at the upper levels, by a verbal vocabulary test.*
N—*Number Facility: The ability to work with numbers, to handle simple quantitative problems rapidly and accurately, and to understand and recognize quantitative differences. At the lower grade levels the N scores are determined by a pictorial test that requires no reading. Addition problems are also used. At the upper levels arithmetical reasoning problems are included.*
P—*Perceptual Speed: The ability to recognize likenesses and differences between objects or symbols quickly and accurately. This ability is important in acquiring reading skills, but tends to plateau at a relatively early age. For this reason it is included only with the three batteries designed for the lower grades.*
S—*Spatial Relations: The ability to visualize objects and figures rotated in space and the relations between them. The test measuring this ability appears in every level of the PMA and is important throughout the school years. (p. 4)*

The total time for the test is a little over one hour. The manual recommends that the test be divided in half, one part being given on one day and the second on the following day.

Each child is given a test booklet and one colored marking pencil. To illustrate the directions and tasks the child encounters, sample problems of the Verbal Meaning Test with the accompanying directions are presented in Figure 22.

Figure 23 contains a sampling of items from the other three sections of the test.

The Spatial Relations Test requires the child to find the part that completes a picture. For example, S5 is part of a square and the child must find the part that completes it. The Number Facility Test requires the child to write the answer to the problem on the line. The ability to recognize similar objects or pictures is required in the Perceptual Speed Test. Here the child is asked to mark X's on the two pictures that are exactly alike.

The test is scored by counting all the correct answers in each section. Raw scores (number of correct answers) are converted to quotient equivalents and percentiles. Norms for each section are given as well as for a total score (in quotient equivalents and percentiles).

Another widely used instrument is the Kuhlmann-Finch Scholastic Aptitude Tests (Kuhlmann and Finch, 1952; Finch, 1956). This series contains

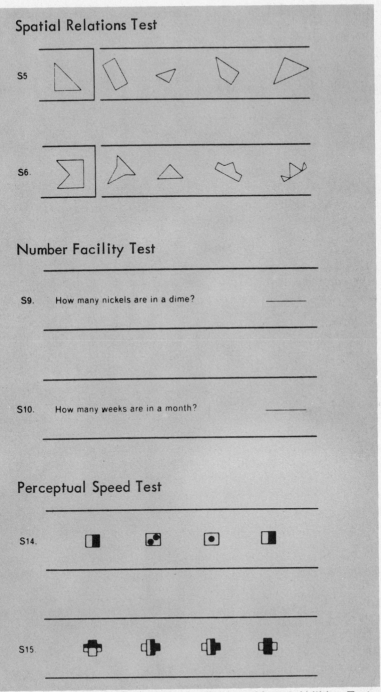

Figure 23. Selected sample items from the Primary Mental Abilities Test. (From *PMA Primary Mental Abilities, Examiner's Manual,* for Grades 2–4. © 1963, Thelma Gwinn Thurstone. Reprinted by permission of the publisher, Science Research Associates, Inc.)

tests for grades 1–12. Over 40,000 pupils in selected schools in thirty states were included in the standardization. Total time for administration is a little over thirty minutes. The test is largely nonverbal and the publishers claim it is "fair to individuals of varying cultural backgrounds." In grades 4–12, answers may be written in test booklets or on separate answer sheets. Figure 24 presents sample items from Test V, which is for fifth-grade students. It consists of five subtests, each of which is five minutes long. Subtest 1 requires the student to find the word that belongs in the second pair. Subtest 2 asks the student to find the picture with arms held like the first picture. A has both arms up; B has right arm up. Subtest 3 requires the student to study the first five numbers in each row to find out what number should come next. Subtest 4 presents three pictures in each row. The student looks at them and chooses the one of five possibilities that goes together with the three pictures. Subtest 5 requires the student to find the word that does not belong with the other four.

The raw score is converted to a standard IQ and mental age. The publishers offer a complete scoring service ("one-week service") providing rank order or alphabetical listing with the mental age and standard IQ.

Otis-Lennon Mental Ability Test is a scholastic aptitude test that has had wide use and acceptance since its initial publication in 1936, when it was called the Otis Quick Scoring Mental Ability Test. The Otis-Lennon is its replacement.

The Otis-Lennon samples a broad range of cognitive abilities from the last half of kindergarten through college and adult. Norms are presented by age, with deviation IQs (a mean of 100, standard deviation of 16), percentile ranks, and stanines. Norms for grade-percentile ranks and stanines are presented through grade 12. There are mental-age norms for primary and elementary levels. The Primary tests take thirty minutes to administer, whereas the others take forty to forty-five minutes.

A well-known and respected series of scholastic aptitude tests is the School and College Ability Tests (SCAT). These tests were first published in 1956 and revised in 1966 as the SCAT Series II. When STEP Series II was standardized (see Chapter 9, p. 254) in 1970, SCAT Series II was renormed in order to have comparable batteries of ability and achievement tests with norms from a single representative population of pupils. Therefore, the latest norms have a 1970 date, although the 1966 test items themselves have not been changed.

The SCAT Series II tests were designed to measure verbal and quantitative ability at four different levels. These levels are: grades 3 Spring–6 Fall; grades 6 Spring–9 Fall; grades 9 Spring–12 Fall; and grades 13 Fall–14 Spring (Educational Testing Service, 1973a). The format of all grade levels is essentially the same, differing only in difficulty of subject matter. Each has parallel forms comparable in content coverage and difficulty. Students record their responses on separate answer sheets. Figure 25 presents sample items from the SCAT Series II Form 4A (grades 3–6).

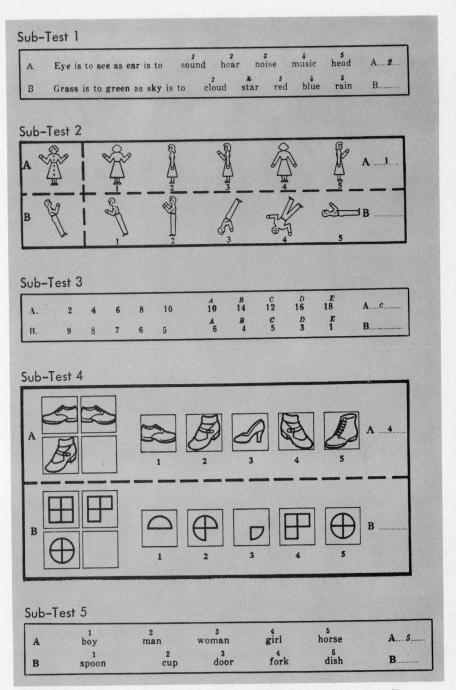

Figure 24. Sample items from the Kuhlmann-Finch Tests, Test V. (By Frederick Kuhlmann and Frank Finch. Copyright 1952 by American Guidance Service, Inc. Reproduced by permission of the publisher.)

Part I Directions

Each question begins with two words. These two words go together in a certain way. Under them, there are four other pairs of words lettered **A, B, C,** and **D.**

Find the lettered pair of words that go together in the same way as the first pair of words.

Then, find the row of boxes on your answer sheet which has the same number as the question. In this row of boxes, mark the letter of the pair of words you have chosen.

See how these examples are marked:

EXAMPLE 1   **calf : cow ::**

     A puppy : dog
     B nest : bird   **Answer**
     C horse : bull
     D shell : turtle   E 1 ■ B C D

In the first pair of words (**calf : cow**), calf goes with cow in this way— a calf is a young cow.

The only lettered pair of words that go together in the same way is **puppy : dog.** A puppy is a young dog.

Box **A** is marked because the letter in front of **puppy : dog** is **A.**

EXAMPLE 2   **minute : second ::**

     A time : clock
     B mile : travel   **Answer**
     C hour : measure
     D foot : inch   E 2 A B C ■

Part II Directions

Each of the following questions has two parts. One part is in Column A. The other part is in Column B.

You must find out if one part is greater than the other, or if the parts are equal.

Then, find the row of boxes on your answer sheet which has the same number as the question. In this row of boxes, mark:

     A if the part in Column A is greater,
     B if the part in Column B is greater,
     C if the two parts are equal.

	Column A	Column B	Answer
EXAMPLE 1	10	9	

The part in Column A (10) is greater than the part in Column B (9). Box A is marked because the part in Column A is greater.   1 ■ B C

	Column A	Column B	
EXAMPLE 3	The value of 5 cents	The value of 1 nickel	

The part in Column A is 5 cents. The part in Column B (1 nickel) is also equal to 5 cents. Box **C** is marked because the parts are equal.   3 A B ■

Figure 25. Directions and example questions from Part I and Part II of the School and College Ability Test. (From School and College Ability Test, Series II-Form 4A. Copyright © 1966 by Educational Testing Service. All rights reserved. Reprinted by permission.)

The SCAT yields three scores: Part I (Verbal), Part II (Mathematical), and a Total. The scores for Parts I and II are obtained by counting the number of right answers, and the total score is calculated by combining both parts. The raw scores are converted to percentile bands (for example, 86th to 96th percentile) and percentile ranks (for example, 92nd percentile). The publishers state that the verbal section of the SCAT Series II correlates .69 with the English grade and the mathematical section .58 with the mathematics grade, and the total score correlates .68 with the grade-point average of fifth-grade students in five selected schools (Educational Testing Service, 1973a, p. 68).

Figure 26 presents items representative of the type of questions found on most scholastic aptitude tests. For a more complete listing of available tests and their evaluations, see the latest edition of the *Mental Measurements Yearbook*.

College admissions tests are also scholastic aptitude tests. These tests will be presented and analyzed in Chapter 11. Tests that yield a scholastic aptitude test score but are also intended for vocational and other uses will be discussed in the following section along with professional tests.

Special Aptitude Tests

This section will discuss vocational aptitude tests and batteries and special tests in art and music. In addition, a brief review of professional aptitude tests will be presented.

The main function of the aptitude test is to measure the potential capacity of an individual. Its job is not to measure what has been learned, but what can be learned. Although aptitudes are generally thought of as being completely apart from training, it is impossible to isolate any aptitude from some kind of learning experience. Thus aptitude tests may indirectly measure what has been learned, as well as what can be learned. Their main objective, however, is to measure the *potential to learn*, whether in school, the creative arts, or vocational pursuits.

Aptitude and interest are often thought of as being equivalent. They are not. The youngster who likes to fix things around the house, the adolescent who takes apart an automobile, and the boy or girl who spends time playing the piano or painting a picture are showing interests. Whether they are revealing abilities or talents is another question. On the other hand, the individual who takes apart an automobile or practices the piano develops skills that enhance ability. Adults may indeed pursue vocations that coincide with their interests, abilities, and skills. Children, however, have not generally experienced enough different activities to judge their own particular abilities and interests adequately. Also, a child or adult may persist in an activity simply because he has developed some skill (learned ability) in that activity, although he has neither high ability nor interest. One job of the school is to expose the child to new experiences and activities so that he may "try

Verbal—Meaning (Vocabulary)
Underline the word that means the *same* as the first word.
   QUIET   a. Blue   b. Still   c. Tense   d. Watery

Verbal—Analogies
Hat is to head as shoe is to _____.
   a. Arm   b. Shoulder   c. Foot   d. Log

Sentence Completion
The sun sets in the _____ and rises in the east.
   a. Summer   b. Morning   c. West   d. End

Reasoning
Study the series of letters below. What letter should come next?
   A B A B A B A B
   a. B   b. D   c. A   d. E

Numbers Series
What number should come next to continue the series: 1 2 4 7
11 16?
   a. 18   b. 19   c. 20   d. 21   e. 22

Number
Add the following columns of numbers and underline *R* for right and
W for wrong.

(1)	16	R W		(2)	42	R	W
	38				61		
	45				83		
	99				176		

Arithmetic Reasoning
Four $10 bills are equal to how many $5 bills?
   a. 20   b. 40   c. 10   d. 2   e. 8

Abstract Reasoning
All four-footed creatures are animals. All horses are four-footed.
Therefore: a. Creatures other than horses can walk.
              b. All horses can walk.
              c. All horses are animals.

Figure 26. Items similar to those found on scholastic aptitude tests.

them on for size," hoping that something will fit, and he may choose a career in which his interests, skills, and abilities coincide. The objective aptitude test provides a measure that may add a new dimension to declared interests and teacher observations in order to help guide a student to his own unique talent and potential.

In addition to helping the student discover his vocational and artistic aptitudes, the school and guidance staff need to know the answers to such questions as, "When should a child start in a reading program?" and, "Is this student ready to begin his study of algebra?" The school must have meaningful data about its student body. It especially needs to know about individual differences. Information is required to help in adjusting the levels of instruction to the needs and abilities of the pupils, who may differ widely in their range of talents. In addition, information on the strengths and weaknesses of each pupil presents a valuable background for individual vocational and personal counseling.

It is extremely important for a person's future adjustment that his educational and vocational planning be made intelligently. Many cases of educational and vocational maladjustment could have been avoided if proper guidance had been available. Many times, students at the ninth or tenth grade seem to have no real problem in making vocational decisions. Their plans seem intelligent enough from the viewpoint of the school, their family, and themselves. Others, however, are not as fortunate, and they often realize it, although some are not aware of their situation. Many adults state, "If only I had known"; the school attempts to avoid this feeling in future adults by helping the child "know" while there is time to make an intelligent decision. Other students may be unhappy about their achievement but believe their status is inevitable.

Thus it is obvious that the school needs not only to have all possible information on each individual student for program planning but also to know each student's abilities in order to provide personal counseling. An aptitude test or battery of tests can help in this work. The counselor who has objective data about a youngster's aptitudes can help the child work toward a constructive utilization of his abilities.

Vocational Aptitude Tests

Aptitude was previously defined as the ability to learn. Thus vocational aptitude tests attempt to measure a youngster's ability to learn in certain occupations. They do not pinpoint a person's exact career; however, they do provide answers to such questions as, "Is it realistic to consider medicine as a career?" "Can Mary consider a job as a secretary?" "Would Bill be better suited to be a mechanic or an office worker?" "Should John go to college, and if so, what type of school—technical or general?"

The school needs to have information on a youngster's aptitudes to guide him intelligently into various educational programs and occupations in which he has a realistic chance of succeeding. It is important to remember, however, that aptitude tests will not make the decisions for an individual but will provide useful data in planning future objectives.

Clerical Aptitude Tests

Test instruments designed to measure clerical aptitude all have in common an emphasis upon perceptual speed. Bingham (1935) described three aspects of clerical work: doing it, checking it, and supervising it. Most clerical aptitude tests combine perceptual speed and Bingham's second phase of "checking." These tests attempt to measure abilities needed in office work—typewriting, bookkeeping, and related activities.

General intelligence, as well as specific clerical aptitude, is also needed. Super and Crites (1962) feel that the minimum IQ required for successful clerical activities is between 95 and 100. They state further that, "When promotability is a factor to be considered in the counseling or selection of potential clerical workers, intelligence should be heavily weighted; when, on the other hand, success in a routine clerical job is in question, intelligence exceeding the minimum requirement is all that is needed, other factors then being the decisive ones" (p. 160).

Detailed studies of clerical jobs reveal that speed, accuracy, motor ability, and dexterity are very important. Our discussion will be focused on tests that mainly measure speed and accuracy.[1]

The Minnesota Clerical Test [2] (The Psychological Corporation) is one of the better known and more widely used tests of clerical aptitude. It was originally constructed for adults (girls seventeen and over, and boys nineteen and above). Its suitability for younger groups was studied by many investigators. Today the range is from the seventh grade and above for both sexes.

The Minnesota Clerical Test is an instrument that attempts to measure speed and accuracy in checking 200 pairs of numbers and 200 pairs of names.

In number checking there are two columns of numbers; in name checking, there are two columns consisting of pairs of names. The person checks the two members of each pair to see whether they are exactly the same. There is a very short time limit, and the results are scored for speed and accuracy. Items that are similar to the tasks on this test follow:

Number Checking

7345	7354
31789	31789
85634	85634

---

[1] The reader who is interested in a more detailed discussion of clerical tests, both paper-and-pencil and psychomotor, should consult Super and Crites (1962).
[2] Originally called the Minnesota Vocational Test for Clerical Workers.

Name Checking

John G. Smith	John C. Smith
The Chase Fuel Co.	The Chase Fuel Co., Inc.
Alger R. MacDonald	Alger R. MacDonald

Another well-known test of clerical aptitude is the General Clerical Test (GCT). On this test there are four separate scores—clerical, verbal, numerical, and total. These scores are derived from nine subtests. The first two tests, checking and alphabetizing, are designed to measure speed and accuracy. The verbal score is ascertained by combining spelling, reading, comprehension, vocabulary, and grammar, and the numerical score is obtained by tests of arithmetic, computation, error location, and arithmetic reasoning.

Many more tests of clerical aptitude could be mentioned; however, our two examples serve as illustrations of the basic format of the clerical aptitude test. In our discussion of the Differential Aptitude Tests later in this chapter, we shall review one other clerical test contained in that battery.

Super and Crites' (1962) comments on the Minnesota Clerical are quite germane for most clerical tests. They state,

> *When appraising clerical promise it is well to use tests of both perceptual speed and intelligence. . . . When the test is used at the junior high school level for curricular guidance purposes, grade norms are to be preferred. . . . It seems wise to use adult norms even with high school juniors and seniors. . . . In using the adult norms, emphasis should be on the occupational rather than on the general norms. . . . As a rule speed on this type of test is a good measure of accuracy. But there are occasional exceptions, and one subject will make a given score by working rapidly with errors, whereas another will make the same score by working more slowly without errors. For this reason the psychometrist or counselor should examine the responses to each test, and take the error score into account in making his interpretation. (pp. 178–79)*

Mechanical Aptitude Tests

In the United States the emphasis is on college training, and yet there is a large segment of our student population who, because of ability, interest, or other reasons, will not attend college. These youngsters may have mechanical ability and they should not be forgotten by their community, for society needs mechanical craftsmen as well as doctors and lawyers. The school that plans programs for these youngsters needs some basis of objective appraisal in selecting students and arranging appropriate courses of study. The mechanical aptitude test can serve this end and other vocational needs very well.

It has been discovered that some mechanical jobs require the ability to see spatial relationships and the ability to visualize actual objects from a drawing or picture, including being able to see how a whole figure can be assembled from its parts, how an object would appear when looked at from a different point of view, and how movements of one part affect movements of another. Test questions that measure this type of ability will be illustrated later in the chapter, when we discuss test batteries.

It is important to remember that different functions or abilities are sometimes placed under the heading of mechanical aptitude. Some instruments such as mechanical information tests depend upon past experience with mechanical objects, whereas other tests do not call upon past experience to the same degree. There is also a difference in performance on these tests between boys and girls.

Some teachers and counselors are confused by the results of mechanical aptitude tests. They assume, for example, that high scores mean a student is slated to be an engineer, whereas others interpret the same results as indicative of lower scholastic ability. These assumptions are fraught with possible errors. First, mechanical aptitude is only one of many abilities an engineer needs to be successful. In addition to mechanical aptitude, the aspiring engineer must have a good background in science and mathematics, as well as general scholastic ability. Second, the tendency for some people to think of mechanical ability as the lowest rung on the scholastic ladder is erroneous. Further, a child's doing poorly in school is no reason to assume he will do well in mechanical work. Mechanical aptitude tests, therefore, must be interpreted in connection with other tests and school achievements.

Many varieties of mechanical aptitude tests have been developed. The majority fall into two main areas: those that are administered individually and require actual manipulation of mechanical objects and those that require only paper and pencil and can be given to many children at the same time.

INDIVIDUAL TESTS

Individual mechanical tests are made up of items that require the subject to use tools and materials and/or blocks, as well as to assemble such devices as a push button or a doorbell. Motor ability and manual dexterity are important ingredients in some of these tests.

One of the most widely used and best-known tests of dexterity is the Minnesota Rate of Manipulation Test. The age range for this test is from thirteen to fifty. The test consists of a form board that has four rows of identical holes, with fifteen holes in each row. There are sixty identical discs a little larger than a checker which fit into the holes. The flat sides of the discs are painted differently from the board. The examiner places the discs in their correct positions and then turns them over and asks the subject to place them in their holes. The examination is administered in four trials. The total testing time is from six to eight minutes.

Another widely used test is the O'Connor Finger and Tweezer Dexterity Tests. These tests are used with adolescents and adults. The Finger Dexterity Test consists of a shallow tray beside a metal plate that has 100 holes arranged in ten rows of ten holes each. Every hole is big enough to contain three metal pins, 1 inch long. The Tweezer Dexterity Test uses the opposite side of the boards and also has 100 holes, but these are just slightly larger than the pins, which allows the subject to place one in each hole. A pair of tweezers is used to pick up the pins.

In the Finger Dexterity Test the subject picks up three pins and places them in each hole, whereas in the Tweezer Test he picks up one pin at a time and attempts to place it in a hole. The score is computed on the basis of the total time required to complete the tasks.

Another test that is very popular with counseling psychologists is the Purdue Pegboard. The Purdue Pegboard is a 12- by 18-inch rectangular board with four cups which hold the test materials at one end and two rows of holes straight down the middle. The examiner first administers the test by asking the subject to put metal pins in the holes one at a time with his right hand. After completing this assignment, the subject is asked to do it again with his left hand. The examiner then asks him to do it with both hands simultaneously. The final task is to assemble the metal pin, metal washer, metal collar, and washer using the right and then the left hands and then both. Scoring is computed on the basis of the number of pins placed in thirty seconds and the number of assemblies made in sixty seconds.

Generally speaking, motor tests have been most successful in the prediction of performance on assembling and machine-operating jobs (see Fleishman, 1953). It should be noted, however, that jobs requiring less repetitive tasks demand more perceptual and intellectual abilities. The important thing to remember in assessing the predictive validity of these instruments is the relationship of the test tasks to the actual job specifications.

PAPER-AND-PENCIL TESTS

Because of their convenience, paper-and-pencil tests of mechanical ability are used much more widely than individual tests in schools. Among the better tests of this type is the Bennett Test of Mechanical Comprehension. This test is made up of drawings concerned with the application of physical principles. If a student has not studied physics, he will not be at a disadvantage in this examination because knowledge of mechanical equipment is not being tested.

There are sixty-eight items in the test. The new alternate forms S and T, are a replacement of three earlier forms dating back to 1940. These new forms have a wider range of difficulty and better reliability. Forms S and T are timed tests and have a thirty-minute limit. The final score is the number of right answers (Bennett, 1969).

According to Bennett (1969), the test is "suitable for male applicants for industrial jobs and for high school students; . . . male applicants for mechanical jobs, men already employed in mechanical jobs, candidates for engineering schools, and other adult male groups of comparable ability and education;

and for women competing on these levels and for the same kind of jobs" (p. 1). The author states that women tend to do less well than men. This is attributed to cultural influences rather than innate ability.

Percentile norms are presented for a number of different groups such as "electrical inspector, construction trades, academic high school, technical high school," and so forth. The reliability coefficients of each form are from .81 to .93, depending on the groups. There are data that show good validity.

Either form may be given, using tape-recorded instructions and questions in English or Spanish for poor readers. There is also a complete Spanish edition. Figure 27 presents sample items from the Spanish edition.

It should be noted that the Mechanical Reasoning Test of the Differential Aptitude Tests (which is presented later in this chapter) is very similar to the Bennett Mechanical Comprehension Test.

The McQuarrie Test for Mechanical Ability is a very old test originally developed as a rough measure of mechanical and manual aptitude. It is a battery of seven subtests, each designed to evaluate different factors assumed to be important in mechanical jobs. The first three—Tracing, Tapping, and Dotting—are measures of manual dexterity; the next three—Copying,

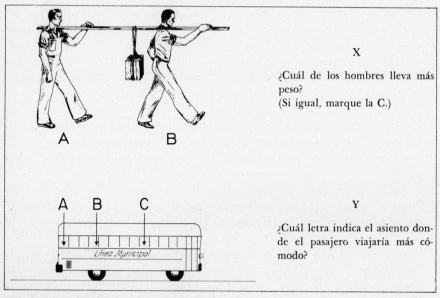

X

¿Cuál de los hombres lleva más peso?
(Si igual, marque la C.)

Y

¿Cuál letra indica el asiento donde el pasajero viajaría más cómodo?

Figure 27. Sample items from the *Test de Comprensión Mecánica Bennett.** (Reproduced by permission. Copyright 1940, renewed 1967; 1941, renewed 1969; 1942, renewed 1969; © 1967, 1968 by The Psychological Corporation, New York, N.Y. All rights reserved.)

* Bennett Mechanical Comprehension Test. Question X asks, "Which man carries more weight?) (If equal, Mark C.)" Question Y asks, "Which letter shows the seat where a passenger will get the smoothest ride?"

Location, and Blocks—are tests of spatial perception. The last subtest, Pursuit, is a test of perceptual speed and accuracy. These differences in content have tended to make most users of the test treat each part separately in validation studies (Super and Crites, 1962).

This group test requires about a half hour for administration. For a detailed examination of this test and other group and individual mechanical tests, see Super and Crites (1962, pp. 219–74).

Test Batteries

Test batteries have been developed to measure many things, including intelligence, general school achievement, and different vocational aptitudes. We shall confine our attention here to the batteries primarily concerned with vocational prediction.

Many studies concerning vocational prediction have been made. In one such study, a group of high school students were given a vocational test battery. Two years after they completed high school, a comparison of their educational and vocational situation and their test scores was made. The study revealed that premedical students had scored very high on all the tests in the battery. Workers in mechanical and electrical trades were above average on the mechanical test and average or below on the other types of tests. This study revealed no definite evidence of success or failure in specific occupations based on aptitude tests. Many studies, however, do show certain trends that can give us some clues for vocational guidance. For example, successful workers in skilled trades do well on certain tests, whereas successful clerical workers generally have high scores on different tests.

Teachers and counselors should be very cautious in interpreting aptitude test results. It should be remembered that aptitude test results are most valid when other tests, such as group tests of intelligence, achievement scores, and the general performance record of the student in school and at home, are taken into consideration.

There are numerous vocational aptitude batteries. However, the battery that teachers are most likely to come in contact with is the Differential Aptitude Tests (DAT). There are two very good reasons for this. First, the DAT lends itself to a school setting in terms of its format and norms. It also yields a scholastic aptitude score, which makes the test useful in another area and eases the financial burden of purchasing an additional instrument. The second reason for the DAT's wide use is its careful attention to standardization procedures and the many excellent reviews of its merits by testing experts. For these reasons we will devote our attention to the DAT. The reader who is interested in reviewing other test batteries should consult the *Mental Measurements Yearbooks*.

The DAT was originally developed in 1947 to provide a scientific procedure for evaluating the capabilities of boys and girls in grades 8–12. The intended use was for educational and vocational guidance. Since that time the tests have also been used for counseling young adults and in the selection of employees. The DAT has been revised and restandardized in 1962 and in 1972. The 1962 revision was mainly an attempt to make administration and scoring easier. The 1972 revision kept the earlier changes and significantly modified test items in five of the eight tests. The basic nature of the battery, however, has remained unchanged (Bennett, Seashore, and Wesman, 1974).

The revised 1972 edition included over 64,000 students throughout the United States. An attempt was made to sample a representative population of all students, both public and parochial, in grades 8–12, with reference to size of school, socioeconomic level of community, scholastic achievement, and ethnic composition. This sampling included a representation of minority groups.

The DAT consists of eight tests and is available in two forms, Form S and Form T, with each form confined to a single booklet. The Form S test booklet is printed in red and black while the Form T booklet is blue and black. The tests of Form T are also available in eight different booklets. In addition, there is a Verbal Reasoning and Numerical Ability combination booklet that may be used as a separate measure of scholastic aptitude. Test booklets are reusable. Answer sheets can be scored either by hand or by machine. These answer sheets can be scored by five different types of test-scoring machines.

Designed for use in the junior and senior high school as an aid in educational and vocational guidance, the DAT is based on the assumption (backed by some research findings) that "intelligence" is not a single ability, but a combination of several abilities. The battery yields nine scores based on the eight tests. (Two of the eight scores combined yield an index of scholastic aptitude.) A great deal of research on the DAT has been reported, some of which may be found in the manual (Bennett et al., 1974). We shall explore each of the tests to obtain some insight into their content and use in vocational and educational guidance.

Figures 28 and 29 present sample items from the various tests of the DAT. The Verbal Reasoning test requires the student to choose from among five pairs of words the correct combination to complete the blanks. In the Numerical Ability test, five answers follow each problem. The student's task is to pick the correct answer or "none of these" if the correct answer is not given. The Abstract Reasoning test consists of "problem figures" and "answer figures." The four "problem figures" make a series. The student is required to find out which one of the "answer figures" would be the next, or the fifth, one in the series. The Clerical Speed and Accuracy test is a test to see how quickly an individual can compare letter and number combinations. Each test item contains letter and number combinations. These same combinations are on a separate answer sheet but are in a different order. In each test item, one of the five is underlined. The student's job is to look at the underlined combination, find the same one on the separate answer sheet, and record his answer.

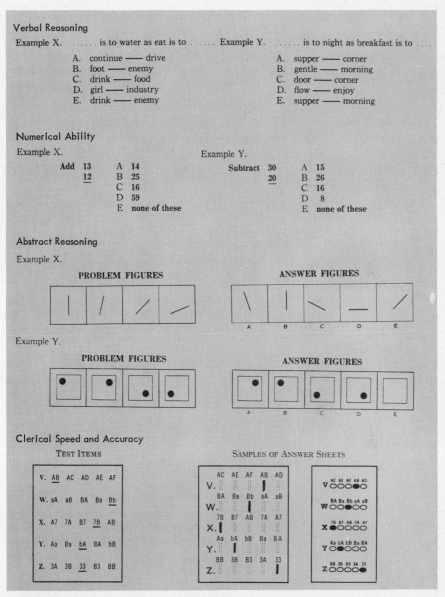

Verbal Reasoning

Example X. ...... is to water as eat.is to ......   Example Y. ...... is to night as breakfast is to ....

A. continue —— drive
B. foot —— enemy
C. drink —— food
D. girl —— industry
E. drink —— enemy

A. supper —— corner
B. gentle —— morning
C. door —— corner
D. flow —— enjoy
E. supper —— morning

Numerical Ability

Example X.

Add 13
12

A 14
B 25
C 16
D 59
E none of these

Example Y.

Subtract 30
20

A 15
B 26
C 16
D 8
E none of these

Abstract Reasoning

Example X.

PROBLEM FIGURES   ANSWER FIGURES

Example Y.

PROBLEM FIGURES   ANSWER FIGURES

Clerical Speed and Accuracy

TEST ITEMS   SAMPLES OF ANSWER SHEETS

V. <u>AB</u> AC AD AE AF

W. aA aB BA Ba <u>Bb</u>

X. A7 7A B7 <u>7B</u> AB

Y. Aa Ba <u>bA</u> BA bB

Z. 3A 3B <u>33</u> B3 BB

Figure 28. Sample items from the Differential Aptitude Tests, Form S. (Reproduced by permission. Copyright © 1972 by The Psychological Corporation, New York, N.Y. All rights reserved.)

The Mechanical Reasoning test consists of pictures which require the student to make judgments concerning the "truth" of certain situations involving balance, weight, and other mechanically related problems. The Space

MECHANICAL REASONING

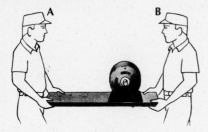

Example X.

Which man has the heavier load?
(If equal, mark C.)

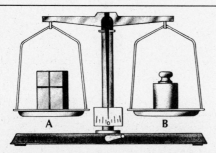

Example Y.

Which weighs more?
(If equal, mark C.)

The correct answer for example X is B.
The correct answer for example Y is C.

SPACE RELATIONS

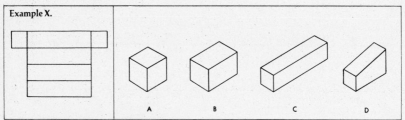

Which of the four figures, A, B, C, or D can
be made from the pattern at the left?

The correct answer is C.

Figure 29. Sample items from the Differential Aptitude Tests, Form S.
(Reproduced by permission. Copyright © 1972 by The Psychological
Corporation, New York, N.Y. All rights reserved.)

Relations test is made up of patterns which can be folded into figures. Four
figures are shown for each pattern. The student is asked to decide which one
of the figures can be made from the pattern shown.

The Spelling test presents a series of words, some of which are correctly
spelled and some of which are incorrectly spelled. In the grammar section
the student is confronted with a series of sentences divided into four parts
(A, B, C, and D). The task is to look at each sentence and decide which
part is grammatically in error. If the entire sentence is free of error, the
student marks "E" on his answer sheet.

The publisher of the DAT has produced a pamphlet entitled "Your Aptitudes as Measured by the Differential Aptitude Tests," which contains an excellent description of each of the tests and what they measure. It is also a good source for understanding any aptitude test battery and is written for students, parents, teachers, and counselors. The reader is encouraged to read the following partial reproduction of this pamphlet carefully, not only for its description of the DAT but also as a general guide to what many vocational (and some scholastic) aptitude batteries measure.

What Is Aptitude [3]

Simply—aptitude is the capacity to learn. You take aptitude tests in order to be able to make better predictions of how you can expect to develop in school and in a job.

Your DAT scores, then, are measures of your capacities to learn—to profit from various courses of study or from training required for jobs you may seek.

These tests give you a way of comparing your abilities—as of now—with those of boys and girls in your grade. The test results will help you evaluate your relative strengths and weaknesses in a variety of aptitudes which are important to your educational progress and your career choices.

Think of the DAT scores simply as useful bits of information. You will want to consider these test scores along with all sorts of other information about you that have already piled up—in your mind, in the school records, and in your family's thinking. Of course, you will want to take into consideration such facts as your school grades and other test scores; the things you like most, hobbies, and out-of-school interests; what courses are available in your school; your ambitions; your qualities of character and traits of personality such as curiosity, skill in getting along with others, and ability to stick with duties and hard tasks; job requirements; health; college entrance requirements; and so on. There are a great many things to take into account.

Aptitude tests will not pinpoint for you exactly what your career should be. These tests do *not* provide specific prescriptions or answers to such specific questions as: *Can I be a plumber? Should I plan to become a physician? Should I be a dress designer?*

But, if you and your counselors will study your DAT scores along with other information, you *can* get answers to some more general questions such as: *Is it reasonable for me to consider medicine as a career? Which would be the better job for me—mechanic or office worker? What are my particular assets and liabilities to be considered if I am thinking of becoming a secretary? Would I profit from a college education? What type of college?*

Information on your aptitudes can start you off on a meaningful study of the various educational programs and occupations you might want to consider. The freedom you have in planning your future places on you considerable responsibility for realistic thinking about yourself.

Verbal Reasoning

Verbal reasoning is important in all academic and most non-academic subjects in high school. If you were to take only one test, VR would be the best all-around predictor of how well you can do in school, especially in the academic subjects. Students who score average or better should seriously consider college; those well up in the top quarter may consider the highly selective colleges.

Students above the bottom quarter on VR but without a college education may be acceptable for various supervisory and managerial jobs in business and industry. Other things being equal, for instance, the employee with more verbal reasoning ability than his fellow workers has a better chance of being selected for special training in technical work or in supervision.

Students not planning for college who have VR as the peak on their profile should consider preparing for such verbal occupations as salesman, credit manager, order taker, complaint clerk. These job names will help you think of others also in which verbal reasoning and understanding are essential.

People who do poorly on the Verbal Reasoning test should perhaps plan on going into some work that will call for less verbal ability. A person can be successful doing clerical work in an office without trying to become head of a department, or successful doing production work in a factory without expecting to become production manager. If the bars for Spelling or Language Usage are below (and do not overlap with) the bar for VR on the profile chart, there is a real chance that you aren't able to use your verbal reasoning ability up to its full capacity. Talk with your counselor and teachers about what you can do to improve your writing, reading, and other language skills.

Numerical Ability

Numerical ability is especially important in such high school subjects as mathematics, physics, and chemistry.

Students who do well on this test are also likely to do well in the arithmetic and measuring so common in business offices, factories, service shops, and stores.

Scores on this test predict, to some extent, success in nearly all high school and college courses. Numerical ability is one element of all-around ability to master academic work.

An above-average score in NA suggests planning for college or other post-high school education. A student who wants to major in such fields as mathematics, physics, chemistry, or any branch of engineering, may expect to encounter some difficulty if his NA score is not in the top third or top quarter.

Numerical ability is also useful in technical careers not requiring a college degree. A score in the second or third quarter on this test, especially if scores on Verbal Reasoning and/or the two Language Usage tests are noticeably *lower* than the NA score, suggests looking at technical training programs either in companies or in training institutes for trades and crafts.

Numerical ability is useful in such jobs as laboratory assistant, bookkeeper, statistical clerk, foreman, or shipping clerk. Many of the jobs in the skilled trades in manufacturing or construction work require considerable numerical ability.

VR + NA

Your combined score on these two tests provides a good estimate of your scholastic aptitude—your ability to complete the college preparatory courses in your school and to succeed in college.

In general, anyone with a rating in the upper quarter (75th percentile or better) should consider himself capable of performing well in college courses. Depending on your current ambitions and your choice of college, a second quarter rating on VR + NA also indicates college potential. Whether students ranking in the third quarter should enter regular liberal arts and science programs is arguable. Are you doing very well in high school? Are you prepared to work harder than your college mates? What college and what courses are you considering? Some students in the third quarter and a few in the fourth quarter who want some post-high school education will find it practical and satisfying to enter one-year or two-year junior college programs in applied arts and sciences, business training, and the like.

Besides predicting academic success, the VR + NA score gives some indication of aptitude for jobs that require more than the average level of administrative and executive responsibility.

Abstract Reasoning

Using diagrams, the Abstract Reasoning test measures how easily and clearly you can reason when problems are presented in terms of size or shape or position or quantity or other non-verbal, non-numerical forms. The repairman trouble-shooting an unusual breakdown, the chemist, physicist or biologist seeking to understand an invisible process, the programmer planning the work of an electronic computer, the systems engineer—all find this ability useful. Carrying out a logical procedure in your mind is important here.

Abstract Reasoning teams up with the next two tests—Space Relations and Mechanical Reasoning—in prediction of success in many kinds of mechanical, technical, and skilled industrial work.

Students standing high on Verbal Reasoning and Numerical Ability have added confirmation of their college ability if they are also above average on Abstract Reasoning. But, if VR and NA are high and AR is below average, they usually may rely on the verbal-numerical combination to see them through.

Students scoring rather low on VR but fairly high on AR have evidence of ability to reason in certain ways despite a verbal shortcoming. Vocabulary building, remedial reading, and similar exercises may help strengthen verbal reasoning power.

Clerical Speed and Accuracy

Clerical Speed and Accuracy measures how quickly and accurately you can compare and mark written lists such as of names or numbers. This is the only one of these tests that demands fast work. It is very easy to get the right answer; speed in doing a simple task is what counts. Girls tend to score higher than boys on this test.

While CSA measures an ability that is useful in many kinds of jobs, it is not really needed or expected in most high school courses. In most school work it is more important to do your work correctly than to do it quickly. But a *very* low score sometimes indicates a source of difficulty with homework or exams.

Have you done well on others of the Differential Aptitude Tests but not very well on this one? If so, perhaps you did not work as fast as you could have worked. By practicing, you may be able to speed up quite a bit without sacrificing accuracy on tasks that you understand well.

Aptitude for CSA is important in many kinds of office jobs, such as record-keeping, addressing, pricing, order-taking, filing, coding, proofreading, and keeping track of tools or supplies. Secretaries, whose most important skills must be in stenography and office services, are better if they also can work fast and accurately on routine clerical tasks.

In most scientific research and much professional work mistakes in recording or copying can be very serious. But speed is needed, as well as accuracy. A good score on CSA is desirable, then, for a job handling data in a laboratory as well as for a job in bookkeeping or in a bank.

Mechanical Reasoning

Students who do well on the Mechanical Reasoning test usually like to find out how things work. They often are better than average at learning how to construct, operate, or repair complicated equipment. While VR and NA are the best predictors of science and engineering grades in college and technical institutes, a high MR score is added evidence of ability in these fields.

Students who do well on this test but whose VR and NA scores suggest that a college engineering course might be very difficult, should look into opportunities in high school technical courses, apprentice training, and post-high-school technical institutes. Men in industry who become technicians, shop foremen, and repair specialists tend to be at least average in MR.

People who do poorly on this test may find the work rather hard or uninteresting in physical sciences and in those shop courses which demand thinking and planning, rather than just skill in using one's hands. Many types of work in the construction and manufacturing trades also require one to understand machinery and other uses of physical forces as well as to have manual skills.

Girls score considerably lower than boys on the MR and SR tests. Therefore a girl who does quite well on these tests, as compared with the average girl, may still be far below the average boy. A girl interested in mechanical or engineering work should ask her counselor to figure her MR and SR percentiles in comparison with boys as well as with girls.

Space Relations

Space Relations measures your ability to visualize, to imagine the shape and surfaces of a finished object before it is built, just by looking at the drawings that would be used to guide workmen in building it. This ability makes some kinds of mathematics easier—solid geometry, for example.

To a person who does poorly on Space Relations, an architect's plans for a house or an engineer's plans for a bridge or a machine might look like nothing but several flat drawings. But how about a person who does well on this test? Such a person looking at those same plans can "see" the finished house, or bridge, or machine. He could probably "walk around" the finished structure—mentally, that is—and "see" it from various angles.

Students who do well on SR should have an advantage in work such as drafting, dress designing, architecture, mechanical engineering, die-making, building construction, and some branches of art and decoration. A good machinist, carpenter, dentist, or surgeon needs this sense of the forms and positions of things in space.

Students planning for careers not requiring college training should consider their SR score in comparison with their other aptitudes in deciding whether to look for jobs (or training courses) that deal with real objects—large or small, watches or skyscrapers—rather than with people or with finances, for example.

Spelling

Spelling measures how well a person can spell common English words. The ability to spell correctly is an important skill needed for written reports in any school or college subject. It is one of the best predictors of the ease and speed with which one can learn typing and shorthand. The ability to spell is important for any job requiring the use of writing skills, e.g., secretary, technical writer, and editor.

If you do well on this test and on Language Usage, as well as on Verbal Reasoning, you should be able to do almost any kind of practical writing, provided you have a knowledge of your topic and a desire to write about it.

Girls tend to score somewhat higher than boys on both Spelling and Language Usage.

Language Usage

Language Usage measures sensitivity to correct sentence structure, punctuation, and the fundamental rules of formal, written communication. It is among the best general predictors of course grades in high school and college. It is especially important for courses which require written reports.

Many careers, such as writing, teaching, editing, law, and journalism, call for a high degree of competence in English. In addition, most careers requiring college-level education require good language skills, as do many office and managerial jobs.

Both Language Usage and Spelling are really short achievement tests. Scores on these tests reflect your mastery of the basic skills of spelling and written communication. If your Verbal Reasoning score is much higher than your score on either or both of these two tests, you might profit from special study or tutoring in English to raise your language skills up to the level indicated by your VR score.

The validity data available on the DAT are staggering. The coefficients are high. Reliability coefficients are also very high.

To help in educational and vocational guidance there is a DAT Career Planning Program. This program uses DAT scores and student answers to a Career Planning Questionnaire. This questionnaire elicits from the student information concerning his favorite school subjects, activities, grades, and interest in various occupations.

Figure 30 presents a DAT Career Planning Report. This report is a computer printout that includes the student's DAT scores, explanations, and statements that correlate the DAT scores with the student's record interests and plans.

The student of measurement should keep in mind the fact that *vocational aptitude batteries alone will not solve educational and vocational problems.* They will, however, provide valuable information for students and others in planning future goals when interpreted in conjunction with other evaluative criteria.

Prognostic Tests

The aptitude tests used to predict school and artistic success or failure are called *prognostic tests* by psychologists. The inquiring student may rightfully ask whether this type of special test is better than an academic aptitude test. The answer is not easy. Many testing people feel that some day the general aptitude test, such as the Differential Aptitude Tests, will take the place of aptitude tests designed for special fields. Today, however, prognostic tests have an important place in the school's testing program. Prognostic tests are especially useful in spotting children who may be able to perform in special academic areas. The important thing to remember is that special aptitude tests can predict failure more accurately than success, for success is in part determined by motivation, social pressures, and other factors. In general terms, we may state that a person with superior intellectual endow-

DIFFERENTIAL APTITUDE TESTS

G. K. Bennett, H. G. Seashore, and A. G. Wesman

Ψ.

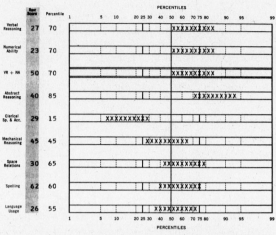

Name	School	Year*	Form	Grade	Sex
MURPHY JAMES L	CENTRAL	1973 F	S	9	M

YOUR PROFILE OF DAT SCORES

The numbers that tell how you did on each test are in the column marked "Percentile." Your percentile tells where you rank on a test in comparison with boys or girls in your grade in numerous schools across the country. If your percentile is 50, you are just in the middle—that is, one-half of the students in the national group did better than you and one-half did less well.

If your percentile on one test is 80, you are at the top of 80 percent of the group—only 20 percent made higher scores than yours. If you scored in the 25th percentile, this means about 75 percent of the group did better than you on the test. These percentiles indicate your relative standing among students of your sex and grade. They do NOT tell you how many questions (or what percent of them) you answered correctly.

On your profile, a bar of X's has been printed in the row for each test you took. The percentile you earned is at the middle of the bar, except when the bar has been shortened in the case of an extremely high or low percentile so as not to run off the chart. (The reason for the bar instead of a single X is that a test is not a perfect measure of your ability; however, you can be reasonably sure that you stand somewhere within the area covered by the bar.)

HOW BIG A DIFFERENCE IS IMPORTANT?

Since tests cannot be perfectly accurate, you should not overestimate the importance of small differences between two percentiles in comparing your aptitudes. The bars of X's help by indicating the more important differences.

Look at the bars for any *two* tests and notice whether or not the ends of the bars overlap. If they do not, chances are that you really are better in the kind of ability represented by the bar farther to the right. If they overlap but not by more than half their length, consider whether other things you know about yourself agree with this indication; the difference may or may not be important. If they overlap by more than half their length, the difference may be disregarded; so small a difference is probably not meaningful. This method of looking at the overlap of bars works for any two abilities you want to compare, whether they are listed next to each other or several rows apart on the chart.

*F — first (fall) semester testing and percentiles; S — second (spring) semester testing and percentiles.

YOUR CAREER PLANNING REPORT

The report printed below is based on your answers to the *Career Planning Questionnaire* and on your aptitudes as measured by the *Differential Aptitude Tests*. Remember that this report tells you how things look at the present time, and that your interests and goals may change. To aid you in understanding the report, descriptions of the tests are printed on the reverse side of this form, followed by the groups of school subjects and activities, and the groups of jobs and occupations.

MURPHY JAMES L

IN YOUR CAREER PLANNING QUESTIONNAIRE YOU INDICATED THAT YOU ARE 14 YEARS OLD, A BOY IN THE 9TH GRADE AND THAT YOU EXPECT TO GRADUATE FROM A FOUR-YEAR COLLEGE. FURTHERMORE YOU SAID THAT YOUR GRADES PUT YOU IN THE SECOND QUARTER OF YOUR CLASS. AMONG THE GROUPS OF SCHOOL SUBJECTS AND ACTIVITIES, YOU SAID YOU LIKED THE FOLLOWING: TECHNICAL SUBJECTS; PHYSICAL SCIENCES; CRAFTS.

YOU INDICATED THAT YOUR FIRST CHOICE OF CAREER GOALS WAS IN THE GROUP CALLED: BUSINESS--SALES AND PROMOTION.
    MOST PEOPLE WHO DO THIS KIND OF WORK HAVE HAD SCHOOL INTERESTS WHICH ARE NOT LIKE THOSE YOU REPORTED. HOWEVER, THEY HAVE HAD THE AMOUNT OF EDUCATION YOU PLAN TO GET, AND THEY HAVE APTITUDES LIKE YOURS. WHILE THIS CHOICE SEEMS REASONABLE IN TERMS OF YOUR TESTED ABILITIES AND YOUR EDUCATIONAL PLANS, YOU MAY WANT TO ALSO THINK ABOUT THE POSSIBILITY OF SOME FIELD OF WORK CLOSER TO YOUR EXPRESSED INTERESTS.

YOU INDICATED THAT YOUR SECOND CHOICE OF CAREER GOALS WAS IN THE GROUP CALLED: ENGINEERING AND APPLIED SCIENCE.
    THE OCCUPATIONAL GROUP THAT YOU HAVE NAMED MATCHES THE SCHOOL SUBJECTS AND ACTIVITIES THAT YOU LIKE. THE EDUCATIONAL PLANS YOU DESCRIBE ARE ALSO APPROPRIATE. YOUR PATTERN OF TESTED APTITUDES, HOWEVER, INDICATES THAT YOU MAY HAVE DIFFICULTY IN MEETING THE EDUCATIONAL REQUIREMENTS. IN REVIEWING THIS OCCUPATIONAL CHOICE, YOU MAY WISH TO CONSIDER OTHER OCCUPATIONAL AREAS MORE IN LINE WITH YOUR ABILITIES.

YOU INDICATED THAT YOUR THIRD CHOICE OF CAREER GOALS WAS IN THE GROUP CALLED: MEDICALLY RELATED.
    PEOPLE WHO PURSUE THIS KIND OF CAREER HAVE SCHOOL INTERESTS LIKE YOURS. THEY USUALLY GET THE KIND OF EDUCATION YOU PLAN. THEY HAVE APTITUDE TEST SCORES LIKE YOURS. ON ALL THESE COUNTS THIS LOOKS LIKE AN OCCUPATIONAL FIELD WHICH MATCHES YOUR ABILITIES AND INTERESTS WELL.

CONSIDERING PRIMARILY YOUR TESTED APTITUDES, AND TO A LESSER EXTENT YOUR SCHOOL SUBJECT AND ACTIVITY PREFERENCES, YOU MAY WANT TO LOOK ALSO INTO THE FOLLOWING OCCUPATIONAL GROUPS: VISUAL AND PERFORMING ARTS; MEDICAL AND LIFE SCIENCES; EDUCATION AND HUMAN WELFARE. THIS IS ONLY A PARTIAL LIST OF THE OCCUPATIONAL AREAS WHICH COINCIDE WITH YOUR ABILITIES AND SCHOOL SUBJECT PREFERENCES.

Any lack of agreement of your present occupational goals with the kinds of school subjects and activities you like, or with your tested aptitudes, suggests that you might reconsider your career plans. The *Occupational Outlook Handbook* (published by the U.S. Department of Labor, and available in most public and school libraries), your school counselor, your parents, and other interested and informed adults may be useful sources of information and helpful to you in making decisions about what to try out and what to aim for.

Figure 30. DAT Career Planning Report. (Reproduced by permission.
Copyright © 1972, 1973 by The Psychological Corporation, New York, N.Y.
All rights reserved.)

ment may or may not be successful in college, but we can be fairly certain
that an individual with very low ability will be unable to succeed academically.
Let us look at some of these special aptitude tests.

SCHOOL READINESS TESTS

Older tests of school readiness were called reading readiness tests. These
tests focused on the specific skills that are necessary for reading, such as
recognizing symbols. In the past ten years a monumental amount of research
has been conducted in the area of early childhood and specifically the cognitive development of the child. One result of this research has been the
realization that readiness for school involves more than the attainment of
specific skills necessary for reading. Thus a new genre of tests has been
developed which assesses the preschool child in a more global manner.

The trend in American education is to include in the public system the
child of five and in some cases four years of age. As the importance of the
early educational experiences becomes more apparent, the trend will probably
continue to include younger and younger children.

As a school psychologist, counselor, or teacher working with young children,
you will be asked many times to help make a decision as to whether a child
should begin first grade or would benefit more from an additional year in
kindergarten. Decisions such as this are not easy ones to make, and tests
can help in making them. The final decision, however, is based on a synthesis
of information from objective tests and clinical impressions by teacher and
parent. It is important that the parents share in this decision making.

In the past, institutions used informal checklists to ascertain the readiness
of a child to learn. This was often couched in terms of the child's maturity.
Recent experience with disadvantaged children has revealed that many of
these children approach school without the basic concepts which teachers
have taken for granted that all children have. This conceptual lack is
hypothesized to result from a paucity of experience, primarily language interaction with adults. Several instruments have recently been developed to assess
the conceptual level of the child.

One of the most recent tests for this purpose is the Tests of Basic Experiences (TOBE). The TOBE is designed to measure basic concepts in the
areas of mathematics, language, science, and social studies. There are two
levels, and the test is designed for preschool, kindergarten, and first-grade
children. It is given as a group test and the lack of understanding of directions
may impair the validity of the test. The manual suggests a proctor for every
four to six children in kindergarten and for every six to ten older children.
There are twenty-eight items and administration time is twenty-five minutes
for each test. Administration consists of verbal direction by the examiner

and the marking of one of four pictures by the child. There is a Spanish edition available.

A similar test is the Boehm Test of Basic Concepts (BTBC). This test is narrower in scope than the TOBE and is designed to assess basic cognitive concepts such as over, under, before, after, and so forth. The test consists of fifty items arranged in two test booklets and is designed for children in grades K, 1, 2, and 3. Third graders, however, on the average pass 90 per cent of the items. Therefore, the instrument appears most useful at the K or first-grade level.

The major technical drawback of the BTBC is the lack of validity studies. None is reported, except content validity. While it seems reasonable that these basic concepts are necessary for educational progress, no data verifying this assumption are given. Since the instrument is new, perhaps such data will be forthcoming in the future.

There are methodological problems inherent in any testing with young children. Anyone testing young children should be aware of these and interpret the results in this light. These problems include being sure that the child understands the procedure, that the child tries his best, and is paying attention, as well as the possibility that the items are ambiguous. These two tests attempt to handle such problems, but the evaluator of young children must keep these sources of variance in mind.

An instrument of the checklist type is the Barclay Early Childhood Skill Assessment Guide (Barclay and Barclay, 1973). This instrument is in a convenient format for preschool, kindergarten, and first grade. The instrument is based on the premise that skills such as attending-responding, task-order, and social interaction underlie learning. The checklist is designed to pinpoint deficits in these areas. The areas covered are Sensory Level, Motor-Perceptual, Environmental Exploration, Visual and Auditory Imitation, Sensory and Memory Discrimination, Self-concept, Attending-Responding, Task-Order Skills, and Social Interaction. As a checklist, it is criterion-referenced rather than norm-referenced, although the authors suggest that local norms may be useful.

The newer instruments owe a great deal to the older developmental schedules and checklists. These range from the elaborate tests given at the Gesell Institute of Child Development to simple checklists of maturation. Let us briefly turn our attention to some of these.

The developmental examination tests administered at the Gesell Institute of Child Development (Ilg and Ames, 1965) fall into seven different parts:

1. The initial interview. *Questions about age, birth date, birthday party including favorite activity and present received; siblings—names and ages; father's occupation.*
2. Pencil and paper tests. *Writing name or letters and address; numbers 1 to 20; copying six basic forms (circle, cross, square, triangle, divided rectangle, diamond in two orientations), and two three-dimensional forms (cylinder and cube in two orientations); completing Incomplete Man figure and giving his facial expression.*

3. Right and left (adaptation of Jacobson's Right and Left tests). *Naming parts and sides of body, carrying out single and double commands, responding to a series of pictures of a pair of hands in which two fingers are touching. Response is first verbal and then motor.*
4. Form tests. *Visual One (Monroe)—matching forms; Visual Three (Monroe) —memory for designs; projection into forms.*
5. Naming of animals for 60 seconds.
6. Concluding interview. *Reporting on what child likes to do best in general, at school indoors and outdoors and at home indoors and outdoors.*
7. Examination of teeth. *Recording of both eruption and decay or fillings.* *(p. 35)*

These separate tests give a complete picture of the child's readiness to learn. They are quite elaborate and time consuming and, of course, are not practical for everyday use in the public schools. On the other hand, the maturation checklist is a more practical school-oriented device. A good example of this approach is Banham's (1959) Maturity Level for School Entrance and Reading Readiness, a checklist for kindergarten and first grade.

There are twenty-five statements divided equally into five developmental areas. Each area begins with "The child can" and it is the examiner's job to check each statement that is representative of the child's maturational performance. Given below are the five areas and representative questions from the checklist.

Bodily Coordination [4]

The child can . . .
_____ 1. Hop on one foot.
_____ 2. Walk three yards on toes without touching heels on the floor.

Eye-Hand Coordination
The child can . . .
_____ 3. Cut out pictures neatly, following straight lines, angles and curves.
_____ 4. Draw a recognizable man of head, body, arms, and legs without copy.

Speech and Language Comprehension
The child can . . .
_____ 5. Pronounce compound consonants correctly in words such as basket, bottle, tree, green, please, thank, sister, brother. Baby talk is outgrown.
_____ 6. Count the five fingers on each hand and add both together to make the correct total of ten.

Personal Independence
The child can . . .
_____ 7. Care for self at the toilet, requiring no assistance with paper or clothing.
_____ 8. Tell own full name and address on request.

---

[4] From "Individual Record Check List—Maturity Level for School Entrance and Reading Readiness." By Katharine M. Banham, Ph.D., Minneapolis, Minnesota: Educational Test Bureau, copyright 1959, by American Guidance Service, Inc. Reproduced by permission.

Social Cooperation
The child can . . .
_____ 9. Recite verses or sing a complete song, and will do so for the entertainment of others.
_____10. Play competitive, active games with other children and keep the rules in such games as: hide and seek, hop-scotch, or cowboys and Indians.

Scoring of this checklist is based on the number of statements true for an individual child. If, for example, twenty of the twenty-five statements are true, the child is ready for first grade; fifteen to twenty true statements indicate readiness within three to six months. If a child scores under fifteen points, the manual recommends attendance at kindergarten or nursery school and more definitive testing (Banham, 1959).

READING READINESS TESTS

Reading readiness tests are generally used in the beginning of a child's first year in school. They help the school in gaining some indication of the child's ability to progress in reading. For example, Miss Smith, a first-grade teacher, wants to know which children are ready for reading and which children may have difficulty. She decides to use a reading readiness test to help answer this question. Upon reviewing the test scores, she finds that some children are ready to read and others are not. With this knowledge she can divide the children into groups of similar readiness and have each group work at its own level. She can use the results of the tests as a guide in starting a formal reading program and in deciding what type of prereading activities she may provide for the children.

Teachers should not feel that the scores their students receive on a reading readiness test will necessarily be an indication of the child's final level of reading achievement. A reading readiness test is used mainly to predict the ability of a child to learn from reading instruction in the first year of school and many times only in the first few months. Actually, a better source for the prediction of final reading achievement is a scholastic aptitude test. In addition, it must be remembered that each child's rate of development is different. For example, Bill may start walking at an earlier age than his brother Jim—even though Jim may start to talk earlier than Bill. In the same way, some children are ready to read at five years of age or even sooner, whereas others are not ready until they are seven or eight years old. It must be remembered also that there is an age difference of as much as eleven months among individual children placed in the same group at the first-grade level. At this age, a few months makes a great deal of difference in physical and intellectual maturity, and thus affects what each child is capable of learning.

There are many reading readiness tests, each having different kinds of tasks. Some require rhyming or matching sounds, and others use oral vocabulary with pictures. For example, in the latter type of problem, the child is asked to identify a picture of an object that the teacher names. The teacher may say "cat" and ask the children to circle the picture of a cat from among pictures of a cat, a dog, a horse, and a bicycle. Almost all the reading readiness tests require the child to be able to match figures or simple words by sight. The test item may show a star and beside the star four figures: a star, a circle, a square, and a diamond. The child must be able to "memorize" the star and pick the star figure from among the other four figures to get the item right.

The Metropolitan Reading Readiness Test is one of the widely used readiness tests. It is made up of six tests. The first is called Word Meaning. The person doing the testing presents four pictures to the child and verbalizes a word that would identify one of the pictures. The child is then asked to point to the picture that is the same as the word. In the second test the examiner shows the child four pictures, but this time instead of calling out a word, a phrase or sentence is stated. The child is then asked to point to the picture that is the same or means the same as the phrase or sentence. This test is called Sentences. The third test, Information, is similar to the first two tests, except that here the child is called upon to point out objects in terms of what they do. The child may, for example, be presented with pictures of four objects including a camera and be asked to "mark the one you would take a picture with." The fourth test, called Matching, requires the child to show ability to recognize similarities and differences in pictures of objects, numbers, and letters. The fifth test, Numbers, consists of simple arithmetic problems. In the sixth and last test, Copying, the child is asked to copy simple forms, numbers, and letters. This test attempts to find out about a youngster's physical and intellectual maturity.

Another example of a readiness test is the Metropolitan Readiness Test. This test is designed to assess prereading skills in kindergarten and first-grade students. The test has two levels; Level I for use at the beginning and middle of kindergarten, and Level II for use at the end of kindergarten and beginning of first grade. Both levels are available in forms P and Q and may be hand or machine scored. Level I covers seven areas: Test 1, Auditory Memory; 2, Rhyming; 3, Letter Recognition; 4, Visual Matching; 5, School Language and Listening; 6, Quantitative Language. Level II covers eight areas: Test 1, Beginning Consonants; 2, Sound-Letter Correspondence; 3, Visual Matching; 4, Finding Patterns; 5, School Language; 6, Listening; 7, Quantitative Concepts; 8, Quantitative Operations. Level II also includes a sample of the child's printing.

Since this is a paper-and-pencil test and children of this age are not very adept at this skill, careful attention is given to teaching the child the correct way to mark the test booklet. The child is given a practice booklet for this purpose. The teacher draws two rectangles on the chalkboard similar to those which the pupils must mark. She shades these on the upper left and lower right corners, and the child is instructed to draw a diagonal line guided by these shadings. The teacher begins by saying, "Now open your booklet and fold it like this. (*Demonstrate.*) You should see some flowers here at the

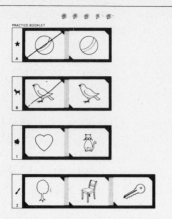

Check to see that all pupils have done this correctly and are on page 2. SAY:

A. Put your finger on the little black STAR, and keep it there while I tell you what to do. Look at the BALL with the line across it. Do you see the little black corners in that box? (Point to the shaded corners of the box on the chalkboard.) Now take your pencil and mark the other BALL in the same way. Draw a line from one little black corner to the other. Make your line across the BALL like this. (Demonstrate on the chalkboard.)

Check to see that all pupils have made the line correctly so that it touches the black corner spaces and is reasonably straight. THEN SAY:

B. Now put your finger on the little black DOG. Look at the BIRD with the line across it. Make a long line just like that one across the other BIRD. Remember to make your line from one black corner to the other one.

Figure 31. Sample Directions from Metropolitan Readiness Tests Level 1, Form P. (Reproduced from Metropolitan Readiness Tests, Level 1, Form P. Copyright © 1976 by Harcourt Brace Jovanovich, Inc. Reproduced by special permission of the publisher.)

top of the page." Figure 31 from the Practice Booklet continues these directions in teaching the child to mark a rectangle.

MATHEMATICAL APTITUDE

For the appraisal of aptitude in mathematics there are many tests; among these are tests of algebra and geometry. Mainly, these tests attempt to predict how well a student will do in his or her first courses in algebra and geometry. That is, they are tests used by the school to find out if a child is ready to start higher mathematics. Some children need more work in arithmetic, and many times it is best if they have a year of general mathematics before starting algebra. The results from these tests, plus the child's past academic record and teacher recommendations, help guide the school in placing the child in the course suited to his or her needs and talents.

Many of the tests of algebra aptitude contain problems of addition, subtraction, multiplication, and division. Some have problems dealing with percentages and the use of United States currency. Others have problems that require abstract reasoning and the ability to use simple arithmetical and algebraic procedures.

FOREIGN LANGUAGE APTITUDE

To assist our schools in helping place students in foreign language courses, the professional test publishers have increased the quality of tests in this field. Basically, these foreign language aptitude tests are designed to provide an indication of a student's probable success in learning a foreign language.

Teachers and counselors may wonder what ability is actually needed to learn a foreign language. According to most authorities in this field, any person who is able to speak English in everyday life can learn a foreign language, given the time and opportunity to do so. Of course, this statement is too general to have much meaning. After all, "given the time" could mean forever. Thus the testing of foreign language aptitude assists in placing students in foreign language study who have the most chance of success. The language aptitude test measures learned capabilities that seem important to rapid success in learning a language.

The guidance counselor will use the results of the foreign language aptitude test in placing an individual in a class best suited to his or her abilities. Of course, as we have mentioned before, the results from one test are never used exclusively. They are used along with other test data and a child's academic record.

One of the prominent foreign language aptitude tests is the Modern Language Aptitude Test (MLAT). The MLAT can be used to measure not only modern language aptitude but also such ancient languages as Latin or Greek. There are five parts to the test. The first part is concerned with memory. The second part deals with the ability to learn speech sounds. The third part measures sound-symbol association ability and calls for knowledge of English vocabulary. The fourth part is devoted to sensitivity to grammatical structure. The fifth part deals with rote memory. In administration of the test a tape recorder presents the instructions and test questions.

Tests such as the Modern Language Aptitude Test do not suggest specific languages for study but only that a person has or has not a general language aptitude.

MUSICAL APTITUDE

In the fields of music and art, the need for tests that can measure ability is self-evident. Many parents have spent much money on their child's music lessons only to find out years later that the child is tone-deaf or has little musical ability. There is no single test that can measure the desire of the child to express himself musically or his willingness to practice every day. In music, as perhaps in no other endeavor, the motivation to stick to the task and devote time to learning the skills each and every day is necessary. It does not matter how much talent a person has; if he or she does not have this desire to perform and the ability to stick to it, the talent will never be realized.

Most musical aptitude tests include questions aimed at discovering perceptive and interpretive abilities—that is, telling the difference in pitch and loudness. In addition, the person is tested in esthetic judgment of a melody or harmony and a rhythmic pattern. The test most widely used by music educators and our schools is the Seashore Measures of Musical Talents. There are six parts to this test, all of which are on phonograph records, each testing a different aspect of musical ability. In the first test, the person is asked to judge which of two tones is higher in pitch. In the second, the judgment is the louder of two sounds. In the third, time intervals are presented, and the student is asked to judge which of two is longer. In the fourth, rhythm is presented, and the individual is asked to tell if one of two rhythms is different or if they are both the same. In the fifth, the task is to judge which of two tone qualities is most pleasing. The sixth test is concerned with tonal memory; that is, the student is asked to judge whether two melodies are the same or different. In each test the judgments become increasingly harder with each item.

Many musicians and other critics have complained that the Seashore tests are not related to the musical activities of the musician. That is, the ability to tell fine differences in time and pitch is not needed by the musician. Be that as it may, the Seashore Measures of Musical Talents remains our best test of musical ability, and if used with other forms of evaluation, it can give some indication of musical talent. In the final analysis, however, you should bear in mind that the actual musical achievement and rate of progress of the person is probably the best predictor of future musical achievement.

ARTISTIC APTITUDE

In the field of aptitude in visual art, several types of tests are available. There are tests of esthetic judgment, design, and actual drawing. Critics of art tests have admitted that these tests can show differences between art students and other groups. However, they contend that this is because of achievement rather than ability. Thus they state that we are measuring what the person has learned rather than his ability to learn or do well in the future.

One of the most widely used art aptitude tests is the Meier Art Judgment Test. This test consists of items presenting a pair of pictures of art objects. One picture is a recognized masterpiece and the other is the same picture with some slight change. The change usually affects the compositional balance of the picture as a whole. The student taking the test is asked to choose the better picture in each pair.

Other tests, such as the Horn Art Aptitude Inventory, require actual drawings. In this test, lines and dots are given from which the person must make a sketch.

As in the test of musical ability, teachers and counselors should consider other factors such as the child's interest, achievement, and his or her art instructor's rating along with the test results before counseling students in definite terms. (See Super and Crites, 1962, Chapters 12 and 13, for a thorough and definitive discussion of musical and artistic aptitude tests.)

Graduate School Tests

The tests in the graduate school area are basically a combination of scholastic aptitude and achievement tests for college graduates. The Graduate Record Examination (GRE) is a very popular and widely used test for admission to graduate school. Part of the GRE is nothing more than a general intelligence or scholastic aptitude test, whereas other sections evaluate achievement in terms of specific subject-matter areas.

Another widely used test, especially in psychology and education, is the Miller Analogies Test. This test consists of analogies whose content is drawn from many different academic fields. The administration of the test is restricted to licensed centers (as is the GRE) and very rigid controls are applied to prevent leakage of content. Percentile norms are given for different groups of graduate students, including those in engineering, language and literature, physical science, social sciences, theology, business administration, psychology, and education. Students in the physical sciences and psychology, as a group, usually receive the highest scores.

In addition to these tests, special examinations are given to applicants to professional schools such as schools of law, dentistry, medicine, and so forth. For a complete list of testing programs for special purposes, see Educational Testing Service (1974).

Using the Results of Aptitude Tests

It is extremely important that the individual, as well as his parents, teachers, and counselors, be aware of his assets and limitations. The school counselor works with many different young people with different kinds of problems.

The results of aptitude tests help in guiding such youngsters as, for example, the student with average ability who hopes to be a nuclear scientist, the student whose parents view him or her unrealistically and aspire either above or below his or her abilities, the person who performs poorly in academic areas but is talented mechanically, the girl or boy with superior intelligence who is not aware of her or his potential, the boy or girl from a poor economic background who is willing to settle for an occupation below the one in which success would be probable, and so forth.

The aptitude test and/or battery can provide a basis for assisting not only in personal counseling but also in sound curricula planning. The school needs to know what courses to offer and who should take them. The data provided by aptitude test results help determine an appropriate course of action.

To illustrate the actual use of aptitude tests in everyday school terms, let us listen to Mr. Sanders, a high school counselor, explain the use of aptitude tests to a group of parents. He has just finished his introductory remarks concerning aptitude testing.

Mr. Sanders: Are there any questions?

Parent: Yes, Mr. Sanders, I have a question. You said that our school gives algebra and foreign language aptitude tests to incoming freshmen to help place them in the types of courses that are suited to their abilities. Does this mean that if my son does poorly on one of these tests he cannot take these subject?

Mr. Sanders: No, Mrs. Smith, that isn't exactly what I meant. We can only advise you and in the final analysis you and your son must make the decision. Besides, these tests do not mean that your son or daughter should never attempt algebra or a foreign language. What they do signify, however, is that the chances for success or failure, at this particular time, are greater with certain students. And it would probably be best if the child who does poorly on these tests waits at least until his sophomore year before attempting to take courses in the particular subjects. The results of these tests are not to hurt or bar students from their right to education, but only to help them make wise choices that are in line with their talents. In the long run, the child is much happier, for he need not experience failure in areas where his talents are not as great.

Parent: Do you mean to say that my child hasn't the right to try a subject, if you think he may fail?

Mr. Sanders: No, not at all. In a democratic society people have the right to fail as well as to succeed. In the school the same situation is true. The point is that the school attempts to educate everyone, and different children have varied abilities. You wouldn't want to push a child into the water who couldn't swim, though it is possible he could learn while in the water—but also he might drown. In the same way we do not want to start a child in algebra if the chances are he will fail. Isn't it best to first teach the child in swimming or in algebra the essentials of these skills before expecting him to perform?

Parent: I see your point. In other words, tests help to determine the most profitable areas of study for the child to enter at this time.

Mr. Sanders: Exactly, but a child is always given the chance to try these subjects in his second year, or even his first, if he and his parents want to go against the recommendations. Of course, we hope that the parents and child will go along with our recommendations, because the purpose of our tests is not to penalize the child but to help him.

Parent: Mr. Sanders, may I change the subject a little?

Mr. Sanders: Certainly.

Parent: My son's cousin is in high school and he has had aptitude tests in art and music. Why don't you give such tests?

Mr. Sanders: We do give tests of musical and artistic aptitude. However, we give this type of test when we feel it is needed. By this I mean that these tests are not given to all students. They are given only when the counselor feels a student's interests may possibly lie in these areas. Or when a child is interested in discovering his abilities and is not yet sure of what he wants to do in life.

Parent: Is this also true for vocational tests?

Mr. Sanders: Yes and no. If you mean general vocational aptitude, yes—we do give all our students a test battery that includes tests of mechanical, clerical, and other skills needed for certain vocations. If you mean individual tests of vocational skills—no. For example, your children are given a test battery called the Differential Aptitude Tests. This test is given in the freshman year of high school and again in the junior year. This test battery gives us a general idea of the aptitudes your child may have in certain general vocational areas. In addition, it also gives us some idea of his general scholastic ability. This helps us help your child in specific vocational and collegiate planning. If these data aren't enough, then we administer an individual test in, for example, mechanical skill.

Parent: Don't you think we are testing our kids to death?

Mr. Sanders: No, not necessarily. The more information we have on your child, the better we are able to help him. Tests are not always correct in their assessment of ability. Therefore, the more tests given, the less chance of error. Again, let me stress, we give tests only to get information to help us guide your youngster. Of course, there is a point when too many tests can be a waste of time and money. But at Jones High School, we give what we feel is necessary. As I stated, not all types of tests are given to every child. *Different tests for different reasons are given to different youngsters.*

Teachers and counselors, of course, may find that their school has different ideas from those of Mr. Sanders or they may discover that financial resources to support an ideal testing program are lacking. Today, with federal and state aid, however, most school districts can arrange to have an adequate testing program. If certain tests are needed for an individual pupil that are not available in a particular school system, it may be possible to refer the student to a public agency or a psychologist in private practice.

The important questions to keep in mind are the following:

1. What information does the school need to provide the best education for its particular students in its particular educational and geographical setting?
2. What information is needed to help each child develop his or her own unique potential?

Aptitude tests help provide the answers to these very important questions.

Achievement Tests

In Chapter 8 we talked about aptitude tests and how they help the school in planning educational programs and guiding each individual youngster to realize his or her fullest potential. We stated that the primary objective of the aptitude test was to measure an individual's potential to learn or succeed, in school, at a vocation, or in an artistic endeavor. Simply stated, then, an aptitude test attempts to measure what a person can do. In this chapter we discuss tests that measure what a person has done.

The primary goal of the achievement test is to measure past learning, that is, the accumulated knowledge and skills of an individual in a particular field or fields. As we have stated, achievement and aptitude tests overlap. Can we test achievement without also testing capacity or ability? In a purely theoretical sense, we cannot. The difference between aptitude and achievement tests is one of degree or objective. Achievement tests emphasize past progress, whereas aptitude tests are primarily concerned with future potentialities. Lindeman (1967) presents the differences between aptitude and achievement tests quite well when he states,

> The primary distinction between aptitude and achievement tests is one of purpose rather than of content. Both are basically achievement tests; but one is used for prediction, whereas the other is used for assessing present knowledge and abilities. Differences in content and format between the two kinds of tests are thus due primarily to differences in the types of validity that each must have. In the case of aptitude tests, this is quite clearly predictive validity, and hence, items are selected on the basis of their prediction of future performance. In the case of standardized achievement tests, items are selected on the basis of content validity for the assessment of previously specified content and objectives. (pp. 107–108).

The achievement tests used most frequently by a teacher are those he develops himself. Most teachers and principals, however, find that published standardized achievement tests and batteries can be of unique importance in many areas of the total school program.

A standardized achievement test or battery is an instrument produced by a test publisher for national use. It is developed through the efforts of professional test experts and is designed to examine educational objectives and goals. The standardized test differs from the classroom examination in its scientific development. A classroom achievement test is made up by a teacher for her own pupils and may or may not be used again. The teacher does not have the time, facilities, or training to investigate the value of her tests in a scientific manner. On the other hand, standardized achievement tests are subjected to rigorous scientific procedures to ensure their worth. In this chapter our attention will focus on the standardized achievement test.

Construction of Achievement Tests

The construction of an achievement test entails a careful analysis of the field to be examined. First, the reasons for the construction of the instrument must be clearly evident. Second, an exhaustive and definitive outline of the subject matter to be used is made. Third, the reasons for construction and an outline of the content are reviewed with such specialists as classroom teachers, educators, and test makers.

The fourth step is to compose test items for each part of the content outline, and then to ask representative educators to comment on their importance, clarity of expression, and representativeness of subject matter. During this step some test items are modified, some are thrown out, and new items are added. The test is then administered to a sample group of children and their performance is analyzed. Let us now focus in detail on some of these steps.

Reasons and Objectives

The first step in the construction of a standardized achievement test is to state with clarity the reasons and objectives behind the instrument. Let us look at some of the stated objectives of the Cooperative Primary Tests (Educational Testing Service, 1967) as an example of this first step.

1. *The tests will focus on skills and concepts basic to future development in reading, writing, listening, and mathematics. They will test understanding and thinking, in addition to memory or matching skills.*
2. *Since learning is the major goal of our schools, the tests will be clearly related to instructional processes, so that teachers can make direct use of the results with individuals and groups.*
3. *The tests will be designed to measure attainment of major educational objectives, regardless of particular curriculum programs and methods.*

4. The tests will minimize the dependence of one skill upon another, for more definitive descriptions of pupil development. For example, no reading will be required on the Listening tests.

5. Every effort will be made to engage the interest of young children and secure valid responses and meaningful demonstrations of their ability.

6. The test will be as convenient as possible for busy teachers to give and score. (p. 6)

Content Outline

The second step involves an exhaustive and definitive outline of the subject matter to be tested. Doren (1973) has outlined the skills necessary to read effectively. Her test is diagnostic and attempts to locate causes of reading difficulty. The following outline of skills is stated in the Doren Diagnostic Reading Test (Doren, 1973).

Skill 1. Letter Recognition [1]
  A. The ability to recognize the same letter when it occurs again and to distinguish it from a letter of similar configuration.
  B. The ability to recognize the capital and lower case forms of the same letter.
  C. The ability to recognize the same letter when presented in different type or style, in both printed and cursive forms.

Skill 2. Beginning Sounds
  A. The ability to match beginning sounds in different words.
  B. The ability to choose the correct beginning sound for a word in context.

Skill 3. Whole Word Recognition
  A. The ability to identify two matching words.
  B. The ability to discriminate between two words similar in both sound and appearance.

Skill 4. Words Within Words
  A. The ability to recognize smaller known words when they form a compound word.
  B. The ability to find small words within larger words which are not compound.
  C. The ability to decide when a word within a word is helpful in word sounding.

Skill 5. Speech Consonants
  A. The ability to identify a new word from the auditory perception of a speech consonant.
  B. The ability to identify a word in context from the visual perception of a speech consonant.

Skill 6. Ending Sounds
  A. The ability to identify a word from its ending sound by auditory discrimination.

[1] From M. Doren, *Doren Diagnostic Reading Test of Word Recognition Skills: Manual.* Circle Pines, Minnesota: American Guidance Service, Inc., Copyright 1973. Reprinted with permission.

B. The ability to choose the correct word in context from words with variant endings.

C. The ability to choose the correct plural form of irregular nouns.

Skill 7. Blending
The ability to apply known blends to independent word selection in context.

Skill 8. Rhyming
A. The ability to recognize words that rhyme by auditory perception.
B. The ability to recognize words that rhyme by visual perception.
C. The ability to recognize that look-alike words do not always rhyme.
D. The ability to recognize that unlike words may rhyme.

Skill 9. Vowels
A. The ability to distinguish a word by its vowel sound from a group of otherwise identical words.
B. The ability to select the letter form of the vowel sound heard, whether in its long or short form.
C. The ability to determine the sound a vowel should be given in words that conform to spelling rules.
D. The ability to recognize long and short vowels by auditory discrimination.
E. The ability to recognize the correct vowel sound in words in which spelling is contrary to the rules.
F. The ability to determine which vowel is sounded when two vowels occur together.
G. The ability to determine whether a vowel is long or short when two vowels occur together.
H. The ability to recognize a diphthong as a new vowel sound and recognize its sound variations.
I. The ability to recognize that the printed vowel may have the sound of a different vowel.

Skill 10. Discriminate Guessing
The ability to supply missing words from clues in the context.

Skill 11. Spelling
A. The ability to spell phonetic words.
B. The ability to spell non-phonetic words.

Skill 12. Sight Words
The ability to read sight words and identify their pronunciation by their phonetic spellings.

Sample Administration

After the standardized achievement test is constructed, it is given to a sample group of children. The results are then analyzed to find out whether the test is measuring what it is supposed to measure. For example, the authors of a social studies test have decided to construct a test that will measure the student's understanding of the currents of history that led up to the Industrial Revolution. They want to know whether they are measuring this area of knowledge or whether they are measuring reading ability, spelling, and so forth. In addition, they analyze the results to see whether children, upon retaking the test in another form, show similar scores. If they find that the test is meeting their objectives and is doing so consistently, they then consider publishing it.

This process is not merely based on inspection or intuition. After the administration of the test, usually to a thousand or more students, an analysis of each test item is made. The requirements each item must meet are (1) *easiness*, (2) *discrimination*, and (3) *distribution*. Let us briefly examine each of these.

Easiness

Analysis of easiness is concerned with the percentage of students who answer an individual item correctly. If, for example, 100 students took an examination and thirty of them answered a specific item correctly, we would state that 30 per cent answered correctly.[2] Here is a list of sample items with percentages of students answering each item correctly.

The preceding items reveal certain characteristics. Items 3, 5, and 9 seem to be relatively easy, whereas items 2, 6, 7, and 8 seem to be quite difficult. Items 1, 4, and 10 are between these extremes.

It is necessary to estimate percentages in an item analysis because very easy or very difficult test items tell us little about the subjects being examined. These easy items only serve to differentiate a very few students from the others. Statistically speaking, the ideal item is one that 50 per cent of the students answer correctly and 50 per cent miss. Thus it provides the greatest number of discriminations. Why? The 50 per cent are composed of different students on each item. Thus one student may answer all items correctly and another may miss all of them. Test producers usually remove items that 80 per cent or more answer correctly or 20 per cent or less miss.

Item Number	Percentage
1	50
2	10
3	80
4	35
5	92
6	8
7	3
8	1
9	95
10	45

[2] To find the percentage on each test item, simply tally the number of students who get a given item correct, divide by the total number of students taking the test, and multiply by 100.

DISCRIMINATION

Discrimination analysis is used in all standardized test construction to determine the degree to which each test item measures the same thing as the total test in which it is included. First, the top 25 per cent of students (total test scores) and the bottom 25 per cent are found. Then an analysis of each item is made by tallying the number of the top and bottom students who answered the item correctly. The percentage of the bottom group is then subtracted from the percentage of the top group. The resulting data indicate the extent to which a given item discriminates. The larger the difference, the better the item.

If a test item does not differentiate between the bottom and top groups, it is not discriminating and is of little use. A negative difference (when the bottom group answers the item correctly more times than the top group) reveals a poor item that is probably ambiguous and is penalizing the students who know the most. Most authorities consider twenty percentage points as the minimum difference for an item that discriminates.

DISTRIBUTION

Distribution analysis is similar to easiness analysis except that all alternative answers to each item are studied. The percentage of students who mark each alternative is computed, not just the ones who obtained the correct answer; for example:

1. The sum of 40 and 40 is

	PER CENT CHOOSING ANSWER
a. o	1
b. 80	58
c. 70	16
d. 40	25

An inspection of our example reveals several important factors. First, this is statistically a fairly good item in that a little over half (58 per cent) of the students obtained the correct answer. Second, we can see whether some of the answers are too easy and should be replaced by new answers that are better alternatives. This is obviously true of the "a" alternative, which was marked by only 1 per cent of the students.

Ambiguous items may be identified by this kind of analysis. If, for example, two alternatives, one of which is the correct answer, produce an equal or near-equal response percentage, there is a good chance that students have a good reason for choosing the incorrect alternative.

Standardization and Norms

After a careful statistical analysis of the data, the test is administered to thousands of children throughout the United States who represent a cross section of the population in terms of age, grade, geographical location, and, in some cases, race and socioeconomic status. Norms are obtained from this analysis and are reported in the form of percentiles, grade equivalents, and so forth. After all this is done, a manual for administering, scoring, and interpreting the test is written. It is obvious from what has been stated to this point that a standardized achievement test is quite time-consuming and expensive to construct.

The following sections from the Norms Booklet of the Stanford Achievement Test (Madden et al., 1973) present a whole, but brief, picture of what actually takes place in constructing an achievement test. A more definitive and complete description of the construction of the Stanford Achievement Test can be found in the technical data report of the Manual (Madden et al., 1975).

Rationale and Purpose [3]

As with each of the prior revisions, the decision to produce a new edition of *Stanford Achievement Test*, superseding the previous edition, rested primarily upon two considerations: (1) the significant changes that had occurred in the elementary school curriculum in the intervening years, and (2) the need for updating the norms. Periodic revisions of achievement tests are a generally accepted practice, but rapid curriculum changes over the past ten years made it essential to prepare a new edition within a shorter interval than had previously been the case.

The first major task undertaken by the authors was to review the entire structure of the *Stanford Achievement Test* series with respect to its two major dimensions, extension over grade levels and across curricular areas. After due consideration, revision of the 1964 edition with respect to both of these dimensions was deemed essential.

Preparation and Editing of Items

In preparing this latest edition of *Stanford Achievement Test*, a major goal was to make sure that the content of the test would be in harmony with present instructional objectives and measure what is actually being taught in today's schools. To make certain that the test content would be valid in this sense, the construction of the new edition was preceded by a thorough analysis of (1) the most widely-used series of textbooks in the various subject areas, (2) a wide variety of courses of study, and (3) the research literature pertaining to children's concepts, experiences, and vocabulary at successive ages or grades.

Prior to the time that items were written for the test, two basic decisions were reached with respect to the general nature of the items. First, it was decided that new items should be written for the 1973 edition—with exceptions, such as questions regarding very elementary facts such as 2+2, or the spelling of a minimal vocabulary. Secondly, it was decided that the multiple-choice format would be employed throughout. On the basis of the analyses of textbooks, courses of study, and research literature, the test specifications or "blueprints" in terms of instructional objectives were prepared jointly by the authors with the assistance of curriculum specialists. Each author assumed special responsibility in areas of his competence and interest. All items recommended for inclusion in the series reflect instructional objectives which are available from the publisher. Responsibility for item writing was also divided among the authors. Within each author's assigned domain, items were written by the author himself and by colleagues who were experts in the particular fields. Each author also did one or more tryouts of the items in his assigned subtests in local school systems in order to check his judgment on performance of various item types and item difficulties.

As complete sets of items were written, they were turned over to the editorial staff of the Test Department of Harcourt Brace Jovanovich, Inc. From this point on the items were edited by five different groups of individuals. First, the items were edited by experts within the various curricular areas being tested. The primary focus of attention for these editors was the correctness of item content. Second, the items were edited by experts within the field of measurement; the major concern of these editors was the application of the rules of good item writing. Third, items were edited by a group of general editors—individuals with considerable experience in editing various types of materials. Their special interest was in the wording of items, grammatical structure, and related matters. Fourth, the items were reviewed and edited by groups of persons with various minority backgrounds. The special concern of these persons was appropriateness of the content for special cultural groups. Besides these groups, teachers involved in the item tryout program were asked to criticize the items, and they constituted a fifth group who shared in the editing process.

Sufficient materials were developed for five exceedingly long forms at each level. Fifty percent more material was tried out than was ultimately retained.

Experimental forms were prepared for each level. These forms were designated, T-1, T-2, T-3, T-4, and T-5. At the three upper levels the five forms were separated into 25 "miniforms," identical in terms of number of items in each subtest. This innovative design had several advantages. It permitted: broader sampling across schools and thus more representative results; better school cooperation, since tests would require shorter administration time; tryout of a great number of items at each level; better test data on items that otherwise would have come at the end of a long test; and the use of a type of matrix sampling for tryout which has implications for future preparation of such tests.

National Tryout of Items

The Item Tryout program is of great importance in that it shapes the subsequent development of the test. It is at this stage that items which have been written, edited, and reviewed are actually tried out in a representative sample of schools. The authors and publisher of the test use the information they gather from a tryout to select the items that will comprise the final published test. The tasks of the test developer at this point may be grouped into two broad categories: (1) selection of a sample of pupils to be tested that accurately reflects the demographic characteristics of the pupils in the country as a whole, and (2) selection of items to be included in the final version of the test that best measure the various areas of achievement being tested.

The first step was the selection of an appropriate sample of schools in which to administer the tests. This process involved a study of various population statistics of the United States such as city size, geographic location, median family income, median years of schooling, and school enrollment. Schools with the desired characteristics were invited to take part in the item tryout program. Positive responses to these invitations resulted in a sample of 61,000 pupils in 1445 classrooms in 47 school systems throughout the country tested in the fall of 1970. Summary statistics concerning this population will be found in the *Technical Data Report.*

The job of selecting the best items involved many criteria. Among the most important were: (1) coverage of all of the instructional objectives in the blueprint for each subject area, and (2) the building of a subtest so that it contained items with a difficulty range from fairly easy to hard. Some items fail to meet all the requirements; it is for this reason that many more items are tried out than are finally used.

Some items which authors considered appropriate for a specific grade proved to be too easy or too difficult for that grade, but fit well at another grade level. For this reason, each level of the test was given not only at the intended grade(s), but also to the grade above and the grade below.

Every pupil who took *Stanford Achievement Test* in the item tryout program took the *Otis-Lennon Mental Ability Test* also. The latter test was administered for the purpose of defining the Stanford tryout population in terms of mental ability. Item performance on Stanford was evaluated against an established scale of measurement.

Schools administering the tests were asked to return the following materials along with the tests:

1. lists of textbooks used at each grade for each subject
2. a test evaluation form
3. a record of time taken to complete each subtest.

The first helped the test authors select items that measure material included in the major textbooks used in the schools. The test evaluation form asked the teacher to respond to questions regarding ease of administration, ambiguities in directions or items, completeness of coverage, and also asked for any suggestions for change. The records of time were used in setting final time limits. In the item tryout program, testing was conducted without time limits in order to allow nearly all children to attempt all items and to enable the administrators to gain an idea of the length of time it took most pupils to complete each test. In this way time limits can be set to make this a power, not a speed test.

In Grades 1 and 2 an end-of-year tryout was conducted to obtain data at the lowest level of the test. Thirteen systems tested a total of 6809 students in Grades 1 and 2 with Primary Level I of the Item Tryout Edition of *Stanford Achievement Test.*

Construction of Final Forms

A variety of statistical data was obtained from the item tryout program for each of the items. These data consisted of the percent of all pupils at each grade level selecting each option in each item and the percent omitting the item. Similar data were also derived for the upper 27% of pupils and for the lower 27%. Item discrimination indices based on the "upper" and "lower" 27% groups were also obtained for the three primary level batteries and biserial correlations were calculated for all the upper level batteries. In addition, preliminary estimates of the reliability of each test at each grade level were obtained.

The content of the final forms of each test was selected in such a way that the final tests conform to the original specifications with respect to such criteria as objectives measured and relative emphases, appropriateness of difficulty in the grades for which the tests are intended, and comparability in content and difficulty among the forms of each battery.

At all levels through Intermediate II a practice test was administered a few days prior to the administration of *Stanford Achievement Test*. This served the purpose of familiarizing the pupils with the type of questions and the method of marking their answers in the answer booklet.

Standardizations

The usefulness of the *Stanford Achievement Test* norms depends largely on the nature of the groups from which they were derived and upon the extent to which these may be considered representative of a larger reference population. The intent has been to provide normative data descriptive of current achievement in the nation's schools. It is believed that the Stanford norm data approximate this goal very closely, though it is impractical to attempt to demonstrate that any norm sample is completely representative of the national school population. The paragraphs which follow describe the sample of pupils on which the norms are based, and the programs conducted for the purpose of obtaining these norm data.

The Standardization Programs

The *first* step in planning for the standardization of *Stanford Achievement Test* was to determine the number of separate standardization programs to be undertaken and the time of the year these programs were to be conducted. The decision was made to have two major standardization programs: one near the end of each grade (May '72), and one near the beginning of each grade (October '72). It was decided also that for the Primary Level I and Level II Batteries a mid-year standardization (February '72) would pinpoint the rapid achievement growth during Grades 1 and 2.

A *second* step in planning for the standardization programs was the decision to standardize the three forms (A, B, and C) simultaneously in both the spring and fall programs.

The *third* step in the standardization programs was the establishment of specifications for the norm groups with respect to such characteristics as geographic distribution, types of school systems to be included, numbers of pupils desired per grade, and the extent of participation within cooperating systems. The distribution according to region and size of system was established in such a way that the norm samples would duplicate these characteristics for pupils in average daily attendance in public and private schools throughout the country. It was decided further that in all participating buildings every pupil in a sample of regular classes in at least eight consecutive grades would be included in the standardization program so that there would be no question of selection from grade to grade.

The desired representation in terms of number and kinds of systems was worked out on a state-by-state basis. Invitations were extended for each program to school systems in the various states meeting the desired specifications. A sufficiently large number of systems was invited to avoid undue influence by any one system. All participating school systems administered Forms A, B, or C of *Stanford Achievement Test* to pupils included in the standardization samples. Each system also administered the *Otis-Lennon Mental Ability Test* to all pupils who took Stanford. All answer documents used in the standardizations were electronically scored, therefore, all pupils completing each battery were included in the norms or in the other research data.

A total of 109 school systems drawn from 43 states participated; over 275,000 pupils were tested in the three standardization programs. The *Technical Data Report* lists all systems participating in the various Stanford research programs.

The standardization samples were selected to represent the national population in terms of geographic region, size of city, socioeconomic status, public school and non-public schools.

A special socioeconomic index based on median family income and median years of schooling for adults in communities was used for selecting the Stanford standardization samples.

Once the test data were available they were weighted to permit the construction of norm groups by grade level that were comparable in mental ability to the norm groups for the *Otis-Lennon Mental Ability Test* (OLMAT). This provided a Stanford norm group for each grade level with a normal distribution of mental ability, a mean OLMAT DIQ (deviation intelligence quotient) that rounds to 100 and a standard deviation that rounds to 16.

Overlapping of Batteries Programs

In addition to the three standardization programs described above, two independent "overlapping of batteries (scaling) programs" were conducted, one in May 1972 and one in October 1972. In these programs each battery was administered one grade above and one below the appropriate grades as well as at the levels for which the battery was intended. The purpose of these programs was to determine the equivalence of scores across the batteries, these data to be used first, in drawing, plotting, and reading continuous grade equivalent lines across all levels of *Stanford Achievement Test*; secondly, to set up a continuous scaled score for the Stanford series from *Stanford Early School Achievement Test* (SESAT) through *Stanford Achievement Test* to *Stanford Test of Academic Skills* (TASK); and thirdly, to provide data for reporting estimated percentile ranks and stanines for a wider range of grades for each level than those tested in the actual standardization programs.

Although one overlapping program at a given testing period might be considered to be adequate for establishing grade equivalents and scaled scores, it was felt that data from two testing periods would provide valuable information for a more refined determination of the grade equivalence lines and for a more accurate estimate of growth through the use of scaled scores especially at the extremes of the range.

After a careful study of the data from each of the overlapping programs, it was decided to do the actual scaling on the fall data. This decision was basically made in order to extend the scales down to the beginning of Kindergarten.

Determining Equivalence of Forms

The programs to determine the equivalence of the three forms were actually incorporated directly into the standardization programs since the three forms were administered simultaneously in each of the two major standardization programs. Forms A and B were administered randomly by class within the same systems and Form C was administered to matched groups of classes in parallel systems. Each population was further equated by the normalization of each *Otis-Lennon Mental Ability Test* distribution by grade and by form to a distribution with a mean IQ of 100 and a standard deviation of 16, as was done in the case of all standardization distributions. This meant that the range of ability for each group was strictly controlled.

It was first planned to administer Forms A, B, and C randomly by class, all within the same systems. However, due to the fact that Forms A and B contain all of the tests of the Complete Battery at each level and Form C contains only the Reading and Mathematics tests, the original pattern was modified in order to simplify administration within the standardization communities. The groups of systems invited to take part in each program were carefully matched and checked for comparability of socioeconomic data and school characteristics.

All forms of each test in the different batteries were built to be equivalent in terms of item content and original item difficulties. However, such factors as the position of an item in the tryout forms and in the final forms usually accounts for slight variations in the point by point relationship of raw scores on different forms. It is for this reason that raw score equivalents are checked at the time of standardization and that raw scores for each form are translated into interpreted scores. The relationship of the raw scores on the various forms of the Stanford tests are in general found to be very close, but because of customary slight variations raw scores should never be compared, even from one form of a certain test to another. In some instances, however, raw scores may be used to rank pupils on a single test within a classroom. (pp. 7–10)

The reader should again note that the preceding selection was a summary. Test publishers produce technical manuals or supplements that contain in detail all the steps in the construction of the test. For example, the technical data report of the Stanford tests requires 77 pages (Madden et al., 1975).

Differences Between Teacher-Made and Standardized Tests

1. The standardized test is based on curricular content and objectives common to representative schools throughout the nation. The teacher-made test is based on the content and objectives of one classroom or in some instances of a department within a school.
2. A teacher-made test may be constructed for a limited topic, whereas a standardized test encompasses large areas of content or skills.
3. Professional educators, psychologists, classroom teachers, and statisticians develop standardized tests. The teacher-made test is usually created by one or a limited number of teachers.
4. The teacher-made test can be evaluated only in terms of a single classroom or school. The standardized test provides evidence of the performances of different groups of children in different educational and geographical settings.
5. The standardized test is created, developed, and constructed by various educators and test specialists who attempt to follow scientific procedures.[4] The teacher-made test is usually constructed by a person untrained in measurement and without much experience with scientific techniques.

[4] *Scientific* here refers to use of the scientific method and measurement procedures that attempt to gauge validity, reliability, standard error of measurement, and so forth.

The standardized test has obvious advantages over the teacher-made test; however, some of the unique attributes of the standardized test are also disadvantages. The consensus of professional experts on curricular objectives, along with a careful analysis of textbooks and courses of study, presents a good general picture, but it does not allow for individual differences in terms of local school goals and student populations. It is at best a compromise—a blending of the best thinking, a consensus, an average—not a tailor-made evaluative instrument for a given educational setting. In addition, a published test is fixed at the point in time when it was developed and published and is not flexible to new situations and educational change. It cannot measure limited local needs. It can, of course, be revised, and the better tests are, as educational goals are changed and modified.

The chief value of the standardized test resides in its national scope, which enables the school district to compare its progress with that of other schools throughout the country. It enables the guidance staff to compare student progress with potentiality as indicated by aptitude tests. The norms presented in the standardized test manual make these comparisons possible.

Ebel presents three common fears or misconceptions educators have regarding standardized achievement tests. The first of these is the feeling that the goals of education are too subtle and complex to be effectively measured. Ebel (1968), in discussing this, states,

> *Teachers of young children know that the development of skills in the tool subjects and the establishment of solid foundations for understanding and interest in the major fields of human knowledge are concrete, specific, important objectives. But some of them may feel that tests, especially objective standardized tests, fail "to get at" the real essentials of achievement in these skill and foundation subjects. This mystical devotion to a hidden reality of achievement which is more essential than overt ability to perform has never satisfied the research worker. He wants to know the nature of this hidden reality and what evidence there is that it is important. (p. 257)*

The second fear is "overconcern" with possible anxiety and stress caused the child by testing. Ebel (1968) feels that it is more conducive to mental health for the child to know how he is really progressing than to shield him from the educational facts of life. "In education, as in medicine and justice, an excess of present sympathy can postpone or even defeat the procedures necessary for an individual's future welfare" (p. 259).

Ebel's third point is the overemphasis on the uniqueness of the school's objectives compared to the objectives outlined in a standardized test. He suggests that what constitutes a good education in Maine is not radically different from what constitutes a good education in California. He states that a teacher should not expect a standardized test to reveal data on how well he or she has taught everything, "but only on the things that all teachers ought to have taught." On the other hand Ebel concludes with the very important point that, "For those achievements which are truly and rightly unique to a particular school or teacher, locally constructed tests are the best answer" (pp. 259–60).

In weighing the advantages and disadvantages of standardized achievement testing, the student of measurement should not think in black or white terms. The teacher-made test is a valuable and important gauge of day-to-day classroom progress. The standardized test allows the teacher and school to see the student's and institution's achievement in a national perspective. The use of both the teacher-made and standardized tests provide a whole educational picture of the student and school.

Thus the user of standardized achievement tests can make broad comparisons between schools or classes or between areas of achievement and aptitude. In addition to the national norms furnished by the test publisher, each school with a complete testing program may develop local norms. Over a period of years, the guidance counselor or principal of a specific school will be in a position to say what the scores mean for his or her particular school.

Types of Achievement Tests

Standardized achievement tests can be divided into three groups. The first group consists of *general achievement test batteries*, which are tests that cover many of the basic subject-matter areas of a school's program, as well as study skills. In using these batteries the school does not have to administer separate tests, nor does it have to scan the market for tests in each subject field. The authors of the general batteries attempt to produce an instrument that will cover the general needs of an achievement testing program for our schools. This type of achievement test is used from elementary school through high school and even at the college level. The second kind of achievement test covers single subject areas, such as social studies, science, or mathematics. The third kind of achievement test is limited to specific areas within general subject-matter fields, such as ancient history, biology, and algebra.

The general achievement battery is the basic type of evaluative instrument used in the elementary schools. The single achievement test covering broad or specific subject areas is used along with the general achievement battery at the junior and senior high school level. We shall examine achievement batteries and tests covering different subject-matter areas and at different grade levels.

Achievement Test Batteries

The general achievement test battery provides the best all-around evidence concerning academic progress. Some authorities recommend that they be administered every year if the school can afford it. We shall have more to say on this subject in our discussion of school testing programs. However, decisions on when and how often any test should be administered are dependent on the local school and its unique needs.

Table 23. Stanford Achievement Test—Subtests for Various Grades

Subtests	Primary Level I Gr. 1.5–2.4	Primary Level II Gr. 2.5–3.4	Primary Level III Gr. 3.5–4.4	Intermediate Level I Gr. 4.5–5.4	Intermediate Level II Gr. 5.5–6.9	Advanced Level Gr. 7–9.5	Task Level I Gr. 9–10	Task Level II Gr. 11–12
Vocabulary	X	X	X	X	X	X	X	X
Reading Comprehension	X	X	X	X	X	X		
Word Study Skills	X	X	X	X	X			
Mathematics Concepts	X	X	X	X	X	X	X	X
Mathematics Computation	X	X	X	X	X	X		
Mathematics Applications		X	X	X	X	X		
Spelling	X	X	X	X	X	X		
Language				X	X	X	X	X
Social Science		X	X	X	X	X		
Science		X	X	X	X	X		
Listening Comprehension	X	X	X	X	X			

Scope and Content

Achievement test batteries differ from one another in (1) their breadth of coverage and (2) level of understanding required. General achievement batteries cover subject-matter and school skills from the primary grades through high school. Table 23, for example, illustrates the range of content and subtests employed in the various forms of the Stanford Achievement Test. Now we turn our attention to the specific content in widely used batteries and discuss what each subtest attempts to measure.

Word Meaning. Almost all achievement batteries have a subtest concerning word knowledge.[5] The batteries, however, vary in the degree to which they measure word meaning. Some evaluate word understanding in the context of a paragraph, whereas others measure it more directly and yield a separate word knowledge or vocabulary score. Others combine both approaches and yield paragraph-reading and vocabulary scores. Two of the most widely used methods, in the multiple-choice format, are shown in the following examples. (In the primary grades, pictures are used.)

1. *Boy* means almost the same as
   a. girl
   b. man
   c. woman
   d. child
2. *Boy* means the opposite of
   a. girl
   b. child
   c. man
   d. woman

Reading. Reading, a basic content area common to all general achievement batteries, presents the student with connected passages from a story or event. The tests vary in types of questions and length of passages. Some are based on passages from fifty to 100 words, with two or three questions on each passage. Others have a small number of long passages (500 or more words), with as many as twenty test questions referring to a single passage. Figure 32 illustrates some sample questions from the Reading Test of the Cooperative Primary Tests for grades 1 and 2, each illustrating different methods of evaluating reading achievement. The children are instructed to read what is in the arrow, then mark the box that goes best with it. Question 1 attempts to evaluate comprehension by having the student identify an illustrative picture with a word stimulus. Question 2 also evaluates comprehension, but the stimulus is an entire sentence rather than a single word. A sentence, being a complete thought, requires a higher level of comprehension than a single word. The student must use various other experiences in order to correctly identify the picture from the sentence.

---

[5] A notable exception is the Sequential Tests of Educational Progress (STEP), a widely used and respected battery of tests.

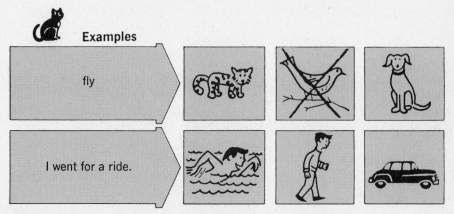

Figure 32. Example questions from Reading, Cooperative Primary Tests, Form 12A. (Copyright © 1965 by Educational Testing Service. All rights reserved. Reprinted by permission.)

In our example, the student is presented with the sentence, "I went for a ride." In order to mark the correct answer, he or she must differentiate among three means of going: swimming, walking, and riding. The child must have had experiences with a car, walking, and swimming in order to be able to choose the correct association with "ride." Not only is experience with these modes necessary, but also the intellectual connection must be made between the experience, the written sentence, and the pictures representing these experiences. Thus, reading becomes a complex and abstract process.

The above examples deal with concrete objects and concrete experiences. Reading skill becomes more complex with the increasing complexity of the material students of higher age and grade levels are required to comprehend. Tasks become more difficult and more abstract as students are required to make inferences and to draw conclusions.

An example of a test item based on two paragraphs and questions measuring more complex types of reading achievement follows.[6] In the actual test there are a total of ten questions on the two paragraphs.

If a nation is a group of people sharing common language, history, customs, beliefs, and land, then the mid-Eastern people known as the Kurds are a national entity. However, their homeland, Kurdistan, has been divided among Turkey, Iran, Iraq, Syria, and the Soviet Union. Of the 5½ million Kurds, 2½ million live in Turkey, and 1½ million live in Iraq. The land has many rivers and streams that make other nations want Kurdistan as a source of water for irrigation and electric power. And, of even greater importance, Kurdistan has one of the richest oil supplies in the world.

[6] From *Reading* of the *High School Placement Test*. Copyright, 1975, by the Scholastic Testing Service, Inc. Used by permission of the Scholastic Testing Service, Inc.

Although the Kurds share the Muslim religion of their neighbors, they have a unique culture and their own language. The Kurds maintain their traditional feudal society—the Kurd owes his <u>allegiance</u> to his chief, or agha, and not to the president or shah. This allegiance has often resulted in severe clashes that have flared into civil war.

(1) Which of these best describes the attitude of the ruling nations toward the Kurds?
    a) "Leave well enough alone"
    b) "Divide and conquer"
    c) "One man, one vote"
    d) "Freedom of choice"

(2) <u>National entity</u>, as underlined and used in this passage, most nearly means
    a) republic.
    b) constitution.
    c) nation.
    d) land.

(3) Most of the Kurds are ruled by
    a) the law of supply and demand.
    b) Kurdistan.
    c) Turkey.
    d) Iraq.

(4) What would probably happen to the five ruling nations if the Kurds achieved independence?
    a) Their governments would collapse.
    b) Their economic position would be weakened.
    c) They would be unaffected.
    d) Other minority groups would rise up in rebellion.

Arithmetic. As with reading, all achievement batteries attempt to appraise arithmetic skills and understanding. The batteries differ in their degree of emphasis on computational skills, problem solving, concepts, and understanding.

One of the difficulties that test authors encounter in appraising arithmetic ability, especially in the area of problem solving, is the separation of reading achievement from mathematical skill. The mathematics section of the Sequential Tests of Educational Progress (STEP Series II) attempts to overcome this obstacle. The Mathematics Basic Concepts tests evaluate elementary mathematical concepts, abilities, and skills that are supposed to be a segment of a general mathematics education. They are number and operation; measurement and geometry; relations, functions, and graphs; proof; probability and statistics; mathematical sentences; sets and mathematical systems; and applications. The pupil is called upon to show an understanding of these concepts by recalling facts, performing mathematical manipulations, and demonstrating one's own technique for solving a problem or generalizing and making logical inferences (Educational Testing Service, 1971).

In addition to the concepts tests there are mathematics computation tests. These measure computational skills such as fractions, decimals, and per cent; estimation; evaluation of formulas; solving simple inequalities; and manipu-

Directions

Each question in this test is followed by four suggested answers.

Read each question and then decide which one of the four suggested answers is best.

Find the row of spaces on your answer sheet which has the same number as the question. In this row, mark the space having the same letter as the answer you have chosen.

EXAMPLE

A 48-inch rope was shortened by cutting 2 inches from each end. How long is it now?

A 44 inches
B 45 inches
C 46 inches
D 47 inches

Answer

█ B C D

The correct answer to this question is lettered **A,** so space **A** is marked.

Note: Figures which accompany problems in this test are intended to provide information useful in solving the problems. They are drawn as accurately as possible EXCEPT when it is stated in a specific problem that its figure is not drawn to scale. All figures lie in the plane unless otherwise indicated.

In this test, all numbers used are real numbers.

STOP. Wait for further directions.

Figure 33. Directions and Sample Item from Sequential Tests of Educational Progress, Mathematics Basic Concepts. (From *Sequential Tests of Educational Progress, Series II, Form 2A.* Copyright © 1969 by Educational Testing Service. All rights reserved. Reprinted by permission.)

lations with exponents. There is very little reading. The mathematical tests, as the other tests in the battery, go from grade 4 to grade 14. It should be noted that there are no mathematical computation tests for grades 13 and 14. Figures 33 and 34 illustrate directions and sample items from the subtests

Directions

Each problem in this test is followed by four suggested answers.

Read each problem and then decide which one of the four suggested answers is correct.

Find the row of spaces on your answer sheet which has the same number as the problem. In this row, mark the space having the same letter as the answer you have chosen.

EXAMPLE

54
− 48

A   6
B   7
C   16
D 102

Answer

■ B̤ C̤ D̤

The correct answer to this problem is lettered **A,** so space **A** is marked.

STOP. **Wait for further directions.**

Figure 34. Directions and Sample Item from Sequential Tests of Educational Progress, Mathematics Computation. (From *Sequential Test of Educational Progress, Series II, Form 2A.* Copyright © 1969 by Educational Testing Service. All rights reserved. Reprinted by permission.)

Mathematics Basic Concepts and Mathematics Computation of the STEP. The Stanford Achievement Test battery provides different mathematical items under different subtests. Figure 35 presents samples from the Intermediate Level I Battery of this test. The Mathematics Concepts Test corresponds to the content of contemporary mathematics texts, which are a combination of "modern" and the "traditional" aspects of mathematics. This test stresses geometry, sets, the clock module, function, and the concept of an average. The Mathematics Computation Test attempts to measure mathematical reasonings that occur in everyday life. Problems cover graphs, advertising displays, buying and selling, and so on. Six of the problems are concerned primarily with the process rather than with a correct answer (Madden et al., 1973).

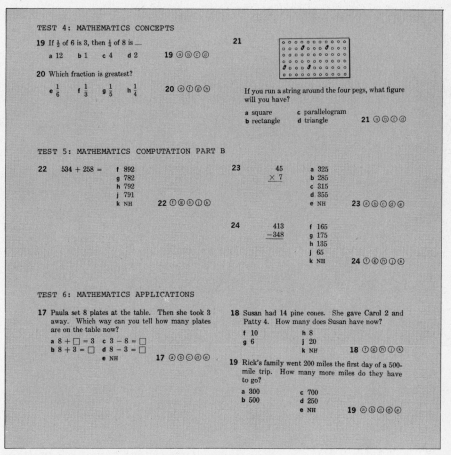

TEST 4: MATHEMATICS CONCEPTS

19 If $\frac{1}{2}$ of 6 is 3, then $\frac{1}{4}$ of 8 is —

   a 12   b 1   c 4   d 2   19 ⓐⓑⓒⓓ

20 Which fraction is greatest?

   e $\frac{1}{6}$ f $\frac{1}{3}$ g $\frac{1}{5}$ h $\frac{1}{4}$ 20 ⓔⓕⓖⓗ

21

If you run a string around the four pegs, what figure will you have?

   a square   c parallelogram
   b rectangle   d triangle   21 ⓐⓑⓒⓓ

TEST 5: MATHEMATICS COMPUTATION PART B

22 534 + 258 =

   f 892
   g 782
   h 792
   j 791
   k NH   22 ⓕⓖⓗⓙⓚ

23   45
    × 7

   a 325
   b 285
   c 315
   d 355
   e NH   23 ⓐⓑⓒⓓⓔ

24   413
   −348

   f 165
   g 175
   h 135
   j 65
   k NH   24 ⓕⓖⓗⓙⓚ

TEST 6: MATHEMATICS APPLICATIONS

17 Paula set 8 plates at the table. Then she took 3 away. Which way can you tell how many plates are on the table now?

   a 8 + □ = 3   c 3 − 8 = □
   b 8 + 3 = □   d 8 − 3 = □
          e NH   17 ⓐⓑⓒⓓⓔ

18 Susan had 14 pine cones. She gave Carol 2 and Patty 4. How many does Susan have now?

   f 10   h 8
   g 6   j 20
          k NH   18 ⓕⓖⓗⓙⓚ

19 Rick's family went 200 miles the first day of a 500-mile trip. How many more miles do they have to go?

   a 300   c 700
   b 500   d 250
          e NH   19 ⓐⓑⓒⓓⓔ

Figure 35. Sample Items from Stanford Achievement Test, Intermediate Level I Battery, Form A. (Reproduced from the *Stanford Achievement Test, Intermediate Level I, copyright* © 1973, by Harcourt Brace Jovanovich, Inc. Reproduced by special permission of the publisher.)

Language Skills. Another almost universal area in most achievement batteries is the section dealing with skills in using language. The detailed coverage of the batteries varies somewhat, but in general they include material on capitalization, spelling, punctuation, case, number, and tense. Some examples of items similar to those found in the batteries follow.

Usage

1. My little sister _____ walk yet.
   a. doesn't
   b. don't
   c. neither

2. Did Bob and Mary play _____ together?
   a. good
   b. well
   c. neither

Capitalization
Directions: Underline the words that should be capitalized:

on february 22, 1732 the father of our country, George washington was born. He was the first president of the united states. thomas jefferson was born in the same state as George washington. thomas jefferson was our third president. Do you know what states washington and jefferson were born in? john adams was our second president. George washington and thomas jefferson were born in virginia.

Punctuation
Directions: In the sentences below, certain spaces are underlined. Insert the correct punctuation marks only where you think they are needed. Remember, *not all* the underlined spaces need punctuation marks.

Mrs___ Robert Jones
2548 Lansdowne Ave___
Springfield___ Illinois
Dear Mrs___ Jones___
 I have recently seen ___ your collection of paintings in the museum at Chapel Hill___ North Carolina___ Do you plan to sell any in the near future___ If so___ please advise___ since I am interested in purchasing some of them___

Spelling
 Some tests provide the teacher with a list of standardized words which are to be read to the students. The student writes the words as the teacher pronounces them. Other tests use the multiple-choice format as illustrated below:
The table was *there* very own.   Right   Wrong
Mark the word that is misspelled
_____desk
_____chair
_____cup
_____cecret
Bill enjoyed his class in
 a. psology
 b. psychology
 c. pschology

Study Skills. Educators, especially since the 1920s, have stated that one of the major purposes of schooling is to provide individuals with the tools for learning on their own after formal schooling has been completed. Consequently, most schools devote considerable time to developing study skills and techniques. Most of the achievement batteries appraise such skills by presenting such tasks as reading graphs, charts, maps, and tables and finding information in reference sources. Some tests incorporate these tasks in content areas such as mathematics and social studies.

The SRA Achievement Series labels these areas as Use of Sources. The following are some sample questions from the SRA Achievement Series for grades 6 and 7.

Use of Sources [7]

Directions: This is a test of how well you have learned to use source materials. The test has two tables of contents, two dictionary entries, two indexes, a library catalog card, and a story for you to study, and questions about them for you to answer. Special directions within the test will identify the different sections and tell you how to complete them. Other questions are about single topics. Here is an example of one type of question:

TABLE OF CONTENTS

Chapter	Page
1. Types of Sailboats	3
2. Learning How to Sail	12
3. Dressing the Part	20
4. Safety Precautions	26

S1. Which chapter would probably tell you about different kinds of sailboats?

A. Chapter 1
B. Chapter 2
C. Chapter 3
D. Chapter 4

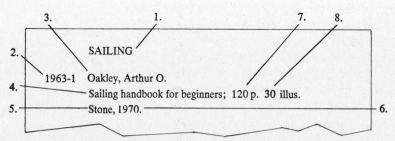

Special Directions: The card above is an example of a library catalog card. Several parts of the card have been numbered. Use this information to answer questions 21 through 24.

---

[7] From *SRA ACHIEVEMENT SERIES Form E/Green Level* by Robert A. Naslund, Louis P. Thorpe, and D. Welty Lefever. © 1971, Science Research Associates, Inc. Reprinted by permission of the publisher.

21. It would be best to look up a card like the one above when you

   A. know only the name of the author of the book
   B. know the title of the book
   C. need a book about sailing
   D. know that Stone is a good publisher

23. Another kind of card for this book should be found in the catalog drawer marked

   A. NEE to OAT
   B. HAN to INT
   C. BEG to CAT
   D. A to ART

Content Areas. The areas we have been concerned with so far are common to the educational core of early childhood and intermediate school and to some extent are relevant for high school and college. In the upper grades less emphasis is placed on core areas and more on subject or content fields. Students learn not only science, for example, but specific fields within science, such as biology and physics. We call these content areas.

In recent years content areas have played a lesser role in standardized testing. This is because many educators and testing people feel that items of information are less common to curricular objectives throughout the United States than are skills. It is, therefore, very difficult to construct content areas that are representative of most schools.

Social studies and science are the areas generally presented in achievement batteries when content areas are appraised. Social studies generally includes history, civics, and geography, and science usually contains subtests in physics, biology, and astronomy.

Survey Achievement Tests

The underlying theory of survey achievement tests is basically the same as for the subtests in general achievement batteries. A survey reading test, for example, includes most of the same kinds of items and materials found in the reading subtest of a general battery. The basic difference between a survey test and a general battery resides in the depth and extent of coverage. The survey test usually concentrates in much more detail on a single area than does the general battery. Further, general batteries do not usually include special subjects, and even when they do, it is at a superficial level as compared to the survey test. This is especially true in areas such as chemistry, biology, physics, algebra, and economics.

When to Use Survey Tests

Survey achievement tests should not be used except for some special reason. The general battery, especially at the early childhood and intermediate school level, is the usual instrument of choice. This is because the general battery and the various subtests are standardized on the same students and developed on the same underlying philosophy. Thus evaluation of student scores on different subtests is based on the same principles and normative population. When using survey tests in arithmetic and reading, for example, it is more difficult to determine the pupil's relative status in these areas because discrepancies in scores could be due to differing degrees of academic progress or to differences in educational principles and the student population used for test standardization.

In certain situations, however, the survey test is the best choice. There are four basic types of special situations that may call for the use of a survey test.

1. *To provide more definitive data on a student who does poorly on a specific subtest of a general achievement battery.* If, for example, a student does poorly on the arithmetic subtest of a general battery and the school wants more detailed information on strengths and weaknesses, they may obtain a more complete picture by administering a survey or special test for arithmetic.
2. *To measure special areas of the high school curriculum that are not covered or are only briefly presented in a general achievement battery.* For example, if a school wants an index of achievement in biology, they will have to use a survey test of biology rather than a general battery that appraises general achievement in science.
3. *To help students plan future educational courses within the school.* For example, does the student have enough mathematical background to take a second year of algebra? An algebra survey test in conjunction with other data could assist the student in making a sound decision.
4. *To help counsel students for college.* If, for example, a student is planning to enroll in a premedical course of study, it would be helpful to him to know his achievement in chemistry, biology, mathematics, and physics as compared to other students throughout the country. Survey tests in these areas could provide this kind of data.

Of course, the preceding situations are only guidelines and are subject to varying circumstances. Special situations not covered by our four basic types may arise. On the other hand, there will be situations that call for the use of a survey test in theory but do not in actual practice. Factors such as time, money, and the need for certain information must be weighed in each individual case.

A great many different kinds of survey tests are available. They range from tests in Greek and Hebrew to agriculture and driver education. We shall therefore focus our attention on reading tests, which should serve as a representative sample.

An Example: Survey Reading Tests

The survey reading test is one of the most widely used types of standardized tests. It is very similar to the reading subtests of general achievement batteries.

Typically covered are (1) ability to read paragraphs and answer questions concerning their content, (2) understanding of word and sentence meaning, and (3) speed of reading.

The basic difference between the survey reading test and a reading subtest of a general battery is, as mentioned earlier, that the survey test attempts to appraise reading skills in greater detail. The survey reading test is therefore generally longer and takes more time to administer.

The major reason for administering a survey reading test is to obtain data for planning group reading activities and individual remedial and developmental reading instruction. If a general battery is administered, a survey test is still needed to secure additional detailed information about pupils who reveal reading problems on the general battery.

Let us turn our attention to an actual survey reading test. The Iowa Silent Reading Tests is representative of many of the survey tests used in our schools. The tests attempt to survey the areas in which the pupil must have gained competency in order to read efficiently. These areas are vocabulary, reading comprehension, use of reference materials, skimming and scanning for actual data, and rate of reading with comprehension (Farr, 1973a,b). There are three levels of the Iowa Silent Reading Tests. They are grades 6–9 (which is also used for high school students reading below grade level) and grades 9–14 (with norms that are different according to post-high school plans). The latter is used for academically talented eleventh and twelfth graders as well as college students. Sample items from each of the four areas of Level I follow.

Test 1: Vocabulary [8]

Directions: For the questions . . . [below] . . . you are to choose the word that is closest in meaning to the first word.

(1) **build**
    (a) fix
    (b) make
    (c) stack
    (d) fill

(2) **arid**
    (e) tough
    (f) dry
    (g) dense
    (h) bitter

(3) **durable**
    (a) practical

[8] The following items are reproduced from *Iowa Silent Reading Tests*, copyright © 1972, by Harcourt Brace Jovanovich, Inc. Reproduced by special permission of the publisher.

(b) tidy
(c) lasting
(d) precious

Test 2: Reading Comprehension Part A

Directions: Read each passage. Then read each question about the passage. You are to find the best answer to each question.

A donkey and a rooster were in a barnyard together, when a hungry lion sneaked up on them. The lion was ready to attack the donkey when the rooster, realizing what was about to happen, began to crow loudly. The lion, frightened by the sound, ran away as fast as he could.

The donkey was very surprised that the lion was frightened so much by the mere crowing of a rooster. Suddenly feeling very brave, the donkey chased after the fleeing lion. He had not run very far, however, when the lion turned around, seized the foolish animal, and killed him without further ado.

(1) The lion became frightened because he —
    (a) was being chased by the donkey
    (b) found himself in a strange barnyard
    (c) heard a strange noise
    (d) was being attacked by the rooster

(2) The donkey was surprised that the —
    (e) rooster had crowed so loudly
    (f) lion had sneaked up on him
    (g) lion had run away
    (h) rooster had not flown away

(3) What did the donkey do when the lion first entered the barnyard?
    (a) He did nothing.
    (b) He warned the rooster.
    (c) He ran away.
    (d) He attacked the lion.

Test 3: Directed Reading Part A

Directions: Below you see part of a page from a dictionary that contains made-up words. Since you have never seen the words before, you will have to use this dictionary and the Pronunciation Key in order to answer questions 1 through 8.

---

involitude

in·vil·car·tal [in·vil′kär·təl] *n.* 1 A sign or symbol used to represent numbers. 2 The act of representing numbers by symbols or signs. 3 A list or note to assist memory. 4 *In medicine*, the chart of a patient's daily progress.

in·vil·dase [in·vil′dās] *adj.* Experiencing a severe or

PRONUNCIATION KEY: add, āce, câre, pälm; end, ēqual; it, īce; odd, ōpen, ôrder; to͝ok, po͞ol; up, bûrn; ə = a in *above*, e in *sicken*, i in *possible*, o in *melon*, u in *circus*; yo͞o= u in *fuse*; oil; pout; check; ring; thin; t͟his; zh as in *vision.*

SAMPLE
(S) Which definition of the word *invilcartal* best describes a shopping list?
  (a) 1   (c) 3
  (b) 2   (d) 4

---

(1) The "a" in *invildase* is pronounced like the "a" in the word—
  (a) above   (c) care
  (b) ace   (d) add

(2) What part of speech is *invilcartal*?
  (e) Verb   (g) Adjective
  (f) Noun   (h) Adverb

  Which one of the definitions given for *invilcartal* is best illustrated by the following sentence?
  "The patient's temperature was entered on her *invilcartal*."
  (a) 1   (c) 3
  (b) 2   (d) 4

Test 4: Reading Efficiency

Directions: As you read through each of the passages below, you are to mark the space to the left of the word that best fits the passage. Work as QUICKLY and as ACCURATELY as you can.

SAMPLE
(S) This test tells how quickly and accurately you
  ○ speak.   ● read.   ○ walk.

---

(1) From the moment he begins to breathe, the newborn baby can do an amazing number of things. He can see, hear, smell, and feel when touched. If he is turned around, he seems to realize his change in

  ○ position.   ○ motion.   ○ address.

(2) Taste is the only one of the five senses that is not immediately ready to function when the baby is

  ○ rocked.   ○ spanked.   ○ born.

(3) When only two hours old, a baby's eyes will follow a moving light; and, if someone touches his left cheek, he will usually turn his head in that same

○ direction.   ○ room.   ○ manner.

Standard scores are translated into percentiles and stanines on the four tests plus a Reading Power score, which is obtained by combining Vocabulary and Reading Comprehension tests.

Different reading tests stress different facets of reading skills and are represented in various tests in varying proportions. The test user should examine the actual test items in order to determine what skills the test is really measuring—not only with reading tests but with all achievement tests or batteries. Only the test consumer, after critically examining the test items, can gauge the validity of the achievement test for his own objectives. The same general principles that guide the use of reading survey tests are also generally relevant for other types of survey tests.

The survey test, then, is a measure of the skills and knowledge that comprise a given subject. Certain areas are represented within each test. Emphasis is sometimes directed in slightly different ways within each test. The test should be chosen that best serves the particular purposes and needs of the student and school.

Diagnostic Achievement Tests

The diagnostic achievement test attempts to measure in detail academic strengths and weaknesses in a specific area, in contrast to the survey test, which attempts to measure overall progress. Many teachers will find diagnostic achievement tests to be familiar friends, because a great deal of a teacher's time is spent in diagnosing the work habits and special academic problems of her students. The diagnostic achievement test attempts to do the same thing.

The diagnostic test indicates specific aspects of a child's educational development. For example, a survey reading test shows that Priscilla, who is in sixth grade, has an overall reading level equal to that of children beginning the third grade. Diagnostic reading tests reveal that Priscilla tends to make reversal errors in reading, for example, substituting *was* for *saw*. Her word recognition is fairly good. Her ability to recognize short vowels and to apply known consonant blends is very poor. These findings, along with other classroom and standardized test data, help in planning concrete educational treatment.

The diagnostic achievement test is an extension of what most teachers attempt to do in their everyday practice. The diagnostic test presents exercises and problems that provide opportunities for students to reveal skills and work habits. It provides the teacher with a systematic technique for evaluating these skills and habits. We shall examine some of the unique features of the reading and arithmetic devices.

READING

There are several types of diagnostic reading tests. Some have specialized subtests yielding scores for different aspects of total reading ability. These are similar to the survey subtests such as those for rate and comprehension, and location of information. Another approach is the diagnostic oral reading test. Gray's Oral Reading Paragraphs is a good example of this technique. This test consists of a standard set of twelve short paragraphs, ranging in difficulty from first to eighth grade. The pupil is given a copy of the standardized paragraphs and directed to read them orally when the examiner gives the signal. A record is kept of the time required to read each paragraph and the errors made. If a word is wholly or partially mispronounced, the examiner notes this. Omitted words, substitutions, and repetitions are recorded. The student is allowed to continue reading until he makes seven errors in each of two paragraphs.

The recording of a student's oral reading is valuable because it enables the teacher to understand the actual process of the child's reading. It helps the teacher pinpoint specific trouble areas.

Another type of test is Doren's Diagnostic Reading Test (1973) which was mentioned earlier in this chapter. This test is administered in a clinical manner rather than in the strict standardized approach. The directions are loose and the teacher proceeds to some extent on her perceptions of the children's receptivity to the tasks. For example, the directions for time state:

> Allow ample time for everyone to finish each part of the test. A *stop* sign is placed at the end of each part. It is recommended that the examiner emphasize that no one should go beyond the *stop* sign until new instructions are given. If a large group is being tested, and one or two individuals are causing delay, proceed with the testing. Let the slower ones complete later the parts which they did not finish. There should be no time limit restrictions on anyone. *(p. 9)*

There are twelve subtests, each measuring a different reading skill. See pp. 251–252 for a list of the different skills measured. Doren (1973), in her discussion of diagnostic testing, presents the basic approach to diagnostic testing.

> In contrast to an achievement test, a diagnostic test is not administered with a norm as its attainment goal. Individuals in need of diagnosis have been classified by previous comparison with a norm, or by teacher observation, as in need of more thorough examination. In an achievement test, the number of correct responses is the measure of the degree of success. In a diagnostic test, it is the mistakes which an individual makes that indicate his areas of need. An exact identification of the type of errors will direct the examiner to specific remedial needs. Total score has overall implications of the degree of need, but serves little diagnostic purpose. *(p. 5)*

ARITHMETIC

A good example of the diagnostic test in arithmetic skills is the Buswell-John Diagnostic Test for Fundamental Processes in Arithmetic. The student is presented with a series of problems in addition, subtraction, multiplication, and division. The items are to be orally worked out by the student. The examiner listens while the student verbalizes what he is doing and why he is doing it. The examiner records specific types of errors on a diagnostic chart provided by the test publishers. Figure 36 presents one page of the record chart.

The manual cites various work habits and provides samples of each. Two examples similar to those listed are

Neglecting to Carry

$$\begin{array}{r} \text{Example:} \quad 233 \\ 695 \\ \hline 828 \end{array}$$

Borrowing Error

$$\begin{array}{r} \text{Example:} \quad 648 \\ 74 \\ \hline 674 \end{array}$$

The manual points out that the teacher should not be satisfied with simply making a diagnosis and checking the items. She should also study the pupil's work habits, that is, how he attacks the problem and what processes he uses, and gear her teaching accordingly. This approach is basic to the use of any diagnostic test. Diagnostic tests are given only to children who need special attention because of scholastic difficulties. They are clinical tools and should only be used in that manner. That is, their statistical validation is open to a great deal of error and cannot be thought of as having the same degree of validity or reliability that other instruments, such as the survey and general achievement battery tests, have. Thus the clinical or subjective approach is indicated in using these tests as aids in learning rather than as definitive assessments of academic progress.

Criterion-Referenced Achievement Tests

The preceding discussion has focused on achievement tests that are *norm-referenced*. Norm-referencing is one of the basic ingredients of standardized tests. The student of measurement should know that the basic question of the norm-referenced test is, How do Mary and Gene or their third and fourth grades compare with others? The answers to this kind of question are helpful in establishing levels of performances in class, school, school district, state, and country.

Teacher's Diagnosis
for Pupil ____________

DIAGNOSTIC CHART
FOR
INDIVIDUAL DIFFICULTIES
FUNDAMENTAL PROCESSES IN ARITHMETIC
Prepared by G. T. Buswell and Lenore John

Published by the
Public School Publishing Co.
Bloomington, Illinois

Name__________ School__________ __________ Grade______ Age______ IQ______

Date of Diagnosis: __________ Add.______; Subt.______; Mult.______; Div.______

Teacher's preliminary diagnosis__________

ADDITION: (Place a check before each habit observed in the pupil's work)

—— a1 Errors in combinations
—— a2 Counting
—— a3 Added carried number last
—— a4 Forgot to add carried number
—— a5 Repeated work after partly done
—— a6 Added carried number irregularly
—— a7 Wrote number to be carried
—— a8 Irregular procedure in column
—— a9 Carried wrong number
——a10 Grouped two or more numbers
——a11 Splits numbers into parts
——a12 Used wrong fundamental operation
——a13 Lost place in column
——a14 Depended on visualization
——a15 Disregarded column position
——a16 Omitted one or more digits
——a17 Errors in reading numbers
——a18 Dropped back one or more tens
——a19 Derived unknown combination from familiar one
——a20 Disregarded one column
——a21 Error in writing answer
——a22 Skipped one or more decades
——a23 Carrying when there was nothing to carry
——a24 Used scratch paper
——a25 Added in pairs, giving last sum as answer
——a26 Added same digit in two columns
——a27 Wrote carried number in answer
——a28 Added same number twice

Habits not listed above__________

(Write observation notes on pupil's work in space opposite examples)

(1) 5 + 2; 6 + 3		(5) 6 + 2 = ; 3 + 4 =	
(2) 2 + 9; 8 + 4		(6) 52 + 13; 40 + 39	
(3) 12 + 2; 13 + 5		(7) 78 + 71; 46 + 92	
(4) 19 + 2; 17 + 9		(8) 3 + 5 + 8 + 2; 8 + 7 + 9 + 7	

Figure 36. Example of Record Sheet used in the Buswell-John Diagnostic Test for Fundamental Processes in Arithmetic. (From the *Buswell-John Diagnostic Test for Fundamental Processes in Arithmetic* by G. T. Buswell and Lenore John. Reprinted by permission of the publisher, Test Division of the Bobbs-Merrill Co., Inc., of Indianapolis, Indiana.)

The *criterion-referenced* test is basically helpful in describing the status of pupils with respect to explicit and defined instructional objectives of a school system. It provides data concerning the level of performance of students on items assessing specific educational objectives and on groups of items evaluating closely related objectives.

Tuckman (1975) summarizes the differences quite well when he states, "Thus, norm-referencing gives *summative* results, that is, it tells you where the individual or group is, while criterion-referencing gives you *formative* results, that is, it tells you in what areas to prescribe instruction in order to facilitate the achievement of proficiency. Criterion-referenced tests help the teacher to monitor student progress, diagnose strengths and weaknesses, and prescribe instruction" (pp. 391–92).

STANFORD TEST OF ACADEMIC SKILLS (TASK)

INDEX OF INSTRUCTIONAL OBJECTIVES

LEVEL I   ENGLISH   FORM A

Item No.	Instructional Objective	p Value Beg. Gr.8	Beg. Gr.9	Beg. Gr.10
	First Item Grouping: Learning Skills			
	ITEM FORMAT: Each item consists of a stem and four options in print.			
	The student demonstrates knowledge of			
	A. dictionary usage by identifying:			
2	information contained in a dictionary.	87	87	89
3	a word that contains a given vowel sound.	81	80	80
5	a word that contains a given vowel sound.	84	83	84
7	a symbol for a given vowel sound.	81	82	84
8	a word that contains a given vowel sound.	79	78	78
9	a word formed by use of a suffix.	55	59	60
13	a word formed by use of a prefix.	60	67	71
15	the change in principal stress in two forms of a word.	47	51	54
	B. reference sources by identifying:			
6	a source for vocabulary development.	51	56	61
14	a source for articles in periodicals.	35	42	51
	C. the use and structure of English by identifying:			
1	an appropriate place for slang expressions.	80	81	85
4	the action words in a sentence.	83	83	84

Figure 37. A sample of English instructional objectives of the Stanford Test of Academic Skills. (Reproduced from the *Stanford Test of Academic Skills (TASK) Index of Instructional Objectives, Level I,* copyright © 1973 by Harcourt Brace Jovanovich, Inc. Reproduced by special permission of the publisher.)

STANFORD TEST OF ACADEMIC SKILLS (TASK)

INDEX OF INSTRUCTIONAL OBJECTIVES

LEVEL I   MATHEMATICS   FORM A

ITEM FORMAT: Each item consists of a stem and five options in print; items 18, 19, 20, 42, and 42 contain a graph or diagram.

Item No.	Instructional Objective	*p* Value		
		Beg. Gr.8	Beg. Gr.9	Beg. Gr.10
	First Item Grouping: Numbers, Symbols, and Sets			
	The student:			
3	renames a standard numeral in expanded notation.	75	77	81
9	identifies a standard numeral from its word form.	84	87	88
13	identifies the place value represented by a digit.	85	87	87
22	identifies the definition of a prime number.	67	72	75
29	identifies a relationship between two sets.	46	47	54
32	determines the value of a linear expression with two unknowns, given the value of each.	38	63	71
47	chooses the correct interpretation of a Venn diagram.	60	63	70
	Second Item Grouping: Number Properties and Operations			
	A. Whole numbers			
	The student:			
1	adds a broken column of three numbers.	89	91	90
2	subtracts a three-digit number from a four-digit number, with renaming.	90	91	92

Figure 38. A sample of mathematics instructional objectives of the Stanford Test of Academic Skills. (From the *Stanford Test of Academic Skills (TASK) Index of Instructional Objectives, Level I,* copyright © 1973 by Harcourt Brace Jovanovich, Inc. Reproduced by special permission of the publisher.)

A SAMPLE OF A
CRITERION-REFERENCED TEST

The Stanford Test of Academic Skills (TASK) provides test consumers with a description of the instructional objective measured by each item in the test.

Figure 37 presents some instructional objectives for English, and Figure 38 presents some of those for mathematics. The "*p* value" headings refer to the item difficulty and to what per cent of the same reference group answered the item correctly during the fall standardizations. For example, 87 per cent of the eighth graders in the fall standardization answered the English item 2 in Figure 37 correctly. Thus the p value at the beginning of eighth grade would be 87.

The Stanford Achievement Test serves the dual purpose of a norm- and criterion-referenced test. Every item in the Stanford was designed to measure a specific instructional objective which is stated in behavioral terms. Thus the Stanford reports norm-referenced and criterion-referenced scores.

Figure 39 is a form that is used for reporting criterion-referenced results on the Stanford. This form reports individual performance on each objective by pupil-reference number. It also reports class and school system results and the number of students answering the item correctly in the national sample (p value). This record helps the teacher in the identification of individual and classroom performance on the specific objectives and assessment of these findings in terms of the local school, school system, and nation.

Before we leave criterion-referenced achievement tests, the student of measurement should realize that the criterion-referenced interpretation of test results is usually more helpful to teachers than the normative interpretation because of the specific prescriptive data versus a relative slot compared to some group. Remember this form of achievement test is beneficial only if you choose a test in which the skills and contents are specifically the kind you need.

Uses of Achievement Tests in the School

Our discussion in this section will center on the primary uses of achievement tests in the school setting. It should be noted that only the major uses will be discussed in practical school terms.

Understanding the Student

To guide a youngster properly in his educational planning, an understanding of his level of achievement is extremely important. The school must know his educational achievement to plan for future academic goals, possible remedial assistance, and eventually his or her vocation. In order to present the important role of achievement testing in understanding the individual pupil, let us listen in to an actual counseling situation. Mr. Smith, the junior high school counselor, is talking to Bob Fein, an eighth-grade student who is concerned about his future high school program.

Mr. Smith: Well, Bob, how can I help you today?
Bob: I'm not sure what courses I should take in high school, you know, whether I should start with algebra or not and so forth.

STANFORD Achievement Test or TEST OF ACADEMIC SKILLS — ITEM ANALYSIS

Miss Smythe
Hootville Elem
Hootville Sch Dist Grade 3

Level Primary 3 Form A Date of Testing 04/15/74
National p Values: Grade 3.8

Test: Math Concepts No. of Items 32 Item Format: All dictated
Page 1 of 2 for this Class report

PUPIL REFERENCE NUMBER		
01 Alexis T J	05 Gustovson P H	
02 Bastian K B	06 Halverson B I	
03 Bowles C C	07 Merden C N	
04 Browning E C	08 Quarles T S	

ITEM GROUPING: Instructional Objective	ITEM NO	EXP % COR	RIGHTS DATA CLASS Number	%	SCHOOL %	SYSTEM %	NAT'L p VALUE	OMITS DATA CLASS Number	%	SCHOOL %	SYSTEM %	PUPIL REFERENCE NUMBER 12345678 90123 4
NUMBER: Pupil:												
chooses number which belongs in a given number series	5		12	40*	49	51*	59	0	0	3	5	1+++*33++
ditto	7		5	17*	54*	52*	75	0	0	2	4	2*3333*1
identifies number at particular point on number line	18		10	33	38	35	40	0	0	5	6	2*1*11*1
represents whole number in terms of specified fraction	20		14	47*	59*	65	69	0	0	4	4	4*++*3+*1
identifies set consisting only of even numbers	25		18	60	63	58	56	0	0	3	5	134++++++
indicates position of a number relative to 3 given numbers	27		8	27	37	35	37	1	3	6	8	3+44+4+1
determines point at which given number is located on number line	31		20	67□	53	68□	52	2	6	10	12	3+4!++++1
adds in finite system of clock module	32		5	17*	62□	47□	38	20	67	6	8	300000+1
ITEM GROUP MEAN P-VALUES				39	52	51	53					
NOTATION: Pupil:												
selects numeral for which digit in thousands place has greatest value	1		24	80	83	87	84	0	0	0	0	2*1*3+*1

Figure 39. Item Analysis Report for Stanford Test of Academic Skills. (Reproduced from *Manual Part IV Administrator's Guide for Interpreting Stanford Achievement Test*, copyright © 1973 by Harcourt Brace Jovanovich, Inc. Reproduced by special permission of the publisher.)

Mr. Smith: Well, how do you feel about it?

Bob: I don't know. My problem is this: you told me that I was above average on my aptitude tests in arithmetic and science, but yesterday you said that my achievement tests were not as good. Now, does that mean that I should not take algebra and science my first year in high school?

Mr. Smith: How have you done in your class work?

Bob: Oh, just fair.

Mr. Smith: I see. Just fair?

Bob: What I mean by "just fair" is a little under C.

Mr. Smith: Well, let's examine your whole record, both your test scores and school grades. It seems that you have above-average ability in most areas. However, your class work is below average, and the achievement tests show that you are a little below grade level in reading, arithmetic, and science. Thus it looks like you have the ability to learn, but you haven't been applying yourself.

Bob: Are you saying, Mr. Smith, that I haven't learned as much as I should have by this time?

Mr. Smith: Yes, in a sense I am saying that. What do you think?

Bob: I . . . I don't know. My parents say that I don't study enough. Could this be the reason?

Mr. Smith: It may well be. On the other hand, there could be other reasons.

Bob: I guess so, but what should I do as far as my high school program goes?

Mr. Smith: The final decision, of course, rests with you. I can point out some general guidelines that may be of help. First, there is no doubt that you have the ability to do average or above-average work in school. Second, your class record and achievement scores indicate that you are below your grade level in some important areas of education. This means that even though you have the ability to learn algebra and science, your lack of progress in these areas may prevent you from doing well in these fields in high school. I would recommend, therefore, that you put off algebra and biology until the tenth grade and concentrate on making up your learning deficiencies by taking general math and general science your first year.

Bob: My parents won't like that, especially since all my friends are starting with algebra and biology. My parents and friends will think I'm stupid, won't they?

Mr. Smith: The important thing, Bob, is that you know that you are not stupid. Besides, your future education will benefit by a firm grounding in the essentials. If you take algebra and biology and fail, how will you feel then?

Bob: Not very good.

Mr. Smith: Of course not. You see, Bob, ability and achievement are, many times, quite different. I am sure you know of guys who could make outstanding baseball players, but never perform well because they haven't learned the basic skills in playing the game. If you take a guy who might be another Babe Ruth and put him in the major leagues before he is ready he may never realize his potential. On the other hand, if you put him in the minor leagues and give him the experience to learn, he may become another Babe Ruth. In the same way, if you have the ability to do well in algebra and biology but lack the learned skills, you need some experience in the minor leagues—that is, general math and general science—before you come up to the big leagues. Then you may become a major league performer. Do you understand what I mean?

Bob: I think I do. In other words, you are saying that by trying a subject that I am not ready for, I may fail it.

Mr. Smith: Yes, not only is there a good chance of your failing, but more important, your failing or having extreme difficulty in passing may close that door of learning to you forever. That's one of the reasons we give achievement tests. We want to know how ready you are to learn new subjects based on your past learning.

Bob: Thank you, Mr. Smith, I will tell my parents what you said.

The case of Bob Fein is, of course, only one example of the many uses of achievement tests in helping to understand and guide students. This example reveals the practical importance of the use of achievement test results along with other data in educational guidance.

Identification of Children for Intensive Study

Achievement tests help spotlight those youngsters who need special attention. It is true, of course, that every child should be studied as an individual, and most of our schools attempt to do this. However, every school system has those pupils who need special assistance more than their peers. They are often difficult to distinguish from the others because they do not seek special help, nor do their teachers or parents often know of their problems.

One way of finding out who these children are is to administer an achievement battery.

The child who needs intensive study may show great differences in his performance on different subtests, or he may perform far below his grade or age level. Sometimes his performance, as in the case of Bob Fein, is far below his capabilities as shown by a group scholastic aptitude test. The school counselor or teacher, in studying a student's test performance, thinks of the following questions:

1. Is the student's achievement related to his aptitude? That is, is the child falling behind the level we expect of him?
2. Does he have a reading problem? If so, do we have an indication of the child's academic aptitude based on a nonreading test?
3. Does he have a problem in some specific school subject? If the answer is yes, further study and testing may be needed.

In order to convey the practical usage of the achievement test, let us look at an actual case encountered by one of the authors in the public schools. A fifteen-year-old boy had marked differences in his various test scores and a poor school record. The boy had excellent scores in some of his aptitude tests, such as mechanical reasoning, abstract reasoning, and space relations. His other aptitude scores were extremely low. His group intelligence test showed an IQ at the level of mental retardation. His achievement tests showed great differences, such as a very low score in social studies, an extremely high score in mathematics, an average score in English, and an extremely high score in science.

An individual intelligence test and a reading achievement test were needed. The results of these tests showed that the boy was in the superior range in intellectual ability and was equal to first-year college students in reading achievement. After these tests were administered, the boy was referred to a school social worker for further study. During the counseling sessions with the social worker, certain facts of the boy's life were obtained. It developed that this boy's parents, who were both physicians, had been killed in an automobile accident when the boy was twelve years of age, and since that time he had been living with his uncle.

When confronted with the results of his test performances the boy admitted he had not tried to do his best on certain tests because "I didn't feel they meant anything anyway."

Circumstances outside of the boy's abilities were affecting his performance both in the classroom and on standardized tests. One had to ask, "Why does he feel certain courses are not important?" "Is there a relationship between the auto accident and the loss of his parents to his scattered performances?" These and other questions had to be answered before any progress could be made in counseling the boy. Therefore, it was decided to administer some personality tests. (See Chapter 7 for explanation of projective and personality tests.)

The test results revealed a boy who was suffering from a "burnt child reaction." That is, the trauma of his parents' deaths had acted on him as though someone had pushed him over a cliff. The boy had probably always had personality problems and had always been near the edge of the cliff. The push or shove was the auto accident and the ensuing deaths. He now felt that his goal in life was to replace his parents by becoming a physician himself. This, of course, was understandable. However, the child lost sight of reality in thinking that he could become a doctor without passing courses not directly related to the sciences. This is why he did not work in social studies and did not attempt to do well on achievement tests outside the scientific areas.

Through the use of tests and interviews, a clearer picture was obtained of this boy's problems, which were interfering with his ability to learn and perform in school. In counseling sessions he was helped to think more realistically about his goals and the means of obtaining them. This is an example of a boy whose vocational goals were in line with his aptitudes but who was unable to harness his abilities in all school subjects because of emotional problems.

Of course, the above case is rather rare in the schools, for most children do not experience the shock of losing both parents. However, it is not rare for a child to be placed in a grade or level below his abilities because of poor achievement. Quite often this inability to use his potential is due to emotional problems. A careful comparison of the child's achievement test scores with his scores on aptitude and intelligence tests can help to identify those few youngsters who need intensive study and help.

Teacher Aids in Program Planning

At the beginning of each school year the classroom teacher is usually given a general outline of subject material to be covered, along with educational objectives. Decisions must be made concerning various subject fields and how much time should be given to a review of the previous year's work. In addition, the teacher is faced with the problem of planning independent work for those children capable of going beyond the regular classroom course of study. Most teachers want to form groupings within the class so that students of similar abilities and skills can work together at a common level. For example, the first-grade teacher may want eventually to group her children in reading in three or four sections. Section 1 might be the top group, section 2 might be the average, and section 3 might include students below average in reading. Section 4, if needed, might consist of those children who are not yet ready to learn to read.

In order to carry out these educational plans and goals, the teacher needs to know her students' abilities, skills, and past learning achievements as soon as possible. One way to do this is to administer achievement tests (survey, diagnostic, or battery). The results of the tests will give the teacher an indication of the relative achievement level of her group of children—that is, whether the group is superior, average, or below average in the basic skills she will attempt to develop. The scores will provide clues to the group's strengths and weaknesses. The teacher can then adapt her plans to the group as a whole and to the individuals within the group.

Of course, tests themselves are only one indication or clue for the teacher. The good teacher, in addition to using the results of tests, obtains certain impressions of her students by contact with them. *The deepest understanding of an individual child comes only through working with that child.* Test scores, however, enable the teacher to have an objective frame of reference in addition to a subjective estimation of the group and the individual child.

Planning and Evaluating Schoolwide Programs

In order to provide the best possible education, a school must always examine and reexamine its curriculum and system of instruction. The achievement battery is used as an aid in the evaluation of the curriculum. The results of the tests provide some indication of how well a school or school system is doing in relationship to other schools. For example, Roosevelt Junior High School wanted to find out how its students' test scores compared with the scores of other children throughout the country. Roosevelt therefore averaged its children's test scores and compared them to the national averages provided by the test publisher. In science and social studies Roosevelt's average student was one grade level below the national standard or average. In mathematics and English its students were above the national average. Roosevelt's teachers were thus enabled to find the weak spots in their programs of instruction.

There are, of course, certain dangers in using this method for evaluating a school's course of study. First, this type of evaluation does not give a complete picture. The achievement test can only evaluate the knowledge and skills it covers. Usually these skills are only a small part of the total objectives of our modern school. A danger that is always present in this kind of evaluation is the relative simplicity of giving objective tests and then stating whether or not the curriculum is up to standard. Good school systems use other methods of evaluation in addition to test results, which enables them to gain deeper insights into the whole school program.

One must also remember the problem of local goals and objectives before critically evaluating a school's instructional program. It would be unfair to say that a particular school is not adequate because the students are below the national average. A particular school may place greater emphasis upon certain subjects and delay others because of its particular situation and educational philosophy. For example, one school may stress meanings and understandings of subject matter rather than factual knowledge. If such a school uses an achievement battery that emphasizes factual content, its students may do poorly; yet this does not mean that the school is necessarily doing a poor educational job. The difficulty with national achievement tests is the problem of making the questions appropriate to most schools in the country. Because the curricula of our schools are not controlled by a single administration, this is a difficult task. Therefore, each school must use the battery in the light of its own particular goals and instructional program.

One must also take into account the geographical location of a school or school system. Schools and communities differ in their social and economic levels. Related to these differences are the ranges of abilities of students in the public schools. These factors must be taken into account when achievement is considered. These differences may be lessened by developing local norms for the school or school system. For example, students who attend schools in the north suburban areas of Chicago generally come from privileged homes. That is, they come from affluent families, who have a fairly high cultural level and who are able to provide their children with experiences that many American families cannot afford, such as visiting the many museums in Chicago, attending plays for children, and attending the children's concerts of the Chicago Symphony Orchestra. In this kind of area the average student does better than the average student in other areas of the country. If the local schools in this area applied only national averages, they would not have a complete picture of their instructional programs. But by establishing local averages they can get a picture of how well the child is doing when compared with his fellow students, who share similar backgrounds and experiences. For the same reasons, a disadvantaged area in

Chicago or elsewhere in the country may want local averages as well as national averages to obtain a more complete picture. By using local averages, the disadvantaged area can tell the relative progress of its students, who start out with so much less than the average national student in skills, motivations, and experiences.

Grouping

To group or not to group, is that the question? How do you feel about this question that has concerned educators for close to sixty years? The bandwagon for and against grouping has changed directions many times in those years. Since Sputnik (about 1957), the educational bandwagon has been directed toward grouping children according to abilities and achievement. The last few years, however, have seen some attempts to redirect the wagon in the other direction. Our task here is not to affirm or negate educational grouping, but to present the uses of standardized achievement tests in grouping if you as educators decide on that course of action.[9]

Most grouping of children into separate tracks or classes occurs during junior and senior high school. The achievement test is one of several measurement instruments used in this process. One needs, first, a scholastic aptitude test to obtain an overall picture of school ability, second, a reading test and, third, a record of classroom progress.

The use of these various techniques presupposes, of course, that children are not grouped according to IQ, "good grades," or achievement test scores, but according to specific and particular situations based on the student's whole scholastic potential and achievement. A high IQ, for example, does not mean a student should be placed in an advanced mathematics course. His achievement in mathematics must match his potential in order for him to succeed in advanced mathematics.

Achievement tests help in grouping by presenting a standardized picture of a student's academic progress. They eliminate teacher bias in academic evaluation. They do not, however, provide the sole basis for grouping decisions.

Research

The standardized achievement test is a valuable aid in educational research. For example, Hyde Senior High School wants to know if team teaching is more successful than the standard "one teacher, one class" approach. Two groups of eleventh-grade United States history students are tested with a history achievement test at the beginning of the year. One group continues

[9] The authors are personally very much for grouping because we see it as an instructional technique in helping children learn. Even when grouping is practiced, there is still a range of abilities and achievement in the classroom. It does, however, narrow the range so that the teacher can gear instruction to most of the children.

along the classical pattern, while the other is exposed to team teaching. At the end of the term a parallel form of the same test is given. A comparison between the group scores is then made. If the team teaching group obtains higher achievement scores, one might say that further explorations in this instructional method are indicated. On the other hand, if the one teacher, one class approach group scored as high or higher, one might have some reservations about continuing team teaching.[10]

The achievement test may also be used to evaluate teachers. Yes, some schools do use achievement batteries to evaluate their teachers. The teacher is judged by the performance of his or her class on the achievement tests. How do you feel about this use of achievement tests? What do you think are some possible problems?

Obviously, this procedure has many shortcomings because the achievement of a class is related not only to the teacher's ability but also to the group's educational history. It does not seem fair to hold a teacher solely responsible for his or her group's present achievement level. As has been stated, achievement is based in part upon aptitude as well as experiences not gained in school. An achievement test can measure the success of only a small portion of the goals of schools today.

On the other hand, if we evaluate teachers collectively or in groups rather than as individuals, the achievement test may serve a sound function, that is, if the tests are used in research investigations of teacher effectiveness rather than as definitive guides for the continued employment of a teacher. The school that uses the achievement test for teacher evaluation does not truly understand the limitations of this form of testing and evaluation. If the school administration had insight into these limitations, it would not run the risk of unhappy teachers teaching "for the tests" rather than for the students.

Remember, the achievement survey, battery, and diagnostic tests are only instruments to be used in assessing the whole child. They have no inherent power to provide complete answers by themselves, but when used with other evaluative instruments and the school record they provide valuable insights into the academic achievement of students. In the same way, we can use them to gain insights into the school's national standing and as an evaluative tool in curriculum assessment as long as we remember they are only one part of the whole academic picture. Let us end our discussion of achievement instruments with the following summary statement concerning achievement tests, from Educational Testing Service, one of the nation's largest test publishers.

[10] It should be noted, of course, that other variables in this kind of investigation must be considered. The two groups should be matched not only in terms of how much knowledge they have of United States history before instruction begins but also on the basis of intelligence, school grades, and historical interests. In addition, the experimental design would have to consider teacher differences in terms of effectiveness and skills. Also allowances for the "Hawthorne effect" (that is, the special attention one group receives) would have to be made. Thus it is plain that this example is intended only as an illustration of a use of the achievement test, not as a good example of sound experimental design.

There is no single achievement test or test battery that will be "best" for all pupil populations, all curriculum objectives, all purposes, and all uses. Even tests universally recognized as "good" are not equally "good" for different school settings, situations, and circumstances.

The recommended procedure for achievement test selection then consists of three phases:

1. study of our own school characteristics and testing needs;
2. analysis of characteristics and capabilities of available tests;
3. matching (a) the population of norm groups, or reliability samples, and of validity studies for each test to our own pupil population, (b) the content of each test to our own curriculum content and objectives, (c) the validity evidence, reliability data, scoring system, and interpretive material for each test to our own testing purposes and prospective uses of test scores. (Katz, 1973, p. 12)

Personality, Attitude, and Interest Inventories

chapter 10

The last two chapters have focused on academic potential and performance. These are the basic ingredients of school life. They are not, however, the only elements essential to success in school or life. Children (and adults) must also be able to harness their talents in fields that satisfy their needs. The problem of vocational choice is of paramount importance to the individual student and to the society that needs to utilize the resources of its people. This is where interest inventories may be of assistance.

In addition to helping children become aware of their interests, the school is also concerned with the mental health of its pupils. A child with an emotional problem is sometimes unable to use his abilities and becomes a school failure or dropout. The school is, therefore, vitally concerned in helping its boys and girls find their interest areas and spotting those children who need psychological guidance. This chapter will be devoted to illustrating the nature, use, and reasons for personality, attitude, and interest tests in the school.

Personality Inventories

The word *personality* has different meanings to different people. To some it is another word for *popularity*; the person either has it or lacks it. To many psychologists personality is the total sum of the characteristics and behavior of a person; this includes everything from intelligence to social relations. To other psychologists personality comprises the distinguishing characteristics of a person. Obviously, *personality* is a broad and general term that lay and professional people define differently. It is impossible to define it in exact terms, for the definition is dependent upon the concepts of the individual explaining its meaning.

Educators generally view personality in terms of adjustment. They are concerned with the functioning of the child in the classroom. Is the child well adjusted enough to learn, or does he have problems that interfere with the learning process? When educators need to know the answer to this and other questions of adjustment, personality inventories may be administered in the schools.

Personality inventories are sometimes referred to as personality tests. They are not tests, but self-reports. There are no right or wrong answers to specific items. The student is asked to respond to statements and questions concerning his own feelings, emotions, family and school situation, and personal needs. The questions asked are many times specific: "Do you often feel unhappy?" "Can you make friends easily?" "Do you suffer from headaches?"

Personality inventories are objective self-reports, as contrasted with projective techniques, which are generally administered individually and require subjective interpretation of objective stimuli by the individual. Projective tests are indefinite and require the person to respond in his own unique manner (see Chapter 7). The personality inventory, on the other hand, is structured and is usually presented in an objective format, similar to tests of aptitude and achievement.

There are many personality inventories in use today (also referred to by some as temperament or adjustment inventories). We will briefly review some of these, but our attention will be focused on the most widely used and respected personality inventory, the Minnesota Multiphasic Personality Inventory (MMPI).

Thorndike Dimensions of Temperament

The Thorndike Dimensions of Temperament (TDOT) is an inventory that requests the student to describe himself with respect to ten dimensions of temperament. Table 24 presents these dimensions and a brief description of each. Note that this inventory does not attempt to probe for deep psychopathology; its aim is to describe a person.

The TDOT is appropriate for juniors and seniors in high school, college students, and adults of equal educational levels. The items are printed in a reusable booklet and the responses, which are marked on a separate answer sheet, may be machine- or hand-scored.

The test booklet presents twenty sets (labeled from A to T), each of which contains ten statements. The student is directed to read quickly through the statements and then go back and choose the three that are "most like you." He signifies his response by blackening the answer space marked L (like) beside the number of the item. He is then requested to go back and blacken the answer space marked D (different) beside the three statements that are

SAMPLE SET	SAMPLE OF ANSWER SHEET
1. The program you watch most regularly on television is a news broadcast.	
2. You are likely to keep people waiting for you.	
3. Nothing seems to work out quite right for you.	
4. You often seem to be given the "dirty" job to do.	
5. You would rather read a history book than a novel.	
6. You are usually "on the go."	
7. You tend to "blow up" in an emergency.	
8. You look forward to the years ahead.	
9. You usually plan things well in advance.	
10. You generally find other people enjoyable.	

Figure 40. Sample set of items from Thorndike Dimensions of Temperament. (Reproduced by permission. Copyright © 1963, The Psychological Corporation, New York, N.Y. All rights reserved.)

"most different from you." Figure 40 illustrates the types of items that are presented. Thorndike (1966), in describing his test, states, "Evidence tends to support the contention that the *TDOT* portrays the individual both as he sees himself and as others see him. Though it does not pretend to delve into deep layers of inner personality dynamics, the inventory appears to be quite successful in providing a differentiated picture of the manifest personality" (p. 5).

The norms for each of the ten dimensions of the TDOT are based on 4,008 students in grades eleven and twelve from twenty high schools and 1,493 freshmen from ten colleges. Separate tables are presented for each sex. In addition to examining these students, Thorndike asked each one to complete six questions relating to home and family background and educational and vocational aspirations. Variations in mean scores among certain subgroups were found to be statistically significant.

The following are brief summaries of these findings as reported by Thorndike (1966).

Sociable. The rural respondents appear less sociable than those from towns or cities. There is a suggestion of higher sociability among males majoring or planning to major in business.

Ascendant. Greater ascendance tends to go with town or city residence, with higher parental socio-economic status, with higher parental education, with plans for college education among high school pupils, and with plans for a professional career.

Table 24. Description of TDOT Dimensions *

Dimension	Abbreviation	Positive End	Negative End
1. Sociable	(Soc)	Sociable Likes to be with other people, to do things in groups, to go to parties, to be in the middle of things	Solitary Likes to be by himself, to do things by himself, to read or engage in other kinds of solitary activities
2. Ascendant	(Asc)	Ascendant Likes to be in the center of the stage, to speak in public, to "sell" things or ideas, to meet important people; tends to stand up for his rights or his point of view	Withdrawing Tends to avoid personal conflict, to dislike being in the public eye, to avoid taking the initiative in relation to others, to accept being imposed upon
3. Cheerful	(Che)	Cheerful, Objective Seems to feel generally well and happy; satisfied with his relations with others, accepted by others, at peace with the world	Gloomy, Sensitive Often seems to feel moody, depressed, at odds with himself; sensitive to the criticism of others; prone to worry and anxiety
4. Placid	(Pla)	Placid Even-tempered, easygoing, not easily ruffled or annoyed	Irritable Short-tempered, annoyed or irked by a good many things, inclined to "blow his top"
5. Accepting	(Acc)	Accepting Tends to think the best of people, to accept them at face value, to expect altruism to prevail	Critical Tends to question people's motives, expecting self-interest, conscious of the need for each to look out for himself

		Tough-Minded (Masculine)	Tender-Minded (Feminine)
6. Tough-Minded	(T-M)	Tolerant of dirt, bugs, and profanity; enjoys sports, roughing it, and the out-of-doors; uninterested in clothes or personal appearance; rational rather than intuitive	Sensitive to dirt, both physical and verbal; concerned with personal appearance; aesthetic interests; intuitive rather than rational
7. Reflective	(Ref)	_Reflective_ Interested in ideas, in abstractions, in discussion and speculation, in knowing for its own sake	_Practical_ Interested in doing and in using knowledge for practical ends, impatient with speculation and theorizing
8. Impulsive	(Imp)	_Impulsive_ Carefree, happy-go-lucky, ready to do things at a moment's notice	_Planful_ Careful to plan life out in advance, systematic, orderly, foresighted
9. Active	(Act)	_Active_ Full of energy, on the go, quick to get things done, able to get a lot done	_Lethargic_ Slow, easily tired, less productive than others; likes to move at a leisurely pace
10. Responsible	(Res)	_Responsible_ Dependable, reliable, certain to complete tasks on time, even a little compulsive	_Casual_ Often late with commitments, rushes to meet deadlines; has difficulty getting things done, unpredictable

* From _Thorndike Dimensions of Temperament: Manual_, by Robert L. Thorndike. Reproduced by permission. Copyright © 1966, The Psychological Corporation, New York, N.Y. All rights reserved.

Cheerful, Placid, Accepting. These scales show no clear differences among the groups on any of the breakdowns.

Tough-Minded. This attribute tends to be somewhat higher in rural groups. For boys, there are substantial differences associated with vocational plan, with scores on the trait being high for those planning agricultural careers and low for those planning to enter the professions.

Reflective. This dimension has a number of correlates. Among boys it is associated with an urban environment, professional occupation of father, plans for a college education for self, intention to major in social science, and aspiration to a professional occupation. Among girls it is also associated with high parental education and aspiration for a college education for self, with a planned college major in languages or in arts, and perhaps with aspirations to a professional career.

Impulsive. This trait shows few correlates. It has some tendency to be high for girls who aspire to a college major in arts.

Active. This scale shows no clear group differences.

Responsible. This scale shows only slight differences. There is a suggestion that children of more highly educated parents report themselves to be less reliable. Girls majoring or aspiring to major in arts rate themselves low on this trait. (pp. 27–28)

Overall validity and reliability for TDOT are lower than the reported coefficients of most aptitude and achievement tests. In discussing reliability, Thorndike (1966) readily concedes this and states that the "reliability of TDOT is lower than one is accustomed to expect in tests of ability, but compares favorably with many other personality inventories" (p. 9).

The student interested in pursuing the technical aspects of this test further in terms of validity, reliability, and correlations with other measures is referred to the TDOT test manual (Thorndike, 1966).

Mooney Problem Check List

Another type of personality inventory is represented by the Mooney Problem Check List. The Mooney, along with its sibling inventories, is not a test; it goes one step further, however, in that it yields no scores. Mooney and Gordon (1950), in describing the utility of their test, state that the "usefulness of the Problem Check List approach lies in its economy for appraising the major concerns of a group and for bringing into the open the problems of each student in the group" (p. 3).

Major Uses

Some of the major uses of the Mooney in a school setting are the following:

COUNSELING

To prepare pupils for interviewer by having them think over their own problems.

To facilitate communication between counselor and student.

To save time for the counselor by providing a quick overview of various problems.

RESEARCH

To provide information useful for curriculum planning, individualized instruction, and counseling needs.

To measure the effect of certain school activities and school oriented problems and objectives.

HOMEROOM AND GROUP GUIDANCE

To help students identify personal problems and needs.

To provide material for discussion in group guidance and orientation programs.

The Mooney Problem Check List has four forms to be used for different age levels: junior high school (*J*), high school (*H*), college (*C*), and adults (*A*). They are all self-administering and for counseling purposes require no scoring. It should be noted, however, that for certain objectives, such as research purposes, the problems checked may be summarized by simply counting the total responses in a number of problem areas. These areas differ according to the form. The problem areas and number of items in each for the junior high school and high school and college forms are as follows (Mooney and Gordon, 1950):

JUNIOR HIGH SCHOOL FORM

210 items, 30 in each area
   I. Health and Physical Development (HPD)
  II. School (S)
 III. Home and Family (HF)
  IV. Money, Work, and Future (MWF)
   V. Boy and Girl Relations (BG)
  VI. Relations to People in General (PG)
 VII. Self-centered Concerns (SC)

COLLEGE AND HIGH SCHOOL FORMS

330 items, 30 in each area
   I. Health and Physical Development (HPD)
  II. Finances, Living Conditions, and Employment (FLE)
 III. Social and Recreational Activities (SRA)
  IV. Social-Psychological Relations (SPR)
   V. Personal-Psychological Relations (PPR)
  VI. Courtship, Sex, and Marriage (CSM)
 VII. Home and Family (HF)
VIII. Morals and Religion (MR)
  IX. Adjustment to College (School) Work (ACW) (ASW)

X. The Future: Vocational and Educational (FVE)
XI. Curriculum and Teaching Procedure (CTP)

The usual analyses of validity and reliability are not relevant to this type of instrument. The interested student should consult the manual (Mooney and Gordon, 1950) for specific types of validity, reliability, and norms reported. In addition, a bibliography of research and use of the instrument is presented.

The following are some typical items from the junior high school form:

Directions [1]: Read the list slowly and as you come to a problem which troubles you, draw a line under it.

1. Often have headaches
2. Don't get enough sleep
3. Have trouble with my teeth
4. Not as healthy as I should be
5. Not getting outdoors enough
6. Getting low grades in school
7. Afraid of tests
8. Being a grade behind in school
9. Don't like to study
10. Not interested in books

61. Being teased
62. Being talked about
63. Feelings too easily hurt
64. Too easily led by other people
65. Picking the wrong kind of friends
66. Getting into trouble
67. Trying to stop a bad habit
68. Sometimes not being as honest as I should be
69. Giving in to temptations
70. Lacking self-control

In addition to the 210 items, there are three questions that ask the student to write in his own words about problems troubling him and to say whether he would like to spend some of his school time talking to someone about them. The Mooney, in essence, then, is not a measuring device in the usual sense. Cronbach's (1960) appraisal of it states quite cogently that the "Mooney Problem Check List is of considerable value because it draws attention to specific concerns the client is ready to talk about and wants help with. It is, in effect, a preliminary interview rather than a measuring device" (p. 487).

Minnesota Multiphasic Personality Inventory

The Minnesota Multiphasic Personality Inventory (MMPI) was designed to provide an objective measure of some of the most important personality characteristics that relate to personal and social adjustment. It attempts to provide, in a single test, scores on all the most important aspects of personality (Hathaway and McKinley, 1951).

The MMPI is one of the most respected and widely used personality inventories in existence today. More research has been done with it and on it than any other inventory now available. The diversity of problems that have

[1] Sample items from the *Mooney Problem Check List—Junior High School Form.* (Reproduced by permission. Copyright 1950 by The Psychological Corporation, New York, N.Y. All rights reserved.)

been examined with the MMPI is truly outstanding. In addition to the numerous studies of a psychological and psychiatric nature, studies relating personality characteristics to success in practice teaching, cancer, brain lesions, multiple sclerosis, low-back pain, and characteristics of and criteria for nursing students have also been done. These are only a very small fraction of the various kinds of investigations reported.

The first MMPI investigations appeared in 1940. The test materials and the first formal manual were published in 1943. The number of articles, books, dissertations, and other investigations dealing with the MMPI has been enormous.

FORMAT

The MMPI consists of 550 statements to which the subject is asked to respond in three ways: "true," "false," or "cannot say." The MMPI is given in two forms, individual (card form) and group (booklet). In the individual form, the test administrator presents the subject with a box of 550 small cards with printed statements on each. Instructions are on the cover of the box and ask the subject to sort the cards into three stacks according to the three preceding categories. The group form presents these same 550 statements [2] in a printed format in the usual type of group test booklet.[3] The instructions in the test booklet request the person to "read each statement and decide whether it is *true as applied to you* or *false as applied to you.* . . . If a statement does not apply to you or if it is something that you don't know about, make no mark on the answer sheet" (Hathaway and McKinley, 1943). The subject records his answers on a separate answer sheet, which may be hand- or machine-scored. The MMPI was originally designed for individuals sixteen years of age and over, although it has been used successfully with fourteen-year-old high school students (Hathaway and Monachesi, 1953, 1961). The card form is recommended for testing small groups or individuals and should be used when testing older persons, disturbed persons, hospital patients, or persons with low educational achievement or intellectual ability. The group form yields the same results, however, for high school and college and professional people (Hathaway and McKinley, 1951).

The MMPI items cover broad areas of content ranging from statements dealing with health and psychosomatic symptoms and neurological disorders to sexual, religious, political, educational, and social attitudes. Items similar to those found in the MMPI follow:

I have been healthy during the past three years.
I do not become fatigued easily.
Important sexual facts should be taught to children.

[2] Actually, the booklet presents 566 items, sixteen of which are duplications of the basic 550 items.
[3] A new form (Form R) allows scores to be obtained from only the first 399 items. Numbers 400–566 are designated for research.

I sometimes like to swear.
I definitely lack self-confidence.

SCORES

Clinical Scales. The MMPI provides scores on nine "clinical scales." They are as follows:

1. Hypochondriasis (Hs).
2. Depression (D).
3. Hysteria (Hy).
4. Psychopathic Deviate (Pd).
5. Masculinity-femininity (Mf).
6. Paranoia (Pa).
7. Psychasthenia (Pt).
8. Schizophrenia (Sc).
9. Hypomania (Ma).

The preceding scales consist of statements that differentiate between the following diverse groups: patients in the general wards of the University of Minnesota Hospitals (254 patients who were in the hospital for physical disease); a normal group of individuals who were bringing relatives or friends to the University Clinic (724 cases); precollege high school graduates who came to the University Testing Bureau for precollege guidance (265 cases); and patients (221) in the psychopathic unit of the University Hospitals and the outpatient neuropsychiatric clinic (Hathaway and McKinley, 1956).

Validity Scales. In addition to the basic nine scales, a unique feature of the MMPI is its four "validity scales." They are not validity scales in the usual testing sense but are attempts to note carelessness, malingering, misunderstanding, and test-taking attitudes of the subject. These four scales are the following:

1. THE CANNOT SAY SCORE (?). The "cannot say" score is the total number of statements that the subject responded to by not answering "true" or "false."
2. LIE SCORE (L). "True" responses to statements in the lie scale present the respondent in an unfavorable light; "false" responses present him in a favorable light. Dahlstrom, Welsh, and Dahlstrom (1972), in referring to this scale, state that "these attributes are clear, unambiguous, and generally socially unfavorable. It was assumed that most people would be willing to endorse the statements of the L scale as true about themselves even though the items deal with disapproved actions and feelings" (p. 49).
3. VALIDITY SCORE (F). The validity score is based upon a group of items

rarely endorsed by the original standardization group, including the mentally ill patients. Many of the items relate to peculiar thoughts and beliefs and lack of control over impulses. It is highly unlikely that any subject would exhibit all or a majority of these behavioral patterns. The F score serves as a check on the whole record. A high F score indicates other scores are probably invalid because the subject was careless or did not understand the statements or that possible scoring errors were made.

4. THE K SCORE (K). The K score is the most recent of the validity scales and was developed as a measure of test-taking attitudes that appear either as defensiveness or as a need to represent one's worst features. College students tend, as a group, to have higher K scores (psychological defensiveness and sophistication) than individuals of less sophistication and those who consciously or unconsciously desire to place themselves in a "poor light."

After scoring the MMPI, the examiner reviews the four validity scales before proceeding further. If any or all of these scales are over the designated ceiling, the record is considered suspect; if they are extremely high, it is considered invalid.

In addition to the basic nine scales of the MMPI, a tenth was added, the Social Introversion (Si) scale. Dahlstrom, Welsh, and Dahlstrom (1975) present studies in which a high relationship was found between the Si scale and the number of extracurricular activities participated in by high school and college students.

Over 200 new scales, in addition to those already mentioned, have been developed by independent investigators. Very few of these investigators took part in the original construction of the MMPI. These scales vary widely—for example, Academic achievement (Ac), College achievement (Ae), Aging (Ag), Alcoholism (Al), Adjustment to prison (Ap), Anxiety reaction (Ar), Success in baseball (Ba), Delinquency (De), Ego strength (Es), Low back pain (Lb), and so forth (Dahlstrom et al., 1972). In addition to scale variance studies, graduate schools and professional groups have utilized the MMPI as a basis for characterization of personality and as a screening device (see, for example, Karmel, 1961).

INTERPRETATION

Normally the interpretation of the MMPI is based on only fourteen scales (nine "clinical," plus Si and the four validity scales) and possibly several other "pet" scales of the examiner. Scores are converted to norms based on the original sample and according to sex. These norms are reported in the form of T scores (standard scores) with a mean of 50 and a SD of 10. A score of 70 or higher is generally considered as the point above which psychopathology might be inferred. The skilled examiner, however, is more interested in the total profile configuration and the relative peak scales (highest elevation) than the score per se. On the other hand, in most cases, extremely high

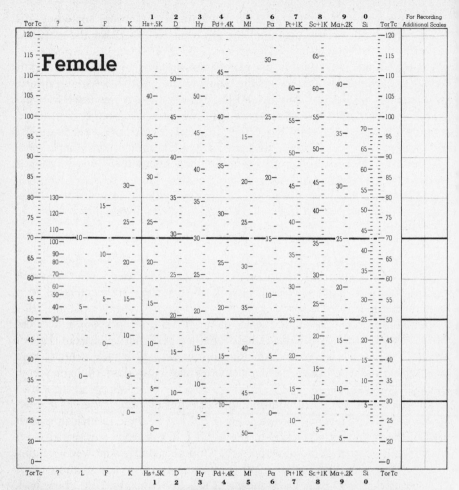

Figure 41. The Minnesota Multiphasic Personality Inventory Profile.
(Reproduced by permission from *The Minnesota Multiphasic Personality Inventory Profile and Case Summary*. Copyright © 1948 by The Psychological Corporation, New York, N.Y. All rights reserved.)

scale scores reveal blatant psychopathology. Figure 41 presents an MMPI profile.

The MMPI can be given by people not trained in psychology; however, it is dangerous for persons not skilled in its use to interpret the results. Usually, the MMPI is given only by the school psychologist and then only after parental permission has been obtained. This is not the kind of test that is given to all students; it should be given only to those who have revealed emotional problems. We will have more to say about this later in the chapter.

The qualified school psychologist in his or her interpretation of the MMPI will use one of several excellent resources as a basis for interpretation. One of the older and staple sources is *An Atlas for the Clinical Use of the MMPI* (Hathaway and Meehl, 1951), which provides coded profiles and short case histories. A more recent aid is the *MMPI Handbook* (Dahlstrom et al., 1972). It is the most comprehensive and usable source for profile interpretations. Another source that is limited to college students is Drake and Oetting's (1959) *MMPI Codebook for Counselors*.

In addition to the use of codebooks, the school psychologist now has at his or her disposal computer interpretations. The Psychological Corporation offers an MMPI reporting service that provides a one-page report of diagnostic and interpretive statements of an individual's personality. Figure 42 presents a sample of this type of report.

The School and Personality Inventories

Educators may well ask, "Why give personality inventories in the school?" This is a legitimate question. Let us first state a basic and very important premise. That is, *personality inventories are not given to all youngsters.* They are administered only to those who have displayed behavior patterns that could indicate emotional problems.

In order to clarify the role of the MMPI in the school, let us take the case of Bill. Bill was referred to the school psychologist by the school social worker because of his inability to get along in the classroom. Bill's test record showed he was in the superior range of school ability. However, his grades were very poor, F's and D's. Bill would spend much of his time drawing pictures and "goofing off." The social worker was unable to come up with a clear diagnosis, so after receiving parental permission, Bill was given the MMPI. The test results showed Bill was the type of boy who was unable to cope with his environment. It was obvious that Bill was sick and needed immediate treatment. Thus the social worker, on the basis of the MMPI and other data, referred Bill to an agency that could help him.

Some Basic Problems in the Use of Personality Inventories

One of the basic problems in administering personality inventories is the amount of reading required. A student who is slow in reading may tire of the test and respond without careful consideration of the test item. In addition to the amount or reading, difficulty with words is a problem. If the vocabulary and abstractness of the ideas are beyond the student's comprehension, the student may respond to the test item in a careless manner. Some tests, like the MMPI, have scales to detect this problem, but most others do not.

Another difficulty is the reluctance of some individuals to be honest in their answers. For most personality inventories, the person must be honest

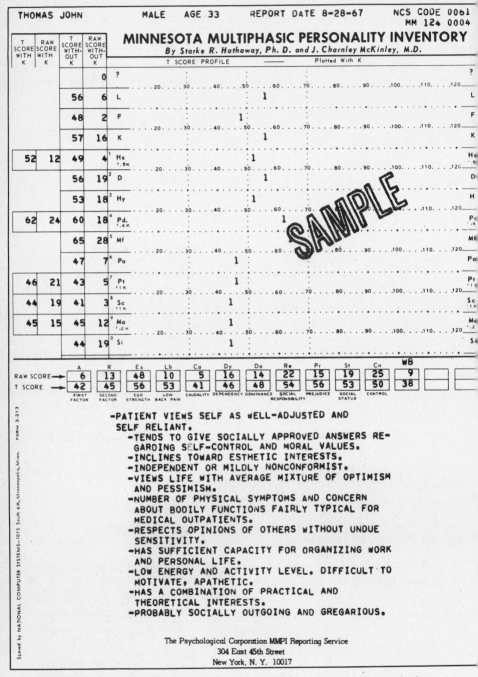

Figure 42. Sample MMPI computer report. (Reproduced by permission. Copyright 1943, 1951, © 1967 by The University of Minnesota. Published by The Psychological Corporation, New York, N.Y. All rights reserved.)

in his or her response in order to get a valid picture. Studies have shown that most personality inventories can be faked. That is, the person with some psychological insight can give whatever picture desired. However, on the MMPI this is not as likely to happen, because there are scales that indicate whether or not a person is responding truthfully.

The problem of faking means that a student's scores on a personality inventory are subject to error, and the interpretation of these scores must be done with extreme caution. For example, let us suppose that a personality inventory is given to a ninth-grade boy who has been giving his teachers a difficult time. To this boy, teachers may be a symbol of authority against which he rebels. Therefore, if the test is given by a teacher or other authority figure, there is good chance that he will not be honest in his answers. Second, one must remember that pupils are taught to do their best on tests in school. This being the case, many children are not going to reveal their personal problems. Besides, some children who reveal a healthy adjustment on an inventory may in actuality be defensive and unable to reveal their real problems.

Remember also that personality inventories are middle class in thinking. Items often have different meanings for different socioeconomic levels and ethnic groups.

The educator should view the use of the personality inventory as only one step in attempting to ascertain the problems that interfere with a student's academic performance. Personality inventories may provide a quick gauge of what troubles the pupil. Most school counselors do not have the training required to administer more complex instruments such as projective devices, and they can use personality inventories as screening instruments in order to make intelligent referrals to appropriate resources in the community. Of all the inventories available, the MMPI is the most reliable and valid. Its judicious use by trained school personnel can facilitate behavioral analysis and lead to the proper handling of disturbed children. (For a technical review of the limitations and assets of personality inventories, see Megargee, 1966, Chapters 5, 6, and 7.)

Attitude Inventories

The attitude inventory is basically a self-report or questionnaire designed to measure a person's bias toward some group, social institution, social concept, or proposed action. One of the most common and primitive forms of this type of appraisal is the opinion poll. In such a poll a group of questions might be presented to a community on a facet of school policy and the results tabulated to express the consensus of community opinion.

The greatest use of attitude inventories has been in research endeavors which attempt to discover attitude differences, kinds of experiences that can change attitudes, and the influence of one's attitudes on his or her view of the world. Thurstone (1959), for example, developed thirty scales for measuring attitudes toward war, Negroes, Chinese, capital punishment, church, censorship, and other practices, issues, and groups of people.

Minnesota Teacher Attitude Inventory

In a more immediate area of concern to educators is the Minnesota Teacher Attitude Inventory (Cook et al., 1951), designed to assess pupil-teacher relations. It is based on ten years of experimentation and standardized on teachers from different communities, schools, and grade levels. It is used in selecting teachers and in counseling student-teacher candidates. The range is from high school seniors through adulthood.

The following items are similar to those found in this inventory:

Most students are resourceful if you leave them on their own.
A teacher should never let his students know that he is ignorant of a topic.

This inventory is especially useful for research purposes, but a great deal of caution must be exercised in any practical usage such as counseling or selection.

Survey of Study Habits and Attitudes

Another attitude inventory of special interest to educators is the Survey of Study Habits and Attitudes (Brown and Holtzman, 1966). This survey was developed to help discover why some students with high scholastic aptitude do poorly in school, whereas others with only average ability do well. The authors recommend its usage as a

1. *Screening instrument.* Administered to twelfth grade or college students at the beginning of the school year. Used later for individual counseling and as a technique to discover students who may need immediate help.
2. *Diagnostic instrument.* Provides format for systematic recording of student's feelings and practices involving schoolwork.
3. *Teaching aid.* In elementary courses in psychology and education to help communicate effective methods of study.
4. *Research tool.* In educational or counseling processes.

The student is presented with 100 statements in the Survey of Study Habits and Attitudes (SSHA) booklet and is asked to respond, in terms of a five-point scale, to each statement by choosing one of the following:

R—*Rarely,* 0 to 15 per cent of time
S—*Sometimes,* 16 to 35 per cent of time
F—*Frequently,* 36 to 65 per cent of time

G—*Generally*, 66 to 85 per cent of time
A—*Almost always*, 86 to 100 per cent of time

The following are some sample statements from the SSHA.[4]

I believe that teachers intentionally schedule tests on the days following important athletic or social activities.
I believe that a college's football reputation is just as important as its academic standing.
With me, studying is a hit-or-miss proposition depending on the mood I'm in.
I am careless of spelling and the mechanics of English composition when answering examination questions.
I believe that one way to get good grades is by using flattery on your teachers.
I think that it might be best for me to drop out of school and get a job.

Figure 43 presents a sample of a diagnostic profile for a college freshman. The profile includes the scales and what they mean.

The Survey is also published in Spanish (Encuesta de Hábitos y Actitudes hacia el Estudio, 1971). It was prepared in Mexico in order to be certain of its suitability for use in other Hispano-American countries. The percentiles are for high school and first-year college students in Mexico.

Survey of School Attitudes

The Survey of School Attitudes (SSA) was created to enable the teacher and administrator to assess the reaction of pupils to four major areas of the school curriculum: reading and language arts, mathematics, science, and social studies.

Items on the SSA were keyed to instructional objectives and daily activities in each curricular area. For example, the Mathematics scale includes geometry, numeration concepts, computation, and so on. Earth science, life science, physical science, and scientific methods are included in the Science scale.

The SSA requests that students indicate preferences toward activities in the four major areas by stating whether they like, dislike, or are neutral toward them. The sum of a student's responses to a given curricular area is considered an indication of the pupil's overall affective reaction to that area (Hogan, 1975).

The SSA is designed for administration by teachers to the entire class, although it can be given individually. There are two forms (A and B) for

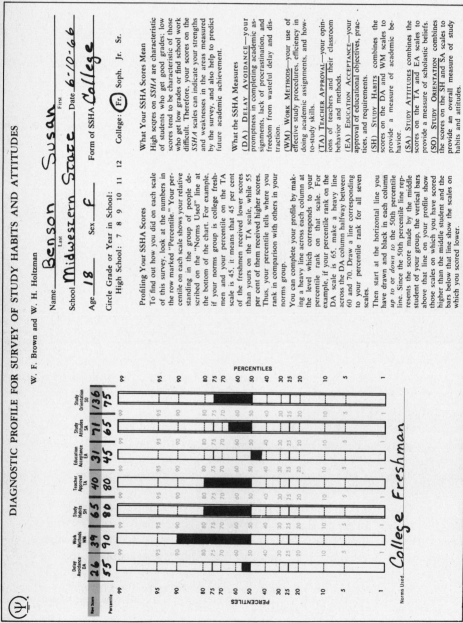

Figure 43. Diagnostic profile for Survey of Study Habits and Attitudes. (Reproduced by permis-

primary and intermediate grades. The primary level is for grades 1–3 and for fourth-grade pupils with reading difficulty. At the primary level, the teacher reads the item "stems" to the students. The intermediate level is designed for grades 4–8. Here the students read and react to the items on their own. The vocabulary level is at or below the fourth-grade level. There is no time limit. Figure 44 presents sample items from the SSA Intermediate level.

The manual presents percentile ranks by grade. Criterion-referenced "level scores" are also presented; thus norm-referenced and criterion-referenced interpretations are possible. Figure 45 presents a sample class report for a seventh grade. Note that this class is lowest in attitude toward mathematics and highest in attitude toward science. Commenting on this seemingly unusual situation, Hogan (1975) states,

> *The contrast between the average scores in Mathematics and Science is itself interesting. This class illustrates the tendency for attitudes toward these two areas to be rather independent at the intermediate and junior high grades. Because of the association between mathematics and science courses at the college level, it is often assumed that children who like (or dislike) mathematics will like (or dislike) science also. In fact, research shows that in the*

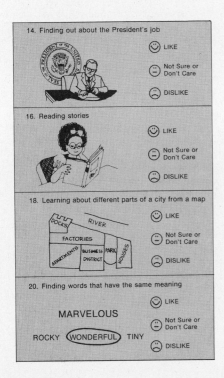

Figure 44. Sample items from the Survey of School Attitudes Intermediate Form A. Reproduced from *Survey on School Attitudes Intermediate Form A,* copyright © 1973, 1975, by Harcourt Brace Jovanovich, Inc. Reproduced by Special permission of the publisher.)

Teacher Mr. Wright
School North Elementary
System Springfield Public Date 10/07/75
Grade 7 Form A
Level Intermediate
Norms Used Grade 7
Class List Report
SSA | HBJ 1
Survey of School Attitudes / Scoring Service
Process Number

Student	Level Scores (RL M S SS)	Percentile Ranks (RL M S SS)	READING / LANGUAGE	MATHEMATICS	SCIENCE	SOCIAL STUDIES	LOCAL	Raw Scores (RL M S SS)
Bise, Ruby	4 3 2 3	76 52 2 17	LnDLLnLLD-LLLnL	nLLLnnDDLDnLDnn	DDnLDDDDDnDDn--D	nDnDDDnLLnnLLDD	LLLnnLLLDn	22 16 7 13
Eicn, Rex	4 3 4 4	85 60 68 48	nDLLnLDLLLLLLLL	LnnLDnLLDnnnnnL	nLnnLLLnLnLLmnL	LLnDnnLLLLDLLDD	LLnLLLLnnL	24 18 23 19
Foster, Marcia	5 4 5 4	92 80 90 77	LLnLnLLnLLLLLnL	nLLLLLnLnnLnnLn	LLLLLLnnLLLLLLn	LnLnnnnLLLLLLLn	LLLLLnLLnL	26 23 27 24
Graszl, Bill	3 2 4 3	20 22 42 21	LnnDnnDDnnDnLDn	DLLLDLnDDDDDDDD	LLnLDLDDLLDLLLD	LnnDnDDLLnDLDDD	LLDLDnnLDD	12 9 19 14
Hajdu, Bob	3 3 4 5	25 60 48 99	LDDnnDDnn-DLnLn	nLn-nLLnnnLD-LD	LLnnnnnnnLnnnLL	LLLLLLLLLLLLLLL	LnLLLLnnD-	13 18 20 30
Harper, Gary	3 1 5 4	20 2 99 54	nDnnDDnnnnnnnnn	DDDDDDnDDDDDDDD	LLLLLLLLLLLLLLL	LDnnLnLLLLnLLDD	LLDDDDLLnL	12 1 30 30
Jackson, Keith	3 5 5 3	42 95 85 42	LnnLDLDnDLnnnDL	nLLLLLLLLLLLnLL	LLLLLnLnLnLLLnL	LnnDnDLnnLnLnnL	LLLLLLLnnL	16 28 26 18
Johnson, Jeff	2 5 4 4	12 89 74 48	LDDnDnnnDnnDnDn	nLnLLLLLLLnnLLLL	nnLnnLLLLLLLnnL	nnLnDDLLnLLnnnL	LLDDDDLDDn	10 26 24 19
Land, Roger	1 1 2 1	1 2 1 1	DDDDDDDDDDDDDDD	DDnDDDDDDDDDDDD	nDDDnDDnnDnDDDD	nDDDDDDDDDDDDDn	nnDDDDDnD	0 1 5 2

	READING/LANGUAGE	MATHEMATICS	SCIENCE	SOCIAL STUDIES
Median Raw Scores	15.5	16.5	23.0	20.0
Percentile Rank of Median Raw Scores	42	56	68	54
Distribution of Level Scores	freq.	freq.	freq.	freq.
5	2	3	6	2
4	6	3	9	12
3	8	6	2	5
2	3	5	2	0
1	1	3	0	1
Data based on following number of students	20	20	19	20

Legend: L = Like, n = neutral, D = Dislike, - = omit

Figure 45. Sample Class List Report. (Reproduced from *Survey of School Attitudes, Manual for Administering and Interpreting, Intermediate Level Forms A and B,* copyright © 1973, 1975 by Harcourt Brace Jovanovich, Inc. Reproduced by special permission of the publisher.)

elementary school years mathematics attitudes are more closely related to reading attitudes than to science attitudes; science attitudes are more closely related to social studies attitudes than to mathematics attitudes.

This example also underscores the value of using both norm- and criterion-referenced score interpretations. Using the level score summary (criterion-referenced), Mathematics is clearly the area of least positive attitudes. However, percentile ranks—a norm-referenced score mode—reveal that this class has the least positive attitude toward the Reading/Language Arts scale, since the PR corresponding to the median raw score is lowest on the Reading/Language Arts scale.

How can this apparent contradiction be explained? The answer lies in the definitions of the two types of scores: the Level scores are absolute scores with the same meaning from grade to grade and scale to scale. Percentile ranks, on the other hand, are relative scores that have a different meaning across grades and scales depending on how the students in the normative groups responded to the items. . . . Therefore, although on an absolute scale the class expressed a rather neutral attitude, the class liked mathematics more than did the students in the norm group. Similarly, although the class expressed generally positive attitudes toward Reading/Language Arts, the students in the norm group expressed even more positive views. (pp. 22–23)

Allport-Vernon-Lindzey Study of Values

A different type of attitude inventory from those thus far cited is the Allport-Vernon-Lindzey Study of Values (1970).[5] The Study of Values was developed to measure the relative prominence of six basic interests, motives, and other evaluative attributes. The classification, based upon Spranger's *Types of Men* (1928), is as follows,

Theoretical. The basic interest of the theoretical type of man is the discovery of truth. In pursuing this objective, he takes a "cognitive" attitude, that is, he is empirical, rational, and critical in his "intellectual" approach to life.

Economic. The economic type of man is characterized by interest in what is useful and practical. This type is very similar to the stereotype of the average American businessman. This is the kind of man who wants education to be practical and looks upon pure research or unapplied data as wasteful.

Aesthetic. The aesthetic type of man places the highest value on form and harmony; his major interest is in the artistic facets of life; each unique experience is encountered from the point of view of grace or symmetry.

Social. The social type man's highest value is altrustic love or philanthrophy.

Political. The political type man is characterized by his dominant interest in power, influence, and renown. This man does not necessarily limit or engage in political activities per se; his power needs can be channelized in all sorts of activities and vocational pursuits.

Religious. The religious type of man is mystical, concerned with the cosmos as a whole and relating himself to its embracing totality.

The actual test is designed for college students and adults (with at least some college education) and consists of items based upon familiar situations to which alternative answers may be chosen. There is no item limit. The authors suggest three basic uses for the Study of Values:

1. Counseling, vocational guidance, and selection.
2. Classroom demonstration. As a teaching aid in beginning courses in psychology, education, and so on.
3. Research. For investigation of group differences, changes in values, comparison with other attitude and interest scales, resemblances between peer groups and family, and so forth.

---

[5] The classification of the Study of Values as an attitude inventory is arbitrary. Actually, it has a great deal in common with interest and personality instruments and could also be included under either designation. It is in fact a combination of all three types.

Two sample items with directions from the Study of Values follow:

Directions:
If the subject agrees with alternative (a) and disagrees with (b) he places 3 in the first box and 0 in the second box or vice versa. If there is only a slight preference for one over the other, they are rated 2 and 1 respectively.

Example [6]:
When witnessing a gorgeous ceremony (ecclesiastical or academic, induction into office, etc.), are you more impressed: (a) by the color and pageantry of the occasion itself; (b) by the influence and strength of the group?

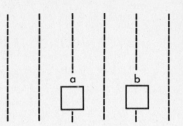

[*Part II.* The subject is asked to rate four possible attitudes or answers in order of personal preference, allocating 4 to the most attractive and 1 to the least attractive alternative.]

Example:
Do great exploits and adventures of discovery such as Columbus's, Magellan's, Byrd's and Amundsen's seem to you significant because—
a. they represent conquests by man over the difficult forces of nature
b. They add to our knowledge of geography, meteorology, oceanography, etc.
c. they weld human interests and international feelings throughout the world
d. they contribute each in a small way to an ultimate understanding of the universe.

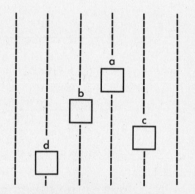

Scoring is an easy task because no key other than the simple instructions on the detachable page of the test booklet is required. Total scores on the six values are plotted on the profile presented on the last page of the booklet (see Figure 46). Final scores are reflective only of *relative* trends, because it is impossible to obtain high or low scores in all areas.

The Study of Values was originally published in 1931. Since that time, continued investigations have resulted in three editions. In 1968, a machine-scorable booklet was made available. In addition, there are now supplementary high school norms (Allport, Vernon, and Lindzey, 1970).

The 1960s saw a renewed concern over the measurement of values. Gordon

(1975) and Holtzman (1975b), for example, reviewed these trends. The Vietnam War, the Flower Children, and so on, all contributed to this re-awakening. The measurement of values, nevertheless, remains an elusive goal in the field of scientific measurement. This is particularly true in the context of the diverse cultural values present in America. The 1960s highlighted this diversity. An even more elusive area is the relationship between moral values and behavior. The problem, of course, is that in an actual situation, people may not act in accordance with their professed values. For centuries philosophers have grappled with moral behavior, but scientists have not attempted this task until very recently. Kohlberg (1969, 1974), following a Piagetian frame of reference, lists and discusses six stages of moral development. These start at a premoral level and proceed through a morality of status quo to the formulation of self-accepted moral principles. Kohlberg states that people want the highest stage of moral development that they can understand. The Moral Judgment Scale makes use of nine contrived dilemmas, presented one at a time. The person taking the test responds to the described behaviors and states reasons for these reactions. The interviewer attempts to encourage detailed explanations by probing questions.

The Scale is a good clinical and possibly research tool but is not an instrument on which one can rely. There is no real standardization to facilitate comparisons from one study to another.

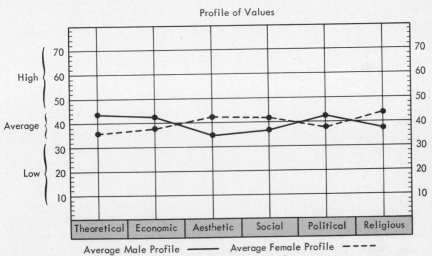

Profile of Values

Average Male Profile ———— Average Female Profile —— —— ——

Figure 46. Average profiles of males and females on the Allport-Vernon-Lindzey Study of Values. (From *Allport-Vernon-Lindzey Study of Values* (3rd ed.), by Gordon W. Allport, Phillip E. Vernon, and Gardner Lindzey. Copyright © 1960 by G. W. Allport, P. E. Vernon, and G. Lindzey. Reproduced by permission of the Houghton Mifflin Co.)

Interest Inventories

Each person makes a variety of decisions regarding the type of activities in which he or she will participate. Some individuals show preferences for sports, and others spend their time in reading or pursuing such hobbies as building model airplanes. Thus each person shows a preference for some activities and little interest in or even aversion to others. Measuring these tendencies to like or dislike certain activities is the main objective of the interest inventory.

Interest inventories are administered in the schools because it has been found that interests are related to academic success, job satisfaction, and eventual adjustment to and pleasure in adult life. For these reasons, it is important that every student have an understanding of his or her relative degree of interest in various activities. The counselor, in helping an individual student, wants the answers to such questions as, What are the interests of this pupil? How does interest in science compare to interest in social activities? How does interest in a certain type of activity compare to those of other persons?

But why give interest tests when all one has to do is to ask the person his or her likes and dislikes? After all, no one knows John as well as John knows himself. John may state that he likes arithmetic or wants to be an engineer, but such expressions of interest are of limited value. Authorities investigating this problem suggest that "single" expressions of interest may be unreliable and lack permanence. An individual's statement of interest in being a fireman may be true at a certain age, but not necessarily true later in life. People's interests are influenced by many factors, and their expressed interests may not represent their true desires and needs.

An adolescent from a middle-class community who is asked whether he or she is interested in going to college may answer affirmatively because it is the thing to do, although there is really little interest in a college education. The answer is yes because the word *college* is a symbol of respect and status. Parental pressures and the desire for the prestige associated with the college graduate may have influenced this answer.

Fowler (1945), in an article dealing with the value of expressed interests of students, states,

> There are two chief arguments, both supported by ample studies, against dependence upon self-estimated interests in choosing an occupation. One of these arguments concerns the factors which interfere with making a realistic choice, factors leading students to declare occupational goals too hard to reach. . . . The second major argument . . . calls attention to the frequent disagreement between self-estimated and measured interests. (p. 1)

In support of the preceding points, one can add the experience of vocational counselors who deal with adults. It is not uncommon for the vocational counselor to see persons who are in occupations in which they claim to have interest but who are actually occupationally misfitted. For example, during a counseling session with a teenage boy concerning future vocational plans, the boy stated, "I want to be in something I like—not like my father." During future counseling sessions the fact of the father's unhappiness in his job as an electrical engineer was repeated over and over. At the conclusion of the counseling sessions with the boy, a conference with the father was arranged.

Mr. Snow, the boy's father, was a well-groomed man in his middle forties. He appeared to be a moderately successful man. He began the interview by asking about the progress of his son and stating, "I don't want my son to be unhappy in the profession he chooses. That's why I asked you to see him and give him tests and guidance. I've seen too many men in jobs they weren't suited for." The counselor asked him if he was happy in his work, and he replied that he was. Noticing an uneasiness in his reply, the counselor waited for him to continue. There was a long pause and then he sheepishly admitted that he wasn't really sure his answer was true. He rather reluctantly agreed to take an interest inventory.

On this particular test, Mr. Snow scored high in the areas of social service and sales. His scientific and mechanical interests were considerably lower. When the results of the tests were discussed with him, he told how he had decided to become an engineer.

His father, who had been an engineer, died when Mr. Snow was in the second grade, and his mother had never remarried. Mr. Snow's mother always held up to her son the fact that his father had been a good man and would have liked his son to become an engineer. Therefore, Mr. Snow never thought of any career but engineering. Because he did well in science and mathematics, it was assumed that engineering was a good vocational choice for him.

After the test results were presented to Mr. Snow, he admitted that he was unhappy in his work and missed the opportunity to work with people. After a series of counseling interviews, Mr. Snow talked to his employer and asked to be given a chance in engineering sales. His employer granted his request, and today Mr. Snow is much happier in his vocational situation. A year after the interviews he said, "I am a new man in this work. For the first time in my life, I can be happy when Monday comes and not dread going to work."

Of course, not all people who rely on self-estimates in selecting their occupations are unhappy with their choices; some are very happy. Self-estimates are, however, often poor indicators for future occupational placement. This is the reason the counselor attempts to look at more than what the individual says he wants to be or do in life.

As we have mentioned, a person's stated interests may not always mirror true feelings. Thus professionals in this field construct their instruments to ask a variety of questions concerning the person's likes and dislikes. Questions such as whether the person would rather read a book or go to the movies are asked rather than whether he or she would rather be a lawyer or a teacher.

In the following discussion of interest inventories, we devote our major attention to the most widely used and respected instruments, the Strong Vocational Interest Blank and the Kuder interest inventories. We also briefly review a newer instrument, the Minnesota Vocational Interest Inventory, which is a departure from the classical models.

Strong Vocational Interest Blank

The Strong Vocational Interest Blank (SVIB) was first published in 1927 after several years of research; it has the longest continuous history of any widely used inventory. It has been revised three times (1938, 1966, 1974) since its initial publication. The 1974 edition of the SVIB is called the Strong-Campbell Interest Inventory (SCII) and is the most extensively modified of all the revisions. The major changes involve the merger of the men's and women's forms into one test booklet and the introduction of a theoretical framework to guide the interpretation of the scores.

The SCII asks the student to answer either "Like," "Indifferent," or "Dislike" to 325 items. Figure 47 reveals some of the items on the SCII which the person responds to in the "Like" (L), "Dislike" (D), or "Indifferent" (I) manner. The items cover the usual range of occupational tasks and daily activities. It takes most students twenty-five to thirty-five minutes to complete the inventory. The reading level is around the sixth grade, although some items are more difficult. The manual (Campbell, 1974)

1 Actor/Actress	46 Editor	91 Orchestra conductor
2 Advertising executive	47 Electrical engineer	92 Pharmacist
3 Architect	48 Electronics technician	93 Photographer
4 Art museum director	49 Elementary school teacher	94 Physician
5 Art teacher	50 Employment manager	95 Playground director
6 Artist	51 Factory manager	96 Poet
7 Artist's model	52 Farmer	97 Police officer
8 Astronomer	53 Fashion model	98 Politician
9 Athletic director	54 Florist	99 Private secretary
10 Auctioneer	55 Foreign correspondent	100 Professional athlete
11 Author of children's books	56 Foreign service officer	101 Professional dancer
12 Author of novels	57 Free-lance writer	102 Professional gambler
13 Author of technical books	58 Governor of a state	103 Psychologist
	59 High school teacher	104 Public relations director

Figure 47. Example of Items from the SCII test booklet Form 325. Reprinted from *Strong-Campbell Interest Inventory* Form 325 of the *Strong Vocational Interest Blank* by Edward K. Strong, Jr., and David P. Campbell with the permission of the publishers, Standard University Press. Copyright © 1974 by the Board of Trustees of the Leland Stanford Junior University. This material may not be copied or reproduced without permission in writing from Stanford University Press.

recommends that seventeen to eighteen years of age and beyond is the most appropriate age range for routine use. This is because interest at this age begins to solidify and the results are most useful for long-range career-planning purposes.

There are seven parts to the test. In the first six parts, a person indicates a preference by marking L, I, or D. The seventh part asks the student to read a statement such as "usually start activities of my group" and to react either "yes," "no," or "?" to the question of whether the statement is an accurate self-description (Campbell, 1974).

The SCII can be scored only by a commercial scoring agency. There are a number of such agencies that have this service. It usually takes several days from receipt of test to return of completed printout profile.

Individual SCII scores are reported on a preprinted profile form. Scores are recorded on this profile by computer. Figures 48 and 49 present parts of the two-page profile booklet. Note that on Figure 48 there are six themes. They are Realistic (R), Investigative (I), Artistic (A), Social (S), Enterprising (E), and Conventional (C). These themes are taken from Holland (1973) and based on thorough research by Holland and other investigators. Each of the themes describes a type of person and the kind of work environment he or she would find consonant.

The results are expressed as standard scores ($M = 50$, SD $= 10$). The normative group, for General Occupational Themes, is the general reference sample consisting of 300 men and 300 women representative of all occupations included in the inventory.

The Administrative Indexes detect carelessness. The two Special Scales were formerly called the Nonoccupational Scales. They are empirical scales that were developed with nonoccupational criteria. The Academic Orientation scale (AOR) was produced by comparing the item responses of good and poor students at the University of Minnesota's College of Science, Literature, and the Arts. It attempts to forecast staying power in high school, college, and graduate school. The Introversion-Extroversion scale (IE) was developed by comparing the item responses of extroverts and introverts as measured by the MMPI. Scores on this scale reflect outgoingness (extrovert—wants to be with people) and people who like to work alone (introvert).

The twenty-three Basic Interest Scales can be seen in Figure 48 grouped under the six General Occupational Themes. They are homogeneous scales and were formed by clustering together items that had high intercorrelations. The scores are not much affected by age except for the Adventure scale, on which teenage boys score eight to ten points higher than adults. The open and shaded bars show the scores of female and male subsamples.

The Occupational Scales (see Figure 49) include 124 scales, 67 from male samples and 57 from female samples. They are more complex than the other scales and include more items with greater diversity of content. On this Scale, some "Dislike" responses are scored positively; for example, if people of a

SVIB-SCII Profile for _____

Date Scored

General Occupational Themes

Theme	Std Score	Result
R-Theme		This is a _____ Score.
I-Theme		This is a _____ Score.
A-Theme		This is a _____ Score.
S-Theme		This is a _____ Score.
E-Theme		This is a _____ Score.
C-Theme		This is a _____ Score.

Administrative Indexes

(for the use of the counselor)

TOTAL RESPONSES
INFREQUENT RESPONSES

Response %
LP   IP   DP

OCCUPATIONS
SCHOOL SUBJECTS
ACTIVITIES
AMUSEMENTS
TYPES OF PEOPLE
PREFERENCES
CHARACTERISTICS
Special Scales: AOR: IE:

Basic Interest Scales

Scale	Std Score	Very Low	Low	Average	High	Very High

R-THEME
- AGRICULTURE
- NATURE — 30 35 40 45 50 55 60 65 70
- ADVENTURE
- MILITARY ACTIVITIES
- MECHANICAL

I-THEME
- SCIENCE
- MATHEMATICS
- MEDICAL SCIENCE
- MEDICAL SERVICE

A-THEME
- MUSIC/DRAMATICS — 30 35 40 45 50 55 60 65 70
- ART
- WRITING

S-THEME
- TEACHING
- SOCIAL SERVICE
- ATHLETICS
- DOMESTIC ARTS
- RELIGIOUS ACTIVITIES

E-THEME
- PUBLIC SPEAKING
- LAW/POLITICS
- MERCHAND'NG
- SALES
- BUSINESS MGMT. — 30 35 40 45 50 55 60 65 70

C-TH
- OFFICE PRACTICES

Figure 48. Portion of SCII Profile. Reprinted from *Strong-Campbell Interest Inventory* Form 325 of the *Strong Vocational Interest Blank* by Edward K. Strong, Jr., and David P. Campbell with the permission of the publishers, Stanford University Press. Copyright © 1974 by the Board of Trustees of the Leland Stanford Junior University. This profile may not be copied or reproduced without permission in writing from Stanford University Press.

Occupational Scales

Code	Scale	Sex Norm	Std Score	Very Dissimilar	Dissimilar	Ave	Similar	Very Similar
RC	FARMER	m						
RC	INSTRUM. ASSEMBL.	f						
RCE	VOC. AGRIC. TCHR.	m						
REC	DIETITIAN	f						
RES	POLICE OFFICER	m						
RSE	HWY. PATROL OFF.	m						
RE	ARMY OFFICER	f						
RS	PHYS. ED. TEACHER	f						
R	SKILLED CRAFTS	m						
RI	FORESTER	m						
RI	RAD. TECH. (X-RAY)	f						
RI	MERCH. MAR. OFF.	m						
RI	NAVY OFFICER	m						
RI	NURSE, REGISTERED	m						
RI	VETERINARIAN	m		15	25	45	55	
RIC	CARTOGRAPHER	m						
RIC	ARMY OFFICER	m						
RIE	AIR FORCE OFFICER	m						
RIA	OCCUP. THERAPIST	f						
IR	ENGINEER	f						
IR	ENGINEER	m						
IR	CHEMIST	f						
IR	PHYSICAL SCIENTIST	m						
IR	MEDICAL TECH.	f						
IR	PHARMACIST	f						
IR	DENTIST	f						
IR	DENTIST	m		15	25	45	55	
IR	DENTAL HYGIENIST	f						
IRS	PHYS. THERAPIST	f						
IRS	PHYSICIAN	m						
IRS	MATH-SCI. TEACHER	m						
ICR	MATH-SCI. TEACHER	f						
IC	DIETITIAN	f						
IRC	MEDICAL TECH.	m						
IRC	OPTOMETRIST	m						
IRC	COMPUTER PROGR.	f						
IRC	COMPUTER PROGR.	m						
I	MATHEMATICIAN	f						
I	MATHEMATICIAN	m		15	25	45	55	
I	PHYSICIST	f						
I	BIOLOGIST	m						
I	VETERINARIAN	f						
I	OPTOMETRIST	f						
I	PHYSICIAN	f						
I	SOCIAL SCIENTIST	m						
IA	COLLEGE PROFESSOR	f						
IA	COLLEGE PROFESSOR	m						
IS	SPEECH PATHOL.	f						
IS	SPEECH PATHOL.	m						
IAS	PSYCHOLOGIST	f						
IAS	PSYCHOLOGIST	m		15	25	45	55	
IA	LANGUAGE INTERPR.	f						
ARI	ARCHITECT	m						
A	ADVERTISING EXEC.	f						
A	ARTIST	f						
A	ARTIST	m						
A	ART TEACHER	f						
A	PHOTOGRAPHER	m						
A	MUSICIAN	f						
A	MUSICIAN	m						
A	ENTERTAINER	f						
AE	INT. DECORATOR	f						

Code	Scale	Sex Norm	Std Score	Very Dissimilar	Dissimilar	Ave	Similar	Very Similar
AE	INT. DECORATOR	m						
AE	ADVERTISING EXEC.	m						
A	LANGUAGE TEACHER	f						
A	LIBRARIAN	f						
A	LIBRARIAN	m						
A	REPORTER	f						
A	REPORTER	m						
AS	ENGLISH TEACHER	f						
AS	ENGLISH TEACHER	m						
SI	NURSE, REGISTERED	f						
SIR	PHYS. THERAPIST	m						
SRC	NURSE, LIC. PRACT.	m						
S	SOCIAL WORKER	f						
S	SOCIAL WORKER	m						
S	PRIEST	m		15	25	45	55	
S	DIR., CHRISTIAN ED.	f						
SE	YWCA STAFF	f						
SIE	MINISTER	m						
SEA	ELEM. TEACHER	f						
SC	ELEM. TEACHER	f						
SCE	SCH. SUPERINTEND.	m						
SCE	PUBLIC ADMINISTR.	m						
SCE	GUIDANCE COUNS.	m						
SER	RECREATION LEADER	f						
SEC	RECREATION LEADER	m						
SEC	GUIDANCE COUNS.	f						
SEC	SOC. SCI. TEACHER	f		15	25	45	55	
SEC	SOC. SCI. TEACHER	m						
SEC	PERSONNEL DIR.	m						
ESC	DEPT. STORE MGR.	m						
ESC	HOME ECON. TCHR.	f						
ESA	FLIGHT ATTENDANT	f						
ES	CH. OF COMM. EXEC.	m						
ES	SALES MANAGER	m						
ES	LIFE INS. AGENT	m						
E	LIFE INS. AGENT	f						
E	LAWYER	f						
E	LAWYER	m		15	25	45	55	
EI	COMPUTER SALES	m						
EI	INVESTM. FUND MGR.	m						
EIC	PHARMACIST	m						
EC	BUYER	f						
ECS	BUYER	m						
ECS	CREDIT MANAGER	m						
ECS	FUNERAL DIRECTOR	m						
ECR	REALTOR	m						
ERC	AGRIBUSINESS MGR.	m						
ERC	PURCHASING AGENT	m						
ESR	CHIROPRACTOR	m						
CE	ACCOUNTANT	m						
CE	BANKER	f		15	25	45	55	
CE	BANKER	m						
CE	CREDIT MANAGER	f						
CE	DEPT. STORE SALES	f						
CE	BUSINESS ED. TCHR.	f						
CES	BUSINESS ED. TCHR.	m						
CSE	EXEC. HOUSEKEEPER	f						
C	ACCOUNTANT	f						
C	SECRETARY	f						
CR	DENTAL ASSISTANT	f						
CRI	NURSE, LIC. PRACT.	f						
CRE	BEAUTICIAN	f						

Figure 49. Portion of SCII Profile. Reprinted from *Strong-Campbell Interest Inventory* Form 325 of the *Strong Vocational Interest Blank* by Edward K. Strong, Jr., and David P. Campbell with the permission of the publishers, Stanford University Press. Copyright © 1974 by the Board of Trustees of the Leland Stanford Junior University. This profile may not be copied or reproduced without permission in writing from Stanford University Press.

certain occupation dislike an activity more than the general population, the "Dislike" reaction to that activity is positively scored. Therefore, a student may receive a high score on an Occupational Scale by having dislikes in common with members of that occupation, as well as by having their likes in common.

After each Occupational Scale is an "f" or an "m," which indicates the sex of the sample used to create the scale. Every respondent is scored on all scales to be sure that complete data are available for everyone. It should be noted, however, that only the scores for the same-sex scales are plotted visually. This is because according to the manual the same-sex scales are more valid for the person than the scale of the opposite sex (Campbell, 1974).

The reader will note that in Figure 49 there are letters preceding each occupational title. These letters point to General Occupational Themes that are predominant in that occupation. The themes, for example, of an engineer are (I) Investigative and (R) Realistic, while a physician has these plus (S) Social. These themes are based both on the mean scores on the General Occupational Theme Scales received by each occupational criterion sample and on the correlations of the Occupational Scales with each of the Theme Scales.

The user of the SCII has the option of utilizing a second type of profile that is generated by computer (see Figure 50). No preprinted form is used. Interpretation of scores as well as the scores are printed out by the computer. The reader will note that the computer report illustrated in Figure 50 is only the first of eight pages.

The SVIB-SCII has had a long history of investigative research. This research has produced a great store of reliability and validity data (see Campbell, 1971, 1974). The *Mental Measurements Yearbook*, Vols. 1–7, list 1,267 entries on the SVIB. These entries only go up to 1972 but are indicative of the extensive warehouse of research data.

The long history of the SVIB has provided an opportunity to compare data on men tested in the 1930s with those on men tested in the 1960s. For example, one study was a comparison between the SVIB profile of 100 bankers who took the inventory in 1934 and a similar 100 bankers (same jobs and exactly the same banks as the 1934 bankers) tested in 1964. The two profiles were very similar, which seems to indicate that bankers of the 1960s share similar patterns to those of the 1930s (Campbell, 1974).

Kuder Interest Inventories

The first Kuder Preference Record was published in 1939. It was a vocational interest inventory constructed to yield seven independent scores on the following scales: Literary, Scientific, Artistic, Persuasive, Social Service, Musical, and Computational. The second record form (Preference Record Form B) rectified many of the faults of the first; for instance, the amount of

```
PAGE 1 OF 8                                              JANUARY 14, 1974

                    STRONG VOCATIONAL INTEREST BLANK
             STRONG-CAMPBELL INTEREST INVENTORY RESULTS FOR


             **SANDY SMITH**

     THE FOLLOWING STATISTICAL RESULTS HAVE BEEN COMPILED FROM YOUR ANSWERS
     TO THIS INVENTORY.

     THREE TYPES OF INFORMATION ARE PRESENTED-

             1) YOUR SCORES ON 6 GENERAL OCCUPATIONAL THEMES.  THESE GIVE
                SOME IDEA OF YOUR OVERALL OCCUPATIONAL OUTLOOK.

             2) YOUR SCORES IN 23 BASIC INTEREST AREAS.  THESE SHOW THE
                CONSISTENCY, OR LACK OF IT, OF YOUR INTERESTS IN EACH OF
                THESE SPECIFIC AREAS.

             3) YOUR SCORES ON 124 OCCUPATIONAL SCALES.  THESE TELL YOU
                HOW SIMILAR YOUR INTERESTS ARE TO THOSE OF EXPERIENCED WORKERS
                IN THE DESIGNATED OCCUPATIONS.


     FIRST, A CAUTION.  THERE IS NO MAGIC HERE.  THIS REPORT WILL GIVE YOU
SOME SYSTEMATIC INFORMATION ABOUT YOURSELF BUT YOU SHOULD NOT EXPECT MIRACLES.
YOUR SCORES ARE BASED SIMPLY ON WHAT YOU SAID YOU LIKED OR DISLIKED.

     MOST IMPORTANTLY---THIS TEST DOES NOT MEASURE YOUR ABILITIES-IT IS CONCERNED
ONLY WITH YOUR INTERESTS.


THE GENERAL OCCUPATIONAL THEMES

          PSYCHOLOGICAL RESEARCH HAS SHOWN THAT OCCUPATIONS CAN BE GROUPED
     INTO SIX GENERAL THEMES.  ALTHOUGH THESE ARE CRUDE, THEY DO PROVIDE
     USEFUL GUIDELINES.  HERE IS AN ANALYSIS OF HOW YOUR INTERESTS
     COMPARE WITH EACH OF THESE THEMES-

     R-THEME- THIS TYPE IS RUGGED, ROBUST, PRACTICAL, STRONG,AND
              FREQUENTLY AGGRESSIVE IN OUTLOOK.  THEY HAVE GOOD PHYSICAL SKILLS
              BUT SOMETIMES HAVE TROUBLE COMMUNICATING THEIR FEELINGS TO OTHERS.
              THEY LIKE TO WORK OUTDOORS AND WITH TOOLS, ESPECIALLY WITH LARGE POWERFUL
              MACHINES.  THEY PREFER TO DEAL WITH THINGS RATHER THAN WITH IDEAS
              OR PEOPLE.  THEY USUALLY HAVE CONVENTIONAL POLITICAL AND ECONOMIC
              OPINIONS, LIKE TO CREATE THINGS WITH THEIR HANDS, AND PREFER
              OCCUPATIONS SUCH AS MECHANIC, LABORATORY TECHNICIAN, SOME
              ENGINEERING SPECIALTIES, FARMER, OR POLICE OFFICER.  THE TERM
              *REALISTIC* IS USED TO SUMMARIZE THIS PATTERN, THUS, R-THEME.


          YOUR ANSWERS SHOW THAT FOR YOUR SEX YOU ARE LOW IN THESE
          CHARACTERISTICS AS YOUR STANDARD SCORE WAS 35.
```

Figure 50. SCII Interpretive Profile printed by computer. Reprinted from Strong-Campbell Interest Inventory Form 325 of the *Strong Vocational Interest Blank* by Edward K. Strong, Jr., and David P. Campbell with the permission of the publishers, Stanford University Press. Copyright © 1974 by the Board of Trustees of the Leland Stanford Junior University. This profile may not be copied or reproduced without permission in writing from Stanford University Press.

reading required for each choice was cut in half. Two scales were also added, Mechanical and Clerical.

The third form (Preference Record C) added a Verification Scale. This scale was composed of responses that almost everyone selects, and a score was derived to find those who did not answer items carefully. Because users of

Form B requested a scale measuring interest in agricultural, naturalist, and outdoor activities, a study was begun to see if such a scale could be developed. The result was a new scale, Outdoor, which was included in Form C (Kuder, 1971).

Two more forms since Form C have been developed and published. Form E came first as a logical continuation of, although not necessarily a replacement for, Form C. Form E used simpler language and was developed with younger children in mind. The items showed little resemblance to Form C (Kuder, 1971). The latest addition is the Kuder DD Occupational Interest Survey (Kuder, 1975). Its format is quite different from that of the other Kuder inventories. It has a new scoring technique and compares a person's interests with those of other persons in specific vocations. We shall briefly review Form C and the Occupational Survey, leaving the bulk of our attention for Form E, which has the most direct meaning for school personnel.

KUDER PREFERENCE RECORD FORM C

Form C has been widely used in the schools for a good many years. It is usually given in the ninth or tenth grade. The inventory consists of 168 questions. Each question is made up of three choices of activity, to which the person taking the test must respond by choosing the one he likes most and the one he likes least. There is no time limit. The average time for high school students has been found to be around thirty minutes to one hour and for college students approximately forty minutes. Scoring may be done by hand if pins are used. The directions are easy to follow and students may score the inventory themselves.

There are two profile sheets available for use in interpreting the nine scales and the Verification Scale. One profile sheet contains the norms for boys and girls in grades nine through twelve and the other presents norms for men and women. The examiner first checks the Verification score to see whether the inventory has been carefully completed. Next, he locates the highest score, the two highest, or in some cases even the three highest. (There are many possible combinations—even no high scores.) He then consults an occupational table that lists the scales and the various possible professions and vocations under that scale, for example,

Scientific
  Professional:
    Chemist
    County Agricultural Agent
    Dentist
  Semiprofessional:
    Aviator
    Weather Observer
  Clerical and Kindred:
    Physician's Assistant

Protective Service:
Detective

Form C may be used to help youngsters identify occupations they are interested in for further study and as a check on their choice of occupation to see whether it is consistent with the type of thing they ordinarily prefer to do (Kuder, 1960).

KUDER E GENERAL INTEREST SURVEY

Form E, according to Kuder (1971), was constructed in response to the need for an interest inventory to be used with younger students, especially at the junior high level. Language was kept to a sixth-grade level. In addition, other innovations were developed such as an improved scale for finding careless responses, lack of understanding, or faking. On the technical side, longer scales were constructed, because younger students' responses tend to be less reliable.

There are 168 items on this form. The instructions and format are very similar to those of Form C. Figure 51 serves as an illustration of Form E's general instructions and items. It generally takes forty-five to sixty minutes to administer; however, there is no definite time limit.

The student can score and plot his own profile by following the directions on the Profile Leaflet provided. The first step is to check the Verification score. Students whose scores on this scale are under a certain number (15) may proceed to construct their profiles. Scores over the prescribed number indicate that the student's responses may not be valid.

Figure 52 presents a portion of the Leaflet for grades 6 to 8. The Profile Leaflet also contains an interpretation of the verification scale. A major portion of this interpretation follows. Note that it is directed to the student to help him understand the meaning of his scores.

Interpreting Your Interest Profile [7]

You are interested in something if you enjoy doing it. Your interest profile indicates whether your interests in the ten areas measured are high, average, or low compared with those of other boys or girls at your grade level across the nation.

A score above the top dotted line in any column is a high score. It means that you have indicated a preference for activities in that area more frequently than most young people at your grade level. (The percentile on the same line as your score for an interest area tells you what percentage of students expressed preference for activities in that area less frequently than you did.) A score between the two dotted lines means that your interest in the area represented is about average. A score below the bottom dotted line is a low score. It indicates that you have not expressed preference for activities in that area as often as most young people.

[7] From *Profile Leaflet Grades 6–8, Kuder E, General Interest Survey* by G. Frederic Kuder © 1976, 1963, G. Frederic Kuder. Reprinted by permission of the publisher, Science Research Associates, Inc., Chicago, Illinois.

NAME_____ AGE_____ SEX_____ GROUP_____ DATE OF TEST_____
   Print   Last   First   Initial   M or F

DIRECTIONS

The *Kuder General Interest Survey* is exactly what its title suggests: a survey of your interests in a wide range of activities. It is not a test. There are no answers that are right or wrong for everyone. An answer is right if it is true for you.

If corrugated paper has been distributed to you, place it in the booklet just before the profile section, page 33.

On each page of this booklet you will see a list of things to do, in groups of three. First read the list of all three activities in a group. Decide which of the three you like *most*. In the answer section there are two circles on the same line as this activity—one in the column marked **M** for *most* and one in the column marked **L** for *least*. Using the pin provided, punch a hole through the left-hand circle following this activity. (Hold the pin straight up and down when you punch your answers.) Then decide which activity you like *least*, and punch a hole through the right-hand circle of the two circles following this activity.

In the examples below, the person answering has indicated for the first group of three activities that he prefers the activity "visit a museum" *most*, and the activity "browse in a library" *least*. For the second group of three activities he has indicated he prefers the activity "collect signatures of famous people" *most*, and the activity "collect butterflies" *least*.

EXAMPLES
Punch your choices for these activities in the section at the right.

P. Visit an art gallery . . . .
Q. Browse in a library . . . .
R. Visit a museum . . . .

S. Collect signatures of famous people . . . .
T. Collect coins . . . .
U. Collect butterflies . . . .

Please pretend that you can do *all* of the things listed, even those that require special training. Make your choices as if you were equally familiar with *all* of the activities. Do not choose an activity just because it is new or different, or because you think others might consider it a good choice.

You may like all three activities in a group, or you may dislike all three. In either case, show what your choices would be if you *had* to choose. *It is important that you answer all questions.* For each group of activities, it is essential that you choose the activity *most* preferred and the activity *least* preferred.

Do not spend a great deal of time on any one group. Do not talk over the questions with anyone. Unless an answer represents what *you* think, it will not contribute to a helpful picture of your interests.

If you want to change an answer, punch two more holes close to the answer you wish to change; then punch the new answer in the usual way.

Each time you turn a page, firmly crease it along the perforation on the left-hand margin of the booklet. Keep the bound spine always pointing to the left. This will assure accurate alignment of the pin-punches for scoring.

Start now and continue working until you have indicated your choices for all pages, columns 1 through 12.

Be sure to put your name, sex (F for female and M for male), age at your last birthday, grade, and today's date—month, day, and year—at the top of this page.

2

Figure 51. Instructions and sample problems from the Kuder E, General Interest Survey. (From Kuder E, *General Interest Survey* by G. Frederic Kuder. © 1976, 1963, G. Frederic Kuder. Reprinted by permission of the publisher, Science Research Associates, Inc.)

Like most people, you probably have scores that are high in some areas, low in some, and average in others. Looking at *all* your scores is important, because most school subjects and jobs involve a combination of two or more interests.

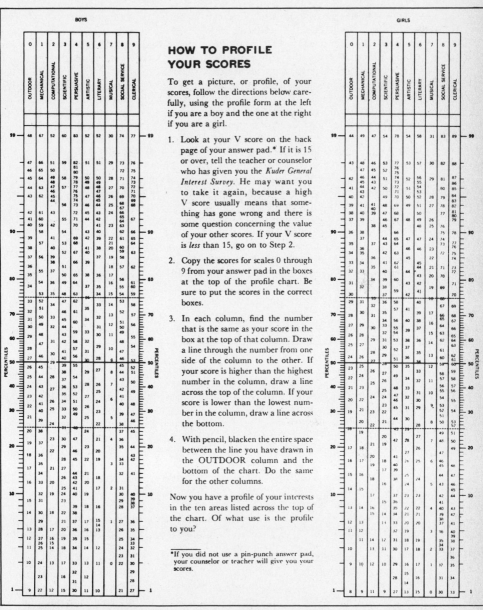

Figure 52. Profile Leaflet for Kuder E, General Interest Survey. (From Kuder E, *General Interest Survey* by G. Frederic Kuder. © 1976, 1963, G. Frederic Kuder. Reprinted by permission of the publisher, Science Research Associates, Inc.)

The more interested you are in a school subject, a job, or anything you do, the greater your chances are for success in it. It is easier and more satisfying to put your efforts into activities you enjoy than into those you dislike. Of course, no one can do *only* what interests him. Studying your interests, however, will help you direct your activities mainly into channels where you are more likely to achieve satisfaction. In addition, such study may help you find some things that appeal to your interests even in chores that you dislike.

An important fact to keep in mind is that low scores sometimes mean that you haven't had enough of an opportunity to develop interests in certain areas. Imagine, for example, a young person whose family and friends are not particularly interested in music, and who has not had an opportunity to learn to play an instrument, to listen attentively to records, or to go to concerts. He may not score as high in musical interest as someone who has had more experience with music. You have to be introduced to or discover an activity before you can like it or dislike it. Participating in something you've decided you might like may in turn tend to strengthen your interest in it. As you mature and are exposed to a variety of new experiences, some of your old interests may change and some new ones may develop.

High interests are not *better* than low interests; nor is one interest better—or worse—than another. What counts is knowing what your interests are and considering them whenever you have an important educational or vocational decision to make.

Here is what the ten interest areas measured by the *Kuder General Interest Survey* mean.

Outdoor interest means preference for work or activity that keeps you outside most of the time—usually work dealing with plants and other growing things, animals, fish, and birds. Foresters, naturalists, fishermen, telephone linemen, and farmers are among those high in outdoor interest.

Mechanical interest means preference for working with machines and tools. If you like to tinker with old clocks, repair broken objects, or watch a garage mechanic at work, you might enjoy shop courses in school. Aviator, toolmaker, machinist, plumber, automobile repairman, and engineer are among the many jobs involving high mechanical interest.

Computational interest indicates a preference for working with numbers and an interest in math courses in school. Bookkeepers, accountants, bank tellers, engineers, and many kinds of scientists are usually high in computational interest.

Scientific interest is an interest in the discovery or understanding of nature and the solution of problems, particularly with regard to the physical world. If you have a high score in this area, you probably enjoy working in the science lab, reading science articles, or doing science experiments as a hobby. Physician, chemist, engineer, laboratory technician, meteorologist, dietitian, and aviator are among the occupations involving high scientific interest.

Persuasive interest is an interest in meeting and dealing with people, in convincing others of the justice of a cause or a point of view, or in promoting projects or things to sell. Most salesmen, personnel managers, and buyers have high persuasive interest. If you have a high score in this area, you may enjoy such activities as debating, selling tickets for a school play or dance, or selling advertising space for the school paper.

Artistic interest indicates a preference for doing creative work with the hands —usually work involving design, color, and materials. If you like to paint, draw, sculpt, decorate a room, design clothes, or work on sets for school plays, you are probably high in this interest. So are artists, sculptors, dress designers, architects, hairdressers, and interior decorators.

Literary interest is an interest in reading and writing. Persons with literary interest include novelists, English teachers, poets, editors, news reporters, and librarians. If you have a high score on the literary scale, English is probably one of your favorite subjects, and you may enjoy writing for the school paper or magazine.

Musical interest usually is demonstrated by persons who enjoy going to concerts, playing an instrument, singing, or reading about music and musicians. Musicians, music teachers, and music critics are among those who have directed high musical interest into a vocation.

Social Service interest indicates a preference for activities that involve helping people. Nurses, Boy Scout or Girl Scout leaders, vocational counselors, tutors, personnel workers, social workers, hospital attendants, and ministers, rabbis, and others in religious service are among those high in this interest area.

Clerical interest means a preference for work that is clearly defined for you— work that involves specific tasks requiring precision and accuracy. If you have high clerical interest, you probably enjoy school subjects and activities that require attention to detail. Jobs such as bookkeeper, accountant, file clerk, salesclerk, statistician, teacher of commercial subjects, and traffic manager fall in this area.

The ten interest areas discussed here are not the *only* ones; nor is the classification system used the only one possible (for example, interests may be classified by specific occupations or by preferences for certain kinds of personal situations). The interest areas described, however, are the ones that will mean most to you in making decisions about school subjects and broad fields of work to explore.

Scores in related interest areas are much higher for some occupations than for others. For example, authors, editors, and reporters are at the 97th percentile in literary interest. Musicians and music teachers are at the 99th percentile in musical interest. Mechanics and repairmen, on the other hand, are at the 65th percentile in mechanical interest—their highest score; and surgeons are at the 75th percentile in scientific interest.

Some occupational groups have scores nearly as high—or higher—in apparently unrelated interest areas as in related areas. In one survey the highest percentile for lawyers and judges was 82, on the literary scale. The next was 61, on both the musical and the clerical scales. In another survey the second-highest interest for surgeons was outdoor interest, with a percentile of 68. Their next-highest interest was literary, with a percentile of 66. The main reason for results of this type is that people often have more than one strong interest. They may go into a career that make uses of their combined interests, or they may direct one or more of their strong interests into a satisfying after-work activity that provides a change of pace and broadens the range of their activities. Businessmen may find relaxation and a chance to get away from people and pressures in such activities as hunting and fishing. One retail salesman, for example, may enjoy many do-it-yourself activities involving high mechanical interest. Another may enjoy fishing or gardening or acting in a community theater. A businessman may, in his free time, play in a string quartet, paint or sculpt, or engage in some other kind of activity not clearly related to the work he performs for a living.

Knowledge of your interests can tell you only what you *enjoy* doing; *it cannot tell you how well you do these things.* What you do well depends on many things besides interest—particularly, your abilities. Your counselor can help you find out whether your abilities measure up to your interests. He can help you with your decisions about what course of study and school subjects to take. Your counselor may also be able to suggest ways in which you can explore and broaden your interests—extracurricular activities you might enjoy, books appropriate to your interests, and kinds of part-time or summer jobs you might want to consider. At various points during your school years—especially before making plans for college or a job—you may want to reexamine your interests. Your counselor can suggest other Kuder interest inventories for this purpose.

The Survey is not intended to be the basis of vocational choice. It is intended as background information to be utilized in the whole process of choosing a career. In the seventh and eighth grades, the Survey can help students choose electives, high school courses, and areas of study, for example, college track or commercial track. In the ninth or tenth grade, the Survey provides the opportunity for the student to reexamine interests or plan a high school program, or, if the student has decided to drop out of school, it can help in choosing immediate vocational pursuits.

The relationship of Form E to Form C was studied. Correlations were obtained ranging from .69 to .82 for boys, with a median of .76; and from .65 to .86 for girls, with a median of .79 (Kuder, 1971). For definitive data on validity, reliability, and other technical information, see the Manual (Kuder, 1971) and Buros (1972).

KUDER DD OCCUPATIONAL INTEREST SURVEY (OIS)

The DD inventory is primarily geared for high school juniors and seniors to help them make immediate vocational or educational choices. It also may be used with college freshmen and adults in employment counseling, placement centers, and Job Corps type programs (Kuder, 1975).

The format of the items is very similar to that of the other Kuder inventories. There are 100 sets of three activities each, and the student is asked to indicate his preference by marking one "most" and one "least" for each set. The scores are reported and plotted on a special table. See Figure 53 for a sample report. The results show the degree to which the student's preferences resemble those typical of people in various occupations and areas of study. About 80 per cent of the people in the occupations and areas of study listed (satisfied with their vocations) obtain scores of .45 or more on the scale for their job or area of study (Kuder, 1975).

An important feature of the OIS is the fact that scores for it represent the correlation of a person's interest with those of people in a number of specifically defined occupations. (The person's scores for these occupations are compared directly with each other.) This is a departure from other Kuder inventories, which are based on a general reference group. (See discussion on technical aspects of inventories at the end of this chapter.) In addition, the verification score is improved and should lead to the identification of faking or misunderstanding.

The decade of the 1970s has seen a great deal of change in terms of male and female opportunities and role identities. Therefore, some may question if separate norms for the sexes are still relevant. According to Kuder (1975),

Report of Scores — Kuder Occupational Interest Survey (Form DD)

NAME: HARE, PETER — LOCATION: ASHLAND H.S. # 000-38928 — DATE OF SURVEY: 04-08-74

OCCUPATIONAL SCALES FEMALE NORMS

Accountant	.51	Nurse	.35
Bank Clerk	.43	Nutritionist	.35
Beautician	.33	Occupational Therapist	.31
Bookkeeper	.45	Office Clerk	.40
Bookstore Manager	.36	Physical Therapist	.39
Computer Programmer	.49	Primary School Teacher	.37
Counselor, High School	.38	Psychologist	.38
Dean of Women	.36	Psychologist, Clinical	.33
Dental Assistant	.42	Religious Education Director	.28
Department Store Saleswoman	.33	Science Teacher, High School	.41
Dietitian Administrative	.40	Secretary	.43
Dietitian, Public School	.40	Social Caseworker	.30
Florist	.34	Social Worker, Group	.30
Home Demonstration Agent	.31	Social Worker, Medical	.31
Home Ec Teacher, College	.41	Social Worker, Pyschiatric	.29
Interior Decorator	.29	Social Worker, School	.29
Lawyer	.36	Stenographer	.41
Librarian	.35	X-Ray Technician	.43
Math Teacher, High School	.47		

COLLEGE MAJOR SCALES, FEMALE

Art & Art Education	.25
Biological Sciences	.40
Business Ed & Commerce	.48
Drama	.25
Elementary Education	.34
English	.32
Foreign Languages	.33
General Social Sciences	.36
Health Professions	.41
History	.34
Home Economics Education	.37
Mathematics	.51
Music & Music Education	.28
Nursing	.33
Physical Education	.39
Political Science	.36
Psychology	.40
Sociology	.30
Teaching Sister, Catholic	.34

OCCUPATIONAL SCALES MALE NORMS

Acc't. Certified Public	.57	Engineer, Electrical	.57	Optometrist	.55	Psychology Professor	.46
Architect	.43	Engineer, Heating Air Cond.	.57	Osteopath	.45	Radio Station Manager	.45
Automobile Mechanic	.40	Engineer, Industrial	.53	Painter, House	.35	Real Estate Agent	.50
Automobile Salesman	.40	Engineer, Mechanical	.58	Pediatrician	.46	Sales Eng. Heating Air Cond	.51
Banker	.52	Engineer, Mining & Metal	.56	Personnel Manager	.42	Science Teacher, High School	.50
Bookkeeper	.56	Farmer	.44	Pharmaceutical Salesman	.40	School Superintendent	.46
Bookstore Manager	.49	Florist	.45	Pharmacist	.48	Social Caseworker	.38
Bricklayer	.43	Forester	.50	Photographer	.47	Social Worker, Group	.37
Building Contractor	.45	Insurance Agent	.48	Physical Therapist	.47	Social Worker, Psychiatric	.35
Buyer	.55	Interior Decorator	.28	Physician	.44	Statistician	.54
Carpenter	.37	Journalist	.39	Plumber	.40	Supv Foreman, Industrial	.51
Chemist	.51	Lawyer	.43	Plumbing Contractor	.49	Travel Agent	.46
Clothier, Retail	.47	Librarian	.41	Podiatrist	.47	Truck Driver	.42
Computer Programmer	.59	Machinist	.43	Policeman	.46	Television Repairman	.54
Counselor, High School	.45	Mathematician	.51	Postal Clerk	.50	University Pastor	.34
County Agricultural Agent	.40	Math Teacher, High School	.58	Printer	.46	Veterinarian	.42
Dentist	.48	Meteorologist	.51	Psychiatrist	.40	Welder	.43
Electrician	.46	Minister	.33	Psychologist, Clinical	.41	X-Ray Technician	.48
Engineer, Civil	.57	Nurseryman	.48	Psychologist, Counseling	.43	YMCA Secretary	.38
				Psychologist, Industrial	.48		

COLLEGE MAJOR SCALES MALE NORMS

Agriculture	.51	Foreign Languages	.44
Animal Husbandry	.48	Forestry	.52
Architecture	.43	History	.44
Art & Art Education	.32	Law (Grad School)	.46
Biological Sciences	.48	Mathematics	.67
Business Acc't & Finance	.63	Music & Music Ed	.40
Business & Marketing	.50	Physical Education	.48
Business Management	.55	Physical Sciences	.59
Economics	.57	Political Science & Gov't	.44
Elementary Education	.50	Premed, Pharm & Dentistry	.54
Engineering, Chemical	.61	Psychology	.52
Engineering, Civil	.60	Sociology	.49
Engineering, Electrical	.64	U.S. Air Force Cadet	.49
Engineering, Mechanical	.59	U.S. Military Cadet	.49
English	.40		

OCCUPATIONAL SCALES FEMALE NORMS Title	Score	COLLEGE MAJOR SCALES FEMALE NORMS Title	Score	OCCUPATIONAL SCALES MALE NORMS Title	Score	COLLEGE MAJOR SCALES MALE NORMS Title	Score
ACCOUNTANT	.51	MATHEMATICS	.51	COMPUTR PROGRAMR	.59	MATHEMATICS	.67
COMPUTR PROGRAMR	.49	BUS ED & COMMERC	.48	ENGINEER, MECH	.58	ENGINEERING, ELEC	.64
MATH TCHR, HI SCH	.47			MATH TCHR, HI SCH	.58	BUS ACCT AND FIN	.63
BOOKKEEPER	.45	HEALTH PROFES	.41	ACCT, CERT PUBLIC	.57	ENGINEERING, CHEM	.61
		BIOLOGICAL SCI	.40	ENGINEER, CIVIL	.57		
BANK CLERK	.43	PSYCHOLOGY	.40	ENGINEER, ELEC	.57	ENGINEERING, CIVIL	.60
SECRETARY	.43	PHYSICAL EDUC	.39	ENG, HEAT/AIR CON	.57	ENGINEERING, MECH	.59
X-RAY TECHNICIAN	.43	HOME ECON EDUC	.37	BOOKKEEPER	.56	PHYSICAL SCIENCE	.59
DENTAL ASSISTANT	.42	GEN SOCIAL SCI	.36	ENG, MINING/METAL	.56	ECONOMICS	.57
HOME EC TCHR, COL	.41	POLITICAL SCI	.36	BUYER	.55	BUS MANAGEMENT	.55
SCIENCE TCHR, HS	.41	ELEMENTARY EDUC	.34			PREMED/PHAR/DENT	.54

V 53

M	.53	S	.61
MBI	.19	F	.55
W	.43	D	.37
WBI	.19	MO	.41

Figure 53. Sample report form for Kuder Occupational Interest Survey. (From Kuder DD *Occupational Interest Survey—General Manual* by G. Frederic Kuder. © 1966, 1968, G. Frederic Kuder. Reprinted by permission of the publisher, Science Research Associates, Inc.)

the reason is that men and women, even in the same occupation, tend to respond differently to certain items in the OIS. For example, 57 percent of men in general but only 35 percent of women in general marked that they would rather go to see a fire than do either of the other activities presented in the same item. Differences of this sort occur most frequently in the manual and lower-skilled occupations, where relatively few women are employed today.

These sex differences in responses appear to be determined mainly by differences in early play experiences, how parents and others expected boys and girls to behave, and other such factors. As these things change and as more women go into skilled trades and more men into occupations such as secretary, primary school teacher, and nurse, men and women may not differ as greatly in the degree to which they like and dislike certain activities.

As they share more and more common experiences, the interests of men and women in general—but particularly of those in the same occupation—should increasingly resemble each other. Right now, however, most men respond differently from most women to certain items. For this reason, although scores are reported on all scales regardless of the sex group on which the scales were developed, subjects should study each set of scores under its own heading. (p. 9)

A Final Word on the Kuder Inventories

A common denominator of all the instruments is the forced-choice format —the student must answer "most" or "least" to three possible activities. They all share a heritage of many years of dedicated research and analysis since the publication of the first inventory in 1939. With all the research done by Kuder and his associates as well as by independent investigators, it is of interest to note the following caution in interpreting the results of any of the Kuder instruments (or any instrument, for that matter),

Factors other than ability may make it unfeasible for people to give serious consideration to occupations or fields of study in which they have high interest scores; for example, a student with a high score on the Farmer scale, for whom moving into a rural area would be undesirable, should not regard farming as a good possibility to explore. In any case students should not feel pressured to pursue investigation of a particular field, regardless of how high their interest scores or how great their abilities in that field. The principal purpose of their scores is to point out promising possibilities for future occupations or studies from the point of view of their own patterns of interests. The scores should help them make decisions by suggesting a variety of choices to explore; they should under no circumstances be regarded as pointing to the only possible paths open. (Kuder, 1975, p. 11)

Minnesota Vocational Interest Inventory

The Minnesota Vocational Interest Inventory (MVII) provides information on the interest patterns of men in *nonprofessional occupations*. It is intended as a guidance tool for counselors working with students and other individuals who are planning vocations in the semiskilled and skilled occupations (Clark and Campbell, 1965). Individual scores represent the similarity of the interests of the person taking the MVII to those of men in a variety of non-professional occupations.

The MVII has 158 sets of three items to which the person responds by choosing the item he would like to do most and the item he would like to do least. The actual format is the same as the Kuder Form C in terms of the triads of three items and the task of selecting one most and one least desired activity (forced-choice method). Figure 54 presents the profile sheet used in plotting the results. The shaded bands reveal the scores of the middle third of a group of skilled tradesmen.

In interpreting the results, a written explanation (on the other side of the profile sheet) is given to help the student understand the meaning of the scales and his scores on them. Scoring may be done by hand or machine. There is no time limit. Most individuals are able to complete the inventory in less than forty-five minutes (Clark and Campbell, 1965).

Practical Implications of Interest Inventories

Many studies concerning the relationship between interest and ability have been made. Most of them show a slight relationship between academic achievement in a field and interest in it. There is also some indication that those of high ability in a certain field will show some interest in it. However, this relationship is too low for us to state that an interest inventory can be used to determine ability or, on the other hand, that an ability or achievement test can reveal interest. The counselor must have both types of information for sound vocational counseling. It is important, therefore, to remember that if a student has a high score in scientific interest, it does not necessarily mean that he has the ability to become a scientist. In making a vocational choice, the interest pattern of a student must be viewed along with his or her past academic record and achievement and aptitude test scores.

Let us examine an actual counseling situation to see how interest inventories are used. Ralph Laine, counselor at Education High School, is thinking about one of his students. The boy, Jerry, is attempting to decide on a career. His highest interest scores are in mechanical and artistic areas. Mr. Laine, after reviewing the results of the interest inventory, looks up Jerry's ability and achievement test scores as well as his class record. He does this because he knows that ability as well as interest is required for success in a vocation. From the class record and test data, Mr. Laine can see that there is a good chance of college for Jerry. He therefore points out to Jerry occupations that utilize his interest and abilities. He discusses with Jerry, for example, the possibility of becoming an architect, an artist, or a teacher of art. In addition, he points out occupations at the semiprofessional level that do not require a college education, such as draftsman, decorator, and taxidermist. He does not, however, go into other fields that do not require even a high school education, such as upholstering or tailoring. Although the

MINNESOTA VOCATIONAL INTEREST INVENTORY

NAME _____ AGE _____ SEX _____ DATE _____

OCCUPATIONAL SCALES	STD. SCORE^a	0	10	20	30	40	50	60
1 BAKER								
2 FOOD SERVICE MANAGER								
3 MILK WAGON DRIVER								
4 RETAIL SALES CLERK								
5 STOCK CLERK								
6 PRINTER								
7 TAB. MACHINE OPERATOR								
8 WAREHOUSEMAN								
9 HOSPITAL ATTENDANT								
10 PRESSMAN								
11 CARPENTER								
12 PAINTER								
13 PLASTERER								
14 TRUCK DRIVER								
15 TRUCK MECHANIC								
16 INDUSTRIAL EDUC. TEACHER								
17 SHEET METAL WORKER								
18 PLUMBER								
19 MACHINIST								
20 ELECTRICIAN								
21 RADIO-TV REPAIRMAN								

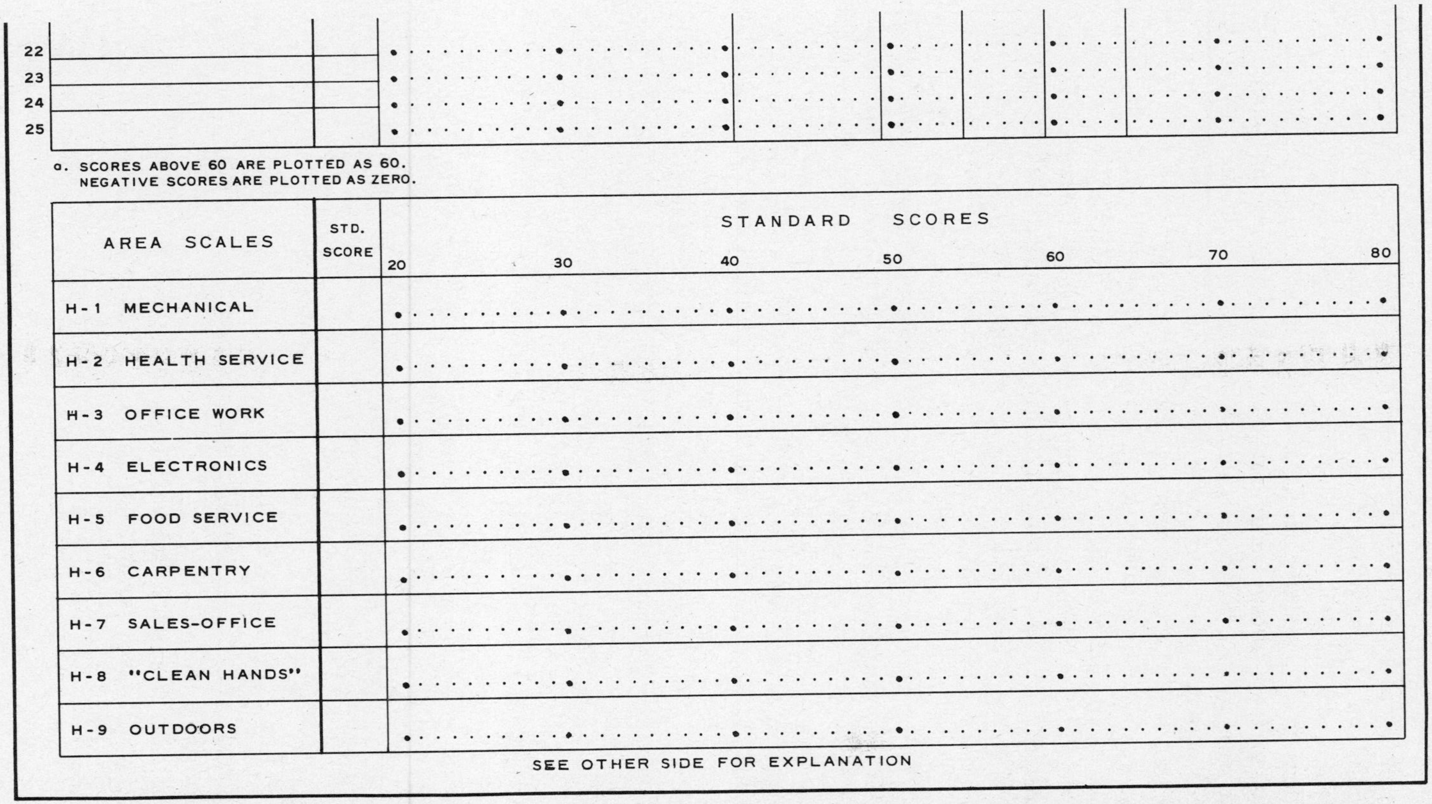

Figure 54. MVII profile sheet. (Reproduced by permission. Copyright © 1965. The Psychological Corporation, New York, N. Y. All rights reserved.)

job is still far from simple, the interest test has narrowed the field, and Mr. Laine and Jerry can now concentrate on the occupations requiring mechanical and artistic activity.

In viewing the interest patterns of a student, there are certain facts in addition to those already mentioned that one must bear in mind. First, interest patterns generally reveal themselves in mature children at the age of fifteen or sixteen. However, some develop definite interests as late as age twenty-two, and others may never develop these patterns. Second, interest patterns generally seem to be established in a person before he or she has had a chance to have extensive occupational experience. Third, because a person has certain interests, we cannot say definitely that he or she will be successful in the areas of interest. Other factors, such as ability, must also be considered. It is self-evident, therefore, that interest patterns *cannot* predict school achievement. Fourth, interest scores may predict the relative happiness or feeling of satisfaction a person may receive from certain types of work. Fifth, most people may be satisfied in many different types of school-work and in a number of different jobs. Sixth, if a person wants to fake interest, this can be done easily. The Kuder has keys that sometimes reveal faking, but they are not foolproof. Of course, most people seeking vocational guidance tend to be honest in their answers, at least at the conscious level. And, seventh, motivation and personality may enter the picture and distort the meaning of the interests of an individual as revealed by an inventory (Carter, 1949; Strong, 1943, 1955; Super and Crites, 1962; Darley and Hagenah, 1955; Campbell, 1968, 1974; Kuder 1971, 1975).

The student of measurement should remember that interest inventories are only systemized surveys of what a person is interested in. *Don't forget the person.* Some people *do not* need to have an interest inventory to point out their vocational choices. They are sure of what they want and where they are going. Whether they are right or wrong is not the point; they have a right to make their own decisions. Interest inventories should not be given on the basis that "it's good for them" but on the basis of the needs of the individual student. (For an excellent discussion of some of the practical problems in interest measurement, see Weitz, 1968.)

Technical Aspects

Most of the major innovations in interest inventories have been based on empirical data. These data have at times been very complete and other times not very extensive.

The Strong Vocational Interest Blank and the Kuder inventories have both been intensively investigated. This is not the place to review their credentials in terms of exact validity and reliability coefficients. The interested student may pursue this by referring to the latest manuals and other references previously cited in this chapter. It can be stated, however, that in general both yield scores that are acceptable in terms of reliability for teen-age individuals or older persons. These inventories reveal reliability coefficients that are fairly comparable to those of ability tests.

The main task in appraising the validity of interest inventories is judging the honesty of the person's responses. As Thorndike and Hagen (1969) state, "There isn't really any higher court of appeal for determining a person's likes and preferences than the individual's own statement" (p. 395). There is no doubt that a person can fake his responses, but as we have stated before if he comes of his own volition there is little reason for a conscious distortion.

In the area of concurrent validity, the situation is different. The occupational-interest scales for the Strong were, for example, devised to distinguish members of occupational groups from people in general. Percentage overlaps [8] for each scale on SVIB were computed. They range from 15 to 52, with a median of 31 per cent overlap, for the men's form; and from 16 to 42, with a median of 34, for the women's form. Thus the scales as a whole are fairly successful in separating the groups (Campbell, 1974). Most of the Kuder (with the notable exception of Kuder's Occupational Interest Survey, 1975) inventories attempt to distinguish between members of vocations and people in general.

Strong's (1955) classical investigation revealed the predictive validity of his instrument. This study showed a high degree of agreement between interest scores in 1927–30 and occupations of these people in 1949. A great deal of accumulated evidence reveals that on the whole both the Strong and Kuder have some validity as predictors of vocational choice.

The validity and reliability of the Minnesota Vocational Interest Inventory are promising but must still await further research before it can take its place next to the Strong and Kuder.

The selection of one interest inventory over another is dependent on pupil needs, age, and occupational horizons. As a general rule, the Strong is never given before the senior year of high school, whereas the Kuder inventories may be first administered in junior high school.

If the teacher or counselor recognizes that the interest inventory is tentative and that it is not a measure of ability but only of declared interests, and uses it along with other data, most students can profit from the experience of taking an interest inventory.

[8] The percentage of scores in one distribution that can be matched by scores in another distribution. If the distributions of the two groups are identical, the overlap is 100 per cent. A complete separation means a zero overlap.

College Entrance Examinations

chapter 11

The American college today is faced with the problem of accommodating large numbers of young people who want a college education. The history of higher education has been different from that of the public schools. Americans have prided themselves on the fact that public schools were for all children no matter what their academic potential or achievement. Colleges and universities, on the other hand, have not attempted to educate all the people; they have accepted only those with the academic abilities to profit from a higher education.[1] Therefore, colleges have always been faced with the problem of selective admissions. As a consequence, colleges used standardized tests and other selective criteria even before the number of college applicants became so large.

Colleges differ as to the testing instruments they use for selection. Some administer their own tests; others prefer to use the services of the College Entrance Examination Board (CEEB) or the American College Testing Program (ACT). The basic difference between the Scholastic Aptitude Test of the CEEB and the ACT lies in the grouping of items and in the scores provided. The ACT provides tests organized into sections and produces scores more nearly related to the traditional disciplines, whereas the Scholastic Aptitude Test is organized in a verbal-quantitative manner.

[1] The reader might quibble with this statement because of "open admission" in some schools such as the City University of New York. However, this program has not been entirely successful and a return to more selective admission is occurring. Additionally, most colleges have never experimented with open enrollment.

Most of our discussion in this chapter will be devoted to the CEEB and ACT, which represent the greatest percentage of admissions testing in the United States. Let us first briefly review some of the other tests used by colleges and administered at the local level.

College-Administered Tests

Among the most prominent tests used by colleges not participating in the CEEB and ACT programs are the following: The College Qualification Tests of the Psychological Corporation, the School and College Ability Tests of the Educational Testing Service, Ohio State University Psychological Test, Form 21 of the Ohio College Association, and the College Classification Tests of Science Research Associates. All of these are similar in terms of what they attempt to measure. The Ohio State University Psychological Test differs from the others in that there is no time limit. The School and College Ability Tests is the same instrument, at the college level, mentioned in Chapter 8. To illustrate the kinds of items generally found on most of the preceding tests, let us look at the College Qualification Tests.

The College Qualification Tests (CQT) is a multipurpose battery that serves as a basis (partial) for college admissions, placement, and counseling. It is also used in some scholarship award programs. There are three tests:

1. *CQT-Verbal.* This section is basically a vocabulary test with synonym-antonym questions. It attempts to measure verbal aptitude, which is an important ability needed for college success.
2. *CQT-Numerical.* This section attempts to measure mathematical skills in arithmetic, algebra, and geometry.
3. *CQT-Information.* This is a test of general information in the areas of science (physics, chemistry, biology) and social studies (history, government, economics, geography). It was constructed to measure the student's general background. This section yields two subscores, Science and Social Studies, as well as a total Information score.

The level of the test ranges from grades eleven through thirteen. The manual presents norms based on freshmen in state universities, private colleges, Southern universities, and junior colleges as well as norms for six different degree programs.

College Entrance Examination Board

One of the oldest and best known of the major selection testing programs is the College Entrance Examination Board (CEEB). The CEEB is a non-profit membership organization composed of more than 2,000 colleges, schools, educational systems, and education associations (College Entrance Examination Board, 1976b). Chauncey and Dobbin (1966), in their discussion of the history of testing, state the basic reason for the creation of the CEEB,

> *The College Board examination program was started at the turn of the century as the result of a proposal that colleges requiring examinations for admission would do both the high schools and the applicants a service by setting a common examination on which an applicant could earn admission to any of a number of colleges. Until the College Board was formed, a student who wanted to enter his application at three colleges had to take three different examinations at three different times and places. The principal of any high school that had many college-going graduates had an exasperating time trying to arrange for and comply with the multitude of examinations his seniors needed to take . . . not to mention preparing the students for the examinations. (p. 17)*

The first tests consisted of essay questions. In 1926 an objective test called the Scholastic Aptitude Test (SAT) was used for the first time. The use of the SAT increased slowly at first, but as more schools began to require it for admission and as the number of college applicants increased, the SAT became a "household name" to aspiring college students. In the years since 1926, thousands of research studies have been conducted by these and other educational institutions, as well as by private investigators, to ascertain the predictive validity of the SAT (College Entrance Examination Board, 1976b).

A service of the College Entrance Examination Board is the Admission Testing Program (ATP). The ATP offers the Scholastic Aptitude Test, the Test of Standard Written English, the Achievement Tests, and the Student Descriptive Questionnaire.

The CEEB has its tests administered at testing centers throughout the world. These centers are usually located in a high school or college. The tests are administered by local qualified personnel at either the high school or college level. There is strict adherence to standardized procedures. The administrator is even required to call long distance for certain types of irregularities.

The centers administer the test and send them back to the CEEB headquarters in their geographical region for scoring. The results are then sent to the student and his or her secondary school as well as to the colleges to which he or she is applying for admission. Score reports are sent free of charge to the first three colleges of the applicant's choice. There is a nominal charge for each additional college.

Test Dates and Schedule. Although dates and number of administrations of the College Board may vary, the usual number is six times during a calendar year. The administration dates are spread out during the year, for example, November, December, January, March, May, and June. There are various restrictions concerning who may take the examination and where it is given;

therefore, it is necessary to check information concerning administration. The administration dates are usually scheduled for Saturdays.

The Preliminary Scholastic Aptitude Test/National Merit Scholarship Qualifying Test

The Preliminary Scholastic Aptitude Test/National Merit Scholarship Qualifying Test (PSAT/NMSQT) is basically a shorter version of the Scholastic Aptitude Test. The PSAT/NMSQT is given to students in their junior year of high school. The College Board investigated students' academic performance in college based on three years of high school, and found that by the time a child is a junior in high school his or her performance in college can be predicted by his or her three years of grades and an aptitude test almost as well as by senior year grades and test scores. Because of this finding, the College Board decided to offer the PSAT/NMSQT to encourage earlier and better college guidance. Thus the College Board recommends the PSAT/NMSQT for juniors. Colleges that are College Board members will consider the PSAT/NMSQT scores in early counseling and in giving advice to prospective students concerning their chance of acceptance and success.

The PSAT/NMSQT is a one-hour-and-forty-minute examination. There are two scores, verbal and mathematical. The scores are reported on a scale ranging from 20 to 80.

Some educators may wonder if the PSAT/NMSQT is really necessary. You may be saying to yourself, "Look here, by the time a student is in his junior year the school already has information useful for counseling him about college plans. I have also read that a pupil's performance in college preparatory courses is the most important indicator of college success or failure. And besides all of the above, what about those standardized tests you have been talking about? Isn't that enough testing? Why is the PSAT/NMSQT needed or helpful anyway?"

The PSAT/NMSQT may be helpful in several ways. For example, the child who gets all A's at one high school may be only a C student at another school. The PSAT/NMSQT helps solve the problem of different standards among high schools by serving as a national yardstick that can be used to measure a student's ability as compared to other boys and girls throughout the nation. In addition, the school counselor will have information concerning the scores needed for admission on this test by various colleges and universities. He, therefore, can help students in early planning for college in a realistic and meaningful manner.

It is not wise, however, to assume that a student's PSAT/NMSQT score is the only factor in predicting college success or failure. Suppose, for example, that John scores below 30 on the PSAT/NMSQT and is thinking of going to college. His academic record is good, and he seems to be motivated to work in school. In addition to these factors, his family can offer him strong financial and moral support. If this is the case, he can probably still gain admission to college if, with the counselor or teacher's support and guidance, a college is carefully selected.

Each student receives one copy of *About Your PSAT/NMSQT Scores*. This booklet contains the scores of the student plus a variety of tables and other information to help students interpret their scores.

Each school is sent two copies of the *Report of Student Scores and Plans*. The report presents test scores and percentile ranks for all the school's students who took the PSAT/NMSQT and biographical data such as projected college major and career preferences. An asterisk to the right of a student's Selection Index indicates that he or she did not meet the requirements for scholarship competitions administered by National Merit Scholarship Corporation (College Entrance Examination Board, 1975a).

SOME TECHNICAL DETAILS

The score range of the PSAT/NMSQT, as was mentioned earlier, is from 20 to 80 and is equivalent to the score scale of the SAT, which ranges from 200 to 800. The placement of a zero after the PSAT/NMSQT score reveals what the student's probable SAT score would have been if he had taken the SAT instead of the PSAT/NMSQT. For example, a PSAT/NMSQT score of 45 is roughly equivalent to a SAT score of 450. It should be noted that relatively low scores are followed by somewhat higher average increases than high PSAT/NMSQT scores. A junior year PSAT/NMSQT score of 30, for example, is usually increased, on the average, to a senior SAT score of 345, whereas a 60 is increased on the average to 610 (College Entrance Examination Board, 1975a).

The equivalency between the two tests lends itself to comparisons of scores between individual students and groups of students tested on different dates in different years. It should be noted, of course, that grade levels must be considered in these comparisons. This is because a junior who has obtained the same score as a senior may actually be a better student.

The PSAT/NMSQT, like any other test, cannot be interpreted as representing the exact college potential of every student. The standard error of measurement for both the verbal and mathematical sections is approximately four points.

The PSAT/NMSQT may also be given to sophomores. The average gain from sophomore to senior will be larger than the junior to senior score gain because of a longer time between tests. For the same reason, sophomore scores tend to be less reliable. It is recommended that these scores be used only as "rough indicators."

NATIONAL MERIT SCHOLARSHIP CORPORATION

Thus far we have talked about the PSAT phase of the equation of PSAT/NMSQT. Let us now turn our attention to the National Merit segment. The National Merit Scholarship Corporation (NMSC) has the responsibility for the administration of the National Merit Scholarship Program and the National Achievement Scholarship Program for Outstanding Negro Students. High School students who take the PSAT/NMSQT finish the first requirement in the yearly competitions NMSC conducts. NMSC is a nonprofit organization that administers the Scholarship Program. The annual competition for undergraduate college scholarships is open to U.S. citizens who are attending high school.

Recent competitions have seen about 3,800 Merit Scholarships worth about $9 million awarded each year. A Special Scholarship is given to the person whose PSAT/NMSQT scores are high but less than the score needed to become a finalist and qualify a Merit Scholarship (College Entrance Examination Board, 1975a). Approximately 475 Special Scholarships estimated to be worth $1.4 million are offered each year by 130 companies that sponsor Merit Scholarships.

The first steps in obtaining eligibility for a scholarship are

1. U.S. citizenship or plans to obtain as soon as qualified.
2. Enrollment as full-time high school student progressing toward completion of high school.
3. Plans to attend an accredited college upon graduation from high school and to enroll full-time in an academic program leading to one of classical degrees.
4. Take PSAT/NMSQT at the proper time.

The program designates "Commended Students." These are students whose scores place them in the top 2 per cent of the nation's graduating seniors. They will not be considered for National Merit scholarships because their Selection Index scores are below merit level.

Semifinalists are those who compete for the scholarships and whose scores put them in the top one-half of one per cent of the country's secondary school seniors in a given year. Designation is on a regional basis so the country as a whole will be represented.

To become a finalist and to be in the running for a Merit Scholarship, a student must meet the requirements given earlier plus the following:

1. Be in the final year of high school and plan to enter a regionally accredited U.S. college during the fall of the following year.
2. A high academic standing verified by a transcript.
3. Endorsed and recommended by high school principal.
4. Complete an NMSC scholarship application.
5. Confirm his or her previous PSAT/NMSQT scores by equivalent scores on the SAT.

The preceding are in essence the general requirements for the NMSC. The reader is referred to the PSAT/NMSQT Student Bulletin (College Entrance

Examination Board, 1975b) or the NMSC [2] for more definitive information.

The Scholastic Aptitude Test (SAT)[3]

The SAT is the oldest examination of the College Entrance Examination Board. This test measures skills basic to schoolwork. Like the PSAT, it has two sections, verbal and mathematical. *It is a test of ability, not of factual knowledge.* The verbal section emphasizes ability to read with understanding and to reason with words. The reading material consists of passages from such academic fields as the humanities, social science, and science. The mathematical section measures the individual's aptitude in solving problems and stresses mathematical reasoning rather than factual recall of high school mathematics.

Verbal and mathematical talents are, of course, related to college success. Usually the scores of any individual on the SAT are closely related to his success as a student. Therefore, one usually finds that a student who has a good academic record will score high on the SAT, whereas the student who has performed poorly in school is very likely to receive a low score. Of course, there are exceptions to every rule; the SAT is far from being a perfect predictive yardstick of collegiate success.

The SAT is a two-and-one-half hour multiple-choice test. It is divided into five thirty-minute sections and is given with the thirty-minute Test of Standard Written English. The test booklets vary in that one student may be answering math questions while another is responding to verbal questions. Several new editions of the SAT are developed each year, each assembled to the same content and statistical specifications. Generally, the easiest questions come first. Each question counts the same and there is only one correct answer. A statistical process called *equating* is used to ensure that the scores a student receives are relatively independent of the particular edition of the SAT taken.

Scores on the SAT, as you remember, are reported in numbers ranging from 200 to 800. About two-thirds of the students taking the SAT score somewhere between 400 and 600. In terms of a general grading system in which zero is at the bottom and 100 is a perfect score, we can state that 200 is equal to zero and 800 is equal to 100. Therefore, an individual cannot receive a score below 200 or one above 800.

The standard error of measurement for both the verbal and mathematical sections is approximately thirty points. The reliability coefficient based on the Kuder-Richardson Formula 20 is .90 for the verbal section and .88 for the mathematical section.

---

[2] National Merit Scholarship Corporation, Department of Educational Services, 990 Grove Street, Evanston, Ill. 60201.

[3] Sources for the descriptions of the various SAT and Achievement tests and other relevant data are College Entrance Examination Board (1976a,b,c,d,e).

Why Take the SAT?

Not all students should take the SAT. The student who does is interested in obtaining admission to a college that requires the SAT as one of the criteria for selection. It helps these schools in evaluating applicants from all over the world by providing them with a uniform frame of reference to judge a variety of college applicants. It helps the student in evaluating the college by comparing his scores with the average student at the college of his choice.

Can Students Study for the SAT?

The best answer to give to the question of whether one can study for the SAT would be to say yes, if the pupil begins in the first grade of school. Though this may sound like an evasion of the question, it is a most honest and logical answer, because school skills are the direct result of practice and instruction over a long period of time. You cannot expect Johnny to study for a few weeks or even months and acquire the skills that he should have learned years before. No one believes that one can learn to play the trumpet or sing or become a major-league baseball player overnight. All these skills require years of practice and development. By the same token, one cannot learn to read well or reason logically in a few hard sessions of cramming.

Research into the problem of preparation for the SAT has shown that cramming or special course preparation does not raise the student's score enough to make it worth while. (See Chapter 5 for a thorough discussion of this problem.) Thus the best preparation for the student is to do his schoolwork in earnest, read widely, and observe and think about his environment throughout his school years. The administrators of the College Board Examinations state that the student should avoid cramming and come to the test well rested. They do state, however, that reviewing math concepts may be of benefit. Each student who plans to take the SAT is given a booklet describing the test. In this booklet, the suggestion is made that the student go over the practice questions carefully so that he or she will understand the directions clearly and not use precious time for this purpose when he or she comes to the actual testing situation.

Sample Questions from the SAT

The following items are similar to those found in the Verbal and Mathematical sections of the SAT.[4] Included is at least one example of each type of SAT question:

---

[4] The following sample questions are reprinted from *About the SAT—Admissions Testing Program of the College Entrance Examination Board 1976–77.* Reprinted by permission of Educational Testing Service, the copyright owner. This booklet, which contains many illustrative examples of the different kinds of questions that are used in the Scholastic Aptitude Test, is revised annually and is supplied without cost to high schools for distribution to students before they take the test. This booklet as well as other CEEB materials may also be obtained on request by writing the College Entrance Examination Board, Box 592, Princeton, N.J. 08540.

VERBAL QUESTIONS

The SAT Verbal section consists of four types of questions: sentence completions, reading passages, antonyms, and analogies. The first two yield a reading comprehension subscore, and the last two yield a vocabulary subscore.

Reading Comprehension: Sentence Completion. In the sentence completion type of question, the student must select words or phrases that are consistent in style or logic with other elements in the sentence.

Directions: Each sentence below has one or two blanks, each blank indicating that something has been omitted. Beneath the sentence are five lettered words or sets of words. Choose the word or set of words that *best* fits the meaning of the sentence as a whole.

Question 1:
From the first the islanders, despite an outward —, did what they could to — the ruthless occupying power.
(A) harmony. .assist (B) enmity. .embarrass (C) rebellion. .foil
(D) resistance. .destroy (E) acquiescence. .thwart

Explanation:
The answer should involve two words that are more or less opposite in meaning, since the word *despite* implies that the islanders acted in one fashion, while presenting a somewhat different impression to the *ruthless occupying power.* (A), (B), (C), and (D) fail to give the sense of opposition that is required. If *outward harmony* existed, to *assist* the occupying power would probably contribute to this state of harmony and strengthen it. If *enmity* existed, *embarrassing* the occupying power would be one method of expressing this feeling. If *rebellion* did exist, then the islanders would be doing what they could to *foil* the occupying power; these words are not opposite in meaning and do not make sense in the sentence. The same logic holds for *resistance. .destroy.* The only choice implying two opposed actions is (E).

Question 2:
High yields of food crops per acre accelerate the — of soil nutrients.
(A) depletion (B) erosion (C) cultivation (D) fertilization
(E) conservation
Answer: (A)

Reading Comprehension: Reading Passages. Questions that require the reading of passages test the student's understanding of the sense of a written excerpt. Comprehension at various levels is tested. The student must be able to interpret and to analyze what is read. Some questions require application of the principles or opinions expressed. The passages are taken from published sources in a variety of fields.

Directions: Read the following passages and then answer the questions on the basis of what is *stated* or *implied* in the passages.
In the searching rhetoric of student action, all idols and ego models toppled. Not even Martin Luther King, Jr. escaped. The students honored King, but they refused to accept his leadership because they did not think he was radical

enough. Borrowing the concept of confrontation and the tactic of direct action from King, the students carried the struggle to a new level, adding mass action to direct action. Above all else, they added the fateful escalator principle, the idea that racial tensions must be raised to the highest pitch. Central to the new orientation of the students was the idea of choice and responsibility. It was necessary, they said, to present communities with clear-cut choices between bias and some other highly cherished value, civic peace or profits, for example. Not until men had to choose once and for all between, say, dollar bills and bigotry, would a breakthrough occur. The theory did not suffer through implementation. In the period from February 1960 to September 1961, the sit-in movement affected 20 states and more than 100 cities.

The new strategy was spelled out in a Nashville jail in the spring of the struggle. In this jail were scores of sit-in students awaiting trial on charges of disturbing the peace. John Lewis, an American Baptist Seminary student who later became national chairman of the Student Nonviolent Coordinating Committee, decided that the moment was appropriate for a sermon. He opened his Bible, peered through the bars at the guards and his fellow students, and announced his text: Matthew 10:34.

> Think not that I am come to send peace on earth:
> I came not to send peace, but a sword.

Question 1:
The strategy on which the student action discussed in the passage was based can best be described as one of
(A) compromise   (B) orientation   (C) confrontation
   (D) responsibility   (E) dialogue

Explanation:
The information given throughout the passage eliminates choices (A), (B), and (E). The students wanted to take direct action and to increase tensions. Choice (D) fails to pinpoint the students' proposed and actual tactics, but (C) does aptly describe them and is therefore the best answer to this relatively easy question.

Question 2:
It can be inferred that John Lewis chose Matthew 10:34 as his text primarily because it
(A) promised that there would be peace on earth
(B) did not advocate passive resistance
(C) contained a reference to the concept of mass action
(D) was not familiar to his listeners
(E) told the story of a person awaiting trial
Answer: (B)

Vocabulary. The vocabulary score is derived from testing knowledge of antonyms and analogies. The Antonyms test is designed to test extent and quantity of vocabulary, while the Analogies test is designed to test understanding of relationships among words and ideas.

Antonyms (Opposites)

Directions: Each question below consists of a word in capital letters, followed by five lettered words or phrases. Choose the word or phrase that is most clearly *opposite* in meaning to the word in capital letters. Since some of the questions require you to distinguish fine shades of meaning, consider all the choices before deciding which is best

Question 1:
   COMPOSURE: (A) analysis   (B) alertness   (C) contrast
   (D) agitation   (E) destruction

Explanation:
   The word *composure* means calmness or self-possession. Choices (A), (C), and (E) can be eliminated, as they are clearly not opposites of calmness. Although choice (B) *alertness* suggests mental activity and attentiveness, its opposite would be a word specifically suggesting lack of attention. The correct answer is, therefore, (D) *agitation*, which means emotional disturbance or excitement.

Question 2:
   SCHISM: (A) majority   (B) union   (C) uniformity
   (D) conference   (E) construction
Answer: (B)

Question 3:
   FINITE: (A) without success   (B) without change
   (C) without end   (D) inexpressible   (E) unfortunate
Answer: (C)

Question 4:
   MALICE: (A) charity   (B) abundant wealth
   (C) complete agreement   (D) vigor   (E) strong feeling
Answer: (A)

Analogies

Directions: Each question below consists of a related pair of words or phrases, followed by five lettered pairs of words or phrases. Select the lettered pair that *best* expresses a relationship similar to that expressed in the original pair.

Question 1:
   SUBMISSIVE:LED:: (A) intolerable:indulged   (B) incorrigible:taught
   (C) wealthy:employed   (D) inconspicuous:overlooked
   (E) condescending:humiliated

Explanation:
   The relationship between *submissive* and *led* can be stated: "Someone who is (submissive) can be easily (led)." The answer is (D) since someone who is (inconspicuous) can be easily (overlooked).

Question 2:
   SNAKE:PYTHON::   (A) bird:starling   (B) flower:blossom
   (C) mammal:reptile   (D) lion:tiger   (E) rat:mouse
Answer: (A)

Question 3:
   GEM:SETTING:: (A) diamond:coal   (B) painting:frame

(C) tree:habitat   (D) novel:epilogue   (E) mountain:valley
Answer: (B)

Question 4:
   CAT:LYNX:: (A) crow:eagle   (B) cow:ox   (C) monkey:man
   (D) leopard:panther   (E) dog:wolf
Answer: (E)

MATHEMATICAL QUESTIONS
The mathematical portion of the SAT consists of two kinds of multiple-choice questions:

(1) Standard multiple-choice questions
     (approximately two-thirds of the test)
(2) Quantitative comparison questions
     (approximately one-third of the test)
The mathematical questions in the SAT measure quantitative abilities closely related to college-level work.
The arithmetic includes the four basic operations of addition, subtraction, multiplication, and division, properties of odd and even integers, and averages. The algebra includes linear equations and exponents, but not quadratic equations or fractional or negative exponents. The geometry includes the properties associated with parallel lines and the informal measurement-related concepts of area, perimeter, volume, the Pythagorean Theorem, and angle measure in degrees. Unusual notation is used only when it is explicitly defined for a particular question.
   Certain questions emphasize nonroutine or insightful problem-solving approaches. For example, the correct solution to certain problems can be obtained once an appropriate insightful approach is discovered, but could be obtained only at the cost of much time and thought if a routine approach were used. Other . . . problems may be solved reasonably by either method, although an insightful approach might still be quicker than a routine one.

The directions and reference formulas that are shown in the sample booklet also appear in the actual test. Thus the student can be familiar with these before the testing session.

Standard Multiple-Choice Questions

Directions: In this section solve each problem using any available space on the page for scratchwork. Then indicate the *one* correct answer in the appropriate space on the answer sheet.
   The following information is for your reference in solving some of the problems.

Circle of radius r:
   Area $= \pi r^2$
   Circumference $= 2\pi r$
   The number of degrees of arc in a circle is 360.
   The measure in degrees of a straight angle is 180.

Triangle:
   The sum of the measures in degrees of the angles of a triangle is 180.

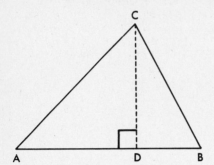

If ∠CDA is a right angle, then

(1) area of △ABC = $\dfrac{AB \times CD}{2}$

(2) $AC^2 = AD^2 + DC^2$

Definitions of symbols:

< is less than	≦ is less than or equal to
> is greater than	≧ is greater than or equal to
⊥ is perpendicular to	‖ is parallel to

Note: Figures which accompany problems in this test are intended to provide information useful in solving the problems. They are drawn as accurately as possible EXCEPT when it is stated in a specific problem that its figure is not drawn to scale. All figures lie in a plane unless otherwise indicated. All numbers used are real numbers.

If $16 \times 16 \times 16 = 8 \times 8 \times P$, then P =
(A) 4 (B) 8 (C) 32 (D) 48 (E) 64
Answer: (E)

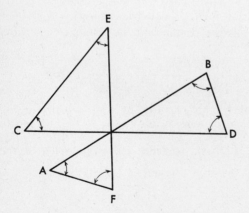

In the triangles above, if AB, CD, and EF are line segments, what is the sum of the measures of the marked angles?
(A) 180° (B) 360° (C) 540° (D) 720°
(E) It cannot be determined from the information given.

This is an example of a moderately difficult question. The ability to reason insightfully in a nonroutine manner is almost essential to solving the problem within a reasonable period of time. One such solution requires discovering that the sum of the measures of the unmarked angles in the three triangles is 180°. Since the sum of the measures of all the angles in the three triangles is 540°, it follows that the sum of the marked angles is 540° − 180°, or 360°.

Answer: (B)

Quantitative Comparison Questions

Each of these questions presents two quantities to be compared, one in Column A and the other in Column B. In general, this type of question requires less time to answer, involves less reading, and requires somewhat less computation than the usual multiple-choice mathematics question. . . . the concepts of greater than (>), less than (<), and equal to (=) [must be used] to decide which choice is correct.

Directions: Each question in this section consists of two quantities, one in Column A and one in Column B. You are to compare the two quantities and on the answer sheet blacken space

A if the quantity in Column A is the greater;
B if the quantity in Column B is the greater;
C if the two quantities are equal;
D if the relationship cannot be determined from the information given.

Notes: 1. In certain questions, information concerning one or both of the quantities to be compared is centered above the two columns.
2. A symbol that appears in both columns represents the same thing in Column A as it does in Column B.
3. Letters such as x, n, and k stand for real numbers.

Questions:

Column A	Column B
1. $3 \times 352 \times 8$	$4 \times 352 \times 6$

2. $\dfrac{1}{x}$ is a negative integer.

Column A	Column B
$-\dfrac{1}{x}$	x

Explanations:

1. Note that 352 is common to both quantities. Since 3×8 equals 4×6, the two quantities are equal and the correct answer is (C). Note also that in arithmetic questions such as this, a (D) answer is impossible.

2. You are given that $\dfrac{1}{x}$ is negative. From this you can conclude that x must be negative and $-\dfrac{1}{x}$ must be positive. Since any positive number is greater than any negative number, the quantity in Column A is greater than the quantity in Column B. Answer: (A)

EXAMPLES		
Column A	Column B	Answers
E1. 2×6	2+6	● Ⓑ Ⓒ Ⓓ

E2. 180 - x.	y	Ⓐ Ⓑ ● Ⓓ
E3. p - q	q - p	Ⓐ Ⓑ Ⓒ ●

Student Descriptive Questionnaire (SDQ)

The SDQ presents a series of questions to students about their interests, experiences, activities, and future plans. Students do not have to answer these questions. The SDQ is an effort to humanize college selection. Thus colleges may see students in terms of strengths, weaknesses, and needs rather than grades and test scores alone. The primary purpose of the SDQ is to help students achieve their post-high school objectives. The data are also used for research, although individual names are never identified.

Student Search Service (SSS)

The SSS is constructed to enable colleges and scholarship donors to identify people with certain characteristics, using data from the SDQ. Students record their interest in being in SSS by answering affirmatively to item number 1 on the SDQ. The SSS provides factual data and opportunities for post-high school planning.

The Test of Standard Written English (TSWE)

The TSWE is a thirty-minute multiple-choice test and is given with the SAT. The items assess the student's ability to perceive standard written English. Many colleges do not require the TSWE, but some may use it to place freshmen in the introductory English course.

The purpose of this test is to evaluate a student's ability to recognize standard written English. Standard written English is defined as the language of most college textbooks and the English that students will probably be expected to use in the papers they write for most college courses.

The . . . test contains 50 multiple-choice questions. In general, the questions are somewhat easier than those in the SAT. The Test of Standard Written Eng-list is not intended to distinguish among students whose command of English is better than average. Scores are reported on a 20 to 60+ scale. Therefore, students who receive a score of 60+ can conclude that the test is not difficult enough to measure the upper limits of their ability.

No question on the test asks [the student] to define grammatical terms like "clause" or "noun" or to identify correct spelling or capitalization. And in only a few questions are punctuation marks like the semicolon or the apostrophe important in arriving at the answer.

The samples that follow illustrate the two types of questions included in the test.

Sample Questions

Usage

Directions: The following sentences contain problems in grammar, usage, diction (choice of words), and idiom. Some sentences are correct. No sentence contains more than one error.

You will find that the error, if there is one, is underlined and lettered. Assume that all other elements of the sentence are correct and cannot be changed. In choosing answers, follow the requirements of standard written English.

If there is an error, select the one underlined part that must be changed in order to make the sentence correct, and blacken the corresponding space on the answer sheet. If there is no error, mark answer space (E).

Question 1:

The Secretary of State, as well as the other members of the cabinet, were summoned suddenly to the bedside of the ailing President. No error
    A   B   C   D   E

Explanation:

The correct answer to this question is (A). The error is one of agreement. In standard written English, the sentence would read: "The Secretary of State, as well as the other members of the cabinet, was summoned . . ." It is important to remember that "as well as" does *not* link words in the same way as "and" does. The underlined words at (B), (C), and (D) are used correctly.

Question 2:

Prefabricated housing is economical because they reduce labor costs
                    A   B   C

considerably. No error.
    D   E
Answer: (C)

Sentence Correction

Directions: In each of the following sentences, some part of the sentence or the entire sentence is underlined. Beneath each sentence you will find five ways of phrasing the underlined part. The first of these repeats the original; the other four are different. If you think the original is better than any of the alternatives, choose answer (A); otherwise choose one of the others. Select the best version and blacken the corresponding space on your answer sheet.

This is a test of correctness and effectiveness of expression. In choosing answers, follow the requirements of standard written English; that is, pay attention to grammar, choice of words, sentence construction, and punctuation. Choose the answer that produces the most effective sentence—clear and exact, without awkwardness or ambiguity. Do not make a choice that changes the meaning of the original sentence.

Question 1:
Eddie was as angry as Linda was when he discovered that thieves had stripped her car.
  (A) Eddie was as angry as Linda was
  (B) Eddie had anger like Linda's
  (C) Eddie's anger was like Linda was
  (D) Eddie's anger was as great as Linda
  (E) Eddie had an anger as great as Linda

Explanation:
This question tests your ability to recognize that, logically, only similar things should be compared with each other. The best choice is (A) because it compares one person with another, as logic demands. (C), (D), and (E) are incorrect answers because they compare a person with an emotion. (B) does compare one person with another, but it uses language not ordinarily used in standard written English ("had anger" for "was angry").

Question 2:
The world-famous actress, Sarah Bernhardt, born in 1844.
  (A) The world-famous actress, Sarah Bernhardt, born in 1844.
  (B) A world-famous actress was Sarah Bernhardt, born in 1844.
  (C) Sarah Bernhardt, the world-famous actress, was born in 1844.
  (D) Born in 1844 was Sarah Bernhardt, being a world-famous actress.
  (E) She was a world-famous actress and Sarah Bernhardt was born in 1844.
Answer: (C)

Achievement Tests

The College Board Achievement Tests are constructed by committees appointed by the College Board that include both college and secondary school teachers. These people work with measurement specialists at Educational Testing Service. The development of the test follows the same procedure inherent in any proper standardized achievement test construction (see Chapter 9).

The College Board Achievement Tests consist of the following one-hour tests:

American History and
   Social Studies
Biology
Chemistry
English Composition
English Literature

Hebrew
Latin
Mathematics, Level I
   (Standard)
Mathematics, Level II
   (Intensive)

European History and	Physics
World Cultures	Russian
French	Spanish
German	

Ten of the fifteen tests are administered at the regular testing dates; the remainder are given at less frequent intervals.[5]

The scores on the achievement tests are reported on the standard 200 to 800 College Board scale. Results are reported in the same manner as the SAT.

In the following discussion of the specific achievement tests, the questions presented represent some of the sample items from the ATP-CEEB booklet (College Entrance Examination Board, 1976c), which is given to students planning to take the achievement tests. The information contained in this booklet is intended to help the student understand the types of questions that will be asked and the manner in which they will be presented.

Sample Test Questions from the Achievement Tests [6]

ENGLISH COMPOSITION

The English Composition Test uses a multiple-choice format. Four aspects of composition are measured. These are (1) relationship between ideas in a sentence, (2) tone and meaning of words, (3) wordiness and ambiguity, and (4) structure and idiom of written English generally acceptable to college teachers.

Directions: The following sentences may contain problems in grammar, usage, diction (choice of words), and idiom.
Some sentences are correct.
No sentence contains more than one error.
You will find that the error, if there is one, is underlined and lettered.

EXAMPLE:

He spoke bluntly and angrily to we spectators.
    A   B   C   D

No error
    E   Answer: Ⓐ Ⓑ ● Ⓓ Ⓔ

---

[5] During the 1976–77 year, European History and World Cultures, Hebrew, Latin, and Russian were given only in December 1976 and May 1977.
[6] The following examples are from *About the Achievement Tests—Admissions Testing Program of the College Entrance Examination Board,* 1976–77. Reprinted by permission of Educational Testing Service, the copyright owner.

Assume that all other elements of the sentence are correct and cannot be changed. In choosing answers, follow the requirements of standard written English.

If there is an error, select the <u>one underlined part</u> that must be changed in order to make the sentence correct, and blacken the corresponding space on your answer sheet.

If there is no error, mark answer space E.

Questions:

1. It is startling <u>to realize</u> that in this rich country thousands of people live out
A

   <u>their life</u> <u>without ever having</u> <u>enough to eat.</u> <u>No error</u>
   B   C   D   E

2. The <u>descent</u> in the number of hatching eaglets <u>is said to be</u> <u>the result of</u> an
A   B   C

   increasing <u>concentration</u> of DDT in the food of the parent birds. <u>No error</u>
   D   E

A second kind of question requires [the student] not only to identify unacceptable usage, but also to choose the best way of phrasing a sentence.

Directions: In each of the following sentences some part of the sentence or the entire sentence is underlined. The underlined part presents a problem in the appropriate use of language. Beneath each sentence you will find five ways of writing the underlined part. The first of these repeats the original, but the other four are all different. If you think the original sentence is better than any of the suggested changes, you should choose answer A; otherwise you should mark one of the other choices. Select the best answer and blacken the corresponding space on your answer sheet.

This is a test of correctness and effectiveness of expression. In choosing answers, follow the requirements of standard written English; that is, pay attention to acceptable usage in grammar, diction (choice of words), sentence construction, and punctuation. Choose the answer that produces the most effective sentence—clear and exact, without awkwardness or ambiguity. Do not make a choice that changes the meaning of the original sentence.

Questions:

1. The reader of "Manchild in the Promised Land" <u>cannot scarcely help but be</u> moved by the experiences Claude Brown describes.
   - (A) cannot scarcely help but be
   - (B) can scarcely help to be
   - (C) can but scarcely help be
   - (D) cannot scarcely help but to be
   - (E) can scarcely help being

2. Henry David Thoreau first saw Walden Pond at the age of five years, which <u>was later to become famous as the setting of his experiment in simple living.</u>
   - (A) Henry David Thoreau first saw Walden Pond at the age of five years, which was later to become famous as the setting of his experiment in simple living.
   - (B) When he was five years old, Henry David Thoreau first saw Walden Pond, which was later to become famous as the setting of his experiment in simple living.

(C) When he was five years old, Henry David Thoreau first saw Walden Pond, and later this became famous as the setting of his experiment in simple living.

(D) At the age of five years, Henry David Thoreau first saw Walden Pond, and this place was later to become famous as the setting of his experiment in simple living.

(E) Henry David Thoreau, being five years old, first saw Walden Pond, later becoming famous as the setting of his experiment in simple living.

A third type of composition question tests the student's command of traditional grammar by having him or her review sentences containing faulty grammar or structure. The student must spot wrong tense, case, or number, failure to maintain parallel structure, misplaced modifiers, and similar errors.

Directions: Read each sentence carefully; then on your answer sheet blacken space
A if the sentence contains faulty diction;
B if the sentence is wordy;
C if the sentence contains clichés or mixed metaphors;
D if the sentence contains faulty grammar or sentence structure;
E if the sentence contains none of these errors.

Questions:
1. The property immediately adjacent to the old mine and next to it is not worth much money and has little financial value.
2. His mother mentioned that he will go to kindergarten next fall, but she will be very much surprised if he liked it.
3. According to the next expert who bombasted, the committee had messed everything up so badly that construction could not initiate for another six months.

LITERATURE

The Literature Test assesses the student's ability to understand and to interpret works of literature. The questions are based on passages from poetry, fiction, drama, and prose written in English. The student is not expected to have read the selections, but is expected to use skills of analysis developed in studying literature. The student may be asked to analyze parts or summarize the meaning or tone of a passage or explain allusions or connotations of words or phrases. Other skills tested are knowledge of elements of style and the relationship of style to meaning, mood, or structure.

Directions: This test consists of selections from literary works and questions on their content, form, and style. After reading each passage, choose the best answer to each question. Read each passage carefully several times before you choose your answers.

Questions:
Learning teacheth more in one year than experience in twenty; and learning teacheth safely when experience maketh more miserable than wise. He hazardeth

sore that waxeth wise by experience. An unhappy master is he that is made cunning by many shipwrecks; a miserable merchant, that is neither rich nor wise but after some bankruptcies. It is costly wisdom that is bought by experience.

1. Which of the following best describes the style of the passage?
    (A) It uses a repeated balancing of parts rather than logical connectives.
    (B) It builds up to a climax by placing subordinate clauses first.
    (C) It is telegraphic in that subjects and occasionally predicates are omitted.
    (D) It uses a great number of long noun clauses to qualify the main statements.
    (E) It imitates conversation by using many parenthetical elements.
2. The effect of the style is best explained as one that
    (A) shows the author as unable to make up his mind.
    (B) reinforces the comparison of learning and experience.
    (C) shows that experience is really more valuable than learning.
    (D) makes the author seem to be an intimate friend of the reader.
    (E) reinforces the nautical imagery by reproducing the rhythm of the tide.

HISTORY AND SOCIAL STUDIES

Two tests in the history and social studies area cover American history (American History and Social Studies Test) and European history (European History and World Cultures Test).

AMERICAN HISTORY AND SOCIAL STUDIES

The American History and Social Studies Test emphasizes United States history of the nineteenth and twentieth centuries. Political history is emphasized, with social, economic, and diplomatic trends less represented. There are some questions dealing with cultural and intellectual history. Other fields of political science and law, economics, sociology, geography, and anthropology are also represented. Particularly emphasized are the concepts, methods, and generalization of these social studies as they affect the study of history. The test has different sections such as knowledge of specifics, inferences drawn from sources, and applications of abstractions to particulars.

Directions: Each of the questions or incomplete statements below is followed by five suggested answers or completions. Select the one which is best in each case. Some questions require knowledge of facts, terms, concepts, and generalizations. They test recall of basic information about significant aspects of American history and the social studies.

1. The predominant religion in colonial New England was
    (A) Anglican   (B) Lutheran   (C) Quaker
        (D) Congregational   (E) Baptist
2. All of the following conditions experienced by free Negroes in the pre-Civil War North were also encountered by black residents of Northern cities in the 1960s EXCEPT
    (A) substandard housing
    (B) legal disfranchisement
    (C) inferior public education
    (D) discrimination in employment
    (E) hostility from white ethnic minorities

Some questions require the ability to select or apply hypotheses, concepts, principles, or generalizations to given data. The questions may begin with concrete particulars and ask for the appropriate concept, or they may begin with a concept and apply it to particular problems or situations. Thus, both inductive and deductive reasoning are part of this category.

3. Over the past sixty years, hours worked have been steadily reduced, while both money wages and real wages have continued to rise. What factor is primarily responsible for this trend?
   (A) A reduction in profit margins
   (B) Minimum wage laws
   (C) Restriction of the labor supply
   (D) Increased output per man-hour
   (E) Right-to-work legislation

MATHEMATICS

There are two tests in mathematics. Level I is for those students who have had three years of college preparatory mathematics. This is usually the test used for college admission. Students with more than three years of math in high school are urged to take Level II.

Below is a diagram of the relative distribution of subject matter on the two tests. Both levels cover the same material but differ in attention devoted to the curriculum areas.

FOREIGN LANGUAGE

There are six tests in the foreign language area. These measure reading comprehension in French, German, Hebrew, Latin, Russian, and Spanish. The publishers recommend that a student should not take an Achievement Test in this area if he has had less than two full years of secondary school study in the language. An example of a vocabulary item from the French test follows:

Directions: This part consists of a number of incomplete statements, each having four suggested completions. Select the most appropriate completion and blacken the corresponding space on the answer sheet.

Questions:
1. Je n'ai pas d'argent. Je vais en . . .
   (A) apprêter   (B) empêcher   (C) emprunter   (D) prêter
2. Le général manoeuvra habilement...protéger ses troupes, tout en menaçant les éléments avancés de l'ennemi.
   (A) de manière à   (B) au moyen de   (C) sur le point de
   (D) en dépit de

SCIENCES

There are three tests in the sciences, covering biology, chemistry, and physics. The tests cover material generally included in high school courses in these subjects. Students are advised not to take the tests unless they have completed or almost have completed a full year of course work. For each science test, questions test knowledge, comprehension, application, analysis, synthesis, and evaluation.

BIOLOGY

The Biology Test covers the following topics: development and growth, ecology (including parasitism and disease), evolution, heredity, morphology, physiology,

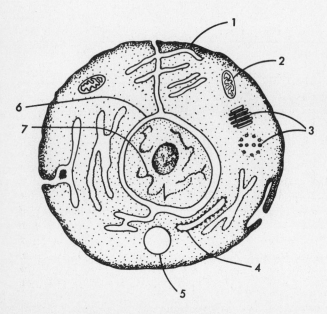

A GENERALIZED ANIMAL CELL

and taxonomy. These topics are covered at subcellular and cellular, tissue and organ, and organism and community levels. There are also a few questions on such topics as scientific methodology and the history of biology. Zoological and botanical materials are utilized in approximately equal amounts.

Questions closely related to the knowledge objective

Directions: The two questions [following] refer to a diagram with certain parts labeled with numbers. Each question is followed by five suggested labels or answers. For each question select the one best answer.

Questions: (see diagram of animal cell p. 360)
1. Aerobic respiration occurs in
   (A) 1   (B) 2   (C) 5   (D) 6   (E) 7
2. The genetic code is carried in
   (A) 1   (B) 2   (C) 4   (D) 5   (E) 7

CHEMISTRY

The Chemistry Test covers the content of a basic chemistry course including molecular theory, the periodic table, formulas and equations, and chemical reactions, as well as higher level application of knowledge. Below is an example of a question requiring analysis.

Directions: Each of the questions or incomplete statements below is followed by five suggested answers or completions. Select the one which is best in each case.

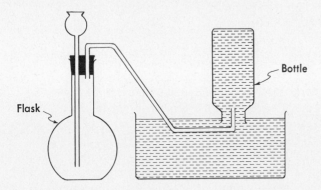

Question:
The apparatus shown above is assembled.
Copper pellets are placed in the flask. When <u>dilute</u> HNO_3 is dropped onto the the copper, the gas in the flask becomes light brown in color and remains that color while a large amount of colorless gas is collected in the bottle. When <u>concentrated</u> HNO_3 is dropped onto the copper, the gas in the flask becomes deep brown in color, and only a small amount of colorless gas is collected in the bottle. In both experiments, if air is mixed with the colorless gas in the bottle, the gas turns brown. A reasonable explanation for the absence of brown gas in the bottle is that this gas
   (A) can be formed only in the presence of copper

(B) is so cooled by the water in the pan that it becomes a liquid
(C) diffuses very slowly
(D) is too dense to be collected over water
(E) is very soluble in water

PHYSICS

The Physics Test measures the content of a good high school physics course. Emphasis is on the use of major principles.

Directions: Each of the questions or incomplete statements below is followed by five suggested answers or completions. Select the one which is best in each case.

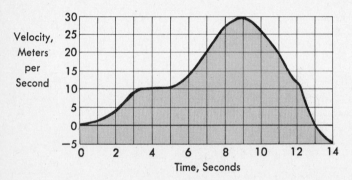

Velocity, Meters per Second

Time, Seconds

Question:
The graph above shows the velocity of a car as a function of time while the car moves along a straight track.
During the 7th second, the car is moving with constant
(A) speed   (B) velocity   (C) acceleration
(D) momentum   (E) kinetic energy

In interpreting achievement test scores it is important to remember that what is considered a good score at one college may not be considered good at another. Colleges differ in the scores they require for admission and placement.

In order to better understand what these scores mean, one must consider several factors. First, because all students do not take all the achievement tests, an individual may be competing with more able students on one test than on another. For example, the average score on the Advanced Mathematics Test is generally around 600, whereas the average Social Studies score is about 500.

Second, a student's foreign language score should be considered in relation to the number of years he has studied the language. It has been found that students taking these tests differ significantly in their scores according to the number of years of foreign language study. According to the College Board, students with three years of a language score eighty points higher than those with two years of study; those with four years of study generally score sixty points higher than those with three years of study.

American College Testing Program

One of the comparatively newer college admissions testing programs is the American College Testing Program (ACT). The ACT is a federation of state programs founded in 1959. It is an independent and nonprofit corporation. The American College Testing Program (1975a) states that its main purposes are to:

help students present themselves as persons with special patterns of educational abilities and needs

provide colleges with student admissions/enrollment data

provide dependable and comparable information for precollege counseling in high schools and for on-campus educational guidance

provide colleges with information about students' high school records

provide students with information about their college choices

provide estimates of students' academic and out-of-class abilities

provide Interest Inventory results to help students select college majors and make educational and career plans

provide information useful in granting scholarships, loans, and other kinds of financial assistance

help colleges place freshmen in appropriate sections in introductory courses in English, mathematics, social studies, and natural sciences

help colleges identify students who would profit from special programs such as honors, remedial, and independent study

help colleges estimate whether a student should be considered for further examination and advanced placement

help colleges examine and improve their educational programs. (p. 2)

There are over 2,400 institutions and agencies throughout the United States and foreign countries in the ACT program. This includes institutions of diverse objectives and curricula such as technical schools, universities, four-year liberal arts colleges, community colleges, and nursing schools (American College Testing Program, 1975a).

The ACT examination is given five times a year in 2,800 test centers in the United States and at about 180 centers in seventy-five foreign countries. The testing dates are in October, December, February, April, and June in the United States and in December, February, and April in foreign test centers.

The ACT Test Battery [7]

The ACT Test Battery is made up of four tests—English Usage Test, Mathematics Usage Test, Social Studies Reading Test, and Natural Sciences Reading Test—which attempt to measure abilities necessary for college work

---

[7] Information contained in the following descriptions of the various ACT tests and other data in the pages to follow are based on literature from the American College Testing Program (1972, 1974, 1975a,b,c, 1976). The interested student should use this information only as a general guide or orientation. For specific, detailed, and current information write to The ACT Program; P.O. Box 168; Iowa City, Iowa 52250.

by appraising how the student can apply what has already been learned. There is no attempt to measure specific and detailed subject matter.

The English Usage Test attempts to measure the student's understanding of capitalization, punctuation, usage, phraseology, style, and organization. This test has eighty items and requires forty minutes to administer. Items and format are similar to the English achievement test of the CEEB.

The Mathematics Usage Test attempts to appraise a student's mathematical reasoning ability. There are forty items; administration time is fifty minutes. The emphasis in the examination is on the solution of practical quantitative problems that are presented in many college mathematics courses. Mathematical techniques used in high school courses are also covered.

The Social Studies Reading Test attempts to measure evaluative reasoning and problem-solving skills required in social studies by appraising student comprehension of reading passages culled from representative social studies materials. In addition, items that test understanding of basic concepts, knowledge of reference sources, and awareness of study skills especially needed in college social studies curricula are measured. There are fifty-two items; the test administration time is thirty-five minutes.

The Natural Sciences Reading Test has fifty-two items; the total time for administration is thirty-five minutes. This test attempts to measure critical reasoning and problem-solving skills needed in the natural sciences. The major emphasis is on the development and testing of hypotheses and the appraisal of scientific reports. A sample passage and questions follow:

Test 4: Natural Sciences Reading [8]

Read the passage through once. Then return to it as often as necessary to answer the questions.

As the cells that make up different tissues and organs differ in structure and function, so also do they differ in their response to radiation. The law of Bergonie and Tribondeau states that the radiosensitivity of a tissue is directly proportional to its reproductive capacity and inversely proportional to its degree of specialization. In other words, immature, rapidly dividing cells will be most harmed by radiation. In addition, three other factors are important: under-nourished cells are less sensitive than normal ones; the higher the metabolic rate in a cell, the lower its resistance to radiation; and cells are more sensitive to radiation at specific stages of division.

Radiation alters the electrical charges of the atoms in the irradiated material, breaking the valence bonds holding the molecules together. For example, radiation passing through a cell is most likely to strike water molecules. The breakdown products from these molecules may combine with oxygen to form bleaches, which in turn can break down protein molecules in the cell. One class of these proteins comprises the enzymes that not only play a role in nearly all biochemical reactions but also control cell division. Such inhibition of cell

---

[8] From *Taking the ACT Assessment—1976–77 Edition*. Copyright 1976 by The American College Testing Program. All rights reserved. Reproduced by permission of the American College Testing Program.

division may permit cells to grow to an abnormal size; when such a cell dies there is no replacement to fill the void in the tissue. If the cell has been altered so that its daughter cells are genetically different from the parent cell, the daughter cells may die before they reproduce themselves; they may continue to grow without dividing; or they may divide at a higher or lower rate than the parent cell.

Because of these possible effects, doctors and scientists have been concerned about the exposure of humans to radiation. A study of the effects of radiation on the human body indicates that the following organ and tissue groups are most affected by radioactivity: (1) blood and bone marrow, (2) lymphatic system, (3) skin and hair follicles, (4) alimentary canal, (5) adrenal glands, (6) thyroid gland, (7) lungs, (8) urinary tract, (9) liver and gallbladder, (10) bone, (11) eyes, and (12) reproductive organs. Although no permissible level for exposure of humans to radiation has been established, data reported in 1957 indicate that 25 roentgens cause no observable reaction, 50 roentgens produce nausea and vomiting, 400 to 500 roentgens give the individual a fifty-fifty chance of survival without medical care, and 650 roentgens are lethal.

Questions:
1. Why is muscle tissue relatively unaffected by radiation?
    A. Its cells contain no water.
    B. It is highly specialized.
    C. It is protected by the bony skeleton.
    D. Its cells have a unique method of reproduction.
2. If radiation can *cause* cancer, as implied in the second paragraph, then which of the following best justifies the use of radiation in treating cancer?
    A. Cancer tissue is highly specialized, hence very sensitive to radiation.
    B. Only the cancer cells receive the radiation.
    C. Cancer cells divide relatively rapidly.
    D. The patient may die anyway, and desperate measures are appropriate in such instances.

ACT Scores and What They Mean

ACT uses two types of scores for reporting test results, standard scores and percentile norms. ACT uses a scale from 1 (low) to 36 (high) as its standard scores. The scale is the same for each of the four tests. Raw scores are obtained by totaling the number of correct responses. These raw scores are then converted into the ACT standard scores. The standard scores are converted into percentile ranks in order to compare students with others in specified groups. In addition to the scores on these four tests, the student will receive another score. This score, called the *composite score,* is an average of the four tests and indicates the student's general ability to succeed in college. Copies of the ACT scores, reported in percentiles, are sent to the student's high school and to three colleges of his choice.

The standard score system of ACT was developed to facilitate test interpretation for teachers and counselors. It was originally constructed for the Iowa Tests of Educational Development (ITED) and modified for ACT use. The basic and major purpose is not only to help convey test scores in a meaningful manner but to be sure that test scores are interpreted with proper respect for errors of measurement inherent in the scores. The probable error of measurement itself was used as the unit of measurement in the scale and is slightly larger for the ACT-tested population than for the ITED. It, of course, varies from test to test.

The student of measurement should remember the following normative characteristics of the ACT:

1. Standard score range: 1–36.
2. Standard deviation: 5–8.
3. Standard error of measurement: 1–2.
4. Mean composite score of college-bound high school students: 19.

It is important in interpreting a student's score to know with whom he or she is being compared. ACT's *College Student Profiles: Norms for the ACT Assessment* (American College Testing Program, 1972) provides norms for ACT scores for the following groups:

Norms for the Total Group of Freshmen
Norms by Institutional Type and Control
Norms by Geographic Region and College Type
Norms by Student Age and College Type
Norms by Student Age
Norms by Curricular Major Chosen
Norms by Degree Sought
Norms by Estimated Family-Income Level
Norms for Selected Groups of "Disadvantaged Students"

To illustrate how percentile rankings derived from different normative groups may help the student understand his scores, let us look at the case of Alan Wagner. Alan's composite score is 18. Alan looks in the ACT Profiles book and finds that colleges and ACT normally are presented according to college type: public, private, nonsectarian, Protestant, and so on. He sees the following classification (American College Testing Program, 1972):

Type 1. Two but less than 4 years of work beyond the 12th grade—includes junior colleges, technical institutes, and normal schools offering at least a 2-year program of college level studies.
Type 2. Only the bachelor's and/or first professional degree—includes those institutions offering courses of studies leading to the customary bachelor of arts or bachelor of science degree and all those degrees which entitle the possessor to enter the profession indicated, e.g., doctor of medicine, bachelor of pharmacy, or bachelor of science in engineering.
Type 3. Master's and/or second professional degree—includes those institutions offering the customary first graduate degree and any degree earned in the same field after the first professional degree or after a bachelor's degree in that field. This type of institution does not offer the doctor of philosophy or equivalent degrees.
Type 4. Doctor of philosophy and equivalent degrees—includes those institutions which are considered to be universities.

Type 5. All postsecondary institutions that cannot be classified in one of the other four type designations, e.g., hospital schools of nursing and technical institutes or vocational schools offering only programs that are less than 2 years in length. (p. 9)

As Alan looks at the norms for these college types, he finds that the meaning of his score of 18 varies tremendously depending on with whom he is comparing himself. At a Type 4 private college, he is at the 12th percentile, but compared to Afro-American students from families with incomes below $7,500 he is at the 83rd percentile, and at the 71st percentile compared to Spanish-American students with the same family income. Compared to college-bound students in general, a score of 18 places him at the 45th percentile. If he chooses a Type 2 Catholic college, his percentile ranking is 19; at a Type 3 private college, 20; at a Type 2 private nonsectarian college, 30; and at a Type 1 private college, he ranks at the 47th percentile.

The preceding cases are only a few norm groups that are presented by ACT. Note the difference in percentile rankings when Alan compares himself to these various groups.

These reference or norm groups are extremely important in selecting an appropriate college. Alan would probably be successful in passing his course work at a Type 1 private college and is about average when compared to the general college-bound high school student. If Alan is of Spanish or Afro-American background and his family income is less than $7,500, he has scored quite well compared to his ethnic-economic peers.

ACT Self-reports

In the actual test setting, the student is requested to report recent grades, before the senior year, in each of the four subject areas to be tested: English, mathematics, social studies, and natural sciences. ACT (1975a) states,

Perhaps the most reliable research findings in education are that high school grades are predictive of college grades and, further, that academic aptitude tests and high school grades combined are a better predictor of college grades than either alone. The self-reported grades collected on the ACT Assessment are reported to the student's secondary school and the colleges of his or her choice. . . . These self-reports are considered estimates of high school academic achievement, because high school grades presumably depend on both academic aptitude and personal characteristics such as persistence and study habits. (p. 4)

ACT Student Profile

The ACT Student Profile is an interesting and unique instrument, based on the assumption that the quality of education a college provides is partly dependent on the amount of relevant data it has about its students. The Student Profile asks for this kind of information. For example, the student indicates vocational plans; probable major area of study; the kind of degree sought; the size of hometown; the kind of housing desired at college; and other data helpful to the college in student guidance. The ACT Student Profiles may be used in admissions, planning freshman courses, advanced placement, scholarship and loan programs, student counseling, and so on.

Although school grades and test scores indicate academic potential, other factors bearing on success in nonacademic activities must also be considered. This is supported by the research literature. For example, Holland and Richards (1965), after studying the relationship of academic and non-academic accomplishment of over 7,000 college freshmen, state,

> *Some of the practical applications of our findings seem clear. If a sponsor is interested only in finding students who will do well in the classroom in college, then high school grades and tests of academic potential are the best techniques available. On the other hand, if a sponsor wishes to find college students who will do outstanding things outside the classroom and in later life, then he should continue to make an effort to secure a better record of the student's competencies and achievements in high school. Our results support some of the items used for this purpose in typical application blanks for admission to college, scholarships, and fellowships, but they also suggest the potential usefulness of a more active effort to secure a more reliable and valid record of each student's past achievement and involvement. (p. 22)*

Research—A Brief Review of Recent Studies

Munday (1965) investigated the predictive validity of the ACT tests with the SAT and SCAT tests for a sample of twenty-one colleges and universities. Grades in specific courses and overall grade averages were studied. It was found that predictive validity varied from school to school and from course to course. It was also found that the ACT and SAT tests possessed about the same relative degree of predictive validity. The SCAT was not found to be as good a predictor as either the ACT or the SAT.

Angoff (1965), in an investigation of talented students, found the SAT to be a good instrument for identifying students of high ability.

Lins, Abell, and Hutchins (1966), in an investigation of the SAT and the ACT, found that they could not equate them. They concluded that because the predictive abilities of neither test were very high, the use of "cutoff" practices by some college admissions offices was open to serious question. Boyce and Paxson (1965), on the other hand, in a study of the predictive validities of eleven tests, including the ACT and SAT, found moderate validities, ranging from .42 through .64. The grade point average of the student at the end of the first quarter was used as the criterion of success or failure.

Barth (1965) found that success on the SAT and CEEB writing sample did not require knowledge of the terminology of present school grammar. He stated, "Only a knowledge of certain questions of usage and a sensitivity to language . . . are required" (p. 9).

Hoyt (1968) in a study of 169 students from four colleges found a great deal of diversity in freshman classes and colleges. Wide differences in grading practices at different institutions were noted. These differences, according to Hoyt, explain the low correlation that he found between the grades and the ACT composite score. The correlation of the mean college grade point average with the ACT was only .34. This finding confirmed earlier studies.

Angoff (1971), in reviewing studies on the effects of fatigue on test scores caused by a full day of testing, found little evidence to support the assumption that fatigue is a major determiner of performance on the achievement tests. For a very complete history of the CEEB and a thorough review of numerous studies, the reader is referred to Angoff (1971).

Angoff and Modu (1973) established score equivalences between the SAT and its Spanish-language equivalent, the College Board Prueba de Aptitud Académica (PAA). Conversion tables resulted from their extensive study so that now PAA verbal and mathematical scores can be converted to SAT verbal and mathematical scores. DuBois (1972) is very high in his praise of the SAT, feeling that it is highly perfected and has reached the "pinnacle of the current state of the art of psychometrics" (p. 646).

Wallace (1972a), commenting on recent research on race and sexual differences, states, "Extensive research has also been focused on the relative validities of the SAT for male versus female students and Negro versus white students. In neither of those sets of comparisons have any important differences been found" (p. 649). This does *not* mean that no differences were found in scores on the basis of sex or race. Score differences are found and have been discussed previously. What it means is that the SAT predicts success in college equally well for male and female and for black and white students.

Wallace (1972b), in comparing the ACT and SAT, states, "ACT suffers by comparison with the SAT in psychometric care and sophistication, is about equal in validity for predicting collegiate success, and excels somewhat in the variety and extent of ancillary services offered" (p. 615).

The reader who is interested in pursuing the research in more depth is referred to Buros (1972) and the current psychological and educational literature. See, for example, Chapter 19 for further help in location of relevant research sources.

Twelve-Year Decline of SAT Scores—Why?

The Admissions Testing Program's annual summary of 1974–75 College Bound Seniors was reported in the *ATP News* (College Entrance Examination Board, 1975c). The results revealed that SAT scores above 600 were less frequent and scores below 400 were more frequent than the previous year. SAT verbal and mathematical score averages were eight to ten points below the previous year. SAT verbal and mathematical score averages have declined significantly since 1962–63, when they stood at 478 and 502, respectively. The average scores in 1974–75 were 434 and 472, respectively. Both male and female scores have declined.

A special advisory panel headed by Will and Writy has been appointed by the CEEB in conjunction with Educational Testing Service to study the problem. Speaking to the problem, Wirty (College Entrance Examination Board, 1976f) stated, "At this time we have no substantial evidence that enables us to attribute the score decline to any single cause or any particular set of causes" (p. 5).

The area in which the decline seems to be the greatest is reading comprehension. These writers feel that this fact is a clue to the phenomenon as well as a major problem itself. We are becoming a nation of TV watchers, and our reading is confined to simple areas of our life such as selecting products from the supermarket shelf. The child learns to read and stops there. If one wants to learn to fly an airplane, one needs practice in flying. An occasional weekend stint is not enough. Even for the pilot who has earned his wings, the need for practice is evident.

There is no continual positive reinforcement for reading. The positive reinforcements of past years such as entertainment, travel fantasy, and exploration of ideas and systems of life are no longer extant. There is little reason to read outside of school work when television presents all the entertainment a child may want. Going to school and reading textbooks alone, however, are not sufficient to develop collegiate reading levels. Certainly this lack of practice in reading may explain the drop in the highest scores (over 600).

The basic point is that as long as reading is important in our society, we must not only teach it, we must also do it. Many people in our society are proceeding under the assumption that the printed word is dead: that we no longer need literacy in a postindustrial age. After all, are not highway signs being changed to international signs and cannot a drivers' license examination be administered orally? There is not a more cruel hoax perpetrated in educational circles today. Literacy is needed more today than at any time in the past. Certainly a person can function on the highway and the supermarket without reading. One soon learns the symbols of the products one likes. In the world of work, however, it is a different matter. The unskilled lower-level jobs are decreasing due to automation and the skilled service jobs are increasing. A service person installing a new piece of equipment *must* be able to read the directions and complete report forms. Those of you who have put together children's Christmas toys with the aid of written directions and diagrams know that this requires a high level of proficiency. If our society finds that reading is obsolete, then our schools and society need to decide what should replace it. We may in the future have examinations to test visual and auditory memory and learning through TV. Then we will need to teach the best method of TV watching and listening.

Since society has not as of this date switched to TV education and methodology, we must focus our scope on reading. Thus it is the authors' strong *opinion* that less TV watching and more reading of all shades and hues will significantly increase not only reading comprehension on the SAT but also overall scores. Today even math requires good reading skills. The key to success in school and success on tests such as the SAT is in reading. The best reading instruction, although necessary, will not alone change the scores. What will change the scores is a combination of basic reading instruction, preferably with the emphasis on phonics, strong community and school support, and a system that rewards reading outside of school with internal rewards of joy and accomplishment.

What do you think? The preceding statement is not scientific fact but is based on an interpretation of research findings in a variety of fields. Future data may indicate other factors such as busing, high rate of divorces, and number of children in the family. In the meantime, we are not waiting. We have and will continue to reinforce our children's reading, from comic books to the classics, over TV watching. What will you do?

The Practical Meaning of College Entrance Examinations

College admissions tests are not perfect, or even close to perfect, in forecasting how a student will perform in college. There is no one device available today to predict with 100 per cent accuracy a student's future success or failure in college. The tests that are available today, however, do present a fairly good indication of a student's chances when coupled with high school performance.

Colleges do not rely on test scores as their sole criterion for admission. The formula used by most colleges in determining admission is the high school record (academic and extracurricular), teacher and counselor recommendations, high school standardized test scores, and, of course, college entrance examinations.

Scores on the CEEB and ACT can only be interpreted in the light of the individual college. A score of 500 on the verbal section of the SAT, for example, may be a satisfactory score for College X and far below what is acceptable for College Y. Soldwedel (1966), in discussing this problem, states,

> Generally you can assume that (1) low test scores may adversely affect chances of admission; (2) high scores will help but do not by themselves guarantee acceptance. The trouble with this generalization is that it does not answer the questions How low? and How high?
>
> How low is bad and how high is good will be determined by whatever the traffic will bear. You may find it difficult to get answers to the questions from admissions people. And there is good reason for the reluctance. What colleges would like to get, in terms of student body performance on standardized tests, and what they actually take are often two different things. Certainly it must be

added that there are institutions with sufficient endowment funds to hold rigidly to a test performance score. These are not in the majority, however. Colleges, faced with the necessity of reaching a certain quota of freshmen, may dip to lower test scores as applicants are sifted. On the other hand, some colleges are reluctant to divulge the minimum test scores they require because all strive for upward mobility and do not want to be saddled with the lowest score from year to year. (p. 51)

Let us take the case of Jane and Bill to illustrate the place of college admissions tests in screening applicants.

Jane is an attractive senior girl at Glen High School. Her high school record shows that she is a good student. Her academic average is B+. She has been a cheerleader for three years and is presently the editor of the school newspaper. Her teachers like her and will give her excellent recommendations. On the Scholastic Aptitude Test she obtained a score of 400 on the verbal section and 350 on the mathematics section. Her achievement scores in English composition, French, and social studies are all somewhere in the 400's. Jane would like to attend an Eastern girls' school, and her parents have money set aside for this.

The standards of the better girls' schools in the east are fairly high, and generally, test scores such as Jane's would not be acceptable to these schools. The Eastern school may feel that Jane has overextended herself in high school and could not live up to their standards. Thus, even though her record is excellent, she may not gain admission to this type of school. Factors such as the type of high school Jane attended would be very important. If Jane's high school is one of excellent academic reputation, she may still gain admission. The important thing to remember is that Jane could be admitted to other colleges in the country. And even with her low college entrance examination scores, she may still gain admission to a highly selective school because of her other outstanding credits. Thus Jane is not "doomed" because of her college entrance examination scores.

Now let us look at a different situation. Bill is a senior at North High School. He is a rebellious boy who is not very interested in school and cares little about homework. Consequently, his grades in school have been rather poor. His grade average is C. He has done little in the way of extracurricular activities and is generally disliked by his teachers. On the College Board examinations, he received the following scores: verbal—650; mathematics—700; English composition—600; French—650; chemistry—700.

These scores indicate that Bill has the ability to succeed in college. Even with these excellent scores, however, he may find some college doors closed to him because of his poor academic record. However, he will probably gain admission to some college because of his promising potential.

The reader can see from the two examples cited that test scores are not the only criteria that the college uses for admission. Certainly most students do not present such extreme cases. However, there are variations, and for this reason the person's whole record is taken into account. In Jane's case, it is possible that she has developed good study skills and has devoted a lot of her time to her homework. The chances are that these habits will carry over in her college work and help her earn higher grades than her College Board scores would indicate—that is, if she has made good grades on quizzes and final examinations in high school and has not received her high grades because of her appearance and ability to get along with her teachers.

In the case of Bill, we may state that in predicting success or failure in college there are certain negative signs even though his test scores are very high. Why? Because Bill has operated below his potential for so long, the chances are that he will continue to do so in college. Study habits have to be developed, and Bill has apparently not done this. In addition, he does not seem motivated to do so. He may state that this will all change in college, but the chances are that he will continue this pattern.

Of course, there are many exceptions to what has been stated. We are speaking in general and in terms of probability, not certainty. There are students like Bill who not only change their school pattern but go on to be scholars and prominent people in the arts and sciences. In general, however, this does not happen. Still, because of the chance that it may, Bill should be encouraged to go on to college, and counseling to ascertain the reasons for his underachievement should be planned.

The important thing for those who are going to deal with students is to remember that college admissions tests are to help students and are not intended to hurt them. Remember that the individual who enrolls in a college that is beyond his abilities may "flunk out" or quit in discouragement. If, on the other hand, he is guided into a college that is commensurate with his needs and abilities, he is more likely to complete his education.

FIVE

Criterion-Referenced Tests and Informal Techniques

Criterion-Referenced Testing

chapter 12

In the foregoing chapters on tests we have primarily discussed norm-referenced tests. In using these tests we have stressed the importance of interpreting an individual's score by comparing it to the performance of the group to which the individual belongs. Using our statistics from Chapter 3, we know from our student's percentile what percentage of students scored above and what percentage scored below this particular student. We know whether he or she was above average or below average and the range of scores in the reference group.

What Is Criterion-Referenced Testing?

Many educators have come to the conclusion that comparison with others is not always the best way to evaluate an individual. Therefore, for several years the trend has been to develop measurement techniques in which individuals are evaluated in relation to self-achievement or to an unchanging absolute standard. One reason for this quest is to diminish the competitiveness that often ensues in group-referenced testing. Experts speculate that competitive comparisons are particularly damaging for the young child.

An instrument with an absolute criterion performance would theoretically allow every child to reach an acceptable level of performance rather than to force 50 per cent to be "below average." Another reason has been an attempt to ameliorate the unfavorable comparison that disadvantaged or slow children suffer when compared with more advantaged or gifted peers. A third reason has been to develop instruments that are less evaluative and more prescriptive in nature.

Criterion-referenced testing is a major conceptual departure from norm-referenced testing. Let us be sure that we understand these differences before proceeding. Norm-referenced tests are predicated on the assumption that the distribution of any trait measured will resemble a normal curve. This, you remember, means that the greatest number of scores fall at the center and there is a spread to each side of this center. A test of this type is judged by certain validity and reliability data. Many mathematical formulations have been developed to support, explain, and interpret norm-referenced tests.

On the other hand, criterion-referenced tests are not based on the normal distribution of a trait but are concerned with actual behaviors that a person can perform. How another person performs on the test is irrelevent to interpreting an individual score.

Criterion-referenced tests may be thought of as having an absolute standard, whereas norm-referenced tests have relative standards. For example, let us suppose you want to judge the skill that a child possesses in identifying the sounds associated with the vowels. For both tests the *content* of the test is similar. Both would have items that reflect all the sounds associated with letters *a, e, i, o,* and *u.* The major difference in the two types of tests would be in the interpretation of results and the resulting information which you receive.

In the criterion-referenced test, you would know that John (or Mary) correctly identified 85 per cent of the sounds of the vowels. Furthermore, an inspection of the test might reveal that John missed those items associated with short *a* and long *i.*

This information tells you how far he has progressed toward mastering a skill you may consider necessary for reading. You also have information to direct you in designing instructional strategies to help John on the road to complete mastery. In this case, the *absolute* standard is the mastery of all the sounds of all the vowels. As a first-grade teacher, you can assume that all the children in your class can reach this, or, you choose a degree of mastery that will enable the child to make reading progress.

From the same test, if the interpretation is norm-referenced, you may know that John performed better than 86 per cent of six-year-olds, 48 per cent of seven-year-olds, and 23 per cent of eight-year-olds. Similarly, 14 per cent of six-year-olds performed better than John, as did 52 per cent of seven-year-olds, and 77 per cent of eight-year-olds. If John is six years old, 86 per cent is pretty good, and you can feel you have done a good job. You do not, however, know where his deficits are.

Thus, in testing, we have two basic approaches to individual measurement: norm-referenced and criterion-referenced. Reference in these two terms has to do with the frame of reference used to interpret an individual's score. In norm-referenced testing, the individual's performance is evaluated according to how it compares to the performance of a similar group. In criterion-referenced testing, the individual is not compared with a group norm, but with an unchanging criterion. An example of criterion-referenced testing is a drivers' license examination. In such an examination you either pass or fail, and it does not matter how you rank compared with others taking the test. Theoretically, every individual could reach an acceptable level of the criterion. A perennial problem with this type of testing, of course, is what to use for a criterion and where to place the cutoff. Let us turn our attention to the problem of the criterion.

The Criterion

If the criterion is to be a standard for absolute judgment, then you'd better be sure it is the right one. Criterion-referenced testing has grown out of the movement of the 1960s stressing instructional objectives. Therefore, it leans heavily on objectives stated as observable behavior. All teachers and counselors should be familiar with this concept. Educators have struggled long and hard with the problem of how specific these behavioral objectives should be. The answer to this question is the razor's edge of instructional strategies. If the objective is too general, it becomes an abstraction, and the evaluation of a child's performance becomes unsure: as, for example, "the child will understand and apply the scientific method." If the objective is too specific, both teacher and child may be bogged down in a mire of detail. Instructional objectives could attain the proportions of a large paragraph and reach a number that even the most competent teacher could not adequately handle.

Thus the first step in choosing the criterion is an adequate description of the instructional objectives. These should be stated in terms of the behaviors that you desire the student to exhibit. These behaviors then are your criteria. The next step is to determine the proficiency of the behavior that will constitute an acceptable criterion. The general rule for mastery seems to be between 80 and 90 per cent accuracy. This means that you will accept two out of ten questions (reflecting a single objective) wrong and judge that child as acceptably proficient. This is not a rule, but a general guideline. For some purposes the criterion must be all or noth'ng, not 90 per cent. The criterion deserves careful thought and scrutiny, for no criterion-referenced test can be better than the criterion.

Types of Criterion-Referenced Testing

Actually, criterion-referenced testing is the most prevalent kind used in the schools. Each time a teacher gives a quiz or examination, she or he is probably using criterion-referenced testing, or measuring actual performance.

This is usually a test of material covered in the instructional period. We will cover this in more detail in Chapters 14, 15, and 16. For now let us look at some of the characteristics and types of criterion-referenced tests.

Mastery Testing

Whenever a unit is taught in a school room and an evaluation procedure is instituted to determine the degree of mastery a student has achieved, it is called *mastery testing.* The assumption is that all children in school will master the skill of reading. Thus, at each level of difficulty, testing can be used to determine the degree of mastery or nonmastery.

Mastery testing is best suited to an evaluation of basic skills in the elementary school. As one goes higher in school, the subject becomes less structured and there is less agreement on the content of the skills involved.

Diagnostic and prescriptive tests among the published tests are illustrative of criterion-referenced tests. At this point, these are generally limited to mathematics and reading at the elementary level. Diagnostic tests diagnose the level on which a child is performing. Prescriptive tests indicate the weaknesses of a child and are used to prescribe further work. See Appendix C for a listing of these tests, and Chapter 9 for a description. The important thing to remember is that the child is judged on the basis of the content of the test and not by being compared to the performance of a group.

Some tests may give data for interpreting test results in relation both to group norms and to an established criterion. An example of this is the 1974 edition of the Stanford Achievement Tests.

Individualized Instruction

A second major use of criterion-referenced testing is in individualized instruction. In individualized instruction the aim is each child's mastery of the subject matter. There are many approaches that reflect this interest, including programmed learning, computer-assisted instruction, and other individualized systems in which the learner sets the pace.

Indigenous to all these programs is a careful statement of objectives expressed in terms of the desired learning outcome. These objectives are then the criteria upon which the performance is judged. The stress on stating desired learning outcomes as behavioral objectives has grown out of the behavioral objectives movement. This will also be discussed further in Chapter 14 on teacher-made tests. For now, it is enough to know that, before a lesson is taught, objectives are set stating exactly the behavior desired and the degree of proficiency to be reached. Thus it may be stated that the child will be able to perform addition operations using three-digit numerals with 80 per cent accuracy. The child who gets seven or fewer out of ten problems correct is sent back through a learning situation for this operation. The child who gets eight, nine, or ten out of ten problems correct has reached the criterion and may proceed to another level. Most individualized instruction procedures are variations of this process. The essential principle is that each child may proceed at a different pace and it is conceivable that each child could be doing somewhat different work. The sequence of learning and testing may either be constructed by the teacher or be constructed by an educational test publisher.

Published Criterion-Referenced Tests

A more recent advance in the partnership between test publishers and classroom teachers is a service offered by educational test publishers that includes custom-made criterion-referenced tests. The test publisher has on file a large number of instructional objectives and test questions designed to measure these objectives. The questions are written by professional test-question writers. A school desiring a test could select from a list of objectives those that correspond to that school's instructional objectives and receive in return a professionally constructed test to measure local objectives. The objectives are specific to subject matter, as, for example, sixth-grade American history. Figures 37 and 38 in Chapter 9 illustrate the degree of specificity present in professionally constructed tests of English and mathematics.

Test publishers also have shown their interest in jumping on the criterion-referenced testing bandwagon by supplying data in test manuals for both norm-referenced and criterion-referenced interpretation of the same test. Educators must be very careful in the use of these tests. There are some basic differences between norm-referenced tests and criterion referenced tests that may preclude the interpretation of the same test from both frames of reference.

Advantages and Disadvantages

There are, of course, advantages and disadvantages to criterion-referenced tests. It has long been a fear that schools would begin "teaching for the test"; that is, that curricula would be dictated by the test publishers. No doubt, the effect of the massive testing in the last fifty years has been a certain uniformness of curricula. Every school wants to be in the upper half of the distribution. When results show that a school or class is scoring below the national average, then the implication is that something is not being done correctly. Subsequently, subtle and sometimes blatant pressures are put on teachers to bring the kids up to the national average. Of course, it is often assumed the way to obtain these scores is to teach the skills and understandings reflected on the standardized test.

We have the same danger of test publishers directing curricula with the newer criterion-referenced tests. It may be that a local system has perfectly legitimate objectives for the situation but that the publisher has no questions to reflect these objectives. The local system may then give up its objectives and accept those that the publisher can test. Thus all the schools that use this service of the publisher are drawing on the same pool of questions. Since unit testing is an integral part of planning a course, the publisher's objectives will no doubt be selected from the cafeteria offerings at the beginning of instruction. This again will exert subtle shaping of local curricula from a national company.

Another danger of such testing is inherent in the behavioral objectives movement. That is that a cardinal principle of writing objectives for classroom instruction is that they be reflected in some objectively measurable behavior. Anyone who has a genuine grasp of learning and the growth and development of children knows that there are elements of understandings, attitudes, and growth that do not lend themselves to objective measurement. The danger then is that schools will stop trying to teach children the broader understandings and that education will consist only of eliciting the "correct" response to a specific stimulus.

There are advantages to criterion-referenced tests. These include emphasis on a more careful statement of objectives and avoidance of the problem of comparison of groups. Each student knows where he stands and where he needs to go, but the comparison with others is avoided.

Much work needs to be done to perfect the theory and application of criterion-referenced tests. New statistics need to be developed to gauge reliability and validity. Work will proceed on this new phase. The full story is not in on this type of testing. The word for teachers and counselors is to approach it with an open but critical mind. You must judge if any test gives you the information you need.

A Special Case of Validity and Reliability

Criterion-referenced tests offer us special problems with validity and reliability. In Chapter 4, we discussed three kinds of validities: construct, criterion-related, and content. The basic purposes of norm-referenced and criterion-referenced tests are different. The statistics of norm-referenced tests depend on a normal distribution and much variability in individual scores. Criterion-referenced testing is not based on these assumptions, and therefore the usual methods of determining validity coefficients are not applicable to this type of test. It is important to understand that criterion-referenced testing and criterion-related validity are two different things and not necessarily related.

Content validity is of special importance to criterion-referenced tests. Consider the case of mastery testing. Obviously, the content of the test must reflect the instruction. This is ascertained by the same procedures that are used with norm-referenced tests. It is a matter of judgment that all processes are measured by the questions and that there are sufficient questions for each process.

There is nothing inherently conflictual in construct validity and criterion-referenced tests. Criterion-referenced tests, however, are designed to measure performance, and often the underlying construct is nonexistent or of little interest. For example, it is difficult to identify a construct underlying driving a car. If statistical evidence is used for construct validity, the data used must not be dependent on an assumption of a normal distribution.

There are times when a criterion-referenced test may be used for predictive purposes. We have already mentioned that the usual validity coefficient is inappropriate for this type of test. What situations would call for use of prediction with criterion-referenced tests? When you use a pretest to determine which children enter a unit of study, you are in effect predicting that these children have a chance of success with the material. In using a posttest to determine which children should proceed to new material, a similar prediction is operative. We need some evidence that these tests are indeed worthy as bases of such decisions. One way to help determine the amount of validity of your test is to use an expectancy table as described in Chapter 4.

Reliability is the ability of the test to consistently measure whatever it does measure. We would like the same kind of consistency for criterion-referenced tests as for norm-referenced tests. The same problem is operative with reliability that we discussed in relation to validity: reliability coefficients are based on correlation procedures which require variability in scores. Criterion-referenced tests do not require this variability, and therefore the procedure is not useful in estimation of reliability of this type of test. Probably in the future statistical procedures will be developed to estimate the reliability of criterion-referenced tests, but for the present we will have to depend on other methods. Gronlund (1976) suggests that the reliability of a test increases as the number of questions measuring a single objective increases. As a rule of thumb, ten items reflecting each specific learning outcome seems to be a satisfactory number.

Informal Techniques: Observation, Self-report, Peer Report

chapter 13

In the preceding chapters we have directed our attention to those techniques and instruments that are standardized; that is, are produced on a large scale, are suitable for a large number of children, and are interpreted with norms supplied by the test publisher. Beginning with this chapter, we will devote our attention to those methods and procedures developed by teachers or counselors for a specific group, child, or situation.

In the previous chapter on criterion-referenced testing, we discussed procedures for adapting tests to the individual child or the particular local situation. In this chapter, we will review informal tools and techniques to evaluate various aspects of development. Then four chapters will be devoted to teacher-made tests and grading.

Rationale for Informal Techniques

This book is written for teachers and counselors and to this point has stressed the objective evaluation of students. With objective instruments, any teacher or counselor should obtain the same or very similar results. This is not the entire picture of measurement, however, for although the instruments may be standardized, neither children nor schools are standard. Thus there are some situations in which information is needed and informal techniques are the only feasible source of this information.

As a teacher or counselor, it is not enough to

evaluate the student on the basis of standardized tests alone. You must put together a whole picture of the student. You must explain discrepancies and supply information not forthcoming from other sources such as observations of the teacher (or counselor), a self-report from the student, or a peer report.

We will cover some of the techniques available to the teacher and review the application of these to various kinds of information needed.

Observations

The teacher sees the child in many different situations and over a long period of time. Standardized tests, on the other hand, cover a few hours in the course of a school year. Thus there are many aspects of development, skills, and attitude for which the teacher is perhaps the best source of information. There are various techniques that may be used in observing students. The key is that observation should be systematic. This means that the teacher decides beforehand the area in which information is to be gathered and notes behavior pertaining to this area.

Anecdotal Records

The first technique we will discuss is anecdotal records. An anecdotal record is a short verbal recording of an incident. The danger of this type of record is that the bias of the teacher may affect what is seen of the child's behavior. If you are going to use anecdotal records, then you must try to be as objective as possible in recording the event. You may interpret the event and offer recommendations, but these should be separated from the interpretation. The actual format used for the anecdotal records varies with the administrative convenience of the school. Records may be kept on 5×7 (or larger) file cards with the incident on one half of the front and the interpretation on the other. You may keep a looseleaf notebook with a section for each child in your class. In that case, anecdotes for each child can be added as they are collected.

What kinds of information are best suited for anecdotal recordkeeping? Obviously, do not gather information that would better be gathered by other means such as a standardized test. If, however, your report card system carries items reflecting character traits such as dependability, responsibility, ability to work with others, or care of materials, then you need a systematic method of gathering information on these areas. If you try to give a rating the night before the parent conference or the night before the report cards go out, you are likely to draw on your own biases involving the child. It is meaningful to tell a parent, "John volunteered to plan and paint the scenery for our puppet show. He planned and carried out the project on his own. I think this shows growth in independent work." Perhaps the parent is not so sure what you mean by "John is doing well on independent work."

But, you say, how can I have cards on all the children? How can I watch them all? Obviously, you can't watch them all all the time. The answer is systematic, rather than haphazard, observation. In systematic observation, decide each day the area and the children to be observed. Set aside a certain time to write the records. For example, you might decide to observe for evidence of social relations with three children. Then, on a particular day, you would notice this area with the chosen children. Of course, you leave open the possibility of recording those unusual events that occur when you least expect them. For example, you have been working with John, trying to get him to consult reference books for information rather than to ask you. One day you notice that he has done just that. This is evidence of growth in an area in which you have been attempting to make progress, and it is deserving of notation. Your systematic approach should extend over the period of a school year. That is, at the beginning you select in advance the areas to be observed. This technique is especially suitable for evidence of development (or lack of it) in the areas of emotions, social relationships, citizenship, appreciations, and attitude. All of these require knowledge and skill on the part of the teacher, and clinical judgment as to the proficiency of the child.

In addition to systematic observation of all students, this technique is valuable in gathering information on the unusual student who may have special problems. These children are those with emotional problems, the physically handicapped, the retarded, the bright underachiever, or the educationally retarded. The children may give cues to the conditions necessary for their growth through their behavior that you could not glean from objective testing.

As a counselor, anecdotal records should be a part of the record that you keep on each counselee. You should take a few minutes after each counseling session to note the date, the problem discussed, and the resolution of the problem (or progress made toward resolution). If the nature of the problem is personal, you could note emotional state, psychological reactions, your interpretation of the incident, and other information.

It is useful to review these records before each interview. If you have 300 counselees, it is hard to remember each one. But it certainly helps with rapport (after looking at your notes) to say, "Last October when I saw you, you were having some trouble with Ms. Mean in science. How are you doing now?" With a record of each visit, you may find that you never see some students, whereas others have a crisis every week.

Rating Scales

In the area of achievement there are skills that can best be measured by actual observation of the behavior involved rather than by paper-and-pencil tests. Can you imagine evaluating a student on running the 100-meter dash by asking,

Which of the following times is closest to that in which you could run the 100-meter dash?
(a) 3 minutes   (c) 6 minutes
(b) 2 minutes   (d) 3.5 minutes

Of course not, you say. The way to judge is to have the student run the distance and time it with a stopwatch. Other areas that are better judged by actual behavior or products include,

1. English: theme writing, speaking, dramatics, oral reading, poetry writing, poetry reading.
2. Science: experiments, especially those involving hypothesis formulation, data collection, hypothesis testing, and conclusions.
3. Art: techniques in use of materials and the products.
4. Music: performance of vocal or instrumental skills, unless the class is music theory.
5. Physical education: performance of the student in various skills, unless you are testing for knowledge of rules of a game.
6. History/social studies: evaluation of assigned projects.

A rating scale has two dimensions—the first describes the characteristics to be judged and the second the degree of proficiency attained by the student. Let us look at an example. Themes written by students are notoriously difficult to grade. With a rating scale, both you and the student have a better knowledge of what is evaluated and how. The students should be aware of the areas to be rated and the standards to be used. You set the rules, but be sure both you and the student are using the same rules. You should also have taught the areas that you evaluate. For example, you are a teacher of high school history and have assigned a term paper to be written. You should decide before the assignment is made how you will evaluate the paper. Your objective is not only to evaluate how well the students can write a theme but also to teach them how to write a theme. Therefore, you need a list of your instructional objectives for the assignment. These become the items on the rating scale for evalaution. Table 25 presents an example of a rating scale for our course in history.

In this table, the left-hand column shows the parts of the theme that are to be graded. Some of the behavioral objectives corresponding to these theme writing skills are the following,

1. The student will demonstrate a grasp of relationships through choice of topic.
2. The student will be able to state in clear, unambiguous terms the theme of the paper.
3. The student will develop the theme in a logical way, using either inductive or deductive reasoning.

Table 25. *Rating Scale for History Theme*

	No Credit 1	Poor 2	Good 3	Excellent 4	Superior 5

1. Choice of topic
2. Statement of theme
3. Development of theme
4. Concluding argument
5. Documentation
6. Bibliography form
7. Style of writing
    Total
    Grand Total					

4. The student will demonstrate knowledge of form of theme writing through documentation, bibliography, and style.
5. The student will be able to state clearly the concluding argument.

Of course, these objectives are stated beforehand and the evaluation of the theme evolves from them. Along the top of Table 25 are the categories for evaluating the theme. In this case, a check under 1 denotes unacceptable work and one under 5 denotes superior work. A rating scale may have varying numbers of categories, usually from three to ten. Three gives some discrimination for quality, and ten probably requires finer discrimination than is possible unless each is carefully defined. Five categories seem a good number, perhaps because it corresponds to the traditional five-point grading system of A to E.

Checklist

A checklist is similar to a rating scale, but does not allow discrimination as to quality of performance. A checklist is useful for checking skill and products on an all-or-nothing basis. For example, in the previous theme you might have a checklist procedure to evaluate form. In this case, it is either right or wrong. (This method utilizes two categories; rating scales begin with three categories.) Below is a partial checklist for form.

CHECKLIST FOR FORM

Title page   _____   Footnotes   _____

Margins   _____   Bibliographic entries   _____

A checklist is most useful for those processes in which one skill must be completed before the next one can be learned. An example of this is skill steps in mathematics. Much programmed learning is systematized in this manner.

Behavior Modification

The modification of behavior depends on a systematic observation of the behavior of the child. This technique is most often used to modify (decrease) unwanted behavior or increase desired behavior. The behavior may be academic, social, or interpersonal. The technique is applicable to any behavior that can be clearly defined. The principle behind behavior modification is that behavior is controlled by its consequences. When a behavior is rewarded (reinforced), it continues or increases. When it is not reinforced, a behavior decreases or is extinguished. When a behavior is punished, it is suppressed. Thus in extinguishing a behavior the problem is to identify the reinforcer and remove it. In increasing a behavior it is a problem of finding a reinforcer and supplying it. Obviously, taken to logical conclusion, one could control all aspects of a child's behavior by the addition or subtraction of reinforcers.

The first step in this technique is the definition of the behavior. In the academic area, for example, you might have a child who has high ability but will not pay attention to his studies. Perhaps you notice that when you give a silent reading assignment he spends a great deal of time looking out the windows and around the room. A child may or may not be reading if he is looking at the book, but he most certainly is not reading if he is *not* looking at the book. Thus we must increase his behavior of attending (directing attention to) the book during silent reading. The first problem is to find out exactly how much time he spends in attending and how much time on distraction. You can measure either frequency of looking away from the book or duration of looking away or looking at the book. If our goal is to increase time attending to the book, we should measure duration of time attending. Suppose in our class we assign silent reading for fifteen minutes each day. We first need to know how much of this time John actually spends attending to the written page. It is here that we begin our data collection. Figure 55 shows these data. The first section is the baseline that establishes the amount of time the child spent looking at the book in the silent reading period.

The next problem is choosing a reinforcer. Anything that the child desires can serve as the reinforcer. It is a question of knowing the child and choosing what is important or desirable to him. The teacher decided in this case that what John really liked best was shooting basketball in the gym. Thus this was chosen as the reinforcer. The teacher then may say to the child something similar to the following: "You spend a lot of our silent reading time looking out the window instead of at your book. I timed you today and you spent only three out of fifteen minutes trying to read. I have a deal for you. For

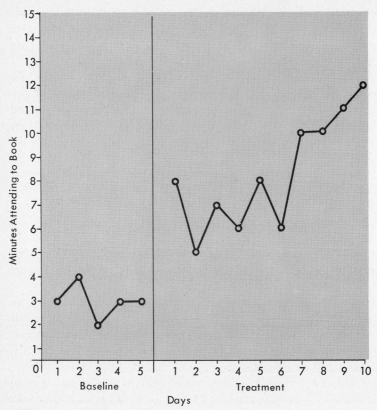

Figure 55. Attending behavior of John —————.

every minute above three that you spend looking at your book, I'll let you spend the same amount of time shooting baskets in the gym." As you can see from Figure 55, in two weeks John was earning nine minutes a day to shoot baskets and had quadrupled the time spent looking at his book during silent reading.[1]

Figure 55 illustrates *duration of behavior*. Another method of data collection is *time sampling*. The idea in time sampling is the same as sampling from a batch of cookies. The assumption is that if you taste one cookie you know how all the cookies taste. You cannot observe a child all the time, so you choose a segment of time to observe. The assumption is that the child will behave in any segment of time as he does in any other. The segments might be the first fifteen seconds of each minute for a specified time, or the first five minutes of each hour. A high-frequency behavior could be observed in the shorter time, while a less frequent behavior would require a longer time.

---

[1] The reader should note that the data in Figure 55 are hypothetical. They do not represent a real incident but are given only for illustrative purposes.

This method is most useful for counting the frequency of a behavior. A data graph would then show number of occurrences of a behavior. Discrete behaviors such as hitting another child, head banging, or shooting spitballs are best measured by frequency count.

Behavior modification is a useful technique, especially with very disruptive behavior and retarded children. The danger is that children may learn to earn rewards rather than learn the skills you are trying to reinforce (Levine and Fasnacht, 1974). Other writers have suggested that extrinsic rewards may decrease learning behavior previously reinforced by intrinsic rewards (Notz, 1975).

Unobtrusive Measures

The last category of observational measures we will discuss is called unobtrusive measures. This means to observe students in such a way that they do not know they are being observed. In dealing with human subjects, experimenters have found that the very act of measuring often changes the factor being measured. An obvious example is in measuring resistance to temptation. You could place a bowl of candy on the table and tell a person, "I want to see how long you can resist taking some candy." Then you might sit watching with a stop watch. You would have quite a different picture, however, if you placed a bowl of candy on the table, said, "Don't eat this candy," left the room, and watched through a one-way mirror.

Unobtrusive measures can also be useful in academic areas. Listening to your students in unguarded conversation gives you a measure of how they actually use the language. If you were there with a checklist of grammatical errors, they would most likely begin to monitor their own speech. If you hear many errors, you should devise instructional strategies to correct this. Schools, after all, are to prepare students to function in the real world, not to prepare them to take tests.

Unobtrusive measures are useful in a variety of situations in the classroom. Any situation that presents the application of classroom learning to real situations is suitable. The areas of social relations, attitudes, and values are especially good for this type of measurement. If you asked people to tell you how they felt about people of different racial backgrounds, they would report one thing; if you actually observed how they acted in free situations, you might have a different picture. Some observations for this attitude might be whom children sit by at lunch or whom they choose for partners for a team. Attitudes toward ecology can be estimated by actions in the school environment. For more information, see Webb (1975) and Webb, Campbell, Schwartz, and Sechrest (1971).

In summary, observational data are useful and are an important part of the total picture for a child. The key, however, is systematic observation. Be sure you have a plan and follow it through.

Self-report

In addition to observing a child, another method of gathering information concerning a child is to ask the child himself. We have reviewed some instruments of this type in Chapter 10, such as the Mooney Problem Check List, interest, and personality inventories. Here, we will review informal methods that the teacher or counselor may devise.

An autobiography is a good source of information about a person. It is relatively unstructured and open-ended, although it is a good idea to give a student an outline of the areas to be covered. These can include family background and history, school history, personal history, interests, attitudes, and hobbies, and vocational plans for the future. An autobiography is similar to the projective devices discussed in Chapter 7 in that there are a past, present, and future. The autobiography is best suited for high school students since their command of written language and their maturity better enable them to convey useful and accurate information.

Students may also supply information about themselves through completing questionnaires. A questionnaire concerning health is an example. A teacher might use a questionnaire concerning study habits, leisure-time activities, and skills. In many cases the most accurate and direct route to gather information is to ask the person about whom you desire information. Although this seems obvious, it is a source often overlooked.

The third category of self-report techniques available is those scales that are devised by the teacher but that employ techniques used in published tests. This type of instrument may be a checklist, a rating scale, sentence completion, or other device. The teacher's knowledge of tests will suggest methods that can be adapted. These instruments are best suited to gather information on attitudes and social or personal problems. They are especially good in gathering data concerning attitudes in which the continuum may extend from *strongly agree* to *strongly disagree* or *strongly like* to *strongly dislike*. These scales are called Likert-type scales. For example, if you were measuring attitudes toward homework, you might have the following item:

It is unfair for a teacher to assign homework over the weekend.

strongly agree	agree	don't care	disagree	strongly disagree

The student is directed to check the blank that most nearly expresses how he or she feels about the statement.

Peer Report

A third source of information about a person is from those people who are members of the same group (peers). It is useful to know how other children view a child. Obviously, other children are not a good source of information concerning the child's academic progress, nor are they a good source of information about the goals, aspirations, values, likes, and dislikes of the student. In the former, the teacher is a better source of information; in the latter, the student himself is a better source. Peers, however, can be a valuable source of information concerning the social adjustment of the child.

One of the oldest and most often used techniques for this purpose is the sociogram. Data gathering for a sociogram may be phrased in an endless number of ways, but the point is to get each person to name whom they consider to be the most desirable person or persons in the group. The hypothetical situation might be the person you would most like to study with, go on a picnic with, have on your team, or sit next to. The directions may ask the child to name two, three, or even four people.

After the data are collected, a diagram is made of the data. Lines indicate those children chosen and who chose them. The sociogram gives much information about the social structure in the class, such as the following,

1. The most popular.
2. The least popular (one whom no one chooses is an isolate).
3. Cliques (a group that excludes other children).
4. Dyads (two children who choose each other).

The information from a sociogram can be used to form new groups, or to break up existing ones. It is up to the teacher how much social manipulation to undertake. A thorough knowledge of group and individual psychology enhances a teacher's effectiveness in handling groups.

Another technique similar to the sociogram is the "Guess Who" technique. In this method, the students are given a series of behavioral descriptions and they then supply the names of their peers who fit the descriptions. There may be a limit to the names for each category, or it may be unlimited. Some examples of behavioral descriptions are

1. A person who is funny and makes other people laugh.
2. A person who works hard in class and usually has the right answers.
3. A person who is really good in sports.

The "Guess Who" technique may also be used to gather negative evaluations. These are dangerous to use as each child knows he is eligible for a negative evaluation by the other students. Young people tend to tell each other who they nominated and eventually find out their own status. This information can affect the self-esteem of children.

In summary, sociometric techniques are one more way of knowing children. The social development is part of the responsibility of the school. These techniques, in the hands of a competent teacher, can aid this development.

Uses of Information

In general, the rule for teachers and counselors is: Get the information you need and use the information you get. Those people who are responsible for the development of young people need to be able to put together a great deal of information into a picture of a complete functioning individual. Human beings are complex in their needs, desires, motivations, aspirations, abilities, and personalities. Each person is an individual, and a teacher or counselor needs a lot of information to help each child grow into what he or she is capable of. You must know what information you need and how to get it. However, that is only half the picture. Information in a file cabinet does no one any good. You must use the information you gather for better advising, better communication with parents, individualizing instruction, and designing strategies for growth of the child in social, emotional, or academic areas. Do not lose sight of the fact that schools exist for children. Information gathered should be used for the benefit of those children.

SIX | Teacher-Made Tests and Grades

Teacher-Made Tests

A very important part of the evaluation process of a school consists of teacher-made tests. As we discussed in the chapter on college entrance examinations, the very best predictor of college success is a combination of a standardized test (college entrance examination) and high school grades (teacher evaluations). These evaluations by teachers are based in large measure on the results of tests that teachers themselves have constructed. As testing people, we think of tests as instruments used to measure aptitudes, knowledge, and skills. Obviously, you must have good instruments to obtain the most accurate measure of a person. This is no less true of teacher-made tests than of standardized tests.

Like it or not, one must measure outcomes of instruction. It is true that experts who specialize in test construction do not always do a good job even though they have the assistance of subject-matter specialists to help them. We have seen the problems of validity and reliability in the construction of standardized tests. How can one, then, expect a classroom teacher who has had one course in testing to do a good job?

It is true that no matter how much you read about classroom tests in this or other books, you will never conceive or produce a test that will really meet the ideal standards of test construction. However, you will probably do well enough for your own purposes if you follow correct test construction methods. Reading the following material will not solve all your test problems, but it should help. Remember, just as the standardized test is a reflection of educational goals and procedures, so is the teacher-made test —and even more so, because the teacher knows what the specific objectives of instruction are and what methods have been employed to reach them.

Table 26. *Advantages and Limitations of Standardized and Nonstandardized Tests of Achievement* *

Criterion	Standardized Advantages	Limitations
1. Validity a. Curricular	Careful selection by competent persons. Fit typical situations.	Inflexible. Too general in scope to meet local requirements fully, especially in unusual situations.
b. Statistical	With best tests, high.	Criteria often inappropriate or unreliable. Size of coefficients dependent upon range of ability in group tested.
2. Reliability	For best tests, fairly high—often .85 or more for comparable forms.	High reliability is no guarantee of validity. Also, reliability depends upon range of ability in group tested.
3. Usability a. Ease of administration	Definite procedure, time limits, etc. Economy of time.	Manuals require careful study and are sometimes inadequate.
b. Ease of scoring	Definite rules, keys, etc. Largely routine.	Scoring by hand may take considerable time and be monotonous. Machine scoring preferable.
c. Ease of interpretation	Better tests have adequate norms. Useful basis of comparison. Equivalent forms.	Norms often confused with standards. Some norms defective. Norms for various types of schools and levels of ability are often lacking.
Summary	Convenience, comparability, objectivity. Equivalent forms may be available.	Inflexibility. May be only slightly applicable to a particular situation.

Standardized Versus Teacher-Made Tests

There should be no battle between standardized and teacher-made tests. Most schools use both types of instruments; each has its own advantages and disadvantages. The real question is when to use the standardized achievement

Nonstandardized			
Essay		**Objective**	
Advantages	*Limitations*	*Advantages*	*Limitations*
Useful for English advanced classes; afford language training. May encourage sound study habits.	Limited sampling. Bluffing is possible. Mix language factor in all scores.	Extensive sampling of subject matter. Flexible in use. Discourage bluffing.	Narrow sampling of functions tested. Negative learning possible. May encourage piecemeal study.
	Usually not known.	Compare favorably with standard tests.	Adequate criteria usually lacking.
	Reliability usually quite low.	Sometimes approaches that of standard tests.	No guarantee of validity.
Easy to prepare. Easy to give.	Lack of uniformity.	Directions rather uniform. Economy of time.	Time, effort, and skill are required to prepare well.
	Slow, uncertain, and subjective.	Definite rules, keys, etc. Largely routine. Can be done by clerks or machine.	Monotonous.
	No norms. Meaning doubtful.	Local norms can be derived.	No norms available at beginning.
Useful for part of many tests and in a few special fields.	Limited sampling. Subjective scoring. Time consuming.	Extensive sampling. Objective scoring. Flexibility.	Preparation requires skill and time.

* From Julian C. Stanley, *Measurement in Today's Schools,* 4th ed., © 1964, pp. 304–305. Reprinted by permission of Prentice-Hall, Inc., Englewood Cliffs, N.J.

test and when to use the teacher-made achievement test. A general rule of thumb is that the teacher-made test is the instrument of choice to appraise outcomes of local classroom instruction. The standardized achievement test provides information of local achievement compared to national norms. Table 26 compares strengths and weaknesses of standardized and teacher-made tests.

Purposes of Teacher-Made Tests

"The test is the message." The teacher, in the most direct and meaningful manner, tells the student what he *really* thinks is important through his tests. Unfortunately, this often results in students studying for a test rather than for what they can learn. Although we can discourage studying only for tests, it is doubtlessly impossible to eliminate it. Therefore, remember that you will communicate your subject-matter emphasis through the tests you give.

Tests serve the teacher with valuable insights into his or her instructional effectiveness. The teacher can ask himself, "Are the students learning what I want them to learn?" and then find the answer in his students' test results.

Tests also provide the teacher with information on individual progress. Without this kind of data, it is almost impossible to make decisions on passing and failing students, grouping, remedial help, or providing enriching experiences for the advanced pupil. Testing also aids in evaluating the class as a whole.

Tests, of course, provide part of the basis for assigning grades. If used properly, they can forestall parental shock at report card time. The parent who has seen his child's test papers knows fairly well what grades his child will receive.

Reviewing tests with parents and teachers can help the child learn the material not yet incorporated into his intellectual and educational storehouse. The teacher can spot the kinds of problems that are troubling the student and work on his areas of weaknesses.

Planning Ahead

There you are, Ms. Fry, your first month of teaching and you've done a pretty fair job so far. Now you have to decide how to evaluate what the students have learned because you must turn in the first report card grades next week. "Now what kind of test should I give these kids?"

Quality tests do not spring forth full blown. They are planned in detail when you detail the overall goals of the course. Questions dealing with the type of test to use, the amount of material to be tested from text and classroom discussions, and so on should be decided before you begin classroom instruction.

Defining Objectives

Defining objectives is not new to those of you who have been exposed to a "methods" course in education. You know that defining goals or objectives is a primary ingredient of the teaching process. Noll and Scannell (1972) state the case very cogently when they say, "To try to teach and evaluate without defining objectives is like starting out on a journey without knowing where to go. It may be pleasant to wander around for a while, but it is doubtful that any sort of progress can be made without some direction" (p. 166).

General Objectives

Usually there are two kinds of objectives, general and specific. For example, many years ago a group of educators set forth objectives that have become known as the *seven cardinal principles* of education (United States Department of Interior, 1918). These general objectives are

1. To promote good health.
2. To teach command of the fundamental processes.
3. To provide for worthy home membership.
4. To aid in the selection of a vocation.
5. To offer civic education.
6. To assure worthy use of leisure time.
7. To promote ethical character.

Another illustration of general objectives is the classical eight-year study of Aikin (1942). These objectives are

1. The development of effective methods of thinking.
2. The cultivation of useful work habits and study skills.
3. The inculcation of social attitudes.
4. The acquisition of a wide range of significant interests.
5. The development of increased appreciation of music, art, literature, and other esthetic experiences.
6. The development of social sensitivity.
7. The development of better personal-social adjustment.
8. The acquisition of important information.
9. The development of good physical health.
10. The development of a consistent philosophy of life.

Another excellent source of ideas for general educational objectives is the *Taxonomy of Educational Objectives* (Bloom, 1956; Krathwohl, 1964). The original conception of the taxonomy was to encompass three behavioral spheres—cognitive, affective, and psychomotor. The cognitive area covers objectives related to recall or recognition of knowledge and problem solving. The affective domain deals with changes in interest, values, and attitudes and the development of appreciation and adjustment. The psychomotor area covers objectives relating to manual and motor skills. Bloom's (1956) work covered the cognitive domain, whereas Krathwohl (1964) dealt with the affective area. Work in the psychomotor domain has not yet been published.

Let us briefly review Bloom and his committee's work as it relates to our concern for objectives. The committee made the following statement concerning their findings for the classroom teacher (Bloom, 1956):

> *Use of the taxonomy can also help one gain a perspective on the emphasis given to certain behaviors by a particular set of educational plans. Thus, a teacher, in classifying the goals of a teaching unit, may find that they all fall within the taxonomy category of recalling or remembering knowledge. Looking at the taxonomy categories may suggest to him that, for example, he could include some goals dealing with the application of this knowledge and with the analysis of the situation in which the knowledge is used. (p. 2)*

The classification of cognitive educational objectives falls into six major categories:

1.00 Knowledge.
2.00 Comprehension.
3.00 Application.
4.00 Analysis.
5.00 Synthesis.
6.00 Evaluation.

These major categories are broken down into subsections. For example, some of the headings under Knowledge are as follows:

1.00 Knowledge.
    1.10 Knowledge of specifics.
        1.11 Knowledge of terminology.
        1.12 Knowledge of specific facts.
    1.20 Knowledge of ways and means of dealing with specifics.
    1.30 Knowledge of the universals and abstractions in a field.

Under every heading there are a definition and a discussion of the meaning of that heading. These are further clarified by illustrations of the kind of educational goals included in the specific category. In addition, at the end of each of the sections there is a review of the types of test items that may be used to test achievement of the various facets of each objective. It is highly recommended that the classroom teacher obtain a copy of Bloom's (1956) *Taxonomy of Educational Objectives,* an excellent resource for preparing classroom units of study and tests.

Krathwohl (1964) and his committee produced the following major categories in their work in the affective domain:

1.0 Receiving. Sensitivity to the existence of certain stimuli.
2.0 Responding. Active attention to stimuli, for example, going along with rules and practices.

3.0 Valuing. Consistent belief and attitude of worth held about a phenomenon.

4.0 Organization. Organizing, interrelating, and analyzing different relevant values.

5.0 Characterization by a value or value concept. Behavior is guided by value.

For a detailed discussion of these objectives, see Krathwohl's *Taxonomy of Educational Objectives.*

Specific Objectives

Taxonomies of educational objectives have been around a long time. They sound pretty good, but the difficulty is that they are in general terms and teachers do not always know how to apply them to specific learning situations. Metfessel, Michael, and Kirsner (1976) have attempted to make these objectives more specific by identifying the verbs that can be used in planning behavioral objectives for each level of learning. Following is an adaptation of these verbs. As active verbs, they indicate the behavior that would reflect a dimension of learning. The reader should understand that this is not a definitive list, and that the classroom teacher should assume responsibility for evolving objectives, perhaps with different verbs.

Knowledge: to acquire, define, demonstrate, distinguish, explain, identify, recall, recognize.

Comprehension (translation): to change, give in own words, illustrate, rephrase, restate, transform, translate.

Comprehension (interpretation): to draw, illustrate, interpret, rearrange, represent, reorder.

Comprehension (extrapolation): to conclude, deduce, estimate, extend, generalize, infer, interpolate, predict.

Application: to apply, calculate, classify, choose, develop, employ, organize, restructure, transfer, use.

Synthesis: to combine, constitute, derive, design, develop, formulate, modify, originate, plan, produce, propose, put together, relate, tell, write.

Evaluation: to appraise, argue, assess, consider, decide, validate.

In the area of specific objectives we are concerned with specific subject matters and the various things that the child does with these represented by the verbs listed. This means skills, concepts, facts, and principles. A good method of setting forth your instructional objectives is to outline them. Note that these specific objectives are stated in behavioral terms. Behavioral terms sometimes seem difficult, but they are merely a method for clarifying thinking on instructional matters. Simply stated, a behavioral objective is a statement of what you want the student to do to show you that he has mastered a concept. Put another way, behavioral objectives are statements of desired learning outcomes. Sounds simple, does it not? The fact of the matter is that educators have been grappling with behavioral objectives for more than fifteen years. There are some learnings that are desirable in a classroom that cannot be stated in behavioral terms.

To the extent that stating desired outcomes in behavioral terms helps the teacher clarify instruction, they are useful. When behavioral objectives become a burden or when the general goals are obscured by the minutia of objectives, they cease to help students to learn. The point is that, however these objectives are stated, the teacher should know *specifically* what is expected of the learner and how this will be evaluated. For readers who want more explicit information on behavioral objectives, see Tuckman (1975), Gronlund (1976), and Popham (1975).

The construction of objectives should not become laborious. Do not be overwhelmed by the process; use it to your advantage. This means construct objectives for units of study, including evaluation methods, in a manageable manner. For example, let us look at a unit on arithmetic.

GENERAL OBJECTIVE
To develop skill in the process of calculating two-, three-, and four-digit problems in addition.

SPECIFIC OBJECTIVES
1. The learner will calculate with 90 per cent accuracy the addition of two-, three-, and four-digit numbers in problems not requiring carrying.
2. The learner will calculate with 90 per cent accuracy the addition of two-, three-, and four-digit numbers in problems requiring carrying.
3. The learner will calculate with 90 per cent accuracy the addition of two-, three-, and four-digit numbers with decimals.

Let us translate our "general" and "specific" objectives in arithmetic to actual test questions:

Set I

15	65	38	633	178
+61	+32	+61	+224	+521

342	3241	1753	5761	6521
+257	+3425	+8245	+1226	+3367

Set II

68	27	57	834	368
+34	+48	+26	+287	+576

819	6351	3847	2139	7635
+314	+4219	+1538	+4513	+2868

Set III

1.5	7.6	6.5	5.33	7.88
+3.7	+8.5	+4.2	+6.11	+1.33

4.63	88.44	13.69	65.78	23.87
+6.15	+16.67	+15.48	+30.29	+36.65

From the foregoing illustration you can see the strong relationship between objectives of an instructional unit and evaluation. We will necessarily emphasize the last phase of the process (testing). You should bear in mind that final evaluation is implicit and sometimes explicit in the first statement of objectives. Obviously some type of instructional strategy intervenes between objective and evaluation. Let us now look carefully at the process of constructing your test.

Steps in Test Construction and Administration

So far we have talked mostly in general terms. Let us now get down to practical situations by outlining, step by step, the actual process of test construction and administration.

1. *"Get ready" stage.*
   a. Secure all the instructional materials bearing on the intended test, for example, books, notes, and content outline or unit objectives.
   b. List the objectives you want your test to measure.
2. *"Get set" stage.*
   a. Plan type of test to be used and the general format of the test.
   b. Write a preliminary draft of the items to be used.
   c. Plan the length of test. How long do you want the test to be—the whole class period, or a shorter time?
   d. Go over test items. Do this several days after you have written the preliminary draft. Take out the items that do not seem relevant and polish others.
   e. Arrange items in order. Rate your items for difficulty and place the easiest first so as not to discourage the students and to give the poorer students some motivation to continue with the test.
   f. Instructions. Be sure you know what you want the students to do and are able to communicate your wishes to them.
   g. Decide on the "Rules of the Scoring Road." Be sure you have written the correct answer before testing. This is as true for essay questions as for objective items.
3. *"Go" stage.*
   a. Time. Whatever you decide upon, be consistent. For example, do not state, "You will have thirty minutes to complete the test," and then

give the slower students an hour. It is not fair to the others who attempted to complete the assignment in the stated time. Generally, allow enough time for at least 90 per cent of the students to finish.

b. Physical Conditions. Try to maintain a quiet, disturbance-free room. Do not walk around the room, tap a pencil, talk to other teachers, and so on.

c. Administration. Do not be hostile in tone or manner when giving directions. Your voice should be clear and instructions should be easily understood by all the students. Testing is difficult for all of us. Do not make it worse by using it as punishment.

Evaluation of Your Test

The reader has already been exposed in earlier discussions to what constitutes a good measuring device. In this section, we will of necessity repeat some of these factors as they relate to teacher-made tests. Ebel (1965, pp. 281–307) has summarized the characteristics of a good test by noting the following ten qualities: [1]

1. *Relevance.* Is your test measuring your educational objectives and actual instruction? This is the validity aspect of the classroom test.

2. *Balance.* How close does your test come to the "ideal"? That is, do your items reflect your stated objectives?

3. *Efficiency.* How much time does your test take to administer? Is it taking too much? A compromise between available time for testing and scoring and other needs must be made.

4. *Objectivity.* There should be agreement by experts on the "right" or "best" answer to a question. Objectivity does not refer to the type of test (for example, multiple-choice or completion items) but is directly concerned with the scoring of the test.

5. *Specificity.* Are you testing the subject matter presented in the classroom? That is, does the test discriminate between those students who have learned the subject matter and those who have not on a better than chance basis?

6. *Difficulty.* The difficulty of test items should be at the level of the group being tested. Generally, we can consider a test appropriate if each item in the examination is passed by half of the students.

7. *Discrimination.* A test item discriminates if more good students answer it correctly than do poor students.

8. *Reliability.* Is the test measuring whatever it does measure consistently?

9. *Fairness.* Does each student have an equal chance to demonstrate his

---

[1] Slight modifications in terms of descriptions, but not qualities—for example, *Relevance* —have been made.

knowledge? The test should be constructed so that each student has an equal chance to "show his stuff."

10. *Speediness.* Are scores influenced by speed of response, and if so to what degree? In testing achievement, speed should play a very minor role in determining a student's score. There should be sufficient time for *almost all* students to finish the test.

Types of Teacher-Made Tests

There are basically two types of teacher-made tests, essay and objective. There are, however, many forms of the objective type, whereas the essay is generally confined to a "short answer" or "discussion" format. The following list of different types of objective teacher-made tests is cited to show the scope and breadth of available formats. Some of these will be discussed in the following chapters.

Objective Tests [2]

1. Simple recall.
   a. Basic.
   b. Problem type.
   c. Maps, charts, and so on.
2. Completion.
   a. Basic.
   b. Matching.
   c. Analogies.
   d. Maps, charts, and so on.
3. Alternative response.
   a. Basic.
   b. Two-clause.
   c. Three alternatives.
   d. Converse.
   e. With correction.
   f. With qualifications.
   g. With diagrams.
   h. With analogies.
4. Multiple choice.
   a. Basic.
   b. Recall.
   c. Common principle.
   d. Results.

[2] Adapted from A. J. Lien, *Measurement and Evaluation of Learning.* Dubuque, Iowa: Wm. C. Brown Company Publishers, 1976.

　　　　e. Causes.
　　　　f. Charts, maps, and so on.
　　　　g. Analogies.
　　5. Matching.
　　　　a. Basic.
　　　　b. Three columns.
　　　　c. Master list.
　　　　d. Analogies.
　　6. Rearrangement.
　　　　a. Chronological.
　　　　b. Order of importance.
　　　　c. Order of difficulty.
　　　　d. Length, weight, logic, and so on.

In the chapters that follow, we will discuss many of the preceding types of teacher-made tests. The reader is already familiar with some from the chapter on achievement tests.

Essay Versus Objective Tests

There are no definitive rules for judging whether the essay or the objective test is better, nor are there rules for when one type should be used in preference to the other. The teacher is in the best position to select one form over the other. The basis for the selection rests with the particular purposes and needs of the classroom setting and, more specifically, with what the teacher wants to measure and the available time for this task. Table 27 presents a summary of a few of the major characteristics of the two types of tests.

The student of measurement should remember that neither the essay nor the objective test alone is completely satisfactory in measuring academic progress. Each has its own advantages and disadvantages, and it is your responsibility to use the right test in the right place for the right purpose.

Teachers, Tests, and Reality

An attempt has been made in this chapter to give some guidelines for constructing tests. In the following chapters, detailed examples and suggestions for developing essay and objective tests will be presented. It should be noted, however, that the time available will be the common denominator in our discussions.

Remember also that no single teacher-made test should be the only basis of important educational decisions. Day-to-day classroom performance, scores on standardized tests, and academic achievement measured by a series of teacher-made tests over a period of time should be considered in the whole

Table 27. *A Comparison of Essay and Objective Tests* *

	Essay	Objective
Abilities measured	Requires the student to express himself in his own words, using information from his own background and knowledge. Can tap high levels of reasoning such as required in inference, organization of ideas, comparison and contrast. Does *not* measure purely factual information efficiently.	Requires the student to select correct answers from given options, or to supply an answer limited to one word or phase. Can *also* tap high levels of reasoning such as required in inference, organization of ideas, comparison and contrast. Measures knowledge of facts efficiently.
Scope	Covers only a limited field of knowledge in any one test. Essay questions take so long to answer that relatively few can be answered in a given period of time. Also, the student who is especially fluent can often avoid discussing points of which he is unsure.	Covers a broad field of knowledge in one test. Since objective questions may be answered quickly, one test may contain many questions. A broad coverage helps provide reliable measurement.
Incentive to pupils	Encourages pupils to learn how to organize their own ideas and express them effectively.	Encourages pupils to build up a broad background of knowledge and abilities.
Ease of preparation	Requires writing only a few questions for a test. Tasks must be clearly defined, general enough to offer some leeway, specific enough to set limits.	Requires writing many questions for a test. Wording must avoid ambiguities and "giveaways." Distractors should embody most likely misconceptions.
Scoring	Usually very time-consuming to score. Permits teachers to comment directly on the reasoning processes of individual pupils. However, an answer may be scored differently by different teachers or by the same teacher at different times.	Can be scored quickly. Answer generally scored only right or wrong, but scoring is very accurate and consistent.

picture of pupil evaluation; as Nunnally (1972) states, "To reach important conclusions about students on the basis of only one teacher-made test would be as unwise as it would be for the prospector to abandon his claim because the first shovelfull was not brimming with gold" (p. 106).

chapter 15

The Essay Test

In 1845, Horace Mann substituted a uniform written examination for the usual oral testing of students in the Boston public schools (Chauncey and Dobbin, 1966). Before Mann's "step forward," the examination of students consisted of interrogation by the teacher or a board of school officials. Since Mann's radical change, the essay test has undergone a great deal of investigation and critical comment. Let us very briefly review some of the studies and comments as they relate especially to reliability. We shall keep them in mind in our later discussion of developing and scoring essay tests. Above all, they should serve as cautionary lights in our use and application of the essay test in the total evaluation of our students.

Reliability

In 1912 and 1913, Starch and Elliott (1912, 1913a,b) produced the first studies on the reliability of grading essay tests. These three classical investigations covered the subject matter of high school English, history, and mathematics.

In the area of English, the investigators selected two English themes of supposed equal quality and asked 142 English teachers to grade them on the basis of 100 per cent. The first paper received grades ranging from 50 to 98, with a median of 80.2. The second paper received grades ranging between 64 and 99, with a median of 88.2 (Starch and Elliott, 1912).

Starch and Elliott (1913a), in their study of history tests, found an even larger discrepancy of grades. The range was over seventy points on the same 100 per cent basis. In their mathematics investigation, they sent a plane geometry paper to 138 geometry teachers for grading, because they thought that mathematics should be more subject to grading consistency. Their results revealed a grade range between 28 and 95 (Starch and Elliott, 1913b).

In a later and more sophisticated investigation, Falls (1928) requested 100 English teachers to grade a paper already evaluated by a committee as excellent. The 100 teachers did not know that a committee had previously evaluated the paper or that the writer, a high school senior, was a reporter for a large city daily paper. Grades on this paper were between 60 and 98. In addition, comments placed the writer's grade level in school from fifth grade to a junior in college. Study after study has confirmed these findings.

Through the years, research designs, methods, and procedures of analysis have become more sophisticated, but the results have generally been the same. For example, in a more contemporary study, Myers, McConville, and Coffman (1966) used 145 readers and 80,000 essays. They found average single reader reliabilities of .41. The average reliability rose to .73 when the number of readers was increased to four. This dramatic increase was achieved under controlled conditions with trained readers who read the essays as a whole and then utilized a four-point scale. This research revealed that if a teacher is going to give essay tests, several graders should be used.

James (1927) attempted to study the reliability of grades assigned by the same instructor. He selected four compositions that were judged to be of the same quality and asked forty-three English teachers to judge them. Two were in good handwriting and two in poor. Two months later, the same themes were presented to the same teachers but with the handwriting reversed—that is, the two that had been in poor handwriting were reproduced in good penmanship and vice versa. The results revealed a one-letter-grade difference in favor of the good handwriting.

Recent research (Coffman, 1971) has also indicated that irrelevant factors such as neatness and handwriting may influence grades. Marshall and Powers (1975) studied grading reliability of 120 prospective teachers enrolled in undergraduate history of American education and educational psychology classes at the University of Missouri. Twelve forms of an essay response were graded. The directions included a statement that the grades were to be based on content only. The graders were given the essay questions, an outline of content that an outstanding response would contain, and a description of the nine-point grading scale to be used. The directions were explicit: "Grade this examination on *content alone* . . . . Disregard everything but the factors relevant to the content outline" (p. 182). The results indicated that graders were influenced by quality of composition and writing neatness.

Most of the research on essay tests has involved the reliability of graders of essay tests. A paucity of data exists concerning the actual reliability of the instrument itself. Cureton (1958), in a discussion of this problem, states that in order to obtain an estimate of essay test reliability, two equivalent forms are necessary at the beginning and they must be administered to the individuals at an optimal time interval. Each reader would have to read all of the answers to a specific question on both forms. If this situation could be created, then a correlation between grades obtained on one form with those obtained on the other could be considered as an estimate of reliability.

Payne (1968) states that one method of increasing the reliability of an essay test "is to increase the number of questions and restrict the extensiveness of the answers. The more specific and more narrowly defined the questions, the less likely they are to be ambiguous to the examinee. This should result in more uniform comprehension and performance of the assigned task, and the reliability of the instrument and scoring should be increased" (pp. 80–81).

Another help in improving reliability is to state the question in enough detail so that students will understand what is wanted. If this is not done, some pupils will give attention to one aspect of the question while others cover different points. If this happens, reliability in scoring will be quite difficult (Educational Testing Service, 1973c).

The teacher who wants to administer essay tests in spite of the research findings on reliability should be very cautious in interpreting the scores. Some of the advice given here on the construction of essay tests should help, but caution should still be the watchword. It should also be noted that the research and implications for the reliability of the essay test that have been made are in reference to evaluation. The educational process, of course, involves more than evaluation. Teachers may feel that the essay test, though not necessarily reliable in the measurement sense, may be an excellent instructional device; that is, it may help the student learn to organize his thoughts and express them in writing. We will have more to say on the advantages of the essay test later in this chapter.

Validity

Achievement tests are validated on the basis of whether or not they cover the subject matter taught and the goals of the unit of study. Validity, as is the case with reliability, tends to be higher as the number of questions is increased. Essay tests necessarily contain a relatively small number of questions. Thus the sampling of the objectives outlined in the unit or course specifications will be small and therefore will tend to lower the validity of the test. It is common after taking an essay test for students to feel that some of their study time was "wasted" because so much of the course was not measured in the four, five, or six essay questions presented to them.

Another problem in the validity of essay tests is the evaluation of more than one area of learning. For example, some instructors reduce the score for poor spelling or grammar on a history paper, thereby lowering the history grade. The resultant grade does not reveal what the student knows about history alone but also what kind of speller and/or grammarian he is. This type of "history" evaluation generally does not serve the cause of history or that of spelling and grammar very well. Our old definition of validity certainly applies here—that is, whether or not the test measures what it is supposed to measure. If you are testing history, *then test history, not English.* If, on the other hand, you feel that educational objectives are best served by evaluating English usage and content, then give two grades—one for English and one for history, but be sure to follow through on the report card. If history alone is on the card, give only the history grade or add the English evaluation so that parents and other school personnel in future years will have a clear understanding of how the pupil was evaluated and in what areas.

There is another case familiar to everyone. This is the tendency of students to expound at length on essay examinations, often without specifically answering the question. An adept student may raise his grade because of this facility, because of a general rather than specific knowledge of the subject matter. The tendency of graders to reward the more verbose students lowers the overall validity of the test.

Advantages and Disadvantages of the Essay Test

The essay test, despite low reliability and validity, is held in high esteem by many teachers from elementary through graduate school. Let us look at some of the common arguments given in defense of essay tests and their merit.

Thorndike and Hagen (1969) state that the "major advantage of the essay type of question lies in its potential for measuring the student's abilities to organize, integrate, and synthesize his knowledge" (p. 77). In a similar view, Tuckman (1975) posits that essay questions enable the person to structure and compose his or her own reactions within a relatively broad area.

Does the essay test in fact present a chance for the student to show his organizational skills? The answer is dependent on the quality of the test. If the test is well constructed, it probably can. The problem, however, is that often the student is not presented with an examination geared to this goal. The student may find himself at a loss in attempting to answer a long discussion question—for example, "Discuss the antecedents of pop art." This type of essay problem does not enhance organizational ability, nor does it call for the student's skill in selecting important facts or ideas. The student faced with our example problem would have to ask himself first of all, "What does the teacher want? Does she want me to start with the Egyptians or primitive period of art or does she want me to trace the development of pop art in the twentieth century?" On the other hand, if the problem was stated as, "Discuss the influence of cubism on pop art," the student would have an idea of where to start and develop his line of reasoning; he would know what the teacher wanted. Similarly, all the students would be dealing with the same problem and therefore give the teacher a better basis for comparison. Used in this manner, the essay test can be useful in evaluating a student's ability to organize, select, and integrate important ideas and trends.

Another hallmark of essay tests is that they require students to answer questions in their own words and handwriting. We have already discussed some of the problems in this area in our review of reliability and validity. You will remember the James (1927) study that revealed that good penmanship usually yielded one grade higher than poor handwriting. In addition, the student who can use the English language effectively will generally do better on discussion questions. The student who may not write as well either in terms of penmanship or English usage may, in fact, actually know more about zoology or history and yet receive a lower grade. It is very difficult not to be influenced by such external factors as neatness, handwriting, sentence structure, spelling, and vocabulary. This is not to state that these factors are not important. On the contrary, they are legitimate and necessary educational objectives. If people cannot communicate their knowledge and ideas, how do we, or how does society in general, know that they possess either? The problem, then, is not the worth of grammar and penmanship but how to evaluate a student's knowledge and understanding of biology or history without evaluating other skills and knowledge.

A pragmatic disadvantage of essay items is time. Brown (1976) states, "The major disadvantage of essay items becomes readily apparent when scoring begins. To read and grade essay items is a time-consuming task" (p. 260).

Another disadvantage of the essay test lies in the scoring. How do you evaluate the answer given? What are the degrees of correctness? Downie (1967), in reviewing the merits and limitations of essay tests, states,

> If we cannot truly assert that essay tests foster skill in writing and answer adult needs better than objective tests, why use the essay test? Probably for most classroom situations they are unnecessary except to evaluate how well a student can write a theme or essay. If we want to assess style, quality, and other aspects of writing, it is obvious that the essay test item has to be used. Even here though studies have shown that objective tests of writing ability can predict achievement in writing, the latter measured by both teachers' estimates and grades received, better than do the essay tests. (p. 202)

Noll and Scannell (1972) agree with Downie when they state, "it seems questionable whether the use of essay questions can play a very substantial role in the improvement of a student's writing ability . . . the proportion of total instructional time spent in taking examinations is too small . . . it seems unlikely that a student under the pressure of an examination will be able to do his best writing . . ." (pp. 200–201).

These writers, although agreeing with the studies of the essay test's poor reliability, cannot go along with the pessimistic views of professors Downie, Noll, and Scannell. Properly constructed essay tests can serve as aids in developing and fostering skills in writing. People learn by doing, not by showing potential to do. One cannot learn to play the piano because one's musical ability is potentially great. One learns to play the piano by playing the piano. One learns to organize and express oneself in written discourse by actual writing experience. In a strict measurement sense the essay test is not the best device for evaluation. In an educational sense, which includes measurement, however, the essay test may be used as a useful instructional tool in facilitating learning.

Construction of Essay Tests

Let us now proceed to the ingredients that make essay tests more useful to classroom evaluation. First, we can improve the essay examination by limiting it to the objectives that it measures best, for example, skills in the selection and organization of important facts and ideas. Second, we grant the deficits of the essay test, such as limited sampling, and go on from there and attempt to write the best essay questions possible. Let us now venture forth into the practical ways of writing good essay questions. The following steps are based on the *judgment* of "test experts," not on experimentally established procedures.

1. What do you want to find out about the student's achievement? If your goal is to determine the degree to which he can apply facts, then phrase your question in a manner that calls upon this process. Write down your evaluation goals and refer to them as you write the questions. Ask yourself continually, "Does this test bring out information that I want?"
2. Phrase your questions in a precise and cogent manner. Avoid cluttering your questions with excessive clauses and difficult words. Remember, use simple sentences that everyone in the classroom can read with ease and understanding.
3. Generally begin your essay questions with such words or phrases as *contrast, compare, present an original example of,* and *state the reasons for.* Do not begin essay questions with such words as *what, who, list,* and *discuss* (unless you detail the concepts you want discussed very specifically and thereby explain what you mean by *discuss*). These words either are too nebulous or are prone to elicit mere recitation of facts.
4. Define and narrow the subject area of the question. For example, in an American history class, one might say, "Describe the various facets of colonial life in America." It would be better, however, to say, "Explain and describe the following facets of American colonial life: (a) the people, (b) the economy, (c) everyday life, (d) intellectual pursuits." The first question is too broad and general to evoke anything but good guesses as to what the teacher wanted. The second approach presents the student with specific facets of colonial life to discuss and explain. In addition, it tells the student that a relatively long time will be required to answer the question, whereas the first question gives no indication of time requirements.

Another example of improving an essay question that is too general is the following:

Poor   Explain why you think the United Nations has been a success or a failure.

Better   An important function of the United Nations is to help settle disputes between nations. Describe how one dispute was handled successfully, pointing out how the settlement illustrates a general strength of the United Nations. Describe also how one dispute was handled unsuccessfully, pointing out how this illustrates a general weakness of the United Nations. Your essay should be about 300–400 words in length (2 or 3 pages in longhand). (Educational Testing Service, 1973, p. 8)

5. Never write essay questions with the words *what do you think, in your opinion,* or *write all you know about.* If a teacher begins a question by stating: "What do you think?" she is probably not interested in the student's opinion but really wants to gauge the student's knowledge as presented by the teacher and/or textbook. Thus the question would be better if asked in terms such as, "Why did the _____?" If the purpose of the essay test is to obtain student attitudes (which are impossible to grade) or to measure the ability of a student to present a logical defense of his position, then *you* or *in your opinion* is permissible. The teacher should, however, be careful in the case of measuring the student's ability to present a sound and rational position to grade on that premise and *not* on the position per se.

6. Construct your questions so that they may be answered at all degrees of competency. Every student should be able to respond to the question. However, the students may reveal varying levels of knowledge and understanding in their responses. Do not present questions that only the top 10 per cent can answer or questions that do not differentiate between the bottom 10 per cent and the top 10 per cent. The difficulty of the question should lie in the response, not in the vagueness or remoteness of the question.

7. Allow enough time for students to respond to the questions. Remember, you are attempting to measure understanding and ability to apply facts, not how fast students are able to write or organize their thoughts. If you give more than one essay question, you might suggest a time allowance for each question.

8. Require all students to respond to the same questions. Do not offer alternative choices among the essay questions presented. For example, if you present six questions and ask the students to choose four to write on, you will not have a common basis upon which to evaluate different individuals within the classroom. Presenting the same questions to all the students gives a common reference point in comparing students and increases the validity of the test.

Grading Essay Tests

Grading essay tests is extremely important. It is as important as, if not more so than, the construction of good questions. Of course, both are needed if we are to be as fair as possible to our students. The following suggested procedures should help in this endeavor:

1. Prepare in advance the "ideal" answer and the number of credit points to be allowed for each question. The model answer will serve as the measurement criterion for each student's answer. Knowing in advance the number of points to be allowed for each question will make scoring consistent from paper to paper.
2. Grade all papers without knowledge of the author. This prevents bias from entering into grading procedures. If you know who wrote the paper, your appraisal of him or her as an individual and student may influence your scoring at either a conscious or an unconscious level. The following procedures can be used in facilitating anonymity. Although some of these procedures may seem overly elaborate or unnecessary, they are devised to help make your tests more valid and fair for all students. The important thing to remember is not the devices per se, but the underlying principle of grading papers with the least amount of bias, prejudice, or halo effect.
   a. Prepare a paper with all of the students' names and an equal list of numbers. Pass the sheet among the students and ask each to select a number and place it before his or her name. After the last student has completed this task, ask him to place the sheet of paper face down in one of your opened desk drawers. Each student will then use the number he has selected on his test, rather than his name. Thus, in grading the papers, you will not know who wrote it. After the papers are graded, you can match the numbers with the names for recording grades and returning papers.
   b. Ask students to write their names on the back of their last sheet of paper.
   c. If the answers are written in a test book with the name on the front, turn back the front cover. Instruct students to place name only on the front cover.
3. Grade only one question at a time for all papers. That is, start with question 1 on the first paper and grade it according to your "ideal" answer and then proceed on to the next paper and grade only question 1. Follow this procedure until you have gone through all the papers then come back and start with question 2 and so forth until all the questions have been read. This enables you to judge the responses of all your students to the same question consecutively. Otherwise, you

may be influenced by what the student has written on a previous question.

4. Write comments as well as awarding grades. Remember that a prime reason for giving the essay test is to facilitate learning. Written analysis or comments on the student's answer for each question will help achieve this goal probably more than a grade.

5. Average two or more graders' ratings. If two or more teachers are using the same test and have agreed upon the scoring procedure, and all the factors are held constant except for different graders, then an average of the scores for each test produces a more reliable rating. This, of course, takes time and would probably be done only in very important situations such as promotion or graduation.

A Case History

The following case history of an essay test and one teacher's approach is presented to illustrate some of the points we have covered in actual practice. After reading it, evaluate what Mr. Frank did and did not do. How would you rate his approach based on our previous discussions?

An Essay Test to Measure a Special Ability in Eighth-Grade American History [1]

Mr. Frank's eighth-grade American history class has been studying the fighting that took place between the Indians and the settlers in the western states. The class had just completed several discussions on the rights of each side.

The major purpose of having these discussions was to improve the pupils' ability to find and express convincingly facts and arguments in support of their opinions.

Mr. Frank decided that he would like to give a test to measure his class's skill in this ability. At first, he considered giving an objective test. He thought he might list a number of arguments presented by both the Indians and the settlers and then ask the class to identify those which were backed up by facts. But then he decided against using this kind of test. An objective test would require the student to select sound arguments: it would not call upon him to develop and present them convincingly as he would do in actual discussion. Accordingly Mr. Frank decided that an essay test would satisfy his purposes best.

Since the subject matter of the test was limited, it was unnecessary for Mr. Frank to prepare a written plan for the test. In a sense, the test questions themselves constituted the test plan. Here is the test he prepared. It had three questions:

    1. *Pretend that you are a settler and give three general reasons why you think your side is right in the war with the Indians. For each of the reasons, describe an actual happening to support your argument.*

    2. *Pretend that you are an Indian and give three reasons why you think your side is right in the war with the settlers. For each of the reasons, describe an actual happening to support your argument.*

[1] From *Making the Classroom Test: A Guide for Teaching.* Copyright © 1959, 1961, 1973 by Educational Testing Service. All rights reserved. Reprinted by permission.

3. *Look at the six reasons given by both sides and decide which one would be most dangerous if everyone accepted this kind of reasoning. Give two examples of how people might do bad things if they accepted this kind of reasoning.*

Before scoring the papers, Mr. Frank analyzed the points which he thought would appear in an ideal response and decided how much he would count for each point. He decided not to take off credit for mistakes in spelling and English usage. But he planned to show the English teacher any paper which was especially poorly written so that the English teacher might give help in composition writing to those pupils who needed it.

After Mr. Frank corrected the papers, he found that most of the pupils had proceeded well on Questions 1 and 2 requiring reasons and examples. However, many of them had floundered on Question 3, which required them to point out the dangerous implications of one argument. Because of their difficulty with Question 3, Mr. Frank decided to organize a series of classroom debates, so that the students would get practice in extending, attacking, and defending an argument.

On an essay test of this sort, scores are not highly reliable. On a second reading, after a little time lapse, Mr. Frank would find it difficult to give every paper the same mark as on the first reading. Furthermore, several teachers grading the same papers would probably not agree very closely with one another. Therefore, Mr. Frank avoided giving an exact numerical score for each paper but instead assigned three general grades: good, average, and poor. However, he wrote many comments on the papers so that the pupils would have a better idea of the strengths and weaknesses of their arguments. He also read several papers to the class for discussion purposes, making full use of the test as an instructional device.

The Objective Test

Horace Mann's "step forward" in 1845, when he introduced a uniform written examination was, as was stated in the previous chapter, a radical departure from the traditional oral examination. Mann's most important contribution to student evaluation was the introduction of the concept of requiring all students to answer the same questions. This idea was basic to later standardized tests. The beginning of the "second step forward" can be seen in the early history of standardized testing. This history has been reviewed earlier, and it need not be mentioned again except to say that teacher-made objective tests grew with, and parallel to, the standardized testing movement. The objective test was developed in order to overcome some of the disadvantages of the essay test. We have already discussed some of the merits and limitations of both kinds of instruments. The critics of objective tests state that they measure only factual recall, emphasize memorization of obscure details, encourage too much guessing, do not deal with conceptualization, and do not present the student with the opportunity to practice writing.

Although we have dealt with the preceding criticisms in part in the previous chapters, in this chapter we will consider them in reference to what constitutes an objective test. Most importantly, however, our main attention will be focused on practical methods of improving and utilizing the objective test for classroom use and analyzing the results.

Characteristics

The objective test is so called because the scoring procedure is determined when the test item is written. That is, the correct answer, usually only one, is completely stated before testing. Thus the grader can be completely objective about the answer. We mentioned that the major drawback of essay tests lies in scoring the test. Objective tests attempt to overcome this deficiency. It should be noted that the word *objective* is in reference only to the rules for scoring. These scoring rules for objective tests are absolutely clear before testing begins. The actual content and coverage of objective tests, however, may be as subjective as those of the essay test. It is possible that the teacher may be wrong in what she designates as the correct answer. The important point to remember is that the teacher must be sure of what she considers to be the correct answer. In an essay test, teachers sometimes have a great deal of difficulty setting up their own standards for the correct answer. The objective test item, however, must have only one correct answer, and this is decided when the item is written, not when it is graded.

The objective test is a structured examination. That is, each examinee is presented with exactly the same problem. The essay question, no matter how well it is phrased, will have different meanings to different students. The objective test, on the other hand, being completely structured, must be answered in a prescribed manner. The student is not called upon to organize his response as he is in the essay format.

The objective test requires the student to *recognize*, not *recall*, the correct answer. This is because most objective tests present given alternatives (with the exception of the completion item), one of which is the correct response. It should be noted, however, that objective items can be constructed to appraise recalling and the use of previously learned information, although in most cases the objective test does not tap this source of knowledge.

In our previous discussions of reliability, we have noted that an increase of items tends to increase the reliability of the test. The objective test lends itself to this task more readily than the essay because each item of the objective test is short and requires less response time. Thus the greater number of items in the objective test can sample more topics.

Scoring the objective test is routine, because a scoring key is established at the time the test is constructed. The score, therefore, will be the same no matter who scores it. The student who is the teacher's pet or the "bad boy," the handwriting expert or the scribbler, will all obtain the same scores if they choose the same responses.

General Rules for Item Writing

The following rules should be observed when writing objective tests:

1. Observe the rules of good English usage. Gear your language to the whole group of students. Attempt to communicate to the students in

readable language that is not stilted or complex. Be sure that even the duller students can understand the items.

2. Avoid questions that do not have answers that would be agreed upon by most experts. Do not use "trick" items in which the correct answer is dependent upon obscure key words.
3. Avoid items that answer other items in the test.
4. Use your test items to tap important, not trivial, areas of knowledge.
5. Identify any authorities cited in your item.

Types of Objective Items

There are many different types of objective items. Our attention will be focused on the most prominent.

True-False Items

Do not use true-false items if at all possible. The true-false item has been very popular with teachers, probably because it is easy to construct and requires little time. Do not allow the ease of construction to lure you into the true-false trap. Good true-false items are not easy to write, and even the good ones have many limitations. The following statements are representative of the major drawbacks of the true-false item:

1. The true-false item tends to be greatly influenced by guessing. If, for example, a true-false test contained 100 items, it is very probable that most students could obtain a score of around fifty by guessing. This restricts the range and meaning of the scores. What is the relationship of John's score to guessing? Can one really say that Mary is a better student than Jane, or is she a better guesser? The longer you make the test, the less chance of measurement error resulting from guessing; however, guessing still has an undue influence on scores.
2. It is almost impossible to make statements either absolutely true or absolutely false. For example, read the following statements and see if either is absolutely true or false.

T   F   Adolph Hitler was responsible for World War II.
T   F   People exist only in relationship to other people.

Although many historians and political scientists would place the major responsibility for World War II on Hitler and Germany, they would also trace the conflict to World War I and the resulting economic sanctions. The answer, of course, would need to be qualified. The second statement might fit neatly into some philosopher's bag or be warmly embraced by the sociologist. Other philosophers and psychologists might disagree entirely with it, or agree only if certain qualifications and nuances are added. Who is right? There are few, if any, ideas in the world of today that are so absolutely certain that simple true-false statements can be applied to them.

3. True-false tests foster poor test-taking habits. Students are clever and will second-guess the teacher who employs the true-false item and discern patterns, such as, "She usually gives more items that are true," or, "Did you notice her true-false tests are in patterns of fives—five true and then five false?"

Granted that the preceding examples are obvious and one-sided, could you disprove their validity? Could the perfect item that you come up with be repeated in different areas over 100 times or more?

If you must write true-false items, bear in mind the following "yellow lights":

1. Stay away from broad generalizations which obviously give the answers away. Statements that include such terms as *never, only, always, all,* and *every* tend to do this.
2. Avoid items that are partly true and partly false.
3. Do not write unusually long and complex statements. Statements of this kind are generally true and many students are aware of this.

Completion Items

Completion items require the student to fill in a blank that completes the sentence or answers a specific question. For example:

1. The Constitution requires that a member of the United States Senate be at least _____ years old.
2. How old does a person have to be in order to be eligible for the United States Senate? _____.

The first statement requires the student to complete the sentence, whereas the second asks the student to supply the answer. The last form is also called by some a short-answer item. For the purposes of our discussion, both will be included under completion items.

The completion item is related to the essay item and serves as a bridge between the objective and essay test. On the one hand, it is objective, in the sense that a prearranged answer can be chosen before testing; on the other hand, it is related to the essay test because the student must produce the correct answer rather than recognize it. The completion item is especially useful for appraising your student's knowledge of facts, such as names and dates. Its major limitation is its major asset; that is, its use to appraise factual knowledge. It does not measure the student's ability to apply or use this kind of information. In addition, it is difficult to phrase items with clarity and yet not confuse students. Also, some areas of study do not lend themselves to the simple task of asking for pure facts.

The following are some suggestions for writing completion items:

1. Write completion items in your own words and be sure that you limit correct responses to your actual achievement goals.
2. Refrain from writing items that can be completed by general intellectual ability rather than knowledge of the subject.
3. Do not give away the answer by varying the blanks according to the number of letters in the word. Blanks should always be of standard length.
4. Do not mutilate a passage with too many blanks.

> *Poor:* In (1917) Puerto Ricans were made (citizens) of the (United States) and given the right to (elect) an upper house with the (President) reserving the (right) to (veto bills) and appoint the governor and certain other officials.

> *Better:* Puerto Ricans were made citizens of the United States and given the right to elect an upper house with the President reserving the right to veto bills and appoint the _____ and certain other officials in the year of _____.

5. The important word or words to be fitted in should be at or near the end of the blank. This allows the student the opportunity to read the problem before the blank is seen.

> *Poor:* _____ _____ was the first United States astronaut.

> *Better:* The name of the first United States astronaut is _____ _____.

6. Construct your specific questions in a direct manner rather than using incomplete sentences.

> *Poor:* Columbus discovered America in _____.

> *Better:* In what year did Columbus discover America? _____.

7. State the words in which the answer is to be given.

> *Poor:* Where does the Congress of the United States hold its sessions? _____.

> *Better:* In what city does the United States Congress hold its sessions? _____.

Matching Items

The matching item's major advantage is that it condenses a great deal of material into a limited amount of space. An example of this type item is as follows:

1. James Fenimore Cooper _____	a.	Compensation
	b.	The Deerslayer
2. Ralph Waldo Emerson _____	c.	Ethan Brand
	d.	Ichabod
3. Nathaniel Hawthorne _____	e.	The Legend of Sleepy Hollow
4. Edgar Allan Poe _____	f.	A Psalm of Life
	g.	The Raven

In the blank spaces students are requested to write the letter of each of the titles on the right that corresponds to the authors on the left.

The matching item is not particularly well suited to measuring the student's ability to conceptualize. It is useful for appraising specific aspects of a subject field, such as dates, leading personalities, definition of terms, meaning of words, and association of authors with titles of books.

The following are some suggestions for writing matching items:

1. All matching items should be presented intact. All items for each set should be on a single page. Do not split the items from one page to another. This may be confusing and time-consuming for the student.
2. The list of answer choices should contain at least two or three more items than the number of problems, which will reduce the effect of guessing. If both lists contained an equal number of items, the student could more easily arrive at the correct response through the process of elimination.
3. Do not mix subject fields. This means, for example, that if you have dates in a response list, you should not mix names or other unrelated items with them.
4. The instructions should clearly state the basis for matching. Students should be told specifically what they are to do. For example, if one answer is to be used more than once, be sure to explain this in the directions.
5. Present response items in a logical order if at all possible—alphabetically, chronologically, or any other format that assists the student in quickly perceiving all the items. For example, note the alphabetical list of authors and titles in our previous example.

Remember that you are attempting to appraise the student's knowledge of the subject field, not his intellectual acumen in figuring out obscure test directions. If your matching items and directions are unclear, you may penalize the student who knows the subject but is not test-wise or skillful at figuring out puzzles.

Multiple-Choice Items

The multiple-choice format is one of the most popular and effective of all the objective tests. It consists of two parts: (1) the stem, which states the problem, and (2) a list of options, one of which is to be selected as the answer. The stem may be stated as a question or as an incomplete statement. It does not matter much which form is used. Most experienced test writers prefer the incomplete statement because it allows the reader a smooth transition from reading the stem to selecting the appropriate item. On the other hand, inexperienced test writers prefer the question form because it is easier to construct and helps the writer to state the problem cogently.

In constructing an incomplete statement item, be very careful in phrasing the options. Each option should follow the stem in a smooth manner. An awkwardly phrased option may be a cue that it is not the correct answer. Examples of both forms follow:

> *Question:* What is one of the important causes of mental retardation?
> A. Poor schools.
> B. Smoking.
> C. Heredity.
> D. Nuclear fallout.

> *Incomplete Statement:* One important cause of mental retardation is
> A. poor schools.
> B. smoking.
> C. heredity.
> D. nuclear fallout.

The multiple-choice item can be used to appraise almost any educational objective with the exception, of course, of student organization and ability to produce answers. Some of the areas it is effective in measuring are the following:

1. Information.
2. Vocabulary.
3. Isolated facts.
4. Cause-and-effect relationships.
5. Understandings.
6. Insight and critical analysis.
7. Solution of problems.
8. Interpreting data.
9. Application of principles.

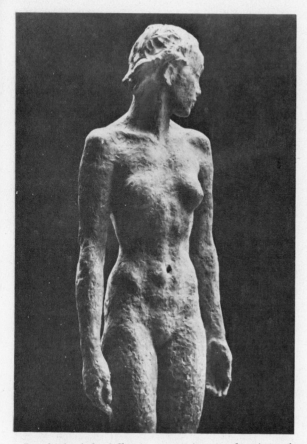

In which of the following centuries was the piece of sculpture shown above most probably produced?
(A)   *The fifth century* B.C.
(B)   *The fourteenth century* A.D.
(C)   *The sixteenth century* A.D.
(D)   *The eighteenth century* A.D.
(E)   *The twentieth century* A.D.

Figure 56. Example of multiple-choice item testing depth of knowledge. (From *Multiple-Choice Questions: A Close Look.* Copyright © 1963, Educational Testing Service. All rights reserved. Reprinted by permission of Educational Testing Service.)

Many people believe that the multiple-choice item is a superficial exercise requiring little thought and no understanding. In order to combat this myth, the Educational Testing Service (1973) prepared a booklet to show in concrete terms the falseness of the charge. Note that in Figure 56 a piece of sculpture is presented and the student is required to place it in its proper time period. Here the student must apply learned data to the situation. It is not simply an exercise or recitation of memorized information.

The multiple-choice item is very versatile and relatively free of some of the problems that afflict other types of objective items. The multiple-choice item does not require that one option or alternative be completely correct. On the contrary, the requirement is only that one option be significantly more correct. The difficulty of a multiple-choice item will depend on the "almost right" aspect of the options.

The construction of a good multiple-choice test item is difficult. Developing plausible incorrect options taxes the ingenuity of the teacher. The end product, however, is well worth the investment of time and energy. It is therefore recommended that you consider using the multiple-choice item for most of your objective tests. It is hoped the following suggestions and examples will help in this endeavor:

1. The stem of a multiple-choice item should pose a clear question or problem. It should not be a series of unrelated ideas, some of which are true and others false.

Poor: In the Midwest
   A. there are many mountains.
   B. tornadoes occur most frequently in the spring.
   C. people are politically more conservative.
   D. Chicago is the largest city.

In the preceding example, note that the stem consists of a vague phrase "In the Midwest." What does that mean? It does not clearly convey the problem to the student. Should the student answer (D), which the teacher intended, or (B), which is also plausible, or how about (C)?

Better: The most heavily populated city in the Midwestern region of the United States is
   A. New York.
   B. Chicago.
   C. Cleveland.
   D. Los Angeles.

Note that if the student chooses (A) or (D) he shows his lack of knowledge of the location of the Midwest, whereas a (C) response would show his knowledge of this but a lack of information of the largest Midwestern city. Most importantly, however, the stem clearly focuses on the most heavily populated city in the Midwest, and only one answer is correct.

2. The stem should include as much of the item as possible. Note the preceding examples. The *poor* example has three words, whereas the

better example has most of its words in the stem and very few in the options. This approach facilitates economy of reading time and communication of the problem to the student.

3. Incorrect options should be logically related to the stem. If you supply obviously incorrect options, the student, by sheer logic and elimination, may obtain the correct response. Note the following examples:

Poor: Schizophrenia is a term used in psychology to characterize
  A. racial discrimination.
  B. a group of children.
  C. a group of psychotic reactions.
  D. a group of Indians.

The student who has read and listened in class at even a very minimal level should be able to guess that (C) is the correct response. He therefore rules out all other options. We have appraised only his intellectual ability to rule out obviously incorrect alternatives.

Better: Schizophrenia is a term used in psychology to characterize a group of
  A. neurotic reactions.
  B. organic disturbances.
  C. psychotic reactions.
  D. manic-depressive reactions.

In the *better* version the student knows that all four options are psychological terms dealing with disturbed behavior. The problem is which alternative best characterizes schizophrenia. The knowledgeable student knows that (A) is incorrect because schizophrenia constitutes a loss of reality. He also knows that schizophrenia may have an element of organicity (physical causes) and sometimes behavior similar to those classified as manic-depressive. He chooses (C) because he knows that the other responses, although related, are separate diagnostic entities and schizophrenia includes a group of psychotic reactions. Thus using all plausible options curtails intelligent guessing.

4. The length of the options should be consistent and not vary with their correctness or incorrectness. If this is not done students will become aware of the fact that the long options are correct or vice versa. Using our previous example, let us modify the options:

Poor: A. neurotic reactions.
  B. organic disturbances.
  C. psychotic reactions which reveal various degrees of ego disintegration.
  D. manic-depressive reactions.

Note that in the changed version the correct answer (C) is longer, whereas in the original (*better* version) all four of the options are consistent in length.

5. The stem should not contain an excessive number of words unless your goal is to evaluate the student's ability to select basic facts, or unless your objective is to play an intellectual variety of hide and go seek. Note the following two examples:

> *Poor:* On March 4, 1801, Thomas Jefferson, leader of the victorious Republican Party, walked from his capital boarding house and took the oath of office. He looked the part of a farmer and, indeed, he was one, for his biggest interest, next to his country, was his affection for his beautiful home and estate in Virginia. He was a philosopher and lover of peace and was happiest when he could think about problems in art, religion, or science. The most important event of his first administration was
>   A. the repeal of the Naturalization Act.
>   B. the purchase of the Louisiana territory.
>   C. the repeal of the excise tax.
>   D. bringing the Barbary pirates to terms.

> *Better:* The most important event of Thomas Jefferson's first administration was
>   A. the repeal of the Naturalization Act.
>   B. the purchase of the Louisiana territory.
>   C. the repeal of the excise tax.
>   D. bringing the Barbary pirates to terms.

Note that in the *poor* example the student had to wade through irrelevant material before arriving at the problem, whereas in the *better* example the stem immediately confronted the student with his task.
6. Maintain correct English usage throughout the item.
7. Place the correct option randomly throughout the test. That is, do not place most of the options in the (A) position, (B) position, and so on. Nunnally (1972) suggested a method that is easy to do and will arrange your items in a random order:

> One way to rearrange the alternatives in a random sequence is by the use of shuffled cards. If, for example, there are five alternative answers for each item, the letters a, b, c, d, and e are written respectively on five cards. These are then shuffled four or five times and dealt out. The letter on the first card determines the position of the first alternative as it appeared when the item was constructed, which ... is usually the correct alternative. The next card dealt determines the position of the first incorrect alternative, and so on until the positions of all five alternatives are determined. When such a random procedure is used, students cannot accurately detect patterns in the ordering of alternatives. (pp. 124–25)

8. Do not use such options as *none of these, both a and c above,* or *all of the above.* The only time you may use such terms is in a mathematical problem requiring mechanical computation. In the following example the use of *none of the above* might penalize the good student who knows "too much." Instead of answering (C), the choice might be (D), because IQ is not necessarily equivalent to intelligence and therefore

on the basis of a test one cannot classify Mary's intelligence. If, on the other hand, we substitute *below average* for *none of the above*, the student is forced to make a decision, and knowing that an IQ of 103 in the general classification system is considered average, will respond appropriately and save his or her dissent or criticism of the item for later discussion.

Poor: Mary has an IQ of 103. Her intelligence is
   A. superior.
   B. genius.
   C. average.
   D. none of the above.

9. Accentuate the positive and eliminate the negative. In a learning situation it is much better to emphasize the positive over the negative aspects of learning. There are times, however, when the only thing one can do is to have students look for an option that does not relate or follow from a given principle. Negative statements used sparingly are acceptable. The problem is, however, that you may be reinforcing learning of erroneous concepts; it is also confusing to students who are geared to looking for correct rather than incorrect responses. If you must use a negative word in the stem it should be set off from the sentence by capitalization or underlining. For example,

According to the United States Constitution, citizens do NOT have the right to
A. free assembly.
B. freedom of religion.
C. make arrests.
D. advocate sedition.

10. Develop your test according to your educational objectives and the rules of good test construction. This last suggestion is obvious but nevertheless needs to be said. Remember that the "ideal" test, following the suggestions that have been made, is meaningless if it does not measure what *you* want. This means that you must judge the skills, understandings, facts, and other factors you consider important within the structure of good test construction. A test ideal from a test maker's point of view may be poor from a teacher's perspective. The important thing to do is to combine both so as to have the best possible instrument to help you help your students in their educational progress.

Mechanical Operations

Thus far our attention has been directed to improving the quality of objective test items. This section will be devoted to the clerical or pedantic aspects of test construction. Though it may not be as glamorous or as creative, it is a necessary part of test production.

Item Writing

Professional item writers use separate 5- by 8-inch cards on which they write their items. This procedure may be of help in putting together the final product. At the bottom of the card, list the area and skills tested by the item. The intended answer key (A, B, C, or D) should be written on the back of the card.

Assembly

You now have a group of items that need to be integrated into a test format. Check the items against your course objectives and make sure you have covered all the areas you consider important. Be sure you have enough items to make your test reliable.

Editing and Arranging

Be sure that your items follow the suggestions for good item construction. Check your English usage to see that it is grammatically correct and that you have not inadvertently misspelled or omitted a word. Next, see if you can arrange for a colleague to read over your test and attempt to answer the questions. Incorporate his suggestions into your test if they seem appropriate.

After you have edited your examination, arrange the questions in order of difficulty. This can be done by establishing categories representing degrees of difficulty—for example: *very hard, hard, average, easy, very easy*. The distribution of item difficulty should be similar to the normal curve distribution. That is, there should be a few *very hard* and a few *very easy* questions. The rest of the items should be of moderate difficulty. There is no point in having items that no students can answer or items that everyone answers correctly. Before you administer the test, of course, you can only estimate the difficulty of items; however, as we shall discuss later, an item analysis of the test results will establish the degrees of difficulty more accurately.

After you have ascertained the degrees of item difficulty, your next step is to arrange the questions in the order that they will be presented to the student. First, be sure not to mix different formats—that is, all multiple-choice items should be in the same section, all matching items should be in the same section, and so forth. Second, within each type of item, arrange your problems by degree of difficulty, starting with the *very easy* and ending with the *very hard* items. It is very important to do this because some students, especially the younger ones, may be discouraged by difficult problems in the beginning and consequently either not finish or not do their best.

This arrangement is also helpful to students who work slowly. These students may know the answers to the easier questions but in a timed test may never reach them. If possible, also try to have topics follow in logical and coherent blocks of questions. Do not present, for example, an item on the Constitution, then one on the Bill of Rights, then one on the Constitution, and so forth. It is much more desirable to group the Constitution questions together and then the Bill of Rights questions together. This presents whole blocks of subject matter together and allows the student to attack the problems from a common frame of reference. (If you arrange according to groups, you will then, of course, place the items within groups from *easy* to *hard*.)

Directions

The detailed nature of test directions will depend on the grade and test sophistication of your students. Explicit and understandable directions are extremely important. You may present your written directions on the front page along with a place for name, date, class, and any other data you deem necessary.

The directions should be completely clear on the exact method to be used in recording the answers. In addition, the student should be told of the proposed scoring procedure and credits to be allowed for each section or item of the test.

The following is an example that may be adapted for most objective tests.

Directions: This is a fifty-minute test. There are seventy-five questions. Mark only *one* answer to each question. Mark the answer you think is correct (see example below) by drawing an "X" through the letter that best corresponds to the correct answer for each problem. Do not make any marks on the test. Make all of your marks on the separate answer sheet.

Do not waste time on questions that seem too difficult. It is better to go on and finish the test and then go back to the difficult questions. Remember it is better to make a careful guess than to spend too much time on any one item or to leave an answer blank. Your score will be based on the number of correct answers you mark.

Example:

Test Problem	Answer Sheet

The first president of the United States was
    A. Abraham Lincoln
    B. George Washington
    C. Benjamin Franklin   A   X   C   D
    D. Thomas Jefferson

Table 28 presents an example of a teacher-made answer sheet.

Physical Layout

Remember, not only should your whole test, questions and language, be geared for student understanding, but also the physical layout should be

Table 28. *Part of a Teacher-Made Answer Sheet*

Name _____ Class _____
Date _____ Name of Test _____

Directions: Mark an X through the letter that corresponds to the best answer in the following way:

Example: A ⊠ C D

Remember, mark only one answer to each question.

Question:	Answer:	Question:	Answer:
1.	A B C D	25.	A B C D
2.	A B C D	26.	A B C D
3.	A B C D	27.	A B C D
4.	A B C D	28.	A B C D
5.	A B C D	29.	A B C D

arranged for your convenience in scoring. Here are some simple suggestions that will help you and your students:

1. Test material and all items pertaining to it should go on the same page. Do not, for example, have the test items that refer to a chart on a separate page, but include the problem, items, and chart on the same page. Do not break up an item by having the stem and one or two options on one page and the rest on the next page.
2. Arrange to have each multiple-choice option on its own line.
3. Arrange your answer sheet (see Table 28) so that the answers are all in one column. This helps if you score by sight and is also convenient if you use a scoring key that can be placed beside the column.

Reproduction

You now have before you the edited and arranged questions, directions, and answer sheet. Now type a rough draft to see how it looks. Decide on your space requirements and other necessary mechanical problems. After you have done this, reproduce the test, using a mimeograph or any other process that is available to you. A good rule of thumb is to produce at least ten extra copies for unexpected needs. Next, duplicate your answer sheets.

Scoring

Prepare your scoring key by marking the correct answers on an answer sheet. Although you could stop at this point and score the tests by comparing the key to the student's answer sheets, you should spend a little more time now to save your eyes and time in the future. A good method to accomplish this is to produce a *scoring stencil*. The scoring stencil is simply an answer sheet with the correct answer punched out; it is placed over an answer sheet, thereby making it possible to count the correct responses. There are many ways of constructing a scoring stencil. One method is to paste a correctly marked answer sheet on a piece of cardboard or a group of five or six papers pasted together, and punch out holes in the marked spaces.

In a large school system you may have an electrical scoring machine such as the IBM 805, which will save a great deal of time. In that case, you will, of course, use standard IBM answer sheets similar to those used with standardized tests. You will then only have to record the correct answers on an IBM answer sheet using a number 2 pencil. This stencil is then placed in the machine. In the past, special pencils were used.

Item Analysis

Many teachers think that after they have developed, produced, administered, and scored a test they are through. This is not the case at all. If you stop after scoring, you will be losing many valuable data about your test and student reactions. Test analysis will give you clues to the achievements of your class and will aid in future teaching objectives. It will also tell you about the weaknesses of your test and help you make improvements in future examinations.

The discussion that follows will be brief because the methods for analyzing test results were already presented in the chapter on achievement tests (Chapter 9). The same methodology of item analysis in standardized achievement tests, for the most part, can be used with your classroom tests.

You will first want to ascertain the degree of difficulty of your items. This can be done in a small classroom (less than forty students) by selecting the top ten and lowest ten students according to their test scores.[1] For each of the ten top students go through the text and mark a 1 next to each response chosen. Do the same for the lowest ten using a different mark, such as an ×. For example, note the following history item and the responses of the top and lowest ten.

The first president of the United States was

× × × × × × × × 1 1 1 1 1 1 1 1 1 1	A.	Abraham Lincoln
	B.	George Washington
×	C.	Benjamin Franklin
×	D.	Thomas Jefferson

An inspection of our example reveals that all the top ten students chose

---

[1] For the most reliable and theoretically correct method that would be needed for larger groups, see Chapter 9.

the correct answer and eight of the lowest ten also responded correctly. These data, although based only on a sampling of the class, would be very valuable to the teacher. On the basis of our example, the teacher might decide that the easiness level is too high and that the item does not discriminate between good and poor students. For larger groups of students and for tests of 100 questions or more, mechanical methods such as scoring and punch cards would need to be used.

In analyzing data, you will look for quest ons that no one answers correctly or that receive the same number of correct responses from "poor" students as from "good" students. The question or the options may be poorly stated.

If you are using a test primarily to rank your students for grading purposes, your questions (ideally) should be so difficult that on a five-option multiple-choice item only 60 per cent of the group obtain the right answer, on a four-option multiple-choice item 62 per cent obtain the right answer, and on each true-false item 75 per cent mark the correct response (Educational Testing Service, 1973b).

A Case History

The following case history is presented as an illustration of some of the concepts, procedures, and problems in objective test construction that face the teacher. In many ways it is a synthesis of our previous discussion placed in an actual school setting.

An Objective Achievement Test on Fifth-Grade Arithmetic [2]

It was near the end of the school year and Mrs. Jackson, fifth-grade teacher, decided to give her pupils an arithmetic test covering the year's work. Her first step was to list the kinds of information she hoped to get from the test. She decided that, most of all, she wanted to get a general picture of class achievement with some indication of over-all areas of strength and weakness. Secondary purposes she listed were (1) to identify those pupils who might be especially weak in a particular arithmetic skill and (2) to measure the relative abilities of her students for purposes of report-card grading.

In trying to get an accurate picture of over-all class achievement, she decided that there were two ways in which she could classify the year's work: one was according to *the kind of computation required*, and the other was according to *the way the problem was presented*.

The kinds of computation required were

1. Multiplication
2. Division
3. Addition and Subtraction of Fractions
4. Measuring (distance, time, weight, temperature, etc.)
5. Decimals

[2] From *Making the Classroom Test: A Guide for Teachers.* Copyright © 1959, 1961, 1973 by Educational Testing Service. All rights reserved. Reprinted by permission.

The ways the problems were presented were

1. Simple computation, such as $21\overline{)\$1.05}$ or $1/2 + 1/3$
2. Problems requiring use of procedures learned previously, such as

   John missed $1/5$ of the twenty words on a spelling test. How many words did he miss?

   or

   A group of twenty-nine children were making programs for a school assembly. They needed 435 programs. How many did each child have to make?

3. Problems requiring original thinking by pupils and use of "number sense." In these problems the pupils could not depend on previously learned procedures for a method of solution but must develop their own procedures for solution. Two problems of this type follow:

   Problem one. Explain how you, as a fifth-grade pupil, using ten blocks, could prove to a fourth-grade pupil that $1/2$ is bigger than $2/5$.

   Problem two. You are standing directly in front of Building A and looking off at Building B in the distance. Here is the way the two buildings look to you:

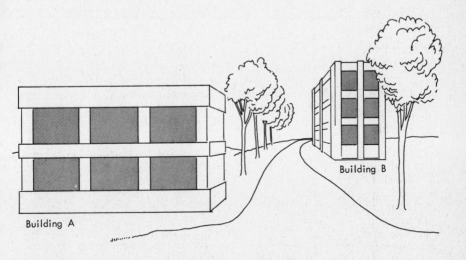

   The rooms in both buildings are the same height. By looking at the windows, decide which of the following is true:

   (A) Both buildings are the same height.
   (B) Building A is two-thirds as high as Building B.
   (C) Building A is one and one-third times as high as Building B.
   (D) Building A is twice as high as Building B.
   (E) You can't tell from looking at the buildings which one is higher.
      (Answer: B)

Using these two ways for classifying the questions (according to the kind of computation required and according to the way the problem was presented), Mrs. Jackson was now ready to make *a written plan* for the test. She intended that this plan would provide for a test *paralleling* the emphasis given to various points in class.

Mrs. Jackson wrote out her test plan in the form of a "two-way grid." In a two-way grid each question is classified in two dimensions.

The two-way grid that Mrs. Jackson made for the arithmetic test is on page 6. Since she planned to allow an hour for the test, she thought 40 questions would be about the right number. The numbers in the boxes represent questions—these questions to be of a type described by the two dimensions of the grid.

Way Problem Presented

Kind of Computation Required	Routine Computa-tion	Thought Problems Following Proce-dures Taught Pre-viously	Thought Problems Requiring Students to Develop New Procedures
Fractions	7	4	1
Multiplication	2	3	1
Division	3	4	1
Measuring	1	5	1
Decimals	3	3	1

After Mrs. Jackson completed the two-way grid, she found it relatively easy to write most of the questions for the test. She was able to write many questions by paralleling questions from the arithmetic textbook itself. However, she found it quite challenging to write the five problems which would require students to develop new procedures.

Mrs. Jackson believed that the test covered understandings and skills in which her pupils had been well prepared. Therefore, she expected the very best students to get all or nearly all of the questions right, and she expected even the below-average students to get a majority of the questions right. She did not, however, make the mistake of deciding in advance that some minimum score—say 28 questions right (70%)—would represent a passing mark. She knew from previous experience that sometimes her questions turned out to be more difficult than they first seemed to her. She decided to wait until she could look at the scores actually made on the whole test and could scrutinize carefully any questions which proved particularly troublesome.

As it happened, most of the students did well on the test, although no one had a perfect paper. On the basis of the test, Mrs. Jackson felt that her class had achieved the objectives of the work in arithmetic. She did notice, however, that a number of students had difficulty with the problems involving decimals. Therefore she decided to spend more time working on decimals in the few weeks remaining in the school year. And then there was one student who failed all the division problems, although he did fairly well on the rest of the test. She arranged to give this student special help in division.

Most of the students had between 30 and 35 questions right. However, there were a few who scored above, and a few who fell below this middle range. Knowing which students were in the middle and which were above or below was useful to Mrs. Jackson in assigning report-card grades. Of course she also took into account each pupil's class work and his standing on other tests.

In evaluating her test, Mrs. Jackson felt it had been reasonably successful in meeting the purposes for which she had planned it. The test had given her a good picture of over-all class achievement and it had pointed up the weakness in decimals. It had not been planned to be highly diagnostic, but it had helped to identify one pupil who was especially weak in division. In addition, although the test did not rank all of her students in the exact order of their arithmetic abilities, it had given her information that was useful for grading purposes.

Grades and Report Cards

chapter 17

Thus far we have primarily devoted our discussions to instruments that attempt to appraise student progress *objectively*. In this chapter our attention will be directed to the assignment of labels to test results and other evidence of pupil achievement. The best-constructed tests will be rendered useless if after reviewing the results the teacher assigns grades without a structured and coherent plan. Grading is subjective, but this subjectivity may be kept to a minimum by appropriate grading practices.

The assignment of report card grades is a difficult task. However, if a logical and rational system is followed, these tasks become less difficult. In addition, if information concerning a student's ability and progress is reported in understandable terms, fewer parents will become irate.

Philosophy

The individual teacher must think about grades in the context of learning and reality, must formulate a philosophy and approach to grades and report cards, and must then act accordingly. In determining this philosophy, questions dealing with the effects of grading on learning and motivation must be answered. These philosophical conclusions must then be translated into the context of the school setting and its own unique demands and realistic problems. If, for example, you decide that grading is inaccurate and unreliable and the school policy is directly in conflict with your ideals, do you completely capitulate or do you, on the other hand, go on strike and refuse to cooperate with the school administration? Or do you work within the system and attempt to modify existing practices?

This chapter is based on the last approach—that grades are with us, like it or not, and our job is to make them as accurate and effective as possible. The teacher who is against grades can in the classroom place more emphasis on the rewards of learning and less on the importance of grades. The teacher can take part in teacher committees formed to review and modify the existing grading policies. This approach incorporates individual philosophy within the reality of the school setting.

Purposes of Grades

Now that we have accepted, rather grudgingly, the need for grades, let us review some of their historical purposes:

1. They provide data for parents on their children's progress.
2. They certify promotional status and graduation.
3. They serve as an incentive to do school lessons.
4. They help in educational and vocational guidance by presenting a realistic basis for future choices.
5. They serve as a reference point for personal development.
6. They provide a basis for awarding honors.
7. They enable the school to ascertain the amount of extracurricular activities, if any, in which the student should participate.
8. They may be used as sources for recommendations to prospective employers.
9. They provide information for curriculum research.
10. They provide data to a school that the student may later attend through transfer or graduation.

These purposes are not sacrosanct, and certainly some, such as "motivation," could possibly be discarded in an ideal situation where students learn "for the sake of learning," but some of the other purposes would be difficult to fulfill without grades or another evaluative device.

Assigning Test Grades

Students need to know how well they perform on a classroom test. They must know the areas of their subject-matter strength and weakness. This can be accomplished by going over the test, item by item, and allowing the students to ask questions. The teacher and his students can together decide whether certain competencies are lacking or whether there was a misunderstanding of the test question. The teacher may decide that a test item was poor and the student's "incorrect" response might be considered correct.

Students also need to know what their final scores mean. Not many students in our American schools will be satisfied to know only how many questions they answered correctly. They want an evaluation: "Is my score good, fair, or bad?" Let us look at some possible approaches.

Norm-Referenced Grading

You will probably remember from our previous discussions (see Chapters 9 and 12) that *norm-referenced* refers to a relative level of achievement, that is, comparing a student's performance with that of a reference group, usually his or her own peers. The student's *relative* place in the group, therefore, will determine the grade. A high grade would indicate high achievement in the group, whereas low achievement in the group would produce a low grade. In this situation, grading is related not only to the student's performance but also to the achievement of the entire group.

The giving of norm-referenced grades is simply the ranking of students in achievement and assigning grades on this basis. A good example of this procedure is the use of the normal curve.

Grading on the curve theoretically assumes a given number of grades, A through F, which are determined by the relative positions of the students in comparison to one another. For example, note the following distribution:

Grade	Percentage of Students
A	10
B	15
C	50
D	15
F	10

This form of grading, which presupposes that achievement will be normally distributed in a given classroom and that therefore a certain number of A's, B's, C's, D's, and F's must be given in relationship to the normal curve distribution, is a *prostitution of statistics* and a poor and unfair way to grade. The classroom does not contain enough pupils for the assumption to be made that there is a normal distribution of students. A much greater number than the usual twenty to forty pupils per class would be needed. Thus the teacher may have a bright or dull class that is not at all representative of different levels of ability. If the teacher follows the curve in this setting, some children in the bright group would be doomed to failure and some children in the dull class would have to receive A's. Promotion and test grades would then be linked to the chance of what group a student found himself in. If an average pupil could arrange to be in the dull group, he probably would graduate in the top of his class. The use of the curve in the upper-middle-class high school and college and graduate school presents a similar problem. In these settings there tends to be a skewed curve; that is, students at the low end may be in the bright range of ability in the general population and students at the top in the very superior classification. If curving were adhered to completely in such situations, bright and superior students might have difficulty in graduating. Thus in a statistical sense the curve is an erroneous method of evaluation because the groups are too small, and in selected groups there is not a representative distribution.

Stanley (1964), in discussing the problems of "grading on the curve," cites an amusing story:

> On the first day of class a graduate professor of Latin informed the seven students taking his advanced course that he had learned of grading on the curve the previous summer and would use it in this class, resulting in certainty that one of the seven students would fail the course. As the students left at the close of class, one of them muttered to the other six, "I'm sure to be the one who fails, so I'm dropping the course right now."
> "But you can't do that," the others exclaimed, "because we don't know which one of us would fail then."
> So the six pitched in and paid the predestined failure to stay in the course and absorb the failing grade. (pp. 326–27)

In addition to its statistical limitations, the curving of grades leads to undesirable attitudes. The quest for grades and the competitiveness among students are greatly increased. The typical student cannot help but hope that his friends will do poorly so as to enhance his own grade.

Still another drawback lies in the position in which it places the teacher. If she assists one student to do better on a test, she is automatically relegating another pupil at least one slot back. In some cases, this may mean helping one student to pass at the expense of another's failure.

Our discussion of norm-referenced grading (grading on the curve) leads to only one conclusion: If this grading method is taken to mean that a set number of students must pass and a given number must fail, then this approach should never be used in classroom evaluation.

Criterion-Referenced Grading

Criterion-referenced grading is as old as teaching. A criterion-referenced approach to grading is the comparison of a student's performance to prearranged standards. Letter grades in this system are given on the basis of an absolute standard of achievement rather than a relative (norm-referenced) one.

The teacher says, "I have my standards and the children must meet them if they want to pass the test. I don't care if everyone passes or everyone fails. They must meet my standards." This approach is not confined to any one discipline, but the number who actually enforce such standards is probably not very large. It is difficult to have absolute standards when dealing with children, because children, like any other group, differ. Not many teachers would give all F's or all A's; nor would principals or parents accept them.

A traditional approach in assigning test grades is arbitrarily to decide that all students who answer 92 per cent of the questions correctly receive an A; those who answer 85 per cent correctly receive a B; 75 per cent correctly receive a C; and so forth. Usually this involves not only arbitrary percentage criteria but also undefined instructional objectives.

Gronlund (1976) suggests that criterion-referenced grading is most helpful when a mastery learning approach is utilized. This is because "mastery learning places special emphasis on delimiting the domain of learning tasks to be achieved, defining the instructional objectives in behavioral terms, specifying the standards of performance to be obtained, and measuring the intended outcome with criterion-referenced instruments" (p. 529). Using these procedures, Gronlund (1976) defines letter grades in a criterion-referenced system as follows:

A = *Outstanding. Pupil has mastered all of the major and minor instructional objectives of the course.*
B = *Very Good. Pupil has mastered all of the major instructional objectives of the course and most of the minor objectives.*
C = *Satisfactory. Pupil has mastered all of the major instructional objectives but just a few of the minor objectives.*
D = *Very Weak. Pupil has mastered just a few of the major and minor instructional objectives of the course. He barely has the minimum essentials needed for the next highest level of instruction. Some remedial work would be desirable.*
F = *Unsatisfactory. Pupil has not mastered any of the major instructional objectives of the course. He lacks the minimum essentials needed for the next highest level of instruction. Considerable remedial work is needed. (p. 529)*

The criterion-referenced marking system has advantages and disadvantages. Let us first look at its advantages. It makes the school faculty focus its educational sights on both instructional process and outcomes, not only on outcomes. It helps modify student academic behavior so that it reflects more knowledge and proficiency. It enables the schools to demonstrate the educational growth of students that has occurred both for the parents and for the community at large. It is to be hoped that, through criterion-referencing, student attitudes will change from competition for grades to internal growth in the acquisition of academic proficiencies (Millman, 1972). On the negative side of the ledger, one must be careful not to lose sight of factors such as attitudes simply because they cannot be easily measured.

Another problem associated with criterion-referenced grading is the choice of proficiency standards. The problem of criteria in general was discussed in Chapter 12. Millman (1972) aptly identifies the problem in stating, "the choice of a proficiency standard is, to a large extent, arbitrary. Whether a student's performance is good enough to permit him to commence instruction in new skills is, in the final analysis, a matter of judgment" (p. 360). The skill, knowledge, sensitivity, and humanity of the teacher must go into this judgment. In many cases the quality of the classroom depends on the quality of these judgments.

The Answer?

There is no easy solution to the assignment of grades on an examination. The fairest approach seems to be an intelligent combination of some of the approaches already mentioned. Absolute standards should be tempered by the performance of the class as a whole. A given amount of material must be learned, and within this frame of reference grades will be decided on the relative merits of the entire class performance. This may sound like curving, and it is in the sense of comparing students to one another. It is not in the sense of predetermining how many people must receive certain grades.

In determining grades for a specific test, one must keep in mind the purposes of the test in relationship to the instructional objectives of the unit. These goals will weigh heavily in the consideration of grade categories. For example, you are teaching arithmetic in fourth grade. One of your basic objectives is to teach children the multiplication tables. A passing grade in fourth-grade arithmetic means partly that a child has learned how to multiply. In this situation an absolute standard in grading is necessary. You cannot certify that a child has learned how to multiply on the basis of his class ranking in a given test or on an arbitrary percentage of the questions answered correctly. Grading must be in line with your educational objectives.

In another situation where there is more latitude in objectives, the teacher may want to allow the B, C, and D grades to be distributed according to the performances of the students. There will, of course, not be a predetermined number of grades. The A and F grades may entail the classical percentages approach, allowing these percentages to be relevant to the specific educational objectives. In an objective examination the minimum level for a passing grade should probably be kept between 40 and 45 per cent, because even poor students will be able to guess some of the answers.

Thus norm-referenced grading and criterion-referenced grading are not dissonant enemies but are part of the same educational team. Both are needed and important in a good educational system.

Individual test grades should be a device to convey relative performance. Of course, the student's test scores throughout the semester or year should be averaged. The final results may be quite different from an assigned grade on one test.

In awarding test grades, what is important is the relationship of these symbols to overall educational concerns and objectives. Combining these with the most appropriate mechanical means for assignment of grades will produce the most equitable evaluation.

Assigning Report Card Grades

The teacher has prepared the educational unit, taught the lessons, and measured the outcomes. Now final grades must be assigned. What factors should be considered? Should classwork as well as tests be counted? How should different sources of evaluation be weighed?

Keeping in mind the educational goals, the teacher must decide what evidence will indicate the accomplishment of these goals. A decision must be made concerning the relative weight to be placed on different types of data, including examinations, quizzes, papers and reports, and classroom participation.

Examinations and Quizzes

All the student's *raw scores*, not his test grades, on the objective tests and quizzes he has taken are totaled. For example, Bill Ross, a student, has obtained scores of 40 and 55 on the two objective tests. Each test had a total of 60 items. The maximum possible score that Bill could receive would be 120. His overall objective test score is 95. The same process is used for grades obtained on quizzes. Each student's scores are tallied in the same manner. These cumulative scores are graded according to the educational goals by using the techniques discussed in the previous section.

Papers and Reports

Reliability in evaluating papers and reports is quite low. However, this work represents an important aspect of the learning process and needs to be considered in the total evaluation. If papers and reports are to receive equal weight with quizzes and/or examinations, a composite grade of all papers may be simply obtained by assigning numbers to the various letter grades given for each paper or report. For example, consider the following table.

Bill Ross's Papers and Reports

	Grades	Composite Grade
Papers	A, B, B	3.3 (B)
Reports	B, C, D	2.0 (C)
(A = 4, B = 3, C = 2, D = 1, F = 0)		

Process:

Papers	Reports
$4 + 3 + 3 = 10$	$3 + 2 + 1 = 6$

$$\begin{array}{r} 3.3 \\ 3 \overline{)10} \\ 9 \\ \hline 10 \end{array} \qquad \begin{array}{r} 2 \\ 3 \overline{)6} \\ 6 \\ \hline 0 \end{array}$$

Classroom Participation

Classroom work is a very important area of evaluation but one of the most difficult to quantify. Questions that need to be answered in this area are, "How well does the student work with others?" "What is his role in class discussions?" "How deep and pertinent are his contributions to these discussions?" "How well does he perform in class projects?" "How well does he perform in class recitations and blackboard work?"

The answers to these questions are not easy and are subject to many distortions. They are nevertheless important. Probably it is best *not* to include them in an overall grade evaluation. They should be noted, however, in the child's cumulative record, and if there is space on the report card for comments, a brief written description and analysis of these traits should be given.

Combining Data from Different Sources

See Chapter 13 for a discussion of anecdotal records and rating scales suitable for evaluating classroom participation. Now we are at the juncture where we must translate our calculations into the form of a letter grade. One of the most feasible methods is to reduce all the scores to a common denominator or numerical scale. If, for example, all our data are to receive equal value in determining the final grade, we can use the method described in the section on papers and reports. Let us look at Bill Ross's record as an example of this method:

Average Scaled Scores

Quizzes	Objective Tests	Papers	Reports	Final Average	Grade
2.4	3.0	3.3	2.0	2.6	B —

In the preceding example the quizzes and objective test grades were assigned the same values as papers and reports, that is, A = 4, B = 3, C = 2, and so forth. These sources of evaluation were given equal weight to simplify the example. If we were to decide to weight different areas differently, the same basic process could be followed but more value would be given to the areas of most importance. For example, if the quizzes and objective tests were to be counted as worth two times as much as the other factors, their value would become 4.8 and 6.0, respectively. (We would then, of course, divide the total by 6 rather than by 4.)

Report Cards

The great majority of report cards contain both grades and a list of check items, especially in the elementary grades. The report card, no matter what its format, should keep subject-matter achievement separate from effort, neatness, citizenship, behavior, and so forth. The report card is an important tool of communication, deserving of the best efforts to provide understandable answers to parental questions such as, "How does my child compare to the other children in reading?" "Does he make friends easily?" "What about his behavior in the classroom?"

There is no one report card that can serve as a model. The local school system must devise the type that best serves its needs. The important thing to remember is that it serves as a line of communication between the teacher and parents. The meaning of the grades and symbols used should be clear.

Evaluation and Reality

All teachers are not going to follow the rules for proper measurement, and, as we have stated before, even if they do we cannot expect perfect tests or grades. What can the teacher do in light of the tenuousness of testing and grading? The answer is easy. The teacher should avoid taking tests or grades too seriously.

On the whole, most teachers do a pretty good job of evaluation. The dramatic exceptions cloud the picture. Think back to your own student days in elementary and high school. How many times did you think you were unfairly graded? How about evaluation in college? Probably your college grades do not seem as valid as your elementary and high school evaluations. If that is true maybe it is because the college professor does not have as many data upon which to base his evaluation—daily recitations, class projects, observations, and so forth.

The important thing to remember in your evaluation is to attempt to minimize personal bias or prejudice in awarding grades. At the same time, one must face reality and admit to students and parents that grades are only an attempt to evaluate performance. Do not be afraid to admit that there is not always a great deal of difference between a C and a B. However, you will usually be confident of the validity of the extremes. That is, an A is awarded on very evident criteria, as is an F so awarded, especially when it means a student will be held back a semester or year in his school life. Try to emphasize learning and deemphasize the importance of grades. Follow your grade evaluations with either oral or written descriptions of student progress, especially with children who are experiencing learning difficulties.

SEVEN | *A*
School
Testing
and
Evaluation
Program

chapter 18

Planning and Using a Testing Program

This chapter deals with the actual mechanics of planning and using standardized tests in a comprehensive school testing program. Our discussion is focused primarily on paper-and-pencil group testing. These tests are generally administered to all pupils in a given grade at the same time. Projective techniques, apparatus-type tests, and other clinical instruments will not be discussed because they are not part of a general group testing program.

The intent, then, of this chapter is to present an outline and discussion of what constitutes a sound testing program in terms of specific and concrete suggestions. These suggestions should not be taken as the final word in testing programs. Test selection and the objectives of a testing program must meet individual needs and be developed in conjunction with the educational goals of a particular school within a particular geographical setting for particular groups of students.

There are, however, general guidelines and essential steps to be taken in the development and implementation of a testing program, as follows:

1. Determine the objectives of the testing program.
2. Select tests that meet these objectives.
3. Arrange a time schedule for administering the tests.
4. Arrange for an in-service test orientation for teachers.
5. Arrange for a pretest orientation for students.
6. Administer the tests.
7. Score the tests.
8. Record the test results.
9. *Use* the test results.

Determining the Objectives

Tests are useful only if they supply the school, the teacher, the student, and the parent with meaningful information. To administer tests because it is fashionable to do so or because the government provides funds for testing is an exercise in futility.

Although it may seem obvious to the reader that tests should be given for specified purposes and then so used, this is not always the case. Many years ago, for example, this writer had occasion to be in a school system that applied for governmental funds for testing. The request was granted and the school staff administered a great many different tests without ever thinking of what they wanted to measure. They had received money and they were going to spend it all. The natural consequences of this "nonthink" action were a great deal of wasted time and energy. After the tests were administered and scored, no one knew what to do with them. They were finally stacked in neat piles and found their last resting place in the school basement. The government had spent money, the teachers had spent time, the students had spent energy, and the test publishers and authors were a little richer. These were the only results of testing in this school.

A Testing Committee

The first step in planning the objectives of a standardized testing program is to involve appropriate personnel. Almost all the school's staff and administration have a vital interest and responsibility in planning the testing program. Personnel at different levels will be able to utilize some or all of the test results.

A standing testing committee is one method of involving staff participation in the development of a schoolwide testing program. This committee should be composed of school personnel who have interest and needs that may be served by testing, and should represent the special interests of various groups within the school. If there is a director of testing or research, he or she should be appointed to give technical assistance. The guidance counselor and/or school psychologist can also serve in an advisory capacity. In addition, representatives from the school administration and instructional staff will need to participate in the committee to voice their special needs and interests. In a large system the directors of instruction and curriculum could serve as representatives. What is important is that the committee represent the various interests within the school system.

The committee's work should not stop when a testing program has been developed. The committee needs to direct its energy toward a continual evaluation of the testing program, making changes, modifications, and additions as the need arises.

The involvement of teachers and other school personnel in the planning and directing of a testing program lessens the likelihood of misuse of tests. Misuse involves not only the filing away of unused test data but also incorrect interpretation of those data. Involving teachers in the planning of a testing program may also help keep them from feeling that outside materials and unnecessary work are being imposed on them.

Practical Aspects

The purposes of a testing program in a given school system should relate directly to that system's own educational goals and needs. First, the needs of the students, the instructional program, and administrative concerns should be surveyed. Research data will evolve from this process. The school testing program should be geared to practical needs, not to what a textbook states or what a consultant thinks is in vogue. Consultants, textbooks, and testing experts have their place and can make valuable contributions. Their assistance, however, should come after the local school has decided on its own unique objectives and practical needs. Theoretical researches dealing with curriculum problems or administrative issues are worthy in themselves of the school's time and energy, but the practical problems of educating children must come first.

Structure

A practical approach must be developed within a rational and cohesive system that provides tools of assessment and defines the limits of the program. In planning a testing program, considerations for administration, scoring, and reporting results must be based on the availability not only of funds but also of personnel. Teachers often complain of delayed feedback of test results. Giving tests in the fall and not making the results available until spring is a good way to lose the support of the faculty. The importance of reporting test results to teachers as soon as possible cannot be over-emphasized. It is much better to have a small program that the school can handle than an elaborate one that causes discontent.

The structure of the program should be definitively geared to specific purposes. The program should state in clear and cogent terms its purposes and range of objectives. For example, the statement "to diagnose instructional problems" is very nice, but to what does it refer? A better statement might be, "to diagnose problems in seventh-grade arithmetic." Thus a specific purpose has been formulated, and further action, such as selection of tests in arithmetic achievement, may be directly formulated.

When to Begin Planning

The testing committee needs to plan for testing well in advance of the intended dates of administration because (1) committees should not be rushed in their important deliberations and (2) selecting, ordering, receiving, and inventorying tests are time-consuming. Lennon (1962), in addressing himself to this problem, states,

> A *testing program should be planned between six months and a year in advance of the time when it is actually to take place, depending somewhat on whether it is a spring or a fall program, on local budgeting practices, on the size of the system and consequent communications and training problems, and similar factors. When a major program is being contemplated, one that covers many subjects at many grade levels with a single battery, it will ordinarily be desirable to think in terms of establishing a program that will be maintained for several years. In giving thought to this type of program, it is well to have in mind such matters as the availability of alternate forms, and the possibility that revised editions of the test in question will be appearing over the period of the proposed program.* (p. 3)

Selecting Tests

Selecting the tests that meet the school's objectives and needs is a difficult task. There are many published standardized tests but only a small number of quality instruments that will be suitable for local needs. The testing committee needs to appraise the intended test not only in terms of suitability for local purposes but also in the technical sphere of validity, reliability, and standard error of measurement. These basic concepts are crucial factors in selecting tests. In addition, practical problems such as cost and time to administer and score the test must be considered. The committee should be aware of these criteria in their test selections. The committee member who is the director of testing or research should direct the technical evaluation. If there is no director of testing and research, then the school psychologist and/or guidance counselor should serve in this capacity. The committee will, of course, have available basic references such as test catalogues, *Mental Measurements Yearbook, Tests in Print, Psychological Abstracts*, and *Standards for Educational and Psychological Tests*, reviewed in Chapter 19. In the following two sections essential types of tests needed at different levels and the rationale for their use will be presented.

Suggestions for a School Testing Program

The recommendations that follow are based on a general core of test needs from kindergarten through twelfth grade. It must, however, be stated once again that the local school should develop its own testing program according to its own needs and objectives. On the other hand, the local school, no matter what its specific needs or problems, should consider certain essential areas in its measurement program. The suggestions that follow are directed to these essential elements.

Kindergarten Through Sixth Grade

The elementary school is primarily concerned with the development of basic skills and tools in the essential areas of reading, writing, and arithmetic. This may sound like an old-fashioned view, but basically the three R's are still the essential ingredients needed to build upon for future educational progress.

It should be noted again that our discussion is confined to paper-and-pencil tests. It is assumed that the teacher will use other techniques to measure such things as citizenship and social adjustment. Our concern here is the measurement of academic promise and achievement. It is also assumed that children have been given physical examinations, including eye and hearing tests.

READING READINESS TESTS (K–1)

The reading readiness test is usually the first test a child encounters in his school career. The reading readiness test has many shortcomings in terms of validity and reliability. Even more important, however, there is a great deal of confusion as to what constitutes readiness. Still, the first-grade teacher needs to know something about her pupils and their readiness to learn. The readiness test, with all its shortcomings, will provide a rough estimate upon which to begin a program of individualized reading instruction. Later, as the teacher becomes better acquainted with her students, she will make appropriate changes based on new data. In the meantime, however, the reading readiness test has served a useful function.

READING TESTS

Television notwithstanding, reading is still the most important learned skill in the education of an individual. The mastery of this skill enables the student to acquire other knowledge to build upon and expand his intellectual horizons. The absence of this basic skill spells academic trouble for the student. If reading is the single most important skill to be learned in the elementary school, it follows that the most important test to be given is the reading test. It should be placed at the top of the testing list of priorities.

Financial resources permitting, a reading test should be administered every year beginning in the second grade. If there are limited funds, the reading test may be administered at the beginning of the third grade to all students. Future testing would focus on students experiencing difficulties in classroom reading. It is best, however, to measure all children's reading growth each year in order to gear the instructional program to individual needs. The reason for testing reading in the beginning rather than at the end of the academic year is that children may go down or up in their reading levels over the summer. The teacher needs to know the level of student reading achievement at the beginning of the school year, not levels three to seven months old.

SCHOLASTIC APTITUDE TESTS

The scholastic aptitude test helps the teacher understand the range of possible student progress. It presents objective data to aid the teacher in understanding individual student achievement both in the classroom and on other standardized tests.

The scholastic aptitude test should not be administered earlier than the end of the second grade or beginning of the third grade. In the first grade, a reading readiness test is generally preferable to the scholastic aptitude test. The assignment of an IQ or "intelligence" score (even if we call it scholastic aptitude, not everyone has received the message) at the beginning of a child's school career may do a great deal of harm. Teachers are likely to be less rigid about a child's maturational level of readiness than they are about his mental ability. Although we delay our testing of scholastic aptitude until the end of the second or third grade, we must remember that even at this point reliability is not very satisfactory.

If a scholastic aptitude test is given at the end of the second grade, we want to administer another test at the end of the fourth or beginning of the fifth grade. If only one test of this type is to be given in elementary school, the fourth or fifth grade is preferable because of the greater reliability of scholastic aptitude tests at this level. If financial resources for testing are plentiful, scholastic aptitude can, of course, be more frequently measured, depending on the needs of the particular school. Additional testing will also serve to increase the reliability of results.

ACHIEVEMENT BATTERIES

A minimal program in grades 1 through 3 would involve measuring achievement in the basic skills. These include reading, arithmetic, language, and listening. If reading skills are adequately appraised by the achievement battery, the school could eliminate the separate reading test or use a different type of test such as an oral reading instrument. If monetary conditions allow, it would be best to begin these tests in the beginning of the second grade and continue testing in the fall of each year. If a school system can afford to administer the battery only once during the elementary program, the beginning of the fourth grade is best. This would enable the school to plan their instructional program for the next three years based on the academic achievement of the children. With these data, provisions can be made for accelerated or enriched programs as well as for remedial instruction for those children who reveal educational retardation.

At the upper grades of elementary school the achievement battery should include tests in content areas such as social studies and science. These more specialized areas should not be included until fifth or sixth grade.

SPECIALIZED TESTS

The four types of tests presented so far form the core of a good testing program. Individual needs of schools and students, however, may necessitate supplementary instruments. For example, the school in a disadvantaged setting may want to include a culture-fair test. If a community has a school psychologist and can afford individual intelligence testing, kindergarten would be an appropriate place for administration. Because the individual intelligence test is much more reliable than the group test, it provides an excellent base for programming individual instruction, if combined with a reading readiness test. However, the vast majority of school systems cannot afford this luxury.

Personality inventories and projective techniques are administered only upon referral from the teacher to the school psychologist. They should never be administered routinely.

Seventh Through Twelfth Grade

In the junior and senior high school the scope of testing enlarges, along with the increase in the number of educational choices and decisions that must be made. Among the most important issues facing the student at this level are what courses to take and when, educational and vocational goals, and whether to go to college or learn a trade. These issues do not replace our previous concern with the basic skills and proficiency in content areas. The specific subject matter broadens as the educational ladder is climbed, but underneath the diversity and complexity of new courses the essentials of reading, writing, and arithmetic remain basic to educational growth and academic sophistication.

Scholastic Aptitude Tests

The scholastic aptitude test is of paramount importance at this level of education, because decisions concerning courses of study and plans for college must be made. The measurement of school abilities of students by the scholastic aptitude test at this level is much more accurate than at lower levels. We can, therefore, consider a single measure of scholastic aptitude at this level more likely to represent the true ability of the student than a single measure obtained at the elementary level.

If only one scholastic aptitude test can be administered during the period between seventh and twelfth grades, the most appropriate time is the eighth or ninth grade. If monetary resources are adequate, a scholastic aptitude test should be administered at the beginning of the seventh grade, at the end of the eighth grade, and again at the beginning of the tenth grade. Those students who are going on to college will probably take the PSAT in the eleventh grade and/or the SAT or ACT in the twelfth grade.

Special Aptitude Tests

Special aptitude tests can provide important information for students who are not planning to go on to college as well as for those who are planning to major in special areas in college. As you know from our previous discussion of special aptitude tests, there are two types: (1) separate tests that measure specific aptitudes and (2) those that combine measures of different aptitudes into a single test battery, such as the Differential Aptitude Test battery (DAT).

If a battery such as the DAT is given, the school may also use it as a scholastic aptitude test. In the ideal situation, however, it would be best to use the scholastic aptitude score from a battery such as the DAT only as a check on other measures.

Special aptitude tests have the most relevance for the student and school beginning with the ninth grade. A test battery such as the DAT is highly recommended. The battery should generally be administered during the time of year in which students will not be taking other tests and early enough in the year that results will be meaningful. Generally, the middle or latter part of the first month of school is a good time. The ninth and eleventh grades seem to be the most propitious levels for administering special aptitude tests, because there is then enough time for the student and school to make decisions on course and vocational plans. The same tests should be given in the eleventh grade as were given in the ninth, using a different form in order to check estimates of aptitude and note changes in performances.

Achievement Tests

Although the teacher's classroom tests will be the final word in estimating grades and school achievement, the standardized achievement test can be of assistance in planning course selection and vocational goals. When achievement tests in specific content areas such as social studies, English, science, and mathematics are used to facilitate educational decisions, they should be administered in the eighth and tenth grades.

If these tests are to be used for administrative purposes rather than guidance, the ninth and eleventh or twelfth grades are most appropriate. From data gathered at these times, the administration has a record of growth and achievement of the student body as a whole. It is of no help, however, for individual guidance to present students with these tests when it is too late to make many changes in their educational plans.

Reading Tests

Reading is as important at the secondary level as it is in the elementary school. The reading test may be used to advise students in course planning. More important, it can help spot children who need special help. Remedial action can then be instituted. The reading test should be given as early as possible in the seventh and tenth grades. This will help ensure immediate attention for those children who need improved reading skills. Seventh and tenth grades were chosen because they are the beginning grades of junior and senior high school. In another system appropriate changes would need to be made.

INTEREST INVENTORIES

Interest inventories provide important supplementary data to be used with aptitude and achievement test results. This wedding of data can assist the student in his vocational planning. A good time to administer the interest inventory is in the ninth grade so that interest patterns may be considered in planning courses of study.

PERSONALITY INVENTORIES

The administration of personality inventories to all students is not recommended, except for research purposes. Personality inventories, along with clinical techniques such as projective devices, should be administered only by a qualified clinical or school psychologist upon referral and with the full knowledge and written permission of both of the student's parents.

Scheduling of Tests

The test committee has been hard at work establishing objectives and selecting tests and appropriate grades for their administration. Now some of the school administrators take charge and help steer the committee into a discussion and plan of *when* and *how* to schedule the administration of the tests. They examine the reasons that most schools usually schedule testing for the fall or spring.

There are a number of reasons for testing in the fall as compared to the spring. The advantages of fall testing are as follows:

1. The test information is current at the beginning of the school year. During the summer some students gain skills and others lose some proficiencies.
2. It presents a complete test record for each student, whereas spring testing requires some make-up testing for new students.
3. Fall testing emphasizes analysis of student progress and problems rather than an assessment of faculty instruction.
4. Recent testing can serve as a basis of grouping.
5. Scores on tests may facilitate using supplementary criterion-referenced tests for specific educational diagnosis.

Spring testing does not have as many advantages as fall testing. It does, however, enable teachers and the guidance staff to base the programming of the following year on objective data. It is also a good time to administer achievement tests, as the school administration is usually attempting to gauge its standing and progress at a national level. The administration may also be interested in data for research concerning the effectiveness of teaching.

The choice of the time of year for testing is also dependent on local conditions and needs. If, for example, a school system is divided into an eight-year elementary and four-year high school plan, the receiving high school will want to test eighth-graders in the early spring in order to make intelligent decisions regarding number and types of courses to offer. In addition, counselors will want to talk to students and parents concerning course selections. This is especially true when homogeneous grouping is practiced.

Scheduling tests is a complex task when the whole school is involved. In an all-school testing program at the senior high school level, classes should be discontinued during the hours of testing. The mornings are generally considered the best time for testing because the students are fresh and probably at their best. The afternoon classes can be held as usual, or all the classes can be scheduled with shortened time periods.

Three hours should be the maximum time for testing at the high school level. At lower levels it is better to spread the testing over a period of several days so as not to tire young children excessively. Consult the test manual for methods of dividing the time properly. Be sure that all the school staff and the students know when testing is scheduled. It is a good idea to reproduce a schedule and hand it out to all teachers and students.

Tests should be administered during normal school hours. Do not give tests before a holiday or the day before a "big" game or dance. Tests should be scheduled at a time when there will be a minimum of distraction.

Test Orientation

General Orientation for Faculty

Each year before testing is to begin, teachers need a refresher course in standardized testing. This orientation should be presented no sooner than two weeks and no later than two days before the tests are to be administered.

The director of this in-service testing program should be a member of the test committee who is especially qualified in testing, such as the school counselor or psychologist. A teacher representative from the test committee should be at the side of the director, helping him to present the materials, and as a symbol that the testing program has been a joint teacher-administrator effort. (See Chapter 2 for a discussion of an in-service testing program.) The program should cover the following essentials:

1. Why the school is administering standardized tests.
2. What these tests mean and what they do not mean.
3. A brief description of each test to be used and its purposes.
4. How tests can help the classroom teacher.
5. Good test administration, including the importance of following directions exactly.
6. Questions from the faculty.

Selection and Orientation of
Test Administrators

Unless a school is exceptionally fortunate to have extra school psychologists and counselors available, the school must rely on teachers to administer the tests. This is not a real problem if teachers are properly prepared. A special in-service program for test administrators should be conducted after the general in-service program previously discussed.

The selection of test administrators in a large system can be made by the department chairman. He or she should be sent a brief communication stressing the importance of testing and the vital role of the test administrator. A list of selection criteria should accompany the communication. These essential criteria are as follows:

1. Reads fluently.
2. Has good pronunciation.
3. Follows directions scrupulously.
4. Thinks on his or her feet.
5. Communicates well with students.
6. Has some interest in doing the job.

The training or orientation of test administrators should encompass the following objectives:

1. Complete understanding and familiarity with the test and manual.
2. Understanding of and appreciation for standardized test procedures.

These objectives may be accomplished by having the test administrators take turns administering the tests to each other. If there are too many teachers to allow enough time for this approach, the director of the in-service program can administer two to four items of each test to the group. This will give them practice in what the test is all about. The director's method of reading the directions and speech pattern can serve as the model for test administration. A full question and answer period should follow.

In Chapter 5 we discussed proper test administration and scoring procedures. Several points are worth noting again.

1. Test administrators must follow the directions verbatim.
2. Questions should be answered within the context of the test directions.
3. Two timepieces should be used—the wall clock and a wrist watch or, in tests with short time limits, a stop watch.
4. Test administrators should circulate around the room after testing has begun to see whether there are any problems.
5. Special care should be taken in scoring—always spot-check scores.

Pretest Orientation for Students

Students should be called together in an assembly-like program. The reasons for testing and what the results may mean for the students should be candidly presented. This general overview of testing may be conducted by one of the specialists.

A follow-up of the assembly on testing should be given in home rooms by representatives from the office of testing or the school psychologist or counselor. This should be an informal question-and-answer session. The importance of testing as an aid to each student should be emphasized.

In the lower grades, teachers may want to use special tests that help a child learn to respond correctly to directions and formats of standardized tests. Still another approach may be movies that explain how to take a standardized test. Educational Testing Service sells and rents such a film.

Recording Test Scores

There should be a test record sheet in a counselor's notebook or a notation of the test and results in the cumulative record of the student. Another copy should be filed in the central administration office for use in case the counselor or teacher misplaces his records. The records in the central administration office should not be open for casual inspection.

In the actual recording of test data extreme care must be taken to achieve accuracy. Not only must the scores be accurate, but they also must convey a meaningful picture to the casual professional glance. A good test record form should include the following data:

1. Full name of the test, including the specific form used.
2. Date administered, including the year, month, and day of testing.
3. Grade of student when test was taken.
4. Norm group used.
5. All scores that are useful and meaningful for analysis.

Reporting Test Results to Students and Parents

Teachers and counselors are faced with the problem of how best to convey test results to students and parents. If they reveal too much, they may psychologically damage the student. If they do not reveal anything, the student and his parents do not benefit from the tests. Besides, many parents will not stand for being excluded from the "test score club." Parents have a right to know about their child's abilities and achievements, and the student has a right to know meaningful information about himself. Durost (1961b), in discussing the problems of telling parents about test results, presents four philosophical premises that should form the basis of school policy:

1. *Parents are entitled to information related to their children's progress in school, especially as it relates to future educational or vocational plans.*
2. *Test information given to parents must be expressed in understandable terms.*
3. *Test results are best revealed in terms of a simple scale broadly based. (Some common means of interpretation, such as intelligence quotients and grade equivalents, appear to be more precise than they really are.)*
4. *The information should have uniform meaning to parent and educator and demonstrated relevance (validity) for the purpose in mind such as grouping, promotion, and guidance. (p. 1)*

Specific IQ scores should be given to parents only when the parents demand their presentation based on legal rights. If this happens, the teacher or counselor should sit down with the parents and explain the "true" meaning of IQ. Included in this should be a brief history of IQ, what it means and doesn't mean, a short but accurate briefing concerning the normal curve, an exploration of standard error of measurement (see Chapter 4), and a summation of the preceding sprinkled with yellow lights of caution such as this "is only one test" (see Chapters 3, 5, 6, and 8). Grade equivalents or placement scores are not a satisfactory means of reporting, because misunderstanding often results from their use (see Chapter 3). Percentiles and stanines are most appropriate for conveying test results to students and parents.

Ricks (1975) poses the question, "Are any numbers necessary?" Although he would not impose a ban on using numbers in reporting test data, he notes that some very good counselors do not present any numerical data at all. Such verbal techniques as, "You score like people who . . ." or, "Your son (or daughter) scores like students who . . ." are an excellent way to communicate information about test scores.

This mode of test interpretation in an actual situation might take the following form:

Counselor (or teacher): Mary, you score like people who have a difficult time in college. On the other hand, your scores reveal a great deal of promise in commercial areas such as filing and typing. You may want to consider a secretarial school after high school graduation.

Counselor (or teacher): Your son Wally scores like students who find the ivy league schools difficult but seem to manage well in smaller private four-year colleges.

Counselor (or teacher): You score like students who do better in algebra if they take general mathematics in the ninth grade and algebra later.

In conveying test data to students and parents, the teacher or counselor should be sure to emphasize that test scores are tentative and that their real meaning lies in using them with other information such as school grades, classroom performance, and teacher evaluation. This does not mean tests should be scoffed at or relegated to an insignificant part in the educational enterprise. It does mean that the accuracy of the scores and what they *probably* signify for the individual must be candidly presented. At the same time, cases that do not bear out test scores may be cited, as, for example, the following case.

Jerry M. was born in Germany during the early 1930s. His father was a professor of history in a well-known German university. One day Jerry's father took him for a walk down the main street. In front of Jerry, who was five years old, were three rather muscular men in brown shirts with swastika arm bands. Jerry, being no different from most young boys, was awed by their uniforms. He ran up to one of the soldiers and greeted him with a salute. The soldier kicked Jerry and sent him sprawling to the gutter. Jerry's father was then beaten into unconsciousness. Jerry and his father were Jews.

Not long after this incident, Jerry and his family emigrated to the United States, where his father was employed as a professor in a well-known university. Jerry was enrolled in the first grade. After a few months, Jerry's teacher found that he was making little progress in reading and learning English. The father was sent for and recommendations were made for individual intelligence testing. Jerry's teacher felt that he was a retarded child. The psychologist's report was in agreement with the teacher. Jerry had a reported IQ of 65. There was no doubt that Jerry should be in a special education class for educable mentally handicapped children. (The astute reader may question the reliability of the tests in that Jerry was still new to the English language. This was no problem, because the psychologist giving the test was also a German immigrant and was able to administer the test in German.)

The father was quite upset about the findings, as most parents would be, and would not accept them. He chose to send Jerry for psychiatric help. The psychiatrist's report showed that Jerry was emotionally disturbed and needed intensive psychotherapy. After five years of psychotherapy, Jerry's IQ score had risen from 65 to 90. Although this was remarkable, Jerry was still far from being a scholar. At the end of the ninth grade, Jerry was only a year behind his class in most of his subjects, and his IQ score had risen to 110.

The last the writer heard of him, Jerry was studying for his Ph.D. in chemistry. Certainly, this is an extreme case and by no means the usual run of affairs. Also, let me point out that psychotherapy is not a cure for mental retardation. Jerry was never mentally retarded; however, the trauma of his life in Germany and other factors prevented him from using all of his intellectual capacity.

This case is obviously a highly unusual situation. For most children tests are fairly accurate in estimating achievement and potential to achieve. However, because we deal with people rather than numbers, the exceptions must always be kept in mind. The reader who is interested in pursuing the effects of emotional problems on intelligence and the expression of mental ability in autistic children can read the extensive writings of Dr. Bruno Bettelheim. In *The Empty Fortress* (Bettelheim, 1967), for example, the problem of determining the intelligence of autistic children is explored.

The teacher and counselor must bridge the gap that separates them from students and parents in order to realize the full effectiveness of tests. This can be done only if a concentrated effort is made to present information in relevant and understandable terms.

Sources of Test Information

Where should you, as a teacher, counselor, or psychologist, go to find information about tests? A student once answered matter-of-factly, "To the librarian; she could tell me where to go." Another student suggested the *Encyclopaedia Britannica*. This was a little better since at least the person would be looking for herself. The *Encyclopaedia* does have extensive coverage of testing, from aptitude tests to personality instruments. It is, however, not meant for professionals but as a source to help lay people.

This chapter is written for the professional test user. This includes by definition all those who utilize psychological and educational testing. Certainly teachers and other school personnel need to know about tests—where to find test information, where to find critiques of tests, where to find testing books for parents, and so on. We will attempt to provide this and other information. In addition, test resource materials will be listed.

Special Resources

We shall discuss three of the most widely used resources in testing, *Standards for Educational and Psychological Tests*, *The Mental Measurements Yearbook*, and *Tests in Print*. These references are the basis for definitive test information in the field of measurement.

Standards for Educational and Psychological Tests

Standards is a forty-page booklet published by the American Psychological Association et al. (1974) and has been frequently mentioned in this book. There is little need to elaborate on its essential characteristics at this point. It is important, however, to state that *Standards* represents the collective opinions of selected psychologists and educators and as such presents the "rules of the testing road" as seen by most test experts today. Although there are no legal requirements to make one adhere to these "rules," one would hope that teachers and other school personnel would take *Standards* quite seriously. Every school should have a copy in its testing library and should make use of it when evaluating a test.

The Mental Measurements Yearbook

The Mental Measurements Yearbook, volumes 1 to 7, edited by Oscar K. Buros (1938, 1941, 1949, 1953, 1959, 1965, 1972), is the most valuable and important single source of information about tests. The *Yearbooks* contain detailed information and critical reviews on thousands of tests. An attempt is made to list, discuss, and criticize every published standardized test. *The Seventh Mental Measurements Yearbook* (1972) is a two-volume edition that lists 1,157 tests.

The critical reviews are written by experts in the general field of measurement and in the specific area of his or her special competency. Thus a measurement specialist in school ability and achievement testing would review tests in that particular area only. The number of reviews for each test is based on the interest which that area of testing generates and the extensiveness of the test's utilization. Some tests of wide general interest and use, therefore, may be reviewed by two or more experts. The reviewers provide frank, detailed, and critical information about each test. The following is an example of the type of review contained in the *Yearbooks*; it is excerpted from a review by Dr. Robert H. Dolliver, one of many reviewers of the Kuder Occupational Interest Survey. Dolliver (1972) states,

> There are two major difficulties in accurately viewing this test. First, it is necessary to understand exactly which of the several Kuder tests and revisions we are talking about. Second, it is important to overcome the tendency to view the Strong Vocational Interest Blank *as an ultimate model of a vocational interest test. This tendency leads to a bias against the Kuder and interferes with an accurate appraisal of it.*
>
> The Kuder Occupational Interest Survey (Form DD) is the elaboration of the Kuder Preference Record—Occupational (Form D). The items are in the same triad format as in Form D; the subject picks his most and his least preferred activity from the three alternatives. Kuder comments that this format keeps potential response bias from operating. Each item can have any of six possible combinations of response. Thus, the 100 test triads become 600 potential patterns of item response.
>
> The major change noticeable to the test user is the addition of scales for college majors (like similar scales which make up the College Interest Inventory). The number of occupational scales has been increased since Form D. New scales have been normed on women for 37 occupations and for 19 college majors. In addition, women receive scores on 20 occupational scales and 8 college major scales which were normed on men. The Verification scale remains the same as

on Form D. Experimental scales (printed on only one of the test report forms) reflect a combination of the factors of sex, age, and the attempt to make a best impression. The scores for each scale are reported as correlation coefficients. And the highest 10 occupational and the 10 top college major correlations are rank ordered at the bottom of the test report. The rank ordering, a very helpful practice, appears to have been inaugurated since the manual was printed.

Kuder DD makes a direct comparison between the scores of the individual test taker and the modal responses of those in each occupation and in each college major. Employing a procedure suggested by Clemans, Kuder reports lambda correlation coefficients (a statistic similar in concept to the biserial correlation). Kuder did comparative studies with his test items and found that lambda scores greatly improved concurrent prediction over the differentiation method.

The rank order of scores, rather than their absolute level, is stressed. But test reports with no scores higher than .31 "should be regarded with caution," and "if there are no scores over .39 and only a few scores in the .32 through .39 range, any interpretation must be highly tentative." The manual reports that, in 30 of the criterion groups which were studied, 80 percent of the subjects obtained scores of .45 or over on their own occupational scale and many scored above .60. (Theoretically, of course, it is possible to score as high as 1.00.) Scores which fall within .06 of the highest score are recommended for primary consideration. It appears that frequently six or eight scale scores would be within that range. Test users may be confused by the seeming frequently limited overall range of the correlations. In the two test reports shown in the test manual, the ranges for the 77 male and the 57 female occupations were .21 to .51 and .24 to .48, respectively. And for the 29 male and 27 female college majors the ranges shown were .29 to .53 and .27 to .64, respectively. The sample test in the interpretive leaflet shows a similarly restricted range.

The Kuder DD is a great improvement over the Kuder D. Present evidence supports Kuder's contention that the lambda correlation scoring will be shown to be highly accurate. But this has not yet been sufficiently demonstrated. (pp. 1427–29)

In addition to test reviews, the *Yearbooks* provide other important and practical items of information such as the test author; test publisher; norms, for example, appropriate grade and/or age levels; prices of tests; publication and revision dates; administration time; and available forms. In addition, references are listed.

Every school or other institution using tests should have at least the last three editions of the *Yearbooks*. The first source that school testing people and testing specialists consult for testing information is the latest edition of the *Yearbooks*. A new test is usually reviewed in the first *Yearbook* that was published after the test was distributed for popular use. Some tests are continually reviewed in subsequent *Yearbooks*; others are not. Thus, for an exhaustive and detailed account, one should have all the *Yearbooks*; for most school purposes, however, the last three *Yearbooks* should suffice.

Tests in Print

An exhaustive and comprehensive listing of all types of tests that are available is *Tests in Print II* (Buros, 1974a). Alongside the *Yearbooks*, this book should be in every school and agency dealing with people and testing. It supplements the *Yearbook* and is an independent guide and index to 70,000 documents and references. The list includes 2,467 tests, 16,574 references on specific tests, 493 test publishers with listings of their tests, indexes that include in-print and out-of-print tests, and many other important features. This book serves primarily as a reference guide to enable you to find out where to obtain critical and detailed data on each listed test. In addition to references for further investigation, it presents data on each test—for example, author, publisher, norms, forms, and any special features.

Mental Measurements Yearbook Monographs

Monographs that group the references and reviews for specific types of tests in the *Yearbooks* are also available. These include tests found in the *Yearbooks* and *Tests in Print*. For example, *Personality Tests and Reviews* (Buros, 1974b) is a two-volume bibliography of nonprojective and projective devices as of 1974. It has reprintings of *Yearbook* reviews, references, and other data. Volume I covers the first six *Yearbooks*, Volume II includes the seventh *Yearbook* and *Tests in Print*. The following are the other monographs:

English Tests and Reviews
Foreign Language Tests and Reviews
Intelligence Tests and Reviews
Mathematics Tests and Reviews
Reading Tests and Reviews
Science Tests and Reviews
Social Studies Tests and Reviews
Vocational Tests and Reviews

Texts and Reference Books

No single textbook can adequately cover in detail all the special areas of testing. Certain texts are written for special areas of testing or for a special audience. The following books have been selected as sources for more detailed investigations and study. It should be noted that the list is not exhaustive.

Intelligence Tests

Harris, D. B. *Children's drawings as measures of intellectual maturity: A revision and extension of the Goodenough Draw-a-Man Test.* New York: Harcourt Brace Jovanovich, 1963. Description of method for measuring intelligence by the use of drawings. An extensive survey of the literature of children's drawings, and a complete test manual including the Draw-a-Woman Scale.

Mataranzzo, J. D. *Wechsler's measurement and appraisal of adult intelligence.*

(5th ed.) Baltimore: Williams and Wilkins, 1972. An updating, revision, and enlargement of Dr. David Wechsler's four previous editions. This new edition not only is directed to and about the Wechsler tests of intelligence but also surveys areas such as nature versus nurture; meaning of intelligence; classification; concepts of mental retardation, average, and superior intelligence; brain-behavior relationships; history of intelligence testing; diagnostic and clinical applications of the Wechsler Scales. It also has excellent references.

Terman, L. M., & Merrill, M. A. *Stanford-Binet Intelligence Scale: 1972 norms edition*. Boston: Houghton Mifflin, 1973. Essentially the manual for the Binet but gives the reader some knowledge of thorough test construction and a detailed idea of what IQ is.

School Tests

Ilg, F. L., & Ames, L. B. *School readiness: Behavior tests used at the Gesell Institute*. New York: Harper & Row, 1965. Combined text and manual presents Gesell Institute's view that children should be enrolled in school on the basis of development, not on chronological age or IQ. Description of tests used and how to administer and use results. One section of book is devoted to teachers, administrators, and parents.

Johnson, O. G., & Bommarito, J. W. *Tests and measurements in child development: A handbook*. San Francisco: Jossey-Bass, 1971. This handbook includes only tests not mentioned in the *Yearbook*. It lists information on assessment devices for children from birth to twelve years, as well as devices for measuring dimensions of parental behavior.

Walker, D. K. *Socioemotional measures for preschool and kindergarten children*. San Francisco: Jossey-Bass, 1973. This is a very specialized list that includes tests of social and emotional development for three- to six-year-old children.

Specialized Psychological Testing

Dahlstrom, W. G., Welsh, G. S., & Dahlstrom, L. E. *An MMPI handbook*. Vol. I, *Clinical interpretation*. Minneapolis: University of Minnesota Press, 1972.

Dahlstrom, W. G., Welsh, G. S., & Dahlstrom, L. E. *An MMPI handbook*. Vol. II, *Research developments and applications*. Minneapolis: University of Minnesota Press, 1975. The authors of these volumes present an excellent resource for clinical interpretation and technical information on the various uses of the Minnesota Multiphasic Personality Inventory (MMPI). These volumes are written by the foremost authorities on the MMPI in the world. Anyone interested in any aspect of the MMPI from interpretation to the thousands of research studies should consult these volumes.

Guidance Counseling

Goldman, L. *Using tests in counseling*. (2nd ed.) Pacific Palisades, Calif.: Goodyear, 1971. A guide to interpretation, test selection, and research findings in measurement. Intended to help school counselors in the uses of tests in counseling.

Mortensen, D. G., & Schmuller, A. M. *Guidance in today's schools.* (3rd ed.) New York: John Wiley and Sons, 1976. An excellent source for integrating measurement into the guidance functions. See especially Chapters 7 and 8.

Vocational Testing

Super, D. E., & Crites J. O. *Appraising vocational fitness.* New York: Harper & Row, 1962. A compilation and evaluation of useful tests for the identification of vocational aptitudes and skills. The book discusses each test in terms of its applicability, contents, administration and scoring, norms, and so forth. Individual case histories and their eventual disposition are also given.

Miscellaneous

Albright L. E., Glennon, J. R., & Smith W. J. *The use of psychological tests in industry.* Cleveland: Howard Allen, Inc., Publishers, 1963. Primarily devoted to selection problems, especially useful as a reference for personnel officers.

Allen R. M., & Jefferson, T. W. *Psychological evaluation of the cerebral palsied person: Intellectual, personality, and vocational applications.* Springfield, Ill.: Charles C Thomas, Publisher, 1962. Significant tests for use with cerebral-palsied persons are outlined and discussed.

Clark, H. H. *Application of measurement to health and physical education.* (4th ed.) Englewood Cliffs, N.J.: Prentice-Hall, 1967. Detailed description of various performance tests in physical education; paper-and-pencil tests for sports knowledge and health education. A measurement classic in the field of physical education.

Evaluation of pupil progress in business education. American Business Education Yearbook, Vol. 17, 1960. New York: New York University Campus Stores, 1960. Especially useful for testing students in business education.

Ismail, A. H., & Gruber, J. J. *Integrated development of motor aptitudes and intellectual performance.* Columbus, Ohio: Charles E. Merrill, 1967. An excellent source book for motor aptitude tests and their relationship to intellectual functioning.

The reader is again cautioned to bear in mind that the preceding list is not exhaustive and is intended only as a further guide to source material in specific areas of testing. Moreover, some of these references may no longer be pertinent when you consult them. Do not reject a new test or any test because it is not listed in this book or one of the references. Remember that authors are selective and present tests they think are valuable. In the final analysis, it is your job to select tests appropriate for your needs.

Test Publishers

One of the most important sources of test information, especially about a specific test, is the publisher. (See Appendix B for a complete list of these publishers and their addresses.) The test publisher, upon request, will send a catalogue of his tests that lists pertinent data such as price, norms, time necessary to administer a given test, and number of available forms. Specific and detailed information may be obtained by requesting a "specimen set" from the publisher. The "specimen set" is generally quite inexpensive or given free of charge. It usually includes the test, answer sheet, scoring stencil, directions for administering and scoring, and manual.

The "specimen set" facilitates evaluation of the test by first-hand inspection. The manual usually contains data on how the test was constructed and standardized, as well as norms and interpretive suggestions. It is the most contemporary source of test information, but of course one must be judicious in evaluating its contents. It is asking too much to expect the test publisher to be unbiased in his reporting of the test's limitations and assets. Test publishers can be very useful as a source of information if used together with your own critical evaluations and those of testing experts like those found in the *Yearbooks*.

Many test publishers, in addition to selling tests, also distribute advisory information concerning the whole field of testing. This information is usually written in an easy-to-understand way and is geared to the practicing school teacher and counselor or anyone else who uses tests in day-to-day practice. These advisory services are almost always objective and unbiased reports of tests and factors affecting tests in terms of construction and use. These publications that deal with commonly encountered measurement problems are available free of charge. Three of the most active of these publishers are listed:

1. The Psychological Corporation; 757 Third Avenue; New York, N.Y. 10017. The Psychological Corporation publishes from time to time the *Test Service Bulletin*. These bulletins generally contain a three- to five-page article on some facet of tests or testing. There are currently over twenty-four bulletins available to teachers, students, and schools. Examples of some of these bulletins are the following: No. 36, "What Is an Aptitude?"; No. 38, "Expectancy Tables—A Way of Interpreting Test Validity"; No. 39, "Norms Must Be Relevant"; No. 54, "On Telling Parents About Test Results"; No. 55, "The Identification of the Gifted"; No. 56, "Double-Entry Expectancy Tables"; No. 57, "Testing Job Applicants from Disadvantaged Groups." Some of the articles are bound together in one bulletin.

2. Educational Testing Service; Princeton, N.J. 08540. This publisher produces a series entitled *Evaluation and Advisory Service Series*. At present, this series includes four booklets: No. 1, "Locating Information on Educational Measurement: Sources and References"; No. 3, "Selecting an Achievement Test: Principles and Procedures"; No. 4, "Making the Classroom Test: A Guide for Teachers"; No. 5, "Short-cut Statistics for Teacher-Made Tests." In addition to these, several

other booklets and materials are provided free of charge to students, teachers, and schools.
3. Harcourt Brace Jovanovich, Inc.[1]; 757 Third Avenue; New York, N.Y. 10017. This publisher produces two series of test advisory publications, *Test Service Notebook* and *Test Service Bulletin*. The notebooks are generally four pages long and focus on subjects related to test theory, administration of testing programs, results of research studies, and correct test usage. Examples of some of the currently available Notebooks are No. 11, "A Comparison of Results of Three Intelligence Tests"; No. 13, "A Glossary of 100 Measurement Terms"; No. 17, "Why Do We Test Your Children?"; No. 20, "Testing in the Secondary School"; No. 23, "The Characteristics, Use and Computation of Stanines"; No. 25, "How Is a Test Built?"; No. 27, "Fundamentals of Testing: For Parents, School Boards, and Teachers."

The *Test Service Bulletin* generally offers brief reports on effective testing programs and discussions of testing concepts. Examples of some of the currently available bulletins are No. 77, "The Intelligence Quotient"; No. 79, "Misconceptions About Intelligence Testing"; No. 91, "Finding Mathematics and Science Talent in the Junior High School"; No. 94, "Aptitude and Achievement Measures in Predicting High School Academic Success"; No. 95, "Testing: Tool for Curriculum Development"; No. 99, "Selection and Provision of Testing Materials"; No. 102, "Test Administration Guide."

Journals

The *Yearbooks*, though very valuable, are published only every five or six years. This means that a more contemporary source of test evaluation is needed. One such source is the professional journals that review new tests. The following journals are of particular interest to test users:

1. *Personnel and Guidance Journal.*
2. *Educational and Psychological Measurement.*
3. *Journal of Consulting Psychology.*
4. *Personnel Psychology.*
5. *Review of Educational Research.*
6. *Journal of Educational Psychology.*
7. *Measurement and Evaluation in Guidance.*
8. *Journal of Educational Measurement.*
9. *Journal of Applied Psychology.*

[1] Note that in 1970 the Psychological Corporation became a subsidiary of Harcourt Brace Jovanovich. In 1975, the two integrated their research, service, and publishing activities. Together, they presented in 1976 two catalogues, one of educational tests and one of psychological tests for clinical counseling and industrial use.

10. *Journal of Clinical Psychology.*
11. *Journal of Counseling Psychology.*
12. *Journal of Projective Techniques and Personality Assessment.*
13. *Journal of School Psychology.*
14. *Psychology in the Schools.*
15. *Psychological Bulletin.*
16. *Psychometrika.*
17. *American Educational Research Journal.*
18. *Journal of Experimental Education.*
19. *Contemporary Psychology.*

Psychological Abstracts and Educational Index

The *Psychological Abstracts* and the *Educational Index* are excellent bibliographic references in their respective fields. The *Psychological Abstracts* serve as the general guidelines for all psychological journals. Each issue contains a brief (abstract) summary of every report in the psychological journals, including the subject and important features of the report. Every year a subject and author index is given for convenience in locating material published in the previous year. The *Psychological Abstracts* also publish monthly listings of new tests. In addition, data concerning research use of tests and resultant findings are also presented.

The *Educational Index* provides a very wide listing of journal articles in the field of education. It includes lay as well as professional materials and discussions. It does not give analyses as detailed as those in the *Psychological Abstracts*. Only references are given. One could find, for example, under "achievement testing" lists of tests and articles dealing with this area or, for that matter, any other sphere of measurement relating to education.

The intelligent use of tests demands the utilization of all appropriate sources of test data. The combination of *Psychological Abstracts* and the *Educational Index*, plus the sources previously mentioned, should provide the test user with the necessary data to make intelligent choices in his or her evaluation and selection of measurement instruments.

EIGHT | Appendixes

Glossary of Common Measurement Terms[1]

appendix A

academic aptitude (scholastic aptitude) A combination of inherited and acquired abilities needed for schoolwork.

accomplishment quotient (AQ) The ratio of educational age to mental age; EA ÷ MA. (Also called *achievement quotient.*)

achievement age The average age on an achievement test. If a child obtains an achievement age of 11 years 8 months on a reading test, his score is equal to those of children of 11 years 8 months, who on the average receive a similar score.

achievement test A test that measures the amount of knowledge or skills that a child has learned in a particular subject field.

age equivalent The age for which a given score is the real or estimated average score.

age norms Values considered as average on a certain test for children of various ages.

age-grade table A table showing the number of students of various ages in each grade.

alternate-form reliability The closeness of correspondence, or correlation, between results on alternate (equivalent or parallel) forms of a test; thus, a measure of the extent to which the two forms are consistent or reliable in measuring whatever they do measure, assuming that the examinees themselves do not change in the abilities measured between the two testings.

aptitude The ability to acquire new knowledge and proficiency with training. It is a combination of inborn capacity or ability and acquired skills.

aptitude test A test that measures the potential ability or capacity of a person to learn various skills and acquire new knowledge.

---

[1] This glossary includes some of the common terms used in measurement. It has been revised and adapted from Test Service Notebook No. 13, by permission. Published by Harcourt Brace Jovanovich, Inc.

arithmetic mean The sum of a group of scores divided by the number of scores, which produces an average.

average A general term applied to measures of central tendency. The three most widely used averages are the *arithmetic mean*, the *median*, and the *mode*.

battery A group of several tests that are comparable, the results of which are used individually, in combination, and/or totally.

behavior rating scale A device to record judgments about the occurrence or type of behavior of a specific person or group.

ceiling The top score or upper limit of a test.

checklist A list of behaviors, observations, or characteristics that are checked or answered yes by a rater or observer when it has been decided that the item has satisfactorily occurred. The item is not checked or answered no when it is judged not to have occurred satisfactorily.

class analysis chart A chart, usually prepared in connection with a battery of achievement tests, that shows the relative performance of members of a class on the several parts of the battery.

coefficient of correlation (r) A measure of the degree of relationship, or "going-togetherness," between two sets of measures for the same group of individuals. The correlation coefficient most frequently used in test development and educational research is that known as the *Pearson (Pearsonian) r*, so named for Karl Pearson, originator of the method, or as the *product-moment r*, to denote the mathematical basis of its calculation. Unless otherwise specified, "correlation" usually means the product-moment correlation coefficient, which ranges from .oo, denoting complete absence of relationship, to 1.oo, denoting perfect correspondence, and may be either positive or negative.

completion item A test question requiring the student to complete or fill in a word or words in a phrase or sentence from which one or more parts have been deleted.

correction for guessing A reduction in score for wrong answers, sometimes applied in scoring true-false or multiple-choice questions. Many question the validity or usefulness of this device, which is intended to discourage guessing and to yield more accurate rankings of examinees in terms of their true knowledge. Scores to which such corrections have been applied—e.g., rights minus wrongs, or rights minus some fraction of wrongs—are often spoken of as "corrected for guessing" or "corrected for chance."

correlation Relationship of "going-togetherness" between two scores of measures; tendency of one score to vary concomitantly with the other, as the tendency of students of high IQ to be above average in reading ability. The existence of a strong relationship—i.e., a high correlation—between two variables does not necessarily indicate that one has any causal influence on the other.

criterion A standard by which a test may be judged or evaluated; a set of scores, ratings, etc., that a test is designed to predict or to correlate with.

criterion-referenced test A designation applied to tests that provide data on specific skills or information on a given student. These tests are constructed to assess the objectives of instruction. The derived scores relate to what the student knows or can do, not how he stands compared to another student or norm group.

decile Any one of the nine percentile points (scores) in a distribution that divide the distribution into ten equal parts; every tenth percentile. The first decile is the 10th percentile, the ninth decile the 90th percentile, etc.

deviation IQ A comparison of a person's score to a score considered average for his age.

diagnostic test A test used to locate specific areas of a child's weakness or strength that determines the kind of weaknesses.

difficulty value The per cent of some specified group, such as students of a given age or grade, who answer an item correctly.

discriminating power The ability of a test item to differentiate between persons possessing much of some trait and those possessing little.

distractor Any of the incorrect choices in a multiple-choice or matching item.

distribution (frequency distribution) A tabulation of scores from high to low, or low to high, showing the number of individuals who obtain each score or fall in each score interval.

educational age (EA) See *achievement age*.

equivalent form Any of two or more forms of a test that are closely parallel with respect to the nature of the content and the difficulty of the items included and that will yield very similar average scores and measures of variability for a given group.

evaluation program Such a program involves the use of testing and nontesting instruments and techniques for the appraisal of growth adjustment and achievement of the child.

extrapolation A process of estimating values of a function beyond the range of available data.

factor In mental measurement, a hypothetical trait, ability, or component of ability that underlies and influences performance on two or more tests, and hence causes scores on the tests to be correlated. The term "factor" strictly refers to a theoretical variable, derived by a process of *factor analysis*, from a table of intercorrelations among tests; but it is also commonly used to denote the psychological interpretation given to the variable—i.e., the mental trait assumed to be represented by the variable, as verbal ability, numerical ability, etc.

factor analysis A statistical technique for analyzing the relationship among a set of scores.

forced-choice item Generally, any multiple-choice item in which the individual is required to make a choice of answers provided him.

grade equivalent A score that indicates a student's average performance in terms of grade and month. A grade equivalent of 7.2 is interpreted as the second month of the seventh grade.

grade norm The average score that a student in a certain grade receives on a test.

group test A test that can be administered to one or more individuals at the same time by one examiner.

individual test A test that can be administered to only one individual at a time.

intelligence quotient (IQ) The ratio of mental age (MA) to chronological age (CA). The formula is $IQ = MA \div CA \times 100$.

interpolation In general, any process of estimating intermediate values between two known points. As applied to test norms, it refers to the procedure used in assigning interpreted values (e.g., grade or age equivalents) to scores between the successive average scores actually obtained in the standardization process. In reading norm tables, it is necessary at times to *interpolate* to obtain a norm value for a score between scores given in the table; e.g., in the table given here, an age value of 12-5 would be assigned, by interpolation, to a score of 118.

Score	Age Equivalent
120	12-6
115	12-4
110	12-2

inventory test As applied to achievement tests, a test that attempts to cover rather thoroughly some relatively small unit of specific instruction or training. The purpose of an inventory test, as the name suggests, is more in the nature of a "stock-taking" of an individual's knowledge or skill than an effort to measure in the usual sense. The term sometimes denotes a type of test used to measure achievement status prior to instruction. Many personality and interest questionnaires are designated "inventories," since they appraise an individual's status in several personal characteristics, or his level of interest in a variety of types of activities.

item A question or exercise in a test.

item analysis The process of evaluating single test items by any of several methods. It usually involves determining the difficulty value and the discriminating power of the item, and often its correlation with some criterion.

Kuder-Richardson formula(s) Formulas for estimating the reliability of a test from information about the individual items in the test, or from the mean score, standard deviation, and number of items in the test. Because the Kuder-Richardson formulas permit estimation of reliability from a single administration of a test without the labor involved in dividing the test into halves, their use has become common in test development. The Kuder-Richardson formulas are not appropriate for estimating the reliability of speeded tests.

mean See *arithmetic mean.*

median The point at which a given group of test scores is divided into two equal parts. Half the scores fall below the median and half above it.

mental age (MA) The age for which a score on an intelligence test is average or normal. For example, if a score of 60 on an intelligence test is equal to a mental age of 7 years 9 months, then 60 is the average score that would be made by a random group of children 7 years 9 months of age.

mode The score that occurs most frequently in a distribution of scores. For example, the mode score is 55 in the following scores of children on a reading test: 10, 30, 35, 55, 55, 55, 55, 60, 67, 69, 72, 72, 78, 79, 84, 85, 88, 90, 94, 96, 98, 99.

multiple-choice item A test item in which the examinee's task is to choose the correct or best answer from several given answers, or options.

multiple-response item A special type of multiple-choice item in which two or more of the given choices may be correct.

N The symbol commonly used to represent the number of cases in a distribution, study, etc.

normal distribution curve This is a method of representing the distribution of various levels of ability and other characteristics within our society. In a normal distribution, scores are distributed symmetrically about the average, with as many cases at various equal distances above the average as below the average, and with cases concentrated near the average and decreasing in number the farther one departs from the average.

norm-referenced test A test that provides data on students relative to one another. Norms for interpretation are usually obtained from a norm group. Scores are, therefore, interpreted on a relative basis rather than in absolute terms.

norms A way of describing, by statistical methods, the test performances of specific groups of students of various ages and/or grades. Norms are used to describe average, below-average, and above-average performances. Grade, age, and percentiles are commonly used types of norms.

objective test A test in which there is no possibility of difference of opinion among scorers as to whether responses are to be scored right or wrong. It is contrasted with a "subjective" test—e.g., the usual essay examination to which different scorers may assign different scores, ratings, or grades.

omnibus test A test (1) in which items measuring a variety of mental operations are all combined into a single sequence rather than being grouped together by type of operation, and (2) from which only a single score is derived, rather than separate scores for each operation or function. Omnibus tests make for simplicity of administration: one set of directions and one overall time limit usually suffice.

parallel-item agreement A reliability procedure used with criterion-referenced tests. Performances on items that are similar and attempt to measure the same objective are compared. Dissimilarity in these may lead to item revision.

percentile A score designating what percentages of the total group of scores equal or fall below it. Thus the person obtaining a percentile rank of 25 is considered as equaling or surpassing 25 per cent of the group taking the same test.

percentile rank The per cent of scores in a distribution equal to or lower than the score corresponding to the given rank.

performance test In a way, every test may be considered a performance test. However, pencil-and-paper or oral tests are not usually regarded as performance tests. Generally, a performance test requires the use and manipulation of physical objects and the use of physical and manual skills not restricted to oral and written answers. The important thing is that the test response is identical with the behavior about which information is desired.

personality test A test that attempts to measure everything that constitutes a person's mental, emotional, and psychological makeup.

power test A test that attempts to measure level of performance rather than an individual's speed in answering questions. There is little, if any, emphasis on time.

practice effect A term test people use in describing the influence of previous experience with a test. For example, Johnny took the same test two months ago. Will his previous experience with this test help him achieve a higher score?

profile A graphic portrait of an individual's test results on several tests.

prognostic technique A test used to predict future success or failure in a specific academic subject or field.

projective test A method of testing to determine personality characteristics. The person is presented with a series of ink blots, pictures, unfinished sentences, and so on. The term *projective* is used because it is believed that a person "projects" into his answers and statements his own needs and feelings.

quartile One of three points that divide the cases in a distribution into four equal groups. The lower quartile, or 25th percentile, sets off the lowest fourth of the group; the middle quartile is the same as the 50th percentile, or median; and the third quartile, or 75th percentile, marks off the highest fourth.

random sample A sample of the people of a population made in such a way that every person of the population has equal chance of being included. This method attempts to eliminate bias.

range The extent of difference between the highest and lowest scores on a test. For example, 98 is the highest score and 10 is the lowest; therefore the range is between 10 and 98.

raw score Usually the number of right answers, or some such formula as rights minus one-half wrongs, which gives a total score.

readiness test A test that measures the degree to which a child has achieved certain skills or information needed for undertaking some new learning activity. For example, a reading readiness test indicates the degree to which a child is at a developmental stage where he may profitably begin a formal program of reading instruction.

recall item An item that requires the examinee to supply the correct answer from his own memory or recollection, as contrasted with a *recognition item*, in which he need only identify the correct answer, e.g., "Columbus discovered America in the year —" is a recall item, whereas "Columbus discovered America in (*a*) 1425, (*b*) 1492, (*c*) 1520, (*d*) 1546" is a recognition item.

recognition item An item requiring the examinee to recognize or select the correct answer from among two or more given answers. See *recall item.*

reliability The extent to which a student would obtain the same score if the test were to be readministered. That is, is the test consistent in measuring whatever it does measure?

reliability coefficient The coefficient of correlation between two forms of a test, between scores on repeated administrations of the same test, or between halves of a test, properly corrected.

representative sample A sample that corresponds to or matches the population of which it is a sample with respect to characteristics important for the purposes under investigation—e.g., in an achievement test norm sample, proportion of pupils from each state, from various regions, from segregated and nonsegregated schools, etc.

scholastic aptitude See *academic aptitude*

skewness The tendency of a distribution to depart from symmetry or balance around the mean.

Spearman-Brown formula A formula giving the relationship between the reliability of a test and its length. The formula permits estimation of the reliability of a test, lengthened or shortened by any amount, from the known reliability of a test of specified length. Its most common application is in the estimation of reliability of an entire test from the correlation between two halves of the test (*split-half reliability*).

speed test A test that measures an individual's performance by the number of questions he can answer in a certain amount of time.

split-half coefficient A coefficient of reliability obtained by correlating scores on one half of a test with scores on the other half. Generally, but not necessarily, the two halves consist of the odd-numbered and the even-numbered items.

standard deviation (SD) A measure of the variability or dispersion of a set of scores. The more the scores cluster around the mean, the smaller the standard deviation.

standard error (SE) An estimate of the magnitude of the "error of measurement" in a score—that is, the amount by which an obtained score differs from a hypothetical true score. The standard error is an amount such that in about two thirds of the cases the obtained score would not differ by more than one standard error from the true score. The *probable error (PE)* of a score is a similar measure, except that in about half the cases the obtained score differs from the true score by not more than one probable error. The probable error is equal to about two thirds of the standard error. The larger the probable or the standard error of a score, the less reliable the measure.

standard score A general term referring to any of a variety of "transformed" scores, in terms of which raw scores may be expressed for reasons of convenience, comparability, ease of interpretation, etc.

The simplest type of standard score is that which expresses the deviation of an individual's raw score from the average score of his group in relation to the standard deviation of the scores of the group. Thus:

$$\text{Standard score } (z) = \frac{\text{raw score } (X) - \text{mean } (M)}{\text{standard deviation (SD)}}$$

By multiplying this ratio by a suitable constant and by adding or subtracting another constant, standard scores having any desired mean and standard deviation may be obtained. Such standard scores do not affect the relative standing of the individuals in the group or change the shape of the original distribution.

More complicated types of standard scores may yield distributions differing in shape from the original distribution; in fact, they are sometimes used for precisely this purpose. *Normalized standard scores* and *K-scores* (as used in Stanford Achievement Test) are examples of this latter group.

standardized test A test that has definite directions for administering, scoring, and use.

stanines A nine-point scale. It divides the norm population into nine groups. The mean score from 1 to 9 is 5.

survey test A test that measures general achievement in a given subject or area, usually with the connotation that the test is intended to measure group status, rather than to yield precise measures of individuals.

test-retest coefficient A type of reliability coefficient obtained by administering the same test a second time after a short interval and correlating the two sets of scores.

true-false item A test question or exercise in which the examinee's task is to indicate whether a given statement is true or false.

true score A score entirely free of errors of measurement. True scores are hypothetical values never obtained by testing, which always involves some measurement error. A true score is sometimes defined as the average score of an infinite series of measurements with the same or exactly equivalent tests, assuming no practice effect or change in the examinee during the testings.

validity A term used to designate the extent to which a test measures what it is supposed to measure. For example, is the reading test measuring Bill's reading ability or his knowledge of science?

Publishers of Standardized Tests[1,2]

American Orthopsychiatric Association, Inc.
1790 Broadway
New York, New York 10019
212-586-5690

American College Testing Program (ACT)
P.O. Box 168
Iowa City, Iowa 52240
319-356-3711

American Guidance Service, Inc.
Publishers' Building
Circle Pines, Minnesota 55014
612-786-4343

Behavioral Publications, Inc.
2852 Broadway
New York, New York 10025
212-246-6000

The Bobbs-Merrill Company, Inc.
4300 West 62nd Street
Indianapolis, Indiana 46206
317-291-3100

Bureau of Educational Measurements
Emporia Kansas State College
Emporia, Kansas 66801
316-343-1200

Bureau of Educational Research and Service
C-6 East Hall
State University of Iowa
Iowa City, Iowa 52240
319-353-2121

[1] Test catalogues are sent free of charge on request.

[2] For a complete list of test publishers, see Publishers' Directory in the latest *Mental Measurements Yearbook*.

California Test Bureau
West of Mississippi (main office)
Del Monte Research Park
Monterey, California 93940
408-649-8400

East of Mississippi:
206 Bridge Street
New Cumberland, Pennsylvania
17070
717-774-0430

Center for Psychological Service
1835 Eye Street, N.W.
Washington, D.C. 20006
202-541-4465

Committee on Diagnostic Reading
Tests, Inc.
Mountain Home, North Carolina
28758
704-OXford 3-5223

Consulting Psychologists Press, Inc.
577 College Avenue
Palo Alto, California 94306
415-326-4448

CPS, Inc.
P.O. Box 83
Larchmont, New York 10538

Education-Industry Service
1225 East 60th Street
Chicago, Illinois 60637

Educational and Industrial Testing
Service
P.O. Box 7234
San Diego, California 92107
714-222-1666

Educational Records Bureau
21 Audubon Avenue
New York, New York 10032
212-535-0307

Educational Testing Service
Princeton, New Jersey 08540
609-921-9000

Western office:
1947 Center Street
Berkeley, California 94704
415-849-0950

Midwestern office:
990 Grove Street
Evanston, Illinois 60201
312-869-7700

Follett Publishing Company
1010 West Washington Boulevard
Chicago, Illinois 60607
312-665-5855

Grune and Stratton, Inc.
381 Park Avenue South
New York, New York 10016
212-741-6800

Guidance Testing Associates
6516 Shirley Avenue
Austin, Texas 78752
512-472-7087

Harcourt Brace Jovanovich, Inc.
757 Third Avenue
New York, New York 10017
212-754-3100

Harvard University Press
79 Garden Street
Cambridge, Massachusetts, 02138
617-495-2600

Hay Associates
1845 Walnut Street
Philadelphia, Pennsylvania 19103
215-561-7000

Houghton Mifflin Company
1 Beacon Street
Boston, Massachusetts 02107
617-725-5000

Institute for Personality and Ability
Testing (IPAT)
1602 Coronado Drive
Champaign, Illinois 61820
217-352-4739

Kaplan School Supply
600 Jonesboro Road
Winston-Salem, North Carolina 27103
919-768-4450

NFER Publishing Co., Ltd.
2 Jennings Bldgs.
Thames Avenue
Windsor, Berks.
SL4 IQS, England

Ohio Testing Services (Ohio
Scholarship Tests)
Division of Guidance and Testing
State Department of Education
965 South Front
Columbus, Ohio 43212
614-466-4590

The Psychological Corporation
757 Third Avenue
New York, New York 10017
212-754-3500

Psychological Test Specialists
Box 1441
Missoula, Montana 59801

Psychology Research
Box 14, Technology Center
Chicago, Illinois 60616

Psychometric Affiliates
Box 3167
Munster, Indiana 46321
219-836-1661

Saul Rosenzweig
8029 Washington Street
St. Louis, Missouri 63114

Scholastic Testing Service, Inc.
480 Meyer Road
Bensenville, Illinois 60106
312-766-7150

Science Research Associates, Inc.
259 East Erie Street
Chicago, Illinois 60611
312-266-5396

Sheridan Psychological Services, Inc.
1332 East Collins Avenue
Beverly Hills, California 90213
213-639-2595

C. H. Stoelting Company
1350 South Kostner Avenue
Chicago, Illinois 60623
312-522-4500

Teachers College Press
Teachers College
Columbia University
New York, New York 10027
212-678-3929

Charles C Thomas, Publisher
327 East Lawrence Avenue
Springfield, Illinois 62703
217-789-8980

United States Employment Service
(See local U.S. Employment Service)

University Bookstore, Purdue
University
360 State Street
West Lafayette, Indiana 47906
317-749-8111

University of London Press Ltd.
Little Paul's House, Warwick Square
London E.C.4, England

Western Psychological Services
12031 Wilshire Boulevard
Los Angeles, California 90025
213-478-2061

Representative Tests

appendix C

This appendix includes representative tests in areas of concern to the teacher and school counselor. Tests such as projective devices that require specialized training are not listed.

This test list is by no means exhaustive. The reader *should not* construe the listing of a test to mean approval by the authors, nor should he interpret the omission of one as their disapproval.

The names of tests, grade ranges, publishers, and *Mental Measurements Yearbook* (MMY) volume and page citation or test publication dates are presented for reference research. (See Chapter 19 for a discussion of sources of information.) The reader should refer to Appendix B for the addresses of publishers.

Name of Test	Grade Range* (or age)	Publisher	MMY (or date)
Individual Intelligence Tests			
AAMD Adaptive Behavior Scale	3 yrs. & up	American Association on Mental Deficiency	7-37
Cattell Infant Intelligence Scale	3–30 mos.	Psychological Corporation	6-515
Columbia Mental Maturity Scale	3–11 yrs.	Harcourt Brace Jovanovich	6-517 (1972)
Concept Assessment Kit— Conservation	4–7 yrs.	Educational and Industrial Testing Service	7-437
Full Range Picture Vocabulary Test	2 yrs. & up	Psychological Test Specialists	6-521
Haptic Intelligence Scale for Adult Blind		Psychology Research	7-409
McCarthy Scales of Children's Activities	2½–8½ yrs.	Psychological Corporation	(1972)
Minnesota Preschool Scale	1–6 yrs.	American Guidance Service (Educational Test Bureau)	6-528
Peabody Picture Vocabulary Test	2–18 yrs.	American Guidance Service	7-417
Pictorial Test of Intelligence	3–8 yrs.	Houghton Mifflin	7-418
Porteus Maze Test	3 yrs. & up	Psychological Corporation	7-419
Quick Test	2 yrs. & up	Psychological Test Specialists	7-422
Stanford-Binet Intelligence Scale	2 yrs. & up	Houghton Mifflin	7-425 (1973)
Van Alstyne Picture Vocabulary Test	2–7 yrs.	Harcourt Brace Jovanovich	6-537
Wechsler Adult Intelligence Scale (WAIS)	16 yrs. & up	Psychological Corporation	7-429
Wechsler Intelligence Scale for Children—Revised (WISC-R)	5–15 yrs.	Psychological Corporation	7-431 (1974)
Wechsler Preschool and Primary Scale of Intelligence (WPPSI)	4–6 yrs.	Psychological Corporation	7-434
Developmental Scales			
Arthur Point Scale of Performance Tests:	4 yrs. & up		4-335
Form I		Stoelting	
Form II		Psychological Corporation	
Bayley Infant Scales of Development	2 months– 2½ yrs.	Psychological Corporation	7-402
Denver Developmental Screening Test	2 weeks– 6 yrs.	Ladocer Project and Publishing Foundation, Inc.	7-405

* Note that numbers indicate grade range, whereas age is specifically designated by years or the letter A (adult).

Name of Test	Grade Range (or age)	Publisher	MMY (or date)
Gesell Developmental Schedules	4 wks–6 yrs.	Psychological Corporation	6-522
Learning Accomplishment Profile	1–6 yrs.	Kaplan School Supply	

Readiness and Preschool Tests

Name of Test	Grade Range (or age)	Publisher	MMY (or date)
Analysis of Readiness Skills: Reading of Mathematics	K–1	Houghton Mifflin	(1972)
Boehm Test of Basic Concepts	K–2	Psychological Corporation	7-335
Circus: Assessment Preprimary to (SPRING) beginning primary	N (Fall)–K K–1 (Fall)	Educational Testing Service	(1974) (1976)
Cooperative Preschool Inventory—Revised Ed.		Educational Testing Service	7-404
(English & Spanish editions)	N–3	Educational Testing Service	(1975)
Let's Look at Children	Nsry–1 K–1	Harcourt Brace Jovanovich	7-751 (1976)
Metropolitan Readiness Tests		Harcourt Brace Jovanovich	7-28
Stanford Early School Achievement Test (SESAT) (English & Spanish editions)	K–1		
Tests of Basic Experiences (TOBE)	Nsry–1	California Test Bureau McGraw-Hill	7-33

Aptitude Test Batteries

Name of Test	Grade Range (or age)	Publisher	MMY (or date)
Academic Promise Tests (APT)	6–9	Psychological Corporation	7-672
Differential Aptitude Tests (DAT)	8–12, A	Psychological Corporation	7-673 (1974)
Flanagan Aptitude Classification Tests (FACT)	9–12, A	Science Research Associates	7-675
General Aptitude Test Battery (GATB)	16 yrs. & up & 9–12, A	U.S. Employment Service	7-676
Multiple Aptitude Tests, 1959 Edition	7–13	California Test Bureau	6-776
SRA Primary Mental Abilities, Revised	K–12	Science Research Associates	7-680

Scholastic Aptitude Tests

Name of Test	Grade Range (or age)	Publisher	MMY (or date)
American College Testing Program Examination	12 & Jr. Coll.	American College Testing Program	7-330
California Test of Mental Maturity, 1963 Revision	4–16, A	California Test Bureau	7-338

Name of Test	Grade Range (or age)	Publisher	MMY (or date)
College Entrance Examination Board Scholastic Aptitude Test (SAT)	11 & up	Educational Testing Service (for CEEB)	7-344
College Qualification Tests	12 & up	Psychological Corporation	7-345
Cooperative Primary Tests	1–3	Educational Testing Service (Cooperative Test Division)	7-10 (1967)
Cooperative School and College Ability Tests (SCAT) also Series II, 1968)	4–16	Educational Testing Service (Cooperative Test Division)	7-347 (1973)
Culture Fair Intelligence Test	4–13 yrs. & 10–16, A	Institute for Personality and Ability Testing	6-453
Goodenough-Harris Drawing Test	3–15 yrs.	Harcourt Brace Jovanovich	7-352 7-353
Graduate Record Examinations (GRE)	16–17	Educational Testing Service	7-667
Henmon-Nelson Tests of Mental Ability, 1973 Revision	3–17	Houghton Mifflin	6-462 (1973)
Kuhlmann-Anderson Intelligence Tests, Seventh Edition	K–12	Personnel Press, Inc.	6-466
Lorge-Thorndike Intelligence Tests (multilevel edition)	K–12	Houghton Mifflin	7-360
Miller Analogies Test	Grad. Sch.	Psychological Corporation	7-363
Ohio State University Psychological Test, Forms 21 and 23	9–16, A	Science Research Associates	5-359
Otis-Lennon Mental Ability Test	1–16	Harcourt Brace Jovanovich	7-370
Pintner General Ability Tests—Revised	K–12 & up	Harcourt Brace Jovanovich	5-368 (1966) (1968)
Progressive Matrices	5 yrs. & up	H. K. Lewis & Co., Ltd. (U.S. distributor: Psychological Corporation)	7-376
SRA Tests of Educational Ability, 1962 Edition (TEA)	4–12	Science Research Associates	7-382
Tests of General Ability (TOGA)	K–12	Science Research Associates	6-496

Special Aptitude Tests

Mathematics

Lee Test of Geometric Aptitude, 1963 Revision	Hi. Sch.	California Test Bureau	6-647
Mastery: An Evaluation Tool, Mathematics	3–9	Science Research Associates	(1975)

Name of Test	Grade Range (or age)	Publisher	MMY (or date)
Orleans-Hanna Algebra Prognosis Test	Hi. Sch.	Harcourt Brace Jovanovich	7-510
Orleans-Hanna Geometry	Hi. Sch.	Harcourt Brace Jovanovich	7-539
Foreign Languages			
Modern Language Aptitude Test	9–16, A	Psychological Corporation	7-254
Modern Language Aptitude Test— Elementary	3–6	Psychological Corporation	7-255
Pimsleur Language Aptitude Battery	6–12	Harcourt Brace Jovanovich	7-256
Mechanical Aptitude Tests			
Revised Minnesota Paper Form Board Test	9–16, A	Psychological Corporation	7-1056
SRA Mechanical Aptitudes	9–12, A	Science Research Associates	4-764
Test of Mechanical Comprehension (Bennett)	9 & up	Psychological Corporation	7-1049
Motor Tests			
Purdue Pegboard	9–16, A	Science Research Associates	6-1081
Stromberg Dexterity Test	A	Psychological Corporation	4-755
Clerical Aptitude Tests			
Minnesota Clerical Test	8–12, A	Psychological Corporation	6-1040
Short Employment Tests	*	Psychological Corporation	6-1045
Short Tests of Clerical Ability	*	Science Research Associates	6-1046
Artistic Aptitude Tests			
Horn Art Aptitude Inventory	12–16, A	Stoelting	5-242
Meier Art Tests 1. Art Judgment 2. Aesthetic Perception	7–16, A	Bureau of Educational Research and Service, University of Iowa	7-240
Musical Aptitude Tests			
Musical Aptitude Profile	4–12	Houghton Mifflin	7-249
Seashore Measures of Musical Talents, Revised Edition	4–16, A	Psychological Corporation	6-353
Wing Standardized Tests of Musical Intelligence	8 yrs. & up	NFER Publishing Co.	6-354

* No specific grade or age range.

Name of Test	Grade Range (or age)	Publisher	MMY (or date)
Elementary Achievement Test Batteries			
Iowa Tests of Basic Skills	3–9	Houghton Mifflin	6-13 (1974)
Metropolitan Achievement Test	1–12	Harcourt Brace Jovanovich	7-14
Sequential Tests of Educational Progress (STEP)—Series II	4–14	Educational Testing Service (Cooperative Test Division)	6-25 (1971)
SRA Achievement Series	1–9	Science Research Associates	7-18 (1971)
Stanford Achievement Test	1–9	Harcourt Brace Jovanovich	7-25 (1973)
High School Achievement Batteries			
Iowa Tests of Educational Development	9–12	Science Research Associates	6-14 (1972)
Metropolitan Achievement Test	1–12	Harcourt Brace Jovanovich	7-14
Sequential Test of Educational Progress, Series II (STEP)	4–14	Education Testing Service (Cooperative Test Division)	6-25 (1971)
Stanford Achievement Test: High School Battery	1–9	Harcourt Brace Jovanovich	7-25
Special Achievement Tests			
Blyth Second-Year Algebra Test—Revised Edition	Hi. Sch.	Harcourt Brace Jovanovich	7-497
Cooperative Science Tests	6–12	Educational Testing Service (Cooperative Test Division)	7-787
Cummings World History Test	9–13	Harcourt Brace Jovanovich	5-817
Dunning-Abeles Physics Test	11–13	Harcourt Brace Jovanovich	5-753 (1967)
MLA Cooperative Foreign Language Tests	Hi. Sch.	Educational Testing Service (Cooperative Test Division)	7-254
Modern Math Understanding Test	4–9	Science Research Associates	(1966)
Nelson Biology Test— Revised Edition	9–13	Harcourt Brace Jovanovich	7-819
Reading Tests			
Davis Reading Tests	8–13	Psychological Corporation	6-786
Diagnostic Reading Scales	1–8	California Test Bureau	7-717 (1972)

Name of Test	Grade Range (or age)	Publisher	MMY (or date)
Diagnostic Reading Tests	K–13	Committee on Diagnostic Reading Tests, Inc.	6-823
Durrell Analysis of Reading Difficulty, New Edition	1–6	Harcourt Brace Jovanovich	5-660
Gates-McKillop Reading Diagnostic Tests	2–6	Teachers College Press	6-824
Gilmore Oral Reading Test		Harcourt Brace Jovanovich	7-737
Iowa Silent Reading Tests	6–Col.	Harcourt Brace Jovanovich	6-794 (1973)
Mastery: An Evaluation Tool, Reading	3–9	Science Research Associates	(1975)
Nelson-Denny Reading Test	9–16, A	Houghton Mifflin	6-800
Skills Monitoring System Reading	3–5	Harcourt Brace Jovanovich	(1975)
1976 Stanford Diagnostic Reading Test	1.5–9.5	Harcourt Brace Jovanovich	(1976)

Interest Inventories

Gordon Occupational Check List	Hi. Sch.	Harcourt Brace Jovanovich	7-1019
Guilford-Zimmerman Interest Inventory	10–16, A	Sheridan Psychological Services	6-1057
Holland Vocational Preference Inventory	Col. & A	Consulting Psychologists Press	6-115
Kuder General Interest Survey	6–12	Science Research Associates	7-1024
Kuder Occupational Interest Survey	9–16, A	Science Research Associates	7-1025
Kuder Preference Record—Personal	9–16, A	Science Research Associates	6-132
Kuder Preference Record—Vocational	9–16, A	Science Research Associates	6-1063
Minnesota Vocational Interest Inventory	Hi. Sch. & A	Psychological Corporation	7-1026
Ohio Vocational Interest Survey (OVIS)	8–13	Harcourt Brace Jovanovich	7-1036
Strong-Campbell Interest Inventory (SCII), 1974 edition of Strong Vocational Interest Blank (SVIB)	11–12, Col. & A	Stanford University Press	7-1037 (1974)

Personality and Attitude Inventories

Adjustment Inventory (Bell)	9–16, A	Consulting Psychologists Press	6-59
California Psychological Inventory (CPI)	13 yrs. & up	Consulting Psychologists Press	7-49

Name of Test	Grade Range (or age)	Publisher	MMY (or date)
California Test of Personality	12–16, A	California Test Bureau	6-73
Edwards Personal Preference Schedule (EPPS)	Col. & A	Psychological Corporation	7-72
Eysenck Personality Inventory	Hi. Sch., Col., A	Educational and Industrial Testing Service	7-76
Gordon Personal Inventory	8–16, A	Harcourt Brace Jovanovich	6-102
Gordon Personal Profile	9–16, A	Harcourt Brace Jovanovich	6-103
Guilford-Zimmerman Temperament Survey	12–16, A	Sheridan Psychological Services	6-110
IPAT Children's Personality Questionnaire	8–12 yrs.	Institute for Personality and Ability Testing	7-96
Jr.-Sr. High School Personality Questionnaire	7–12	Institute for Personality and Ability Testing	7-97
Minnesota Multiphasic Personality Inventory (MMPI)	16 yrs. & up	Psychological Corporation	7-104
Minnesota Teacher Attitude Inventory	12–17	Psychological Corporation	6-699
Mooney Problem Check List	7–16, A	Psychological Corporation	6-145
Personality Inventory (Bernreuter)	9–16	Consulting Psychologists Press	6-157
Sixteen Personality Factor Questionnaire	15 yrs. & up	Institute for Personality and Ability Testing	7-139
Study of Values	13 & up	Houghton Mifflin	7-146
Thorndike Dimensions	11 & up	Psychological Corporation	7-154

Projective Techniques *

Bender-Gestalt Test		American Orthopsychiatric Association	7-161
Blacky Pictures		Psychodynamic Instruments	6-204
Children's Apperception Test (CAT)		CPS Inc.	6-206 (1971)
Gerontological Apperception Test		Behavioral Publications, Inc.	(1971)
Holtzman Inkblot Technique		Psychological Corporation	7-169
H-T-P: House-Tree-Person		Western Psychological Services	6-215
Kent-Rosanoff Free Association Test		Stoelting	6-226
Machover Draw-a-Person Test		Charles C Thomas	6-229 7-165
Make a Picture Story (MAPS)		Psychological Corporation	6-230

* Unless specifically identified in the title of the Projective Technique (e.g., Children's Apperception Test), the technique may be used for any age or grade classification.

Name of Test	Grade Range (or age)	Publisher	MMY (or date)
Piotrowski's Automated Rorschach (PAR)		Hay Associates	(1974)
Rorschach		Grune and Stratton (U.S. distributor)	7-175
Rosenzweig Picture-Frustration Study (P-F Study)		Saul Rosenzweig	6-238
Rotter Incomplete Sentences Blank		Psychological Corporation	6-239
Senior Apperception Technique		CPS Inc.	(1973)
Szondi Test		Grune and Stratton (U.S. distributor)	6-243
Thematic Apperception Test (TAT)		Harvard University Press	7-181

Values of the Correlation Coefficient for Different Levels of Significance

df	P = .10	.05	.02	.01
1	.988	.997	.9995	.9999
2	.900	.950	.980	.990
3	.805	.878	.934	.959
4	.729	.811	.882	.917
5	.669	.754	.833	.874
6	.622	.707	.789	.834
7	.582	.666	.750	.798
8	.549	.632	.716	.765
9	.521	.602	.685	.735
10	.497	.576	.658	.708
11	.476	.553	.634	.684
12	.458	.532	.612	.661
13	.441	.514	.592	.641
14	.426	.497	.574	.623
15	.412	.482	.558	.606
16	.400	.468	.542	.590
17	.389	.456	.528	.575
18	.378	.444	.516	.561
19	.369	.433	.503	.549
20	.360	.423	.492	.537
21	.352	.413	.482	.526
22	.344	.404	.472	.515
23	.337	.396	.462	.505
24	.330	.388	.453	.496
25	.323	.381	.445	.487
26	.317	.374	.437	.479
27	.311	.367	.430	.471
28	.306	.361	.423	.463
29	.301	.355	.416	.456
30	.296	.349	.409	.449
35	.275	.325	.381	.418
40	.257	.304	.358	.393
45	.243	.288	.338	.372
50	.231	.273	.322	.354
60	.211	.250	.295	.325
70	.195	.232	.274	.302
80	.183	.217	.256	.283
90	.173	.205	.242	.267
100	.164	.195	.230	.254

From Table VII of Fisher and Yates, *Statistical Tables for Biological, Agricultural and Medical Research,* published by Longman Group Ltd., London (previously published by Oliver and Boyd, Edinburgh), and is used by permission of the authors and publishers.

References

Aikin, W. M. *The story of the eight-year study, with conclusions and recommendations.* New York: Harper & Row, 1942.

Ainsworth, M. Some problems of validation of projective techniques. *British Journal of Medical Psychology,* 1951, 24, 151–61.

Airasian, D. W. & Madaus, G. F. Criterion-referenced testing in the classroom. *National Council on Measurement in Education,* 1972, 3, 1–8.

Allport, G. W., Vernon, P. E., & Lindzey, G. *Study of values: Manual.* (3rd ed.) Boston: Houghton Mifflin, 1970.

American College Testing Program. *Assessing students on the way to college. Volume II. College student profiles: Norms for the ACT assessment.* Iowa City, Ia.: American College Testing Program, 1972.

American College Testing Program. *Your college-bound students: Interpretive guide to the ACT high school profile service.* (4th ed.) Iowa City, Ia.: American College Testing Program, 1974.

American College Testing Program. *Using ACT on the campus, 1975–76 edition.* Iowa City, Ia.: American College Testing Program, 1975. (a)

American College Testing Program. *ACT assessment student's booklet: Understanding and using assessment results in planning for college, 1975–76 edition.* Iowa City, Ia.: American College Testing Program, 1975. (b)

American College Testing Program. *Announcement of the ACT research services for colleges and universities, December 1975 edition.* Iowa City, Ia.: American College Testing Program, 1975. (c)

American College Testing Program. *Taking the ACT assessment, Eastern region edition, 1976–77.* Iowa City, Ia.: American College Testing Program, 1976.

American Educational Research Association and National Council on Measurements Used in Education, Committee on Test Standards. *Technical recommendations for achievement tests.* Washington, D.C.: National Education Association, 1955.

American Personnel & Guidance Association. *Ethical standards.* (Rev. ed.) Washington, D.C.: American Personnel & Guidance Association, 1974.

American Psychological Association. *Technical recommendations for psychological tests and diagnostic techniques.* Washington, D.C.: American Psychological Association, 1954.

American Psychological Association. Revised ethical standards of psychologists. *APA Monitor,* March, 1977, pp. 22–23. (a)

American Psychological Association. *Standards for providers of psychological services.* Washington, D.C.: Author, 1977. (b)

American Psychological Association. Ethical standards of psychologists. *American Psychologist,* 1963, *18,* 56–60.

American Psychological Association. *Ethical principles in the conduct of research with human participants.* Washington, D.C.: American Psychological Association, 1973.

American Psychological Association, American Educational Research Association, and National Council on Measurement in Education. *Standards for educational and psychological tests.* Washington, D.C.: American Psychological Association, 1974.

Anastasi, A. *Differential psychology.* (3rd ed.) New York: Macmillan, 1958.

Anastasi, A. Some current developments in the measurement and interpretation of test validity. In A. Anastasi (Ed.), *Testing problems in perspective.* Washington, D.C.: American Council on Education, 1966. Pp. 307–17. (a)

Anastasi, A. Some implications of cultural factors for test construction. In A. Anastasi (Ed.), *Testing problems in perspective: Twenty-fifth anniversary volume of topical readings from the invitational conference on testing problems.* Washington, D.C.: American Council on Education, 1966. (b)

Anastasi, A. *Psychological testing.* (4th ed.) New York: Macmillan, 1976.

Angoff, W. H. The College Board SAT and the superior student. *Superior Student,* 1965, *7,* 10–15.

Angoff, W. H. (Ed.). *The College Board Admissions Testing Program: A technical report on research and development activities relating to the Scholastic Aptitude Test and Achievement Tests.* New York: College Entrance Examination Board, 1971.

Angoff, W. H. & Modu, C. C. *Equating the scales of the Prueba De Aptitud Académica and The Scholastic Aptitude Test: Research report 3.* New York: College Entrance Examination Board, 1973.

Armstrong, M. A. S. Children's responses to animal and human figures in thematic pictures. *Journal of Consulting Psychology,* 1954, *18,* 67–70.

Arthur, G. *A point scale of performance tests.* Vol. II. *The process of standardization.* New York: Commonwealth Fund, 1933.

Arthur, G. *A point scale of performance tests. Vol. I.* (2nd ed.) Chicago: Stoelting, 1943.

Arthur, G. *A point scale of performance tests. Revised Form II. Manual for administration and scoring the tests.* New York: The Psychological Corporation, 1947.

Atkinson, J. W. Motivational determinants of risk-taking behavior. *Psychological Review,* 1957, *64,* 359–72.

Atkinson, J. W. (Ed.). *Motives in fantasy, action, and society.* Princeton, N.J.: Van Nostrand, 1958.

Banham, K. M. *Maturity level for school entrance and reading readiness: for kindergarten and first grade.* Minneapolis: American Guidance Service, Inc., 1959.

Barclay, L. K. & Barclay, J. R. *The Barclay early childhood skill assessment guide.* Lexington, Ky.: Educational Skills Development, Inc., 1973.

Barth, C. A. Kinds of language knowledge required by college entrance examinations. *English Journal*, 1965, 54, 824–29.

Bayley, N. Consistency and variability in the growth of intelligence from birth to eighteen years. *Journal of Genetic Psychology*, 1949, 75, 165–96.

Bayley, N. Development of mental abilities. In P. H. Mussen (Ed.), *Carmichael's manual of child psychology.* New York: Wiley, 1970.

Beck, S. J. *Rorschach's test: 1. Basic processes.* New York: Grune & Stratton, 1961.

Bellak, L. *The TAT, CAT, and SAT in clinical use.* (3rd ed.) New York: Grune & Stratton, 1975.

Bellak, L. & Bellak, S. S. *Manual: Senior apperception technique.* Larchmont, N.Y.: C.P.S., 1973.

Bellak, L. & Hurvich, M. S. A human modification of the Children's Apperception Test (CAT-4). *Journal of Projective Techniques and Personality Assessment*, 1966, 30, 228–242.

Bender, L. *A visual motor gestalt test and its clinical use.* New York: The American Orthopsychiatric Association, 1938.

Bennett, G. K. *Manual forms S and I: Bennett Mechanical Comprehension Test.* New York: The Psychological Corporation, 1969.

Bennett, G. K., Seashore, H. G. & Wesman, A. G. *Differential Aptitude Tests Forms S & T, Manual.* (5th ed.) New York: The Psychological Corporation, 1974.

Benton, A. L. Influence of incentives upon intelligence test scores of school children. *Journal of Genetic Psychology*, 1936, 49, 494–96.

Bettelheim, B. *The empty fortress.* New York: The Free Press, 1967.

Biehler, R. F. *Psychology applied to teaching.* (2nd ed.) Boston: Houghton Mifflin, 1974.

Bingham, W. V. Classifying and testing for clerical jobs. *Personnel Journal*, 1935, 14, 163–72.

Black, H. *They shall not pass.* New York: William Morrow, 1963.

Bloom, B. S. (Ed.). *Taxonomy of educational objectives. Handbook 1: The cognitive domain.* New York: David McKay, 1956.

Blum, G. S. *The Blacky Pictures: A technique for the exploration of personality dynamics.* New York: The Psychological Corporation, 1950.

Borgatta, E. & Bohrnstedt, G. Review of equality of educational opportunity. *American Educational Research Journal*, 1968, 5, 260–65.

Boyce, R. W. & Paxson, R. C. The predictive validity of eleven tests at one state college. *Educational and Psychological Measurement*, 1965, 25, 1143–47.

Brown, F. G. *Principles of educational and psychological testing.* (2nd ed.) New York: Holt, Rinehart and Winston, 1976.

Brown, W. F. & Holtzman, W. H. *Survey of Study Habits and Attitudes: Manual.* New York: The Psychological Corporation, 1966.

Buck, J. N. *H-T-P: House-Tree-Person Projective Technique.* Los Angeles: Western Psychological Services, 1964.

Buros, O. K. (Ed.). *The 1938 mental measurements yearbook.* New Brunswick, N.J.: Rutgers University Press, 1938.

Buros, O. K. (Ed.). *The nineteen forty mental measurements yearbook.* New Brunswick, N.J.: Rutgers University Press, 1941.

Buros, O. K. (Ed.). *The third mental measurements yearbook.* New Brunswick, N.J.: Rutgers University Press, 1949.

Buros, O. K. (Ed.). *The fourth mental measurements yearbook.* Highland Park, N.J.: Gryphon Press, 1953.

Buros, O. K. (Ed.). *The fifth mental measurements yearbook.* Highland Park, N.J.: Gryphon Press, 1959.

Buros, O. K. (Ed.). *The sixth mental measurements yearbook.* Highland Park, N.J.: Gryphon Press, 1965.

Buros, O. K. (Ed.). *Seventh mental measurements yearbook.* Highland Park, N.J.: Gryphon Press, 1972.

Buros, O. K. (Ed.). *Tests in print II.* Highland Park, N.J.: Gryphon Press, 1974. (a)

Buros, O. K. (Ed.). *Personality tests and reviews* (Vols. I and II) Highland Park, N.J.: Gryphon Press, 1974. (b)

Burt, C. The inheritance of mental ability. *The American Psychologist,* 1958, 13, 1–15.

Burt, C. Inheritance of general intelligence. *American Psychologist,* 1972, 27, 175–90.

Campbell, D. P. Stability of interests within an occupation over thirty years. *Journal of Applied Psychology,* 1966, 50, 51–56.

Campbell, D. P. Changing patterns of interests within the American society. *Measurement and Evaluation in Guidance,* 1968, 1, 36–49.

Campbell, D. P. *Handbook for the Strong Vocational Interest Blank.* Stanford, Calif.: Stanford University Press, 1971.

Campbell, D. P. *Strong Vocational Interest Blank: Manual for the Strong-Campbell Interest Inventory.* Stanford, Calif.: Stanford University Press, 1974.

Carter, H. D. *Vocational interests and job orientations: A ten year review.* Stanford, Calif.: Stanford University Press, 1949.

Casey, M. L., Davidson, H. P. & Harter, D. I. Three studies on the effect of training in similar and identical material upon Stanford-Binet test scores. *Twenty-seventh yearbook, national social studies on education* (Part 1). 1928, 431–39.

Caspari, E. Genetic endowment and environment in the determination of human behavior: Biological viewpoint. *American Educational Research Journal,* 1968, 5, 43–55.

Cattell, J. M. K. Mental tests and measurements. *Mind,* 1890, 15, 373–80.

Chase, C. I. *Elementary statistical procedures.* New York: McGraw-Hill, 1967.

Chase, C. I. *Measurement for educational evaluation.* Reading, Mass.: Addison-Wesley, 1974.

Chauncey, H. & Dobbin, J. E. Testing has a history. In C. I. Chase and H. G. Ludlow (Eds.), *Readings in educational and psychological measurement.* Boston: Houghton Mifflin, 1966.

Clark, K. E. & Campbell, D. P. *Minnesota Vocational Interest Inventory: Manual.* New York: The Psychological Corporation, 1965.

Cleary, T. A., Humphreys, L. G., Kendrick, S. A. & Wesman, A. Educational uses of tests with disadvantaged students. *American Psychologist,* 1975, 30, 15–41.

Coffman W. E. Essay examinations. In R. L. Thorndike (Ed.), *Educational measurement.* (2nd ed.) Washington, D.C.: American Council on Education, 1971.

Coleman, W. & Ward, A. Comparison of Davis-Eells and Kuhlmann-Finch scores of children from high and low socioeconomic status. *Journal of Educational Psychology,* 1955, 46, 465–69.

College Entrance Examination Board Trustees. A statement by the college board trustees on test "coaching." *College Board News,* 1959, 5, 2–3.

College Entrance Examination Board. *Effects of coaching on scholastic aptitude test scores.* New York: College Entrance Examination Board, 1968.

College Entrance Examination Board. *1975 PSAT/NMSQT interpretive manual for counselors and administrators.* Princeton, N.J.: College Entrance Examination Board, 1975. (a)

College Entrance Examination Board. *1975 PSAT/NMSQT student bulletin.* Princeton, N.J.: College Entrance Examination Board, 1975. (b)

College Entrance Examination Board. *ATP news.* Princeton, N.J.: College Entrance Examination Board, 1975. (c)

College Entrance Examination Board. *Student bulletin 1976–77.* Princeton, N.J.: College Entrance Examination Board, 1976. (a)

College Entrance Examination Board. *Guide for high schools and colleges 1976–77.* Princeton, N.J.: College Entrance Examination Board, 1976. (b)

College Entrance Examination Board. *About the achievement tests, 1976–77.* Princeton, N.J.: College Entrance Examination Board, 1976. (c)

College Entrance Examination Board. *Your student report, 76–77.* Princeton, N.J.: College Entrance Examination Board, 1976. (d)

College Entrance Examination Board. *About the SAT admissions testing program of the College Entrance Examination Board, 1976–77: A description of the SAT and Test of Standard Written English.* Princeton, N.J.: College Entrance Examination Board, 1976. (e)

College Entrance Examination Board. *The college board news.* New York: College Entrance Examination Board, January 1976. (f)

Committee on Test Standards, American Educational Research Association; National Education Association; and National Council on Measurements Used in Education. *Technical recommendations for achievement tests.* Washington, D.C.: The National Education Association, 1955.

Conrad, H. S. & Jones, H. E. A second study of familiar resemblance in intelligence. *Original studies and experiments, thirty-ninth yearbook of the national society for the study of education, part II.* Chicago: University of Chicago Press, 1940.

Cook, W. W., Leeds C. & Callis, R. *The Minnesota Teacher Attitude Inventory.* New York: The Psychological Corporation, 1951.

Crane, V. R. & Heim, A. W. The effects of repeated retesting: III. Further experiments and general conclusions. *Quarterly Journal of Experimental Psychology,* 1950, 2, 182–97.

Cronbach, L. J. Further evidence on response sets and test design. *Educational and Psychological Measurement,* 1950, 10, 3–31.

Cronbach, L. J. *Essentials of psychological testing* (2nd ed.) New York: Harper & Row, 1960.

Cronbach, L. J. *Essentials of psychological testing* (3rd ed.) New York: Harper & Row, 1970.

Cronbach, L. J. Five decades of public controversy over mental testing. *American Psychologist*, 1975, *30*, 1–14.

Cronbach, L. J. & Meehl, P. E. Construct validity in psychological tests. In C. I. Chase & H. G. Ludlow (Eds.), *Readings in educational and psychological measurement*. Boston: Houghton Mifflin, 1966.

Cross, O. H. A study of faking on the Kuder Preference Record. *Educational and Psychological Measurement*, 1950, *10*, 271–77.

Cureton, E. E. Definition and estimation of test reliability. *Educational and Psychological Measurement*, 1958, *18*, 715–38.

Dahlstrom, W. G., Welsh, G. S. & Dahlstrom, L. E. *An MMPI handbook*. Vol. 1, *Clinical interpretation*. Minneapolis: University of Minnesota Press, 1972.

Dahlstrom, W. G., Welsh, G. S. & Dahlstrom, L. E. *An MMPI handbook*. Vol. II, *Research developments and applications*. Minneapolis: University of Minnesota Press, 1975.

Darley, J. G. & Hagenah, T. *Vocational interest measurement: Theory and practice*. Minneapolis: University of Minnesota Press, 1955.

Davis, A. Socioeconomic influences upon children's learning. *Understanding the Child*, 1951, *20*, 10–16.

DeLong, A. R. Emotional effects of elementary school testing. *Understanding the Child*, 1955, *24*, 103–107.

Dempster, J. J. B. Symposium on the effects of coaching and practice in intelligence tests: III. Southampton investigation and procedure. *British Journal of Educational Psychology*, 1954, *24*, 1–4.

Department of Labor. *The Negro family—The case for national action*. Office of Policy Planning and Research, Department of Labor, March 1965.

Dolliver, R. H. Likes, dislikes, and SVIB scoring. *Measurement and Evaluation in Guidance*, 1968, *1*, 73–80.

Dolliver, R. H. Kuder occupational interest survey. In O. K. Buros (Ed.), *The seventh mental measurements yearbook*. Highland Park, N.J.: Gryphon Press, 1972.

Doren, M. *Doren Diagnostic Reading Test of Word Recognition Skills: Manual*. Circle Pines, Minn.: American Guidance Service, Inc., 1973.

Downie, N. M. *Fundamentals of measurement: Techniques and practices*. (2nd ed.) New York: Oxford University Press, 1967.

Drake, L. E. & Oetting, E. R. *An MMPI codebook for counselors*. Minneapolis: University of Minnesota Press, 1959.

Droppelt, J. E. *How accurate is a test score?* Test Service Bulletin, No. 50. New York: The Psychological Corporation, 1956.

DuBois, P. H. College Board Scholastic Aptitude Test. In Oscar K. Buros (Ed.), *The seventh mental measurements yearbook* (Vol. I). Highland Park, N.J.: The Gryphon Press, 1972.

Durost, W. N. *The characteristics, use, and computation of stanines*. Test Service Notebook, No. 23. New York: Harcourt Brace Jovanovich, 1961. (a)

Durost, W. N. *How to tell parents about standardized test results*. Test Service Notebook, No. 26. New York: Harcourt Brace Jovanovich, 1961. (b)

Dyer, H. S. Does coaching help? *College Board Review*, 1953, *19*, 331–35.

Ebbinghaus, H. Uber eine neue Methode zur prüfung geistiger Fähigkeiten und ihre Anwendung bei Schulkindern. *Zeitschrift für Psychologie*, 1897, 13, 401–59.

Ebel, R. L. *Measuring educational achievement*. Englewood Cliffs, N.J.: Prentice-Hall, 1965.

Ebel, R. L. Standardized achievement tests: Uses and limitations. In W. L. Barnette (Ed.), *Readings in psychological tests and measurements*. (Rev. ed.) Homewood, Ill.: The Dorsey Press, 1968.

Ebel, R. L. Criterion-referenced measurement: Limitations. *School Review*, 1971, 79, 282–88.

Educational Testing Service. *Cooperative Primary Tests: Handbook*. Princeton, N.J.: Educational Testing Service, 1967.

Educational Testing Service. *Sequential Tests of Educational Progress Series II Handbook*. Princeton, N.J.: Educational Testing Service, 1971.

Educational Testing Service. *School and College Ability Tests Series II Handbook 1973 revision*. Princeton, N.J.: Educational Testing Service, 1973. (a)

Educational Testing Service. *Making the classroom test: A guide for teachers*. Princeton, N.J.: Educational Testing Service, 1973. (b)

Educational Testing Service. *Multiple-choice questions: A close look*. Princeton, N.J.: Educational Testing Service, 1973. (c)

Educational Testing Service. *ETS publications and audiovisual materials 1974*. Princeton, N.J.: Educational Testing Service, 1974.

Eells, K., Davis, A., Havighurst, R. J., Herrick, E. & Tyler, R. *Intelligence and cultural differences*. Chicago: University of Chicago Press, 1951.

Engelhart, M. D. Obtaining comparable scores on two or more tests. *Educational and Psychological Measurement*, 1959, 19, 55–64.

Engelhart, M. D. *Using stanines in interpreting test scores*. Test Service Notebook, No. 28. New York: Test Department, Harcourt Brace Jovanovich (n.d.).

Entwisle, D. R. To dispel fantasies about fantasy-based measures of achievement motivation. *Psychological Bulletin*, 1972, 77, 377–91.

Erlenmeyer-Kimling, L. & Jarvik, L. Genetics and intelligence: A review. *Science*, 1963, 142, 1477–79.

Eysenck, H. J. *The IQ argument*. New York: The Library Press, 1971.

Falls, J. D. Research in secondary education. *Kentucky School Journal*, 1928, 6, 42–46.

Farr, R. (Ed.). *Manual of directions level 1: Iowa Silent Reading Tests*. New York: Harcourt Brace Jovanovich, 1973. (a)

Farr, R. (Ed.). *Guide for interpretation and use level 1: Iowa Silent Reading Tests* New York: Harcourt Brace Jovanovich, 1973. (b)

Ferris, F. L., Jr. Testing in the new curriculum: Numerology, "tyranny," or common sense. *The School Review*, 1962, 70, 112–31.

Fifer, G. Social class and cultural group differences in diverse mental abilities. In A. Anastasi (Ed.), *Testing problems in perspective: Twenty-fifth anniversary volume of topical readings from the invitational conference on testing problems*. Washington, D.C.: American Council on Education, 1966.

Finch, F. *Manual Kuhlmann-Finch Scholastic Aptitude Tests*. Circle Pines, Minn.: American Guidance Service, 1956.

Findley, W. G. The Occupational Interest Survey. *Personnel and Guidance Journal*, 1966, 44, 72–77.

Fisher, S. & Fisher, R. A test of certain assumptions regarding figure drawing analysis. *Journal of Abnormal and Social Psychology*, 1950, 45, 727–32.

Fitzgibbon, T. J. *The use of standardized instruments with urban and minority-group pupils.* New York: Harcourt Brace Jovanovich, 1972.

Flanagan, J. C. The development of an index of examinee motivation. *Educational and Psychological Measurement,* 1955, 15, 144–51.

Fleishman, E. A. Testing for psychomotor abilities by means of apparatus tests. *Psychological Bulletin,* 1953, 50, 241–62.

Fowler, F. M. Interest measurement questions and answers. *School Life,* 1945 (December).

Fowler, W. L. *A comparative analysis of pupil performance on conventional and culture-controlled mental tests.* Unpublished doctoral dissertation, University of Michigan, 1955.

Frank, L. Projective methods for the study of personality. *Journal of Psychology,* 1939, 8, 389–413.

Frankenburg, W. K., Camp, B. W. & Van Natta, P. A. Validity of the Denver Developmental Screening Test. *Child Development,* 1971, 42, 475–85.

French, J. W. An answer to test coaching: Public school experiment with SAT. *College Board Review,* 1955, 27, 5–7.

French, J. W. & Dear, R. E. Effect of coaching on an aptitude test. *Educational and Psychological Measurement,* 1959, 19, 319–30.

Furuno, S. & Connor, A. Use of non-professional personnel for health screening of Head Start children. Paper presented at annual meeting of the Orthopsychiatric Association. San Francisco, Calif., March 1970.

Furuya, K. Responses of school-children to human and animal pictures. *Journal of Projective Techniques,* 1957, 21, 248–52.

Gamble, K. R. The Holtzman Inkblot Technique: A review. *Psychological Bulletin,* 1972, 77, 172–94.

Games, P. A. & Klare, G. R. *Elementary statistics: Data analysis for the behavioral sciences.* New York: McGraw-Hill, 1967.

Garrett, H. E. A note on the intelligence scores of Negroes and whites in 1918. *Journal of Abnormal and Social Psychology,* 1945, 40, 344–46.

Garrett, H. E. The SPSSI and racial differences. *American Psychologist,* 1962, 17, 260–63.

Garry, R. Individual differences in ability to fake vocational interests. *Journal of Applied Psychology,* 1953, 37, 33–37.

Gaudy, E. & Spielberger, C. D. *Anxiety and educational achievement.* New York: Wiley, 1974.

Gehman, W. S. A study of ability to fake scores on the Strong Vocational Interest Blank for Men. *Educational and Psychological Measurement,* 1957, 17, 65–70.

Gesell, A. & Amatruda, C. *The psychology of early growth.* New York: Macmillan, 1938.

Gesell, A. & Amatruda, C. *Developmental diagnosis: Normal and abnormal child development.* (2nd ed.) New York: Hoeber, 1947.

Gesell, A. et. al. *The first five years of life: A guide to the study of the preschool child.* New York: Harper & Row, 1940.

Gesell, A. et al. *Gesell developmental schedules.* New York: The Psychological Corporation, 1949.

Goldfried, M. R., Stricker, G. & Weiner, I. R. *Rorschach handbook of clinical and research applications.* Englewood Cliffs, N.J.: Prentice-Hall, 1971.

Goldman, L. *Using tests in counseling.* (2nd ed.) Pacific Palisades, Calif.: Goodyear, 1971.

Good, W. R. Misconceptions about intelligence testing. In C. I. Chase & H. G. Ludlow (Eds.), *Readings in educational and psychological measurement.* Boston: Houghton Mifflin, 1966.

Goodenough, F. L. *Measurement of intelligence by drawings.* New York: Harcourt Brace Jovanovich, 1926.

Goodenough, F. & Maurer, K. *The mental growth of children from two to fourteen years: A study of the predictive value of the Minnesota Preschool Scales.* Minneapolis: University of Minnesota Press, 1942.

Gordon, E. M. & Sarason, S. B. The relationship between "test anxiety" and "other anxieties." *Journal of Personnel,* 1955, 23, 317–23.

Gordon, L. V. *The measurement of interpersonal values.* Chicago: Science Research Associates, 1975.

Gordon, L. V. & Durea, M. A. The effect of discouragement on the revised Stanford-Binet scale. *Journal of Genetic Psychology,* 1948, 73, 201–207.

Goslin, D. A. The search for ability: *Standardized testing in social perspective.* New York: Russell Sage Foundation, 1963.

Gourevitch, V. *Statistical methods: A problem-solving approach.* Boston: Allyn and Bacon, 1965.

Greensboro Daily News. Scientists agree race, intelligence not related. Greensboro, N.C.: *Greensboro Daily News,* Feb. 22, 1976.

Griffin, P. M., Sanford, A. R. & Wilson, D. C. *Learning Accomplishment Profile: Examiner's manual.* Winston-Salem, N.C.: Kaplan School Supply Corp., 1975.

Gronlund, N. E. *Preparing criterion-referenced tests for classroom instruction.* New York: Macmillan, 1973.

Gronlund, N. E. *Measurement and evaluation in teaching.* (3rd ed.) New York: Macmillan, 1976.

Grooms, R. R. & Endler, N. S. The effect of anxiety on academic achievement. *Journal of Educational Psychology,* 1960, 51, 299–304.

Guilford, J. P. *Fundamental statistics in psychology and education.* (4th ed.) New York: McGraw-Hill, 1965.

Gustad, J. W. Test information and learning in the counseling process. *Educational and Psychological Measurement,* 1951, 11, 788–95.

Harmon, L. W. Optimum criterion group size in interest measurement. *Measurement and Evaluation in Guidance,* 1968, 1, 65–72.

Harris, C. W., Alkin, M. C. & Popham, W. J. (Eds.). *Problems in criterion referenced measurement.* CSE Monograph series in evaluation, No. 3. Los Angeles: Center for the Study of Evaluation, University of California, 1974.

Harris D. B. *Children's drawings as measures of intellectual maturity: A revision and extension of the Goodenough Draw-a-Man Test.* New York: Harcourt Brace Jovanovich, 1963.

Hathaway, S. R. & McKinley, J. C. *Booklet for the Minnesota Multiphasic Personality Inventory.* New York: The Psychological Corporation, 1943.

Hathaway, S. R. & McKinley, J. C. *Minnesota Multiphasic Personality Inventory: Manual.* (Rev. ed.) New York: The Psychological Corporation, 1951.

Hathaway, S. R. & McKinley, J. C. Construction of the schedule. In G. S. Welsh & W. G. Dahlstrom (Eds.), *Basic readings on the MMPI in psychology and medicine.* Minneapolis: University of Minnesota Press, 1956.

Hathaway, S. R. & Meehl, P. E. *An atlas for the clinical use of the MMPI*. Minneapolis: University of Minnesota Press, 1951.

Hathaway, S. R. & Monachesi, E. D. *Analyzing and predicting juvenile delinquency with the MMPI*. Minneapolis: University of Minnesota Press, 1953.

Hathaway, S. R. & Monachesi, E. D. *An atlas of juvenile MMPI profiles*. Minneapolis: University of Minnesota Press, 1961.

Haugh, O. The standardized test—to be or not to be. *English Journal*, 1975, 64, 53–55.

Hebb, D. O. *A textbook of psychology*. Philadelphia: W. B. Saunders, 1958.

Heim, A. W. & Wallace, J. G. The effects of repeatedly retesting the same group on the same intelligence test: II. High grade mental defectives. *Quarterly Journal of Experimental Psychology*, 1950, 2, 19–32.

Herrnstein, R. J. I. Q. *The Atlantic*, 1971, 228, 43–64.

Herrnstein, R. J. *I.Q. in meritocracy*. Boston: Little, Brown, 1973.

Hill, E. F. *The Holtzman Inkblot Technique: A handbook for clinical application*. San Francisco: Jossey-Bass, 1972.

Hoffmann, B. *The tyranny of testing*. New York: The Crowell-Collier Press, 1962.

Hogan, T. P. *Survey of School Attitudes: Manual for administering and interpreting*. New York: Harcourt Brace Jovanovich, 1975.

Holland, J. L. *Making vocational choices: A theory of careers*. Englewood Cliffs, N.J.: Prentice-Hall, 1973.

Holland, J. L. & Richards, J. M. *Academic and non-academic accomplishment: Correlated or uncorrelated?* ACT Research Report No. 2. Iowa City, Ia.: American College Testing Program, 1965.

Holtzman, W. H. Holtzman Inkblot Technique. In A. S. Rabin (Ed.), *Projective techniques in personality assessment*. New York: Springer, 1968.

Holtzman, W. H. New developments in Holtzman Inkblot Technique. In P. McReynolds (Ed.), *Advances in psychological assessment* (Vol. 3). San Francisco: Jossey-Bass, 1975. (a)

Holtzman, W. H. Moral development. *Proceedings of the 1974 Invitational Conference*. Princeton, N.J.: Educational Testing Service, 1975. (b)

Hoyt, D. P. Description and prediction of diversity among four-year colleges. *Measurement and Evaluation in Guidance*, 1968, 1, 16–26.

Hurlock, E. B. An evaluation of certain incentives used in school work. *Journal of Educational Psychology*, 1925, 16, 145–59.

Ilg, F. L. & Ames, L. B. *Child behavior*. New York: Dell, 1955.

Ilg, F. L. & Ames, L. B. *School readiness: Behavior tests used at the Gesell Institute*. New York: Harper & Row, 1965.

Ireton, H., Thwing, E. & Gravem, H. Infant mental development and neurological status, family socioeconomic status, and intelligence at age four. *Child Development*, 1970, 41, 937–45.

James, H. W. The effect of handwriting upon grading. *The English Journal*, 1927, 16, 180–85.

Jenkins, M. D. The upper limit of ability among American Negroes. In J. L. French (Ed.), *Educating the gifted: A book of readings*. (2nd ed.) New York: Holt, Rinehart and Winston, 1964.

Jensen, A. R. Social class, race and genetics: Implication for education. *American Educational Research Journal*, 1968, 5, 1–42.

Jensen, A. R. How much can we boost IQ and scholastic achievement? *Harvard Educational Review*, 1969, 39, 1–123.

Jensen, A. R. IQ's of identical twins reared apart. *Behavior Genetics*, 1970, 1, 133–47.

Jensen, A. R. *Genetics and education.* New York: Harper & Row, 1972.

Jensen, A. R. How biased are culture loaded tests? *Genetic Psychology Monographs*, 1974, 90, 185–244. (a)

Jensen, A. R. The strange case of Dr. Jensen and Mr. Hyde? *American Psychologist*, 1974, 29, 467–468. (b)

Johnson, D. M. Application of the standard-score IQ to the social statistics. *Journal of Social Psychology*, 1948, 27, 217–27.

Johnson, D. G. & Bommarito, J. W. *Tests and measurements in child development: A handbook.* San Francisco: Jossey-Bass, 1971.

Jung, C. G. The association method. *American Journal of Psychology*, 1910, 21, 219–69.

Kardiner, A. & Ovesey, L. *The mark of oppression: A psychological study of the American Negro.* New York: Norton, 1951.

Karmel, L. J. *An analysis of the personality patterns, and academic and social backgrounds of persons employed as full-time counselors in selected secondary schools in the state of North Carolina.* (Doctoral dissertation, University of North Carolina). Ann Arbor, Mich.: University Microfilms, 1961, No. 62–3134.

Karmel, L. J. Effects of windowless classroom environment on high school students. *Perceptual and Motor Skills*, 1965, 20, 277–78. (a)

Karmel, L. J. "Secretarial-psychologist"—A new member of the psychological team? *Journal of School Psychology*, 1965, 4 (3), 64–67. (b)

Karmel, L. J. *Testing in our schools.* New York: Macmillan, 1966.

Karmel, L. J. Do IQ tests discriminate against Negroes in their preparation for the world of work? *New York Personnel and Guidance Bulletin*, 1967, 19 (3), 10–13.

Karmel, L. J. Preparing counselors to use tests. *Counselor Education and Supervision*, 1968, 7, 319–20.

Karmel, L. J. Individual inventory: Definition rationale, and purposes. *The High School Journal*, 1971, 54, 251–64.

Karmel, L. J. & Salt, S. The teacher and the windowless school. *Illinois Education*, 1965, 53, 13.

Katz, M. *Selecting an achievement test: Principles and procedures.* Princeton, N.J.: Educational Testing Service, 1973.

Kaufman, A. S. Factor analyses of the WISC-R at eleven age levels between 6½ and 16½ years. *Journal of Consulting and Clinical Psychology*, 1975, 43, 135–47.

Kaufman, A. S. & Hollenbeck, G. P. Factor analysis of the standardization edition of the McCarthy scales. *Journal of Clinical Psychology*, 1973, 29, 358–62.

Kaufman, A. S. & Kaufman, N. L. Black-white differences at ages 2½–8½ on the McCarthy Scales of Children's Abilities. *Journal of School Psychology*, 1973, 11, 196–206. (a)

Kaufman, A. S. & Kaufman, N. L. Sex differences on the McCarthy Scales of Children's Abilities. *Journal of Clinical Psychology*, 1973, 29, 362–65. (b)

Kent, G. H. & Rosanoff, A. J. A study of association in insanity. *American Journal of Insanity*, 1910, 67, 317–90.

Klineberg, O. *Negro intelligence and selective migration.* New York: Columbia University Press, 1935.

Klineberg, O. (Ed.). *Characteristics of the American Negro.* New York: Harper & Row, 1944.

Klopfer, B. & Kelley, D. M. *The Rorschach technique.* New York: World Book Co., 1946.

Klopfer, B., Ainsworth, M. D., Klopfer, W. G. & Holt, R. R. *Developments in the Rorschach technique.* New York: World Book Co., 1954.

Knobloch, H. & Pasamanick, B. *Developmental diagnosis.* New York: Hoeber-Harper, 1974.

Kohlberg, L. Stage and sequence: The cognitive-developmental approach to socialization. In D. Goslin (Ed.), *Handbook of socialization: Theory and research.* Chicago: Rand McNally, 1969.

Kohlberg, L. The development of moral stages: Uses and abuses. *Proceedings of the 1973 Invitational Conference on Testing Problems.* Princeton, N.J.: Educational Testing Service, 1974.

Koppitz, E. M. *The Bender-Gestalt Test for young children: Research and application, 1963–1973.* New York: Grune and Stratton, 1975.

Krathwohl, D. R., Bloom, B. S. & Masia, B. B. *Taxonomy of educational objectives. Handbook 2: The affective domain.* New York: David McKay, 1964.

Kuder, G. F. *Administrator's manual Kuder Preference Record Vocational—Form C.* Chicago: Science Research Associates, 1960.

Kuder, G. F. *Kuder E General Interest Survey manual.* Chicago: Science Research Associates, 1971.

Kuder, G. F. *Kuder DD Occupational Interest Survey Interpretive Leaflet Grades 11–12.* Chicago: Science Research Associates, 1974.

Kuder, G. F. *Kuder DD Occupational Interest Survey general manual.* Chicago: Science Research Associates, 1975.

Kuder, G. F. & Richardson, M. W. The theory of the estimation of test reliability. *Psychometrika,* 1937, 2, 151–60.

Kuhlmann, F. A. A revision of the Binet-Simon system for measuring the intelligence of children. *Journal of Psycho-asthenics, Monogram Supplement,* 1912, 1, 1–41.

Kuhlmann, F. & Finch, F. H. *Kuhlmann-Finch scholastic aptitude tests.* Minneapolis: American Guidance Service, 1952.

Lasaga, J. I. Analytic technique. In E. S. Shneidman (Ed.), *Thematic test analysis.* New York: Grune and Stratton, 1951.

Laurendeau, M. & Pinard, A. *Causal thinking in the child: A genetic and experimental approach.* New York: International Universities Press, 1962.

Laurendeau, M. & Pinard, A. *The development of the concept of space in the child.* New York: International Universities Press, 1970.

Lee, E. S. Negro intelligence and selective migration: A Philadelphia test of the Klineberg hypothesis. *American Sociology Review,* 1951, 16, 227–33.

Lennon, R. T. *Selection and provision of testing materials.* Test Service Bulletin, No. 99. New York: Harcourt Brace Jovanovich, 1962.

Lennon, R. T. Testing and the culturally disadvantaged child. Paper read at series on *Problems in Education of the Culturally Disadvantaged,* Boston, February 1964. (Copies may be secured from the Test Department of Harcourt Brace Jovanovich, Inc.; 757 Third Ave.; New York, N. Y.)

Levine, F. M. & Fasnacht, G. Token rewards may lead to token learning. *American Psychologist*, 1974, 29, 816–20.

Levitt, E. E. & Truumaa, A. *The Rorschach technique with children and adolescents: Application and norms.* New York: Grune and Stratton, 1972.

Levy, L. H. *Psychological interpretation.* New York: Holt, Rinehart and Winston, 1963.

Lewis, M. Infant intelligence tests: Their use and misuse. *Human Development*, 1973, 16, 108–18.

Lien, A. J. *Measurement and evaluation of learning.* Dubuque, Ia.: Wm. C. Brown, 1976.

Lindeman, R. H. *Educational measurement.* Glenview, Ill.: Scott, Foresman, 1967.

Lins, L. J., Abell, A. P. & Hutchins, H. C. Relative usefulness in predicting academic success of the ACT, the SAT, and some other variables. *Journal of Experimental Education*, 1966, 35, 1–29.

Lipton, R. L. A study of the effect of exercise in a simple mechanical activity on mechanical aptitude as is measured by the subtests of the MacQuarrie Test for Mechanical Ability. *Psychology Newsletter*, NYU, 1956, 7, 39–42.

Little, K. B. & Shneidman, E. S. The validity of thematic projective interpretations. *Journal of Personality*, 1955, 23, 285–94.

Livingston, S. A. Criterion-referenced applications of classical test theory. *Journal of Educational Measurement*, 1972, 9, 13–26.

Longstaff, H. P. Practice effects on the Minnesota Vocational Test for Clerical Workers. *Journal of Applied Psychology*, 1954, 38, 18–20.

Lord, F. M. & Novick, M. R. *Statistical theories of mental test scores.* Reading, Mass.: Addison-Wesley, 1967.

Loretan, J. O. Alternatives to intelligence testing. *Curriculum and Materials: Board of Education of The City of New York*, 1966, 20 (3), 6–9.

Lorge, I. Difference or bias in tests of intelligence. In A. Anastasi (Ed.), *Testing problems in perspective: Twenty-fifth anniversary volume of topical readings from the invitational conference on testing problems.* Washington, D.C.: American Council on Education, 1966.

Machover, K. *Personality projection in the drawing of the human figure: A method of personality investigation.* Springfield, Ill.: Charles C Thomas, 1949.

Madden, R., Gardner, E. F., Rudman, H. C., Karlsen, B. & Merwin, J. C. *Stanford Achievement Test Intermediate Level I, Manual Part I.* New York: Harcourt Brace Jovanovich, 1973.

Madden, R., Gardner, E., Rudman, H., Karlsen, B. & Merwin, J. *Manual Part V: Technical Data Report Stanford Achievement Test.* New York: Harcourt Brace Jovanovich, 1975.

Magnusson, D. *Test theory.* Reading, Mass.: Addison-Wesley, 1967.

Mandler, G. & Sarason, S. B. A study of anxiety and learning. *Journal of Abnormal and Social Psychology*, 1952, 47, 166–73.

Marshall, J. C. & Powers, J. M. Writing neatness, composition errors, and essay grades. In D. A. Payne & R. F. McMorris (Eds.), *Educational and psychological measurement: Contributions to theory and practice.* (2nd ed.) Morristown, N.J.: General Learning Press, 1975.

Matarazzo, J. D. *Wechsler's measurement and appraisal of adult intelligence.* (5th ed.) Baltimore: Williams & Wilkins, 1972.

McCall, R. B., Hogarty, P. S. & Hurlburt, N. Transitions in infant sensorimotor development and the prediction of childhood IQ. *American Psychologist*, 1972, 27, 728–48.

McClelland, D. C. (Ed.). *Studies in motivation.* New York: Appleton-Century-Crofts, 1955.

McClelland, D. C. The measurement of human motivation: An experimental approach. In A. Anastasi (Ed.), *Testing problems in perspective.* Washington, D.C.: American Council on Education, 1966.

McClelland, D. C., Atkinson, J. W., Clark, R. A. & Lowell, E. A. *The achievement motive.* New York: Appleton-Century-Crofts, 1953.

McCollough, C. & Van Atta, L. *Introduction to descriptive statistics and correlation: A program for self-instruction.* New York: McGraw-Hill, 1965.

McGuire, C. H. Testing in professional education. *Review of Educational Research: Educational and Psychological Testing,* 1968, 38, 49–60.

McKee, P. & Brzeinski, J. E. *The effectiveness of teaching reading in kindergarten.* U.S. Department of Health, Education, and Welfare, Office of Education, Cooperative Research Project No. 5-0371. Denver: Denver Public Schools and Colorado State Department of Education, 1966.

McNemar, Q. Lost: Our intelligence. Why? In C. I. Chase & H. G. Ludlow (Eds.), *Readings in educational and psychological measurement.* Boston: Houghton Mifflin, 1966.

Megargee, E. I. (Ed.). *Research in clinical assessment.* New York: Harper & Row, 1966.

Merrill, M. A. Training students to administer the Stanford-Binet Intelligence Scale. *Testing today.* Boston: Houghton Mifflin (three-page letter to the editor, distributed by Houghton Mifflin, no date).

Millman, J. Reporting student progress: A case for a criterion-referenced marking system. In V. H. Noll, D. P. Scannell & R. P. Noll (Eds.), *Introductory readings in educational measurement.* Boston: Houghton Mifflin, 1972. Pp. 352–363.

Montagu, M. F. A. Intelligence of northern Negroes and southern whites in the first world war. *American Journal of Psychology,* 1945, 58, 161–88.

Mooney, R. L. & Gordon, L. V. *The Mooney Problem Check Lists: Manual.* (Rev. ed.) New York: The Psychological Corporation, 1950.

Mortensen, D. G. & Schmuller, A. M. *Guidance in today's schools.* (3rd ed.) New York: Wiley, 1976.

Munday, L. *Comparative predictive validities of the American College Tests and two other scholastic aptitude tests.* ACT Research Report, No. 6. Iowa City, Ia.: American College Testing Program, 1965.

Murray, H. A. *Explorations in personality.* New York: Oxford University Press, 1938.

Murray, H. A. *Thematic Apperception Test manual.* Cambridge, Mass.: Harvard University Press, 1943.

Murstein, B. Assumptions, adaptation level and projective techniques. *Perceptual and Motor Skills,* 1961, 12, 107–25.

Myers, A. E., McConville, C. & Coffman, W. E. Simplex structures in the grading of essay tests. *Educational and Psychological Measurement,* 1966, 26, 41–54.

Myrdal, G. *An American dilemma.* New York: Harper & Row, 1944.

Newman, H. M. *Multiple human births.* Garden City, N.Y.: Doubleday, 1940.

Nichols, P. L. & Broman, S. H. Familial resemblance in infant mental development. *Developmental Psychology*, 1974, 10, 442–46.

Noll, V. H. Simulation by college students of a prescribed pattern on a Personality scale. *Educational and Psychological Measurement*, 1951, 11, 478–88.

Noll, V. H. & Scannell, D. P. *Introduction to educational measurement.* (3rd ed.) Boston: Houghton Mifflin, 1972.

Notz, W. W. Work motivation and the negative effects of extrinsic rewards: A review with implications for theory and practice. *American Psychologist*, 1975, 30, 884–91.

Nunnally, J. C. *Educational measurement and evaluation.* (2nd ed.) New York: McGraw-Hill, 1972.

Pascal, G. R. & Suttell, B. J. *The Bender-Gestalt Test: Quantification and validity for adults.* New York: Grune and Stratton, 1951.

Payne, D. A. *The specification and measurement of learning outcomes.* Waltham, Mass.: Blaisdell Publishing Co., 1968.

Pike, L. W. & Evans, F. R. Effects of special instruction for three kinds of mathematics aptitude items. *College Entrance Examination Board Research Report, 1,* 1972.

Popham, W. J. *Educational evaluation.* Englewood Cliffs, N.J.: Prentice-Hall, 1975.

Popham, W. J. & Husek, T. R. Implications of criterion-referenced measurement. In D. A. Payne & R. F. McMorris (Eds.), *Educational and psychological measurement: Contributions to theory & practice.* (2nd ed.) Morristown, N.J.: General Learning Press, 1975.

Popham, W. J. & Sirotnik, K. A. *Educational statistics: Use and interpretation.* (2nd ed.) New York: Harper & Row, 1973.

Postman, L. & Keppel, G. *Norms of word association.* New York: Academic Press, 1970.

Quay, Lorene C. Reinforcement and Binet performance in disadvantaged children. *Journal of Educational Psychology*, 1975, 132–35.

Raven, J. *Progressive matrices, Forms, 1938, 1947, 1962.* New York: The Psychological Corporation.

Ricks, J. H. On telling parents about test results. In D. A. Payne & R. F. McMorris (Eds.), *Educational and psychological measurement: Contributions to theory and practice.* (2nd ed.) Morristown, N. J.: General Learning Press, 1975.

Rorschach, H. *Psychodiagnostics* (translated by P. Lemkau and B. Kronenburg). New York: Grune and Stratton, 1942.

Rosen, B. C. The achievement syndrome. *American Sociological Review*, 1956, 21, 203–11.

Rosenberg, L. A. *Scientific racism and the American psychologist.* Paper presented at the meeting of the District of Columbia Psychological Association, Washington, D.C., October 1966.

Rosenzweig, S. *Psychodiagnosis: An introduction to the integration of tests in dynamic clinical practice.* New York: Grune and Stratton, 1949.

Sacks, E. L. Intelligence scores as a function of experimentally established social relationships between child and examiner. *Journal of Abnormal and Social Psychology*, 1952, 47, 354–58.

Salt, S. & Karmel, L. J. The windowless school. *The Clearing House*, 1967, 42, 176–78.

Sarason, S. B. The test-situation and the problem of prediction. *Journal of Clinical Psychology*, 1950, 6, 387–92.

Sarason, S. B. *The clinical interaction, with special reference to the Rorschach.* New York: Harper & Row, 1954.

Sarason, S. B. & Gordon, E. M. The test anxiety questionnaire: Scoring norms. *Journal of Abnormal and Social Psychology*, 1953, 48, 447–48.

Sarason, S. B. & Mandler, G. Some correlates of test anxiety. *Journal of Abnormal and Social Psychology*, 1952, 47, 810–17.

Sarason, S. B., Mandler, G. & Craighill, P. G. The effect of differential instructions on anxiety and learning. *Journal of Abnormal and Social Psychology*, 1952, 47, 561–65.

Sarason, S. B., Davidson, K., Lighthall, F. & Waite, R. A test anxiety scale for children. *Child Development*, 1958, 29, 105–13.

Sarason, S. B., Davidson, K. S., Lighthall, F. F., Waite, R. R. & Ruebush, B. K. *Anxiety in elementary school children.* New York: Wiley, 1960.

Schafer, R. *The clinical application of psychological tests.* New York: International Universities Press, 1948.

Schwartz, E. M. & Elonen, A. S. IQ and the myth of stability: A 16-year longitudinal study of variations in intelligence test performance. *Journal of Clinical Psychology*, 1975, 31, 687–94.

Sears, R. Motivational factors in aptitude testing. *American Journal of Orthopsychiatry*, 1943, 13, 468–93.

Seashore, H. G. & Ricks, J. H. *Norms must be relevant.* Test Service Bulletin, No. 39. New York: The Psychological Corporation, 1950.

Shavelson, R. J., Block, J. H. & Revitch, M. M. Criterion-referenced testing: Comments on reliability. *Journal of Educational Measurement*, 1972, 9, 133–37.

Sherman, M. & Key, C. B. The intelligence of isolated mountain children. *Child Development*, 1932, 3, 279–90.

Shneidman, E. S. (Ed.). *Thematic test analysis.* New York: Grune and Stratton, 1951.

Shneidman, E. S. Projective techniques. In B. B. Wolman (Ed.), *Handbook of clinical psychology.* New York: McGraw-Hill, 1965.

Shockley, W. Negro IQ deficit: Failure of a malicious coincidence model warrants new research proposals. *Review of Educational Research*, 1971, 41, 227–48.

Shuey, A. M. *The testing of Negro intelligence.* (2nd ed.) New York: Social Science Press, 1966.

Sinick, D. Encouragement, anxiety, and test performance. *Journal of Applied Psychology*, 1956, 40, 315–18.

Smith, R. J. & Hansen, L. H. Integrating reading and writing: Effects on children's attitudes. *The Elementary School Journal*, 1976, 76, 238–45.

Soldwedel, B. J. *Preparing for college.* New York: Macmillan, 1966.

Spearman, C. E. *The abilities of man: Their nature and measurement.* New York: Macmillan, 1927.

Spielberger, C. D. (Ed.). *Anxiety: Current trends in theory and research* (Vol. 2). New York: Academic Press, 1972.

Spranger, E. (translated by P. J. W. Pigors). *Types of men.* Halle: Niemeyer Verlag, 1928.

Spuhler, J. N. & Lindzey, G. Racial differences in behavior. In J. Hirsch (Ed.), *Behavior-genetic analysis.* New York: McGraw-Hill, 1967.

Stanley, J. C. *Measurement in today's schools.* (4th ed.) Englewood Cliffs, N.J.: Prentice-Hall, 1964.

Starch, D. & Elliott, E. C. Reliability of grading high school work in English. *School Review,* 1912, 20, 442–57.

Starch, D. & Elliott, E. C. Reliability of grading work in history. *School Review,* 1913, 21, 676–81. (a)

Starch, D. & Elliott, E. C. Reliability of grading work in mathematics. *School Review,* 1913, 21, 254–57. (b)

Stone, L. J. & Church, J. *Childhood & adolescence: A psychology of the growing person.* (3rd ed.) New York: Random House, 1973.

Stott, L. H. & Ball, R. S. Infant and preschool mental tests: Review & evaluation. *Monographs of the Society for Research in Child Development,* 1965, 30 (3, serial No. 101).

Strong, E. K. *Vocational interests of men and women.* Stanford, Calif.: Stanford University Press, 1943.

Strong, E. K. *Vocational interests 18 years after college.* Minneapolis: University of Minnesota Press, 1955.

Stutsman, R. *Mental measurement of preschool children.* New York: World Book Co., 1931.

Super, D. E. & Crites, J. O. *Appraising vocational fitness: By means of psychological tests.* (Rev. ed.) New York: Harper & Row, 1962.

Super, D. E., Braasch, W. F., Jr. & Shay, J. B. The effect of distractions on test results. *Journal of Educational Psychology,* 1947, 38, 373–77.

Symonds, P. M. *Manual for Symonds Picture-Story Test.* New York: Bureau of Publications, Columbia Teachers College, 1948.

Symonds, P. M. *Adolescent fantasy: An investigation of the picture-story method of personality study.* New York: Columbia University Press, 1949.

Terman, L. M. *Measurement of intelligence.* Boston: Houghton Mifflin, 1916.

Terman, L. M. & Merrill, M. A. *Measuring intelligence.* Boston: Houghton Mifflin, 1937.

Terman, L. M. & Merrill, M. A. *Stanford-Binet Intelligence Scale: Manual for the third revision, form L-M.* Boston: Houghton Mifflin, 1960.

Terman, L. M. & Merrill, M. A. *Stanford-Binet Intelligence Scale: Manual for the third revision, form L-M, 1972 Norms edition.* Boston: Houghton Mifflin, 1973.

Thomas, H. Psychological assessment instruments for use with human infants. *Merrill-Palmer Quarterly,* 1970, 16, 179–223.

Thorndike, E. L. *The measurement of intelligence.* New York: Columbia Teachers College, 1927.

Thorndike, R. L. *Personnel selection: Test and measurement techniques.* New York: Wiley, 1949.

Thorndike, R. L. *Thorndike Dimensions of Temperament: Manual.* New York: The Psychological Corporation, 1966.

Thorndike, R. L. & Hagen, E. *Measurement and evaluation in psychology and education.* (3rd ed.) New York: Wiley, 1969.

Thurstone, L. L. *The measurement of values.* Chicago: University of Chicago Press, 1959.

Thurstone, L. L. & Thurstone, T. G. Factorial studies of intelligence. *Psychometrics Monographs,* 1941, No. 2.

Thurstone, T. G. *Examiner's manual: Primary mental abilities for grades 2–4.* Chicago: Science Research Associates, 1963.

Tuckman, B. W. *Measuring educational outcomes: Fundamentals of testing.* New York: Harcourt Brace Jovanovich, 1975.

Tyler, L. *The psychology of human differences.* (2nd ed.) New York: Appleton-Century-Crofts, 1956.

United States Department of Health, Education, and Welfare. *Equality of educational opportunity: Summary report.* Catalog No. FS5.238:–38000. Washington, D.C.: U.S. Government Printing Office, 1966.

United States Department of Interior, Bureau of Education. *Cardinal principles of education.* Bulletin No. 38, 1918.

United States Office of Education. *American Education,* October 1966.

Uzgiris, I. C. & Hunt, J. McV. *Assessment in infancy: Ordinal Scales of Psychological Development.* Urbana, Ill.: University of Illinois Press, 1975.

Vandenberg, S. Contribution of twin research in psychology. *Psychological Bulletin,* 1966, 66, 327–52.

Varble, D. L. Current status of the thematic apperception test. In P. McReynolds (Ed.), *Advances in psychological assessment.* Vol. 2. Palo Alto, Calif.: Science & Behavior Books, 1971.

Vernon, P. E. Symposium on the effects of coaching and practice in intelligence tests: V. Conclusions. *British Journal of Educational Psychology,* 1954, 24, 57–63.

Veroff, J., Atkinson, J. W., Feld, S. C. & Gurin, G. The use of thematic apperception to assess motivation in a nationwide interview study. In J. W. Atkinson, J. O. Raynor, et al. (Eds.), *Motivation & achievement.* Washington, D.C.: Holt, Rinehart and Winston, 1974.

Vincent, J., Bright, R., Dickason, L. & Bussey, I. Effects of the WIST reading readiness on first grade readiness and later academic achievement. *The Journal of Educational Research,* 1976, 69, 250–53.

Waite, R. R., Sarason, S. B., Lighthall F. F. & Davidson, K. S. A study of anxiety and learning in children. *Journal of Abnormal and Social Psychology,* 1958, 57, 267–70.

Walker, D. K. *Socioemotional measures for preschool and kindergarten children.* San Francisco: Jossey-Bass, 1973.

Wallace, W. L. College Board Scholastic Aptitude Test. In Oscar K. Buros (Ed.), *The seventh mental measurements yearbook* (Vol. I). Highland Park, N.J.: Gryphon Press, 1972. (a)

Wallace, W. L. ACT test program of the American College Testing Program. In Oscar K. Buros (Ed.), *The seventh mental measurements yearbook* (Vol. I). Highland Park, N.J.: Gryphon Press, 1972. (b)

Warren, H. C. (Ed.). *Dictionary of psychology.* Boston: Houghton Mifflin, 1934.

Webb, E. J. Unobtrusive measures. In D. A. Payne & R. F. McMorris (Eds.),

Educational and psychological measurement: Contributions to theory and practice. (2nd ed.) Morristown, N.J.: General Learning Press, 1975.

Webb, E. J., Campbell, D. T., Schwartz, R. D. & Sechrest, L. *Unobtrusive measures.* Chicago: Rand McNally, 1971.

Webster's New collegiate dictionary. (6th ed.) Springfield, Mass.: G. & C. Merriam, 1961.

Wechsler D. *Wechsler Intelligence Scale for Children (Manual).* New York: The Psychological Corporation, 1949.

Wechsler, D. *Manual for the Wechsler Adult Intelligence Scale.* New York: The Psychological Corporation, 1955.

Wechsler, D. *The measurement and appraisal of adult intelligence.* (4th ed.) Baltimore: Williams and Wilkins, 1958.

Wechsler, D. *The measurement of adult intelligence.* (4th ed.) Baltimore: Williams and Wilkins, 1960.

Wechsler, D. *Manual for the Wechsler Preschool and Primary Scale of Intelligence.* New York: The Psychological Corporation, 1967.

Wechsler, D. *Manual: Wechsler Intelligence Scale for Children—Revised.* New York: The Psychological Corporation, 1974.

Weitz, H. Some practical problems in interest measurement. *Measurement and Evaluation in Guidance,* 1968, 1, 56–62.

Werner, E. E., Honzik, M. P. & Smith, R. S. Prediction of intelligence and achievement at ten years from twenty months pediatric and psychologic examinations. *Child Development,* 1968, 39, 1963–75.

Wesman, A. G. Intelligent testing. *American Psychologist,* 1968, 23, 267–74.

Wesman, A. G. Testing and counseling: Fact and fancy. *Measurement and Evaluation in Guidance,* 1972, 5, 397–402.

Whaley, D. L. & Malott, R. W. *Elementary principles of behavior.* New York: Appleton-Century-Crofts, 1971.

Wickes, T. A., Jr. Examiner influence in a testing situation. *Journal of Consulting Psychology,* 1956, 20, 23–26.

Williams, F. M., Jones, Q., Roger, M. & Zahradka, P. National tests: Bridges or barriers to minority students. *College and University,* 1975, 50, 562–78.

Winterbottom M. R. The relation of need for achievement to learning experiences in independence and mastery. In J. W. Atkinson (Ed.), *Motives in fantasy, action and society.* Princeton, N.J.: Van Nostrand, 1958.

Wiseman, S. Symposium on the effects of coaching and practice in intelligence tests: IV. The Manchester experiment. *British Journal of Educational Psychology,* 1954, 24, 5–8.

Wiseman, S. & Wrigley, J. The comparative effects of coaching and practice on the results of verbal intelligence tests. *British Journal of Psychology,* 1953, 44, 83–94.

Wolk, R. L. & Wolk, R. B. *Manual: Gerontological Apperception Test.* New York: Behavioral Publications, 1971.

Wood, P. L. & Deal, T. N. Testing the early educational and psychological development of children—ages 3–6. *Review of Educational Research,* 1968, 38, 12–18.

Yerkes, R. M. (Ed.). Psychological examining in the United States Army. *National Academy of Science Memoirs,* 1921, 15.

index